MACROECONOMICS

MACROECONOMICS
Theory and Applications

S.P.S. CHAUHAN

Associate Professor of Economics (Ex), University of Delhi
Former Associate Professor of Business Statistics (MIB) & O.R. (M.Com.),
Deptt. of Commerce, Delhi School of Economics, University of Delhi
Visiting Professor of Economics
Lal Bahadur Shastri Institute of Management (LBSIM), New Delhi,
Fortune Institute of International Business (FIIB), New Delhi,
New Delhi Institute of Management (NDIM), New Delhi,
ICFAI Business School (IBS), (Gurugram), Haryana.

PHI Learning Private Limited

Delhi-110092
2025

In fond memory of ***Shri Asoke K. Ghosh*** *(October 1942–February 2024), Founder Chairman and Managing Director of PHI Learning, whose vision endlessly inspires.*

The Legacy Continues... .

Published by Pushpita Ghosh, PHI Learning Private Limited, Rimjhim House, 111, Patparganj Industrial Estate, Delhi-110092 and Printed by Syndicate Binders, A-20, Hosiery Complex, Noida, Phase-II Extension, Noida-201305 (N.C.R. Delhi).

₹725.00

MACROECONOMICS—THEORY AND APPLICATIONS
S.P.S. Chauhan

ISBN-978-93-5443-964-3 (Print Book)
ISBN-978-93-5443-775-5 (e-Book)

The export rights of the book are vested solely with the publisher.

Contents

Preface .... *xiii*

UNIT-1
INTRODUCTION

1. Introduction to Macroeconomics 3

Introduction 3
1.1 Meaning and Scope of Macroeconomics 4
1.2 Methodology of Macroeconomics 5
1.3 Limitations of Macroeconomic Analysis 5
1.4 Difference between Micro and Macroeconomics 6
1.5 Complementarity of the Two Approaches 7
Key Terms and Concepts 8
Exercises 10

UNIT-2
NATIONAL INCOME AND RELATED AGGREGATES
(Basic Concepts and Measurement)

2. National Income and Related Aggregates—
Basic Concepts and Measurement **15**

Introduction—The Concept of Income 15
2.1 National Income—Meaning and Measurement 16
2.1.1 Income Method 17
2.1.2 Product or the Value Added Method 20
2.1.3 Expenditure Method 27
2.2. Identity of NI, NP, and NE: The Circular Flows of Income, Output and Expenditure 29
2.2.1 Circular Flows in a Two-sector-economy 30
2.2.2 Circular Flows in a Two-sector-economy in Presence of the Financial Institutions 30
2.2.3 Circular Flows in a 3 Sector Economy with Financial Institutions 31
2.2.4 Circular Flows in a Four Sector Economy with Financial Institutions 32

2.3 National Income Aggregates 32
2.4 National Income at Current and Constant Prices 37
2.4.1 National Income at Current Prices 37
2.4.2 National Income at Constant Prices 37
2.5 Private Income, Personal Income and Personal Disposable Income 40
2.5.1 Private Income 40
2.5.2 Personal Income 41
2.5.3 Personal Disposable Income 42
2.6 Per Capita Income 42
2.7 Utility of National Income Estimates 42
2.8 *GNP* Per Capita, *PQLI, HDI* and Social Welfare 43
2.9 Input-output Accounting: Leontief's Input-output Table 52
2.10 Conclusion: Criteria for Determining What to Include and What not in National Income 57
2.11 Consolidated Accounts for the Nation 58
Key Terms and Concepts 59
Exercises 64

UNIT-3
EMPLOYMENT, CONSUMPTION, INVESTMENT AND MODELS OF GOODS MARKET EQUILIBRIUM

3. Introduction to Theory of Employment 77
Introduction: Concepts of Employment and Unemployment 77
3.1 Nature of Unemployment in Developed Countries 77
3.1.1 Cyclical Unemployment 77
3.1.2 Frictional Unemployment 78
3.1.3 Voluntary Unemployment 78
3.2 Nature of Unemployment in Underdeveloped Countries 79
3.2.1 Seasonal Unemployment 79
3.2.2 Underemployment 79
3.2.3 Structural Unemployment 79
3.2.4 Disguised Unemployment 79
3.3 Some Features of Unemployment 80
3.3.1 Urban Unemployment as an Offshoot of the Rural Unemployment 80
3.3.2 Disguised Unemployment as a Potential Source of Capital Formation 80
3.4 Concept of Full Employment: Keynesian and Classical Versions [Figures 3.2, 3.3(a) and 3.3(b)] 81
3.5 Classical and Keynesian Theories of Employment: A Critical Assessment 83
3.5.1 Classical Theory of Employment 83
3.5.2 (a) Basis of Classical Theory and its Implications 84
3.5.2 (b) Keynesian Theory of Employment and its Implications 85
Key Terms and Concepts 90
Exercises 92

4. Consumption Function 94

Introduction 94
4.1 Consumption Function 94
4.2 The Most Common Form of the Consumption Function 97
4.3 Keynesian Psychological Law of Consumption 98
4.3.1 Assumptions of the Psychological Law of Consumption 98
4.3.2 Implications of the Psychological Law of Consumption 99
4.4 Factors Influencing Consumption Demand 100
4.5 Savings Function 102
4.6 Empirical Estimates of Consumption Function 104
4.6.1 Empirical Estimates for Long-run Consumption Function 104
4.6.2 Empirical Estimates for Short-run Consumption Function 104
4.7 Life Cycle of People in General in Relation to Income, Consumption, Saving and Rate of Interest—Some Interesting Observations 108
4.7.1 Fisher's Time Preference: Present or Future Income and Interest 108
4.7.2 Wealth-holder's Consumption and Saving over Life Cycle 111
Key Terms and Concepts 114
Exercises 116

5. Investment Function 119

Introduction 119
5.1 Terminology in Use 119
5.2 Factors Influencing a Firm's Decision to Invest 121
5.3 Factors Influencing NPV 125
5.3.1 Marginal Efficiency of Capital (MEC) 125
5.3.2 *MEC* Schedule and Determination of Capital Stok 126
5.3.3 Factors Influencing MEC 128
5.3.4 Prospective Yield and Short- and Long-term Expectations 128
5.4 Capital Stock and Desired Capital Stock 129
5.5 Estimation of Present Value of a Capital Asset 129
5.6 *MEC* and *MEI* 130
Key Terms and Concepts 133
Exercises 134

6. Determination of Income in Two, Three and Four Sector Models in Goods Market 137

Introduction 137
6.1 Determination of Equilibrium Level of Income in a Two Sector Economy 138
6.1.1 Aggregate Demand (*AD*) Curve 138
6.1.2 Aggregate Supply (*AS*) Curve 140
6.1.3 Determination of Equilibrium Level of Income 140
6.2 Investment Multiplier and Income Generation 143
6.3 Static and Dynamic Multipliers 146
6.4 Paradox of Thrift 148
6.5 Accelerator Principle and Leverage Effect 149
6.5.1 Multiplier–Accelerator Interaction: The Leverage Effect 150

6.6 Limitations of the Multiplier-Process ... 151
6.6.1 Conditions Necessary for Working of the Multiplier ... 152
6.6.2 Leakages from Multiplier ... 152
6.6.3 Reasons for Failure of the Multiplier in the Underdeveloped Countries ... 153
6.7 Determination of Equilibrium Income in an Economy with Three Sectors ... 154
6.7.1 When Taxation is Autonomous ... 155
6.7.2 When Taxation is Progressive/Degressive ... 159
6.7.3 Balanced Budget Multiplier ... 161
6.8 Determination of Equilibrium Level of Income in an Economy with Four Sectors ... 163
6.8.1 When Taxation and Imports are Autonomous ... 163
6.8.2 When neither Import nor Taxation is Autonomous ... 165
Key Terms and Concepts ... 167
Exercises ... 170

7. Money, its Functions, and Money Market Equilibrium ... 175
Introduction ... 175
7.1 Barter and its Drawbacks ... 175
7.1.1 Forms of Money through its Stages of Evolution ... 176
7.2 Definitions and Functions of Money ... 180
7.2.1 Definitions ... 180
7.2.2 Functions of Money ... 181
7.3 Supply of Money ... 184
7.3.1 RBI's Concept of Money Supply ... 184
7.3.2 *H*-Theory of Money Supply ... 186
7.4 Demand for Money ... 189
7.4.1 Classical Approach to Demand for Money ... 189
7.4.2 Keynesian Approach to the Demand for Money ... 190
7.5 Money Market Equilibrium ... 197
7.5.1 Static Equilibrium of Money Market [Figure 7.8(b)] ... 197
7.5.2 Dynamic Equilibrium of Money Market [Figure 7.9 and 7.10] ... 198
7.6 Applications and Implications of *LM*-Curves ... 201
7.6.1 *LM*-curve and Changes in Money Supply (Fixed Price Model, Figure 7.12) ... 201
7.6.2 *LM*-curve and Changes in Money Supply (Variable Price Model, Figure 7.13) ... 203
Key Terms and Concepts ... 204
Exercises ... 205

8. Goods Market Equilibrium ... 208
Introduction ... 208
8.1 Goods Market Equilibrium—The *IS*-Curve ... 209
8.1.1 Algebraic Method of its Derivation ... 209
8.1.2 Four Quadrant Method of its Derivation ... 212
8.1.3 Two Quadrant Method of its Deriving (Figure 8.4) ... 212

8.2 Applications and Implications of *IS*-Curves 213
- 8.2.1 *IS*-curves Undergo a Parallel Shift upwards to Right when Autonomous Investment Increases (Figure 8.5) 213
- 8.2.2 *IS*-curves Undergo a Parallel Shift upwards to Right when Tax Financed Government Expenditures Increase (Figure 8.6) 213

Key Terms and Concepts 215
Exercises 216

9. Simultaneous Equilibrium of Goods Market and Money Market (General Equilibrium) 217

Introduction 217
9.1 Equilibrium through *IS-LM* Framework 218
9.2 *IS-LM* Equilibrium under Fiscal and Monetary Influences 221
9.3 Tracing Path from Disequilibrium to Equilibrium in *IS-LM* Framework [Figure 9.3] 223
9.4 Efficacy of Monetary and Fiscal Policies through *IS-LM* Framework 224
9.5 Assorted Implications and Applications 225
- 9.5.1 Derivation of Aggregate Demand under Fixed Prices 225
- 9.5.2 Effect on Aggregate Demand (*AD*) through *IS-LM* Framework under Variable Prices 229
- 9.5.3 Downward Wage-price Flexibility and the Classical Full Employment Equilibrium through *IS-LM* Framework (Figure 9.12) 231
- 9.5.4 Downward Wage-price Flexibility and Less than Full Equilibrium in Keynesian Model through *IS-LM* Tools (Figure 9.13) 233
- 9.5.5 Keynesian Reasoning for Unattainability of Classical Full Employment through *IS-LM* Tools even with downward Wage-price Flexibility 234
- 9.5.6 Wage Price Flexibility and Pigou Effect 236

9.6 Suggested Remedies for the Problem of Unemployment 238

Key Terms and Concepts 239
Exercises 241

UNIT-4
ECONOMIC POLICIES

10. Monetary Policy 245

Introduction 245
10.1 Objectives of Monetary Policy 245
10.2 Instruments of Monetary Policy 248
- 10.2.1 Quantitative Methods 249
- 10.2.2 Qualitative Methods 251

10.3 Functions of the Monetary Institutions 253
- 10.3.1 Functions of the Central Bank 253

10.3.2 Functions of a Commercial Bank 254
10.3.3 Balance Sheet of a Commercial Bank 258
10.4 Commercial Banks—Creation and Control of Credit 259
10.4.1 Process of Credit Creation by Commercial Banks 259
10.4.2 Limitations to Credit Creation by Commercial Banks 261
10.5 Privatization and Modernization of Indian Banking 262

Key Terms and Concepts 263
Exercises 264

11. Fiscal Policy 266

Introduction: Meaning and Evolution of Fiscal Policy 266
11.1 Objectives of Fiscal Policy 267
11.2 Instruments of Fiscal Policy 268
11.3 Government Budget and its Terminilogy 270
11.3.1 Revenue Budget 270
11.3.2 Capital Budget 271
11.3.3 Overall Budget 271
11.3.4 Concept of Budget Surplus 272
11.3.5 Types of Deficits 273
11.4 Assorted Consequences of Direct and Indirect Taxes 275
11.4.1 Effect of Taxes and Subsidies on (GDP), Employment and Prices 275
11.4.2 Direct Tax and Laffer's Curve 277
11.4.3 Principle of Maximum Social Advantage in Taxation 278

Key Terms and Concepts 280
Exercises 281
Case Study 283

12. Foreign Trade Policy 284

Introduction 284
12.1 Foreign Exchange Rates 285
12.1.1 Nominal Exchange Rates 285
12.1.2 Real Exchange Rates 285
12.2. Strength of a Country's Currency in Relation to the Currencies of its Trading Partners 290
12.3 Balance of Trade and Balance of Payments 293
12.4 Disequilibrium in BOP—Internal and External Imbalances 296
12.4.1 The Mundell-Fleming-Model—Perfect Capital Mobility under Fixed Exchange Rates 296
12.4.2 Mundell-Fleming Model—Perfect Capital Mobility under Flexible Exchange Rates 299
12.5 Trilemma and its Impossibility 301
12.6 Concluding Note 303

Key Terms and Concepts 304
Exercises 306
Case Study 308

UNIT-5
MONEY-EROSION IN ITS VALUE: INFLATION

13. Inflation: Meaning, Theories, Causes and Effects 313

Introduction: Meaning of Inflation..................313
13.1 Definitions of Inflation 313
13.2 Theories of Inflation 314
13.2.1 Quantity Theory of Value of Money Theory..................314
13.2.2 Cost-Push and Demand-Pull Theories 317
13.3 Inflation: Terminologies 322
13.4 Phillips Curve and Inflation..................324
13.5 Measures of Inflation 329
13.6 Effects of Inflation 330
13.6.1 Non-Economic Effects of Inflation 330
13.6.2 Economic Effects of Inflation 330
13.7 Control of Inflation 332
Key Terms and Concepts..................334
Exercises..................336

UNIT-6
GROWTH AND DEVELOPMENT

14. Economic Growth and Development 341

Introduction..................341
14.1 Need for Economic Growth..................342
14.2 Source of Economic Growth 344
14.2.1 Technology and Resources (A) 345
14.2.2 Labour (L)..................345
14.2.3 Capital (K) 346
14.3 Theories of Growth..................349
14.3.1 Harrod-Domar Theory of Growth 349
14.3.2 Neoclassical Theories of Growth—Solow's per capita Growth theory and Lewis Structural Change Theory of Growth..................351
14.3.3 Rostow's Theory of Growth..................355
14.3.4 International Dependence Theory 356
14.3.5 Indian Growth Models: Mahalanobis's Model of Growth and Vakil and Brahmananda Model of Wage Goods..................357
14.4 Economic Development and its Requisites..................357
14.4.1 Measurement of Development..................358
Key Terms and Concepts..................360
Exercises..................361

***Index* 363**

Preface

This book is an attempt to provide a textbook on Macroeconomics to the students pursuing undergraduate, postgraduate and management courses in various universities and management institutions.

Interactions with faculties as also with students reveal that most of us lack clarity of basics of the subject. Contemporary literature takes directly to macroeconomic policies and their terminology a vast majority has no idea of. A number of foreign works on the subject appear no better than class-notes of a student who in his/her bid to miss out no part of the lecture ends up missing quite a bit of the basics. Such works make no sense and fail miserably in making any point. It is not that there are no books that lift the matter from its ground level to the level of its contemporary uses and applications but the ones that exist have gone to such depths that no part of it can be understood without going through the concepts from the very beginning. A reader lacks time and patience to go through the multitude every time in a bid to refer only to a particular aspect of a topic. No doubt, such works are too classic to be practical.

Authors may succeed in proving their intellect as also their command over the discipline but what use is it if they remain the only ones in the know of the things. There is nothing wrong with brief and concise expressions delivered in a piece-meal manner but that requires a sound base possessed by the readers and audiences. Economics is not a discipline woven around the jargon of vocabulary but it is an art of laying the complications of economic affairs bare so that students of economics as also the general public may not be confused by the vested interest while deciding in favour of those who can best represent and serve their interests. The case with general public is perhaps even worse. They know nothing about economic policies their political leaders lure them with. The result is that economic future of a country is often decided by those majorities who know nothing about them. No wonder economic evils take their roots deep instead of getting uprooted.

Textbooks must therefore focus on clarity of concepts before building the discipline over it.

The book in your hands intends to do just that. Clarity of key terms and concepts forms the foundation of this work. Superstructure follows thereafter in simple language. Illustrative case-lets, wherever necessary, are added to drive them home.

It is a pity to see youngsters cramming up definitions and the formulae in a parrot fashion to meet the requirement of the examination.

Apart from what has been said above, care has been taken to establish a scientific link among topics. The reader will find such links in abundance while connecting the topics of his/her prescribed syllabi. The subject matter of this text, therefore, is scientifically organized with utmost care to link the topics to provide the reader a smooth and interesting sailing through the text. To maintain the links, many additional topics have been included, besides covering the syllabus.

A list of 'Key Terms and Concepts' at the end of each chapter is provided for ready reference to them in the chapter they have gone through and can bear them in mind for a quick recall. The list follows Exercises with hints and solutions wherever necessary.

The author is deeply indebted to the students and the teaching fraternities in the university who have gone through the texts on microeconomics for honours and postgraduate students of the university and have prompted the author to undertake one on macroeconomics as well. Well friends, here is what you asked for. I hope it will meet your expectations. Subsequent suggestions from them are highly solicited.

—S.P.S. Chauhan

UNIT-1

INTRODUCTION

Chapter 1: Introduction to Macroeconomics

Chapter 1

Introduction to Macroeconomics

INTRODUCTION

'Economics is a science that studies human behavior as a relationship between ends and scarce resources that have alternative uses' (Robbins).

Ends refer to objectives humans desire to achieve. For an individual who intends to buy a car priced at ₹ 6 lakh, the end is the amount of money needed for the purpose. Resources refer to income or sources of income possessed by the individual. For an individual who possesses a sum of ₹ 4 lakh, his or her resource is ₹ 4 lakhs. The gap between the ends and resources, called the ***resource gap***, is ₹ 2 lakh. The individual in question needs to plug this gap in order to buy the desired product. The problem of raising a sum of ₹ 2 lakh to fill the gap is called an ***economic problem*** and the activities undertaken for the purpose, as ***economic activities.*** Such activities may involve raising of income through production of goods and/or services. This, however, poses a few further problems. In addition to 'what', 'how' and 'for whom' to produce, the individual may have to face the problem of inefficiency in production and distribution. All these problems faced at the individual level, are called the ***micro problems.*** Solutions to the four problems channelize through the *theory of price, theory of production, theory of distribution* and *the welfare economics* which, taken together, provide the subject matter of ***microeconomics***.

Just as the individuals face these economic problems at the individual level, groups of individuals or of individual firms, as also the nation–states, face them at the group level perhaps on a much larger scale. A State requires funds to provide infrastructure, to maintain law and order, to maintain defence forces for security, to provide education and health services to the people, to generate and supply power and to provide a host of other basic amenities for the sake of common cause. Over and above these services, the State has also to act as a producer of a number of goods. This it has mainly to protect the common interest of the common people.

Expenditure incurred by the State on such activities is called ***public expenditure* or *government spending.*** The main source of income of the State is taxation. State taxes the rich to raise income called ***public revenue,*** which it uses to finance public expenditure. Quite often, public revenue falls short of planned expenditure. The gap between the two, analogous to the resource gap of individuals or individual firms, is called the ***deficit or budget deficit*** by governments that draw statements of income and expenditure every year. The only point of difference is that individuals and individual firms can resort to cutting expenditures to the size of income while the governments cannot unless they are prepared to sacrifice some of its social objectives. The governments, therefore, have to raise their income to the size of expenditures planned. Their process of doing this is called ***deficit financing.*** It creates the same sort of economic problems for the State as those faced by the individuals or individual firms.

Thus, problems such as 'what', 'how' and 'for whom' to produce are faced by the state too in its role as a producer of goods and services. It is a different matter that welfare states resort to the ***principle of maximum social advantage***[1] while capitalist states resort to the ***price mechanism*** to solve these problems. In addition, government of a State faces a few other problems too. They are the ***'problem of unemployment'***, ***'problem of growth and development'*** and ***'problem of inflation'***. As a producer, the government also has to face ***problem of inefficiency'*** as well. All these problems are also the problems of several units or sectors lumped together. They are, therefore, also referred to as the ***aggregative problems*** or the ***macro problems***. The reader is advised to refer to author's *Microeconomics*[2] for economic problems and their classification into the broad heads of micro and macro problems.

Solutions to these constitute the subject matter of the micro and macroeconomics respectively. All the economic problems of the nation or of the lumped units (such as industry) fall within the purview of the macroeconomics while all the economic problems of the individuals or of individual firms fall within the purview of the *microeconomics*.

The terms microeconomics and ***macroeconomics***[3] were coined and used by a Norwegian economist, Ragnar Frisch, in 1933. The prefixes *micro* and *macro* meaning *small* and *large* respectively have been derived from Greek language.

However, little attempt was made to analyze the working of the economic system as a whole until the publication of the *General Theory of Employment, Interest and Money* of Prof. John Maynard Keynes in 1936.

1.1 MEANING AND SCOPE OF MACROECONOMICS

According to Kenneth E. Boulding[4], "Macroeconomics is the study of the nature, relationships and behavior of aggregates of economic quantities...".

According to P.A. Samuelson[5], "Macroeconomics is the study of the behavior of the economy as a whole. It examines the overall level of Nation's output, employment, prices and foreign trade."

The definitions given above and a few other similar definitions capture the core of macroeconomics but they do not address to its subject matter. As stated above in the introductory paragraph, *macroeconomics covers a wide range of economic activities and related theories in respect of the lumped or the aggregated units or of the economy as a whole, as to*

(a) How they generate and spend income through production of goods and services,
(b) How human or non-human resources are employed,
(c) How supply and demand of money influence the general price level,
(d) How and what policies regarding production, income, expenditure be formulated for growth and development, and
(e) How and what policies regarding foreign trade be formulated to serve the interest of people at large.

[1] The principle of maximum social advantage refers to the point of intersection of marginal social benefit (MSB) and marginal social sacrifice (MSS). With every rupee of public expenditure incurred by government, the former diminishes while the latter, rises. It is at the point of intersection of the two that the social benefit is maximized.

[2] Chauhan, S.P.S, *Microeconomics, An Advanced Treatise,* Third Edition, (PHI Learning) p. 12.

[3] The nomenclature was coined and used by Ragnar Frisch in his paper 'Propagation Problems and Impulse Problems in Dynamic Economics' in 'Economic Essays in Honour of Gustav Cassel' (London, 1933).

[4] Kenneth E. Boulding, *A Reconstruction of Economics*, John Wiley & Sons, Inc., NY, and Chapman & Hall, London, 1950, p.171.

[5] Paul A. Samuelson, *Economics*, McGraw-Hill, 1989, p.76.

It is difficult to cover the scope of macroeconomics in any single definition. Let us develop another one, a little more informative yet as precise as those of Boulding and Samuelson:

It is a study of national output, income, expenditure, employment, growth and development, demand and supply of money and general price level as also of the nation's foreign trade.

In a much simpler way, *macroeconomics is a study of economic problems of a nation as a whole with a view to analyze ways and means to solve them.*

The definition may not specify the range of the subject matter but it sure points out its domain. It lays down a criterion to list the areas that may or may not fall within its purview.

1.2 METHODOLOGY OF MACROECONOMICS

Macroeconomics deals with great averages and aggregates of the system rather than with particular units in it. Macroeconomics splits up the economy into *big lumps* for the purpose of its study. This, sometimes, is referred to as the *lumping method* involving the analysis of ***general equilibrium***.

Analysis of the product market for determination of equilibrium price and quantity of a product is partial equilibrium analysis based on *ceteris paribus* assumption. It assumes that the conditions of production of the goods and those of employment of the factors of production remain unchanged. Such analysis is microeconomic analysis as it splits one part of the system away from it for the purpose of its intensive or microscopic study under ceteris paribus, meaning every thing else remains unchanged.

As against this, analysis of the system as a whole from the view point of analyzing the likely influences on the equilibrium price and quantity when the production conditions as also those of employment of factors do not remain unchanged any longer. It studies simultaneous equilibria of all the markets including the factor market, the product market and money market. A change in any of these disturbs the rest. For instance, a decrease in supply of factors of production is likely to increase the product price through consequential increase in factor prices followed by that in production costs and a resulting fall in the volume of output produced. Such analysis is macroscopic[1] and hence falls within the purview of macroeconomics.

Microscopic study of an individual or an individual firm followed by generalization of the observations made to reach conclusions about aggregates of such entities or the system as a whole is known as the ***inductive method.*** This is one way of macro-study. The other way is the study of the aggregates without studying its constitute units. To cross check its validity one may deduce conclusions about constituent units. Such deductions comprise ***deductive methods***. Inductive and deductive approaches supplement each other in revealing the truth about aggregates and individuals.

Macroeconomic and microeconomic studies employing these approaches suffer from the limitations these approaches.

1.3 LIMITATIONS OF MACROECONOMIC ANALYSIS

Macroeconomic analysis has been gaining strength ever since the publication of J. M. Keynes' *General Theory of Employment, Interest and Money.* Inductive method has posed the danger of excessive generalization of individual experiences to the system as a whole. Such pitfalls need to be avoided if macroeconomics is to serve as a handmaid of public policy. Let us outline such pitfalls as the limitations of macroeconomic analysis:

[1] The term used by Prof. Dobb, Maurice, *Political Economy and Capitalism.*

1. **Excessive Generalization:** As hinted above, generalization of individual observation to the system as a whole may lead to erratic inferences about the system as a whole. For instance, losses incurred by one firm in the industry do not necessarily imply losses incurring to all of them. Likewise, hospitality shown by one individual does not imply that each and every individual will show the same gesture.
2. **Obsession of Aggregative Approaches:** Excessive thinking in terms of lumping the individual units together may lead to erratic inferences. Individual units possess individualistic traits. They need not be homogeneous in character. One can't add up two apples and three oranges to make any meaningful aggregate.
3. **Fallacy of Deductive Inferences:** Inferences deduced about individual units from the aggregative tendency may not always be true in respect of individual units. For instance, a general rise in prices may not affect all the sections of the community in the same manner and to the same extent. Consumers suffer from rising prices while producers benefit from it.
4. **Inconsistency between Overall and Individual Changes:** A hike in prices of industrial output and a fall in prices of the agricultural products may offset each other to lead to no rise in the general price level. On the basis of stability of the general price level, one who believes that no policy change is called for in the circumstances would certainly jeopardize the cultivators' interests.
5. **Problems of Measurement of Aggregates:** In many cases, measurement of aggregates involves serious problems. You will learn more about such problems in subsequent chapters.

To conclude, macroeconomic analysis, by itself, may not provide a true picture of the economy. It may appear like the top surface of an ocean which appears calm and unruffled from above but harbours quite a few storms underneath it. To locate the trouble spots, it is microeconomic analysis that is called for.

1.4. DIFFERENCE BETWEEN MICRO AND MACROECONOMICS

It is time to summarize the main points of difference between the two branches of economics.

Microeconomics	*Macroeconomics*
1. **Meaning:** Microeconomics may be defined as that branch of economics, which studies the economic behavior of the individual unit, may be a particular household or a particular firm. It is a study of one particular unit rather than of all the units combined together. For example, study of income and expenditure of an individual person or of an individual firm is microeconomic study. Microeconomics, thus, studies the behavior of micro-variables.	1. **Meaning:** Macroeconomics may be defined as that branch of economics, which studies the behavior of not one particular unit, but of all the units taken together. It is a study in aggregates and is often referred to as aggregative economics. It is the study of the economic system as a whole. For example, study of overall production, overall saving, overall consumption and overall investment in the economy is macroeconomic study. It, thus, studies macro-variables.
2. **Methodology:** Microeconomics splits up the entire economy into smaller parts for the purpose of intensive study. This, sometimes, is referred to as the ***Slicing Method*** which forms the ***Partial equilibrium*** analysis based on the *assumption of Ceteris Paribus* (other things remaining unchanged).	2. **Methodology:** Macroeconomics deals with great averages and aggregates of the system rather than with particular units in it. It lumps up the individual units together into *big lumps* for the purpose of study. This is often referred to as the ***Lumping Method*** involving the analysis of ***general equilibrium***.

(Contd.)

Microeconomics	*Macroeconomics*
3. Domain: Microeconomics covers the following: (a) *Theory of Product Pricing*, with its constituents of consumer's behavior and the theory of production and costs. (b) *The Theory of Factor Pricing* with constituents of the theories of wages, rent, interest, and profits. (c) *Theory of Economic Welfare.*	**3. Domain:** Macroeconomics covers the following: (a) *Theory of Income, Output, and Employment* with its constituents of the theory of consumption function, the theory of investment function and the theory of business cycles. (b) *The Theory of Prices* with its constituents of the theories of ***inflation, deflation*** and ***reflation.*** (c) *Theory of Growth* with emphasis on long-term growth of income, employment and output. (d) *Macro Theory of Distribution,* dealing with the relative shares of wages and profits in the total national income.
4. Limitations: Although microeconomic analysis is a very useful component of economics, yet, it has the following limitations: (a) It is true only in case of individual units and may not be true in case of aggregates. Microeconomic observations, thus, cannot be applied to the economy as a whole. For example, saving is a virtue for an individual but the same is not true for the community as a whole. (b) Microeconomic analysis is based on certain assumptions such as the assumption of *ceteris paribus,* and, that of full employment in the economy. In reality, neither of them exists.	**4. Limitations:** Although Macroeconomics is gaining strength, yet there are certain pitfalls that need to be avoided in the interest of public policy. Some of them are as under: (a) Excessive generalization of the individual experience to the system as a whole. (b) Excessive obsession of lumping the sectors together despite the fact that they are not of homogeneous character. For instance, a general rise in prices, may not affect the prices in the same measure in the constituent sectors. (c) The general tendency prevalent in the economy may not get transmitted in equal or the same measure in constituent sectors . (d) The study of the aggregates may reflect stagnation or saturation necessitating a change in economic policy while inter-sectoral comparisons reveal positive symptoms of economic development. For instance, it may appear that national income has been stagnant while inequalities of income distribution have significantly declined. The fact, however, signals economic development
5. Pioneers of Microeconomics: Dr. Alfred Marshall's *magnum opus, "Principles of Economics",* published in 1890 is considered as a leading work of Microeconomics.	**5. Pioneers of Macroeconomics:** John Maynard Keynes' famous work *"General Theory of Employment, Interest and Money,"* published in 1936 is a leading example of Macroeconomics.

1.5 COMPLEMENTARITY OF THE TWO APPROACHES

Micro and macro approaches to economic analysis may appear competitive at the outset but in reality they are complementary to each other. One is of little consequence without the other. Macro observations are observations of individual units lumped together while micro observations are observations about individual unit sliced away from the whole lot. By analogy, while micro study is study of one part of a human body, macro study is the study of the human body as a whole. Study of a human hand is micro study which is not complete without the study of the human body as a whole. If a human hand trembles and is wrinkled, it must belong to an old individual but its converse need not be true. The hand of an old individual may or may not tremble and it may or may not be wrinkled. The use of the word 'may' is deliberate. Hands of every old man do not tremble nor do they have wrinkles for all of them. Whatever is true of one, need not be true for all or whatever is true of all, need not be true for one. Drawing inferences about the lumped lot on the basis an individual observation is known as *generalization* or induction in common man's language and *inductive method* in the language of economics. In like manner, drawing inferences about an individual unit from the observation made about a big lump is known as ***deduction*** in common man's language or *deductive method* in economic analysis.

Generalization of individual traits to learn the traits of the community as a whole could be highly misleading. One needs to study the community as an aggregate to study its traits. This establishes the importance of macro analysis.

Prof. Boulding has driven the point home by citing an apt simile. A forest, as he points out, though an aggregation of trees, yet, it does not exhibit the characteristics and behavior patterns of individual trees. In other words, it would be untrue to say that the behavior patterns of the forest can be obtained by studying the behavior patterns of individual trees. Such an attempt would be highly misleading because an individual tree germinates, grows and decays, while a forest goes on forever with exactly the same composition in respect of the character of the trees that compose it. An individual tree cannot affect the climate of the surroundings in which it grows, but a forest can and it also does.

The two disciplines are complementary rather than competitive in most of the cases of economic analysis. They are so interdependent that neither approach is complete without the other. In other words, we cannot attain complete understanding of the functioning of an economic system unless we integrate the two in a judicious manner. For instance, sales realized by a firm are dependent not only on the price of the product, but more so, on the total purchasing power possessed by the community. In like manner, price of a product depends not only on its demand but also on the costs of production as well as on the prices of other products.

In simple language, the statement that "Indians are very hospitable people" does not imply that a particular Indian, Mr. X, is essentially hospitable. In like manner, the statement that "Mr. Y, an Indian, is very hospitable" does not imply that all Indians are equally hospitable. To be able to comment on the hospitality of the Indians, what one needs is to conduct a survey of a cross-section of Indians and if a majority of them be found hospitable, make a statement that Indians, in general, are hospitable.

KEY TERMS AND CONCEPTS

Economics: It is a science, which studies human behavior as a relationship between ends and scarce resources that have alternative uses. (Robbins).

Economic Problem: It is a problem caused by scarcity of resources in the face of desired ends.

Economic Activity: Activities directed at filling the gap between scarce resource and desired ends. Economic activities must possess the legal and social sanction.

Problem of Unemployment: A situation in which available resources—human or non-human—are not being fully utilized despite the efforts made by the State for the same.

Problem of Inefficiency: A situation in which available resources—human or non-human—are not being utilized to their full productive capacity.

Problem of Growth: A situation in which real income of the country fails to increase at the desired rate year after year.

Problem of Inflation: A situation in which prices of goods and services go on increasing year after year despite the State efforts to contain them. Prices shoot up when active stock of money exceeds the national output of goods and services or when too much money chases too few goods and services.

Inflation and Deflation: Each refers to a state of disequilibrium between the active stock of money and the stock of goods and services available in the nation. When active stock of money exceeds the stock of goods and services in the nation, the outcome is *inflation* and when active stock of money falls short of the stock of goods and services, the outcome is *deflation.*

Reflation: It refers to the inflation of a financial system to restore its previous condition before deflation. The term is coined for the process of refilling the economy with money in the post deflation period to restore the situation that existed prior to the period of deflation.

Slicing Method: It refers to splitting a big lump into individual units for the purpose of analysis of the lump unit by unit. The term has reference to splitting of the economy into smaller individual units with a view to study their working individually.

Lumping Method: It refers to combining individual units into a big lump to study the working of all of them taken together as a single joint unit.

Partial Equilibrium: It refers to the state of balance of opposing forces in one part of a large unit comprising of several such parts inter-linked together. The term has reference to the state of equilibrium in one selected part of a large market structure. For instance, goods market comprises of consumers, producers, and factors of production. All the three are interdependent. The producers hire factors of production, such as labour, from the *factor market* in which demand and supply of factors of production determine the price and the quantity of the factors hired. They then produce that quantity of goods/services that is possible for them to produce under given cost structure, technology and factor productivity. Such production is referred to as the *producers' equilibrium.* Producers sell these products to consumers in the market called the *product market*, the equilibrium of which is governed by the forces of demand and supply of the products. Consumers buy that quantity of a product, which is possible for them under the given disposable income, prices of the product itself and those of the related products. The goods market thus involves at least four equilibria—product market equilibrium, factor market equilibrium, producers' equilibrium and consumers' equilibrium. All the four are highly interdependent. A disturbance in any one of them is transmitted into the rest and disturbs them all. Analysis of changes in any one of them, assuming that the rest of them to remain unaffected by the change, is called the partial equilibrium analysis.

General Equilibrium: The analysis of all of them taken together in respect of how each is affected by a given change in anyone of them is called the general equilibrium analysis.

Inductive Methods: Drawing inferences about a large lump on the basis of the observations made about a single unit in it, is termed as the inductive method. For instance, the inference that the entire electronic industry is making huge profits on the basis of the observation of such profits made by one electronic firm in it is an inference reached through the inductive method or generalization.

Deductive Method: Drawing inferences about a particular unit on the basis of the observations made about a large lump, is referred to as the deductive method. For instance, the process of deducing that each firm in the electronic industry is making huge profits on the basis of the observation that the electronic industry as a whole is making huge profits is referred to as the deductive method.

Scope of Macroeconomics: Macroeconomics covers all the economic problems of a nation as a whole with a view to analyse ways and means to solve them. It thus covers the theories of:

- Determination of national income, output and expenditure.
- Determination of employment.
- International trade.
- Demand and supply of money and their influence on general price level.
- Growth and development.

Limitations of Macroeconomics: Macroeconomics suffers from the following limitations:

- Excessive generalization.
- Obsession of aggregative approach.
- Fallacy of deductive inferences.
- Inconsistency between overall and individual changes.
- Problem of measurement of aggregates.

Microeconomics: Microeconomics may be defined, as that branch of economics, which studies the economic behavior of the individual unit, may be a particular household or a particular firm. It is a study of one particular unit rather than of all the units combined together. For example, study of income and expenditure of an individual person or of an individual firm is microeconomic study. Microeconomics, thus, studies the behavior of micro-variables.

Macroeconomics: Macroeconomics may be defined, as that branch of economics, which studies the behavior of not one particular unit, but of all the units taken together. It is a study in aggregates and is often referred to as *aggregative economics.* It is the study of the economic system as a whole For example; study of overall production, overall saving, overall consumption and overall investment in the economy is macroeconomic study. It is thus study of macro-variables.

Micro and Macro Branches of Economics are Complementary rather than Competitive: Proper analysis of the economy requires micro as well as macro approaches of economics. One is incomplete without the other. In simple language, the statement that "Indians are very hospitable people" does not imply that a particular Indian, Mr. X, is essentially hospitable. In like manner, the statement that "Mr. Y, an Indian, is very hospitable" does not imply that all Indians are equally hospitable. To be able to comment on the hospitality of the Indians, what one needs is to conduct a survey of a cross-section of Indians and if a majority of them be found hospitable, make a statement that Indians, in general, are hospitable.

EXERCISES

A. Short Answer Questions

Distinguish between

1. Microeconomics and macroeconomics.
2. Deductive and inductive methods.
3. Partial equilibrium and general equilibrium.
4. Lumping method and slicing method.
5. Resource gap and budgetary deficit.
6. Economic problems and economic activities.
7. Problem of inefficiency and problem of unemployment.
8. Inflation, deflation and reflation.

B. Long Answer Questions

9. Outline the main limitations of macroeconomic analysis.
10. 'Science is a systematic study involving cause and effect relationships and precision of measurement' How can you justify economics as a science on the basis of these attributes?
11. 'Micro-and-macro-analyses are complementary rather than competitive, Discuss with suitable examples.
12. How are partial and general equilibria interrelated? Give examples to in support of your answer.
13. Would you say that growth and development are one and the same thing? Give arguments in support of your contention.
14. Mention the hazards of excessive generalization and deduction.

UNIT-2

NATIONAL INCOME AND RELATED AGGREGATES

(Basic Concepts and Measurement)

Chapter 2: National Income and Related Aggregates—
Basic Concepts and Measurement

Chapter 2

National Income and Related Aggregates
Basic Concepts and Measurement

INTRODUCTION—THE CONCEPT OF INCOME

The term *income,* in common parlance, refers to the receipts of value in terms of money which the recipient feels free to spend as and when he likes. It implies money value that comes in. That way, even bribes and extortions must be treated as incomes but they are not. It is for this reason that the term *income* needs an appropriate definition.

Income*, in its true connotations, refers to those receipts, cash or kind, that accrue to an individual in exchange for some product, whether tangible like a commodity or intangible like a service, provided such exchange does not violate the prevailing legal and social norms.*

The receipts of a cultivator in exchange for the food-grains (tangible product) and those of a mason in exchange for his services (intangible product) both qualify as incomes to the recipients as neither of them is made in violation of the law of the land or of the social norms. As against this, receipts of value by smugglers in exchange for contraband goods and those by antisocial elements under motivation from an unfriendly country for creating social disharmony fail to qualify as incomes. Likewise bribes received or extorted by corrupt officials fail to pass as their incomes on the grounds that the practice is illegal and hence punishable under law. Even pocket money received by a child from his/her parents, fails to qualify as income on the grounds that the recipient is not expected to forego any value in exchange. As against this, a son washing his father's car every morning for money, usually paid to a menial worker for this kind of service by all means, qualifies as the worker's income. Incomes are, thus, *earned receipts of value* provided they are in the line with the law of the land and the social norms. *All receipts of value that possess the attribute of a quid pro quo*[1] *as also that of a legal and social sanction pass as incomes of the recipients.* Pocket money, scholarships and old-age pensions[2] can't qualify as incomes of the recipients on the grounds that no *quid pro quo* is associated with them. As a result, they are termed as unilateral transfers.

[1] *Quid pro quo means* 'something given in return for something received'.

[2] Old-age pensions, here, refer to ex gratia payments made without any quid-pro-quo. The old citizens are paid by way of charity so that they can afford their subsistence expenses when they are not able to earn through work. Such payments don't qualify as income.

As against such payments, post-retirement pensions of the government employees are treated as their incomes and are subjected to taxation. Such pensions do have a quid-pro-quo though not in simultaneity with the payments but advanced during their service span as services rendered under the contract. Employer contributes 12.5% of the employee's basic salary every month to raise the pension fund. It is thus a deferred income of employees for their services and is duly subjected to income tax whenever received. Employees too are required to contribute a minimum of 12.5% of their basic salary but the same is refunded to them at the time of their retirement. Even private organizations raise such funds, called employees provident fund (EPF), which they pay to the employees usually as a lump-sum at the time of employee's quitting the job or at the time of retirement from it. Except ex gratia old age pensions all other payments are treated as incomes and subjected to taxation.

Understanding the concept of income is crucial for understanding national income. The latter can be regarded as the sum total of the incomes of all the individuals in the nation.

2.1 NATIONAL INCOME—MEANING AND MEASUREMENT

National Income (*NI*) may be defined as the sum total of incomes accruing to the normal residents in the nation. By the expression ***normal residents***, we imply individuals whose economic interest is vested in the country in which they reside. All the enterprises, operating in the country, all the nationals and foreign nationals residing in the country for a year or more, all the nationals abroad who return in less than a year, all the nationals working in foreign institutions located in the country and all the students, scholars, patients staying abroad for education or medical treatment whether for a year or longer fall into the category of normal residents. The essential feature of a normal resident is his/her economic interest that should confine to the country of his/her residence over the period of an accounting year or a part thereof. As against a normal resident, a ***national*** is one who holds the citizenship of the country or holds the country's passport.

A normal resident may have one or more sources of income. Some of them derive income from work while others provide their income earning assets for productive activities. Income from work is known as ***compensation of employees***. Generally it comprises cash payments (salaries, wages, and social security contributions) or kind-compensations (rent free accommodation, free uniform, free medical care, free telephone facility, free furniture, and free education to workers' children, etc.) Income from letting the productive assets comprise rent (on land and building), interest (on liquid assets such as money), dividend (on financial assets such as shares and debentures) and profit (on entrepreneurial activities). Individuals who provide labour or those who provide productive assets are all known as *factors owners*, or simply, ***factors of production.*** Incomes accruing to them are known as ***factor incomes.*** Sum total of factor incomes accruing to normal residents from all types of production is thus known as national income (*NI*).

Factors of production convert basic inputs into finished product called *output.* Hence, the difference of money value of output over that of inputs must be equal to the *factor income* or ***national income (NI).*** The process of conversion of basic inputs into finished products is known as ***value addition***. The total value added at different stages of production by all the factors is also known as the ***national product*** (*NP*). It must represent money value of outputs of all the industries; but for obvious reasons, it doesn't. Outputs of a large number of industries feed several other industries as the latter's inputs. Accounting of outputs of all the industries thus leads to ***double counting*** of those which serve as inputs to other industries. This is so because money value of output of an industry comprises its value addition and the value of inputs consumed by it in the process of production.

One way of avoiding double counting is to include money value of the output of the ***industry of origin*** and the total value added to it by the subsequent industries. By the expression industry of origin we imply the industry where the product originates. Such industries don't use basic inputs. In the chain of cloth industries, farm industry is the industry of origin where raw cotton is grown. Value of the raw cotton is treated as the value addition of the farm industry as the value of its inputs is treated as negligible. Thus value of the product of the cloth industry is the sum of values added by the subsequent industries in the chain to the value addition by the industry of origin.

The other way of avoiding double counting in determination of the national product is to include money values of only those products that are meant for final consumption. Such products are called the ***final goods***. To elaborate, ready to wear garments may be treated as ***final goods*** while raw cotton and cloth, as ***intermediate goods*** which are used as inputs by the garment industry. Whichever the way, money value of the national product (*NP*) is the sum of the values added by all the industries which in turn is the value of total factor income or the national Income (*NI*).

Products are bundles of utility consumers need to satisfy their wants. They are exchanged for money in the market. Thus, expenditure incurred by the consumers on the national product (*NP*) is ***National expenditure (NE).***

In the event of absence of leakages from the circular flow of income and expenditure, we can conclude the following identity:

$$NI = NP = NE.$$

There are thus three approaches to estimate national income:

1. Income Method,
2. Product or Value Added Method, and
3. Expenditure method.

Let us discuss them in their requisite detail below.

2.1.1 Income Method

This method relates to the measurement of *incomes* paid out to the households in return for the supply of productive services and profits retained by the firms as reserves for future operations. The aggregate so obtained is called the National Income. The income accruing to the factors of production in an economy for the supply of the productive services is known as the ***Factor Income***. A sizeable part of this income, called the ***Domestic Factor Income (DFI)*** arises from domestic producers and the rest, called the ***Net Factor Income from Abroad*** (*NFI* from abroad) from foreign or non-domestic producers. The latter represents the excess of factor incomes from foreign producers *less* factor incomes to the foreign factors of production operating in the national territory. Net balance may be positive or negative depending on the relative values of the two (See Box 2.1).

BOX 2.1

National Income = Factor Income
Plus
Retained earnings of firms or Undistributed Profits

Factor Income = Domestic Factor Income
Plus
Net Factor Income from Abroad

Net Factor Income from Abroad = Factor Income from Foreign Producers abroad
Less
Factor Income to Foreign Factors at home

Factor incomes, whether from domestic sources or from foreign sources, refer to the incomes of the four factors of production. People in an economy can be classified into the following four categories for the purpose.

1. Labour—skilled or unskilled, technical or non-technical, intellectual or non-intellectual-participating in production process;
2. Capitalists—those owning and contributing capital whether financial or real to the production process;
3. Owners of land–building, contributing the same to the production process; and
4. Entrepreneurs who organize the factors for converting basic inputs into the finished products.

[*Note that an individual may belong to one or more of the above four categories.*]

Incomes accruing to *labour* are known as the salaries, wages and social security contributions. Collectively they are known as the ***compensation of employees***. The expression is used to denote all cash or kind compensations to the employees for their services along with the contributions made by the employers for the social security of the employees. The former includes salaries and wages in cash or in kind while the latter includes the employers' contributions towards the employees' provident fund, pensions, group insurance and family allowances. The kind compensations relate to free accommodation, free uniforms, free education to the school-going children of the employees, free medical care, free telephone facility, free furniture, etc. (Box 2.2 and 2.3).

BOX 2.2

Domestic Income or Domestic Factor Income (*DI* or *DFI*) = Compensation of employees
Plus
Operating Surplus
Plus
Mixed Incomes

Operating Surplus = Rent + Interest + Dividend + Undistributed Profits
Mixed Incomes = Incomes of the self-employed, such as, doctors lawyers, cricketers, musicians, actors, singers, etc.

BOX 2.3

Compensation of Employees = Salaries and wages in cash or kind
Plus
Social security contribution

Salaries or Wages in Kind = Rent-free accommodation, free uniforms, Free medical Care, free telephone facility, free furniture, free education to the school-going children of the employees, etc.

Social Security Contributions = Employers' contributions towards employees' provident fund, pensions, group insurance and family allowances

Income accruing to *capital* is ***interest,*** that accruing to *land and building* is ***rent*** and income accruing to *entrepreneurship* is ***profit.*** Collectively, they are known as ***income from property and entrepreneurship.*** Land–building and capital if provided by the producer entitle the producer to rent and interest. In such cases, they are known as ***imputed rent*** and ***imputed interest*** respectively. In like manner, that part of the profit, which is not distributed as dividends to the subscribers of the financial capital (shares, debenture, etc.), is known as the ***undistributed profit.*** The producer can use imputed rent, imputed interest, undistributed profits and the dividend accruing to himself from his share capital to operate the firm in future or to expand it. Such funds at the disposal of the producers are often termed as ***retained earnings*** or also as ***operating surplus*** (Box 2.4).

BOX 2.4

Operating Surplus (*OS*) = Income from Property + Income from Entrepreneurship
Income from Property = Rent + Interest + Royalty (if any)
Income from Entrepreneurship = Dividend + Undistributed Profits

Royalty refers to the patent rights, if any, held by the producer. He is entitled to a royalty from the firm for allowing the firm to produce the product.

Mixed Incomes refer to the incomes of the self-employed. Incomes of the lawyers, doctors, musicians, dancers, singers, actors, farmers and the like are own-account incomes and fall into the category of the mixed incomes. Such incomes accrue to these individuals for their productive capabilities and are often termed as their fees. Profits and dividends of the unincorporated enterprises also fall into this category.

Thus, the components of the Domestic Factor Income (*DFI*) can be summarized as below (Box 2.5).

BOX 2.5	
Domestic Income or Domestic Factor Income (*DI* or *DFI*) =	Compensation of Employees
	Plus
	Operating Surplus
	Plus
	Mixed Incomes

To arrive at national income, net factor income from abroad (NFI from abroad) needs to be added to the estimate of domestic income arrived in Box 2.5. Thus,

National Income (NI) = Domestic Income + NFI from abroad.

Net Factor Income from Abroad , also termed as Net Factor Income from rest of the world (NFI_{ROW}) refers to the income of the normal residents of a country for factor services rendered by them to the rest-of-the-world *less* incomes of the foreign factors for the factor services rendered by them to the domestic producers (Box 2.6). The term ***'normal resident'*** refers to a resident whose *economic interest* is vested in the country in which he/she resides at least for some time during the accounting year. All the enterprises operating in a country, all the nationals and foreign nationals residing in the country for a year or more, all the nationals abroad who return back in less than a year, all the nationals working in foreign institutions located in the country and all the scholars, students, patients staying abroad for education or for medical treatment, whether for just one year or more, fall into the category of the normal residents. The essential feature of a normal resident is his/her economic interest that should confine to the country of residence for some time in the accounting year from the view point of the national income accounting. As against the normal resident, a national is an individual who holds the citizenship of the country or holds the country's passport.

BOX 2.6	
Net Factor Income from Abroad =	income from factor services rendered by the normal residents of a country to the rest-of-the-world *less* incomes of the foreign factors operating in domestic territory
=	Net Compensation of employees from the rest-of-the-world
	Plus
	Net Income from property and entrepreneurship from rest-of-the-world
	Plus
	Net retained earnings of the resident companies abroad.

From the view-point of Domestic Income, domestic territory also needs a definition. Domestic Territory, in the current context, is the region within the political boundaries of a nation, comprising of the main land-mass and the territorial waters around it, if any, to a specified stretch. From the view-point of income, it covers the activities of the people within the domestic territory as also those of national embassies, consulates, high commissions and military establishments operating abroad along with those of the domestic owners of the aircrafts, ships, fishing vessels, floating platforms, etc. and natural gas rigs operating within the domestic territories.

National income or Net National Income at factor cost (NNI_{FC}) can thus be summarized as in the Box 2.7

BOX 2.7

Net National Income at factor cost (NNI_{FC}) = compensation of employees
+ operating surplus
+ Mixed incomes
+ net factor income from abroad

[Note that NNI_{FC} refers to national income at factor cost or at the cost of factors of production, that is, without levy of commodity taxes]

2.1.1.1 Problems with the income method of National Income

Estimation of National Income by income method poses a few problems. Some of them are listed below:

1. **Difficulties of Estimation of Mixed Incomes:** Estimation of mixed incomes poses two types of problems. *First,* the problem related to the estimation of the incomes of the self-employment. A great many professionals don't maintain proper accounts. Their word alone has to be relied for the purpose. Many times they get away with under-disclosures of incomes despite investigations conducted by the income tax authorities. *Second,* the problem related to the allocation of the mixed incomes of the owners of property. For instance, incomes accruing to the owners of the buildings, farms and financial assets are often treated as factor incomes as rent and interest while such owners are unincorporated enterprises whose incomes should be treated as the mixed-incomes. The only way-out is accounting for their expenditures to cross check the incomes declared by them.
2. **Difficulty of Estimation of the Wage Income:** Many organizations compensate their employees in such a way that a sizeable part of the compensation of employees is shown as an expenditure incurred in the course of duty. Transfer expenditure, touring expenditure and unreported cash compensation at regular intervals are a few examples. The exercise is intended to evade taxation of income by the employers and employees both.
3. **Difficulty of Estimation of the Compensation in Kind:** Compensations in kind may be estimated in two ways. *First,* at its cost to the employers, and *second,* at its cost to the employees if they were to avail the same elsewhere in open market. The two costs are widely different. At which rate should the compensation in kind be then estimated?
4. **Difficulty in Allocation of the Dividends:** While dividends to the households are treated as factor incomes, those inter-corporate, are not.
5. **Problems of Estimation of the Undistributed Profits:** Dividend disbursed to the share-holders may not match with what actually is paid to them. Records may show whole of the profit as disbursed to the share-holders leaving nothing to show as the undistributed profits while in reality it may not be so.

2.1.2 Product or the Value Added Method

This method relates to the measurement of the value of the goods and services produced in an economy at the market price. The estimate so obtained is adjusted for inter-industry sales to avoid double counting. To maintain its identity with national income, the resulting estimate is further adjusted for ***net indirect taxes*** as the term ***national income*** is commonly used for net estimates of income at factor cost (factor price). In fact, value of goods and services referred to above by output method is not only at market price but also in gross terms without any corrections for them. It is thus known as gross value of output at market price. To reach an alternative measure of national income, what we need is the net value of the national product at factory price or at what is known as the factor cost. For this the following three adjustments to the gross value of the output at market price are thus a must:

1. **Adjustment of Depreciation:** Depreciation refers to loss of value of the productive assets due to wear and tear in the process of production. It is also known as the ***consumption of fixed capital*** in production and is treated as a cost. It is, therefore, subtracted from the gross estimates so as to obtain net estimates (Box 2.8).

BOX 2.8
Net Value of the Output at Market Price = Gross Value of the Output at Market Price *Less* Depreciation or consumption of fixed capital

2. **Adjustment of Market Price:** Market Price refers to the price inclusive of net indirect tax which means ***indirect taxes** less **subsidies***. Indirect taxes refer to the commodity taxes such as the sales tax, excise duty, service tax, etc., levied by the government on some products at the time they are placed in the market for sale. Such taxes when levied raise the factory price (or factor cost) of the product to what is called the market price. In the same way, subsidy represents that part of the factory price (factor-cost) of a product which is paid to the producer by the government so that the market price of the product may fall below the factory price (factor cost). Government bears a part of the factory price of essential products so that the other-wise costlier product may be made affordable to the buyers. This, a welfare oriented government does either to protect the industry or to protect the consumers. For instance, government grants subsidy on *KHADI* products in India so that the otherwise costlier *KHADI* products may enjoy enough demand and the industry may survive. This is essential for the cause of sustaining employment of workers in the *KHADI* industry. In like manner, government subsidizes the otherwise costlier fertilizers so that cultivators may afford them. This is essential for better crop yields. Subsidies reduce the market price while indirect taxes raise it. However the two are never applicable to the same product. Some products are subsidized while others are taxed. The net income accruing to the government from these two is called the ***Net Indirect Tax (NIT),*** which represents the excess of the indirect taxes levied over the subsidies granted (See Box 2.9).

BOX 2.9
Net Indirect Tax (NIT) = Indirect tax – subsidies. Market Price = Factor cost + NIT. Gross Value of Output at market price = Gross Value of output at factor cost + NIT

3. **Adjustment of Inter-industry Sales:** Inter-industry sales refer to that part of the product or output which is sold by one producer to another for the latter's use as an input. Buyers of these inputs make the money value of these inputs (input cost) a part of the money value

of their output. While estimating national income by product method if the money value of each industry's output be included, value of that part of it which is bought as input by other industries gets included more than once leading to what is known as ***double counting*** as mentioned already. For example, a part of the cotton produced by farmers is sold to the cloth mills, which use it as an input for producing cloth. While estimating national income by product method, money value of the products of farm and cloth industries if included without appropriate adjustment, it would lead to double counting of that part of the raw cotton which is used by cloth mills as their input as also pointed out earlier. One way to avoid it is to treat inputs consumed in production as ***intermediate consumption*** and subtract the value of input from that of the output. The method is known as the ***value added method.*** The other way of avoiding double counting is to consider the money value of only those outputs which are meant for final consumption.

The former is known as the *value added method* of estimating national product and the latter, as the ***final product method*** of it.

To arrive at the national product, we need net product from abroad on the lines of net factor income from abroad. Net product from abroad is the value of product from the rest of the world (*ROW*) *less* value of the product to the rest of the world. It is the same as the net factor income from abroad (See Box 2.10).

BOX 2.10

Gross Value Added (*GVA*) = Value of the Gross output
Less
Intermediate Consumption
= Sum of the Values added by all the producers
= Sum of (Output-Input) for all the producers.

Net Value Added (*NVA*) = Gross Value Added
Less
Depreciation or consumption of fixed capital

Net Domestic Product at factor Cost (NDP_{FC}) = Net Value Added at Factor Cost (NVA_{FC})
= Gross Value Added at Factor Cost (GVA_{FC})
Less
Depreciation or consumption of fixed Capital
= Gross Value Added at Market Price (GVA_{MP})
Less
Net Indirect Taxes
Less
Depreciation or Consumption of fixed Capital

National Product (NP_{FC}) = Net Domestic Product at Factor Cost (NDP_{FC})
+ Net Factor Product from Abroad (*NFP* from Abroad)

The value of the output is estimated net of depreciation, indirect taxes and net of inter-industry sales so that it may represent the amount paid to the factors of production. In other words, the equality of domestic product to domestic income and hence that of national product to national income may be preserved to the extent that either may be used to represent the other.

Determination of Value Added by Firms: The value added by a firm can be determined by taking difference of the firm's output over its inputs as stated above. Since the same has a reference to an accounting year, some adjustments need to be made on account of stocks of the previous year and stocks in hand at the end of the current year. Stock in the beginning of the accounting year is referred to as the ***Opening Stock*** while that at the end of the current year, as the ***Closing Stock***. Closing stock *less* the opening stock represents the change in the stocks over the accounting year. The stock here has reference not only to the stock of the finished (unsold) goods but also to that of the semi-finished goods as well as that of raw-materials. Value Added by a firm is Sales *plus* ***changes in stocks*** (ΔS) *less* intermediate consumption as shown below (See Box 2.11) Let us have some illustrations of how certain values of the outputs lead to double counting and how the two methods help to rectify the same.

BOX 2.11

Changes in Stock, ΔS = Closing Stocks – Opening Stock
= [Closing Stock of Finished but unsold goods
+ Closing Stock of Semi-finished Goods
+ Closing Stock of raw-materials]
Less
[Opening Stock of Finished but unsold goods
+ Opening Stock of Semi-finished Goods
+ Opening Stock of raw-materials]
= Changes in Stock of the Finished but unsold Goods
+ Changes in Stock of the Semi-finished Goods
+ Changes in Stock of the Raw-materials

Value Added by the Firm = [Output Sold (sales) + Changes in Stocks]
– Intermediate Consumption
= [Sales + Closing Stock]
– [Intermediate Consumption + Opening Stock]

ILLUSTRATION 2.1: Suppose cotton worth ₹ 10,000 crores originates from the farm-industry. Of this, cotton worth ₹ 4,000 crores is sold to the households for filling cushions, pillows, quilts and the rest, worth ₹ 6,000, is sold to the cloth mills which use it to produce cloth worth ₹ 15,000. Of this, cloth worth ₹ 7,000 is sold to the households for its use as bed covers, curtains, etc. and the rest, worth ₹ 8,000, is sold to the ready-made garment industry which uses it as its input for the manufacture of garments. The value of the garments sold to the households is ₹ 25,000. Assuming that these are the only flows related to the garment industry, estimate the contributions made by this industry to the national product.

Solution: If we include the money values of the outputs of each of the three industries, namely, the farm-industry, the cloth mills and the ready-made-garments-industry, the value of the output would work out at ₹ 50,000 (10,000 of the farm industry + 15,000 of the cloth mills + 25,000 of the ready-made-garment-industry) A little in-depth analysis reveals that a part of the farm output, worth ₹ 6,000 that was bought by the cloth mills, has been counted thrice—once as a part of the farm produce, then as a part of the product of the cloth mills and finally as a part of the output of the ready-made-garment-industry. In like manner, another part of the value of the output of the cloth mills, worth ₹ 8,000, has been counted twice—once as a part of the cloth mills output and then as a part of the output of the ready-made-garment-industry. The total value thus stands over-stated at ₹ 50,000! Inclusion of any part of the value of any output more than once in the product method is called the ***double counting*** as mentioned above.

The error can be rectified in two ways. *First,* count the values of only those outputs which are sold to the households for final consumption (not for further production of other goods). The total volume of sales to the households is ₹ 36,000 [₹ 4000 + ₹ 7000 + ₹ 25000]. Thus by final product method, contribution of this industry is ₹ 36,000, which amounted to ₹ 50,000 due to double counting.

Employing the alternative method the, value added method, we observe that value added by industry origin is ₹ 10,000 [10000 – 0], that by cloth mills is ₹ 9000 [15000 – 6000] and that by ready-made garment-industry, ₹ 17,000 [25,000 – 8,000]. Total value added works out as ₹ 36,000 [10,000 + 9,000 + 17,000]. Both the methods lead to the same contribution to national product. Depicting it through a flow chart (Box 2.12), we see:

BOX 2.12

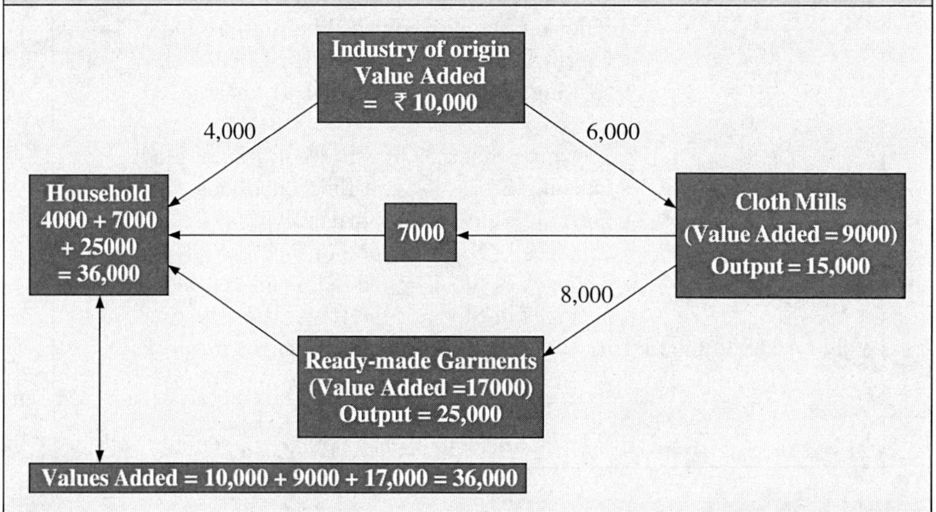

ILLUSTRATION 2.2: Data pertaining to a firm in respect of the accounting year ending 2004-05 are as given below:

Sales: 2,57,537
Closing Stock of Finished goods: 37,432
Closing Stock of Semi-finished goods: 19,476
Closing Stock of Raw-materials: 29,345
Opening Stock of Finished goods: 17,432
Opening Stock of Semi-finished goods: 9,476
Opening Stock of Raw-materials: 19,345
Expenditure on Raw materials & Intermediate Goods: 80,000
Determine the value added by the firm.

Solution: Changes in stocks of finished but unsold goods = 37,432 – 17,432
= 20,000

Changes in stock of semi-finished goods = 19,476 – 9,476
= 10,000

Changes in stock of raw-materials = 29,345 – 19,345
= 10,000

Total changes in stocks = [20,000 + 10,000 + 10,000]
= 40,000
Raw-materials and intermediate goods bought = 80,000
Value Added by the firm = Sales + changes in stocks – intermediate consumption
= 2,57,537 + 40,000 – 80,000
= 2,17,537

Alternatively:

Value of the output = sales + increase in stocks of finished and semi-finished goods
= 2,57,537 + [(37,432 – 17,432) + (19,476 – 9,476)]
= 2,87,537

Value of inputs consumed
= Opening stock of raw-materials + raw-materials bought – closing stock of raw-materials
= 19,345 + 80,000 – 29,345
= 70,000

Value Added = Value of the output – intermediate consumption
= 2,87,537 – 70,000
= 2,17,537.

Net Domestic Product at Factor Cost (NDP_{FC}) or ***Net Value Added at Factor Cost*** (NVA_{FC}) is treated as Net Domestic Income (at factor cost) and is commonly known as Domestic Income. Adding Net Factor Income from Abroad (*NFI* from Abroad) to NDP_{FC} leads to ***Net National Product at Factor Cost*** (NNP_{FC}). In like manner, adding *NFI* from Abroad to Net Domestic Income at Factor Cost (NDI_{FC}) gives **Net National Income at Factor Cost** (NNI_{FC}). In sum, it implies that the income and the value added approaches lead to the same estimate of National Income (See Box 2.13).

We have seen that value to the inputs is added by the four factors of production. The factor-incomes taken together, therefore, are equal to the Net Value Added at Factor Cost (NVA_{FC}). NVA_{FC},

BOX 2.13

Net Domestic Product at Factor Cost (NDP_{FC})
= Net Value Added at Factor Cost (NVA_{FC})
= Compensation of employees
Plus
Operating Surplus
Plus
Mixed Incomes.

Net National Product at Factor Cost (NNP_{FC})
= Net Domestic Product at Factor Cost (NDP_{FC})
Plus
Net Factor Income from Abroad (*NFI* from Abroad)
= Net Domestic Income at Factor Cost (NDI_{FC})
Plus
Net Factor Income from Abroad (*NFI* from Abroad)
= Net National Income at Factor Cost (NNI_{FC}).

Net National Product at Factor Cost (NNP_{FC}) = *NP*
Net National Income at Factor Cost (NNI_{FC}) = *NI*

can thus be estimated indirectly as the sum of the compensation of employees, operating surplus and mixed Incomes.

For the purpose of determination of the national product of an economy, it is divided into the following three major sectors:

1. Primary Sector, comprising of agriculture, forestry, mining and quarrying, fishing and animal husbandry.
2. Secondary Sector, comprising of manufacturing and water, power and gas supply.
3. Tertiary Sector, comprising of services like insurance, banking, transport, communication, real estates, public administration, etc.

A more common classification of the economy for the purpose is not to group various sectors under the broad heads, as given above. Instead, it is to divide the economy into the following fourteen sectors:

(i) Agriculture
(ii) Mining
(iii) Fishing
(iv) Construction
(v) Manufacturing
(vi) Trade
(vii) Finance
(viii) Water, gas and power supply
(ix) Ownership of dwellings and other real estates
(x) Service industry, trade and arts
(xi) Professions
(xii) Domestic Services.
(xiii) Public Administration
(xiv) Private non-profit making organizations.

National product is estimated as the sum of the net value added by each of these sectors.

2.1.2.1 Problems in estimation of National Product (NP)

The product or the output method of estimation of the national product involves the following difficulties:

1. **Difficulty of Evaluation of Products Held for Self-consumption by the Producers:** It is very difficult to find out the value of the products held by the producers for their own consumption.
2. **Difficulty of Choosing the Price:** While estimating the national product at the market price, the main difficulty arises in choice of the price. Prices of products need not be same everywhere. Factor costs vary from one place of production to another and so may be the case with indirect taxes.
3. **Difficulty of Estimation of the Depreciation:** Estimation of depreciation poses a few problems partly due to fluctuations in the capital prices and partly due to subjectivity in consumption of capital which varies from firm to firm and from use to use.
4. **Difficulty of Availability of Reliable Data:** Data available about output in unorganized sector are highly unreliable.

2.1.3 Expenditure Method

It refers to the expenditure incurred on goods and services. A part of the expenditure is incurred on the ***consumer goods*** and the rest on the ***producer's goods***. National product itself is partly meant for consumption and partly for production. Consumer goods are either ***single use consumer goods*** (like bread, butter, etc.) or ***semi-durables*** (like pen, stationary, etc.), or ***durables*** (like cars, refrigerators, etc.). In like manner, producers' goods such as raw materials (***single use-producers' goods***), stationary, equipment, etc. (***semi-durables***) and plant, machinery, etc. (***durable producers' goods***) are meant for production of other goods. Expenditures are incurred on consumer goods by the house-hold sector as also by the government. The former is called the ***private final consumption expenditure*** (C_h) and the latter, ***government final consumption expenditure*** (C_g). Likewise, expenditures incurred on the producers' goods are those ones that are incurred on the inventory, residential constructions and the fixed capital formation. Such expenditures are called the ***Net Domestic Capital Formation*** (*NDCF*) and are given as the difference of ***Gross Domestic Capital Formation (GDCF)*** over Depreciation. *GDCF* has two components—***changes in the stocks*** (ΔS) of the inventories and the ***Net Domestic Fixed Capital Formation*** (*NDFCF*) (See Box 2.14).

BOX 2.14

Net Domestic Expenditure (*DE*) = Domestic Expenditure on Consumers' Goods and Producers' Goods

$= [C_h + C_g] + [NDCF + \text{Net Investment Abroad } (X–M)]$

$= C_h + C_g + \Delta S + NDFCF + (X–M).$

Domestic Expenditure on Consumers' Goods

= Private Final Consumption Expenditure
+ Government Final Consumption Expenditure

Net Domestic Expenditure on Producers' Goods

= [Net Domestic Capital Formation (*NDCF*)]
+ Net Investment Abroad (*X–M*)
= [Gross Domestic Capital Formation (*GDCF*) – Depreciation]
+ Net Investment Abroad (*X–M*)
= [Gross Domestic Fixed Capital Formation (*GDFCF*)
+ Changes in Stocks of Inventories (ΔS) – Depreciation]
+ Net Investment Abroad (*X–M*)[1]
$= [GDFCF + \Delta S - \text{Depreciation}] + (X–M)$

National Expenditure = Expenditure on Domestic Product
+ Net Expenditure on Foreign Product
= Domestic Expenditure + Net Factor Income from Abroad

A little explanation of the components of the expenditure on domestic product would be in order here.

Private Final Consumption Expenditure refers to the expenditure incurred by the households on consumption of final goods and services. Final goods, as stated earlier, are goods that are not meant for further production of other goods and services. Instead, they are meant for ultimate consumption by the households. All consumer goods-whether semi-durables, durables or single use-are final goods. Bread (single use), stationery (semi-durable use), refrigerator, TV (both durables) provide a few examples. From the view-point of national income accounting, they are however treated as consumed the very

[1] Beckerman, Wilfred, *"An Introduction to National Income Analysis"*, Second Edition p. 86.

moment they are sold. As against the final goods, ***Intermediate goods*** are those goods that are meant only for further production of other goods and services. The same goods if bought by the producers assume the role of the ***capital goods*** and are not treated as consumed the moment they are bought. Instead, their value is spread over their life span from the view-point of national income accounts.

The households also consume certain final services such as those provided by the public transport, hospitals, educational institutions, etc. Consumption expenditure of the households on final goods and services can be determined as the sum of money spent by the households on them (See Box 2.15).

BOX 2.15
Private Final Consumption Expenditure (C_h) = Expenditure incurred by the households on final goods and services = Expenditures incurred on consumer goods and those incurred on final services such as those of hospitals, public transport, etc.

Government Final Consumption Expenditure refers to expenditures incurred by government on final goods such as those mentioned above . In addition, being the largest service provider, government also consumes certain services of individuals. Expenditures incurred on such services are known as the government final consumption expenditures (C_g) (See Box 2.16).

BOX 2.16
Government Final Consumption Expenditure (C_g) = Expenditures incurred by the government on final goods and services from domestic territory as well as from the rest of the world

Gross Domestic Capital formation refers to stockpiling of:

(i) the new productive assets such as plant, machinery, equipment, etc.
(ii) New buildings and new residential constructions,

BOX 2.17
Gross Domestic Capital Formation (*GDCF*) = Gross Domestic Fixed Capital Formation (*GDFCF*) *Plus* Changes in Stocks (ΔS) Gross Domestic Fixed Capital Formation (*GDFCF*) = Stockpiling New Plant, Equipment, machinery *Plus* New transport equipment such as rail engines, wagons, trucks, aeroplanes *Plus* New buildings and residential constructions Changes in stocks = Closing stocks of raw-materials, semi-finished and finished but unsold goods *Less* Opening stocks of raw-materials, semi-finished and finished but unsold goods

(iii) New transport equipment such as production of aeroplanes, rail-engines, wagons, trucks, etc., and

(iv) Changes in stocks of raw-materials, semi-finished and finished goods. It refers to the excess of the closing stocks of these over their opening stocks (See Box 2.17).

Net Investment Abroad refers to the excess of exports over imports. Total investment thus is gross domestic capital formation *plus* net investment abroad (See Box 2.18).

BOX 2.18

Total Investment (gross) is thus constituted as

$$I = GDCF + X\text{–}M$$

= Gross Domestic Capital Formation

Plus

Net Investment Abroad

2.1.3.1 Problems of estimation of national income by expenditure method

There are a few problems associated with the expenditure method as well. They are related to estimation of capital formation, expenditure of government and expenditure on durable and semi-durable goods. Capital formation does not include financial capital. Likewise expenditures incurred by the government on old-age pensions, scholarships, etc. are transfer payments which may lead to additional final consumption demand made by the recipients but they are not a part of the government final consumption expenditure. Likewise, resale of durables and semi-durables is only a transfer of ownership, not a part of the final consumption expenditure.

2.2. IDENTITY OF NI, NP, AND NE: THE CIRCULAR FLOWS OF INCOME, OUTPUT AND EXPENDITURE

From the foregone discussions, it is clear that domestic income is identically equal to the domestic product or to the domestic expenditure, all at the factor cost. Adding net factor income/net factor product from abroad to each, the identity transforms to the equality of national income, national product and national expenditure. National income at one point is national product, at the other, national expenditure. Thus flow of income, product and expenditure constitutes a circular flow.

Before proceeding with the circular flows of the income, expenditure and the product, let us distinguish between stocks and flows first.

Stocks and Flows: *Stock* refers to magnitude or quantity of a variable at a particular point of time. *Flow*, on the other hand, refers to the change in the stock over a period of time. For example, suppose a water tap is opened to fill an empty bath-tub at 7:00 AM. Quantity of water at 7:10 AM in the tub was 40 liters and at 7:20 AM, it was 60 liters. Each of these quantities refers to a point of time and hence provides examples of stock. Quantity of water flown into the tub between 7:10 AM and 7:20 AM is 20 liters, which represents flow of water over a period of 10 minutes.

Some of the economic quantities have reference to a point of time and are treated as stocks. For example, capital stock, Stock of wealth, bank balance, foreign exchange reserves, stock of raw materials, etc. Some of them have an explicit mention of the term, while in respect of others, the same is implicit. For example, bank balance always refers to a point of time and hence it is a stock. The term stock is implicit in it. The same is the case with foreign exchange reserves.

In like manner, some economic quantities refer to a period of time either explicitly or implicitly. For instance, salary, investment, national income, capital formation, changes in stock of inventories etc.—all have an implicit reference to a period of time. Salary refers to a period of one month while the rest to a period of one accounting year. Clearly, all of them constitute flows.

Let us now return to the circular flows of income, expenditure and product.

2.2.1 Circular Flows in a Two-sector-economy

Expenditure on the national product is equivalent to the money value of the national product and it is financed by the national income. We can drive the concept home through an illustration. Consider an economy with two sectors: the households' sector and the producers' sector. The households' sector owns factors of production which it provides to the producers' sector for an income, say, ₹ 2000. This is factor income, which can be taken as the national income if it represents the sum of the domestic factor income and the net factor income from abroad. The same represents the service product or the national product at factor cost which is bought by the households' sector in exchange for the income earned by it. Even the entrepreneur belongs to the households' sector. Thus, factor incomes ≡ the money value of the output produced by the factors ≡ the expenditure of the households on the product, assuming no savings (in absence of a financial sector) and no net indirect taxes (in absence of the government sector) exist. Thus, ₹ 2000 worth of factor-services are exchanged for ₹ 2000 worth of income which is given away in exchange for ₹ 2000 worth of product. The transactions are shown below through a flowchart, called ***circular flow in a two-sector-economy*** (See Box 2.19).

BOX 2.19 Circular flow of Income and Expenditure in a Two-sector-economy

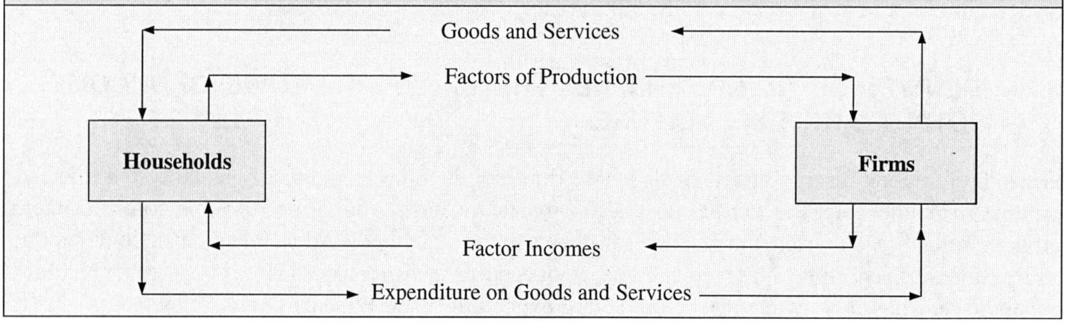

The household sector provides the factors of production to the firms, and in exchange receives incomes called *factor incomes*. Income represents the value of the factor-services. Firms produce goods and services through these factors and sell them to the household sector. Goods and services bought by the household sector represent its *consumption* while money income spent by the household sector on it, represents its consumption-expenditure. The flow of income and expenditure in a two sector economy is complete.

2.2.2 Circular Flows in a Two-sector-economy in Presence of the Financial Institutions

In like manner, the circular flow in a two-sector-economy with financial sector also in operation can be drawn as below. The financial sector here refers to the financial institutions such as banks which mobilize the savings of the firms and the household sectors and use them to finance the firms. In fact, the financial sector is a potential source of plugging the leakages from the circular flow of income and expenditure caused by the savings. Household sector feeds the firms with factor inputs for money income. Thereafter, it saves a part of it and spends the rest on goods and services supplied by the firms. Savings reduce the consumption expenditure and cause accumulation of unsold stocks. Banks mobilize these savings and finance the firms. This helps the firms to maintain their pace of production (See Box 2.20).

BOX 2.20 Circular Flow of Income and Expenditure in a Two-sector-economy in Presence of the Financial Institutions

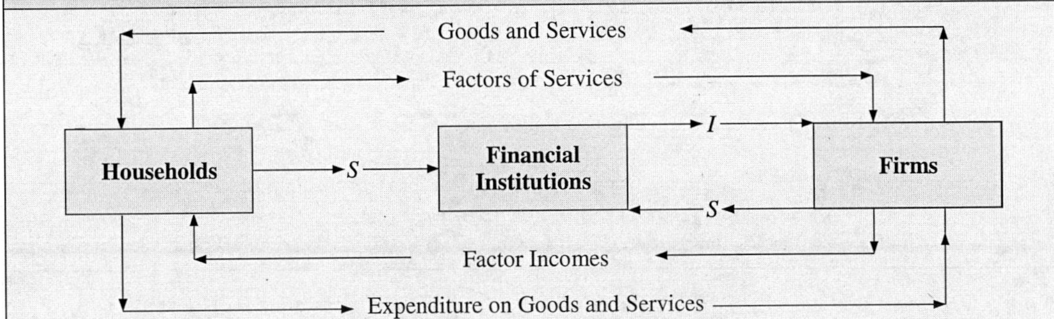

(*Notes*: S ≡ Savings, I ≡ Investment)

2.2.3 Circular Flows in a 3 Sector Economy with Financial Institutions

The third sector is the Government sector. Government also draws productive factors from the household sector to produce services. Thus the household sector derives factor incomes not only from the firms but also from the government. The government derives its income from taxation of products as also the incomes of the individuals. In other words, the sources of income of the government are the direct and the indirect taxes. Government spends its income on purchases of goods from firms, grant of subsidies to firms, transfer payments to the household sector and on factor payments. Income earned by the household sector is partly saved by it and is partly spent on consumption. The financial institutions mobilize savings from households, firms and from government and lend them to the needy firms, households and government.

Goods and services flow from the firms to the household sector and to the government. In exchange for them, the money value of these goods and services flows back to the firms from the household sector and the government. This completes the circular flow of the product.

As regards the flow of income, the household sector derives it in the form of factor incomes from the firms and from the government for the supply of the productive factors. In addition, the household sector also receives transfer payments from government. Income of the firms accrues to them from the sale of goods and services to the household sector and to the government as also from the receipt of subsidies from government (subsidies are that part of the *NIT* which is received by the firms from the government). Income of the government flows to it in the form of the direct taxes (income tax, corporate tax) and indirect taxes (sales tax, excise duty, etc.). It is to be noted that the ***transfer payments*** *are the unilateral transactions, such as old-age pensions, scholarships, etc., that flow from government to the household sector without* any *expectation of a quid pro quo from the recipients.* Likewise, *direct taxes are also unilateral transactions that flow from the household sector*

BOX 2.21 Circular Flows in a 3 Sector Economy in Presence of Financial Institutions

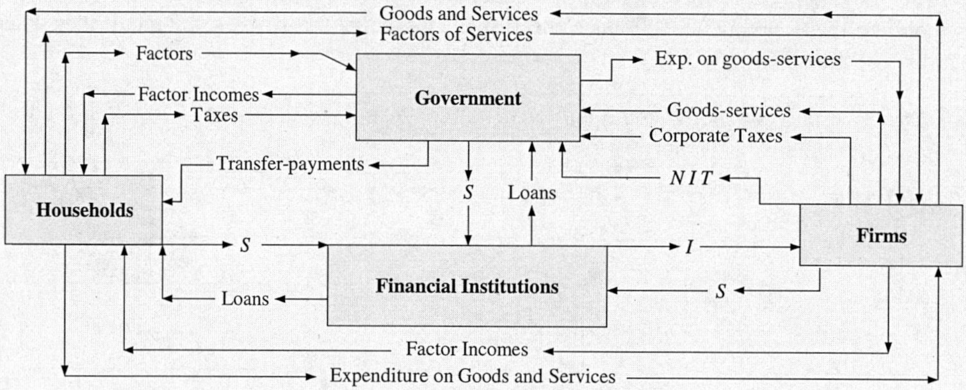

[*Notes*: $S \equiv$ Savings, $I \equiv$ Investment, $NIT \equiv$ Net Indirect Taxes = Indirect Taxes – Subsidies].

to the government without any expectation of a quid pro quo from government. The same is the case with the subsidies that flow from government to firms.

Coming to the flow of expenditures, the household sector incurs them on final consumption of goods and services from the firms, on paying direct taxes to the government and on feeding financial institutions with savings. The firms incur expenditures on paying factor incomes to the productive factors of the household sector, paying direct and indirect taxes to government and on feeding the financial institutions with savings. Government expenditures are incurred on purchasing final goods and services from the firms, paying the factor incomes to the household sector for the factors employed, paying transfer payments to the households, subsidies to the firms and on feeding the financial institutions with savings. Flows from financial institutions go to the firms as investment and to the government and the household sector as loans. ***Circular flows of incomes, expenditures and the products*** have to be balanced due the existence of the contra entries (See Box 2.21).

2.2.4 Circular Flows in a Four Sector Economy with Financial Institutions

The fourth sector is the Rest of the World (*ROW*) sector. *ROW* provides markets for our products and productive factors. In the same way, we provide markets to the *ROW* for its products and productive factors.

Factor incomes from *ROW less* those to *ROW* constitute the net factor income from abroad or from *ROW*. The excess of exports over Imports forms the net exports or the net investment abroad. *ROW* sector, thus, influences the domestic flows of incomes, expenditures and products (Box 2.22).

2.3 NATIONAL INCOME AGGREGATES

There are, in all, ***eight national income aggregates*** often referred to in social accounts. They are, as given below:

1. Gross National Product at market price (GNP_{MP})
2. Gross National Product at factor cost (GNP_{FC})
3. Gross Domestic Product at market price (GDP_{MP})

BOX 2.22 Circular Flows in a Four Sector Economy with Financial Institutions

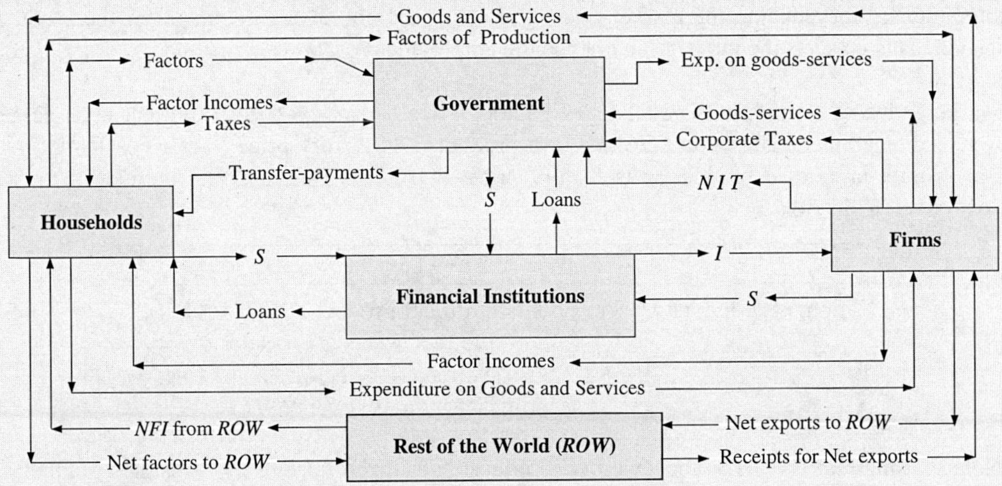

[*Notes:* $S \equiv$ Savings, $I \equiv$ Investment, $NIT \equiv$ Net Indirect Taxes
= Indirect Taxes – Subsidies.
NFI from *ROW* ≡ Net Factor Income from *ROW*
= Factor Income from *ROW* – factor income to *ROW*
Net Exports to *ROW* = Exports to *ROW* – imports from *ROW*
Net factors to *ROW* = factors to *ROW* – factors from *ROW*

4. Gross Domestic Product at factor cost (GDP_{FC})
5. Net National Product at market price (NNP_{MP})
6. Net National Product at factor cost (NNP_{FC})
7. Net Domestic Product at market price (NDP_{MP})
8. Net Domestic Product at factor cost (NDP_{FC})

Note that (NNP_{FC}) has at times a special name of National product (NP); (NDP_{FC}), that of domestic product (DP); (NNI_{FC}), that of national income (NI); (NDI_{FC}), that of domestic income (DI); (NNE_{FC}), that of national expenditure (NE); and (NDE_{FC}), that of domestic expenditure (DE).

(a) Net Indirect Tax (NIT): Excess of Indirect taxes over Subsidies is known as *NIT*. Indirect Taxes, such as Sales tax, Excise duty, cess, etc. are taxes the burden (impact) of which can be shifted to someone else by those on whom they are levied (incidence). Usually the incidence of such taxes falls on the producers of the commodities and services, who in turn, shift a part or the whole of the burden onto the consumers. ***Subsidy***, on the other hand, is a grant of the government of a part of the money value of the product to the producers. The purpose is to protect certain industries so that their product may survive the competition from superior but cheaper substitutes. The best example of subsidy is the coarse cloth *(KHADI)* in India. As mentioned earlier, *KHADI* products require lot of care on the part of the users while mill-made substitutes are not only cheaper but also maintenance-free and convenient to them. The demand for *KHADI* garments in the market, therefore, would be negligible if marketed without price cuts. Such price cuts are likely to cause unbearable loss to the *KHADI* industry, thereby, leading it to its closure. This would affect the employment of millions of workers of the industry. To prevent it all from happening, government compensates the industry for losses caused by price-cuts. *Subsidy* is the name given to such compensations. Grant of subsidy, thus, helps the industry in reducing the market price, generating thereby enough demand for the products in question. This protects the industry and hence the employment of the workers and the other factors of production.

Market Price of a product is equal to its Factory Price (factor cost) *plus* indirect taxes levied *minus* subsidies granted. Thus, Market price of a product = its factory price (factor cost) + Indirect taxes or Market price of a product = its factory price – subsidies. Thus national product at market price can given as in Box 2.23.

BOX 2.23
Thus, National Product at Market Price = National Product at Factor Cost (*FC*) + Indirect Taxes (*IT*) – subsidies = National Product at Factor Cost + Net Indirect Taxes (*NIT*).

Note that indirect taxes are not levied on products subsidized nor are the subsidies granted on products being subjected to indirect taxation.

(b) Depreciation: Also known as the consumption of capital, depreciation refers to wear and tear of the productive assets. All productive assets suffer wear and tear during the production process. The heavier the use, the heavier is the wear and tear and lower is the efficiency and productivity of the asset. To restore its productive potential, its repairs may be frequently required. Thus, expenditures incurred on repairs can serve as a measure of depreciation of the asset in question. Net value of an asset can be found by subtracting depreciation from its gross (original) value (Box 2.24).

BOX 2.24
Gross National Product at Factor Cost (GNP_{FC}) = Net National Product at Factor Cost (NNP_{FC}) *Plus* Depreciation

(c) Net Factor Income from Abroad (NFIA): Excess of the factor incomes earned by the normal residents of a country from the rest of the world over and above the outgoing factor incomes to the rest of the world is called the Net Factor Income from Abroad (*NFIA*) or Net Factor Income from the Rest of the World (*NFI* from *ROW*). The net result could be positive or negative (See Box 2.25).

BOX 2.25
Net Factor Income from Abroad = Factor Incomes from ROW *Less* Factor Incomes to *ROW*.

Income, whether domestic or national, depends on Net Factor Income from Abroad. Product, whether gross or net, depends on depreciation. Likewise, product, whether, at factor cost or at market price, depends on the net indirect taxes to be included as in the former case or excluded as in the latter.

In fact any national income aggregate is equal to the sum of the corresponding domestic aggregate and net factor income from abroad (See Box 2.26).

BOX 2.26
National Income Aggregate = Corresponding Domestic Aggregate *Plus* Net Factor Income from Abroad

In the same way, any gross estimate of a national income aggregate is equal to the net estimate of the corresponding aggregate *plus* depreciation (See Box 2.27).

BOX 2.27
Gross Estimate of a National Income Aggregate = Net Estimate of the corresponding Aggregate *Plus* Depreciation

Finally, any estimate of national income at market price is equal to the corresponding estimate of it at factor cost *plus* the net indirect taxes (See Box 2.28).

BOX 2.28
An Estimate of National Income at Market Price = Corresponding Estimate at Factor Cost *Plus* Net Indirect Taxes

Identity of domestic income, product and expenditure is as shown in shown Box 2.29.

BOX 2.29
Domestic Income = Domestic Product = Domestic Expenditure, Where, *Domestic Income = Net Domestic Income at Factor Cost* (NDI_{FC}) *Domestic Product = Net Domestic Product at Factor Cost* (NDP_{FC}) *Domestic Expenditure = Net Domestic Expenditure at Factor Cost* (NDP_{FC})

Adding Net Factor Income from abroad to each, the identity that results is as given in Box 2.30.

BOX 2.30
National Income = National Product = National Expenditure Where, *National Income = Net National Income at Factor Cost* (NNI_{FC}) *National Product = Net National Product at Factor Cost* (NNP_{FC}) *National Expenditure = Net National Expenditure at Factor Cost* (NNE_{FC}) *(Note how NFIA changes 'domestic' aggregates to 'National' aggregates.)*

Adding 'Depreciation' to each of the above, the identity transforms as in Box 2.31.

BOX 2.31

Gross National Income at Factor Cost (GNI_{FC}) = Gross National Product at Factor Cost (GNP_{FC})
= Gross National Expenditure at Factor Cost (GNE_{FC})

Adding *NIT* to each of the above, the identity transforms as in Box 2.32.

BOX 2.32

Gross National Income at Market Price (GNI_{MP}) = Gross National Product at Market Price (GNP_{MP})
= Gross National Expenditure at Market Price (GNE_{MP}).

Interrelationship in between the national income aggregates can now be summarized as in Box 2.33.

BOX 2.33

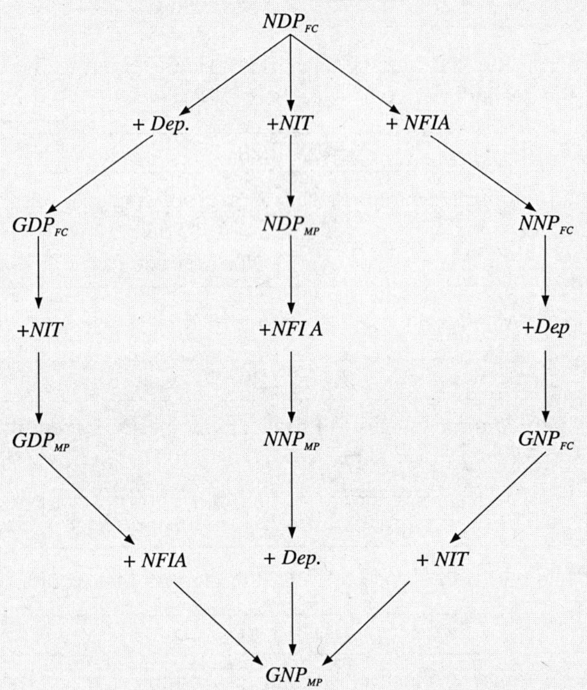

[*Notes: Dep.* = Depreciation, *NIT* = Net Indirect Taxes, *NFIA* = Net Factor Income from Abroad].

(1) $GNP_{MP} = GNP_{FC} + NIT$
(2) $GNP_{MP} = GDP_{MP} + NFIA$
(3) $GNP_{MP} = NNP_{MP} + Dep$
(4) $NNP_{MP} = NDP_{MP} + NFIA$
(5) $NNP_{MP} = NNP_{FC} + NIT$
(6) $NDP_{MP} = NDP_{FC} + NIT$
(7) $GDP_{MP} = GDP_{FC} + NIT$
(8) $GDP_{MP} = NDP_{MP} + Dep.$
(9) $GDP_{FC} = NDP_{FC} + Dep.$

2.4 NATIONAL INCOME AT CURRENT AND CONSTANT PRICES

2.4.1 National Income at Current Prices

National Income at current prices refers to the estimates of national income at the prices prevailing in the economy at the time of estimation. Prices change from day to day, month to month and year to year in every economy due to changes in market forces of demand and supply. National income is estimated every year in terms of prices prevailing at the time of such estimations, i.e., current prices. Such estimates of national income are termed as national income at current prices. Here, the term national income may refer to any of the eight national income aggregates. It should be born in mind, however, that the use of national income in particular, has reference to Net National Income, or more popularly, Net National Product at factor cost.

2.4.2 National Income at Constant Prices

National Income at constant prices refers to conversion of its current estimates in terms of the prices of some particular year of reference (called the base year). To illustrate the point, suppose national income at current prices in respect of some economy is ₹ 10,000 crores. The price index of the current year, with respect to 1991, say, as the base year, is 250. Also suppose that the national income estimate in the base year was ₹ 4,000 crores. One would, at the outset, think that the national income in the current year has more than doubled of what it was in the base year. A little reasoning would, however, show that the inference is not correct. For such comparisons, we need to convert the two estimates in terms of the prices of either the base year or of the current year. It is, however, more convenient to convert the current year's estimate in terms of the base year's prices. The method is known as the ***deflation of the national income***. The current year's estimate of the national income in terms of the base year's prices can be obtained from the *unitary method* or from the expression in Box 2.34.

BOX 2.34

National Income at constant prices

$$= \text{National Income at Current Prices} \times \frac{\text{Base Year's Price Index}}{\text{Current Year's Price Index}}$$

Thus, national income at prices of 1991 = ₹ 10,000 × (100/250)
= ₹ 4,000.

National income at current prices, when expressed in prices of the base year, reduces to the actual income of the current year in this illustration. Thus what appeared to be a sizeable growth from 4,000 to 10,000 (250%) in the nominal terms, actually proves to be zero percent when the current estimate is adjusted for inflation. We observe that it has undergone no change in real terms.

The process of adjustment of the current estimates of national income for inflation, or in simple language, the process of conversion of the current estimates in terms of the base year's prices, is known as ***deflation*** of national income as mentioned above. Thus, current estimates of national income, when deflated, show that the purchasing power of the current national income is no better than that of it in 1991, the base year.

The purpose of deflating national income is twofold:

1. It helps to study the annual growth rate of the national income in historical perspective. This is essential for evaluation of the performance of various growth-oriented economic policies.

2. It helps to compare the purchasing power of the current year's national income with that of any year of reference.

The process of national income deflation can be cut short if national income deflators for different years be given.

National income Deflator

National Income Deflator is a factor used to convert the nominal value of the national income into its real value. The factor is the ratio of the price index of the chosen year (whose nominal national income is to be converted into real terms) to the price index of the base year (See Box 2.35).

BOX 2.35

$$\text{National Income Deflator}^{1} = \frac{\text{Price index of the chosen year}}{\text{Price index of the base year (i.e., 100)}}$$

$$\text{Real National Income} = \frac{\text{Nominal national income}}{\text{National income Deflator}}$$

ILLUSTRATION 2.3: The wholesale price index for 1992–93 in India was 251.00 (1980–81 = 100). *GNP* in billions of rupees for 1992–93 was 61897. Estimate the *GNP* deflator and find out the real *GNP*.

Solution: *GNP* Deflator = (Wholesale Price Index of 1992–93)/(Wholesale price index of 1980–81)
= 251.00/100
= 2.51

Real *GNP* = Nominal GNP of 1992–93/GNP Deflator
= 61897/2.51
= ₹ 24,660.12 Billion.

The actual Value of Real *GNP* in 1992–93 was ₹ 21,870 billions [See Table 2.1]
The discrepancy of ₹ 2790.12 billion is the statistical discrepancy.

GNP Implicit Deflator or Implicit Price Deflator

Another variant of *GNP* Deflator is ***GNP Implicit Deflator*** or ***Implicit Price Deflator.*** It is defined as the ratio of Nominal *GNP* to real *GNP* (See Box 2.36).

BOX 2.36

$$GNP \text{ Implicit Price Deflator} = \frac{\text{Nominal } GNP}{\text{Real } GNP}$$

The expression holds for implicit price deflator of any estimate, be it investment, consumption, or government expenditure. For instance, investment implicit deflator = nominal investment/real investment.

[1] It can be shown that *NI* deflator = Wholesale Price Index of the current year/Wholesale Price Index of the base year.
= National Income in nominal terms/National Income in real terms.
The latter, however, is a variant of *NI* deflator and is called the National Income Implicit Deflator or price implicit deflator.

GNP implicit price deflator can be employed for construction of price indices and measurement of changes in price level. In Illustration 2.3, the nominal *GNP* for the year 1992–93 was ₹ 61,897.00 billions, while the real *GNP* for the same year was ₹ 21,870.00 (Table 2.1)]. The *GNP* implicit price deflator, therefore, is 61,897/21,870 or 2.8302 while *GNP* deflator is 251.00 only. The discrepancy may have arisen from the use of the wholesale price indices in calculation of the *GNP* deflator. To calculate the ***rate of inflation***, we calculate the approximate value of the price-index for the year 1992–93 using the expression,

Approximate Price Index for 1992–93 = GNP implicit price deflator × 100.
= 2.8302 × 100
= 283.02

Rate of Inflation between 1991–92 and 1992–93 is defined as:

$$\text{Rate of Inflation} = \frac{\text{Price index for }(1992-93) - \text{Price index for }(1991-92)}{\text{Price index for }(1991-92)} \times 100$$

$$= \frac{283.02 - 258.7}{258.7} \times 100 = 9.4\ \%\ \text{(approximately).}$$

Here, the price index for the year 1991–92 has been calculated by multiplying the *GNP* implicit price deflator for 1991–92 by 100.

GNP implicit price deflator for 1991–92
= (Nominal *GNP*/Real *GNP*) for the year 1991–92 (Refer to Box 2.36)
= 54,269/20,979
= 2.587

Thus approximate price index for the year 1991–92 is 258.7. (Note that the figures of nominal and real *GNP* and the wholesale price index-number have been taken from the Economic Survey of 1998–99, as given in Table 2.1 for ready reference).

TABLE 2.1 India's Nominal and Real GNP_{FC}—1980–81 to 1996–97

Year	*GNP (in billions of rupees)*		*GNP Growth Rates*[3]		*WPI*[4]
	Nominal[1]	*Real*[2]	*Nominal*	*Real*	*(1980–81 = 100)*
1980–81	12277		19.7	7.3	100.00
1981–82	14326	12993	16.7	5.8	109.80
1982–83	15876	13330	10.8	2.6	114.90
1983–84	18578	14386	17.0	7.9	123.80
1984–85	20711	14926	11.5	3.8	131.80
1985–86	23237	15537	12.2	4.1	137.60
1986–87	25823	16154	11.1	4.0	145.70
1987–88	29223	16812	13.2	4.1	157.60
1988–89	34821	18523	19.2	10.2	169.40
1989–90	40293	19808	15.7	6.9	181.90
1990–91	47027	20850	16.7	5.3	200.50
1991–92	54269	20979	15.4	0.5	228.10
1992–93	61897	21870	14.1	5.2	251.00

(Contd.)

Year	GNP (in billions of rupees)		GNP Growth Rates[3]		WPI[4]
	Nominal[1]	Real[2]	Nominal	Real	(1980–81 = 100)
New Series (Base 1993–94)					
1993–94	79700	78697	16.4	6.2	...
1994–95	93032	94785	18.2	7.7	...
1995–96	108975	91381	17.1	7.8	...
1996–97	127218	98826	16.7	8.1	...

For all practical purposes, *GNP* deflator and *GNP* implicit deflator are the same so long as the nominal and the real *GNP* are taken to define each or so long as the price indices employed in converting the nominal *GNP* into real *GNP* are neither the Consumer Price Indices (*CPI*) nor the Wholesale Price Indices (*WPI*). The consumer price indices account only for consumer goods while the wholesale price indices account only for certain commodities in certain markets and at certain quotations.

2.5 PRIVATE INCOME, PERSONAL INCOME AND PERSONAL DISPOSABLE INCOME

2.5.1 Private Income

Private Income refers to the income of the non-governmental entities from all the sources over a period of one accounting year. It is the income of the firms and the households from all the possible sources. Incomes, under this head, include transfer payments and such other unilateral transactions which empower the private individuals and the entities with the purchasing power.

Box 2.37 lists various components of private income.

BOX 2.37

Private Income = Domestic Product accruing to the Private sector
+ Net Factor Income from Abroad (*NFI* from *ROW*)
+ Net Other Current Transfers from *ROW* (*NOCT* from *ROW*)
+ Transfer Payments (*TP*) + National Debt Interest

Some expressions in Box 2.37 need a brief introduction.

Net Other Current Transfers from ROW such transfers refer to the current transfers from the rest of the world net of the current transfers to the rest of the world. Such transfers are unilateral transactions.

Transfer Payments, such as, old age pensions, scholarships, etc., are unilateral transactions with no compulsions of a *quid pro quo*.

National Debt Interest refers to the interest paid by government on the loans it has taken from financial institutions such as Life Insurance Corporation, Unit Trust of India, etc. The interest finally trickles down to the investors of the household sector and also those of the firms. Employing alternative expressions for domestic product accruing to the private sector, as given below, an alternative expression for the private income can be derived as in Box 2.38.

[1] At current prices.
[2] At 1980–81 prices.
[3] Over the previous year.
[4] The base of the wholesale price index (*WPI*, 1981–82 = 100) published by Economic Survey, *GOI*, 1998–99, changed to *WPI* (1980–81 = 100).

Source: Economic Survey, 1998-99, Government of India, pp. S-3, S-4.

2.5.2 Personal Income

Personal Income is the income of the household sector over an accounting year from all the sources. It is that part of the private income which reaches the individuals of the household sector. It can be given as the private income *less* corporate profit tax *less* undistributed profits.

Corporate Profit Tax is the tax levied on the profits of the business corporations. It does not trickle down to the household sector.

Undistributed profits remain confined to the business firms for business operations in future.

Box 2.40 gives the expression of personal income.

BOX 2.38
Domestic Product Accruing to Private Sector = Net Domestic Product at Factor Cost (NDP_{FC}) – Domestic product Accruing to Government Sector Net Domestic Product at Factor Cost (NDP_{FC}) = Net National Product at Factor Cost – Net Factor Income from Abroad = NNP_{FC} – *NFI* from *ROW* Domestic product accruing to government sector = Income from property and entrepreneurship to government administrative department + Savings of Non-departmental enterprises. Domestic Product accruing to private sector = NNP_{FC} – *NFI* from *ROW* – [Income from property and entrepreneurship to government administrative Departments + Savings of Non-departmental enterprises] = NNP_{FC} – *NFI* from *ROW* – Income from property & entrepreneurship to government administrative departments – savings of non-departmental enterprises

The alternative expression for private income can thus be given as in Box 2.39.

BOX 2.39
Private Income = NDP_{FC} – Domestic Product accruing to the government + Net Factor Income from Abroad + Net Other Current Transfers from *ROW* + Transfer Payments + National Debt Interest = NNP_{FC}– Domestic Product accruing to the government – Net Factor income from Abroad + Net Other Current Transfers from *ROW* + Transfer Payments + Net Factor Income from Abroad + National Debt Interest = NNP_{FC}–Net Factor Income from Abroad – Income from property and entrepreneurship to government administrative department – savings of the non-departmental enterprises + Net Other Current Transfers from *ROW* + Transfer Payments +Net Factor income from Abroad + National Debt Interest = NNP_{FC} – Income from property and entrepreneurship to government administrative department – savings of the non-departmental Enterprises + Net Other Current Transfers from *ROW* + Transfer Payment + National Debt Interest

BOX 2.40
Personal Income = Private Income *Less* Corporate Tax *Less* Undistributed Profits.

2.5.3 Personal Disposable Income

After paying direct taxes (such as income tax), government fees, fines, etc., the income left with household sector is called Personal Disposable Income. The household sector feels free to spend or save or do whatever they like with (Box 2.41).

BOX 2.41
Personal Disposable Income = Personal Income – Direct Taxes, Fees, Fines, etc.

Thus, ***personal disposable income*** is a part of the personal income. It is from this income that a household or a consumer shells out money for consumption and/or savings.

2.6 PER CAPITA INCOME

It is defined as the share of one normal resident in the national income. It can be measured as a ratio of the national income to the population of the normal residents in the country (Box 2.42).

BOX 2.42
Per Capita Income = National Income/Population of the normal residents

In like-manner, ***GNP per capita*** can be defined as the ratio of the *GNP* to the population of the normal residents in the country. The same would be the case with *GDP* per capita. What one needs to do is to take the relevant national income aggregate in the numerator and the population of the normal residents in the denominator. For example, suppose the *GNP* of a country is 20,00,000 Crore of rupees and the population of the normal residents is 100 crores. *GNP* per capita would then work out as ₹ 20,00,000 Crore/100 Crore = ₹ 20,000.

Until recently, *GNP* per capita has been treated as an indicator of economic welfare of a country by a majority of economists all over the world.

2.7 UTILITY OF NATIONAL INCOME ESTIMATES

National income estimates are very important partly as the measuring rod of economic welfare and economic growth of the country and partly as tools of performance appraisal of economic policies, structural changes and comparison of the economic performance of the country vis-à-vis other countries of the world. Let us summarize the utility of national income estimates in the following points:

1. **Indicator of Economic Welfare:** Until recently, *GNP* per capita has served as an indicator of economic welfare of the people in a country. The higher the *GNP* per capita of a country, the higher is the level of the economic welfare of the people in the country.

2. **Measure of Economic Growth and Development:** Economic growth is measured as a percent increase in *GNP* over a period of one accounting year. For instance, if *GNP* increases from ₹ 20,00,000 crores to ₹ 21,00,000 crores over a period of one year, the growth rate for the year would work out as (21,00,000 – 20,00,000)/20,00,000 = 0.05 or 5%. Economic growth leads to economic development. A higher growth would lead to a higher level of economic development, other things remaining the same.
3. **Study and Analysis of Structural Changes in Different Sectors of an Economy:** National income estimates essentially reveal changes in the incomes and outputs of different sectors of an economy. This helps analysis of the relative performance of various sectors of an economy. Most importantly, it helps locating the surplus and the deficit sectors, which is quite crucial for formulation of monetary, fiscal and foreign trade policies.
4. **Comparison of Economic Performance of the Country with that of the other Countries:** National income estimates facilitate the comparison of the economic performance of a country vis-à-vis other countries of the world. For instance, comparing the rate of growth of the national income with that of the other countries tells us how our policies of investment and resource allocation have fared in comparison to those of the other countries of the world. This helps in making decisions whether a policy change is called for.
5. **Significance to Business Policy Formulation:** National income statistics provide data about the past performance of different industries and the likely trends of future demand in respect of these industries. This helps the firms in every industry to chalk out their future plans of production.
6. **Significance to Trade Unions:** Trade unions and labour organizations learn of their contributions to the *GDP* and can accordingly decide in respect of their wages and salaries whether they are on the lower side or on the higher side. This helps them to formulate their strategies for future.

2.8 *GNP* PER CAPITA, *PQLI, HDI* AND SOCIAL WELFARE

GNP per capita

It has been treated as an indicator of economic development and social welfare. For quite some time, a high *GNP* per capita has implied a high level of social welfare and economic development particularly in respect of some advanced countries. On the other hand, developing nations like India have shown signs of impatience about their chronically low growth rates of *GNP*. The obsession of realizing a higher growth of *GNP* is so strong that a number of developing countries have prepared themselves to give up the very objective of social welfare in its pursuance. Creation of employment opportunities, for instance, is a social objective of such economies. It is to achieve such objectives only that a high *GNP* growth is targeted. Nevertheless, quite a few have turned too capital intensive for their cause of growth to care for the very objectives in the process. No doubt a high *GNP*, coupled with its equitable distribution, may help the nation-states in improving the standard of living of the people provided it leads to quality changes in the economy. Let us see what these quality changes are that make *GNP* growth[1] imply economic development too of a nation.

[1] GNP growth refers to the rate at which GNP of a country increases over a period of one year. Development, on the other hand, refers to a state of general well-being of the people in which social evils such as disease, hunger, poverty, illiteracy, epidemics, superstitions stand eradicated, and people lead a life of dignity and self-esteem. Development has more to do with quality of life than with quantity of materialistic achievements. A country is thus a developed one if its people live in self-esteem without a fear of these social evils. A high *GNP* per capita does not necessarily imply a high level of economic development while a high level of economic development essentially ensures a high *GNP* growth. For detailed analysis of growth and development, see chapter 14.

Development refers to ensuring availability of the life-sustaining goods (such as food and shelter), protection from epidemics; provision of educational facilities as also ascertainment of freedom from servitude and dependence. It refers to improving the quality of life of people in general besides liberating them from forces of ignorance and misery. It also refers to striving for material well being of people with individual and national selfesteem.[1] In sum, development is qualitative concept while growth, a quantitative one.

Evidently, a high *GNP* per capita may ensure development provided it percolates among the masses equitably. Kuwait has a very high *GNP* per capita but lacks in equitability of its distribution as also in general level of education, balanced growth of agriculture and industry and in health and medical facilities. It can't be treated as a developed country so long as it lacks in diversification of its *GNP* on the improvement of the living conditions of its people.

Observations such as these about countries like Kuwait, have led to widespread disillusionment of the economists about *GNP* per capita as a measure of economic development and social welfare. The hunt for alternative yardsticks for measurement of economic development has led to the evolution of a wide range of socio-economic indicators for the purpose.

Deficiencies in Measurement of *GNP*

GNP measures suffer from the following deficiencies:

1. **Difficulty in Accounting for Quality Changes in *GNP*:** A low quality house in a congested locality commands a much higher price than what a high quality house in open surroundings does. *GNP*, thus, fails to accommodate the quality changes with the result that it under-estimates the economic welfare of the people.
2. **Commodity Taxes Inflate the Value of the *GNP* without any Increase in the Volume of the Physical Output:** Indirect taxes raise the money value of the *GNP* even when the physical volume of the output remains unchanged. As a result, the measure of welfare is much lower than what the *GNP* estimates indicate.
3. **A Number of Services Remain Excluded from the *GNP* Estimates despite their High Contribution to the Development and Welfare:** In many economies, a number of services such as transport, teaching, laundries, and entertainment are not included in the *GNP* (as has been the practice in some economies) even though their contribution to the development and welfare of the people in the nation is of high significance. *GNP* thus fails to represent a true measure of welfare or development.
4. **Inflation Enhances the Value of the GNP even when Physical Volume of the Output Remains Unchanged:** The effect is the same as that of the commodity taxes. *GNP* if taken as an indicator of welfare, it would show much higher of it than what people actually enjoy.
5. **Problems of Unreported and Illegal Activities:** Illegal activities such as smuggling increase the welfare yet go unreported, and hence, excluded from the estimates of the *GNP*. Welfare is, in reality, much higher than that reflected by the *GNP*.

   Similarly, production of certain goods and services is not reported to the government by their producers with a view to avoid taxation. *GNP* thus gets under-estimated, reflecting much less welfare than that enjoyed by the people.
6. **Not all Activities have a Monetary Value:** Leisure or housewife's services, though making a significant contribution to the people's welfare, fail to be included in the *GNP* mainly due to the problem of assessing their values in the monetary terms. Such activities remain excluded from the *GNP*. *GNP* estimates thus can't reflect the true measure of economic welfare.

[1] Adopted from Denis Goulet, *The Cruel Choice: A New Concept in the Theory of Development* (New York), 1971, pp. 87–94.

7. **Production for Self-consumption Increases Welfare but not Included in *GNP*:** The producers hold a part of the produce back for their self-consumption. This often does not get accounted for in the *GNP*. Production for self-consumption increases the social welfare but fails to enter in the *GNP*-estimates, which thus remain under-estimated.
8. **Increase in Industrial Output Increases Pollution, which Decreases Welfare:** An increase in industrial production increases both *GNP* as well as pollution. An increase in pollution, however, reduces welfare.
9. **A Change in the Composition of the Output may Increase Welfare without Changing the Volume of the Physical Output:** For example, expenditures incurred on the production of destructive missiles or nuclear weapons, if made on promoting better health and education, may increase welfare significantly without any change in the money value of the physical output.
10. **Inequalities in Income Distribution Reduce Welfare of the People:** Existence of inequalities of income distribution adversely affects the welfare of the masses. The richer sections, on the contrary, enjoy surpluses while poorer ones live a life of deprivation.

Discussions above show that *GNP* or *GNP* per capita is an inadequate measure of economic development and social welfare. This has disenchanted the economists about it as a true index of development and welfare.

William Nordhaus and James Tobin[1] developed a ***Measure of Economic Welfare*** (*MEW*) which was adopted by Samuelson[2] and reshaped into what is known as the ***Net Economic Welfare*** (*NEW*). Samuelson's *NEW* can be calculated by subtracting from *GNP* the hidden costs of disamenities of industrialization and by adding to it the values of such items as leisure and housewife's services.

PQLI

A better-known indicator in this regard is the ***Physical Quality of Life Index*** (*PQLI*). It was developed by Morris David Morris[3], an American economist, for Overseas Development Council in the late 1970s. It blends together the three indices:

1. Percentage of the literate population (literacy rate),
2. Infant mortality rate (out of 1000 births)

   Indexed Infant Mortality Rate = [(166 – infant mortality) × 0.625)], and
3. ***Indexed life expectancy*** = ((life expectancy – 42) × 2.7).

Physical Quality of Life Index (*PQLI*) = [Indexed Life expectancy + Average Literacy rate + Indexed Infant mortality rate)]/3

It is calculated on a scale that ranges from 0 to 100.

According to Michael P. Todaro[4], *PQLI* of the 3rd world countries in 1981 are presented in Table 2.2 below. Running across the columns of the table, the following observations become evident:

1. There is no direct correlation between high *GNP* per capita and high *PQLI*. Had it been so, Qatar and Saudi Arabia with per capita *GNP* of \$27,790 and \$12,720 respectively would have had highest *PQLI*.

---

[1] William Nordhaus and James Tobin, *Is Growth Obsolete*, quoted by Paul A. Samuelson, *Economics* (12th edition) p. 119.

[2] Paul A. Samuelson, *Economics* (12th edition) p. 119.

[3] Morris D. Morris, *Measuring the Conditions of the World's Poor: The Physical Quality of Life Index* (London: Frank Cass, 1979).

[4] Michael P. Todaro, *Economic Development in the Third World,* 3rd Edition (Orient Longman Ltd., New-Delhi), p. 104.

2. Countries with very low *GNP* per capita have relatively very high *PQLI.* For instance, Sri Lanka with very low *GNP* per capita of $302 has a *PQLI* as high as 82, China with that of $304 has a *PQLI* of 75, Tanzania with that of $299 has a *PQLI* of 58 and India with a *GNP* per capita of $ 253 has a *PQLI* of 42 while Pakistan and Sudan with *GNP* per capita higher than that of India, have each a *PQLI* lower than that of India.

TABLE 2.2 Comparison of Per Capita GNP and *PQLI* for Selected *LDCS*, 1981

LDCs	*Per Capita GNP ($)*	*PQLI*
Sudan	380	34
Pakistan	349	40
Saudi Arabia	12,720	40
India	253	42
Iraq	3,020	48
Qatar	27,790	56
Tanzania	299	58
China	304	75
Sri Lanka	302	82
Singapore	5,220	86
Taiwan	2,503	87
Costa Rica	1,476	89

At least from the trends in respect of the less developed countries (*LDCs*), it is clear that a country like Sri Lanka can be much happier with a low *GNP* per capita than a number of others with very high *GNP* per capita, provided it has a high life expectancy, a low infant mortality rate and a high literacy rate. This provides sufficient evidence against *GNP* per capita as an indicator of economic development and social welfare. Why than strive for a high *GNP* per capita at the cost of social welfare? Subsidization of health, education, shelter, food and clothing for the poor along with eradication of epidemics, generation of employment opportunities and a trickle-down of national income (large or small, whatever achieved without the sacrifice of the cause of the down trodden) to the lower strata of the society can substantially improve the plight of the general lot of the people as in Sri Lanka and China! Why then countries like India are getting wary of the persistent low growth of *GNP*?

The questions are left for the young readers to ponder upon. It will be in order to quote some of the economists for the reader's assistance in this regard.

According to Schumacher, "The common criterion of success, namely, the growth of *GNP,* is utterly misleading and, in fact, must of necessity lead to phenomena which can only be described as neo-colonialism."[1]

According to J.R. Hicks, "The purpose of income calculation—is to give people an indication of the amount they can consume without impoverishing themselves.[2]

There is a widespread disillusionment among the economists all over the world about the inadequacy and the biasedness of the *GNP* per capita as a measure of economic development and welfare, not only because of the reasons mentioned above, but also so because of the aforesaid problems related to its measurement, concepts and accounting systems as adopted by different countries.

[1] E.F. Sumacher, *Small is Beautiful*, p. 180.

[2] J.R. Hicks,Value and Capital ,Oxford University Press, 1975, p. 172.

HDI

Another index, ***Human Development Index (HDI),*** reported by the United Nations Development Programme **(*UNDP*)** is based on the human development approach, developed by Pakistani economist Mahbub-ul-Haq_anchored in Amartya Sen's work on human capabilities, and often framed in terms of whether people are able to "be" and "do" desirable things in life. Examples include—being well fed, sheltered, and healthy; working, educating, voting, participating in community life. The freedom of choice is central—someone choosing to be hungry (e.g., when fasting for religious reasons) is quite different from someone who is hungry because they cannot afford to buy food, or because the country is in a famine. The index does not take into account several factors, such as the net wealth per capita or the relative quality of goods in a country. This situation tends to lower the ranking of some of the most developed ones such as the G7 members and others.

Published on 4th November 2010 (and updated on 10th June 2010), the 2010 Human Development Report calculated *HDI* combining the following three:

1. *A long and healthy life*: Life expectancy at birth (*LE*).
2. *Education*: Mean years of schooling and expected years of schooling (*MYS* and *EYS*).
3. *A decent standard of living: GNI per capita* (*PPP* international dollars).

In its 2010 report, the *UNDP* began using a new method of calculating *HDI.* Employing the following three indices:

(i) **Life Expectancy Index (*LEI*),**
$LEI = (LE - 20)/(85 - 20)$
$= (LE - 20)/(65).$
(*LEI* is 1.00, when life expectancy is 85 years and zero, when it is 20 years)

(ii) **Education Index(*EI*),**
$EI = (MYSI + EYSI)/2$
(*Mean Years of Schooling Index* (*MYSI*) = *MYS*/15. Fifteen is the projected maximum of this indicator for 2025. *Expected Years of Schooling Index* (*EYSI*) = *EYS*/18. Eighteen is equivalent to achieving a master's degree in most of the countries).

(iii) **Income Index (*II*),**
$II = [\ln (GNI_{PER\ CAPITA}) - \ln (100)]/[\ln (75000) - \ln (100)$
$= [\ \ln (GNI_{PER\ CAPITA}) - ln\ (100)]/[\ln (750)]$, Here, ln ≡ exponential logarithm
(*II* is 1.00 when $GNI_{PER\ CAPITA}$ is \$75,000 and zero when it is \$100).
Finally, *HDI* is reached as the geometric mean of the above three.
That is, $HDI = [LEI \times EI \times II]^{1/3}$

Note here that:

MYS ≡ ***Mean Years of Schooling*** (that is, years that a person aged 15 or more has spent in formal education)

EYS ≡ ***Expected Years of Schooling*** (that is, total expected years of schooling for children under 18 years of age, including, young men and women aged 13–17.

$GNI_{PER\ CAPITA}$ ≡ Gross National Income at purchasing power parity per capita.

Critical Assessment

Disenchantment about *GNP per capita* as a measure of economic development laid emphasis on indicators that employ qualitative measures of development. That way, *PQLI* emerges as the best indicator as it doesn't incorporate *GNP* per capita unlike *HDI,* that does. The latter, though commonly used by economists of the developed world as a measure of economic development, incorporates *GNI* per capita in its computation, which imparts it a bias in favour of high income countries. As discussed above, countries with very high *GNP* per capita show a high *HDI* but lack in development due to inequalities of income distribution and absence of welfare measures.

Let us turn to some illustrations now to show how national income and the related aggregates can be calculated for given data.

ILLUSTRATION 2.4: From the data given below, calculate domestic income, domestic product and domestic expenditure. Are the three the same? (See Box 2.29).

Salaries and Wages = 60,000
Rent = 12,000
Interest = 8,000
Dividend = 2,000
Undistributed Profits = 2,000
Employer's Contribution to Workers' Social Security = 1,000
Indirect Taxes = 3,000
Subsidies = 2,000
Mixed Incomes = 40,000
Consumption of Fixed Capital = 4,000
Govt. Final Consumption Expenditure = 25,000
Private Final Consumption Expenditure = 75,000
Exports = 3,000
Imports = 5,000
Net Factor Income from ROW = (–) 500
Transfer Payments = 2,000
Net Other Current Transfers From ROW = 500
Corporate Profit Tax = 10,000
Direct Personal Taxes = 8,000
Changes in Stocks = 2,000
Gross Domestic Fixed Capital Formation = 20,000
National Debt Interest = 5,000
Sales = 132,000
Intermediate Consumption = 14,000
Domestic Product to Government = 25,000

(All the figures are in Crore of rupees)

Solution: Domestic Income = Compensation of Employees
+ Operating Surplus
+ Mixed Incomes of the Self-employed

Compensation of Employees = Salaries and Wages + Social Security Contribution
= 60,000 + 1,000
= 61,000

Operating Surplus = Rent + Interest + Dividend + Undistributed Profits
= 12,000 + 8,000 + 2,000 + 2,000
= 24,000

Mixed Incomes = 40,000

∴ Domestic Income = 61,000 +24,000 + 40,000 = **115,000**

Domestic Expenditure = [Government Final Consumption Expenditure
+ Private Final Consumption Expenditure
+ Gross Domestic Capital Formation
+ Net Investment Abroad]
Less
[Consumption of Fixed Capital + Net Indirect Taxes]
= [25,000 + 75,000 + (20,000 + 2,000) + (3,000 – 5,000)]
Less
[4,000 + (3,000 – 2,000)] = **115,000**

[Note that Net Indirect Tax = indirect Tax – Subsidies
Net Investment Abroad = Exports – Imports
Gross Domestic Capital Formation = Gross Domestic Fixed Capital Formation + Changes in Stock]

Domestic Product = Sales + Changes in Stock
Less
Intermediate Consumption
Less
Consumption of Fixed Capital
Less
Net Indirect Taxes
= 132,000 + 2,000 – 14,000 – 4,000 – (3,000 – 2000) = **115,000**

It is clear from the calculations that
Domestic Income (*DI*) = Domestic Expenditure (*DE*)
= Domestic Product (*DP*) = **115,000**

ILLUSTRATION 2.5: From the data in illustration 2.4, determine the national income by
(i) Income Method
(ii) Expenditure Method
(iii) Value Added Method
Also determine all the national Income aggregates.

Solution:

(i) National Income by income method is Net national Income at Factor Cost (NNI_{FC}). It is the same as the sum of the domestic income and the net factor income from *ROW*.
NNI_{FC} = DI + Net Factor Income from ROW (*NFIA*).
= 115,000 (As calculated in Illustration 2.4) + (– 500) = **114,500**
(*Note that national income is less than the domestic income. It is so due to the negative balance of the net factor income from ROW*).

(ii) National Income by expenditure method is the Net National Expenditure at factor cost (NNE_{FC}). It is the same as the sum of domestic expenditure and the Net Factor Income/product from *ROW* (*NFIA*).
NNE_{FC} = *DE* + Net Factor Income from *ROW* (*NFIA*)
= 115,000 (As calculated in Illustration 2.4) + (– 500) = **114,500**

(iii) Following the pattern, national income by the value added method,

$NNP_{FC} = DP$ + Net Factor Income from *ROW* (*NFIA*)

= Sales + Changes in Stocks – Intermediate consumption
– Net Indirect Taxes – Consumption of Fixed Capital
+ Net Factor Income from *ROW* (NFIA)
= 132,000 + 2,000 – 14,000 – 1,000 – 4,000 + (– 500) = **114,500**

Apart from NNP_{FC}, there are seven other national income aggregates linked to it. They are:

NNP_{MP}, NDP_{FC}, NDP_{MP}, GDP_{FC}, GDP_{MP}, GNP_{FC}, *and* GNP_{MP}.

$NNP_{MP} = NNP_{FC} + NIT$
= 114,500 + 1000 = **115,500**

$NDP_{FC} = NNP_{FC} - NFIA$
= 114,500 – (– 500) = **115,000**

$NDP_{MP} = NDP_{FC} + NIT$
= 115,000 + 1,000 = **116,000**

$GDP_{FC} = NDP_{FC}$ + Depreciation (Dep.).
= 115,000 + 4,000 = **119,000**

$GDP_{MP} = GDP_{FC} + NIT$
= 119,000 +1,000 = **120,000**

$GNP_{FC} = GDP_{FC} + NFIA$
= 119,000 + (– 500) = **118,500**

$GNP_{MP} = GNP_{FC} + NIT$
= 118,500 + 1,000 = **119,500**

ILLUSTRATION 2.6: From the data in illustration 2.4, calculate

(a) Private Income
(b) Personal Income
(c) Personal Disposable Income
(d) Personal Savings.

Solution:

(a) Private Income = NDP_{FC} – Domestic product accruing to Government
+ *NFIA* + Transfer Payments + National Debt Interest (*NDI*)
+ Net Other Current Transfers from ROW (*NOCT*)
= 115,000 – 25,000 + (–500) + 2,000 + 5,000 + 500 = **97,000**

(b) Personal Income = Private Income – Corporate Tax – Undistributed Profits
= 97,000 – 10,000 – 2,000 = **85,000**

(c) Personal Disposable
Income = Personal Income – personal taxes, fees, fines, etc.
= 85,000 – 8,000 = **77,000**

(d) Personal Savings = Personal Disposable Income
Less
Personal consumption expenditure
= 77,000 – 75,000 = **2,000.**

ILLUSTRATION 2.7: From the data given below, calculate *GNP* at market Price through the Value Added Method:

Value of the output of the primary sector = 10,000
Intermediate consumption in the primary sector = 2,000
Value of the output in the secondary sector = 25,000
Intermediate consumption in the secondary sector = 5,000
Value of the output in the tertiary sector = 45,000
Intermediate consumption in the tertiary sector = 10,000
Net factor income from *ROW* = – 1,000

Solution: *GNP* at Market Price = Value Added by primary, secondary and the tertiary sectors + Net Factor Income from Abroad (*NFIA*)

Value Added by primary sector = Value of its output – its intermediate consumption
= 10,000 – 2,000 = 8,000

Value Added by secondary sector = Value of its output – its intermediate consumption
= 25,000 – 5,000 = 20,000

Value Added by tertiary sector = Value of its output – its intermediate consumption
= 45,000 – 10,000 = 35,000

Total Value Added by all the sectors = 8,000 + 20,000 + 35,000 = 63,000
GNP at Market Price = 63,000 + (–) 1,000 = **62,000.**

ILLUSTRATION 2.8: Industry A sells its product worth 2,000 to Industry B, worth 3,000 to Industry C, worth 5,000 to final demand worth 2,000 to ROW. Industry B sells its product worth 500 to Industry A, worth 3,000 to Industry C, worth 12,000 to final demand and worth 3,000 to ROW. Industry C sells its product worth 1,000 to industry A, worth 3,000 to Industry B, worth 8,000 to final demand and worth 6,000 to ROW. Imports of the three industries from ROW are respectively 1,000, 5,000 and 8,000. Find the contribution of the three industries to the *GDP* at market Price.

Solution: Calculation of contribution of the three industries to the *GDP* at market price can be conveniently done as below:

BOX 2.43

Industry	*Output*	*Input*	*Value Added = output – input*
A	2000 + 3000 + 5000 + 2000 = 12, 000	500 + 1000 + 1000 = 2,500	12,000 – 2,500 = 9,500
B	500 + 3000 + 12000 + 3000 = 18,500	2000 + 3000 + 5000 = 10,000	18,500 – 10,000 = 8,500
C	1000 + 3000 + 8000 + 6000 = 18,000	3000 + 3000 + 8000 = 14,000	18000 – 14000 = 4000
Contribution to GDP_{MP} or Gross Value Added by the Industries at Market Price = **22,000**			

As is clear, inputs of the three industries constitute their intermediate consumption. In fact, inter-industry flows remain confined to the producers' boundary and hence are treated as intermediate inputs. The total value added or the contribution to the GDP_{MP} can also be found by adding up the sales of the industries to the final demand and to the *ROW* (expenditure method). The same is, the result obtained:

Sales to the final demand = 5,000 + 12,000 + 8,000 = 25,000

Sales to *ROW* (net investment abroad) = Exports – Imports
= (2000 + 3000 + 6000) – (1000 + 5000 + 8000)
= 11,000 – 14,000 = (–) 3,000

Thus contribution to the GDP_{MP} = Sales to final demand + Sales to ROW
= 25,000 + (–) 3,000 = **22,000**

The expenditure method and the value added method, both, lead to the same estimate. Note that the estimate here is the domestic product, not the national product. We need net factor income from abroad to add to it to arrive at the national product. Note further that the estimate is at the market price, not at the factor cost. This is so due to the fact that the sales take place at the market price.

2.9 INPUT-OUTPUT ACCOUNTING: LEONTIEF'S INPUT-OUTPUT TABLE[1]

The input-output accounts deal with the inter-industry flows and the table, which records them, is known as the *Input-output Table*. In the language of W. J. Baumol, "Input-output analysis, for which we are indebted to Prof. Leontief, is the name given to the attempt to take account of the *general equilibrium phenomenon in the empirical analysis of production*".

The type of inter-industrial flow, dealt with in illustration 2.8, can be and also is presented best through the table. It is much more than a simple presentation of the inter-industrial flows for which the table is known. Here, we present the structure and the technique of application of the table for the benefit of the reader. The purpose of dealing with the table here is not only to show the reader how simple it becomes to deal with the intertwined inter-industry flows through the table, but also, to enable the reader to grasp the identity of national income, national product and national expenditure, their reconciliation and their links to the producers' boundary.

The table records inputs in columns and outputs in rows and has four quadrants:

(i) Quadrant I (Top-right): Final-demand-quadrant.
(ii) Quadrant II (Top-left): Inter-industry-flow-quadrant.
(iii) Quadrant III (Bottom-left): Primary-inputs-to-industry-quadrant.
(iv) Quadrant IV (Bottom-right): Primary-inputs-to-final–demand-quadrant.

Quadrant I, the final demand quadrant, shows the end use of the finished goods in the form of final consumption of households and government, domestic investment and net investment abroad. Recall that the entries in this quadrant form the components of the GDP_{MP} by the expenditure method.

Quadrant II, the inter-industry-flow quadrant shows the purchases of inputs and supply of the outputs by the industries. It also represents the producers' boundary.

Quadrant III, the primary-inputs-to-the-industry-quadrant, records the components of the gross value added at the market price. Net Value Added at Factor-cost (NVA_{FC}) is one of the components. Recall that all the entries in it are the same as those in the GDP_{MP} by income method. NVA_{FC} represents the net value added at factor cost which is the sum of the compensation of employees, operating surplus (rent, interest, dividend and undistributed profits) and mixed incomes. NVA_{FC} is thus NDP_{FC}. Adding depreciation and *NIT* (Net Indirect Tax) to this gives GDP_{MP} by the income or value added method which is the same as GDP_{MP} by expenditure method.

[1] Prof. W.W. Leontief (1905–99), the Russian–American economist , was awarded the Nobel Prize for Economics in 1973. He is known for his input-output analysis.

Quadrant IV, Primary-inputs-to-final–demand-quadrant, shows the direct purchases of the primary factors for final use. Items recorded in this quadrant are assumed to be negligible for the sake of the simplicity.

Evidently, it is possible to read GDP_{MP} from the table by income, expenditure and by value added methods at the same time. Input output tables and its variant are shown in Tables 2.3 and 2.4

Let us first view the two variants of the table in their requisite detail.

TABLE 2.3 (First Variant)

Output → / *Input ↓*		*INDUSTRY*				*FINAL-DEMAND (F.D)*					*Total F.D*	*Total Output*
		A	*B*	*C*	*Intermediate Outputs*	C_G	C_H	*GDFCF*	*ΔS*	*X–M*		
IN-DUS-TRY	A				P_A						F_A	X_A
	B				P_B						F_B	X_B
	C				P_C						F_C	X_C
Intermediate Inputs		I_A	I_B	I_C	I = P	ΣC_G	ΣC_H	ΣGDFCF	ΣΔS	Σ(X–M)	$F = GDP_{MP}$	X
Depreciation		D_A	D_B	D_C	D						D	
N.I.T		T_A	T_B	T_C	T						T	
NVA_{FC}		V_A	V_B	V_C	V						V	
Primary Inputs		X_a	X_b	X_c	X	ΣC_G	ΣC_H	ΣGDFCF	ΣΔS	Σ(X–M)	$F = GDP_{MP}$	X

Note the difference between the two variants. The first one shows net investment abroad (*X–M*) as a apart of the final demand column while the second one shows exports (*X*) only in place of (*X–M*). In the second variant, *M* is shown as a part of the III quadrant as an input to the industry. All the purchases of the industries, whether from other domestic industries or from the rest of the world sector, constitute their inputs. In the same way, all the sales of the industries, whether to the other domestic industries or to the rest of the world, constitute their outputs. Sales to the rest of the world are recorded as exports in the final demand quadrant. The second variant of the table, thus records imports as inputs (in the columns) and exports as outputs (in the rows) rather than recording net investment abroad (*X–M*) of all the industries in rows as a part of the final demand quadrant.

TABLE 2.4 (Second Variant)

Output → / *Input ↓*		*INDUSTRY*				*FINAL-DEMAND (F.D)*					*Total F.D*	*Total Output*
		A	*B*	*C*	*Intermediate Outputs*	C_G	C_H	*GDFCF*	*ΔS*	*X*		
IN-DUS-TRY	A				P_A						F_A	X_A
	B				P_B						F_B	X_B
	C				P_C						F_C	X_C
Intermediate Inputs		I_A	I_B	I_C	I = P	ΣC_G	ΣC_H	ΣGDFCF	ΣΔS	Σ(X)	F	X
Depreciation		D_A	D_B	D_C	D						D	
N.I.T		T_A	T_B	T_C	T						T	

(Contd.)

Output → / Input ↓	INDUSTRY				FINAL-DEMAND (F.D)					Total F.D	Total Output
	A	B	C	Intermediate Outputs	C_G	C_H	GDFCF	ΔS	X		
NVA_{FC}	V_A	V_B	V_C	V						V	
M	M_A	M_B	M_C	Σ(M)						Σ(M)	
Primary Inputs	X_a	X_b	X_c	X						X	
Total Input	$\mathbf{X_A}$	$\mathbf{X_B}$	$\mathbf{X_C}$	**X**	$\mathbf{\Sigma C_G}$	$\mathbf{\Sigma C_H}$	**ΣGDFCF**	**ΣΔS**	**Σ(X)**	**F**	

An illustration is in order at this stage.

ILLUSTRATION 2.9: An economy has only three producing sectors—Agriculture, Industry and Services. Arrange the information given below in an input-output transaction matrix and calculate the Gross Domestic Product at market prices.

Value of the output of agriculture at market price = 360
Value of the output of industrial sector at market price = 465
Value of the output of service sector at market price = 300

Domestic inputs of industrial sector from
(i) agricultural sector = 120
(ii) service sector = 45

Domestic inputs of services sector from
(i) agricultural sector = 30
(ii) industrial sector = 90

Domestic inputs of agricultural sector from
(i) industrial sector = 60
(ii) service sector = 30

Exports of output of
(i) agricultural sector =120
(ii) industrial sector = 45
(iii) service sector = 90

Imports of raw materials for
(i) agricultural sector = 55
(ii) industrial sector = 95

Household purchases of the output of
(i) agricultural sector = 60
(ii) industrial sector = 120
(iii) service sector = 90

Government purchases of the output of
(i) agricultural sector = 15
(ii) industrial sector = 45
(iii) service sector = 45

Sales to investment by
(i) agricultural sector = 15
(ii) industrial sector = 105

Net Indirect Tax paid by
(i) agricultural sector = 60
(ii) industrial sector = 60
(iii) service sector = 15
Consumption of fixed capital in
(i) agricultural sector = 20
(ii) industrial sector = 20
(iii) service sector = 10

Solution: Let us first make the entries in the ***Second Variant*** of the table (See Table 2.5).

Note that the ***second variant*** maintains the identity of total outputs to total inputs but it fails to maintain that of *GDP* by expenditure and income methods. The reason for that is the fact that net investment abroad (*X–M*) as a component of *GDP* by expenditure method does not figure in the table. In fact, exports of various industries are shown as their outputs in rows and imports as their inputs in columns.

Total output = 1,125
Total input = 1,125
Total output = Total input

The identity of *GDP* by expenditure and income methods for the data in Illustration 2.9 shown in the ***first variant*** of the table (See Table 2.6). This variant is suitable for reading the GDP_{MP} via income and expenditure approaches. Note how the total of the final demand column of the outputs of the three industries gives GDP_{MP} by expenditure method while the total of net value added at factor cost by the three industries as the sum of (NVA_{FC}), depreciation and net indirect taxes (*NIT*) gives GDP_{MP} by income method.

GDP_{MP} by expenditure approach = Total of Final Demand column = 155 + 220 + 225 = 600
GDP_{MP} by income approach = NVA_{FC} + depreciation + NIT = 50 + 135 + 415 = 600
GDP_{MP} by expenditure approach = 600 = GDP_{MP} by income approach
GDP_{MP} by expenditure approach = Total of Final Demand column = 600

The first variant doesn't maintain this identity. However, it maintains identity of total output to total input. In fact total output doesn't includes net investment abroad (*X–M*), instead it includes exports only of the three industries. On the other hand, inputs of the three industrees including their imports make up the total input that equalize total output. Thus total output equals total input in second variant of the Input-output (Table 2.5).

The difference between the two variants is immaterial so long as the reader is able to identify the cause and to make mends to accommodate it. With appropriate accommodation equality of total input to total output and that of GDP_{MP} by expenditure method to GDP_{MP} by income method can each be established from either table.

TABLE 2.5 (Second Variant)

Output → / *Input ↓*		*INDUSTRY*				*FINAL-DEMAND (F.D)*					*Total F.D*	*Total Output*
		A	*B*	*C*	*Intermediate Outputs*	C_G	C_H	*GDFCF*	ΔS	*X*		
IN-DUS-TRY	A	–	120	30	150	15	60	15	–	120	210	360
	B	60	–	90	150	45	120	105	–	45	315	465
	C	30	45	–	75	45	90	–	–	90	225	300
Intermediate Inputs		90	165	120	375	105	270	120	–	255	750	1125
Depreciation		20	20	10	50						50	
N.I.T		60	60	15	135						135	
M		55	95	–	150						150	
NVA_{FC}		135	125	155	415						415	
Primary Inputs		$X_a = 0$	$X_b = 0$	$X_c = 0$	X = 0						X = 0	
Total Input		**360**	**465**	**300**	**X = 1125**							

Now let us turn back to Illustration 2.8 and work it out again employing the first variant of the table to determine contributions of the three industries to the GDP_{MP}.

Table 2.7 demonstrates the process. The NVA_{FC} row and the primary inputs row record the balancing entries. No mention of depreciation and *NIT* in the illustration indicates that both of them in the respective columns of the three sectors may be taken as zero.

Sales to final demand represent the collective values of C_G, C_H, GDFCF and ΔS. The contribution to GDP_{MP} is 22,000 and the total output net of imports is 34,500 and so is total input net of imports.

The entries as made in the first variant of the input-output table are shown in Table 2.7.

TABLE 2.6 (First Variant)

Output → / *Input ↓*		*INDUSTRY*				*FINAL-DEMAND (F.D)*					*Total F.D*	*Total Output*
		A	*B*	*C*	*Intermediate Outputs*	C_G	C_H	*GDFCF*	ΔS	*X–M*		
IN-DUS-TRY	A	–	120	30	150	15	60	15	–	65	155	305
	B	60	–	90	150	45	120	105	–	(–)50	220	370
	C	30	45	–	75	45	90	–	–	90	225	300
Intermediate Inputs		90	165	120	375	105	270	120	–	105	600	975
Depreciation		20	20	10	50							50
N.I.T		60	60	15	135 600							135
NVA_{FC}		135	125	155	415							415
Primary Inputs		$X_a = 0$	$X_b = 0$	$X_c = 0$	X = 0							X = 0
Total Input		**305**	**370**	**300**	**975**							

TABLE 2.7

Output → / *Input ↓*		*INDUSTRY*				*FINAL-DEMAND (F.D)*					*Total F.D*	*Total Output*
		A	*B*	*C*	*Intermediate Outputs*	C_G	C_H	*GDFCF*	*ΔS*	*X–M*		
IN-DUS-TRY	A	–	2000	3000	5000	←		5000	→	1000	6000	11000
	B	500	–	3000	3500	←		12000	→	– 2000	10000	3500
	C	1000	3000	–	4000	←		8000	→	– 2000	6000	10000
Intermediate Inputs		1500	5000	6000	12500	←		25000	→	– 3000	22000	34500
Depreciation		–	–	–	–							–
N.I.T		–	–	–	–	22000						–
NVA_{FC}		9500	8500	4000	22000							22000
Primary Inputs		$X_a = 0$	$X_b = 0$	$X_c = 0$	X = 0							X = 0
Total Input		**11000**	**13500**	**10000**	**34500**							

2.10 CONCLUSION: CRITERIA FOR DETERMINING WHAT TO INCLUDE AND WHAT NOT IN NATIONAL INCOME

It has been seen that a particular product can be a part of the national product, provided it is meant for final consumption. In other words, *it is a part of the national product if it has crossed the **producers' boundary***. In the like manner, any receipt of money value qualifies as a part of the national income, provided there is a *quid pro quo* associated with it. In other words, *it is a part of the national income if some product or service has changed hands to neutralize the receipt of value*. Finally, *a product or service is a **final product** if it is deemed to be a non-essential one for the economy*. An essential product or service is one without which productive activities can't proceed. For instance, power is essential for a factory in the sense that the factory-work comes to a standstill without it. Streetlights are not essential in that sense. Economy can do without streetlights but not without industrial power supply. Power supply to industries is, thus, an intermediate product while streetlights are final products. A national income estimator has to include expenses on streetlights in national expenditure but has nothing to do with expenditures incurred on power supply to the industries. Such expenditures are accounted for by the industrial units themselves in the form of costs incurred on value addition. Thus, to determine whether a product is a part of the national product or an expenditure as a part of the national expenditure or money income as a part of the national income, one should ask oneself the following three questions:

(i) Has the product crossed the producers' boundary? If the answer to this question is in affirmative, the product is a final product and must be included in the national product.

(ii) Is there a *quid pro quo* associated with the receipt of money income? If the answer to this question is in affirmative, the said receipt should be treated as a part of the national income.

(iii) How essential the product in question is for the economy? If the answer to this question is 'very', it is an intermediate product and expenses incurred on it are not to be taken into account by the national income estimator.

2.11 CONSOLIDATED ACCOUNTS FOR THE NATION

The accounts that furnish in a nutshell the information on various flows in the economy are the following four accounts collectively referred to as the *Consolidated Accounts* of the Nation:

(a) *Account–1:* ***Gross Domestic Product and Expenditure Account:*** This account shows GDP_{MP} by income method on the left side and by expenditure method on the right side. Thus, compensation of employees, operating surplus, mixed incomes, *NIT* and depreciation appear on the left side while government and private final consumption expenditures $(C_{G\,+}C_H)$, Gross Domestic Capital Formation (*GDCF*) and net investment broad (*X–M*) on the right side.

(b) *Account–3:* ***National Disposable Income and its Appropriation Account:*** This account records *Net National Disposable Income at market price* by income method on the right side and by expenditure method on the left side. Net National Disposable Income at market price by income method includes NNP_{MP} (Compensation of employees + Operating Surplus + Mixed incomes + *NIT* + Net factor income from abroad) and Net Other Current Transfers from *ROW*. Net National Disposable Income at market price by expenditure method includes government and private final consumption expenditures $(C_G + C_H)$ and Savings $(S_F + S_H + S_G)$. S_F, S_H & S_G represent savings of firms, households and of government. Note that these savings finance net domestic capital formation (*NDCF,* which is *GDCF* less depreciation) and net investment abroad (*X–M*). Gross National Disposable Income at market price can be obtained by adding depreciation to Net National Disposable Income at market price.

(c) *Account–5:* ***Capital and Finance Account:*** This account records sources of financing the capital formation on the right side (Savings, depreciation and capital transfers from *ROW*) and capital accumulated on the left side. Capital accumulated comprises of *GDCF* $(GDF_{CF} + \Delta S)$ and net purchases of intangible assets from *ROW.*

(d) *Account–6:* ***External Transactions Account:*** This account records Net Exports (*X–M*), Net Factor Income from Abroad (*NFIA*), net other current transfers from *ROW* $(NOCT_{ROW})$ and net capital transfers from *ROW* on the left and net purchases of intangible assets from *ROW* on the right side. Let us tabulate them below.

Account 1: Gross Domestic Product and Expenditure Account

GDP_{MP} *(Income Approach)*	GDP_{MP} *(Expenditure Approach)*
1. Compensation of employees	1. Private Final Consumption Expenditure (C_H)
2. Operating Surplus	2. Government Final Consumption Expenditure (C_g)
3. Mixed Incomes	3. Gross Domestic Capital Formation (*GDCF*)
4. Net Indirect Taxes (*NIT*)	4. Net Investment Abroad (*X–M*)
5. Depreciation	5. Statistical Discrepancy

Notes: Compensation of employees =All Cash and kind compensations of employees; Operating Surplus = Rent + Interest + Undistributed profits; Mixed Incomes = Incomes of the self-employed; *NIT* = Indirect taxes – Subsidies; Depreciation = Consumption of fixed capital; *GDCF* = Gross Domestic Fixed Capital Formation (*GDFCF*) + Changes in Stocks (ΔS); Statistical Discrepancy = Balancing Entry.

Account 3: National Disposable Income and Appropriation Account

Appropriation of Net Disposable Income at Market price	*Net Disposable Income at Market price*
Net National Disposable Income at Market Price by Expenditure Method = $[(C_G + C_H) + (S_F + S_H + S_G) + (X–M)$	Net National Disposable Income at Market Price by Income Method = (Compensation of employees + Operating Surplus + Mixed Incomes + *NIT* + Net factor income from abroad) and Net Other Current Transfers from *ROW*

Notes: *See how some of the entries on the right side of Account 1 appear on the left side of account 3 and some of those appearing on* the left side of Account 1 appear on the right side of Account 3. Savings of Firms (S_F), Savings of Households (S_H) and Savings of Government (S_G) finance Net Domestic Capital Formation (*NDCF*), which is *GDCF* – Depreciation. Note also that Compensation of Employees + Operating Surplus+ Mixed Incomes + *NIT* + Net Factor Income from Abroad comprise Net National Product at Market Price (NNP_{MP}).

Account–5: Capital and Finance Account

Accumulations of Capital	*Sources of Capital Finance*
Capital accumulated comprises of *GDCF* ($GDF_{CF} + \Delta S$) and net purchases of intangible assets from *ROW*.	Savings, Depreciation and Capital Transfers from *ROW*)

Note: *GDF_{CF} represents Gross Domestic Fixed Capital Formation **and ROW,** Rest of the World*

Account–6: External Transactions Account

Acquisition	*Appropriation*
Net Exports (*X–M*) + Net Factor Income from Abroad (*NFIA*) + Net Other Current Transfers from *ROW* ($NOCT_{ROW}$) + Net Capital Transfers from *ROW*.	Net Purchases of Intangible Assets from *ROW*

KEY TERMS AND CONCEPTS

Income: It refers to earned income. Value received *in lieu* of some service rendered or some utility foregone.

Factor Income: It refers to income accruing to the factors of production for providing factor services.

Domestic Factor Income: Income accruing to domestic factors of production from their operations in the domestic territory.

Domestic Territory: Domestic Territory, in the current context, is the region within the political boundaries of a nation, comprising of the main land-mass and the territorial waters around it, if any, to a specified stretch. From the view-point of income, it covers the activities of the people within the domestic territory as also those of national embassies, consulates, high commissions and military establishments operating abroad along with those of the domestic owners of the aircrafts, ships, fishing vessels, floating platforms, etc. and natural gas rigs operating within the domestic territories.

Normal Residents: The term '*normal resident*' refers to a resident whose *economic interest* is vested in the country in which he/she resides at least for some time during the accounting year. All the enterprises operating in a country, all the nationals and foreign nationals residing in the country for a year or more, all the national abroad who return back in less than a year, all the nationals working in foreign institutions located in the country and all the scholars, students, patients staying abroad for education or for medical treatment, whether for just one year or for more than that, fall into the category of the normal residents.

National: A national is an individual who holds the citizenship of the country or holds the country's passport.

Net Factor Income from Abroad: It is the excess of factor incomes from foreign producers accruing to domestic factors over the factor incomes accruing to foreign factors from their operations in the domestic territory of ours.

Compensation of Employees: It refers to the cash or kind rewards of the factor labour, skilled or unskilled, accruing to it for providing the factor services along with social security contributions made by the employers. The former refers to salaries and wages in cash or in kind while the latter includes the employers' contributions towards the employees' provident fund, pensions, group insurance and family allowances. The kind compensations relate to free accommodation, free uniforms, free education to the school-going children of the employees, free medical care, free telephone facility, free furniture, etc.

Operating Surplus: It refers to income from property and entrepreneurship accruing to the entrepreneurs for ownership of certain factors as also for their management. Examples are rent, interest, dividend and undistributed profits.

Mixed Incomes: Incomes of the self-employed, such as doctors, actors, dancers, lawyers, chartered accountants, etc. are called the *mixed incomes.*

Transfer Payments: All unilateral transactions, such as scholarship to the students, old-age pensions, pocket money to youngsters paid by parents, etc. are known as transfer payments.

Private Income: Private Income refers to the income of the non-governmental entities from all the sources over a period of one accounting year. It is the income of the firms and the households from all the possible sources. Incomes, under this head, include transfer payments and such other unilateral transactions, which empower the private individuals and the entities with the purchasing power. It includes domestic product accruing to the private sector, net factor income from abroad, transfer payments, national debt interest and net other current transfer payments from the rest of the world. Private Income = Domestic Product accruing to the Pvt. Sector+ *NFIA*+*TP*+ *NDI*+ *NOCT* from *ROW.*

National Debt Interest: It is the interest paid by government on its borrowings, called public borrowings, to the sources it borrows from. Such interest accrues to financial institutions who purchase government bonds and is ultimately passed on to the individuals who invest with the financial institutions. It contributes to the purchasing power of the households and firms.

Net Other Current Transfer from Rest of the World: Such transfers refer to the current transfers from the rest of the world net of the current transfers to the rest of the world. Such transfers are unilateral transactions.

Personal Income: It is the income of the household sector over an accounting year from all the sources. In practice, it is the private income *less* Corporate Profit Tax *less Undistributed Profits.*

Personal Income = Private Income – corporate profit Tax – Undistributed Profits.

Corporate Profit Tax: Corporate Profit Tax is the tax levied on the profits of the business corporations. It does not trickle down to the household sector. In the same way, undistributed profits remain confined to the business firms for business operations in future.

Personal Disposable Income: After paying direct taxes (such as income tax), govt. fees, fines, etc., the income left with household sector is called the *Personal Disposable Income.* The household sector feels free to spend or to save it.

Personal Disposable Income = Personal Income – Direct Personal Taxes, Fees, Fines, etc.

Problems of Estimation of National Income by Income Method: Estimation of National Income by income method poses a few problems. Some of them are listed below:

1. Difficulties of Estimation of Mixed Incomes
2. Difficulty of Estimation of the Wage Income
3. Difficulty of Estimation of the compensation in kind
4. Difficulty in Allocation of the Dividends
5. Problems of Estimation of the Undistributed Profits.

Double Counting: It refers to the error of including the value of intermediate products more than once while estimating the national product by method. It leads to over-estimation of the national product.

Depreciation: It refers to loss of value of the productive assets due to wear and tear in the process of production. It is also known as the *consumption of fixed capital* during production. It is treated as a cost of production.

Obsolescence: It refers to loss of value of a productive asset due to the obsoleteness of its technology Obsolescence differs from depreciation in one respect. Depreciation is loss of value of the productive asset due its use, wear and tear in the process of production but obsolescence is loss of value of the productive asset due to obsolete and outdated technology and not due to its use in production. For example, a completely unused machine may be as good as new but if its technology is outdated, it looses a sizeable part of its value. The loss of value due depreciation is a cost of production but that due to obsolescence is not.

Final and Intermediate Goods: Final goods refer to goods meant for ultimate consumption and not for further production of other goods and services. Intermediate goods, on the other hand, refer to goods meant for further production of other goods and services and not for final consumption. In other words, final goods are meant for household-consumption while intermediate goods are meant for producers. That is why final goods are referred to as *the consumer goods* while intermediate goods are referred to as *the producers' goods*. The distinction is functional. A loaf of bread, if bought by a household for its consumption is a final good while the same loaf would have served as an intermediate good had it been bought or used by a hotel or restaurant for its use as an input for the food products. A refrigerator, if used by a household, is a durable-use-consumer-good but the same is a producers' good if used by food joints for storing food or by chemists for storing medicines.

Economic, Non-economic and Free Goods: Economic goods are those goods that are scarce in supply and hence, command a price in the market. Free goods, on the other hand, are those goods that are abundant in supply, and hence, are not exchanged for a price. For example, air and sunshine are free goods. Non-economic goods are those goods which are highly invaluable and scarce but not available on exchange due to lack of their monetization. For example, services of a housewife, care of a mother, concern of a friend are all invaluable and scarce yet they are not economic goods because there can't be a price tag attached to any of them.

Real and Financial Capital: Real Capital refers to the tangible productive assets that directly participate in the process of production. For example, plant, machinery and equipment directly participate in the process of production and hence constitute the real capital. Financial capital refers to paper titles to the real capital that help procurement or use of real capital in the process of production but do not directly take part in it. Currency notes, shares, bonds and debentures are all examples of financial capital. By themselves, they are as useless as a five-hundred-rupee-note in providing transportation on a day of strike of buses, taxis, scooters and all other means of transport.

Real Income and Nominal Income: Income in terms of money is nominal income while the basket of goods and services it is worth at a point of time is the real income. Magnitude of real income depends on the prices of the goods and the services. Suppose, an individual has ₹ 100. This is his nominal income.

Now suppose that the price of apples is ₹ 20 per kg. The real income possessed by the individual at this price is 5 kg. of apples. If the price of apples falls to ₹ 10 per kg., the real income of the individual would rise to 10 kg. of apples despite no change in the nominal income of the individual.

National Income at Current and at Constant Prices: National income at current prices refers to money value of the goods and services at the prices prevailing in the current period. The same expressed in terms of the prices that prevailed in some year of reference (the base year), would be known as the national income at prices of the base year. If all the estimates of the national income were made each year in terms of the respective prices that prevailed in each of these years, the series so obtained would form a series of national income at current prices. But when all these estimates were converted into the prices that prevailed in the base year with a view to analyze the changes in national income with reference to the base year, the transformed series of national income estimates would be termed as the series of national income estimates at constant prices. Conversion of the national income at current prices into that at the base year's prices is done through the price indices of the current year and the base year. For example, suppose national income of a country in the year 2005 is ₹ 10,000 crores while the price index for 2005 is 250 (with respect to the base year 2001, i.e., base year's price index =100), the current national income when expressed in terms of the base year's prices would be termed as the national income at constant prices which would work out to be (100 × 10,000)/250 or simply ₹ 4,000.

National Income Deflator and National income Implicit Deflator or Implicit price Deflator: National income deflator is defined as the ratio of the price index of the chosen year to that of the base year.

$$\text{National Income Deflator} = \frac{\text{Price Index of the Chosen Year}}{\text{Price Index of the Base Year}}$$

Here, *National Income Deflator* = 250/100 or 2.50. It deflates the national income at current prices into that at constant prices. The current estimate needs to be divided by the national income deflator for the purpose. Hence, 10,000/2.50 = 4,000 is the national income at the base year's price or the national income at the constant price. National income implicit deflator or implicit price deflator is defined as the ratio of the nominal income to the real income. Thus,

$$\text{Implicit Price Deflator} = \frac{\text{Nominal Income}}{\text{Real Income}}$$

Note that *NI* deflator and the implicit price deflator amount to the same thing. The only point of difference is the definition.

Intermediate Consumption: Inputs consumed in production are referred to as the *Intermediate Consumption.*

Gross and Net Value added: Gross Value Added (*GVA*) is defined as the excess of value of the gross output over the intermediate consumption.

Gross Value added = Value of the gross output – Intermediate Consumption = Output–Input.

Net Value Added, on the other hand, is defined as the excess of the gross value added over the consumption of fixed capital.

Net Value Added (*NVA*) = Gross Value Added – Depreciation or consumption of fixed capital

Determination of the Value Added: Value added by all the producers can be determined by clubbing together for all the firms the excess of the values of their outputs over their inputs.

Problems of Estimation of National Income by Value Added Method: The product or the output method of estimation of the national income involves the following difficulties:

1. Difficulty of evaluation of products held for self-consumption by the producers
2. Difficulty of choosing the price
3. Difficulty of Estimation of the Depreciation
4. Difficulty of availability of reliable data.

Private Final Consumption Expenditure: It is defined as the expenditure incurred by the households at the market price on all the consumer goods, including single use, semi-durables and durables.

Government Final Consumption Expenditure: It is defined as the expenditure incurred by the government at the market price on all the consumer goods, including single use, semi-durables and durables.

Gross Domestic Private Investment: It is also known as Gross Domestic Capital Formation (*GDCF*), it comprises of the Gross Domestic Fixed Capital Formation (*GDFCF*) and changes in stocks (ΔS) of raw materials, semi-finished and finished but unsold goods. *GDFCF* refers to stockpiling fixed capital assets, such as plant, equipment, machinery, etc., for production.

Net Investment Abroad: It refers to the excess of exports over imports.

Problems of Estimation of National Income by Expenditure Method: There are a few problems associated with the expenditure method. They are related to estimation of capital formation, expenditure of government and expenditure on durable and semi-durable goods. Capital formation does not include financial capital. Likewise expenditures incurred by the government on old-age pensions, scholarships, etc. are transfer payments, which may lead to additional final consumption demand made by the recipients but they are not a part of the government final consumption expenditure. Likewise, resale of durables and semi-durables is only a transfer of ownership, not a part of the final consumption expenditure.

Domestic Income (*DI*): Also known as NDI_{FC} or NDP_{FC}, DI refers to the factor income from domestic sources. It is equal to the sum of the compensation of employees, operating surplus and mixed incomes.

Domestic Income = compensation of employees + operating surplus + mixed incomes
= compensation of employees + rent + interest + dividend + undistributed-profits + mixed incomes.

Domestic Product (*DP*): Also known as NDP_{FC}, it refers to the net value added at factor cost by all the domestic firms. It is equal to Net Value Added at factor cost.

Domestic Expenditure (*DE*): Also known as the NDE_{FC} or simply as NDP_{FC}, it refers to the domestic expenditure incurred on final goods. In other words, it represents sales to the final-demand, which comprise of government and private final consumption expenditures at factor cost, net domestic capital formation and net investment abroad.

Domestic Expenditure (*DE*) = Government Final Consumption Expenditure + Pvt. Final Consumption Expenditure + *NDCF* + $(X - M)$ – *NIT*

$$= C_G + C_H + [GDF_{CF} + \Delta S - \text{Depreciation}] + (X - M) - NIT$$

Circular Flows of Income and Expenditure: Production is the source of income, which must return back to the source ultimately so that production may maintain its pace. This is known as the circular flow of money or of income. The income that accrues to the household sector for its factor-services is spent by it partly on consumption and partly on investment. It reaches back the producers' sector after its circular flow. The part of it that is held back by the household sector is termed as the leakage from the circular flow. Such leakages lead to accumulation of the unsold stocks of the output, which in turn, lead to depression. Plugging of the leakages from the circular flows is must for sustenance of production.

National Aggregates: NDP_{FC}, the domestic income, is one of the eight national income aggregates. The other seven may be derived from it by adding one or more of depreciation, *NFIA* and/or *NIT* in varying combinations. Addition of depreciation transforms *net* estimates into *gross* estimates; *NFIA* transforms the domestic estimates into national estimates and NIT transforms factor price estimates into market price estimates. Different relationships are shown below:

1. $GNP_{MP} = GNP_{FC} + NIT$
2. $GNP_{MP} = GDP_{MP} + NFIA$
3. $GNP_{MP} = NNP_{MP} + Dep.$
4. $NNP_{MP} = NDP_{MP} + NFIA$
5. $NNP_{MP} = NNP_{FC} + NIT$
6. $NDP_{MP} = NDP_{FC} + NIT$
7. $GDP_{MP} = GDP_{FC} + NIT$
8. $GDP_{MP} = NDP_{MP} + Dep.$
9. $GDP_{FC} = NDP_{FC} + Dep.$

Per Capita Income: It is defined as the share of one normal resident in the national income. It can be measured as a ratio of the national income to the population of the normal residents in the country.

$$\text{Per Capita Income} = \frac{\text{National Income}}{\text{Population of the normal residents}}$$

In a like-manner, *GNP* per capita can be defined as the ratio of the *GNP* to the population of the normal residents in the country. The same would be the case with *GDP* per capita. What one needs to do is to take the relevant national income aggregate in the numerator and the population of the normal residents in the denominator.

Utility of National Income Accounts: National income estimates are very important partly as a measuring rod of economic welfare and economic growth in the country and partly as tools of analysis of economic policies, structural changes and of comparison of the economic performance of the country vis-à-vis other countries of the world. Let us summarize the utility of national income estimates in the following points:

1. Indicator of Economic Welfare
2. Measure of Economic Growth and Development
3. Study and Analysis of Structural Changes in Different Sectors of an Economy
4. Comparison of Economic Performance of the Country with that of the other Countries
5. Significance to business policy formulation
6. Significance to trade unions.

GNP Per Capita as a Measure of Economic Welfare: There is a widespread disillusionment among the economists about *GNP* per capita as a measure of economic welfare. Countries like Kuwait have a very high *GNP* per capita yet enjoy a very low level of economic welfare whatever the reasons. This has initiated economists to look for alternative measures of economic development and welfare. Measure of Economic Welfare (*MEW*), Net Economic Welfare (NEW), Human Development Index (*HDI*) and Physical Quality of Life Index (*PQLI*) are some of the alternatives arrived at in consequence. *PQLI* has so far proved the most practical and the most realistic measure of economic welfare. It has shown why countries like Kuwait enjoy low welfare despite high *GNP* per capita and why countries like Sri Lanka enjoy a high level of welfare despite low *GNP* per capita. *PQLI* is obtained by blending together the indices of life expectancy, literacy rate and infant mortality rate in equal measures (weights). Human development index (*HDI*) as calculated by *UNDP* in the post 2010 period is the geometric mean of Life expectancy index, education index and income index.

Leontief's Input-output Matrix: Inter industrial flows of output and those beyond the producers' boundary, are best depicted in a compact and precise manner through the input-output matrix developed by Prof. Leontief. The table helps recording Domestic Expenditure, Domestic Product and Domestic Income simultaneously in a compact manner at market prices as well as at factor cost. It helps instant knowledge of various domestic income aggregates and at the same time depicts the interindustrial flows of inputs. In a nutshell, it provides a bird's eye-view of the domestic income accounts. Not only this, it also helps the industries to develop their technology matrices so important for them to determine the input requirements for producing a given level of output.

Net National Disposable Income at Market Price: It is the sum of the Net National Product at market price and the Net Other Current Transfers from *ROW*. Thus,

$$\text{Net National Disposable Income at Market Price} = NNP_{MP} + NOCT \text{ from } ROW.$$
$$= NDP_{MP} + NFIA + NOCT \text{ from } ROW.$$

Gross National Disposable Income at Market Price: It is the sum of the Net National Disposable Income at Market Price and the depreciation. Thus,

Gross National Disposable Income at Market Price

$$= \textit{Net National Disposable Income at Market Price} + \textit{Depreciation}$$
$$= NNP_{MP} + NOCT \textit{ from } ROW + \textit{Depreciation}$$
$$= NDP_{MP} + NFIA + NOCT \textit{ from } ROW + \textit{Depreciation}.$$

National Capital: It is defined as that part of the national wealth, which is engaged in current production of goods and services. It comprises of all the structures, plants, machinery, equipments, monetary gold and silver and net assets abroad. Structures refer to fixed productive assets such as national stadia.

Thus, National Capital = Structures + Plant + Machinery + Equipment + Monetary Gold and Silver + Net Assets Abroad

EXERCISES

A. Short Answer Questions

1. Outline components of net factor income from abroad.
2. Enumerate items that comprise compensation of employees.
3. Name the components of the operating surplus.
4. Who is a normal resident?
5. Enumerate important problems faced in estimation of national income by income method.
6. What is double counting? Why should it be avoided?
7. Define depreciation. How is it different from obsolescence?
8. How can market price be obtained from the factor cost?
9. What is meant by gross value added? How does it differ from net value added?
10. What are the intermediate goods? How do they differ from final goods?
11. Name are the major problem encountered in estimation of national income by product method?
12. Define private final consumption expenditure.
13. What are the components of gross domestic capital formation?
14. Define net investment abroad.
15. What is the major difference between domestic income and national income?
16. Define private income. Enumerate its components.
17. How does personal income differ from private income?
18. How does personal income differ from national disposable income?
19. What is meant by the transfer payments (*TP*)? How is it different from transfer income?
20. Define National Debt Interest (*NDI*). Is it a liability or an asset?

21. Define net other current transfers from the rest of the world.
22. What is corporate tax? How is it different from personal tax?
23. What are the components of undistributed profits?
24. Name the major problems faced in estimation of national income by expenditure method.
25. What is meant by per capita income? How can it be determined?
26. Define National Income Deflator. What is its utility?
27. Define National Income Implicit Deflator. Is it the same as national income implicit deflator? Give reasons in support.
28. Name the domestic income aggregates. How are they interrelated?
29. Name the national income aggregates. How are they interrelated?
30. Name gross national income aggregates. How are they interrelated?
31. Briefly outline the circular flows of national income and expenditure in an economy with 3 sectors.
32. Outline the circular flows of income and expenditure in an economy with 4 sectors.
33. What is meant by income from property and entrepreneurship? Explain.
34. How is *GNP* per capita an inadequate measure of economic welfare?
35. What is *PQLI*? How is it determined? How does it compare with *GNP* per capita?
36. What is *HDI*? How is it calculated? Would you rank it better than *PQLI*?
37. Which method is the better way of rectifying the double counting?
38. Outline the major drawbacks of *GNP* estimation.
39. What are the components of final Demand? What is its utility?
40. What makes *NI* at current prices different from that at constant prices?

B. Long Answer Questions

41. Distinguish between the following:
    (a) A national and a normal resident
    (b) Depreciation and obsolescence
    (c) National income at current prices and national income at constant prices
    (d) Market price and factor cost
    (e) Final goods and intermediate goods
    (f) Domestic income and national income
    (g) Gross value added and net value added
    (h) Gross operating surplus and net operating surplus
    (i) Private income and personal income
    (j) Personal income and personal disposable income
    (k) GNP_{MP} and NDP_{FC}
    (l) NNP_{FC} and NDP_{FC}
    (m) National income deflator and implicit price deflator
    (n) NDP_{FC} and GDP_{MP}
    (o) Intermediate consumption and final consumption.
42. Define net factor income from abroad. Calculate net factor income from abroad from the following data: (in crores of rupees)

    Compensation of employees from *ROW* = 600
    Income from property from *ROW* = 400
    Income from entrepreneurship from *ROW* = 500
    Compensation of employees to *ROW* = 800
    Income from property to *ROW* = 500
    Income from entrepreneurship to *ROW* = 600
    Remittances from *ROW* = 80
    Remittances to *ROW* = 100
    Net incurrence of foreign financial liability = (–) 300

Solution:

Net compensation of employees from *ROW*

= Compensation of Employees from *ROW* – Compensation of employees to *ROW*

= 600 – 800 = (–) 200

Net income from property from *ROW*

= 400 – 500 = (–) 100

Net income from entrepreneurship from *ROW*

= 500 – 600 = (–) 100

Net factor income from *ROW*

= Net compensation of employees from *ROW*

+ Net income from property from *ROW*

+ Net income from entrepreneurship from *ROW*

= (–) 200 + (–) 100 + (–) 100 = (–) **400.**

43. How would you treat the following in national income:

(i) Pocket money received by children.

(ii) Scholarship paid to bright children.

(iii) Old-age-pensions received by retired people.

(iv) Total amount received at maturity of an insurance policy, including the amount paid by way of premium and amount accrued by way of interest/dividend, etc.

(v) Lottery of one crore won by an individual.

(vi) Purchase of a new car by an individual.

(vii) Purchase of a second-hand car by individual and commission paid to the dealer.

(viii) Purchase of an old house by an individual and brokerage paid by him to the property dealer.

(ix) Income tax paid by an individual to government.

(x) Expenditures incurred on street-lights and that on power supply to the industries.

(xi) Purchase of old stock (shares) by an individual.

[Ans: (i), (ii), (iii) & (v) are not to be included in national income as each is a transfer payment. (No *quid pro quo* is associated with any of them).

(iv) The amount assured is a capital transfer and hence it is not to be included in NI. Additional amount accruing by way of interest/bonus, etc. is to be included in *NI* on the grounds that it is a factor income.

(vi) It is to be included in national expenditure as it forms a purchase of a consumer durable by the household. Had a firm bought the same, it would not enter into the national expenditure on the grounds that the firm is to treat it as its capital investment and is to include it in the values of its outputs.

(vii) Expenditure incurred on a second-hand car is not to be included in the national expenditure as it is nothing more than a transfer of ownership. Its value has already been included in the national expenditure in the year the car was bought a-new. The dealer's commission, however, is to be included in the national expenditure as the same forms a factor payment for the factor services of the dealer.

(viii) Expenditure on an old-house does not enter into the national expenditure for the same reason as that in (vii) but brokerage paid to the dealer certainly does, again for the same reason as that in part (vii).

(ix) Income tax paid by an individual is a transfer payment from the view point of government as there is no *quid pro quo* associated with it. It can be treated as a negative transfer payment on the grounds that it is received, not paid by the government. Hence it is not a part of the national expenditure. From the view point of the tax payers, it is a part of their past income which is already accounted for in the past.

(x) Expenditure incurred on street-lights is an expenditure on a final product and hence is to be included in the national expenditure but that incurred on the power-supply to the industries is not a part of the national expenditure as it is made on intermediate consumption by the industries, which make it a part of the price of their products.

(xi) Purchase of old stock (shares) is nothing more than a transfer of ownership. Its value is already accounted for in capital formation at the time of its issue.]

44. What are the components of the operating surplus? From the data given below, estimate the value of the operating surplus in each of the following cases:

Rent = 10,000
Interest = 5,000
Dividend = 6,000
Undistributed profits = 4,000

Given that

(i) the building is a rented one
(ii) the building is owned by the entrepreneur and rent is paid to him as imputed rent
(iii) the interest has to be paid to a banker
(iv) the interest has to be paid to the entrepreneur as imputed interest
(v) None of the rent and the interest accrues to the entrepreneur
(Treat each of the above cases independently).

[Ans: The operating surplus refers to the residual income accruing to the owner for ownership and management of certain factors of production such as land-building and capital. The other name given to it is income from property and entrepreneurship accruing to the owner. Such surpluses are at the disposal of the owner who may feed them back into his venture for its operation or for its expansion. Operating Surplus thus has the following possible components:

Operating Surplus = Rent + interest + dividend + undistributed profits

(Undistributed profits are also known as savings of the firms or as retained earnings of the firms)

(i) When rent does not accrue to the owner of the firm, the Operating Surplus,
OS = interest + dividend + undistributed profits
= 5,000 + 6,000 + 4,000 = **15,000.**

(ii) When rent accrues to the owner of the firm, the Operating Surplus,
OS = rent + interest + dividend + undistributed profits
= 10,000 + 5,000 + 6,000+ 4,000 = **25,000.**

(iii) When interest does not accrue to the owner of the firm, the Operating Surplus,
OS = rent + dividend + undistributed profits
= 10,000 + 6,000 + 4,000 = **20,000.**

(iv) When interest accrues to the owner of the firm, the Operating Surplus,
OS = rent + interest + dividend + undistributed profits
= 10,000 + 5,000 + 6,000 + 4,000 = **25,000.**

(v) When none of the rent and the interest accrues to the entrepreneur, the Operating Surplus,
OS = dividend + undistributed profits
= 6,000 + 4,000 = **10,000.]**

45. What are mixed incomes? Suggest a method of estimating them.

46. What is double counting? Demonstrate with the help of a hypothetical example. Show how the problem double counting can be rectified by

(a) the value added method
(b) the final product method

47. Draw the circular flow of income for an economy with only two sectors, namely, the household and the producers' sectors.

48. How would your answer change if the financial sector were also present in the previous question?

49. Enumerate various national income aggregates and show how they are interrelated.

50. Enumerate the components of private and personal incomes. Calculate private and personal incomes from the following data by two alternative approaches:

Domestic Product accruing to private sector = 8,000
Net factor income from abroad = (–) 500
Transfer Payments = 800
National Debt Interest = 600
Net other current transfers from ROW = 400

Corporate profit tax = 100
Undistributed profits = 200
NDP_{FC} = 12,000
Income from property & entrepreneurship to Government administrative departments = 3500
Savings of non-departmental enterprises = 500
Personal Taxes = 100
Personal Savings = 150.

[Ans: Private Income = **9,300**
Personal Income = **9,000.]**

51. Estimate personal consumption expenditure from the data given in question 50. **[Ans:** 8,750]

[Hint: Personal consumption expenditure = Personal disposable income – personal savings
= Personal income – personal taxes – personal savings]

52. Estimate national income (NNP_{FC}) from the data given below by income and expenditure methods (all figures in crores of rupees):

Salaries and wages = 12,000
Social security contributions = 1,000
Rent = 2,000
Interest = 1,800
Private final consumption expenditure (C_H) = 16,000
Govt. final consumption expenditure (C_G) = 5,000
Gross Domestic Fixed Capital Formation(GDF_{CF}) = 3,000
Changes in stocks (ΔS) = 1,000
Exports = 3,500
Imports = 2,000
Dividend = 1,000
Undistributed profits = 1,200
Mixed incomes = 6,500
Net Factor Income from Abroad ($NFIA$) = (–) 500
Consumption of fixed capital = 1,000

[Ans: NNP_{FC} by income method = **25,000**
NNP_{FC} by expenditure method = **25,000.]**

53. Data pertaining to a firm in respect of the accounting year ending 2004–05 are as given below:

Sales = 2,50,000
Closing Stock of Finished goods = 30,000
Closing Stock of Semi-finished goods = 20,000
Closing Stock of Raw-materials = 30,000
Opening Stock of Finished goods = 20,000
Opening Stock of Semi-finished goods = 10,000
Opening Stock of Raw-materials = 20,000
Expenditure on Raw materials & Intermediate Goods = 80,000
Consumption of fixed capital = 15,000
Net Indirect taxes = 10,000

Determine the gross and the net values added at market price and at factor cost.

[Ans: Gross Value Added at market price = **20,000**
Intermediate consumption = **70,000**
Gross Value Added at market price = **200,000**
Gross Value Added at factor cost = **190,000**
Net Value Added at factor cost = **175,000**
Net Value Added at market price = **185,000.]**

54. From the data given below, calculate GDP_{MP} by (a) Expenditure Method (b) Income Method: (₹ in crores)

Personal consumption expenditure = 1,000
Salaries and wages = 1,000

Social security contribution = 200
Gross business fixed investment = 100
Profits = 200
Gross residential construction investment = 100
Government purchases of goods and services = 500
Gross public investment = 100
Rent = 100
Inventory investment = 100
Exports = 200
Imports = 100
Interest = 100
Net Factor Income from Abroad (NFIA) = – 50
Mixed Incomes = 200
Depreciation = 100
Indirect taxes = 150
Subsidies = 50

[Ans:

(a) GDP_{MP} by Expenditure Method = **2,000**
(b) GDP_{MP} by Income Method = **2,000.]**

55. From the data given below, calculate

(i) GDP_{FC}
(ii) National Income
(iii) Net and Gross National Disposable Income
(iv) Private Income
(v) Personal Income
(vi) Personal Disposable Income
(vii) Personal Savings

GDP_{MP} = 2,000
Net Other Current Transfers from *ROW* = 200
National Debt Interest = 100
Income from property and entrepreneurship to government administrative department = 400
Savings of non-departmental enterprises = 100
Transfer Payments (*TP*) = 150
Savings of the firms = 50
Corporate profit tax = 50
Personal taxes = 100
Net Factor Income from Abroad (*NFIA*) = – 50
Net exports = 100
Depreciation = 100
Net Indirect Taxes (*NIT*) = 100

[Ans:

(i) GDP_{FC} = **1,900**
(ii) National Income = **1,750**
(iii) Net National Disposable Income at Factor Cost = **1,950**
Net National Disposable Income at Market Price = **2,050**
Gross National Disposable Income at Factor Cost = **2,050**
Gross National Disposable Income at Market Price = **2,150**
(iv) Private Income = **1,650**
(v) Personal Income = **1,550**
(vi) Personal Disposable Income = **1,450**
(vii) Personal Savings = **450]**

56. What are the components of national capital? From the data given below for the year 2004–05, estimate national capital (₹ in crores)

Structure = 4,000
Plant, Machinery, Equipment = 2,000
Monetary Gold and Silver = 1000
National Productive Assets Abroad = 800
Foreign Productive Assets in the Nation = 1,000
Value of Shares = 2,000
Cash with the financial institutions = 1,000
Cash with the public = 1,000

[**Ans:** National Capital comprises of National Structures, Plant-machinery-equipment, Monetary-gold, silver and Net Assets Abroad. Paper titles such as shares, cash, etc. don't form a part of the national capital. Thus, National Capital = 6,800]

57. Estimate all the national income aggregates from the data given below:

NDP_{FC} = 50,000

Depreciation = 5,000

Net Indirect Taxes = 500

Net Factor Income from Abroad = – 500

[**Ans:** NDP_{MP} = 50,500; GDP_{MP} = 55,500; GNP_{MP} = 55,000; NNP_{MP} = 50,000; NNP_{FC} = 49,500; GNP_{FC} = 54,500; GDP_{FC} = 55,000]

58. From the data given below, estimate capital stock of an economy, as on 1st Jan., 2005: (₹ in crores)

Capital stock on 1st Jan., 2004 = 65,578
GDP_{MP} for 2004–05 = 25,000
Pvt. Final consumption = 10,000
Govt. final consumption = 6,000
Net exports = **2,000**

[**Ans:** ₹ 72,578 crores = 7,000
Capital formed during 2004–05 (*GDCF*) = 7,000
Capital stock on 1st Jan., 2005 = 72,578.]

59. Estimate the values added by firms A and B, from the data given below: (₹ *in lakhs*)

Purchases by Firm A from rest of the World = 50
Sales by Firm B =100
Purchases by Firm A from Firm B = 80
Sales by Firm A =120
Exports by Firm A = 40
Opening stock of Firm A = 40
Closing stock of Firm A = 25
Opening stock of Firm B = 50
Closing stock of Firm B = 30
Purchases by firm B from Firm A = 50

[**Ans:** Value added by Firm A = **15**
Value added by Firm B = **30.]**

C. Easy Type Questions

60. Draw the circular flow of income and expenditure for a three-sector, with financial sector also present.

61. Draw the circular flow of income and expenditure for a four-sector-economy with financial sector also present.

62. Outline various difficulties of estimating national income by various methods.

63. Explain some of the important utilities of national income estimates.

64. Assuming that the economy comprises only of industries A, B and C, estimate national income by income as well as by expenditure methods from the data given below. Also determine private income, personal income, personal disposable income and all the other seven national income aggregates:

Sales of firm A to

(i) Firm B = 250
(ii) Firm C = 25
(iii) Household final consumption = 250
(iv) Govt. final consumption = 150
(v) Investment = 100
(vi) *ROW* = 25

Sales of Firm B to

(i) Firm A = 200
(ii) Firm C = 75
(iii) Household final consumption = 275
(iv) Govt. final consumption = 50
(v) Investment = 125
(vi) *ROW* = 40

Sales of Firm C to

(i) Firm A = 150
(ii) Firm B = 15
(iii) Household final consumption = 25
(iv) Govt. final consumption = 25
(v) Investment = 50
(vi) *ROW* = 35

Consumption of fixed capital by

(i) Firm A = 30
(ii) Firm B = 20
(iii) Firm C = 10

Imports of raw material for

(i) Firm A = 30
(ii) Firm B = 10
(iii) Firm C = 10

Net Indirect Taxes paid by

(i) Firm A = 20
(ii) Firm B = 10
(iii) Firm C = 10

Income from property and entrepreneurship to govt. administrative departments = 150
Savings of non-departmental enterprises = 50
Current transfers from govt. administrative:

Departments = 35
Corporate tax = 10
Direct taxes on households = 15
Interest on National Debt = 15
Net other current transfers from *ROW* = 30
Net factor Income from Abroad = – 50
Savings of firms = 45

[Ans: GDP_{MP} by Expenditure Method = **1100**
GDP_{MP} by Income method = **1100**
National Income (NNP_{FC}) by Expenditure Method = **950**
National Income (NNP_{FC}) by Income Method = **950**
National Disposable Income = **1020**
Private Income = **830**

Personal Income = **775**
Personal Disposable Income = **760**
GDP_{MP} **= 1100 ;** GDP_{FC} **= 1060 ;** GNP_{MP} **= 1050 ;** GNP_{FC} **= 1010 ;** NNP_{FC} **= 950 ;**
NNP_{MP} **= 990;** NDP_{FC} **= 1000 ;** NDP_{MP} **= 1040]**

The solution to this problem can be best-understood and worked out through Leontief Input-output Table. The answer for verification is given on in Table 2.8.

TABLE 2.8

Output → / *Input* ↓		*INDUSTRY*				*FINAL-DEMAND (F.D)*					*Total F.D*	*Total Output*
		A	B	C	*Intermediate Outputs*	C_G	C_H	*GDFCF*	ΔS	*X–M*		
IN-DUSTRY	A	–	250	25	275	150	250	←100→		– 5	495	770
	B	200	–	75	275	50	275	←125→		30	480	755
	C	150	15	–	165	25	25	← 50 →		25	125	290
Intermediate Inputs		350	265	100	715	225	550	←275→		50	1100	1815
Depreciation		30	20	10	60							
N.I.T		20	10	10	40 1100							
NVA_{FC}		370	460	170	1000							
Primary Inputs												
Total Input		**770**	**755**	**290**	**1815**							

65. "*GNP* per capita is a biased index of welfare measure," discuss.

66. From the data given below, estimate

(a) *NNP* at factor cost
(b) Private income
(c) Personal income
(d) Personal disposable income
(e) Operating surplus
(f) Compensation of employees

Savings of the households = 5,000
Savings of the firms = 4,000
Savings of non-departmental enterprises = 200
Income from Property and Entrepreneurship to Government Administrative Departments = 3,000
Transfer Payments = 200
National Debt Interest = 400
Net Other Current Transfers from *ROW* = 100
Net Factor Income from Abroad = 100
Corporate profit Tax = 200
Consumption of Fixed Capital = 1,000
Net Indirect Taxes = 500
Personal Consumption Expenditure = 10,000
Mixed Incomes = 5,000
Rent = 2,000
Interest = 1,000
Dividend = 2,000
Personal Taxes = 5,000

[**Ans:** Personal Disposable Income = **15,000**
Personal Income = **20,000**
Private Income = **24,200**
National Income (NNP_{FC}) = **26,700**
Operating Surplus = **9,000**
Compensation of Employees = **12,600.**]

67. Human Development Index (*HDI*) incorporates Life Expectancy Index (*LEI*), Education Index (*EI*) and Income Index (*II*) all over the world with effect from 2011. Given below the relevant data for countries A and B, compare them on their *HDI*s:

LEI of country A = 65.5 years,
Mean schooling years in Country A = 12 years.
Expected schooling years in country A = 15 years.
GNI per capita in Country A = $1500
LEI of country B = 69.5 years,
Mean schooling years in Country B = 14 years.
Expected schooling years in country B = 16 years.
GNI per capita in Country B = $750

[**Ans:** *HDI* of Country A = **0.6161**
HDI of Country B = **0.4715.**]

68. The data for a hypothetical economy are as given below:

Compensation of employees = 80,000
Operating surplus = 40,000
Mixed incomes = 30,000
Depreciation = 30,000
Indirect Taxes = 50,000
Subsidies = 20,000
Govt. final consumption expenditure = 30,000
Private final consumption expenditure = 70,000
Gross domestic fixed capital formation = 100,000
Changes in Stocks = 20,000
(X – M) = (–) 20,000
Savings ($S_F + S_H + S_G$) = 120,000
Net factor income from abroad =10,000
Net other current transfer from *ROW* = 10,000
Net purchases of intangible assets = 90,000
Net capital transfers from *ROW* = 60,000

Prepare the four consolidated accounts of the nation, that is, Account 1, Account 3, Account 5 and Account 6.

[**Ans:** **Account 1:** GDP_{MP} = 210,000 (Expenditure side Statistical discrepancy = + 10,000)
Account 3: National Disposable Income = 200,000
Account 5: Capital: 210,000
Account 6: Accumulation = 90,000]

UNIT-3

EMPLOYMENT, CONSUMPTION, INVESTMENT AND MODELS OF GOODS MARKET EQUILIBRIUM

Chapter 3: Introduction to Theory of Employment
Chapter 4: Consumption Function
Chapter 5: Investment Function
Chapter 6: Determination of Income in Two, Three and Four Sector Models in Goods Market
Chapter 7: Money, its Functions, and Money Market Equilibrium
Chapter 8: Goods Market Equilibrium
Chapter 9: Simultaneous Equilibrium of Goods Market and Money Market (General Equilibrium)

Chapter 3

Introduction to Theory of Employment

INTRODUCTION: CONCEPTS OF EMPLOYMENT AND UNEMPLOYMENT

Employment, in common parlance, refers to a state of occupation in which an eligible and willing individual is engaged at existing wage rate. Evidently, the individual's eligibility refers to his physical, mental and educational eligibility for the job. Willingness refers to the individual's desire for the job. For instance, a duly qualified individual from an affluent family or one with abundance of wealth may not want to work. Existing wage-rate refers to the market rate of wage. Thus, an eligible and willing individual engaged at market rate of wage is said to be in employment and if engaged at wage rate below the market rate or below his/her full potential (that is, as a part timer), is a type of unemployment called underemployment.

The concept of employment is better explained through that of unemployment. An individual is said to be unemployed if he fails to get a gainful occupation at the wage rate prevailing in the market despite desired eligibility and willingness. The problem of unemployment is rampant all over the world. Its nature and magnitude, however, may vary from country to country. While the developed countries suffer from cyclical and frictional unemployment, the Less Developed ones (*LDCs*) suffer from the seasonal, disguised and structural types of unemployment along with the commonly prevalent underemployment. Let us discuss these main types of unemployment that prevail in the developed and less developed countries in a little more detail.

3.1 NATURE OF UNEMPLOYMENT IN DEVELOPED COUNTRIES

As stated above, the developed countries suffer mainly from two types of unemployment:

3.1.1 Cyclical Unemployment

This type of unemployment, a common trait of developed countries, is caused by trade cycles, which refer to the phenomena of ***upswing*** and ***downswing*** that appear and disappear in trade and business. An upswing begins with the stage of ***recovery*** and ends with the stage of ***boom.*** It is marked for hectic activity and overwhelming optimism. In consequence, rising levels of employment, income, production, prices as also demand become common observations. On the contrary, the downswing follows the stage of boom and ends with ***depression.*** The downswing, also known as recession is characterized for the existence of low level of business and trade activities leading to widespread pessimism. It is marked for declining levels of production, investment, employment, income, prices and receding demand. When depression finally sets in, markets get flooded with stocks of unsold goods, and the household sector gets under widespread and massive unemployment. Such a state of unemployment is referred to as the ***cyclical unemployment.***

Examine the trend-line in Figure 3.1. Segment *AB* marks the phase of prosperity; segment *BC*, that of recession; *CD* that of depression and *DE* marks the phase of recovery. Economic activity rises in Phase *I*, falls in Phase *II* and *III* and rises again in Phase *IV*. Employment rises, falls and rises again accordingly. Such changes in employment are attributed to trade cycles, a common feature of the developed world, and unemployment so caused by them, the cyclical unemployment.

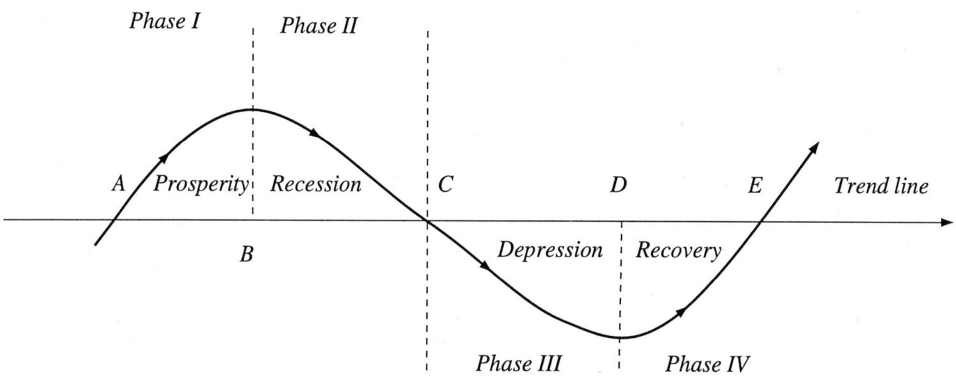

FIGURE 3.1 Trade Cycle: Examine the trend-line. Segment AB marks the phase of prosperity; segment BC, that of recession; CD that of depression and DE marks the phase of recovery. Economic activity rises in Phase *I*, falls in Phase *II* and *III* and rises again in Phase *IV*. Employment rises, falls and rises again accordingly. Such changes in employment are attributed to trade cycle and unemployment so caused as cyclical unemployment.

3.1.2 Frictional Unemployment

This type of unemployment is again a common trait of the developed world. It refers to the state of joblessness of the people in-between two successive jobs. A worker quits a job to look for a better one and remains unemployed until the desired opportunity is found. The joblessness during the intervening period is referred to as the ***frictional unemployment.*** The practice is common only to the developed world where workers possess reserves of income saved by them in the past to finance their needs in the intervening period.

3.1.3 Voluntary Unemployment

A high level of incomes accruing to the workers of the developed world help them in accumulating income-earning assets. A few others, born with a silver-spoon in their mouth, possess plenty to spend upon their subsistence. As a result, they feel no need of work and are said to be in ***voluntary unemployment***. It arises mainly due to affluence of some wealthier sections of the society in the developed world.

3.2 NATURE OF UNEMPLOYMENT IN UNDERDEVELOPED COUNTRIES

The following are the main types of unemployment that prevail in the Less Developed Countries (LDCs):

3.2.1 Seasonal Unemployment

When workers of the *LDCs* remain jobless during certain seasons every year, they are said to be in ***seasonal unemployment.*** For example, a large number of the workers in the primary sector fail to get work during the off-season-period. The reference here is to the period of summers and rains during which activities in the primary sector come to lull. The sufferers are the landless workers in agriculture in India.

The phenomenon is not uncommon even in other sectors of *LDCs.* It is generally common to the labour community but may also be found in other communities as well. It is so because some activities are seasonal activities. Those suited to such activities or engaged in them by choice or compulsion are said to be in seasonal unemployment.

3.2.2 Underemployment

A large number of workers in *LDC*s, either work below their full capacity, or work at wages below the market rate of wage. In the former case, they work as part-time workers, failing to avail gainful employment for normal hours of work every day or certain days every week or certain weeks every month or certain months every year. In the latter case, they fail to avail jobs at wage rates prevailing in the market. An individual with postgraduate degree in marketing management serving as a salesman or a qualified engineer working in a supervisory capacity provide examples of underemployment.

3.2.3 Structural Unemployment

This type of unemployment is caused by backwardness of the economic structure of less developed countries due to which, the LDCs fail to generate sufficient job opportunities to match the rate of growth of job seekers in the country. In other words, the rate of creation of the new job opportunities is much below the rate of growth of the labour-force. In such countries, the rate of the resource utilization is very low due to inadequacy of capital and technology on the one hand and low quality of the work force, on the other. Apart from leading to high growth rate of such labour force, a high population growth leads to heavier social costs causing misallocation of productive resources. This aggravates generation of employment opportunities even further. The type of joblessness of masses is referred to as the ***structural unemployment.***

3.2.4 Disguised Unemployment

Employment of people without contributing any thing to the total product is referred to as the **disguised unemployment.** As the term suggests, it is actually unemployment in the guise of employment. For example, suppose 10 workers produce 100 tons of wheat and on employing another 5 of them, if the output remains unchanged at 100 tons, the contribution of the additionally employed 5 workers to the total product is zero. They are thus in *disguised unemployment.* Technically speaking, a worker is said to be in disguised unemployment if his/her marginal product, or more appropriately, marginal productivity is zero. The marginal-productivity of these 5 additionally employed workers being zero, they are said to be disguisedly employed. In countries like India, the magnitude of disguised unemployment is very high in public sector as also in primary sector like the one of agriculture.

3.3 SOME FEATURES OF UNEMPLOYMENT

3.3.1 Urban Unemployment as an Offshoot of the Rural Unemployment

The nature and quantum of unemployment in urban areas of *LDCs* is often different from what it is in the rural sector. Unemployment is comparatively lower in quantum in urban areas than that in rural areas. The reasons include a comparatively lower rate of growth of the population in the urban areas on the one hand, and concentration of industries generating more job opportunities in these areas, on the other.

Unemployment in rural areas refers to the joblessness of the landless manual and menial workers. Most often, it is these workers who move to urban areas in search of greener pastures. This makes the matters worse for the urban sector not only in respect of employment but also in respect of provision of housing, transport, medical care and schooling apart from those of hygiene. Demands of such amenities rise sky high in consequence. Besides, flight of the rural workers to the urban sectors, there is a sizeable proportion of the rural youth migrating to the urban areas initially for higher education and subsequently for the charms of the city-life and better job prospects. All these factors combine to make the employment scenario worse in the urban sector. Moreover, getting used to the city life, they refuse to return back to their ancestral occupations thereby adding a host of other problems to the urban world besides those of unemployment.

All this contributes a sizeable number of the educated unemployed to the urban sector. The charm of city life adds fuel to fire as mentioned already. Slow progress urbanization of the rural areas is to be blamed for this. The flight of the rural population for various reasons to the urban sectors has aggravated not only the problem of unemployment in the urban sector but also that of civic life.

The reasons for rural flight to urban regions may be summarized in the following points:

1. Rate of growth of the rural population is much higher than that the rural resources can support. As a result, agricultural land per capita decreases significantly.
2. The progress of urbanization of rural regions moves as a snail's pace in *LDCs*. This retains the rural life to the primitive levels.
3. Availability of power and proximity to markets help industries to concentrate in and around cities and townships. Menial and manual work opportunities caused by them in these areas attract rural labour that have negligible or no means of subsistence.
4. Lack of security of life and belongings in rural areas compel the rural rich to shift to urban areas in part or full.
5. Schools, colleges and institutions of modern education and training often cluster in and around the urban regions with little or no similar recourse for the rural youth except to the obvious one of migrating to the urban townships.
6. Cultivation in *LDCs* continues to involve the same risk factors and uncertainties as it did in primitive periods. Besides, it is too much strenuous and too little rewarding to compel the ambitious rural youth to take to wings.

All these factors make urban unemployment an offshoot of rural unemployment.

3.3.2 Disguised Unemployment as a Potential Source of Capital Formation

As pointed out in Sub-section 3.2.4, disguised unemployment is unemployment in the guise of employment. In other words, workers disguisedly employed get paid for it while their contribution to production is nil. Total output remains same even when these workers were retrenched as their marginal product works out is zero. Often they manage such employment for themselves employed even when there is no need for them in the organization. A large number of workers in the public sector and even a larger number of them in agricultural sector are in this type of employment. Economists believe that the disguised unemployment can provide a potential source of capital formation in a capital-deficient *LDCs*. The arguments forwarded by them in defence are mainly two:

1. If the disguisedly employed workers were withdrawn from such employment, a sizable amount of funds would be released from their wasteful use. In other words, non-productive expenditures incurred on their salaries and perks if released, can be utilized to finance the capital formation.
2. Workers released from the disguised unemployment can be utilized in sectors where their productivity is non-zero. In the *LDCs*, there are many sectors where such workers could be of immense utility in production. They can thus draw their salaries from the productive work, which would no longer be a part of the non-productive expenditures.

Either way, the national product is bound to go up. If we look at it from the first angle, funds that get released from the non-productive expenditures can be utilized to finance capital formation. This would go a long way to boost the national output.

On the contrary, if we look at it from the second angle, the non-productive expenditures get converted into the productive ones, leading to higher output. Hence disguised unemployment as a potential source of capital formation, is well founded.

3.4 CONCEPT OF FULL EMPLOYMENT: KEYNESIAN AND CLASSICAL VERSIONS [FIGURES 3.2, 3.3(A) AND 3.3(B)]

From the discussions so far, it is clear that some unemployment always exists in every economy whether it is a developed one or an underdeveloped one. Existence of at least voluntary unemployment is an admitted fact in almost every economy. If we exclude voluntary unemployment from the category of unemployment on the grounds that it causes no problems to an economy, the question that arises is whether the other forms of unemployment are possible to eliminate, or, in other words, is full employment possible if the voluntary unemployment be treated of little consequence?

According to the classical school of thought, existence of the full employment in an economy is a normal situation. The classical economists, however, did not deny the possibility of unemployment in an economy but this to them is an abnormal situation, which gets eliminated as soon as the unemployed agree to work at lower wages (downward wage flexibility). The classical economists contend that they would eventually agree for that rather than remain jobless. This, according to them would induce fresh demand for the workers. Consequently, the level of employment begins to rise until the state of the full employment is reached. Figure 3.2 shows full employment equilibrium as a normal state of an economy according to them.

J. M. Keynes, on the contrary, denied the downward flexibility of money wages and the possibility of existence of full employment equilibrium in an economy. According to him, economies eventually attain equilibrium at less than full employment [Figures 3.3(a) and (b)]. No economy can thus ever reach full employment under rigid money wages. Given the price level, money wages can't be flexible

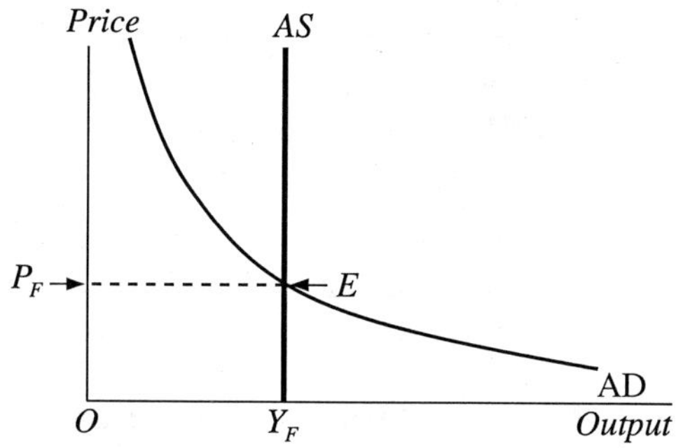

FIGURE 3.2 The full employment equilibrium of the Classical Theory in Simple Terms: It can be explained through the tool of price mechanism, portraying the total output demand, termed aggregate demand (*AD*), as an inverse function of price[1]. It is thus a rectangular hyperbola which is unitary elastic at every point on it. The total supply, termed aggregate supply (*AS*), a perfectly inelastic function of price in a normal state, the full employment equilibrium of classical theory can be represented at point *E,* where *AD* and *AS* intersect each other. Note that the vertical *AS* curve is a consequence of classical assumption of downwardly flexible money wages and prices[2]. Full employment output is Y_F and price, P_F (Note that the slope of the *AS* curve is more introspective than empirical).

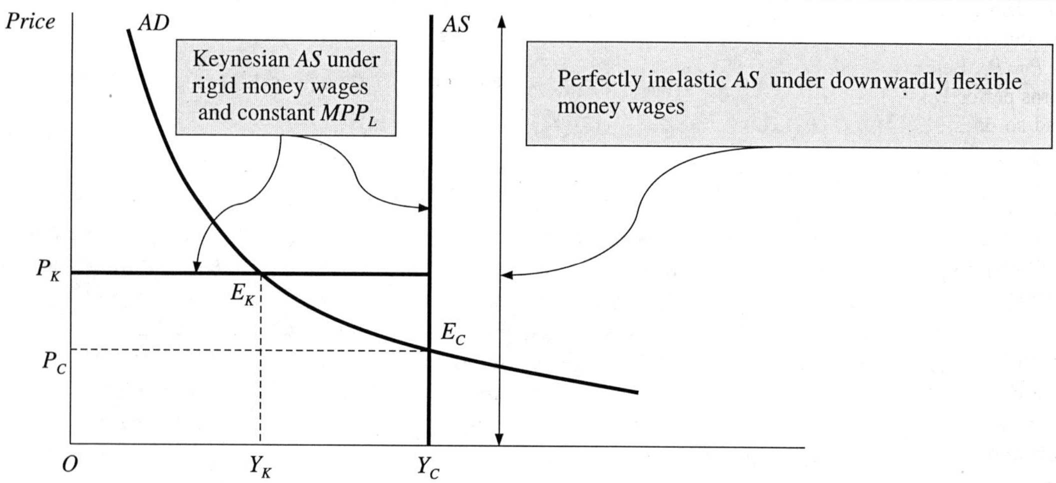

FIGURE 3.3(a) Less than full employment equilibrium of Keynesian theory under rigid money wages and constant MPP_L till Y_c: Portraying *AD* curve on the lines of Figure 3.2, Keynesian less than full employment equilibrium can be explained with *AS* curve partly elastic and partly inelastic under fixed money wages and fixed MPP_L (real wage, $W/P = MPP_L$). It is therefore perfectly *elastic* until full employment and perfectly *inelastic* at full employment. Keynesian equilibrium takes place at E_K, which is less than full employment equilibrium while classical equilibrium can be considered to take place at E_C.

[1] According to Quantity Theory of Money, price level varies directly with money supply, that is $P = MV/Y$, with M standing for money supply, P for price level, V for velocity of circulation of money and Y for outputs transacted (See Chapters 9 and 13 of the book).

[2] The contention implied downwardly flexible money wages as the main plank of full employment equilibrium. Money wage $W = MPP_L \times P$, Where, MPP_L is the marginal physical product of labour and P, the product price. For given MPP_L money wages can be downwardly flexible only when product price is (which to Keynes is not true).

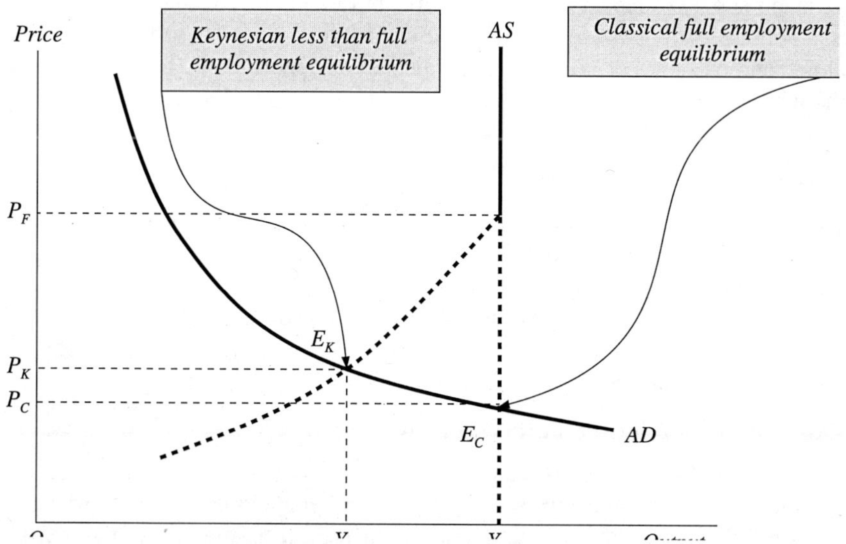

FIGURE 3.3(b) Less than Full Employment Equilibrium of Keynesian Theory under Rigid Money Wages and Diminishing MPP_L Till $Y_{C:}$ Falling MPP_L would result in curtailment of output as also its supply (see that the AS curve is no longer horizontal indicating less supply than when MPP_L is constant). The stage would terminate at $P = P_F$. Below it, *AS* is elastic (but not perfectly) as shown by the dotted portion of *AS*-curve and above it, *AS* turns perfectly inelastic. Given rigid money wages, and diminishing MPP_L production cost rises with employment and so does the Price ($W = MPP_L \times P$). In consequence, firms curtail employment at $P= P_F$ and above. Thus, Keynesian equilibrium takes place at E_K which relates to less than full employment equilibrium while classical equilibrium takes place at F_C. (*AD* follows its derivation on the lines of Figure 3.2).

downward whether MPP_L of labour is constant or diminishing with employment. The latter, Keynesian theory treated as a reality and established the existence of less than full employment equilibrium.

Even if we attempt to wipe off all other types of unemployment through wage-cut, the element of voluntary unemployment would always persist. Moreover, the classical contention of attainment of full employment through wage-cut collapses as soon as we recognize the consequences of a wage-cut. It is so because attainment of full employment through wage-cut reduces income which in turn reduces demand for the output. A fall in demand for the output leads either to the emergence of unsold stocks or to a fall the output-prices.

Full employment, to classical economists, results through downwardly flexible wages which J.M. Keynes rejected. Keynes established less than full employment equilibrium through his assumption of rigid money wages or downwardly inflexible wages. Note, however, that existence of voluntary and frictional unemployment is compatible with the notion of full employment.

3.5 CLASSICAL AND KEYNESIAN THEORIES OF EMPLOYMENT: A CRITICAL ASSESSMENT

3.5.1 Classical Theory of Employment

J.M. Keynes, in his General Theory of Employment, *Interest and Money* (1936), referred to the pre-depression economists as the *Classical Economists.* Classical theory of employment refers to a set of their assumptions regarding certain macroeconomic issues such as employment, production, supply of goods, demand-supply of labour and the state of equilibrium in the economy. J.M. Keynes referred to these assumptions as the ***postulates of the classical economists.*** These postulates were based on deductive logic and had little or no empirical evidence to support them. The main foundation of the classical thought was the Say's Law of Markets. Let us introduce these postulates briefly below to summarize the main contention of the classical school of thought:

3.5.1.1 Existence of full employment

According to classical economists, existence of full employment of productive resources is a normal situation. Deviations from it, if any, disappear in the long-run through the adjustment process. In the event of unemployment, workers agree to wage cuts rather than remain unemployment. Fresh demand for them so created ensures full employment. Downward flexibility of wages is the main plank of full employment. In classical view, full employment means employment of all the resources except those in frictional and voluntary unemployment.

3.5.1.2 Existence of equilibrium in the economy

Just as full employment is a normal situation, so is the state of general equilibrium in the long-run. This is again due to the automatic adjustment process. Full employment attained through a wage cut, leads to overproduction resulting in unsold stocks which clear as soon as a price cut is introduced by the firms. Such price cuts are not inconvenient to the firms under cost-cut caused by wage cut. Unemployment clears through downward wage flexibility and overproduction, through downward price flexibility. Thus the assumption of downward wage price flexibility of classical economists restores normalcy in equilibrium of labour and product markets both.

Both the postulates of the classical theory are based on the assumptions of *existence of perfect competition and laissez-faire (free-trade) system.* Perfect competition ensures the free play of the price mechanism and the laissez-faire system ensures free flow goods and services across the territorial boundaries.

3.5.1.3 Neutrality of money

For classical economists, money has no other function except to serve as a medium of exchange. It facilitates the transactions and that is almost all. Determination of the outputs and the employment are almost independent of money supply and demand.

3.5.2 (a) Basis of Classical Theory and its Implications

Say's Law of Markets is the main plank of the classical theory of employment. The law named after the French economist J. B. Say (1767–1832), states that '*supply creates its own demand*'. Accordingly, all that is supplied gets sold ultimately. In the event of overproduction or underconsumption, a price cut comes to rescue of the firms. Unsold stocks clear off as soon as a price cut is introduced by firms. As held earlier, a price cut is not inconvenient to the firms under cost cut caused by wage cut. Automatic adjustment process of price mechanism and *laissez-faire (free-trade) system* take care of everything.

It would be in order to outline the ***main implications*** of the classical theory of employment:

(a) **Full Employment is a Normal Situation:** If a deviation from full employment ever occurs, it cannot last long. The adjustment process induces willingness among the unemployed to work at lower wages. This creates fresh demand for and full employment is restored.

(b) **All that is Produced and Supplied Gets Sold:** As a deviation, if unsold stocks ever result, they soon get cleared when the adjustment process induces a price cut. A cut in price creates fresh demand for the unsold goods and the apparent overproduction or underconsumption soon disappears.

Assumption of *laissez-faire* system lent further strength to the law of markets. It is the specialization and the division of labour that may lead to overproduction. The *laissez-faire* (free-trade)} system helps to clear the surplus produce, if any, under the barter trade when excess output is exchanged for deficient one (underproduction). Every economy specializes production of goods it is best suited for and produces these goods at its optimal capacity. If the output is much more than what it can consume itself, which may be the usual case, the surpluses can be exchanged under barter for other goods from the foreign countries for which these countries are best suited. The two assumptions were believed to lend strength to the law of markets, which seemed to be a reality until it was challenged during the period of the Great Depression when both these assumptions failed to serve their purpose. Say's Law of Markets collapsed when overproduction flooded the markets in the form of the unsold stocks despite price cuts introduced by the producers in an attempt to recover the sunk costs and wage cuts volunteered by the retrenched workers in an attempt to regain employment. The classical theory virtually collapsed when *wage-price cuts* or ***downward wage price flexibility*** proved to no avail in upholding the ***Say's Law of Markets***. The household sector felt depressed due to loss of employment and the producers sector felt depressed due to mounting stocks of the unsold goods.

3.5.2 (b) Keynesian Theory of Employment and its Implications

During the period of depression, the classical theory faced a serious challenge when downward wage-price flexibilities failed to sustain the ***law of markets***. J. M. Keynes, in his *General Theory of Employment, Interest and Money (1936),* turned the law upside down and held that *it is not the supply that creates its own demand; instead, it's demand, rather* ***effective demand*** *(ED) that creates its own supply.* Deficiency of demand, therefore, deserves more attention. To eliminate the deficiency, leakages from the circular flow of income and expenditure need to be plugged through injections. Sources of leakages are withdrawals such as savings (S), taxation (T), and expenditures on imports (M) while those of injections, investments (I), government expenditures (G) and the earnings from the exports (X) (See Box 3.1).

BOX 3.1

Total leakage from the circular flow = $S + T + M$
Total injection into the circular flow = $I + G + X$

Box 3.1: The four sector model of the circular flow of income and expenditure (See Box 2.22, Chapter 2) shows the locations of leakages (S, T, M) and those of Injections (I, G, X).

Effective Demand, the sole determinant of employment, is determined by two factors which Keynes called "***Aggregate Demand Function****(ADF)* "and "***Aggregate Supply Function (ASF)***" respectively. It may be defined as *the level of employment at which the Aggregate Demand Function (ADF) is equal to the Aggregate Supply Function (ASF).* Aggregate Demand Function (*ADF*) may be defined as *a schedule of various amounts of money, which entrepreneurs in an economy expect from the sale of their output at varying levels of employment.* It represents the *receipts*, which the entrepreneurs taken together *expect* from the sale of output. Aggregate Supply Function (*ASF*), on the other hand, may be defined as *a schedule of various amounts of money, which the entrepreneurs in an economy must receive from the sale of output at varying levels of employment.* It refers to the *costs*, which the entrepreneurs have incurred on production of the output. At any particular level of the output, if *receipts* are less than the *costs*, the producers shall stop production and refuse to retain in employment that particular level of the workers. It goes without saying that so long as the *costs* remain less than the *receipts*, the employment in an economy shall go on increasing till both of them are equalized.

In Layman's language, effective demand refers to that level of demand, which can be matched by the producers without having to change their pace of production. For instance, demand of 120 units or that of 80 units cannot be matched by the producers, currently producing 100 units, without a change in their pace of production. Hence these levels of demand do not represent effective demand. Instead, demand of exactly 100 units is the effective demand as the producers can conveniently meet it without a change in their pace of production.

Aggregate Demand Function (ADF) represents the expected receipt of the producers from the sale of their output. Such receipts must include implicit and explicit costs so that the producers find the production remunerative enough to continue.

On the same lines, *Aggregate Supply Function (ASF)*, on the other hand, refers to costs which form the minimum receipts of the producers from the sales of the output that are must for the producers so that they do not discontinue production. For the sake of simplicity, let us take *ADF* as 'price' and *ASF* as 'cost'. Taking both of them on vertical axis and employment on horizontal axis, we can represent the point of effective demand diagrammatically as in Figure 3.4.

ASF schedule registers slow growth at the initial stages but picks up very fast at higher levels of employment. It becomes almost vertical after a certain level of employment. On the contrary, *ADF* schedule grows very fast at the initial levels of employment, but as the employment is raised, its rate of growth begins to decline. At sufficiently higher levels of employment, *ADF* becomes almost horizontal. The two schedules intersect each other at the point *E*, called the point of *effective demand*. At this point, *ADF* = *ASF* and the corresponding level of employment is *ON*. By definition, *ON* measures the volume of effective demand. Treating *ADF* as the demand price and *ASF* as the supply price, or more appropriately, as the cost of supply, the excess of *ADF* over *ASF* may be taken as the

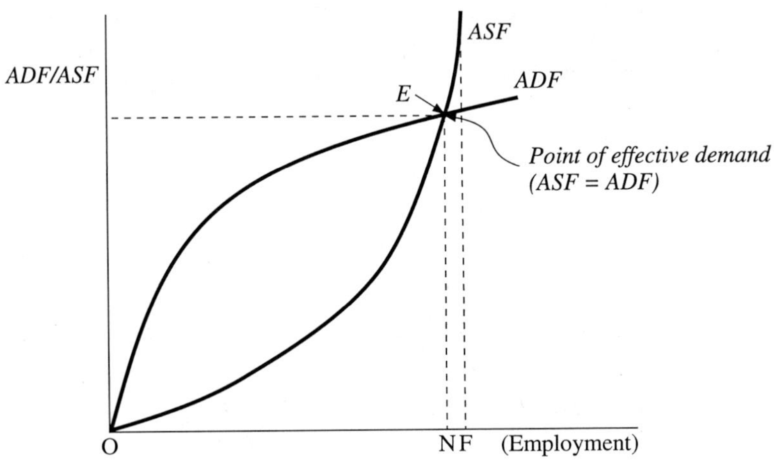

FIGURE 3.4 *ADF* (receipt concepts) and *ASF* (cost concept) are both represented on the vertical axis while level of employment, on the horizontal axis. *ADF* schedule registers sharp increase at the initial levels of employment but tends towards saturation at the higher levels. *ASF* schedule, on the other hand, is slow to rise initially but quite fast at higher levels of employment. The two intersect at *E*, the point of *Effective Demand.* It corresponds to '*ON*' level of employment. This level of employment measures the effective demand.

producer's margin of profit. Area between the two would then represent the total profits. Thus total profit is maximum when the level of employment is at *N*. If the producers employ at a level less than *N*, total profit (area between the two curves), would decline and if they employ at a level higher than *N*, *ASF* exceeds *ADF* and loss begins to accrue to them. Total profit is thus maximized at *ON* level of employment which can thus be treated as equilibrium level of employment.

J.M. Keynes had evolved the concept of effective demand while studying the causes of depression that had gripped the entire Europe during the decade of nineteen-thirties (1930s). The cause of depression, as held by J.M. Keynes, comprised the leakages from the circular flow of income and expenditure. These leakages, also known as withdrawals, comprised savings (*S*), Taxation (*T*) and imports (*M*) which taken together led to the deficiency of demand with the result that markets got flooded with the unsold stocks. This exercised a downward pressure on price to prevent which, producers resorted to supply–cuts. In their bid to do this, producers resorted to the retrenchment of productive factors affecting income of the factor-owners adversely and aggravating, in consequence, the prevailing demand-deficiency even further. Depression dawned upon the producers and the householders alike.

BOX 3.2

ADF or simply aggregate demand (*AD*) = Consumption demand (*C*) + Investment demand (*I*)

BOX 3.3

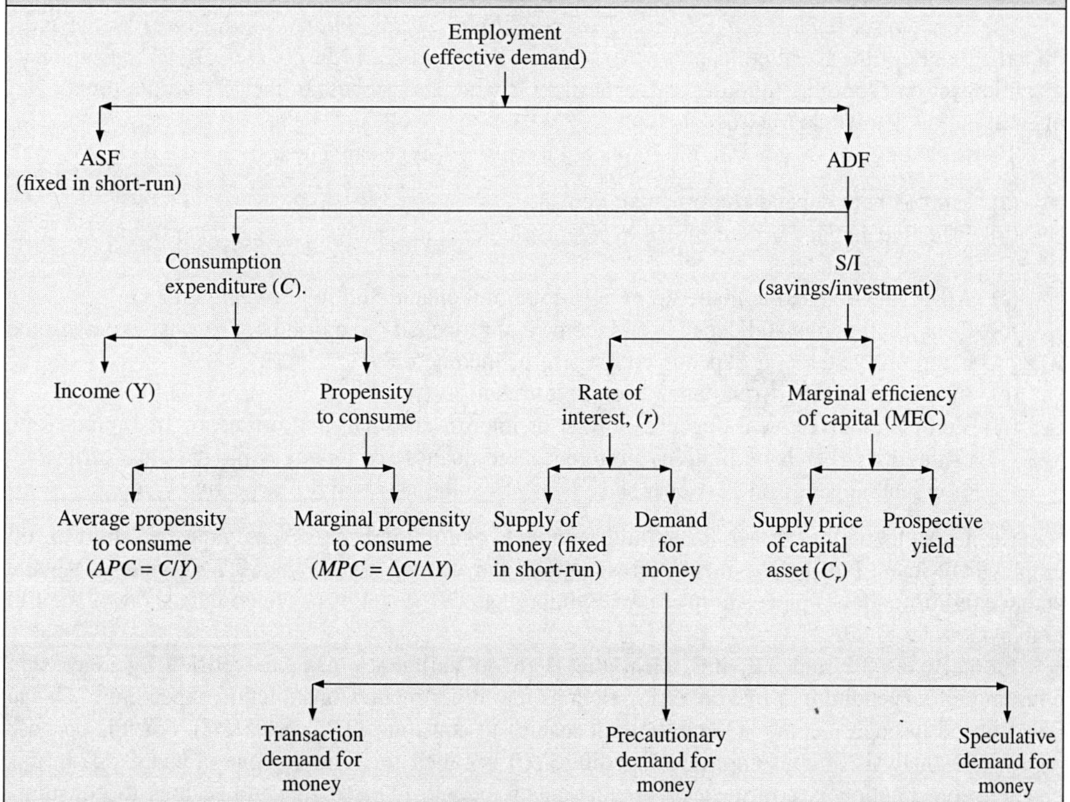

Producers felt depressed when price-cuts failed to clear the unsold goods and householders felt depressed when wage-cuts failed to retain them in employment. The period of depression shattered the existing belief in the *Say's Law of Markets,* which collapsed in consequence when none of its implications could stand on their own to lend any strength to it any more.

To study Keynesian theory, let us begin with the effective demand and its two essential components of *ADF* and *ASF.* The latter assumed constant in short-run by Keynes, the former depended solely on *ADF* in short-run. *ADF* or total demand, for outputs, comprised of the consumption demand (*C*) and investment demand (*I*).

According to Keynesian theory, effective demand has to be as high as possible to keep depression at bay. To raise it, either the consumption demand should be raised to its level, or, savings should be converted into investment.

For the consumption to be high, income and the propensities to consume should all be high. For conversion of the savings into the investment, the marginal efficiency of capital should be greater than the rate of interest. For the rate of interest to be as low as possible, demand for liquidity needs to be cut down. Transaction and precautionary components of demand being interest-inelastic, the only way left is to control speculative demand. This is the crux of the Keynesian theory of employment. It can be presented schematically, along with its components (Box 3.3).

In chapters 4 and 5 that follow, we'll see how consumption and the investment demands can be suitably influenced to boost the effect demand. In chapter 6, we'll examine several models of determining the national income in an economy with two, three and four sectors.

Implications of Keynesian Theory can be summarized as below:

The economists regard *The General Theory of Employment, Interest and Money* as the most important work of the twentieth century. No other work except Karl Marx's *Das Capital* has made as much impact on economic thinking as Keynesian General Theory has. In fact, it laid the foundation of what is now known as Macroeconomics.

The following are, in general, the implications of the Keynesian Theory:

(a) Employment depends on effective demand.
(b) Effective demand is determined by aggregate demand function, as aggregate supply function is relatively stable.
(c) Aggregate demand is made up of consumption demand and investment demand.
(d) Consumption demand depends on income and propensity to consume. Propensity to consume being fairly stable, it depends on the size of income only.
(e) Income in the short-run depends on investment.
(f) Volume of investment depends on rate of interest and marginal efficiency of capital. Rate of interest depends on liquidity preference and quantity of money while marginal efficiency of capital depends on cost of replacement of capital assets and prospective yields.

Keynesian theory has shown that equilibrium level of employment is usually reached short of full employment level. Full employment corresponds to the vertical part of the *ASF* (Figure 3.4) while actual equilibrium takes place short of it at *E*, implying '*ON*' level of it, which falls short of the full employment level '*OF*.'

From Boxes 3.2 and 3.3, it is clear that demand deficiency can be rectified by increasing consumption expenditure or by converting savings into investment. Consumption expenditure (*C*) can be regulated through income (*Y*) and the propensities to consume (*APC* and *MPC*). For this purpose an in-depth analysis of consumption expenditure (*C*) is called for. This is done in chapter 4. In this chapter, consumption is portrayed as a function of income (*Y*) and the propensities to consume.

Consumption is high when income and the propensities to consume are high. In the same way, an indepth analysis of investment expenditure (*I*) is must so that savings (*S*) may be converted into it. This is done in chapter 5. In this chapter, investment (*I*) is portrayed as a function of the rate of interest (*r*) and income (*Y*). Investment is high when rate of interest is low and it is low when rate of interest is high. Equilibrium level of income (*Y*) calls for the equality of Savings (*S*) to Investment (*I*), or more generally, for that of withdrawals (*S*) to injections (*I*). It would be taken up in Chapter 8. Such equilibrium, known as the ***Goods Market Equilibrium***, forms a major segment of the ***general equilibrium.*** The other segment is the ***Money Market Equilibrium.*** This will be taken up in Chapter 7. Money Market Equilibrium is as important for the general equilibrium as is the Góods Market Equilibrium for it. This is so because the money market influences both—the *rate of Interest, r,* and the general price-level, *P*. Rate of interest (*r*), in turn, influences investment (*I*), which in turn, determines *Output* (*Y*). For instance, if rate of interest (*r*) is lower than the ***Marginal Efficiency of Capital*** (*MEC*), as is clear from Box 3.3, Savings (*S*), in all likelihood, would get converted into Investment (*I*). A higher investment implies a higher output, a higher employment, a higher income and a lower price level in the long-run. Rate of interest, as is clear from the Box 3.3, is governed by the forces of demand and supply of money. To ensure that the rate of interest (*r*) is lower than the marginal efficiency of capital (*MEC*), demand for liquidity (money form of assets) has to be kept low while supply of it, high in general. An indirect way of doing the same is to raise the marginal efficiency of capital (*MEC*), high enough, so that the rate of interest automatically falls below it. Managing the *MEC* for this purpose would require a high prospective yield of the capital and a low supply price of it, as may be evidenced from Box 3.3. A high prospective yield requires, among other things, a high level of demand for the outputs. When demand is low, *MEC* can't be high enough to exceed the rate of interest. As a result, the savings component of the withdrawals (leakages) would increase and so would the unsold stocks of the goods. The same would be the effect when consumption is low. Such demand deficiencies lead to depression. The *Great Depression of Thirties* that gripped Europe for a decade was caused by the demand deficiencies. That was the reason why Keynes emphasized demand or effective demand as the only remedy to depression.

Chapter 9 would focus on general equilibrium or simultaneous equilibrium of the money and the goods markets. That would almost wind up the Keynesian Theory. Subsequent chapters would be devoted to issues related to institutions and their policy matters that tend to influence the simultaneous equilibrium of the money and the goods markets in an economy. Such institutions are, *firstly*, the monetary institutions comprising of the bank of issue, the Central Bank, and a number of collaborating institutions like the Commercial Banks, also called the financial institutions, and, *secondly*, the government departmental and non-departmental organizations that intervene into the process 10, 11 and 12 under the heads of the monetary, the fiscal and the foreign trade policies respectively. Problem of inflation is taken up in Chapter 13 while that of growth and development in Chapter 14.

The reader can see that Keynesian Theory is a highly logical formulation on which the foundations of Macroeconomics are laid. Macroeconomics is, thus, a science, not a Pandora Box of policy tools with little or no logical foundations to which many authors have reduced it. No wonder works of such authors drive the young minds to resort to mugging instead of grasping the otherwise interesting concepts of the science of economics.

KEY TERMS AND CONCEPTS

Unemployment: A state of joblessness in which physically and mentally capable workers fail to get jobs at the prevailing rate of wage.

Voluntary Unemployment: A state of joblessness in which physically and mentally capable workers don't offer themselves for work due to affluence.

Involuntary Unemployment: A state of joblessness in which physically and mentally capable workers fail to get jobs at the prevailing rate of wage despite all sorts of attempts made by them.

Full Employment: A state in which no more factors of production are available for employment with the result that output remains stagnant.

Underemployment: A state in which a worker works either at a wage less than the prevailing market rate of wages or is employed below his/her full potential. For example, a worker getting only a part-time job at existing wage rate or getting a full time job at less than the market rate of wage.

Seasonal Unemployment: When a worker remains unemployed over certain season(s) every year, the state of unemployment is referred to as the seasonal unemployment. Some farm labour, for instance, remains unoccupied most of the times except at the harvest times and the sowing times.

Cyclical Unemployment: It refers to massive unemployment caused by the depression phase of the trade cycle. When trade and business are in their lowest ebb, workers get retrenched on a large scale. Such retrenchments lead to involuntary unemployment called cyclical unemployment. It is a feature of unemployment common to advanced countries.

Frictional Unemployment: Workers in advanced countries often quit the current job to look for a better or more suitable job for themselves. In-between two successive jobs, there is always a period of joblessness called the period of frictional unemployment.

Structural Unemployment: When the economic structure is backward enough to generate new jobs at the rate at which job-seekers multiply, the workers left unemployed are said to be in structural unemployment.

Disguised Unemployment: Employment of people without contributing any thing to the total product, is referred to as the disguised unemployment. As the term suggests, it is actually unemployment in the guise of employment. For example, suppose 10 workers produce 100 tons of wheat and after employing another 5 of them, if the output of wheat remains unchanged at 100 tons, the contribution of these additionally employed 5 workers to the total product is zero and they, thus, are in *disguised unemployment.*

Classical Theory of Employment: Full employment is a normal situation, according to this theory. If unemployment arises in any economy at any point of time, it clears off as soon as the unemployed workers lower their wages to regain employment. According to the classical school of thought, workers can't remain jobless for long. They accept wage cuts sooner or later and regain employment. Full employment is thus restored through wage cut. The theory is based on Say's Law of Markets.

Keynesian Theory of Employment: According to Keynesian theory, full employment is not possible.

A section of people always remains unemployed voluntarily due to affluence, if not due to any other reasons. The theory is based on the concept of effective demand.

Neutrality of Money: For classical economists, money has no other function except to serve as a medium of exchange. It facilitates the transactions and that is almost all. Determination of the outputs and the employment are almost independent of money.

Say's Law of Markets: Named after the French economist J. B. Say (1767–1832), Say's Law of Markets, states that *supply creates its own demand.* Some of the implications of this law are:

(a) *Full employment is a normal situation:* If a deviation from full employment ever occurs and unemployment appears, it cannot last long. The adjustment process induces willingness among the unemployed to work at lower wages. This creates fresh demand for the unemployed and full employment is restored.

(b) *All that is produced and supplied gets sold:* As a deviation, if unsold stocks ever result, they soon get cleared when the adjustment process induces a price cut. A cut in price creates fresh demand for the unsold goods and apparent overproduction or underconsumption soon disappears.

Withdrawals: They refer to leakages from the circular flow of income and expenditure and comprise of savings (S), taxation (T) and import spending (M).

Injections: They refer to pumping of funds into the circular flow of income and expenditure through the channels of investment (I), government spending (G) and export earnings (X). In a state of equilibrium,withdrawals always equal injections.

Effective Demand: In a Layman's language, effective demand refers to that level of demand which can be satisfied by the producers without a change in their pace of production. In other words, effective demand is the level of demand which is equal to the level of output. In the language of Keynes, it refers to that level of employment at which aggregate demand function (expected receipt from the sale of output) is equal to the aggregate supply function (minimum receipt from the sale of the output which is must for the producers to continue to operate).

Aggregate Demand Function (ADF): It refers to what producers expect from the sale of their output. Aggregate Demand Function (ADF) may be defined as *a schedule of various amounts of money, which entrepreneurs in an economy expect from the sale of their output at varying levels of employment.* It represents the *receipts*, which the entrepreneurs taken together *expect* from the sale of output.

Aggregate Supply Function (ASF): It may be defined as *a schedule of various amounts of money, which the entrepreneurs in an economy must receive from the sale of output at varying levels of employment.* It refers to the *costs*, which the entrepreneurs have incurred on production of the output.

At any particular level of the output, if *receipts* are less than the *costs*, the producers shall stop production and refuse to retain in employment that particular level of the workers.

Liquidity Preference: It refers to the preference of the people to hold their assets in the liquid form (cash). It varies inversely as the rate of interest, that is, when rate of interest is high, liquidity preference is low and when the rate of interest is low, liquidity preference is high.

Marginal Efficiency of Capital: In the Layman's language, it refers to the rate of return on capital investment and can be defined as the rate of discount, at which, if the annual income streams (annuities) arising from a capital investment were discounted, the discounted values so obtained add up to the supply price of the capital asset. In other words, it is the rate of discount that renders the present values of a series of annuities equal to the cost of the capital asset.

Marginal Propensity to Consume (MPC): It refers to the increase in consumption expenditure per unit increase in consumer's income. In other words, it is the ratio of the increase in the consumption expenditure to the increase in consumer's income.

$$MPC = \frac{(\text{Increase in consumption expenditure, } \Delta C)}{(\text{Increase in income, } \Delta Y)} = \frac{\Delta C}{\Delta Y}$$

Thus, if a consumer increases his consumption expenditure by ₹ 1600 in consequence to an increase in his income from ₹ 10,000 to ₹ 12,000; the marginal propensity to consume is 1600/2000 = 0.80 or 80%.

Average Propensity to Consume (APC): It is defined as the proportion of the consumption expenditure to the income at a point of time. In other words, it is the ratio of the consumption expenditure to the income.

$$APC = \frac{\text{Consumption expenditure, } C}{\text{Income, } Y}$$

Thus, if the consumption expenditure ₹ 9,000 when the consumer's income is ₹ 10,000; the average propensity to consume is 9,000/10, 000 = 0.90 or 90%.

Goods Market Equilibrium: It refers to the equality of the quantity demanded to that supplied so that no unsold stocks of goods exist.

Money Market Equilibrium: It refers to the equality of the quantity of money demanded to that supplied so that there exists a stable rate of interest in the money market.

Equilibrium Level of Income: It refers to that level of income (or output) which corresponds to the simultaneous equilibrium of the money and the goods markets.

Economic Policies: They refer to the policies of the government that influence national output, national income, national expenditure, general price level, level of employment and the foreign trade of the country. There are mainly three components of the economic policies:

1. *Monetary Policy,* referring to all the policies of the central bank in relation to the supply of money.
2. *Fiscal Policy,* referring to all the budgetary policies of the government in relation to taxation and public expenditure.
3. *Foreign Policies,* referring to all the trade policies of the government in relation to the nation's imports and exports.

Consumption Function: The consumption expenditure expressed as a function of income is called consumption function. It may be expressed as $C = f(Y)$. Consumption expenditure varies directly with income in general.

Investment Function: The general form of an investment function is $I = f(Y, r)$, where Y is income and r, the rate of interest. In short-run, in which, income (Y) remains constant investment can then be defined as an inverse function of rate of interest, r, that is, $I = f(r) = I_a - hr$.

EXERCISES

A. Short Answer Questions

1. Briefly introduce the components of economic policies.
2. What is meant by goods market equilibrium? Under what conditions can it be ascertained?.
3. What is meant by money market equilibrium? Under what conditions can it be ascertained?.
4. What is consumption function? On what factors does it depend?
5. What is investment function? On what factors does it depend?
6. What are marginal and average propensities to consume? How do they affect consumption function?
7. Define marginal efficiency of capital. Why should it be higher than the rate of interest?
8. What is liquidity preference? How does it affect the effective demand?
9. What is meant by effective demand?
10. What are withdrawals? Why should they be converted into injections? Outline components of each.
11. What is meant by aggregate demand and aggregate supply functions? How they differ from aggregate demand and aggregate supply?
12. State Say's Law of Markets. What are its implications?
13. What is meant by neutrality of money?
14. Is full employment possible?
15. What in crux is the Classical theory of employment?
16. What in crux is the Keynesian theory of employment? What are its implications?
17. Define disguised unemployment. How can it serve as a potential source of capital formation?
18. Outline the main types of unemployment commonly characterizing *LDCs*.
19. Outline the main types of unemployment characterizing the advanced countries?
20. On what factors does the investment expenditure depend?
21. On what factors does the rate of interest depend? Explain each briefly.
22. If consumption of an individual increases from 900 to 1050 in consequence to an increase in his income from 1000 to 1200, determine

    (i) *MPC*

    (ii) Change in *APC*.

    [Ans:

    (i) $APC = C/Y = 900/1000 = 0.90$. It changes to $1050/1200 = 0.875$.

    (ii) $MPC = \Delta C/\Delta Y = (1050 - 900)/(1200 - 1000) = 0.75$]

23. Why is the aggregate demand curve a rectangular hyperbola with unitary elasticity at every point on it?
24. With the help of an sketch, show how classical theory depicted existence of full employment?

B. Long Answer Questions

25. How did Keynes depict the existence of less than full employment equilibrium? Draw diagrams when
    (i) MPP_L is constant
    (ii) MPP_L diminishes with employment.
26. Write a comprehensive note on the components of effective demand ? How can effective demand be made as high as possible through them?

Chapter 4

Consumption Function

INTRODUCTION

As discussed in chapter 3, if the consumption expenditure were raised to the level of income, the leakage from the circular flow of income and expenditure would disappear. In consequence, there would be no demand deficiency and hence there would be no accumulations of the unsold stocks that initiate forces of depression. This establishes the importance of consumption expenditure for economies that intend to steer clear of it. The nature of the consumption expenditure and the factors that influence it are often studied under the head of the ***Consumption Function.***

In this chapter, let us, therefore, learn all about consumption function so that an important cause of the demand deficiency may be understood fully with an objective of exercising appropriate control over it. It may be recalled here that the main sources of the leakage from the circular flow of income and expenditure are savings, taxation and imports. In this chapter, we focus mainly on consumption, which automatically involves savings, one of the main sources of the leakage. In the next chapter, we will take up investment function, an important component of injections, with a view to see how savings can be converted into investment as a measure of plugging the leakages.

4.1 CONSUMPTION FUNCTION

The algebraic relationship between the consumption expenditure, C, and the factors such as income (Y) on which it depends is known as the consumption function. Consumption expenditure varies directly with income, i.e. as income increases, so does the consumption expenditure in general. In other words, consumption expenditure is an increasing function of income (Y). The functional relationship of the consumption expenditure with income takes the following three forms:

(i) Short-run Consumption Function: In short-run, consumption expenditure is not a simple proportion of the income. It is not zero when income is zero. In other words, a consumer has to incur some expenditure on consumption even when his income is zero. This expenditure is known as the *subsistence or* ***autonomous consumption*** (C_a). It is a must for every individual to meet the minimum basic needs irrespective of the level of income enjoyed. Expenditure incurred on consumption over and above C_a bears a proportional relationship with the disposable income (Y^d). A typical consumption function of this type is referred to as a non-proportional consumption function and is given as:

$$C = C_a + b \cdot Y^d \tag{4.1}$$

Where, $C \equiv$ Consumption expenditure

$C_a \equiv$ Autonomous consumption expenditure

$b \equiv$ A positive constant, between 0 and 1

$Y^d \equiv$ Consumers' disposable income, which is equal to the excess of income over Net Direct Taxes (direct taxes *less* transfer payments). Direct taxes (T) refer to personal taxes such as income tax paid and transfer payments (R) refer to unilateral transfers such as old-age pensions, scholarships, etc. ***Net Direct Taxes*** are thus equal to (T–R).

$= Y–(T–R)$

= Income consumers feel free to dispose off any way they like.

Graphically, the relationship in equation (4.1) is portrayed as in the diagram below (Figure 4.1). Disposable Income Y^d is measured on the horizontal axis and consumption expenditure (C) on the vertical axis. When Y^d is zero, C is C_a. In a two-sector model, disposable income, $Y^d = Y$, as tax and the transfer payments are non-existent due to the absence of the government sector.

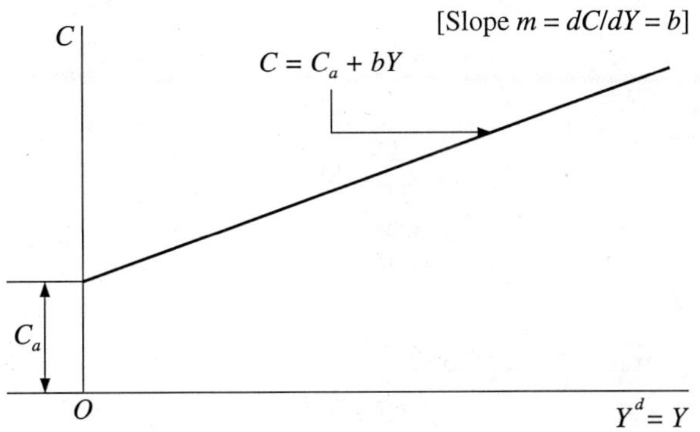

FIGURE 4.1 A short-run or non-proportional Consumption Function, $C = C_a + bY$, has an intercept C_a on the vertical axis indicating consumption expenditure when consumers' income is zero. The slope of the curve is equal to $b = \Delta C/\Delta Y$ or dC/dY for changes in C and Y being infinitesimally small.

The graph is a straight line with an intercept on the vertical axis. For the consumption function in question, ***average propensity to consume*** (APC) can be defined as consumption expenditure incurred per unit of income, i.e.,

$$APC = \frac{\text{Consumption Expenditure } (C)}{\text{Income } (Y)}$$

$$= \frac{C_a + bY}{Y}$$

$$= \frac{C_a}{Y} + \frac{bY}{Y}$$

$$= \frac{C_a}{Y} + b$$

Thus, when $Y = \infty$; $APC = b$, and when Y has finite value, $APC > b$,. In general,

$$APC \geq b \tag{4.2}$$

In like manner, ***Marginal Propensity to Consume*** (*MPC*), defined as an *increase in the consumption expenditure* (ΔC) *per unit increase in income* (ΔY) of the consumers, can be expressed as

$$MPC = \frac{\text{Increase in Consumption Expenditure (X)}}{\text{Increase in Income } (\Delta Y)}$$
$$= \Delta C/\Delta Y \text{ or } dC/dY$$

MPC can thus be obtained for this consumption function through simple differentiation of *C* with respect to *Y*.

$$\begin{aligned} MPC &= dC/dY \\ &= 0 + b \\ &= b \end{aligned} \tag{4.3}$$

Alternatively, let initial and final levels of consumptions be C_1 and C_2 at income levels of Y_1 and Y_2 respectively. Then,

$$C_1 = C_a + bY_1, \text{ and}$$
$$C_2 = C_a + bY_2.$$

Subtracting,

$$C_2 - C_1 = b(Y_2 - Y_1)$$

$\Rightarrow$ $\Delta C = b\Delta Y$ (where, $C_2 - C_1 = \Delta C$ and $Y_2 - Y_1 = \Delta Y$)

$\Rightarrow$ $\Delta C/\Delta Y = b$

$\Rightarrow$ $= MPC.$

For this consumption function, therefore,

$$APC \geq MPC.$$

(From equations 4.2 and 4.3)

(ii) Long-run Consumption Function or Proportional Consumption Function: In the long-run, consumption expenditure is proportional to the income of the consumers. It may be given as:

$$C = bY \tag{4.4}$$

Consumption expenditure, in this case, is zero when income is zero. Average and marginal propensities can be shown to be identical for this type of the consumption function.

$$\begin{aligned} APC &= C/Y \\ &= bY/Y \\ &= b \end{aligned} \tag{4.5}$$

Likewise,

$$\begin{aligned} MPC &= \Delta C/\Delta Y \\ &= b \end{aligned} \tag{4.6}$$

For the long-run consumption function, therefore, the autonomous consumption (C_a) is zero. This type of consumption function relates to the long-run tendency of consumption expenditure (Figure 4.2).

(iii) Non-linear Consumption Function: This type of consumption function is non-linear. It represents the pattern of consumption in the advanced countries or of affluent sections. The algebraic expression may take the following form:

$$C = C_a + bY + cY^2 \tag{4.7}$$

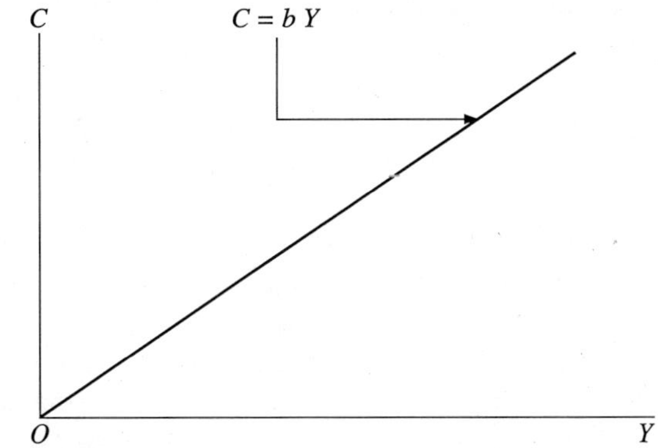

FIGURE 4.2 Long-run Consumption Function: In long-run, consumption expenditure bears a simple proportion with Income *Y*. When $Y = 0$, $C = 0$ and $MPC = APC = b$.

None of the *APC* and *MPC* is constant. Each one is a function of income. For instance,

$$APC = C_a/Y + b + cY$$
$$MPC = b + 2\,cY$$

MPC is a linear function of *Y* while *APC* is non-linear function of it. Figure 4.3 portrays the nature of the curve represented by equation 4.7.

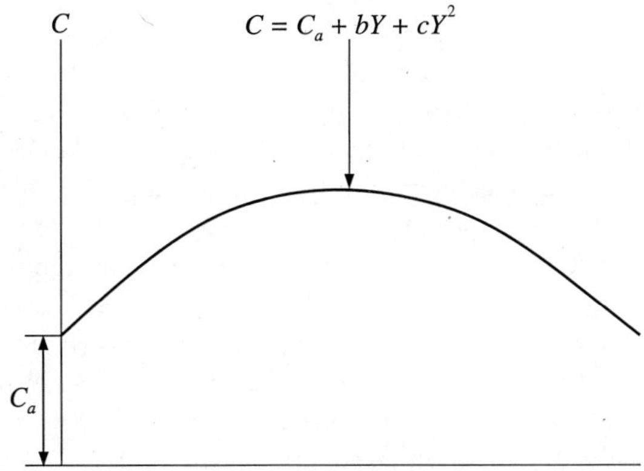

FIGURE 4.3 A **Non-linear consumption function** depicting consumption pattern of the affluent.

4.2 THE MOST COMMON FORM OF THE CONSUMPTION FUNCTION

Of the three, the *first one* is the most common form of the consumption function used in analysis of the national income. There are several reasons for this.

1. It portrays the short-run tendency of the consumption expenditure. It is this tendency that is treated as most appropriate to reflect the pattern of consumption of vast majorities of people in most of the nations whether developed or underdeveloped.

2. When the purpose of analysis is measurement of consumption either at a point of time or over a period of one year with a view to chalk out appropriate policy-mix of consumption for future, it is the short-run consumption function that is found most suitable.
3. C_a is more likely to be non-zero. The period before one gets to earn is generally the same in all the countries whether developed or underdeveloped. One normally starts one's earning life after the age of 20 years on an average. During this period, income is zero but consumption is not.
4. In many Less Developed Countries (*LDCs*), the extent of unemployment is quite high. Incomes of vast majorities are thus zero or low but consumption expenditure is not. Such expenditures are financed either from accumulated savings of the past or from borrowings from anticipated future incomes but more often, they are provided for by relatives and parents.
5. The short-run consumption function thus represents the most common trend of consumption all over the world. Empirical studies conducted in this regard conclude that a consumption function with stable (constant) *MPC* and declining *APC* with increasing income is the most appropriate description of individual consumption. These empirical observations are in line with the short-run consumption function. The statement is consistent with Keynesian belief that the consumption function should have a positive intercept on the vertical axis. The short-run consumption function ($C = C_a + bY^d$ or $C = C_a + bY$ in case the economy has only two sectors, namely, the household sector and the producers' sector) thus, possesses all the requisites expected of the most common consumption function.

4.3 KEYNESIAN PSYCHOLOGICAL LAW OF CONSUMPTION

Keynesian psychological law of consumption is generally considered to comprise the following three related propositions:

1. *When aggregate income increases, consumption expenditure also increases but by somewhat smaller amount:* No doubt, a consumer wants more satisfaction but that does not require that whole of the additional income be spent on additional consumption. What is more consistent with the objective of utility maximization of consumer is to save a portion of income as soon as a satisfactory level of consumption is reached. This may be necessitated by several other objectives such as security for old-age, accumulation of wealth for social status, etc. which the consumers always cherish and are tempted to pursue.
2. *An increase in income is divided in some proportion between savings and consumption, although that proportion can be worked out in practice only after a comprehensive empirical study:* This proposition follows from the first proposition. It is evident that when entire increase in income is not spent on consumption, the residual is saved.
3. *An increase in income is unlikely to lead to less consumption spending or less saving than before:* In other words, if income increases, so do spending and saving.

4.3.1 Assumptions of the Psychological Law of Consumption

The psychological law is based on the following three main assumptions:

1. *The existing psychological–institutional complex remains unchanged:* Keynes assumes that the existing framework of tastes, preferences, habits, beliefs etc. as well as the existing framework of institutional factors such as price-levels, income-distribution, availability of credit, etc. remain unchanged.

2. *The circumstances remain normal:* The assumption implies that the circumstances in the country are not abnormal. For instance, there is no war going on nor is there any revolution, any political upheaval, any state of hyperinflation, or any cyclical depression prevailing in the economy. In other words, the circumstances are just the normal ones. It is evident that the law is applicable only to the short-run as the circumstances do change in the long-run drastically.
3. *The country is having rich, prosperous, capitalistic mode of production based upon the laissez-faire system:* In other words, the country is a developed one and is following a policy of the *laissez-faire* (free trade) system.

   The three assumptions are very essential for the psychological law to operate. Under abnormal circumstances and rapidly changing economic environment, the law fails to have any sanctity.

4.3.2 Implications of the Psychological Law of Consumption

The following are some important implications of this law:

1. *The law highlights the consumption expenditure, in particular, the propensity to Consume:* As the consumption expenditure depends on the level of income of the consumers, the consumption function is highly stable. This leads to a gap in income and consumption expenditure. The gap is equal to the volume of savings or ***withdrawals***, *i.e.,*

   Saving = income-consumption expenditure

   Or, $S = Y - C$

   This gap of income over consumption-expenditure leads to deficiency of demand which if not plugged with injections would lead to depression. In other words, savings need to mobilized and injected back into production-system. Such injections are called ***investment.*** Thus,

   $$I = S = Y - C,$$

   for equilibrium. If injections (I) lags behind the withdrawal (S), depression is not far behind. If S is not properly mobilized and injected back, the only alternative is to increase C, which is possible only through average and marginal propensities to consume. Both need to be very high for this purpose.

   $$Y = C + S$$
   $$\Rightarrow \quad Y/Y = C/Y + S/Y. \text{ (Dividing by } Y \text{ on both the sides)}$$
   $$\Rightarrow \quad 1 = APC + APS \tag{4.8}$$

   where, $APC \equiv$ average propensity to consume (C/Y) and, $APS \equiv$ ***average propensity to save*** (S/Y).

   Thus, APC must be very high and APS very low if the mobilization and injection of savings is low. In like manner, even MPC must be as high as possible and ***marginal propensity to save*** (MPS) as low as possible, so that $MPC + MPS = 1$, as shown below:

   At an initial stage, let $Y_1 = C_1 + S_1$

   At a later stage, let $Y_2 = C_2 + S_2$

   Subtracting, $Y_2 - Y_1 = C_2 - C_1 + S_2 - S_1$

   $$\Rightarrow \quad \Delta Y = \Delta C + \Delta S$$

$$\Rightarrow \qquad \Delta Y/\Delta Y = \Delta C/\Delta Y + \Delta S/\Delta Y$$

$$\Rightarrow \qquad 1 = MPC + MPS \tag{4.9}$$

Note that high values of *MPC* and *APC* (ideally, 1 each) ensure low (ideally, 0) level of leakages from the circular flow of income and expenditure. Recall that Keynesian theory holds that the leakage from the circular flow is responsible for the onset of depression. In other words, if *MPC* and *APC*, each unitary (*i.e., APS* and *MPS* are each zero), the circular flow of income and expenditure is perfect and the question of onset of depression would never arise. Since increase in consumption expenditure lags behind the increase in the income, the marginal efficiency of capital experiences a downward pressure due to lack of consumption demand. This affects the profitability and hence investment, adversely.

2. *The law explains the turning points in the trade cycles:* A downturn from the boom begins when increase in the consumption expenditure is much less than an increase in income. In the same way, an upturn from depression begins when the consumption expenditure cannot be reduced in the same proportion in which peoples' income decreases.
3. *Income of the people does not increase in the same proportion in which the supply of money increases because people do not increase consumption expenditure in the same proportion in which income increases:* It would be in order to demonstrate the relationships between average and marginal propensities to consume and save here for proper understanding of the two (Table 4.1).

TABLE 4.1 Relationship Between Average and Marginal Propensities to Consume and to Save

Y	*C*	*S*	*APC* *C/Y*	*APS* *S/Y*	*APC* + *APS*	Δ*Y*	Δ*C*	Δ*S*	*MPC* Δ*C*/Δ*Y*	*MPS* Δ*S*/Δ*Y*	*MPC* + *MPS*
(1)	(2)	(3)	(4)	(5)	(6)	(7)	(8)	(9)	(10)	(11)	(12)
0	100	– 100	∞	– ∞	–	–	–	–	–	–	–
100	190	– 90	1.90	– 0.90	1.00	100	90	10	0.90	0.10	1.00
200	280	– 80	1.40	– 0.40	1.00	100	90	10	0.90	0.10	1.00
400	420	– 20	1.05	– 0.05	1.00	200	140	60	0.70	0.30	1.00
500	480	+ 20	0.96	+ 0.04	1.00	100	60	40	0.60	0.40	1.00
1000	800	+ 200	0.80	+ 0.20	1.00	500	320	180	0.64	0.36	1.00
1200	900	+ 300	0.75	+ 0.25	1.00	200	100	100	0.50	0.50	1.00
1500	900	+ 600	0.60	+ 0.40	1.00	300	0	300	0.00	1.00	1.00

Explanation: Column (1), (2) and (3) record levels of income, consumption and savings. Column (4) and (5) show how APC and APS are calculated for given levels of income, consumption and savings. Column (6) shows the sum of APC and APS. Note that APC may be higher than 1.00. Whenever this happens, APS must be negative, indicating dissavings. With change of income, consumption and savings both change. MPC and MPS are calculated in columns (10) and (11). Their sum is shown in column (12).

4.4 FACTORS INFLUENCING CONSUMPTION DEMAND

As is evident from the definition of the consumption function, consumption expenditure is a stable function of income. The fact is also supported by statistical evidence. The data on consumption expenditure and income from all over the world testify the stability of the relationship between the two. Nevertheless, factors other than income cannot be overlooked as insignificant in respect of their influence on the consumption expenditure. Keynes himself has observed in his General Theory that the amount that the community spends on consumption obviously depends:

1. Partly on the amount of its income,
2. Partly on the other objective attendant circumstances, and
3. Partly on the other subjective needs of the psychological propensities and habits of the individuals composing it and the principle on which the income is divided.

1. Income: The consumption expenditure, as seen earlier, is a function of income. It varies directly with income of the consumers. The higher the income, the higher is the consumption expenditure except at its sufficiently high levels at which the consumption expenditure reaches a saturation point and even begins to decline beyond it. Exceptional behavior of the consumption expenditure is witnessed in advanced countries or among the rich when the consumers attain the desired level of living standard.

2. The Objective Factors: Among the objective factors are the following ones:

(a) *Distribution of Income:* The national income remaining same, the consumption expenditure would depend on income distribution in the economy in question. People with lower incomes spend everything on the consumer goods.

Their income level is either below the level of subsistence or at par with it. On the contrary, the rich enjoy incomes much higher than their desired levels of consumption, and therefore allocate smaller parts of their incomes on consumption. Despite the wasteful expenditures, the rich are thus able to save quite a lot. If a redistribution of income takes place so that the surplus income with the rich is equitably distributed among the poorer sections of the community, the aggregate consumption expenditure would certainly rise and the level of savings would significantly fall. Income distribution, thus, has a significant role to play in influencing the magnitude of the consumption expenditure.

Alternatively, if the consumption expenditure is low and savings, high the latter must be mobilized properly so that they can finance investments.

(b) *Stock of Wealth:* Wealth is accumulated by the people either to provide for the uncertainties of life or for expenditures anticipated in future or simply for the sake of demonstration. However, successive units of wealth accumulated follow the law of diminishing marginal utility. As a result, the desire for additional accumulation, at a certain level, is overtaken by the desire for enjoying current consumption. Thus consumption expenditure continues to be low up to its desired level after which it may assume a rising trend.

The argument, however, is based on Pigou's model of consumer behavior which was not supported by any empirical evidence.

(c) *Capital Gains:* The capital gains usually do not make a part of the income used as a source of financing the consumption expenditure even though they constitute a significant component of the disposable income of the consumers.

Most of the economists, except Jan Tinbergen[1], ignored capital gains as one of the sources of financing the consumption expenditure. Prolonged American consumption expenditure boom of late 1920s that contained a large part of capital gains stand testimony to the views of Jan Timbergen.

(d) *Availability of Consumer Credit:* It is a common observation that a large number of the households procure credit facility to acquire consumer durables such as automobiles, *TVs*,

[1] Jan Tinbergen, *Statistical Testing of Business Cycle Theories,* Vol. II, pp. 35–40.

refrigerators, etc. In the absence of such credit facility, the expenditure on the consumer durables would decline significantly. Thus, consumer credit has a significant bearing on consumption expenditure.

(e) *Rate of Interest:* According to the classical economists, rate of interest is the sole determinant of the size of the savings. The higher is the rate of interest, the higher is the tendency among the people to save. Thus a rise in the rate of interest increases the volume of savings and hence decreases the consumption expenditure. J. M. Keynes, however, rejected the classical contention and held that the volume of savings depends on the volume of income. A large number of the economists are in agreement with Keynes but they are not so certain about their convictions. It is, nevertheless, true that borrowings for acquisition of consumer durables get discouraged at higher rates of interest. Equally true is the observation that higher rates of interest serve as an incentive to save for higher returns. The notion cannot, however, be applied uniformly on all the individuals. Some of them reserve their savings for future consumption. Quite a few empirical studies have shown inverse variation of consumption expenditure with the rate of interest,

$$C = C_a + b \cdot Y^d - hr \tag{4.10}$$

3. Subjective Factors: Subjective factors vary from individual to individual and are not quantifiable like the objective factors. J.M. Keynes identified certain motives that compel individuals to exercise restraint on their consumption expenditure. Some of them are mentioned below:

1. Motive of Precaution: To raise reserves against unforeseen contingencies.
2. Motive of Enterprise: To raise reserves for business or speculation.
3. Motive of Avarice: To satisfy miserliness or inhibitions against acts of expenditure.
4. Motive of Pride: To bequeath a fortune.
5. Motive of Improvement: To enjoy gradually increasing expenditure for improvement of standard of living.
6. Motive of Independence: To acquire a sense of economic independence.
7. Motive of Calculation: To ensure appreciation for higher real consumption later.
8. Motive of Foresight: To provide for old-age, children's education or for their marriage.

J.M. Keynes himself has called these motives as the motives of precaution, enterprise, avarice, pride, improvement, independence, calculation and foresight respectively. Motives for saving by the state, public sector and by the private sector corporations are, according to Keynes, the motives of enterprise, motives of liquidity, motives of improvement, and the motives of the financial prudence.

4.5 SAVINGS FUNCTION

Functional relationship between saving and income is known as the *saving function.* Savings vary directly with income, that is, they are high when income is high and low when income is low. In other words, an increase in income leads to an increase in savings.

From the psychological law of consumption, savings represent that part of the disposable income of the consumers which is not spent on consumption. Thus, savings function can be derived from the consumption function.

$$\text{Saving} = \text{Income} - \text{Consumption}$$

Or,

$$S = Y - C$$
$$= Y - (C_a + bY)$$

$$= Y - C_a - bY$$
$$= - C_a + (1 - b)Y \quad (4.11)$$

When $Y = 0$, $S = - C_a$. That means savings are negative when income of the consumer is zero. Negative saving is known as ***dissaving***, that is, withdrawing from the past savings or borrowing against higher income anticipated in future. When unemployed, a consumer borrows from his accumulated savings to finance his subsistence consumption. In case he has no such reserves, he resorts to borrowing from available sources and repays such loans from future savings.

The expression, $(1 - b)$ can be identified as $(1 - MPC)$, which represents the ***Marginal Propensity to Save (MPS)***, as discussed earlier (Equation 4.9). *MPS* is defined as the increase in savings per unit increase in income. Mathematically,

$$MPS = \Delta S/\Delta Y$$
= Change in the level of savings per unit change in income.

The saving function for an economy with two sectors, namely, the household and the producers', has been derived in Equation 4.11 above from the relevant consumption function. The same is portrayed in Figure 4.4.

Recall that the consumption function for an economy with Government as the third sector is

$$C = C_a + b\,Y^d \quad (4.12)$$

Here, Y^d is disposable income or income at the disposal of the consumer which is obtained after deducting net direct taxes $(T - R)$ from it. Thus,

$$Y^d = Y - (T - R)$$
$$= Y - T + R \quad (4.13)$$

In absence of the government sector, $T = R = 0$, and,

$$Y^d = Y \quad (4.14)$$

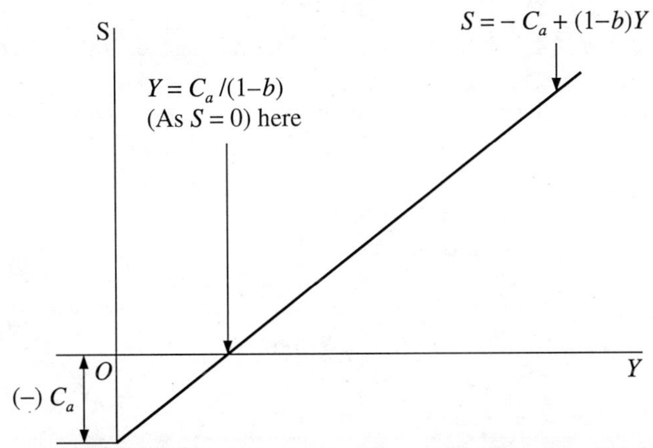

FIGURE 4.4 The savings function makes a negative intercept on the vertical axis, indicating dissaving to the tune of (Ca) when consumer's income is zero. At income level of *Ca*/(1–b), *S* = 0. The slope of the savings function, (1–b), gives the marginal propensity to save (MPS).

4.6 EMPIRICAL ESTIMATES OF CONSUMPTION FUNCTION

The Keynesian psychological Law of Consumption was based on his intuition rather than on empirical evidence. A number of economists after J.M. Keynes tried to estimate the consumption function on the basis of the empirical data. They reached conflicting results about the relationship between consumption expenditure and income for short-run and long-run estimates. We summarize their observations below separately for long-run and short-run.

4.6.1 Empirical Estimates for Long-run Consumption Function

Studies of long-run time series data for U.S. economy over the period of 1948–84, suggested that the average and the marginal propensities to consume (*APC* and *MPC*) were both equal and were somewhere between 0.9 and 1.0. The consumption function, as per these estimates, was of the type:

$$C = 0.9\ Y^d;\ \text{where, } Y^d \equiv \text{Disposable Income.}$$

The result indicates that the consumption expenditure is almost equal to the income. The result evidently did not fit in Keynesian framework. The consumption function of this type is often referred to as the long-run consumption function or even as proportional consumption function due to the fact that it passes through the origin.

4.6.2 Empirical Estimates for Short-run Consumption Function

The short-run time series data were however consistent with the Keynesian theory. The short-run estimates showed that the consumption function has a positive intercept on the consumption axis and that the value of *MPC* is smaller than that in the long-run consumption function. The short-run consumption functions for U.S. economy over the period of 1929–41 in terms of the 1954 prices, as per estimates, was:

$$C = 26.5 + 0.75\ Y^d \tag{4.15}$$

Three immediate implications of this consumption function are:

1. The value of the *MPC* is less than 1.00. In fact it is less than the value *MPC* for the long-run consumption function.
2. The value of *APC* varies inversely as the income. In fact it declines as the income increases. The fact can be easily evidenced by dividing both the sides of the equation by Y^d.

$$APC = \frac{C}{Y^d}$$
$$= \frac{26.5}{Y^d} + 0.75$$

   In fact, when $Y^d = \infty$, $APC = 0.75 + 0 = MPC$.
3. $APC \geq MPC$,
   $APC = MPC$, when $Y^d = \infty$, and
   $APC > MPC$, when Y^d is finite.

Clearly, the estimated short run consumption function was in line with Keynesian contention. Simon Kuznets, on the contrary, contradicted Keynesian hypothesis on consumption in his studies of U.S. national income over the period of 1869–1938.

According to Kuznets, there was no evidence in support of the argument that *APC* declines as the disposable income (Y^d) increases. He found it rather reasonably stable over the entire period of his analysis.

There is a clear discrepancy between the long-run and the short-run estimates of the consumption function. To reconcile, a number of hypotheses have been suggested from time to time. The most important ones of them are briefly discussed below:

1. Relative Income Hypothesis: The relative income hypothesis argues that the fraction of the family income devoted to the consumption expenditure depends on the level of its income relative to the income of the other families with which it identifies itself[1]. In its focus, the relative income hypothesis emphasizes the imitative or the emulative nature of consumption. A family with given level income will typically spend more on consumption if it lives in a community in which its income is relatively lower than if it lives in a community in which its income is relatively higher. This tendency arises in part from the pressures on the family to *"keep up with the Joneses"* and in part from the fact that as the family observes what seem to be the superior goods of other families it will be tempted to spend as a result of what James S. Duesenberry calls *the **demonstration effect.*** Moreover, Duesenberry argues that *"when **absolute income** increases, **absolute consumption** increases but when absolute income decreases, the households do not allow their consumption to fall in proportion to the fall in their incomes."* The latter, in particular, Duesenberry calls as the ***Ratchet Effect.*** *According to Duesenberry, "the ratchet keeps the economy from slipping back all the way and losing all the gains in income acquired during the preceding boom".* The households get used to certain standard of living as well as to a certain level of consumption. As a result, when income falls, the consumption expenditure does not fall in the same proportion in which income does. The relative income hypothesis, therefore, points more towards a non-proportional consumption function.

2. The Permanent Income Hypothesis: ***Permanent Income Hypothesis*** was introduced by Milton Friedman[2] in 1957. According to this hypothesis people tune their consumption expenditure to their permanent income. The term permanent income refers to the mean (average) value of the expected income over a long period of time, which a consumer treats as permanent. Denoting it as Y_p and the corresponding consumption expenditure as C_P, the hypothesis states that C_P is proportional to Y_p.

Thus,

$$C_P = bY_p \tag{4.16}$$

If plotted with Y_P on *x*-axis and C_P on *y*-axis , the consumption schedule so obtained is a straight line passing through origin (Figure 4.5) with a slope of '*b*' [See also Figure 4.2 and Equation 4.4]. Use of, and, emphasis on the term 'permanent' was intended by Friedman to depict long-run trend of consumption expenditure. As regards variations in income, whether positive or negative, Milton Friedman referred to them as ***transitory components*** of income that may be denoted by Y_t. Income in a particular period with this component included is called the ***measured income*** in that period and may be denoted as Y_m. Thus,

$$Y_m = Y_p \pm Y_t \tag{4.17}$$

According to the hypothesis, transitory component is temporary, uncorrelated and unexpected, like windfall gains. Its expected value over a long period of time (in relation to the permanent income) is, therefore, zero. Hence, $Y_m = Y_p$ over the period in question. The possibility of short-run consumption expenditure in presence of Y_t can be expressed as

[1] S. Duesenberry, *Income, Saving and the Theory of Consumer Behavior,* Harward University Press, 1949.

[2] M. Friedman, *A Theory of Consumption Function,* Princeton Univ. Press, 1957.

$$C_m = C_a + b' \, Y_m \tag{4.18}$$

where, $C_m \equiv$ measured consumption expenditure, $C_a \equiv$ autonomous consumption, $Y_m \equiv$ measured income and $b' \equiv$ slope of the consumption function in short-run.

The graph of measured consumption expenditure makes an intercept of C_a on the vertical axis and has a slope of b' (Figure 4.5).

Rejecting the possibility of such behavior of consumption expenditure, the hypothesis specifies that unexpected deviations of income from the permanent income need not reflect in the consumption expenditure of that very year in which they accrue. Instead, the chances are that the transitory component of income (windfall gains) are quite likely to be saved or invested. Moreover the expected value of transitory income over the entire period being zero, the long-run consumption trend (permanent consumption expenditure) depends on permanent income with fairly stable average propensity to consume.

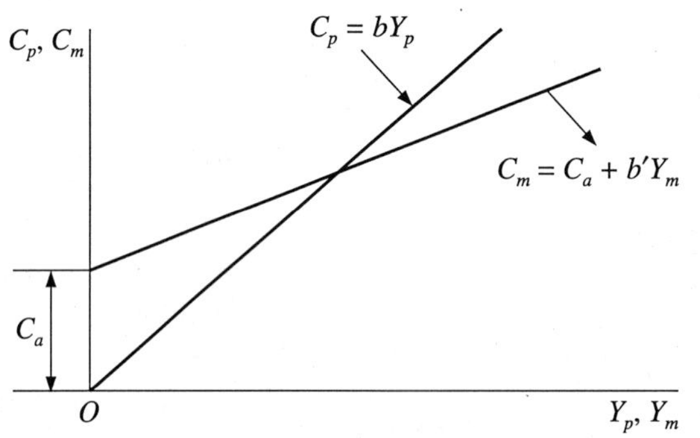

FIGURE 4.5 Representing permanent income (Y_p) and measured (observed) income (Y_m), both, on x-axis and permanent consumption (C_p) and measured (observed) consumption (C_m), both, on y-axis; we plot permanent consumption as a function of permanent income ($C_p = bY_p$) and measured consumption as a function of measured income ($C_m = C_a + b\,Y_m$) as shown. According to Friedman's permanent income hypothesis, permanent consumption is directly proportional to permanent income while measured consumption is a linear function of measured income with an intercept on the y-axis. The latter shows that measured consumption is non-zero at all the income levels while permanent consumption is zero at $Y_p = 0$.

To demonstrate, suppose the average annual income from wages accruing to a factory worker is ₹ 96,000. His average monthly income, then, is ₹ 8,000 which is treated as his permanent income. Now suppose that the worker receives a bonus of ₹ 2,000 in a certain month. The measured income of the worker in that month is ₹ 10,000 of which ₹ 8,000 is the permanent income component while ₹ 2,000 is the transitory income component. Receipt of bonus may not be a regular feature for the worker. In the like manner, a loss of ₹ 2,000 to the same worker may result in some other month due to absence from work on the grounds of illness or long leave taken otherwise. The measured income for the worker in that month would be ₹ 2,000 less (*i.e.*, 6000) The transitory income to the worker is positive in the former case while it is negative in the latter case. In the like manner, Friedman classifies the measured Consumption expenditure (C_m) into two components:

(a) Permanent consumption component, C_p, and
(b) Transitory consumption component, C_t.

Accordingly, $C_m = C_p \pm C_t$ (4.19)

In Figure 4.5, we have shown measured consumption as a function of the measured income. The curve is a straight line with a positive intercept on the consumption axis (can be compared with the short-run consumption function, $C = C_a + bY$, or with $C = C_a + bY^d$, discussed earlier. In the same figure, we have shown the permanent consumption, C_p, as a function of the permanent income, Y_p, which yields to a straight line passing through origin (can be compared with the long-run consumption function $C = bY$, or with, $C = bY^d$, (discussed earlier). What Milton Friedman asserted was that the consumption, or, permanent consumption depends only on the permanent income, with a stable *MPC*. Even Dornbusch, Fischer and Startz[1] hold that "*MPC out of income that is permanent is high, just as in earlier models, but MPC out of transitory income is close to zero.*"

3. The Life Cycle Hypothesis: This hypothesis, developed by Franco Modigliani, Richard E. Brumberg, and Albert Ando[2], is like Friedman's permanent income hypothesis in that the individual's consumption in any given time period does not depend to a significant extent on his income during that period but on the present value of his expected income or his wealth. As suggested by the name given to it, the ***life-cycle hypothesis*** is based on the argument that "*the rate of consumption in any given period is a facet of a plan which extends over the balance of the individual's life, while the income accruing within the same period is but one element which contributes to the shaping of such a plan*[3]" In Figure 4.6, incomes of a consumer and the levels of his consumption maintained by him throughout his life are portrayed. The consumer maintains roughly a constant or slightly increasing

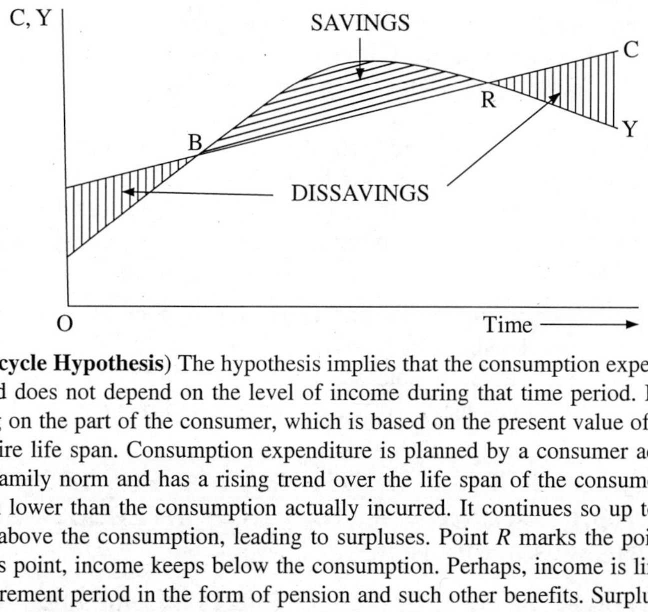

FIGURE 4.6 (Life-cycle Hypothesis) The hypothesis implies that the consumption expenditure of a consumer in a given time period does not depend on the level of income during that time period. Instead, it depends on consumption planning on the part of the consumer, which is based on the present value of his income or wealth expected over the entire life span. Consumption expenditure is planned by a consumer according to his tastes, preferences, and his family norm and has a rising trend over the life span of the consumer. His income, at the initial stages, is much lower than the consumption actually incurred. It continues so up to point B. Thereafter, income shoots much above the consumption, leading to surpluses. Point *R* marks the point of retirement from active work. After this point, income keeps below the consumption. Perhaps, income is limited to that accruing to him in the post-retirement period in the form of pension and such other benefits. Surpluses earned during the peak period finance the deficiency of the consumption in the initial and the final stages of life.

[1] Dornbusch, Fischer and Startz, *Macroeconomics,* Eleventh Edition, McGraw Hill Companies fourth reprint, McGraw Hill Education (India) 2015, page 321.

[2] F. Modigliani and R.E. Brumberg, "Utility Analysis and the Consumption Function: An Interpretation of Cross–section Data," in K. Kurihara, edn., *Post-Keynesian Economics,* Rutgers University Press, 1954, and A. Ando and F. Modigliani, "The Life- Cycle Hypothesis of Saving: Aggregate Implications and Tests, in *American Economic Review,* March 1963, pp. 55–84.

[3] Modigliani and Brumberg, pp. 39–92.

level of consumption over his entire life-cycle, although his income demonstrates quite a different pattern over the same years. It is below the consumption levels in he initial years of the life cycle as well as in the final years of it. In-between, income is far above the corresponding levels of consumption.

The crux of the hypothesis is that people do not consume the amounts earned the same time such amounts accrue to them.

People do not want to consume over their life-times at precisely the same times the amounts they earn. Thus they save and dissave so as to consume incomes over their lifetime in the pattern they want. Typically the hypothesis argues, they will save while working and then use the savings to finance spending in their retirement years. To what extent the aforesaid hypotheses resolve the conflict of the long-and short-run consumption functions, is not very easy to comment upon. It appears that no single conclusion is possible, except that most of the empirical observations and most of the consumption hypotheses confirm that the consumption function is linear with an increasing trend. Moreover, it would not be beyond a reasonable extent to conclude that the linear consumption function with a positive intercept on the vertical axis is the most appropriate description of the consumption pattern in general.

4. Absolute Income Hypothesis: Economists such as Arther Smithies and James Tobin[1], hold that the long-run income-consumption relationship is of non-proportionality with consumption-income ratio (C/Y) falling with rising income. They argue that consumption-income relationship is one of non-proportionality while time series data reveal a relationship of proportionality when the basic non-proportional consumption function keeps shifting upwards with passage of time due to changes in various factors other than income. According to these economists such factors are:

1. In consequence to the accumulated wealth, households tend to spend a larger proportion of their income leading to an upward shift in the non-proportionsal consumption function.
2. Due to flight of labour from rural to urban sectors, non-proprtional consumption function shifts upwards because propensities to consume are higher for factory workers than that for rural workers.
3. Due to rise in proportion of the old in the population, pattern of their consumption shifts the non-proportional consumption function further upwards even without income.
4. With innovations and technological progress old consumer durables get replaced with new high tech ones, implying higher expenditures. This shifts the non-proportional consumption function further up.

Figure 4.7 portrays the deviation of the conclusions drawn from the time series data from those of Arther Smithies and James Tobin.

To have a better picture of various hypotheses, let us understand life cycle of salaried and business people in general in relation to income, saving, consumption and rate of interest in Section 4.7.

4.7 LIFE CYCLE OF PEOPLE IN GENERAL IN RELATION TO INCOME, CONSUMPTION, SAVING AND RATE OF INTEREST—SOME INTERESTING OBSERVATIONS

4.7.1 Fisher's Time Preference: Present or Future Income and Interest[2]

The *Time Preference Theory of Interest* is associated with the name of Irving Fisher who defined interest as an index of the community's preference for a dollar of current income over a dollar of future income. Time preference, is thus preference of having a certain amount today than at a point of time

[1] Arther Smilies, "Forecasting Post War Demsand ", *Econometrica, JAN. 1965* and James Tobin, *"Relative Income Hypothesis and Saving,* published in Money, Trade and Economic Growth, Macmillan, 1951, pp. 135–156.

[2] Chauhan, S.P.S.; *Microeconomics–An Advanced Treatise,* PHI Learning, 2nd Edition (2016); pp. 199–202.

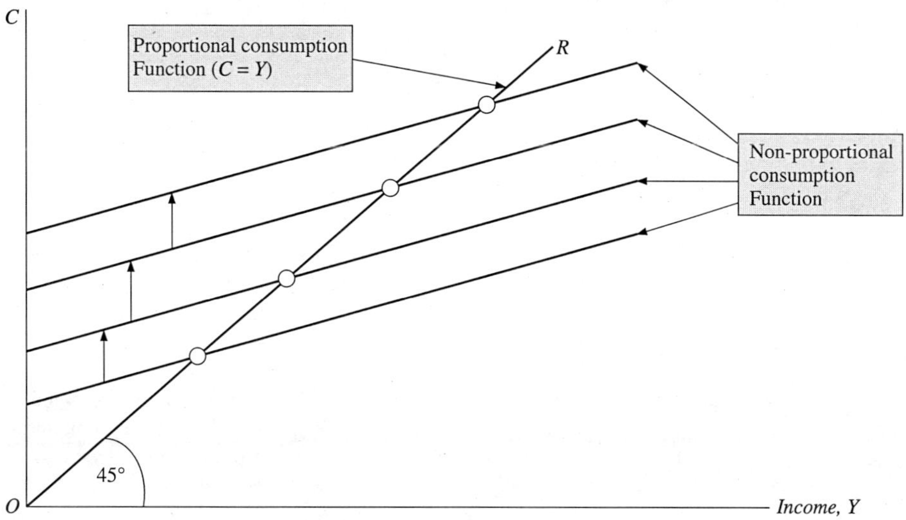

FIGURE 4.7 Absolute Income Hypothesis—The hypothesis of non-proportionality of consumption function forwarded by Arther Smithies and James Tobin stands rejected as explained by the time series data collected and analysed by a number of economists. Accordingly, the long-run consumption function must be one of proportionality, with 45° inclination to the two axes.

in future or having it in future than having it now. Interest is the price of enjoying future income in the present. It is determined by "***marginal rate of time preference***" and "***marginal return over cost***." The former is known also as the rate of willingness, which reflects willingness to borrow. If the rate of willingness is higher than the rate of interest, the tendency to borrow would be high and that to lend, low and if it is lower than the rate of interest, the tendency to borrow would be low and that to lend, high. The rate of return over cost or the marginal return over cost is the discount rate at which the net present values of the alternative future incomes from current investment get equalized. If the

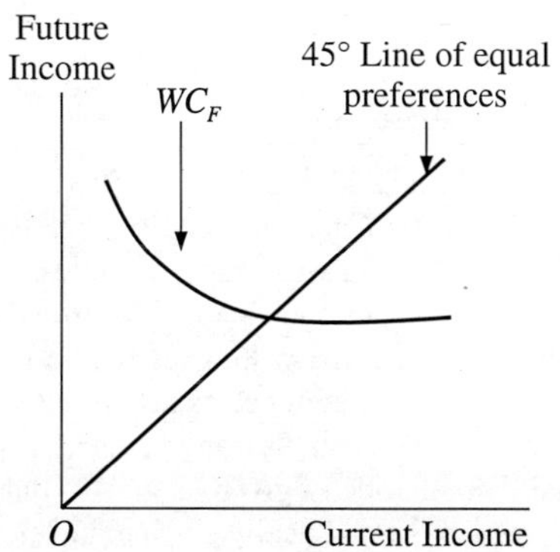

FIGURE 4.7(a) ***The willingness curve (WC_F)*** for those who prefer future income to current income. WC_F, thus, defines negative time preference. Note that WC_F is more or less a quasilinear *IC*.

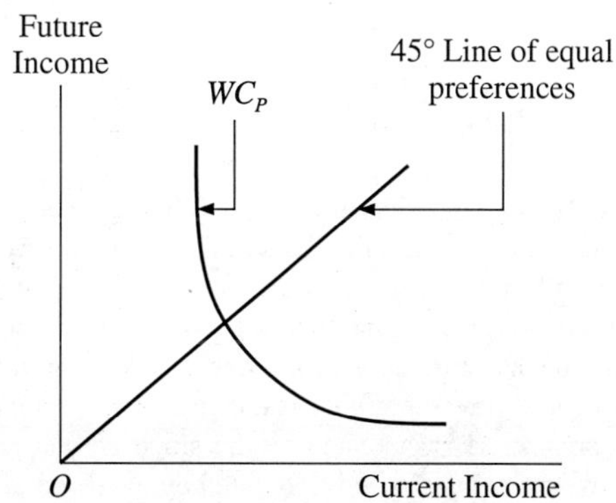

FIGURE 4.7(b) ***The willingness curve (WC_P)*** for those who prefer current income to future income. WC_P, thus, defines positive time preferences. Note that WC_P is more or less a quasilinear *IC*.

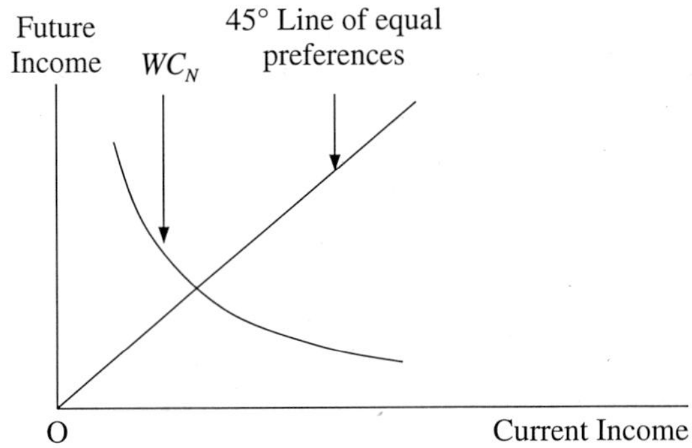

FIGURE 4.7(c) Willingness curve for neutral time preferences (WC_N) between the current and the future incomes is symmetric about the 45°–line which marks equality of preferences between the current and the future incomes, that is, if more of one is preferred, more of the other also has to be preferred or vice-versa.

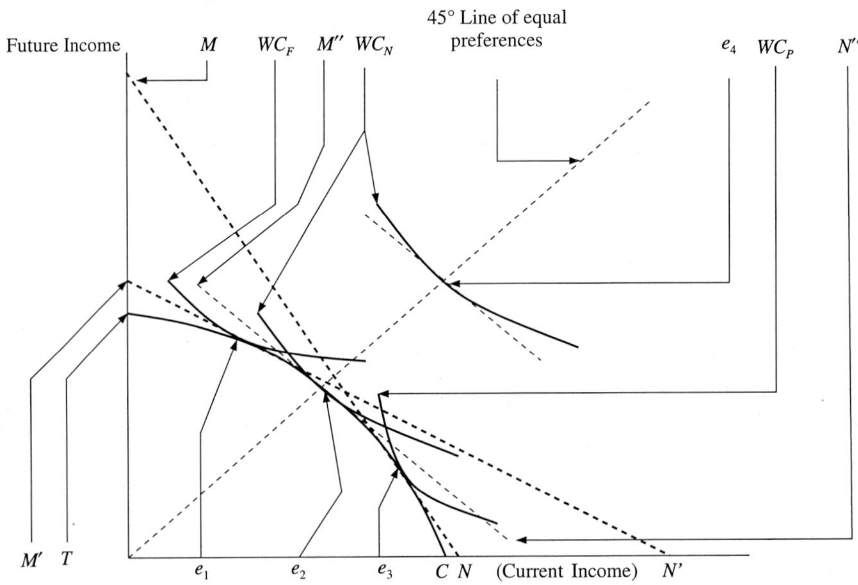

FIGURE 4.7(d) ICs and Fisher's Time Preference Theory of Interest: If the willingness curve is WC_P, it touches the transformation curve, *TC*, at point e_3. At this point, willingness is positive and so is the rate of interest. If the willingness curve is WC_N, it would touch the transformation curve at point e_2 (also shown separately as e_4 for clarity), indicating neutrality to time preference as also to interest rate. If the willingness curve is WC_F, it would touch the transformation curve at point e_1 indicating negativity to time preference as also to interest rate.

Neutral time preference is indicated by the slope of WC_N at e_2 or e_4, which is numerically given as 1; positive time preference is indicated by the slope of WC_P at point e_3, which is numerically given as greater than 1 and negative time preference is indicated by the slope of WC_F at point e_1, which is numerically given to be less than 1.

[Note that *MN* represents the slope of *TC* and WC_P at e_3, *M′N′*, that of *TC* and WC_F at e_1 and *M″N″*, that of *TC* and WC_N at e_2 or at e_4. At e_1 individuals prefer future income to present income, at e_3, they prefer present income to future income while at e_2, they prefer neither, that is, they have neutrality of preference to present or future incomes.]

rate of return over cost is higher for an investment opportunity than the market rate of interest, the tendency to invest is high and that to lend, low. Under Fisher's time preference theory of interest, therefore, we require two tools:

(i) **The Willingness Curve:** It is an indifference curve representing various combinations of the present and the future incomes each of which offers the same level of utility to an individual. It is to be noted that some individuals prefer future income to present income while others prefer present income to future income. For instance, people from business community in general prefer future income to present income. It is so because their present income level is high but the future prospects of it are low. As a result, they prefer to invest for future returns. Unlike the alaried class, they don't have any income assuring schemes like old-age pensions. They are thus the potential sources of loans. Unlike them, there is the salaried class that prefers present income to future income. Individuals in this category feel secure due to old-age pension, provident fund, gratuity and the like. Such expectations assure them a secure future. Besides, their monthly salary has a rising trend as they proceed towards their retirement. The main problem of the people in this category is too low a pay at the entry stage to enjoy desired luxuries of consumer-durables. They invariably tend to borrow to buy the durables such as cars, flats, *TVs*, etc. and thus serve as the potential consumers of loans. The willingness curves for people who prefer future income to present income and those who prefer present income to future income are shown in Figure 4.7(a) and (b) in that order. Both depict quasilinear preferences. For those who are neutral to present and future incomes, their willingness curves resemble the shape of the *IC* as in Figure 4.7(c). All the three depict convex preferences.

(ii) **The Transformation Curves (TCs):** The rate of return over cost or the marginal return over cost is represented by the ***transformation curves*** depicting the rate at which one type of income is transformed into the other. A transformation curve, like a production possibility curve, represents various combinations of the present and the future incomes that are possible to realize with given endowment. As expected, transformation curves are concave to origin. Figure 4.7(d) shows how rate of interest can be determined by Fisher's time preference with the help of these tools. In the figure, *TC* is the transformation curve which represents various combinations of the present and the future incomes that are possible with given endowment. It is concave to origin and its slope is given by the marginal rate of transformation of future income into present income. The ray *OR* depicts the points of balanced preferences between the present and the future incomes. WC_F represents negative time preferences (preference to the future incomes over the present incomes), WC_P represents the positive time preferences (preference to the present incomes over the future incomes) and WC_N represents the neutral time preferences (also shown separately for clarity). The rate of interest is determined at the point of tangency between the transformation curves and the willingness curves.

4.7.2 Wealth-holder's Consumption and Saving over Life Cycle[1]

In the time preference theory of interest [Figure 4.7(d)], we employed willingness curves to represent a wealth-holder's preferences for present and future incomes. A willingness curve was defined as a locus of different combinations of present and future incomes that offer same level of utility to the wealth-holder. One combination of the two incomes is as good as another, so much so, that the wealth-holder turns indifferent in-between them.

[1] Chauhan, S.P.S., *Microeconomics – An Advanced Treatise,* PHI Learning, 2nd Edition (2016); pp 219–222.

The willingness curve therefore was none other than a wealth-holder's indifference curve between present and future incomes. An indifference curve such as the willingness curve may be described as

$$U = \alpha x y + \beta \tag{4.20}$$

where, $x \equiv$ current income; $y \equiv$ future income; and α, β are constants.

The slope of the utility function of Equation 4.20 can be given as

$$\begin{aligned} dy/dx &= -\ [(\partial U/\partial x)/(\partial U/\partial y)] \\ &= -\ \alpha y/\alpha x \\ &= -\ (y/x) \end{aligned} \tag{4.21}$$

We can extend our notion of willingness curve to analyse how a rational individual plans his consumption and savings over his life-span. Preference to current income implies preference to current consumption while preference to future income implies preference to future consumption. The former leads to dissavings while the latter, to savings. An individual preferring current consumption tends to borrow or dissave while another preferring future consumption tends to curtail his current consumption in order to save for future consumption.

The former may be a worker suffering from low levels of current income but expecting high levels of it in future, while the latter, a trader enjoying a high level of current income but fearing tough days in old age. Denoting, for simplicity, future as a period 1 year from now, current consumption as c_1, consumption 1 year from now as c_2, current income as y_1 and income 1 year from now as y_2, the expression for current consumption of an individual preferring present income to income 1 year from now may be given as

$$c_1 = y_1 + [y_2/(1 + r)] \tag{4.22}$$

where, r is the rate of interest and $[y_2/(1 + r)]$ is the discounted value of income 1 year from now.

That is, the individual prefers to consume not only his current income y_1 but also the discounted value of his income y_2 accruing to him 1 year from now. One can also look upon $[y_2/(1 + r)]$ as the amount borrowed now at $100r$ percent per annum compounded annually, which may be paid off 1 year from now from the then income of y_2.

For an individual who prefers future consumption, c_2, to current consumption of $c_1(= y_1)$, the expression may be given as:

$$c_2 = [y_1(1 + r)] + y_2 \tag{4.23}$$

where, $[y_1(1 + r)]$ is the amount the individual would get 1 year from now by investing his current income y_1 at $100r$ percent per annum compounded annually. But if $c_1 < y_1$, $s_1 = y_1 - c_1$, and supposing that he consumes whole of the income during his life span only, the future consumption would be

$$\begin{aligned} c_2 &= s_1(1 + r) + y_2 \\ &= (y_1 - c_1)\ (1 + r) + y_2 \end{aligned}$$

$$\Rightarrow \quad c_2 + (1 + r)c_1 = y_1(1 + r) + y_2 \tag{4.24}$$

Expression 4.24 represents a straight line when c_1 is represented on x-axis and c_2 on y-axis. The expression assumes that current consumption is less than the current income and whole of the future income along with the current savings as also the interest on these savings are to be consumed in future.

If $c_1 > y_1$, the individual would borrow in the current period and repay his borrowings along with interest in future from the future income y_2. In such a case,

$$c_2 = y_2 - (c_1 - y_1)\ (1 + r)$$

$$\Rightarrow \quad c_2 + c_1(1 + r) = y_2 + y_1(1 + r) \tag{4.25}$$

Expressions 4.24 and 4.25 are both identical, each yielding a straight when plotted with c_1 on x-axis and c_2 on Y-axis. If $c_1 = 0$, $c_2 = y_2 + y_1(1 + r)$, which is the same as that given by Equation 4.23. And, if $c_2 = 0$, $c_1 = y_1 + [y_2/(1 + r)]$,

which is the same as that given by Equation 4.18.

Thus, Equation 4.24 or 4.25 would represent the consumer's budget line with a slope of

$$dc_2/dc_1 = -[1 + r] \quad (4.26)$$

Substituting c_1 for x and c_2 for y in Equations 4.20 and 4.21 we have,

$$U = \alpha c_1 c_2 + \beta$$

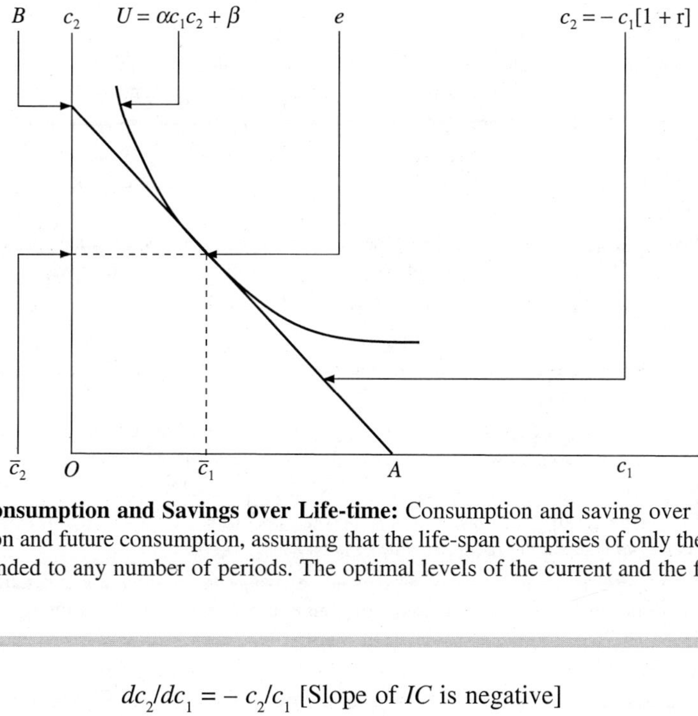

FIGURE 4.8 Consumption and Savings over Life-time: Consumption and saving over life-time, viewed as current consumption and future consumption, assuming that the life-span comprises of only these two periods. The model can be extended to any number of periods. The optimal levels of the current and the future consumptions are $[\bar{c}_1, \bar{c}_2]$.

$$\Rightarrow \quad dc_2/dc_1 = -c_2/c_1 \text{ [Slope of } IC \text{ is negative]} \quad (4.27)$$

For optimality of the combination (c_1, c_2), the budget line should be tangential to the *IC* (Figure 4.8). This requires that the slope of the indifference curve must be equal to that of the budget line. That is,

$$dc_2/dc_1 = -c_2/c_1 = -[1 + r]$$

$$\Rightarrow \quad c_2/c_1 = [1 + r]; \text{ or , } c_2 = c_1 \times [1 + r] \quad (4.28)$$

The analysis above is based on the assumption that 'future' refers to a period one year from now. It can be extended to any period 'n' years from now by replacing the term $[1 + r]$ by $[1 + r]^n$, y_2 and c_2 by y_n and c_n.

In either case, salaried individuals tend to borrow at the early stages of their employment because their current incomes are low and future incomes, high. The business people tend to lend because their current incomes are high while their future incomes, uncertain or low. The latter want to enjoy the same propensity to consume in their old age while the former want a higher propensity to consume in the current period as they are sure of a higher income in their old age.

KEY TERMS AND CONCEPTS

Circular Flow: Circular flow refers to the inflow and outflow of income and expenditure through products. People provide factor services for factor incomes which they spend on products and services. Money income reaches back to the very source of its origin. It is true in all the sectors of an economy.

Leakages from the Circular Flows: When some part of the money income originating from its source fails to reach back the source, it is said to be a leakage from the source. Savings (*S*), taxation (*T*) and import (*M*) are its three channels. They affect production, income and employment adversely unless they are plugged with injections of investment (*I*), government spending (*G*) and exports (*X*).

Injections into the Circular Flow: Injections into the circular flow comprise investment spending (*I*), government spending (*G*) and export-earnings (*X*). They must make up for the loss caused by the leakages so that production, employment and income may continue without an adverse affect.

Consumption Function: Generally consumption expenditure expressed as a function of its determinants, such as, income, average and marginal propensities to consume is called the consumption function. That is, consumption (C) = $C_a + b\ Y$, where, Y is income, C_a autonomous consumption, and *b,* marginal propensity to consume.

Empirical studies have shown that the rate of interest is yet another determinant of the consumption expenditure. Thus, consumption (C) = $C_a + b\ Y - h\ r$, where, all the symbols have their usual meaning except the last one of *hr, with h being a constant of proportionality and r the rate of interest.* The empirical consumption shows that *C is a decreasing function of r.*

Saving Function: Saving expressed as a function of income and propensity to save is called the saving function. A typical saving function is $S = -C_a + (1 - b)Y$, where, Y is income, $(1 - b)$ is marginal propensity to save, $-C_a$ is dissaving.

Short-run Consumption Function: A consumption function of the type $C = C_a + bY$ is the non-proportional or short-run consumption function.

Long-run Consumption Function: A consumption function of the type $C = bY$ is the proportional or long-run consumption function.

Average Propensity to Consume (*APC*): Consumption expenditure incurred per unit of income is called the average propensity to consume (*APC*). It may be expressed as the ratio of the consumption expenditure (C) to the income (Y). Thus, $APC = C/Y$.

Average Propensity to Save (*APS*): Saving per unit of income is defined as the average propensity to save (*APS*). It may be expressed as the ratio of saving (S) to income (Y). Thus, $APS = S/Y$.

Marginal Propensity to Consume (*MPC*): It is defined as the change in consumption expenditure per unit change in income. It may be expressed as a ratio of change in consumption expenditure (ΔC) to the change in income (ΔY). Thus, $MPC = \Delta C/\Delta Y$.

Marginal Propensity to Save (*MPS*): It is defined as the change in savings per unit change in income. It may be expressed as a ratio of change in savings (ΔS) to the change in income (ΔY). Thus, $MPS = \Delta S/\Delta Y$.

Keynesian Psychological Law of Consumption: The psychological law of consumption states:

1. When aggregate income increases, consumption expenditure also increases but by somewhat smaller amount.
2. An increase in income is divided in some proportion between savings and consumption, although that proportion can be worked out in practice only after a comprehensive empirical study.
3. An increase in income is unlikely to lead to less spending or less Saving than before.

Assumptions of the Psychological Law of Consumption: The psychological law is based on the following three main assumptions:

1. The existing psychological–institutional complex remains unchanged.
2. The circumstances remain normal.
3. The country is having rich, prosperous, capitalistic mode of production based upon the *laissez-faire* system.

Implications of the Psychological Law of Consumption: The following are some important implications of this law:

1. The law highlights the identities,

(a) $1 = APC + APS$

where, $APC \equiv$ Average Propensity to Consume (C/Y) and, $APS \equiv$ Average Propensity to Save (S/Y). Thus, APC must be very high and APS very low if mobilization of savings to serve the cause of injection is low. (b) $MPC + MPS = 1$, that is, MPC must be as high as possible and MPS, as low as possible.

2. The law explains the turning points in the trade cycles. A downturn from the boom begins when increase in the consumption expenditure is much less than increase in income. In the same way, an upturn from depression begins when the consumption expenditure cannot be reduced in the same proportion in which peoples' income decreases.
3. Income of the people does not increase in the same proportion in which the supply of money increases because people do not increase consumption expenditure in the same proportion in which income increases.

Factors Influencing the Consumption Expenditure: Consumption expenditure is influenced by the following factors:

1. Income,
2. The Objective Factors, such as
   (a) Distribution of Income,
   (b) Stock of Wealth,
   (c) Capital Gains,
   (d) Availability of Consumer Credit, and
   (e) Rate of Interest.
3. Subjective Factors, such as,
   (a) Motive of Precaution: To raise reserves against unforeseen contingencies.
   (b) Motive of Enterprise: To raise reserves for business or for speculation.
   (c) Motive of Avarice: To satisfy miserliness or inhibitions against acts of expenditure.
   (d) Motive of Pride: To bequeath a fortune.
   (e) Motive of Improvement: To enjoy gradually increasing expenditure for improving standard of living
   (f) Motive of Independence: To acquire a sense of economic independence.
   (g) Motive of Calculation: To enjoy interest appreciation for larger real consumption at a later date.
   (h) Motive of Foresight: To provide for old-age, children's education or for their marriage.

J. M. Keynes himself has called these motives as the motives of precaution, enterprise, avarice, pride, improvement, independence, calculation and foresight respectively. Motives for saving by the state, public sector and by the private sector corporations are, according to Keynes, the motives of enterprise, motives of liquidity, motives of improvement, and the motives of the financial prudence.

Empirical Estimates of the Long-run Consumption Function: Studies of long-term time series data for U.S. economy over the period of 1948–84, suggested that the average and the marginal propensities to consume (APC and MPC) were both equal and were somewhere between 0.9 and 1.0. The consumption function, as per these estimates, was of the type:

$$C = 0.9Y^d;\text{ where, } Y^d \equiv \text{Disposable Income.}$$

The result indicates that the consumption expenditure is almost equal to the income. The result evidently did not fit in Keynesian framework. The consumption function of this type is often referred to as the long-run consumption function or even as proportional consumption function due to the fact that it passes through the origin.

Empirical Estimates of the Short-run Consumption Function: The short-run time series data were, however, consistent with the Keynesian theory. The short-run estimates showed that the consumption function has a positive intercept on the consumption axis and that the value of MPC is smaller than that in the long-run consumption function. The short-run consumption functions for U.S. economy over the period of 1929–41 in terms of the 1954 prices, as per the estimates, was:

$$C = 26.5 + 0.75\ Y^d$$

This consumption function is in line with Keynesian concept of the consumption function with an intercept on the vertical axis.

Relative Income Hypothesis: According to J.S. Duesenberry, the relative income hypothesis argues that the fraction of the family income devoted to the consumption expenditure depends on the level of its income relative to the income of the other families with which it identifies itself.

Permanent Income Hypothesis: Milton Friedman asserted that the consumption or permanent consumption depends only on the permanent income and has a stable APC.

Life-cycle Hypothesis: This hypothesis, developed by Franco Modigliani, Richard E. Brumberg, and Albert Ando implied that an individual's consumption in any given time period does not depend to a significant extent on his income during that period but on the present value of his expected income or his wealth. The consumer maintains roughly a constant or slightly increasing level of consumption over his entire life-cycle, although his income demonstrates a quite different pattern over the same years.

Absolute Income Hypothesis: Economists hold that the long-run income-consumption relationship is one of non-proportionality with consumption income ratio (C/Y) falling with increasing income. They argue that consumption income relationship is one of non-proportionality while time series data reveal their proportionality as non-proportional consumption function shifts upwards with passage of time as a result of changes in certain factors other than income.

EXERCISES

A. Short Answer Questions

1. Give a numerical example to demonstrate the effects of income (Y), and marginal propensity to consume, (b) on consumption expenditure.
2. Demonstrate the effects of marginal propensity to consume, (b) and rate of interest, (r) on consumption expenditure.
3. Define average and marginal propensities to consume. Is it true that $APC \geq MPC$?
4. For the function, $C = C_a + bY$, show that
   (i) $APC + APS = 1$
   (ii) $MPC + MPS = 1$
5. Can average propensity to consume be greater than one? Give reasons for your answer.
6. A consumer's income is ₹ 2,000 and his consumption expenditure is ₹ 1,500. If the remainder is saved by the consumer, calculate the average propensities to consume and to save.
   [Ans: $APC = 0.75$: $APS = 0.25$]
7. In question 6, if the consumer's income changes to ₹ 2,400 and consumption expenditure to ₹ 1,750, calculate:
   (a) consumer's average propensities to consume and to save, and
   (b) consumer's marginal propensities to consume and to save. **[Ans:** (a) 0.73; 0.27 (b) 0.625; 0.375]
8. Explain how leakages from the circular flow of income and expenditure affect income, employment and production in an economy. What would happen to these parameters if injections were inadequate?
9. Explain the main sources of depression of 1930s that gripped the entire Europe?
10. With the help of neat sketches, outline the main variants of the consumption function. Which one of them is treated as most appropriate for macroeconomic analysis and why?
11. What is meant by the relative income hypothesis of consumption? How relevant it is in the modern life style?
12. Explain the implications of the permanent income hypothesis of consumption through an example.
13. What is meant by the life-cycle hypothesis of consumption? How do consumers plan their consumption over their life-span? Use a neat sketch in support.
14. An individual's consumption expenditure is related to his income through the function:

$$C = 1000 + 0.8Y$$

   Estimate his consumption expenditure when his income is (a) 1,000, (b) 1,500.
   Calculate his average propensities to consume and to save in each case and show that the Identity, $APC + APS = 1$ holds in each case.
   [Ans: (a) $APC = 1.80$; $APS = -0.80$
   (b) $APC = 1.467$; $APS = -0.467$].

15. Calculate *MPC* and *MPS* for the data given in question 14. Do your answers satisfy the identity, $MPC + MPS = 1.00$?

[**Ans:** MPC = **0.80,** and
$\Delta Y = 1500 - 1000 =$ **500)**
MPS = **0.20**
(Note that $\Delta S = -700 - (-800) = +$ **100,** and
$\Delta Y = 1500 - 1000 =$ **500)**
Yes, $MPC + MPS = 0.80 + 0.20 =$ **1.00.]**

16. Name three factors on which consumption expenditure depends. How does the rate of interest influence the consumption expenditure?
17. Outline and explain any three objective factors that influence the consumption expenditure.
18. Outline and explain any three subjective factors that influence the consumption expenditure.
19. Give an example to show how availability of the consumer credit influences the consumption expenditure?
20. What is the main difference between the effects of the subjective and objective factors upon consumption expenditure?
21. What is a saving function? What is the significance of '$-C_a$' in a savings function? Explain with the help of a neat sketch.
22. What is the essence of the psychological law of consumption?

B. Long Answer Questions

23. Explain the Keynesian psychological law of consumption. On what assumptions is it based? What are its implications?
24. Explain the role played by the leakages in the onset of economic depression. How can its ill-effects be rectified?
25. "Saving is a virtue for an individual but a vice for the nation'. Comment.
26. From the data given in the table below, calculate *APC, APS, MPC,* and *MPS* each time income changes and hence complete the table.

Income (Y)	*Consumption (C)*	*Savings (S)*	*APC*	*APS*	*MPC*	*MPS*
0	2000	– 2000	–	–	–	–
1,000	2,800	–	–	–	–	–
2,000	3,600	–	–	–	–	–
3,000	4,400	–	–	–	–	–
5,000	6,000	–	–	–	–	–
10,000	10,000	–	–	–	–	–
15,000	14,000	–	–	–	–	–
20,000	18,000	–	–	–	–	–
25,000	22,000	–	–	–	–	–

C. Essay Type Questions

27. What is meant by a consumption function? Give a critical account of the factors that influence the consumption expenditure.
28. Show that the *APC* is always greater than or equal to the *MPC* irrespective of whether the consumption function relates to the short run or to the long-run. Also deduce that $APC = MPC$ when income is infinitely large. What can you say for the two when consumption function is a second degree function of income (*Y*) portraying the pattern of consumption in the affluent societies.

29. How do various hypotheses resolve and reconcile the discrepancy between short-run and long-run consumption functions? What conclusions would you draw from your analysis about the most appropriate form of the consumption function?
30. With help of a neat sketch explain the notion of permanent income hypothesis of consumption.
31. What role does the Fisher's time preference theory of interest play in planning of life-time consumption. Why do some segments of consumers tend to borrow and others to invest or lend?
32. With the help of a sketch show how a wealth holder depends on the rate of interest while planning his/her current and future consumption expenditures?

Chapter 5

Investment Function

INTRODUCTION

In common parlance, investment means commitment of funds to acquisition of any assets that appreciate in time or generate surpluses. Purchase of shares, land, building, and the like-all constitute investment for most of us provided their sale promises some surplus. Commitment of funds to acquisition of goods is likely to generate surpluses when sold. People call it an investment. Likewise, procurement and accumulation of productive assets, whether they are new assets or old ones, are all treated as investment by most of us. The criteria for any expenditure to qualify as investment for a layman is the likelihood of a surplus it may generate in return at a point of time usually in future.

Not all these expenditures qualify as investment in economic sense. Let us see what investment in economics really means. As regards its definition, *investment refers to acquisition and use of new productive assets for production of good and services.* If we split the definition into its components, the first one is acquisition of productive assets, the second one is their use in production of goods and services and the third one is that the assets in question are new assets. Another one implicit in the definition is direct participation of the asset in the process of production. Not all expenditures mentioned above qualify as investments when tested on these parameters The discussion may be yet simpler if we transform the definition into an elaborative one. For instance, *investment refers to acquisition and use of new machinery, equipment, plant, etc. that participate directly in the process of production of goods and services.* If such assets are acquired but not used in current production, the activity is called ***capital formation*** or ***capital accumulation*** but not investment. The instant such capital accumulation is put to use in production of goods and services, it transforms into investment. In sum, acquisition and use of new and tangible productive assets for production of goods and services is termed as investment in economic sense. Thus, a positive change in the stock of productive assets is *capital formation while inducting it in production process, investment.*

Determination of magnitude of investment as also the factors that affect it forms the subject matter of this chapter. Its magnitude is estimated in monetary units at prices that prevail at the time of its induction in production. The value of capital assets acquired in past but inducted in production now must be indexed before such induction. Likewise, factors that influence the value of investment refer to all those determinants that tend to increase or decrease it. The chapter is devoted to such discussions as well.

5.1 TERMINOLOGY IN USE

(i) Gross and Net investment: ***Net investment*** refers to the money value of productive assets at the current prices while **gross investment** refers to the money value of the assets at the time they were inducted in production. The two differ from each other only by the magnitude of depreciation which accounts for the wear and tear of the asset during its use in production.

Thus,

$$\text{Net investment} = \text{Gross Investment} - \text{Depreciation}$$

Depreciation represents loss of value of productive assets in the process of production. Due to wear and tear suffered during production, such assets suffer a loss in their efficiency. Expenditures incurred on their maintenance serve as a measure of depreciation. Firms set aside an amount called depreciation allowance each year in the beginning.

(ii) Autonomous and Induced Investment: ***Autonomous investment*** is that investment which is income and interest inelastic. All the investments made by governments in the public sector are of autonomous character. Such investments are essential for provision of amenities and other measures of social welfare. A welfare oriented state incurs them regardless of the source it gets them from. Private investment may or may not of autonomous in nature. It could be autonomous provided it is made for reasons other than those of making profits. Contributions made by firms to the provident fund of the workers qualify as one example of autonomous investment and medical facility for them, another. Such investments are mandatory for the firms due to labour legislation in most of the countries.

Induced investment is an investment that is income elastic or income sensitive. Such investments increase with an increase in the income of the investor. It may be zero at low level of income, and high at high levels of it. It arises from investor's income and aims for higher levels of the same.

The distinction between the autonomous and induced investments is demonstrated through Figure 5.1. The former gives a horizontal line at all levels of income while the latter, an upward sloping one.

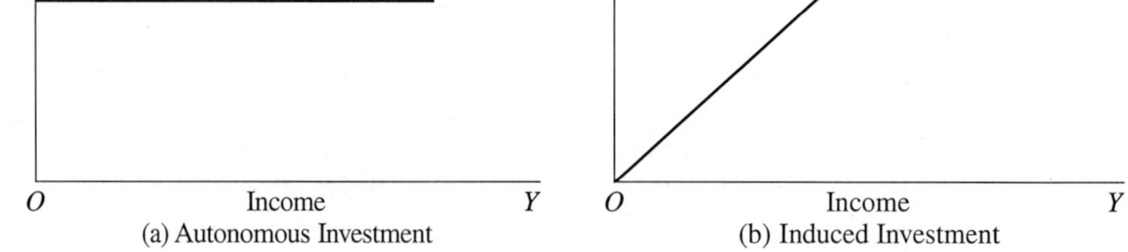

FIGURE 5.1 Autonomous investment (I_a) is independent of income Y, as portrayed in panel (*a*). As against this, induced investment (I_Y) varies directly with income as shown in panel (*b*) Marginal propensity to invest for induced investment, dI/dY can be obtained through differentiation of I_Y with respect to Y and is given as '*i*' The same is zero for autonomous investment, *i.e.* $dI_a/dY = 0$.

Total investment function can be derived through vertical summation of the autonomous investment and the induced investment. That is,

$$I = I_a + I_Y = I_a + iY \tag{5.1}$$

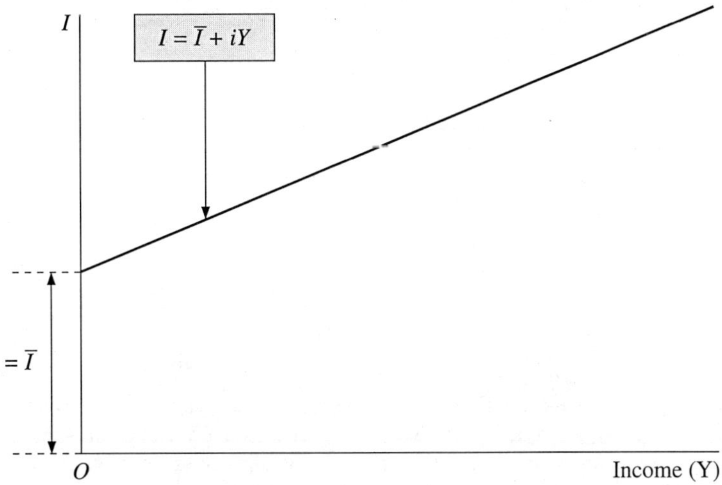

FIGURE 5.2 Total investment as a vertical summation of the autonomous and induced investments is portrayed as a function of income. It makes an intercept on the vertical axis equal in magnitude to the autonomous investment.

where, $I_a \equiv$ autonomous investment $I_Y \equiv$ Induced Investment (iY), 'i' $\equiv$ a constant of proportionality, defined as ***marginal propensity to invest*** *(MPI = dI/dY)* like other propensities of consumption and savings. It implies change in investment per unit change in income.

Investment is portrayed here as a function of income and may be called an ***investment function***.

However, the general form of an investment function is $I = f(Y, r)$, where Y is income and r, the rate of interest. In short-run, in which, income (Y) remains constant, investment can be defined as an inverse function of rate of interest, r, that is,

$$I = f(r) = I_a - hr \tag{5.2}$$

where, I_a is autonomous investment, 'r' *is* rate of interest and 'h', a constant of proportionality. Graphically, investment function given by Equation 5.2 can be portrayed as in Figure 5.3.

(iii) Private and Public Investment: Investment made by individuals in the private sector is known as ***private investment***. The purpose of such investment is the profit. On the contrary, investment made by the government is known as the ***public investment***. The objective of public investment is social welfare, not profit. Government invests huge amounts in activities of public utilities such as construction of roads, stadia, structures for housing schools, colleges, hospitals, etc. They are all public utility projects in which a welfare oriented government invests large chunks of money raised through taxation.

5.2 FACTORS INFLUENCING A FIRM'S DECISION TO INVEST

A firm's investment decisions depend on the Net Present Value (*NPV*) of the investment. It is given as the excess of the present value of returns of an investment over its cost. The net present value of an investment can thus be expressed as

NPV = Sum of the present values of the future income streams from the investment *less* cost of the investment.

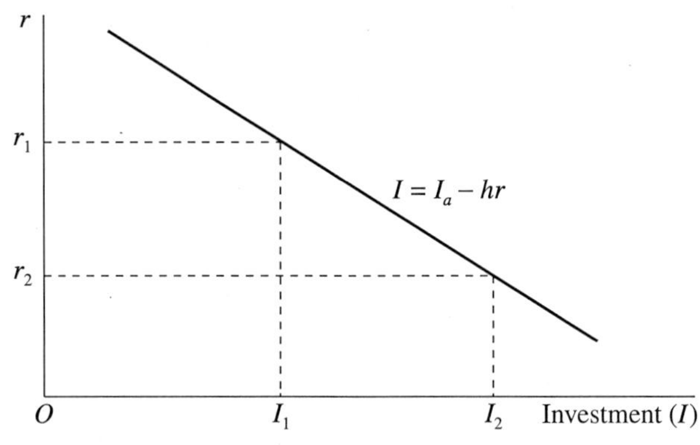

FIGURE 5.3 In short-run, when income Y is constant, investment I varies inversely with the rate of interest r. When the rate of interest is high, investment is low and vice-versa. The inverse variation of 'I' with 'r' can be explained through Keynesian theory that people commit their savings to lending or to speculating rather than to acquisition and use in productive activities when rate of interest 'r' is higher than marginal efficiency of capital (MEC).

For an illustration, suppose that an investor acquires a machine for ₹ 4,000. The life span of the machine is, say, three years. The machine yields an income of ₹ 1,100 at the end of the first year, ₹ 2,420 at the end of the second year and ₹ 1,331 at the end of the third year. Thereafter it reduces to scrap. Also, suppose that the market rate of interest is 10% per annum and it remains stable at least over the life span of the machine.

The present value of an income expected after 'n' years, assuming the rate of interest to remain unchanged at 'r' percent per annum throughout the period, may be treated as the principal 'P' that is lent out now at 'r' percent per annum compounded annually over 'n' years. The amount (A) accruing to the lender, in consequence, may be treated as the income expected (A) by an investor after 'n' years of purchase and use in production of a capital asset of the same value as the principal (P) and generating profit at the same rate as the rate of interest. In other words, A can be given by the compound interest formula,

$$A = P(1 + r/100)^n \tag{5.3}$$

For instance, suppose that a moneylender lends ₹ 10,000 (P) for a period of 3 years (n) at 10% (r) compounded annually. Substituting P = ₹ 10,000; r = 10% or 0.10; and n = 3 years in Equation 5.3, we have

$$\begin{aligned} A &= 10{,}000\ (1 + 0.10)^3 \\ &= 10{,}000\ (1.331) = ₹\ 13{,}310 \end{aligned}$$

Let us repose the problem in a slightly different way. Suppose the moneylender wants to know as to how much to invest on a machine so as to receive a sum of ₹ 13,310 after 3 years at 10% per annum compounded annually. The answer is an obvious one— ₹ 10,000! Rewriting Equation 5.3 as:

$$P = \frac{A}{(1+r)^3} \tag{5.4}$$

and making substitutions, we have

$$P = \frac{13{,}310}{(1+0.10)^3} = ₹\ 10{,}000.$$

That is, an amount of ₹ 10,000 today is the same as that of ₹ 13,310 three years hence so-long-as the rate of interest is stable at 10% per annum. The former is known as the *present value* of the latter. If the amount of 13,310 is due after 4 years and the rate of interest continues to be 10%, its present value may be given as

$$P = \frac{13,310}{(1+0.10)^4} = ₹\ 9091$$

Note that *the present value has decreased due to an increase in the time period, other things remaining same*. The present value, thus, varies inversely with the time period of investment. In like manner, if the rate of interest is 12% instead of 10%, the present value of ₹ 13, 310 expected three years hence would be

$$P = \frac{13,310}{(1+0.12)^3} = ₹\ 9474.$$

That is, *the present value has decreased also due to an increase in the rate of interest, other things remaining the same*. The present value, thus, varies inversely with the rate of interest. It can also be shown that the present value varies directly with the amount expected, other things remaining the same.

$$P = \frac{15,000}{(1+0.10)^3} = ₹\ 11,270$$

That establishes the following observations:

1. the present value of an expectation varies inversely with time period, all else same,
2. the present value of an expectation varies inversely also with the rate of interest, all elase same, and
3. the present value of an expectation varies directly with the amount expected, other things remaining the same.

NPV, as defined already, can be given for each value of *A*—expected after *n* years at *r* %,

1. *NPV* (When *A* = 13,310, *r* =10%, *n* = 3 years) = 10,000–10,000 = 0
2. *NPV* (When *A* = 15,000, *r* =10%, *n* = 3 years) = 11,270–10,000 = 1,270
3. *NPV* (When *A* = 13,310, *r* =10%, *n* = 4 years) = 9091–10,000 = (–) 909
4. *NPV* (when A = 13,310, *r* = 12%, *n* =3 years) = 9474–10,000 = (–) 526

Suppose the investor has to make a choice from the above. Clearly, the investor's first choice is the second option and the second, the first one. A capital investment that generates annual incomes A_1, A_2,..., A_n respectively after 1, 2, ..., *n* years and has a scrap value of '*S*' at the end of its life span of '*n*' years, given the rate of interest as stable at '*r*' percent per annum, the expression for the sum of the present values of the entire income stream can be laid down as

$$\Sigma PV = \frac{A_1}{(1+r)^1} + \frac{A_2}{(1+r)^2} + \frac{A_3}{(1+r)^3} + \ldots + \frac{A_n}{(1+r)^n} + \frac{S}{(1+r)^n} \tag{5.5}$$

where, $\Sigma PV \equiv$ the sum of present values of the income streams

'r' $\equiv$ the rate of interest compounded annually.

$S \equiv$ the scrap value of the capital asset at the end of its life span of '*n*' years.

Returning back to the illustration in the beginning of this section, the income stream comprises

A_1 = 1100, after 1 year from now,
A_2 = 2420, after 2 years from now,
A_3 = 1331, after 3 years from now.

when the rate of interest is 10%, the sum of the present values can be calculated as

$$\begin{aligned}\Sigma PV &= [1100/(1 + 0.10)^1] + [2420/(1 + 0.10)^2] + [1331/(1 + 0.10)^3]\\ &= [1100/1.10] + [2420/2.42] + [1331/1.331]\\ &= 1{,}000 + 2{,}000 + 1{,}000\\ &= 4{,}000.\end{aligned}$$

$$\begin{aligned}\therefore \quad NPV &= \text{Sum of the } PVs\text{—Cost of the machine.}\\ &= 4{,}000-4{,}000\\ &= 0.00\end{aligned}$$

If the scrap is disposed off for ₹ 500 to a scrap vendor at the end of the life-span of the machine, it would lead to a further addition to the *PV* of $[500/(1 + 0.10)^3 = 375.66]$.

The total *PV* would then work out as ₹ 4375.66 [4,000 + 375.66]. The *NPV* in that case would be 375.66 higher.

Investment in a capital asset is *not* viable when $NPV < 0$, viable $NPV > 0$; and it is neither when $NPV = 0$. In case, the expected annual amounts of income, also called as the *annuities*, be fixed, i.e., $A_1 = A_2 = A_3 = \ldots = A_n = A$; and the life span of the machine be infinitely long (*i.e.,* $n \to \infty$) with no scrap value (i.e., $S = 0$), expression in Equation 5.5 can be laid down as

$$\begin{aligned}\Sigma PV &= \frac{A}{(1+r)^1} + \frac{A}{(1+r)^2} + \frac{A}{(1+r)^3} + \ldots + \frac{A}{(1+r)^n}\\ &= A/(1 + r)\,[1+ \{1/(1 + r)\} + 1 + \{1/(1 + r)\}^2 + \ldots, + \{1/(1 + r)\}^{n-1}] \qquad (5.6)\end{aligned}$$

It can be shown by summing up to infinity the terms of the geometric progression in 5.6 with common ratio $|1/(1 + r)| < 1$ that the sum of the present values of the infinitely extending income stream is

$$\Sigma PV = (A/r)^1 \qquad (5.7)$$

Expression in Equation 5.6 follows from equation 5.5 with $S = 0$. In case the rate of interest changes from year to year and even annuities are not the same, the expression for the present values can be written as below:

$$\Sigma PV = \frac{A_1}{(1+r_1)} + \frac{A_2}{(1+r_1)(1+r_2)} + \frac{A_3}{(1+r_1)(1+r_2)(1+r_3)} + \ldots + \frac{A_n}{(1+r_1)(1+r_2)(1+r_3)\ldots(1+r_n)} \qquad (5.8)$$

Investment decisions of a firm therefore depend on the value of the *NPV*. The profitability of an investment project depends on the non-negative value of *NPV*.

[1] Proof: $\Sigma PV = A/(1 + r) + A/(1 + r)^2 + \ldots\ldots + \ldots\ldots + A/(1 + r)^n$
$= A/(1 + r)\,[1 + 1/(1 + r) + 1/(1 + r)^2 + \ldots. + 1/(1 + r)^{n-1}]$
$= A/(1 + r)\,[1 + R + R^2 + \ldots + \ldots + R^{n-1}]$,
[Where, $R = 1/(1 + r)$]
$= A/(1 + r)\,[1\,\{1 - R^n\}/(1 - R)]$
$= A/(1 + r)\,[1\,\{1\}/(1 - R)]$ [$\because$ $R^n \to 0$ as $n \to \infty$, as $|R| < 1$]
$= A/(1 + r)\,[1/(1 - R)]$
$= A/(1 + r)\,[1/\{r/(1 + r)\}]$ [Re-substituting, $(1 - R) = 1 - \{1/(1 + r) = r/(1 + r)\}$]
$= [A/(1 + r)]\,[(1 + r)/r]$, [$\because$ $1/(1 - R) = 1/\{r/(1 + r)\} = (1 + r)/r$]
$= A/r$.

5.3 Factors Influencing Npv

Given the cost of investment, *NPV* depends on the present value (*PV*) of the annuities arising from it. The present value, in turn, depends on the rate of discount (*r*), future incomes (prospective yields) generated by the capital asset and its lifespan. Under the condition of equality of *PV* to the cost of investment, that is, zero *NPV*, the rate of discount was identified by J.M. Keynes as ***marginal efficiency of capital*** (*MEC*). In the illustration mentioned in the beginning of Section 5.2, the prospective yields after 1st, 2nd and 3rd year were respectively 1100, 2420 and 1331 while cost of investment was 4000. When discounted at 10% the prospective yields gave *PVs* of 1000, 2000 and 1000 which upon addition gave a sum of 4000. The rate of discount (10%), according to Keynes, must be *MEC* as it rendered the sum of the discounted values of the prospective yields equal to the supply price of the capital asset.

The prospective yields or ***annuities*** refer to the returns generated by the capital asset in future. In general, *PV* varies inversely on the rate of discount, given the prospective yields and the life span and directly on the prospective yields, given the rate of discount and the life span. Given the prospective yields, *PV* is high when *'r'* is low and it is low when *'r'* is high. In the same way, given the rate of discount, *PV* is high when the annuities are high and it is low when annuities are low. Calculations in the previous section vouch for the statements.

5.3.1 Marginal Efficiency of Capital (MEC)

J. M. Keynes has defined the marginal efficiency of capital (*MEC*) in the following words:

"I define MEC as that rate of discount which would make the present value of the series of annuities given by the returns expected from the capital asset during its life just equal to its supply price"[1].

In other words, *MEC* refers to that rate of discount which equalizes the sum of the present values of the prospective yields (annuities) to the supply price of the capital asset. Thus, in a nut shell, *MEC* is that rate of discount at which *NPV* = 0.

Let us examine the examples worked out in Section 5.2 for *MEC*. In the first one, the rate of discount of 10% equalizes the sum of *PVs* (1000 + 2000 + 1000) of the annuities (1100 + 2420 + 1331) to the supply price of the mason's machine (4000). Therefore the rate of discount, 10%, qualifies as Keynesian *MEC*. In simpler words, the rate rendering the NPV of an investment zero is thus Keynesian *MEC*.

In the next one, the discount rate of 10% fails to qualify as *MEC* because it fails to equalize the *PV* (9091) of the single annuity of 13,310 accruing after 4 years to the supply price (10,000) of the capital asset. That shows that the life span of the capital asset is yet another factor on which *NPV* depends.

Likewise, discount rate of 12% also fails to qualify as *MEC* because it fails to equalize the *PV* (9474) of the single annuity of 13,310 accruing after 3 years to the supply price (10,000) of the capital asset.

Finally, discount rate of 10% also fails to qualify as *MEC* because it fails to equalize the *PV* (11,270) of the single annuity of 15,000 accruing after 3 years to the supply price (10,000) of the capital asset.

The purpose of all these illustrations is to impress the following attributes of the relationships among *MEC*, rate of discount and annuities upon the reader:

1. Every rate of discount can't serve as the *MEC*.
2. For a higher *MEC*, annuities too must be higher so that, their discounted values may sum up to the given cost of the capital asset.

[1] Keynes, *The General Theory.., p. 315.*

3. For a lower *MEC*, annuities too must be lower so that their discounted values may sum up to the given cost of the capital asset.
4. The longer the life span of the capital asset, annuities too must be higher so that, their discounted values may sum up to the given cost of capital asset.

Expressions like $[1/(1 + r)^1]$, $[1/(1 + r)^2]$, $[1/(1 + r)^3]$,..., $[1/(1 + r)^n]$, when multiplied respectively to the annuities A_1, A_2, A_3,..., A_n, that reduce each to their respective present values P_1, P_2, P_3,..., P_n; are known as the ***discounting factors.*** Thus, $1/(1 + r)^n$ is the *discounting factor for the year, n,* at the discount rate of '*r*'. Supply price of capital asset is the cost of its replacement, *C*[1]. It is possible to find the *MEC* that equates the sum of the discounted annuities (sum of the present values) to the supply price of the capital asset by computing the value of the discounting factor for given period at given rate of discount. Such values are also available in tabular form in logarithmic tables or even in the statistical tables for ready reference. Table 5.1 is one such table for ready reference of the reader.

TABLE 5.1 Discounting Factor

Period (Year) / *Interest Rate*	*(1)* 1 Year	*(2)* 2 Years	*(3)* 3 Years	*(4)* 4 Years	*(5)* 5 Years	*(6)* 10 Years	*(7)* 20 Years	*(8)* 30 Years
0.01	0.990	0.980	0.971	0.961	0.951	0.905	0.820	0.742
0.02	0.980	0.961	0.942	0.924	0.906	0.820	0.673	0.552
0.03	0.971	0.943	0.915	0.888	0.863	0.744	0.554	0.412
0.04	0.962	0.925	0.889	0.855	0.822	0.676	0.456	0.308
0.05	0.952	0.907	0.864	0.823	0.784	0.614	0.377	0.231
0.06	0.943	0.890	0.834	0.792	0.747	0.558	0.312	0.174
0.07	0.935	0.873	0.816	0.763	0.713	0.508	0.258	0.131
0.08	0.926	0.857	0.794	0.735	0.681	0.463	0.215	0.099
0.09	0.917	0.842	**0.772**	0.708	0.650	0.422	0.178	0.075
0.10	0.909	0.826	0.751	0.683	0.621	0.386	0.149	0.057
0.15	0.870	0.756	0.656	0.572	0.497	0.247	0.061	0.015
0.20	0.833	0.694	0.579	0.482	0.402	0.162	0.026	0.004

Table 5.1 Extreme left column records rates of interest and extreme top row records time period. An entry in a cell, records the value of the discounting factor corresponding to the rate of interest in the extreme left column and the time period in the extreme top row. For instance, entry 0.772 is the value of the discounting factor at $r = 0.09$ and over a period of 3 years. Likewise, 0.482 is the value of the discounting factor at $r = 0.20$ over a period of 4 years.

5.3.2 *MEC* Schedule and Determination of Capital Stok

The *MEC* schedule refers to the functional relationship between the ***capital stocks*** and the marginal efficiency of capital. When stock of capital is low, *MEC* is high. This is so because low capital stock leads to low output, low supply, high market price, and to a high profit margin, which in turn, leads to a high in *MEC*. A similar reasoning explains why *MEC* is low when capital stocks are high. A high capital stock would lead to high output, high supply, low market price, and to a low profit margin,

[1] Keynes, *The General Theory*, p. 315.

which in turn, would lead to a low *MEC*. This shows that *MEC* varies inversely with the capital stock. An alternative explanation for diminishing *MEC* rests in the law of diminishing returns that sets in production in the long-run. The inverse variation of *MEC* with the capital stock is known as the ***MEC-schedule,*** which slopes downwards as shown in Figure 5.4.

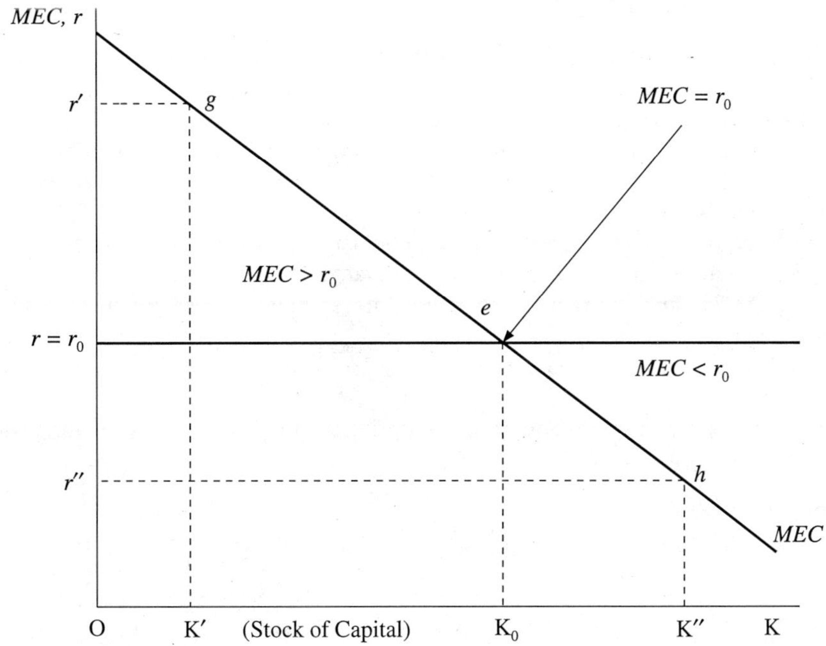

FIGURE 5.4 Representing *MEC* and rate of interest (*r*) both on the vertical axis and capital stock on the horizontal axis, we observe that *MEC* schedule slopes downward, indicating inverse variation of *MEC* with the stock of capital. A low capital stock (*OK*′) implies low output, low supply, high product price and a high profit margin. As a result, *MEC* is as high as *r*′. This initiates entry of new firms and/or expansion of the plant size by the old ones. New productive assets are acquired for production, in consequence. Capital investment raises stocks of productive capital. Output increases and so does supply. This affects profitably and product price adversely. In consequence, *MEC* declines to as low as *r*″ at a capital stock of *K*″. This explains the downward slope of the *MEC* schedule.

Equilibrium level of capital stock is K_0 determined at *e*, where $MEC = r_0$. When $MEC > r_0$, say *r*′, capital stock increases by $[K_0 - K']$. When $MEC < r_0$, say *r*″, saving of funds would take place for a higher return of r_0 interest. Thus when $MEC > r_0$, savings get converted into capital investment but when $r_0 > MEC$, savings get diverted to interest earning.

When *MEC* is high, the high rate of return from the capital investment initiates the investor to induct more capital in production. As the capital stocks increase, so do outputs produced and supplied. As a result, product prices and profit margins both fall and so does the *MEC*. Given the market rate of interest over the period of the life span of the capital asset, it is not difficult to determine the equilibrium level of the capital stock. In the figure above, equilibrium level of the capital stock is determined at the point '*e*' where the *MEC* schedule intersects the horizontal line at the level of the interest given for the life span of the capital asset.

5.3.3 Factors Influencing *MEC*

There are a number of factors that influence *MEC*. For the sake of simplicity, they are grouped as short-run and long-run factors. We discuss them briefly here:

5.3.3.1 Short-run factors

The short-run factors that influence *MEC* are:

1. *Expected Demand:* *MEC* depends on the market demand of the product. When demand is high, so is the *MEC* and when demand is low, *MEC* is low.
2. *Cost and Price Expectations:* If the costs are expected to decline and prices to go up in future, the expectations of the entrepreneurs about the rate of return from investment will go up. In the opposite case, these expectations go down. *MEC*, in each case, would get affected significantly.
3. *Propensity to Consume:* A rise in the propensity to consume raises consumption demand and hence the total demand. This raises the value of *MEC*.
4. *Change in Income:* An increase in income stimulates the investment and a decrease discourages it.
5. *Current Expectation:* The rate of return on current investment influences the future investment and hence *MEC*.
6. *Business Expectations:* The state of optimism or that of pessimism, influences the investment and hence *MEC*.

5.3.3.2 Long-run factors

Following are the long-run factors that influence the value of *MEC:*

1. *Growth Rate of Population:* The rate of growth of population, if experiencing an up-trend, product demand is expected to go up with it and so is the *MEC*. The opposite is the effect of an anticipated fall in population growth.
2. *Development of New Areas:* In case the economy is planning economic development of new areas or that of the underdeveloped ones, all of the activities such as income, investment, production, consumption, etc. will go up, raising *MEC* in the process.
3. *Technological Progress:* An improvement in the technique of production or, a development of a better technology also helps the *MEC* to go up.
4. *The Current Level of Utilization of the Productive Capacity:* If the productive capacity is currently underutilized, the long-run tendency would be its full utilization. This would necessitate investment which in turn would influence *MEC*.
5. *Level of Current Investment:* If the level of investment is already high in an industry, there is little scope for further investment. In the like manner, if the level of investment is currently low, there is a bright chance of it to go up in future. In either case *MEC* is likely to change depending on the current level of investment.

MEC is thus influenced by a number of factors. It is therefore possible to influence it appropriately to get rid of the undesirable effects of the trade cycles. Apart from the above, short- and long-term expectations of the investors also influence *MEC* by influencing prospective yields. The paragraph below would make it clear.

5.3.4 Prospective Yield and Short- and Long-term Expectations

Short-term expectations refer to the sales proceeds of the existing plant where as long-term-expectations refer to the sales proceeds which an entrepreneur can hope for by changing the size of the plant or by building up an entirely new plant. In respect of the short-term expectations, plant size is assumed to be fixed. What varies is the output of the plant. In respect of the long-term expectations, everything is variable—be it the plant size or be it its output.

According to Dudley Dillard[1], short-term expectations are more stable than the long-term expectations. This is so due to the fact that the realized results of the recent past serve as better guides to what is going to happen in the near future whereas no such guiding experience is available in respect of distant future. In short-run, the factors such as consumers' demand, their tastes, their preferences, etc., that influence the current output, are all stable.

Short-run expectations, however, are of little consequence as the capital assets have a much longer life span. Acquisition of a capital asset, therefore, invokes a concern for the long-term factors. Thus the long term expectations play a crucial role in the determination of the prospective yields of the capital assets. However, unstable nature of the long-term expectations, leaves the investor with little alternative except to lay more weightage on what he thinks is going to happen. Thus, the state of confidence of the investor is the primary factor in making the investment decisions.

In sum, investment decisions depend on the *NPV*, which in turn, depends on the *PV* of the prospective yields. The *PV* depends on the values of the annuities and the *MEC*, apart from the duration of the life of capital asset. The higher the *PV* of a given capital investment, the higher is the value of the *NPV*. The higher the value of the *NPV* of a capital investment, the higher is the tendency among the investors to invest.

5.4 CAPITAL STOCK AND DESIRED CAPITAL STOCK

Capital Stock refers to the stock of capital at any point of time. This stock may be of any volume or of any size. It may be more than what is needed or less than what is required. It represents just whatever capital is available at a particular point of time. In other words, it is the existing capital stock.

As against this, the ***desired capital stock*** *refers to the stock of capital that firms would like to have in the long-run, abstracting from the delays they face in adjusting their use of capital.*

Dornbusch and Fischer[2] have employed the concept of the marginal product of capital and that of the rental cost of the capital to define the desired capital stock. Note that marginal product of capital refers to increase in output by inducting one more unit of it in production while rental or user cost of capital is the cost of using one more unit of it in production.

Desired Capital Stock is the capital stock at which the value of the marginal product of capital equals its rental cost (Figure 5.5).

5.5 ESTIMATION OF PRESENT VALUE OF A CAPITAL ASSET

Estimation of the value of a capital asset, at a point of time during its life span is important for the estimation of the national capital. Among a number of methods in use, the present value method is believed to be one of the most logical methods employed for the purpose. The present value of a capital asset is the sum of the discounted annuities of the capital asset over its life-span, as given by Equation 5.5, Section 5.2. To illustrate, suppose a machine has a life span of 5 years. The prospective yields of the machine at the end of the first, second, third, fourth and the fifth years are respectively ₹ 11,000, ₹ 24,200, ₹ 26,620, ₹ 14,641, and ₹ 16,105. Thereafter, the machine turns to scrap and is disposed off to the scrap vendor for ₹ 8,052.50. Assuming the rate of discounting to remain stable

[1] Dudley Dillard, *The Economics of John Maynard Keynes*, (London: Gosby Lockwood & son Lt., 1950, pp. 142–143.

[2] Dornbusch and Fischer, *Macroeconomics*, 6th International Edition, McGraw Hill Inc. pp. 333–335.

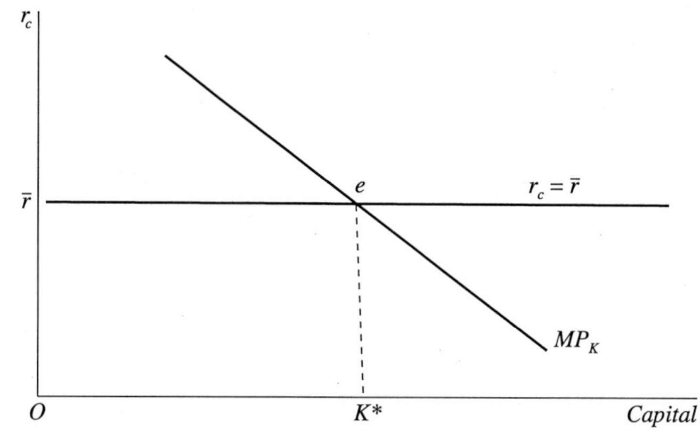

FIGURE 5.5 The marginal product of capital diminishes as the stock of capital in use increases. Thus the schedule of the marginal product of capital slopes downward from left to right. Given the rental cost of capital as $\overline{r}$, the equilibrium level capital stock is K^*, given by the condition, $MP_K = \overline{r}$. Evidently, K^* is the desired capital. It is a function of $\overline{r}$ and the level of the output, Y. Thus, $K^* = f(\overline{r}, Y)$ where, $\overline{r}$ is the rental cost of capital, Y, the output, and K^* is the desired stock of capital.

at 10% throughout the life span of the machine, its present value can be determined from Equation 5.5 as below:

$$\Sigma PV = \frac{A_1}{(1+r)^1} + \frac{A_2}{(1+r)^2} + \frac{A_3}{((1+r)^3} + \ldots + \frac{A_n}{(1+r)^n} + \frac{S_n}{(1+r)^n}$$

$$= \frac{11{,}000}{(1+0.10)^1} + \frac{24{,}200}{(1+0.10)^2} + \frac{26{,}620}{(1+0.10)^3} + \frac{14{,}641}{(1+0.10)^4} + \frac{16{,}105}{(1+0.10)^5} + \frac{8{,}052.5}{(1+0.10)^5}$$

$$= 10{,}000 + 20{,}000 + 20{,}000 + 10{,}000 + 10{,}000 + 5{,}000$$

$$= 75{,}000$$

In general, the present value of a capital asset with a life span of 'n' years and with the respective annuities of $A_1, A_2, A_3, \ldots, A_n$ at the end of 1, 2, 3, …, n years of its life span, can be computed from Equation 5.5 when the rate of discount is stable at 'r' and the scrap value of the machine is S.

In case the rate of discount changes from year to year, Equation 5.8, given below, with adjustment of S, can be used

$$\Sigma PV = \frac{A_1}{(1+r_1)} + \frac{A_2}{(1+r_1)(1+r_2)} + \frac{A_3}{(1+r_1)(1+r_2)(1+r_3)} + \ldots + \frac{A_n}{(1+r_1)(1+r_2)(1+r_3)\ldots(1+r_n)} + \frac{S}{(1+r_1)(1+r_2)(1+r_3)\ldots(1+r_n)}$$

5.6 *MEC* AND *MEI*

As discussed in Section 5.3, MEC is the rate of discount that makes the sum of the discounted annuities of a capital asset equal to the supply price or the replacement cost of the capital asset. At low levels of capital stock, *MEC* is high but as its stock increases, *MEC* declines due to diminishing returns that set in production. *MEC* schedule slopes downwards as shown in Figure 5.6.

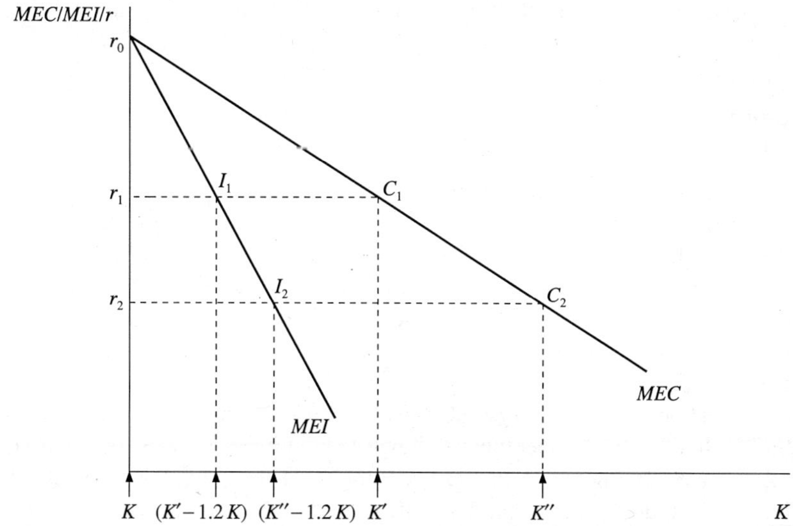

FIGURE 5.6 Let the initial capital stock in the economy be K, when rate of interest is r_0. Assume that $MEC = MEI = r_0$ at this point. The desired capital stock at this point being K and the net investment is zero. Let us assume that depreciation is 20% of the initial capital stock. The producers of the capital goods, therefore, plan their plant-size to produce quantity $K/5$ of the capital goods each year to meet the replacement demand. Assume that they also plan enough reserve capacity to supply capital goods beyond the replacement demand so that none of the additional demands of capital goods, if made, may go unfulfilled. Now suppose interest rate falls to r_1. The desired capital stock at this rate is K' (at point C_1), which is $(K' - K)$ higher in comparison to what it was when the market rate of interest was r_0. The additional demand for capital goods, $(K' - K)$, represents the gross investment demand, which is made up of two components—(a) the replacement demand component of $K/5$, and (b) the net investment demand $[(K' - K) - K/5]$ or $(K' - 1.2K)$. The point it corresponds to at the interest rate of r_1 is point I_1. To demonstrate, let the capital stock K be worth ₹ 1000 Crore at $r_0 = 24\%$. Depreciation being 20%, the replacement demand for capital goods works out worth ₹ 200 Crores for the first year. Now let the rate of interest fall from an initial high of $r_0 = 24\%$ to $r_1 = 18\%$. The resulting demand for the capital stock, according to the *MEC*-schedule, is K' = ₹ 1300 crore (say) at point C_1. The gross investment demand then is worth ₹ 300 $(K' - K)$. The replacement demand component being worth ₹ 200 Crores, the net investment demand component is worth ₹ 100 Crore which can be verified to be equal to $(K' - 1.2K)$ at point I_1.

Now let the rate of interest fall further to $r_2 = 12\%$. The corresponding demand for capital goods, according to the *MEC* schedule is, say, K'' = ₹ 1600 Crore at point C_2. The gross investment demand now is $K'' - K$ = ₹ 600 Crore, of which, the replacement demand component is worth ₹ 200 $(K/5)$ and the net investment demand component is worth ₹ 400 $(K'' - 1.2K)$ marked at point I_2. Joining the points I_1 and I_2, we obtain the *MEI*-schedule which is steeper than the *MEC*-schedule.

Had we not assumed the reserve capacity of the capital goods, with the producers, capital prices would have shot up in the wake of the net investment demand and it would have fallen below the calculated levels. In the result, the *MEI*-schedule would have been non-linear with its concavity towards the origin.

Marginal efficiency of investment *(MEI), on the other hand, relates the rate of return on* ***net investment*** *spending per time period to the market rate of interest.* Like *MEC*, *MEI* is a rate of return. While *MEC* is a stock concept, *MEI* is a flow concept. The formers to the rate of return at a particular level of capital stock, while the latter, to the rate of return at a particular level of the net investment spending. *Note that investment is a change in capital stock over a period of time.* For instance, if the capital stock changes from K' to K'' over a period of one year, the change,

$\Delta K(K'' - K')$, which measures the gross investment over the period of one year. A part of the gross investment is meant for replacement of the worn-out capital assets and is called the replacement investment. The rest is meant for acquisition of new productive assets and is called the net investment. Net investment, thus, is the difference of the Gross investment over the replacement investment.

Net Investment = Gross Investment – Replacement Investment
(Note that replacement investment can be treated as depreciation).

MEI is the rate of return on the net investment. Measuring *MEI* on the vertical axis and the net investment on the horizontal axis, we can portray the relationship between the two. *MEI* has a downward slope just like that of the *MEC* schedule. For the *MEC* schedule, it is the capital stock that is taken on the x-axis and the market rate of interest along with the *MEC* on the vertical axis while for the *MEI* schedule; it is the net investment that is taken on the x-axis and the market rate of interest along with the *MEI* on the vertical axis. The distinction between the two can be understood best from the Figure 5.6.

The *MEC*-schedule, thus, portrays the overall demand for capital in an economy at given values of *MEC*. A linear *MEC*- schedule, as shown in Figures 5.6, owes its linear shape to the fact that the supply of the capital goods in the economy fails to match its demand due to limitation of the capital goods industry to expand its plant size to match the demand for capital goods. If we take into consideration the demand for capital goods of a single firm, it would not be as large as that of an economy as a whole, and can be met from the stocks of the inventories. The *MEC*-schedule for a single firm has a stair-case formation as shown in Figure 5.7(a). While for a firm having a large number of the investment projects with varying *MEC* has a smooth schedule as shown in Figure 5.7(b).

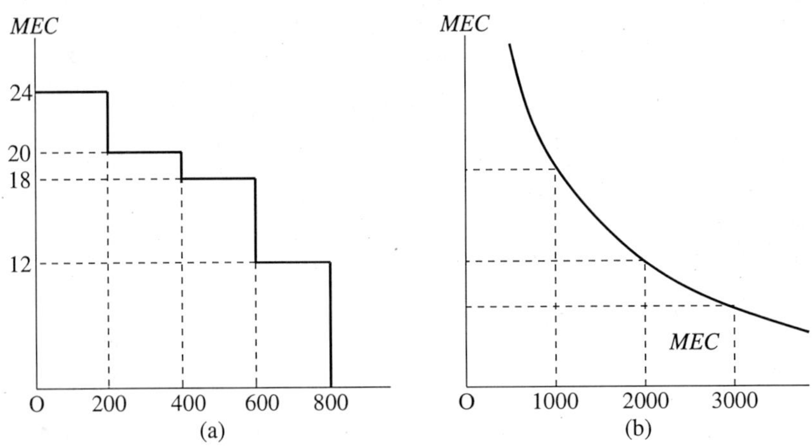

FIGURE 5.7 The left panel shows *MEC*-schedule of an individual firm with four projects. The schedule has a stair-case formation due to a fixed value of the *MEC* for each of the four projects. Each project requires an investment worth ₹ 200 Crore and has each a definite value of the *MEC*. The right panel shows *MEC*-schedule for an individual firm having multiple projects with continuously varying *MEC* and investment demand. *MEC* changes from one level of capital stock to another in a continuous manner yielding a smooth curve with convexity towards the origin. The *MEC*-schedule for all the firms in the economy taken together would have a linear schedule due to the failure of the capital goods industry to match the rising capital demand as depicted in Figure 5.6.

Investment, as a source of plugging the leakages from the circular flow of income and expenditure, thus, depends on a number of factors apart from *MEC* and the market rate of interest. A sustained growth of investment leads to growth of output and employment in the economy and a steady decline in it, retards the economic activities and brings in depression.

KEY TERMS AND CONCEPTS

Capital Stock: It refers to stock of real productive assets at a point of time.

Investment: It refers to procurement of additional real assets for their use in production. It generally refers to period of time.

Gross and Net Investment: Gross investment refers to the sum of replacement investment (depreciation) and net investment. On the other hand net investment refers to additional productive assets at current prices. The two differ from each other only by the magnitude of depreciation.

Net investment = Gross Investment – Depreciation

Depreciation: It represents loss of value of the productive assets due to wear and tear during production.

Autonomous and Induced Investment: Autonomous investment is that part of investment which is income inelastic while induced investment is the rest of it which is income elastic. The latter changes with changing income. of the investor.

Marginal Propensity to Invest: It may be defined as an increase in investment spending per unit increase in income. In other words, it is the ratio of increase in investment spending to increase in income ($\Delta I/\Delta Y$).

Investment Function: It refers to the mathematical relation of investment spending with its determinants—the income and the market rate of .interest. Thus, $I = f(Y, r)$. Investment varies directly with income (Y) and inversely with rate of interest (r).

Private and Public Investment: Investment made in the private sector is known as the private investment. The purpose of such investment is the profit. On the contrary, investment made by the government is known as the public investment .The purpose of public investment is social welfare, not profit.

Annuities: It refers to annual income or returns on commitment of value.

Prospective Yield: It refers to expected inflow on capital investment.

Net Present Value (*NPV*): It refers to excess of the sum of the present values of the annuities over the cost of the investment.

Present Value: It is the discounted value of an income expected in future.

Discount Rate: It is the rate, generally the rate of interest, at which a sum expected in future is reduced to its current equivalent. In the presence of inflation, it is adjusted for the rate of inflation. The adjusted rate is called the *Real Rate of Discount* .

Discounting Factor: The expression $[1/(1 + r)^n]$, which needs to be multiplied to the sum expected in future after n years to convert it into its present value.

Determination of Present Value (*PV*): Present value (*PV*) of a sum expected after n years is given as the sum × discounting factor, that is,

$$PV = A_n/(1 + r)^n$$

where, A_n is the sum expected after 'n' years, $[1/(1 + r)^n]$ is the discounting factor and r, the rate of discount.

Marginal Efficiency of Capital (*MEC*): *MEC* is the rate of discount that makes the sum expected after n years from the capital asset equal to its present value.

Factors Influencing *MEC*: Factors influencing *MEC* are grouped as short-run and long-run factors.

(a) Short-run factors:

1. Expected Demand
2. Cost and Price Expectations
3. Propensity to Consume:

4. Change in Income
5. Current expectation
6. Business Expectations

(b) Long–run factors
1. Growth rate of population
2. Development of new areas
3. Technological Progress
4. The current level of utilization of the productive capacity
5. Level of current investment

Marginal Efficiency of Investment (*MEI*): It refers to the rate of return on net investment. *MEI* schedule slopes downward, indicating inverse variation of *MEI* with the net investment. It is steeper than the *MEC* schedule.

***MEC* and *MEI*:** *MEC* is a stock concept while *MEI*, a flow concept. *MEC* is the rate of return on capital stock at a point of time while *MEI* is the rate of return on net investment over a period of time. *MEI* schedule is steeper than that of the *MEC*. The latter in general is linear for the economy as a whole while it has a stair-case formation for a single firm. It assumes a non-linear shape with convexity towards the origin when the firm in question has multiple plants in operation, each with a different value of the *MEC* that varies continuously with the level of the capital stock in it. *MEI* schedule also has a linear shape in general when capital goods industry possesses reserve capacity to the extent that it can increase the supply of the capital goods without hiking their prices but it is non-linear with its concavity to the origin when capital goods industry has a fixed plant size leading to rising capital prices with rising demand for assets of net investment.

Factors Influencing the Prospective Yield: They comprise of short-run and long-run expectations. Short-term expectations refer to the sales proceeds of the existing plant whereas long-term expectations refer to the sales proceeds which an entrepreneur can hope to earn by changing the size of the plant or by building up an entirely new plant. In respect of the short-term expectations, plant size is assumed to be constant. What varies is the output of the plant. In respect of the long-term expectations, everything is variable—be it the plant size or be it its output. Short-run expectations are quite stable because tastes and preferences of the people are stable. Long-run expectations have no such stability because every thing changes in long-run.

Factors Influencing Investment Decisions: Investment decisions depend largely on the *NPV* of the investment. Given the cost of the investment project, investment decision depends on the present value of the prospective yield (*PV*). *PV*, in turn, depends on the prospective yield and the rate of discount. Thus, investment decisions depend on the prospective yield and the rate of discount as also duration of investment.

Actual and Desired Capital Stock: Actual stock refers to the stock of capital at a point of time possessed actually by the firms. On the other hand, desired capital stock is that stock of capital at which the marginal product of the capital (MP_K) is equal to the rental cost of the capital (r_C).

EXERCISES

A. Short Answer Questions

1. Investment in economic sense is different from what it is in common parlance. Comment.
2. What is an investment function? Distinguish between autonomous and induced investments.
3. What are the main points of difference between gross and net investments?
4. Define marginal propensity to invest. Obtain an expression for it from the investment function.
5. Distinguish between private and public investments.
6. What is meant by annuities? How do they differ from prospective yields?
7. Define present value. On what factors does the present value of an income stream depend?
8. Define net present value. What role does it play in investment decisions?
9. Net present values of five investment options in lakhs of rupees are 2000, 1000, 0, – 1000 and – 2000. Arrange them in order of preference in which you would advise an investor to treat them. Give reasons in support of your answer. **[Ans:** 2000, 1000, 0, – 1000, – 2000**]**

10. What is meant by the rate of discount? An investment of ₹ 10,000 today means an income of ₹ 11,000 after one year. What according to you must be the rate of discount? **[Ans:** 10%]
11. What is a discounting factor? Calculate the value of the discounting factor for the data in Q.10? **[Ans:** $1/(1 + 0.10)^1$ or 0.9090]
12. What is meant by the marginal efficiency of capital? Can the rate of discount in Q.10 be treated as the marginal efficiency of capital? Give reasons in support of your answer. **[Ans:** Yes]
13. In Q.10, if income expected after one year is ₹ 12,000 instead of ₹ 11,000; how would your answer to Q.10, 11 and 12 change? **[Ans:** Rate of discount as also the *MEC* in Q12 is 10%; In this case, *MEC* changes to 20%]
14. Outline and introduce briefly the short-term factors that influence the *MEC*.
15. Outline and introduce briefly the long-term factors that influence the *MEC*.
16. How do the short-run expectations differ from the long-run expectations in respect of the prospective yields?
17. What is meant by the desired stock of capital? How does it differ from the actual stock of capital?
18. Distinguish between *MEC* and *MEI* with the help of a neat sketch.

B. Long Answer Questions

19. Given the market rate of interest as 10% and the *MEC* schedule as $r = 20 - 0.01K$, determine the equilibrium level of capital stock. **[Ans:** 1,000. In equilibrium, market rate of interest = *MEC*. Therefore, $10 = 20 - 0.01K \Rightarrow K = 1{,}000$]

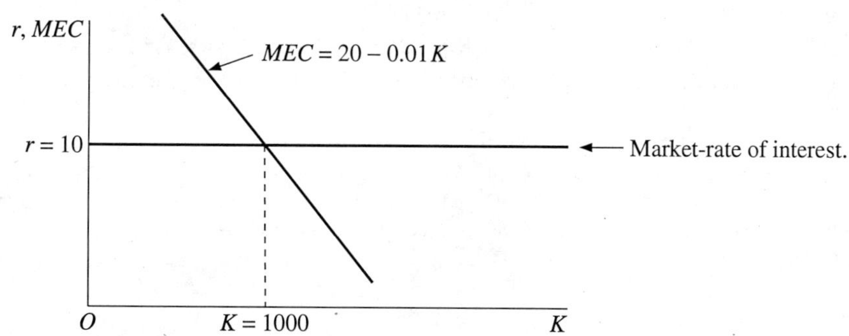

FIGURE 5.8 Equilibrium level of capital stock is determined at the intersection of the *MEC* schedule with the horizontal line representing the market-rate of interest.

20. The schedule for the marginal product of capital is as given below:

$$MP_K = 40 - 0.01\ K$$

The rental cost of the capital is fixed at $r_C = 20$. Determine the desired stock of capital. **[Ans:** 2,000]

21. Is the discount rate always the same as the *MEC*? Give reasons for your answer.
22. Outline the factors that influence the *MEC*. Briefly explain them also.
23. Outline the factors that influence the prospective yield. Briefly explain them also.
24. On what factor in main do the investment decisions depend? Comment on the role of the prospective yield and the rate of discount in investment decisions.
25. How can the *PV* of a capital asset be determined? Explain. An insurance policy assures a sum of one crore after 20 years. If the rate of discount is stable at 10%, what is the *PV* of the sum? On what conditions would your decision to purchase the policy depend? Would you go for it if the *PV* of annual premia is also 14.8644 lakh? **[Ans:** 14.8644 lakh]

26. What is the present value of a machine that yields ₹ 2200, ₹ 4840 and ₹ 2662 at the end of respectively 1st, 2nd and 3rd year of its life span. Given the rate of discount as 10% and that the scrap value of the machine is ₹ 1331. **[Ans:** $PV = \{2200/(1 + 0.10)\} + [4840/(1 + 0.10)^2\} + \{2662/(1 + 0.10)^3\} + \{1331/(1 + 0.10)^3 =$ ₹ 9,000.]

27. A government bond has a face value of ₹ 1000. It is issued as a perpetual bond at a fixed rate of dividend. Given that the rate of dividend is 10% and the market rate of interest is 20%, determine the present value of the bond. **[Ans:** $PV = A/r$. A = 10% of the face value of the bond = 0.10 × 1000 = 100, r = 20% = 0.20. Therefore, PV = 100/0.20 = ₹ 500]

C. Essay type Questions

28. What would the likely shape of the *MEC* schedule be for each of the following:

(a) Single firm,

(b) Single firm with multiple projects of continuously variable *MEC*,

(c) Economy as a whole.

29. How can an *MEI* schedule be derived from the corresponding *MEC* schedule? Explain. Why is the *MEI* schedule steeper than the *MEC* schedule?

30. An individual has two alternative options of investment available to him. The first option requires an investment of ₹ 7, 000 but yields ₹ 2200 at the end of the first year, ₹ 4840 at the end of second year and ₹ 2662 at the end of the third year. The second option requires an investment of ₹ 3,000 but generates a perpetual income stream of ₹ 500. If the market rate of interest is stable in each case and is 10% per annum, which of the two alternative options would you recommend for the investor?

[Ans: Second, *NPV* of the first option is ₹ 1000 while that of the second option, it is ₹ 2,000]

31. Consumption function for an economy with two sectors is given as:

$C = 2{,}000 + 0.80\,Y$, Where, C = consumption expenditure in Crore of rupees, and Y = national income.

The condition for the equilibrium level of income is the equality of savings and the investment. The investment function is given as

$$I = 500 - 100\,r, \text{ Where, } I = \text{investment, and } r = \text{rate of interest.}$$

Obtain the condition of equilibrium level of income in terms of '*r*' and '*Y*'. Find the equilibrium levels of income when the rate of interest is 10%, 15% and 20%. With '*r*' on the vertical axis and '*Y*' on the horizontal axis, plot these data and show that the curve obtained slopes downward from left to right.

[Ans: $r = 25 - 0.002Y$]

Chapter 6

Determination of Income in Two, Three and Four Sector Models in Goods Market

INTRODUCTION

In chapter 2, we saw how national income can be estimated through income, expenditure and value added methods. Our concern, there, was much the same as that of an accountant rather than that of an economist. An accountant concerns with whatever comes in and whatever goes out without bothering for the reasons behind its coming in or going out. He credits the incoming funds and debits the outgoing ones. He records transactions without much concern with questions of cause and effect. It is the economist who questions where they came in from and why and where they are heading to and for what purpose? Would they succeed or not in their purpose or what they would need to succeed?. An economist, therefore, analyses sources, channels and destinations of the flows of such transactions with a view to comment on their adequacy or inadequacy. In simpler terms, an accountant records transactions as they stand while an economist explains the reasons behind such state. The former is concerned with accounting of 'whatever is' while the latter is concerned with 'why it is whatever it is' and 'what it should have been for the desired purpose'. Determination of national income is one thing and determination of the equilibrium level of income, another. An accountant is concerned with estimation of national income while an economist is concerned with adequacy or inadequacy of it to suit the needs of stable equilibrium. In this chapter, we look at the flows of national income and expenditure from the latter's point of view.

Equilibrium level of income or output refers to that level at which total demand (***aggregate demand***, *AD*) for it equals its total supply (***aggregate supply***, *AS*) of it. We have seen in chapter 2 that the money value of the final goods produced in a year is equal to the factor incomes accruing to the factors of production in that year. Thus, national product for a year is equal to the national income in that year. It is for this reason that the terms 'income' and 'output' are often used interchangeably in national income accounts. Aggregate Demand (*AD*) refers to total demand for output. One part of it is the consumption demand (*C*) and the other is investment demand (*I*). Thus,

$$AD = C + I \tag{6.1}$$

Demand for consumption comprises the household's demand (C_h) and the government's demand (C_g) for final goods and services. Thus,

$$\textbf{\textit{Consumption demand,}}\ C = C_h + C_g$$
$$= C + G \tag{6.2}$$

C_g is commonly denoted as G and C_h as C. Goods demanded for consumption are final goods which are not to be used for further production.

Investment demand, on the other hand, refers to demand for intermediate goods which are used in further production. This component of aggregate demand refers to demand for inventories (comprising demand for raw materials, semi-finished and finished but unsold goods), fixed capital (comprising of demand for plant, machinery and equipment) and residential constructions (housing) in the domestic territory as well as abroad. Domestic investment demand is known as Gross Domestic Capital Formation (*GDCF*), which is made up of ***Gross Domestic Fixed Capital Formation*** (*GDFCF*) and ***changes in stocks of inventories***(ΔS). Denoting ***Foreign investment demand*** for our productive goods as X and ***domestic investment demand*** of foreign productive goods as M, the ***net foreign investment demand*** can be given as $(X - M)$. Thus,

$$\text{Investment demand } (I) = \text{Domestic Investment Demand } (GDCF)$$
$$+ \text{ Net Foreign Investment Demand}$$
$$= GDFCF + \Delta S + (X - M) \tag{6.3}$$

$$\therefore \quad \text{Aggregate Demand (AD)} = \text{Consumption Demand} + \text{Investment Demand}$$
$$= C + I$$
$$= (C_h + C_g) + GDFCF + \Delta S + (X - M) \tag{6.4}$$

$$\Rightarrow \quad AD = C + GDCF + (X - M), \text{ where, } GDCF = GDFCF + \Delta S \text{ and } C = (C_h + C_g)$$

In like manner, Aggregate Supply (*AS*) refers to total supply of the output, of which, one part is sold for its use in consumption and the other, not bought for consumption. The latter equals the magnitude of savings (S) and direct taxes (T) paid by consumers. Consumers save a part of their disposable income ($Y^d = Y - T$). Thus, goods not bought for consumption can be measured as savings plus direct taxes paid by consumers.

$$\text{Aggregate Supply } (AS) = C + S + T \tag{6.5}$$

The technique of determining the equilibrium level of income in economies with two, three and four sectors is demonstrated in the Sections 6.1, 6.7 and 6.8 respectively.

6.1 DETERMINATION OF EQUILIBRIUM LEVEL OF INCOME IN A TWO SECTOR ECONOMY

In an economy with only two sectors—the household sector and the producers' sector—the *AD* and the *AS* curves can be obtained as below:

6.1.1 Aggregate Demand (*AD*) Curve

In an economy with the household and the producers' sectors, output is demanded by the household sector for final consumption and by the producers' sector for domestic investment. In absence of the government and the rest-of-the-world sectors, G (C_g), T, R and $(X–M)$ are each treated zero. Assuming that the investment in a two sector economy is wholly of autonomous character, the expression for *AD* from Equations 6.1 and 6.4, can be written as:

$$AD = C + I_a$$

[G and $(X - M)$ are each zero and $I = I_a$, the autonomous investment]

$$= C_a + bY^d + I_a \text{(From equation 4.1)}$$

$$= C_a + bY + I_a \quad (6.6)$$

($\because$ $Y^d = Y - T + R = Y$, as T & R are each zero in absence of the government sector. Aggregate demand curve can thus be obtained by plotting equation 6.6 with Y on the x-axis and AD on the vertical axis. The graph would turn out to be a straight line with an intercept of $(C_a + I_a)$[1] on the vertical axis and would have a positive slope 'b' as shown in Figure 6.1.

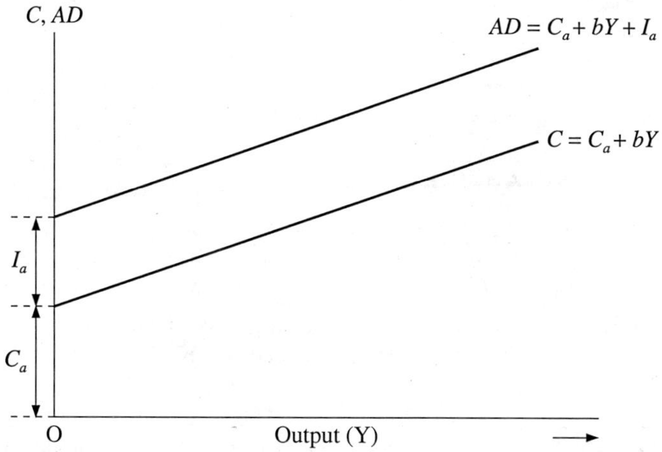

FIGURE 6.1 Aggregate Demand (AD): AD curve is a vertical shift of the consumption function (equation 4.1) through a distance of I_a. In other words, it is a vertical summation of consumption and investment functions. The curve slopes upwards with a slope of 'b'. A numerical illustration in Table 6.1 explains the process of the vertical summation.

To demonstrate the mechanism of derivation of the AD curve, let us take a numerical example with $C_a = 2000$, $I_a = 1000$ and $b = 0.80$ (See Table 6.1).

TABLE 6.1 AD as a vertical summation of C and $\overline{I}$

Income Y	*Autonomous Consumption* $C_a = 2{,}000$	$bY(b = 0.80) = 0.80Y$	$C = C_a + bY$	$I_a = 1{,}000$	$AD = C + I_a$
(1)	(2)	(3)	(4) = (2) + (3)	(5)	(6) = (4) + (5)
1,000	2,000	800	2,800	1,000	3,800
2,000	2,000	1,600	3,600	1,000	4,600
3,000	2,000	2,400	4,400	1,000	5,400
5,000	2,000	4,000	6,000	1,000	7,000
6,000	2,000	4,800	6,800	1,000	7,800
10,000	2,000	8,000	10,000	1,000	11,000

(Contd.)

[1] Some authors use $\overline{A}$ for $(C_a + I_a)$.

Income Y	*Autonomous Consumption* $C_a = 2{,}000$	$bY(b = 0.80) = 0.80Y$	$C = C_a + bY$	$I_a = 1{,}000$	$AD = C + I_a$
(1)	(2)	(3)	(4) = (2) + (3)	(5)	(6) = (4) + (5)
20,000	2,000	16,000	18,000	1,000	19,000
25,000	2,000	20,000	22,000	1,000	23,000

Table 6.1: Different levels of income are shown in Column (1). and autonomous consumption (C_a) = 2000 in column (2). Induced consumption, b Y, is computed in column (3). It is obtained by multiplying entries in column (1) by marginal propensity 'b' = 0.80. Column (4) shows consumption demand (C) which is obtained as the sum of the corresponding entries in columns (2) and (3) at each level of income in column (1). In column. (5) autonomous investment of $I_a = 1000$ is shown which is fixed at all levels of income, Y. In column (6). AD is obtained as the sum of columns (4) and (5). With Y on X-axis and C and AD on vertical axis, the graphs show the consumption demand $C = C_a + bY$ and the $AD = C_a + bY + I_a$. The curves obtained from actual plot would look very much like those in Figure 6.1.

6.1.2 Aggregate Supply (*AS*) Curve

Aggregate Supply (*AS*) refers to the money value of the total output supplied to the market for sale. If money value of the output be represented on the horizontal axis and the aggregate supply (*AS*) on the vertical axis, a 45°–line representing the identity $AS = Y$ is obtained. Goods and services are produced for satisfaction of human needs, including the needs of the producers who form a part of the household sector back home. All, the output produced is a part of the *AS whether it is meant for self consumption or for market needs.* Money value of goods and services produced, therefore, has to be equal to the total supply of goods and services. Hence the identity $AS = Y$. Plotting *AS* as a function of *Y*, we get a 45°–line, called the *AS* curve. The identity remains intact even if a part of *Y* remains unsold. That way, *AS* = output sold + output lying unsold = *Y*. In other words, *AS* represents the value of goods sold and those lying unsold. Unsold goods have the same value in money as the savings (*S*), Thus, output supplied (*AS*) or that produced (*Y*), in monetary terms, is equal to the sum of income spent on consumption as well as that saved

$$AS = Y = C + S \tag{6.7}$$

(Alternatively, put $T = 0$ in Equation 6.5 to account for the absence of the government sector). Portraying Equation 6.7, we get the *AS* curve as shown in Figure 6.2.

6.1.3 Determination of Equilibrium Level of Income

Equilibrium level of income is that level of income/output at which $AD = AS$. Superimposing the two curves into the same space as shown in Figure 6.3, equilibrium level of income can be found at the point where $AD = AS$. Mathematically, this implies that

$$C + I_a = C + S$$

$$\Rightarrow \qquad I_a = S^1 \tag{6.8}$$

This gives the condition of equilibrium. Expression for the equilibrium level of income can be derived by setting $AS = AD$, where $AS = Y$ and $AD = C + I_a$. Thus,

[1] Investment and savings are at times referred to as *Ex Ante* (planned) and *Ex Post* (realized). The reference becomes essential when *Ex Ante* and *Ex Post* estimates differ from each other.

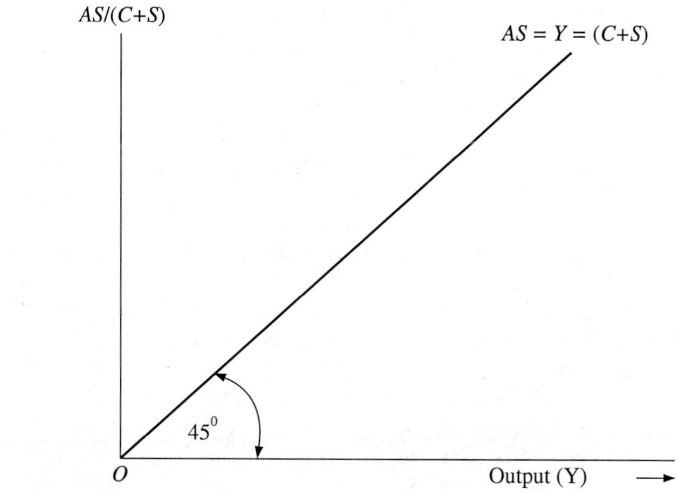

FIGURE 6.2 *AS* curve is a 45°–line representing the identity $AS = Y = C + S$.

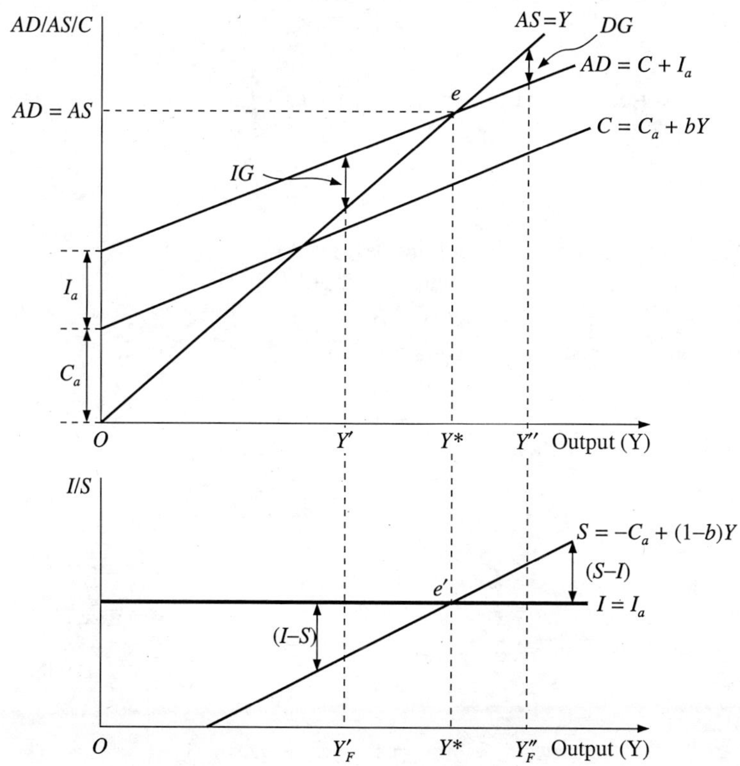

FIGURE 6.3 In the upper panel, $AD = AS$ at point *e*. The level of income at this point is Y^* which is the level of income also determined through the equality of *I* to *S*. Savings function, $S = -C_a + (1-b)Y$ with a negative intercept $(-C_a)$ on the vertical axis. (For savings function, see Equation 4.10 and Figure 4.4). Investment is autonomous (Contd.)

FIGURE 6.3 Contd.

and hence fixed, leading to a horizontal line. Investment and savings-functions intersect each other at point e' lying exactly below e of the upper panel. Equilibrium level of income through the equality of AD to AS (upper panel) or I to S (lower panel) is the same (Y^*).

If full employment is reached at an output $Y_F (Y_F < Y^*)$, $AD > AS$ by $(I_a - S)$. The gap $(I_a - S)$ between AD and AS at output Y_F is called the ***Inflationary Gap*** (IG). It is called so because it causes price-rise (inflation) in the economy. Prices continue to rise until $AD = AS$ at e. Inflationary Gap (IG) may be defined as the ***excess demand*** ($AD > AS$) at full employment level of output. Prices go up at Y_F because output can't be increased to match AD as no more factors of production are available due to existence of full employment.

If full employment is reached at an output $Y'_F (Y'_F > Y^*)$, $AD < AS$ by $(S - I_a)$. The gap of $(S - I_a)$ between AS and AD at output Y'_F is called the ***Deflationary Gap*** (DG). It is called so because it causes prices to fall (deflation) in the economy. Prices continue to fall until $AD = AS$ at e. Deflationary Gap (DG) may be defined as the ***deficient demand*** ($AD < AS$) at full employment level of output. Prices go down at Y'_F because demand is much less than supply at this point. At e, AS is reduced to the level of AD through a cut in the supply price.

Excess and deficient demands can be corrected respectively by decreasing and increasing the AD. This can be accomplished through adjustment of injections and withdrawals. We will discuss these policies as the monetary, fiscal and foreign trade policies in chapters 10, 11 and 12 respectively in their requisite detail.

$$Y = C + I_a$$
$$= C_a + bY^d + I_a$$
$$(\because C = C_a + bY^d)$$
$$= C_a + bY + I_a$$
$$(\because Y^d = Y - T + R = Y \text{ as Tax } T = 0 = \text{Transfers } R \text{ for a two sector model})$$

$$\Rightarrow \quad Y - bY = C_a + I_a$$

$$\Rightarrow \quad Y = \frac{1}{(1-b)}[C_a + I_a] \tag{6.9}$$

Equation 6.9 gives an expression for the equilibrium level of income.

Differentiating equation $C = C_a + bY$ with respect to Y, we have

$$dC/dY = b$$

But, dC/dY = Marginal Propensity to Consume (MPC)

and,
$$1 - b = 1 - MPC$$
$$= MPS \quad \text{(From Equation 4.9)}$$

Equation 6.9 can thus also be written as

$$Y = \frac{1}{(1 - MPC)}[C_a + I_a] \tag{6.10}$$

or, as

$$Y = \frac{1}{(MPS)}[C_a + I_a] \tag{6.11}$$

Alternatively, from Equation 6.8, we have

$$I_a = S$$
$$= Y - C$$
$$= Y - (C_a + bY)$$
$$= Y - C_a - bY$$

$$Y = \frac{1}{(1-b)}[C_a + I_a]$$

$$= \frac{1}{(1 - MPC)}[C_a + I_a]$$

$$= \frac{1}{MPS}[C_a + I_a] \quad (6.12)$$

Equations 6.10, 6.11 and 6.12 represent the same thing. Equation 6.12 is arrived at by equating injections (I) to withdrawals (S) while 6.10 and 6.11 by equating $AD = AS$.

6.2 INVESTMENT MULTIPLIER AND INCOME GENERATION

Keynesian theory of employment had evolved at a time when whole of the Europe was in the grip of severe depression. A number of economists treat the theory as a short-run analysis focusing on the causes and remedies to the prevalent depression in Europe. As stated earlier on several occasions, the theory shifted emphasis on demand from that prevalent on supply under classical theory. To revive demand, J.M. Keynes emphasized generation and propagation of income through injections of investment, government spending and export earnings. He believed that such injections had a multiplying effect on income generation and propagation. In other words, the injections lead to generation of income many more times their magnitude. The number of times of the magnitude of the injection the income increases is known as the ***multiplier***. It is named after the particular injection it multiplies in a multiplier process. For instance, if it multiplies investment, it is called ***investment multiplier;*** if it multiplies the government spending, it is called the ***government expenditure multiplier*** and if it multiplies the export earnings, it is called the ***export multiplier***. To demonstrate, let us take the investment multiplier. It may be defined as the ratio of a change in income to a change in investment spending. In alternative language, it is the magnitude of the increase in income per rupee increase in the investment spending. Thus, investment multiplier, K_{Ia}, can be expressed as

$$K_{Ia} = \frac{\text{Change in income}}{\text{Change in investment spending}}$$

$$= \frac{\Delta Y}{\Delta I_a} \quad (6.13)$$

At a point of time, $\Delta Y/\Delta I_a$ is measured better as a derivative of Y with respect to I_a, that is, as dY/dI_a). For example, investment multiplier for an economy with two sectors, at a point where its equilibrium income is given by Equation 6.8, can be obtained by differentiating[1] the equation with respect to I_a.

$$K_{Ia} = \frac{dY}{dI_a} = \frac{1}{(1 - b)} \quad (6.14)$$

[1] For those who prefer to avoid the use of differential calculus, following simple algebraic treatment is recommended for the derivation of the expression for K. Let the income, consumption and investment in the initial phase be Y_1, C_1 and I_a' while the corresponding values for the final phase be Y_2, C_2 and I_a''. Then, the following identities emerge:

$Y_1 = C_1 + I_{Ia}'$ and, $Y_2 = C_2 + I_a''$ (at the equilibrium, $C + I_a = AD = Y$)

Subtracting, $Y_2 - Y_1 = C_2 - C_1 + I_a'' - I_a'$

$\Rightarrow$ $\Delta Y = \Delta C + \Delta I_a$

$\Rightarrow$ $\Delta Y/\Delta Y = \Delta C/\Delta Y + \Delta I_a/\Delta Y$

$\Rightarrow$ $1 = MPC + \Delta I_a/\Delta Y$ ($\because \Delta C/\Delta Y = MPC$)

$\Rightarrow$ $1 - MPC = \Delta I_a/\Delta Y$

Thus, $K = \Delta Y/\Delta I_a = 1/(1 - MPC) = 1/(MPS)$

Thus, for an infinitesimally small change (dI_a) in investment spending from the existing level of I_a, the income would change by K_{Ia} times (dI_a).

$$dY = K_{Ia} \cdot (dI_a) \tag{6.15}$$

[Note that I_a is a constant at a point of time but if a change is caused from its initial value, differentiation with respect to I_a should not be confused with that with respect to a constant].

If 'b' = 0.80, $K_{Ia} = 1/(1 - b) = 1/(1 - 0.80) = 1/(0.20) = 5.00$.

Now suppose investment increases to ₹ 1010 crore from its initial value of ₹ 1000 crore. Clearly, dI_a = ₹ 10 crore. Additional income generated in consequence would be $K_{Ia} \times (dI_a) = 5.00 \times 10 =$ ₹ 50 crore. Thus, an increase of ₹ 10 crore in investment spending when marginal propensity to consume is 80% would lead to an increase in income by ₹ 50 crore over the multiplier period. This is five times the increase in investment spending. The question that arises is the length of the multiplier period. How long is the multiplier period? Is it in months or years or decades? Well, nothing can be said about the precise length of this period. In fact it may even be infinitely long. We will discuss more about it later in this section while discussing the dynamic multiplier.

Multiplier can be estimated in a number of ways. Much depends on the data provided. We have already seen one way of its estimation above. When *MPC* or *MPS* is given, multiplier can be calculated as

$$K = \frac{1}{(1-b)} = \frac{1}{(1-MPC)} = \frac{1}{MPS} \tag{6.16}$$

Another way of calculating it is to use its very definition. That is, when change in income due a given change in investment is given, multiplier, K_{Ia}, can be calculated from Equation 6.13. To illustrate, suppose that the initial level of income is ₹ 1000 crore of which ₹ 900 crore is spent on final consumption and ₹ 100 crore is retained as savings to finance investment. Now suppose that the income increases to ₹ 1200 crore and consumption increases to ₹ 1050 crore. Clearly, savings or investment would increase to ₹ 150 crore. Thus,

$$\begin{aligned} \Delta Y &= 1200 - 1{,}000 = 200. \\ \Delta C &= 1050 - 900 = 150. \\ \Delta S &= \Delta I_a = 150 - 100 = 50 \\ \therefore K_{Ia} &= \Delta Y/\Delta I_a \\ &= 200/50. \\ &= 4.00 \end{aligned}$$

This implies that if the investment increases by 50, the increase in income would be four times as much, i.e., income would be 4 × 50 or 200. The relationship between K_{Ia} and *MPC* or *MPS* can be understood from Table 6.2.

TABLE 6.2 Relationship Between *K*, *MPC* and *MPS*

MPC	*MPS*	*K* = 1/(1–*MPC*)	*K* = 1/*MPS*	*MPC*	*MPS*	*K* =1/(1–*MPC*)	*K* = 1/*MPS*
0.00	1.00	*K* = 1.00	*K* = 1.00	0.50	0.50	*K* = 2.00	*K* = 2.00
0.20	0.80	*K* = 1.25	*K* = 1.25	0.75	0.25	*K* = 4.00	*K* = 4.00
0.25	0.75	*K* = 1.33	*K* = 1.33	1.00	0.00	*K* = ∞	*K* = ∞

Table 6.2 A high *MPC* means a low *MPS* and a high investment-multiplier. Thus for a high value of investment multiplier, *MPC* must be high or *MPS* must be low. It can be shown that a higher multiplier leads to higher income propagation or a faster recovery of the economic systems from the state of depression.

Alternatively, K_{Ia} can be determined through Equation 6.16 as well. What we need for the purpose is the marginal propensity to consume, *b,* which is defined as

$$b = \Delta C/\Delta Y$$
$$= 150/200$$
$$= 0.75.$$

Then,

In $$K_{Ia} = 1/(1 - b)$$
$$= 1/(1 - 0.75)$$
$$= 4.00$$

ILLUSTRATION 6.1: For a hypothetical economy with two sectors has following specifications:

Consumption Expenditure, $C = 2000 + 0.80Y$

Investment expenditure, $I_a = 500$

(All the figures are in crores of rupees)

Determine:

(a) Equilibrium level of income
(b) Consumption expenditure at equilibrium
(c) Investment multiplier, K_{Ia}
(d) Increase in income when investment increases to 600
(e) Obtain savings function, *MPS* and the value of savings at the equilibrium.

Solution:

(a) $AD = C + I_a$

$AS = Y$

$\therefore\ Y = C + I_a$

($AD = AS$ in equilibrium)

$= C_a + bY + I_a$

$\Rightarrow\ (1 - b)Y = (C_a + I_a)$

$$\Rightarrow \quad Y = \frac{1}{(1-b)}[C_a + I_a]$$

$$= \frac{1}{(1-0.80)}[2000 + 500] \qquad \text{(On substituting given data)}$$

$$= \frac{1}{0.20}[2500]$$

$= ₹\ 12, 500$

(b) Consumption expenditure at equilibrium level of income can be calculated by substituting the value of the equilibrium income in the given consumption function. Thus,

$$C = 2000 + 0.80\ (12{,}500)$$
$$= 2000 + 10000$$
$$= ₹\ 12{,}000$$

(c) Investment multiplier,

$$K_{Ia} = \frac{dY}{dI_a}$$

$$= 1/(1 - b)$$
$$= 1/(1 - 0.80)$$
$$= 1/0.20$$
$$= 5.00$$

(d) Given ΔI_a = ₹ (600 – 500) = ₹ 100
We have to find ΔY when $K_{Ia} = 5.00$

$$\Delta Y = K\,(\Delta I_a)$$
$$= 5.00 \times 100$$
$$= ₹\ 500 \text{ crore}$$

(e) Savings function (S) is given as

$$S = Y - C$$
$$= Y - C_a - bY$$
$$= -C_a + (1 - b)Y$$
$$= -2000 + (1 - 0.80)Y$$
$$= -2000 + 0.20\,Y$$
$$MPS = dS/dY$$
$$= 0.20$$

Value of savings at equilibrium

$$S = -2000 + 0.20\,(12{,}500)$$

(Substituting for Y, the equilibrium income, in the savings function)

$$= ₹\ 500 \text{ crore.}$$

This figure can also be obtained by subtracting the equilibrium value of consumption expenditure from the equilibrium level of income, i.e.,

$$S = 12{,}500 - 12{,}000$$
$$= ₹\ 500 \text{ crore.}$$

ILLUSTRATION 6.2: How would your answers change in illustration 6.1 if investment were to change from ₹ 500 crore to ₹ 400 crore?

Solution: The only change is $\Delta I_a = -100$.
Substitute – 100 instead of + 100 for (ΔI_a) in illustration 6.1 and work out all the answers.

[**Ans:** (a) ₹ 12,500 crore.
(b) ₹ 12,000 crore.
(c) $K_{Ia} = 5.00$
(d) $\Delta Y = K_{Ia} \times (\Delta I_a) = 5.00 \times (-100) = (-)$ ₹ 500 crore (a decrease).
(e) $S = -2000 + 0.20$ Y; $MPS = 0.20$; Equilibrium level of S is ₹ 500 crore.]

6.3 STATIC AND DYNAMIC MULTIPLIERS

Investment multiplier discussed so far is called the ***static investment multiplier***. The other relevant static multipliers are *static government expenditure multiplier* ($\Delta Y/\Delta G$ or $d\,Y/dG$) and *static export multiplier* ($\Delta Y/\Delta X$ or dY/dX), where G and X are government expenditure and exports respectively. The main drawback of a static multiplier is that its effect on income can be estimated only at the end of the multiplier period. As stated earlier, there is no definite limit to the length of the multiplier period. Thus static multiplier is of little use to a finance minister who wishes to know the effects of various injections (I_a, G or X) on income soon after making them so that he could amend the magnitude of injections to bring about the desired level of income generation at a desired point of time. For such purposes, it is the ***dynamic multiplier*** that comes to the finance minister's rescue. A dynamic multiplier gives the effect on income of a given change in one of the injections at any point of time before the expiry of the multiplier period. The expression for the dynamic multiplier is as given below:

$$K_D^1 = (1 - b^n)/(1 - b) \tag{6.17}$$

here, $K_D \equiv$ Dynamic Multiplier; $b \equiv$ Marginal Propensity to Consume (MPC), $n \equiv$ time period after which the effect on income generation of a change in any of the injections is required to be studied.

As the reader is already aware, 'b', the marginal propensity to consume, is less than 1 numerically. When 'n', the multiplier period, is infinitely large as in case of the static multiplier, the dynamic multiplier reduces to the static multiplier. This can be seen using the theorems on limits. As $n \to \infty$, we know that $b^n \to 0$ as $|b| < 1$. As a result, $(1 - b^n) \to 1$ and $K_D \to K_{Ia}$.

To demonstrate the working of the static and the dynamic multipliers, let $b = 0.80$. The static multiplier, $K_{Ia} = 1/(1 - b) = 1/(1 - 0.80) = 5.00$. The additional income generated at the end of the multiplier period is ₹ 500 when investment is increased by 100. That is the overall effect of the static multiplier. Now suppose that the finance minister wants to know the effect on income of the multiplier process after one year of its operation. Using the dynamic multiplier, the income generated after one year (ΔY_1) is

$$\begin{aligned}\Delta Y_1 &= K_{D.}\,\Delta I_a \\ &= [\{1 - (0.8)^1\}/(1 - 0.8)] \times 100 \\ &= 100\end{aligned}$$

In like manner, income generated after 2 years (ΔY_2) is

$$\begin{aligned}\Delta Y_2 &= K_{D.}\,\Delta I_a \\ &= [\{1 - (0.8)^2\}/(1 - 0.8) \times 100 \\ &= 180.\end{aligned}$$

Proceeding likewise, $\Delta Y_3 = 244$, $\Delta Y_4 = 295.20$, $\Delta Y_5 = 336.16$, and so on. It can be verified that the dynamic multiplier for 1st year is 1.00, for first 2 years it is 1.80, for first three years it is 2.44, for first four years it is 2.952 and for first 5 years it is 3.36. Income generated after infinite number of years is $\Delta Y_\infty = 500$ as also given by the static multiplier.

---

[1] To obtain the expression, suppose an increase of ΔI_a in investment is initiated in an economy with $MPC = b = \Delta C/\Delta Y$. The increase, ΔI_a, in investment initiates an equal increase in demand for capital goods, generating an additional income, ΔY_1 equal to ΔI_a for the producers of capital goods. Recipients of ΔY_1 initiate consumption demand, ΔC_1 equal to $b\,\Delta Y_1$ or $b\,\Delta I_a$. This creates an additional income , $\Delta Y_2 = \Delta C_1$ or $b\,\Delta I_a$ for the producers of consumer goods. Recipients of ΔY_2 initiate consumption demand, ΔC_2 equal to $b\,\Delta Y_2$ or $b\,(b\,\Delta I_a) = b^2\,\Delta I_a$ creating income ΔY_3 equal to $b^2\,\Delta I_a$ for producers of consumer goods. Recipients of ΔY_3 initiate consumption demand $\Delta C_3 = b\,(\Delta Y_3)$ or $b^3\,\Delta I_a$ and creating an income of ΔY_4 equal to $b^3\,\Delta I_a$ for the producers of consumer goods. The process of income propagation continues generating income ΔY_n equal to $b^{n-1}\,\Delta I_a$ for the producers of consumer goods in the nth stage. Total income so generated can be expressed as

$$\begin{aligned}\Delta Y &= \Delta Y_1 + \Delta Y_2 + \Delta Y_3 + \Delta Y_4 + \ldots + \ldots + \Delta Y_n \\ &= \Delta I_a + b\,\Delta I_a + b^2\,\Delta I_a + b^3\,\Delta I_a + \ldots + \ldots\, b^{n-1}\,\Delta I_a \\ &= [1 + b + b^2 + b^3 + \ldots + \ldots + b^{n-1}]\,\Delta I_a \\ &= \frac{(1 - b^n)}{(1 - b)} \times \Delta I_a\end{aligned}$$

(Sum of n terms of a geometric progression ($G.P.$) with first term $a = 1$ and common ration $r = b$)

In sum, dynamic multiplier helps measurement of income generated at any point of time during the multiplier period while the static multiplier helps its measurement only at the end of the multiplier period which is infinitely long.

6.4 PARADOX OF THRIFT

Savings have different significance for the individual households and the development planners. An individual household regards habit of saving a part of its income as a *virtue* because savings lend it a feeling of security against the unforeseen. True, savings provide a protective umbrella to it against bad spells. That is why individuals lay stress on savings and spend a great deal of effort on inculcating habits of thriftiness among their young ones. For them, it is like most other good habits that need to be inculcated among the young during their upbringing.

For development planners, however, the matter is the other-way round. For them thriftiness of the people is a *vice* because it affects national investment and hence national income adversely. Figure 6.4 demonstrates the point.

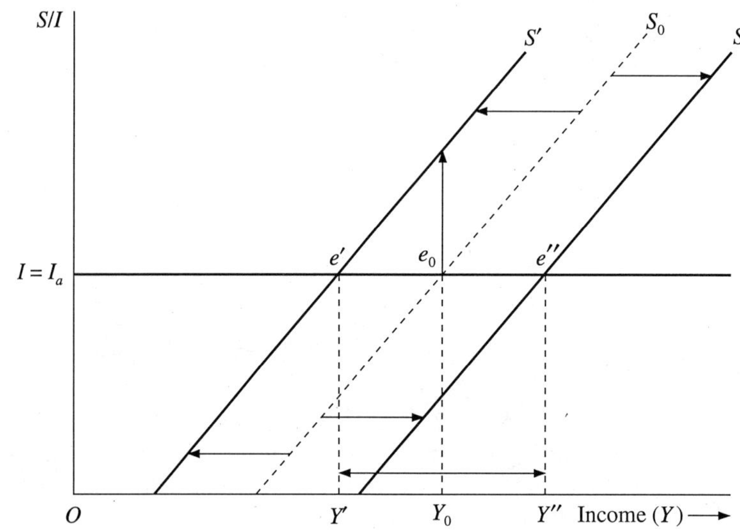

FIGURE 6.4 From the lower panel of Figure 6.3, equilibrium income can be determined through the equality of investment and savings. In this figure equilibrium takes place at e_0 where investment function $I = I_a$ intersects the savings function $S_0 = -C_a^0 + (1 - b)Y_0$, giving equilibrium income Y_0. Now suppose that thriftiness among people increases leading to an upward-to-left shift in the saving function. Note that an increase in thriftiness, implying higher savings at a given level of income, would shift every point on S_0 vertically upward to a corresponding point on S_1 as shown by the upwardly pointing arrow at e_0. The shift results in a fall in the national income from Y_0 to Y'. This shows how an increase in thriftiness reduces national income. It is for this reason that thriftiness, a virtue for the households, is considered a vice for the development planners. A household's mutton is the nation's poison. Savings thus have different implications for households and for the economy. This is what is known as the ***paradox of thrift.***

In like manner if savings or thriftiness decreases among the households, the savings function undergoes a downward to right shift from S_0 to $S''[-C_a'' + (1 - b)Y'']$. In consequence, national income increases from Y_0 to Y'' However, the households' sector feels less secure with less savings to provide a cushion. Again, nation's mutton proves to be the households' poison.

The figure shows how nation's mutton turns households' poison and households' mutton, nation's poison. Savings that serve as a boon to the thrifty households serve as a bane to the nation or vice versa. Different implications of thriftiness to different entities at a point of time are referred to as ***Paradox of Thrift.***

The problem can be resolved if the households possess highly developed banking habits and the banking network is wide and effective in mobilizing their savings. In that case, savings deposits with the banking sector can be used to finance national investment for growth of national income and its development without making the households to feel insecure. Bankers can assure the households of perpetual liquidity of their deposits through their *ATM* and internet facilities and can deploy the idle vault cash to finance productive ventures through their credit creating instruments (see Section 9.4 for details). One such instrument is the credit multiplier defined as the ratio of the total deposits to the available primary deposits (Vault cash left after meeting the cash needs, if any, of the household savers). To demonstrate, suppose a household deposits ₹ 100 per month in a savings deposit and withdraws only 80% of it on an average each month. The proportion of the deposits retained by the bankers as vault cash is known as the ***cash reserve ratio,*** *r*, which gives the ***credit multiplier***, *K*[1] = *1/r*. It is 5.00 when $r = 20\%$. With credit multiplier of 5.00, the total volume of subsequent deposits generated by the lending activity of the bankers is *K* times the primary deposit, i.e., 5 × 100 = 500. This may serve the households' cause of thriftiness and the nation's cause of investment in productive activities in simultaneity.

6.5 ACCELERATOR PRINCIPLE AND LEVERAGE EFFECT

The principle of ***accelerator*** is older than that of the multiplier. It is associated with the name of an American economist, J.M. Clark, though it seems to have been propounded first by a French economist, Albert Aftalion, in an unrefined and an unpolished form at the turn of the 20th century. Accelerator may be defined as the *ratio of an increase in investment to an increase in the consumption expenditure.* Thus, accelerator,

$$\alpha = \Delta I_a/\Delta C$$

For instance, If an increase in consumption demand by 10.00 crore results in an increase in the investment by 20.00 crore, the accelerator,

$$\alpha = 20/10$$
$$= 2.00.$$

Multiplier shows the effect of a change in investment on the income while accelerator shows the effect of a change in consumption spending on the investment. Multiplier, $K_{Ia} = \Delta Y/\Delta I_a$, while accelerator, $\alpha = \Delta I_a/\Delta C$. To demonstrate the working of the accelerator, suppose that 100 machines are required to produce 1000 units of consumer goods. Each one of these machines has a life span of 10 years. That is, one-tenth part of the machine is consumed in production process every year. Assuming that the demand for the consumer goods is stable at 1,000 units, the replacement demand for machines would be (1/10) (100) = 10 machines every year. Now suppose that the demand for consumer goods increases by 10%, that is, it changes to 1100, the requirement of the additional machines would be 100/10 = 10 machines, because one machine produces 10 units as is evident from the fact that 100 machines are required to produce 1000 units of the consumer goods. Hence the investment demand increases from 10 machines to 20 machines (of which 10 machines are demanded as replacement investment and the other 10, as induced investment), registering an increase of 100%. $\alpha = \Delta I_a/\Delta C$ = 100%/10% = 10.

[1] See Section 9.4 for credit creation by commercial banks.

6.5.1 Multiplier–Accelerator Interaction: The Leverage Effect

Prof. Hansen[1] has combined Keynesian Multiplier and Aftalion's accelerator to explain the interaction between investment and consumption as follows. The growth of primary or as he terms it, autonomous investment, has a magnifying effect on total employment and income, and hence, a magnifying effect on the demand for articles of personal consumption (the multiplier effect). This, in turn, again leads to an increase in investment as new means of production become necessary for satisfaction of the enhanced demand for consumer goods (the accelerator effect). The derived investment initiates the multiplier mechanism again and magnifies the hike in employment and income, which in turn, leads to a wave of induced investments. Prof. Hansen calls the effect of the combined action of the multiplier and the accelerator as the ***leverage effect***[2] (Table 6.3).

TABLE 6.3 Multiplier–Accelerator–Interaction: The Leverage Effect ($b = 0.50$, $\alpha = 2.00$)

Multiplier Period	*Initial Investment*	*Induced consumption (ΔC)*	*Induced investment (ΔI_a)*	*Aggregate increase in National income (ΔY)*
1.	20	0.00		20.00
2.	20	10.00	20.00	50.00
3.	20	25.00	30.00	75.00
4.	20	37.50	25.00	82.50
5.	20	41.25	7.50	68.75

Table 6.3 The table has been drawn on the assumption that $MPC = 0.50$ and accelerator, $\alpha = 2.00$. It explains the process of income generation through the interaction of the multiplier and accelerator. Let the initial investment be ₹ 20 crore. Induced consumption is zero and so is the induced investment as neither the multiplier nor the accelerator has been initiated so far. Aggregate increase in income (ΔY) is ₹ 20 crore which is the sum of the initial investment (20), induced consumption (0.00) and induced investment (0.00). Since $MPC = 0.50$, $\Delta C = 0.50 \times \Delta Y = 0.50 \times 20 = 10.00$. Hence induced consumption in period 2 is ₹ 10.00 crore. Increase in the induced consumption is $10 - 0.0 =$ ₹ 10 crore. Therefore, Induced investment $\Delta I_a = \alpha \times \cdot \Delta C = 2 \times 10 =$ ₹ 20 crore. The aggregate increase in the income in period 2 is ΔY = initial investment (20) + induced consumption (10.00) + induced investment (10.00) = ₹ 50 crore. This leads to an induced consumption of $(MPC \times \Delta Y) = 0.50 \times 50 =$ ₹ 25.00 crore in period 3. The increase in the induced consumption, ΔC is ₹ 15 crore (= 25 – 10). Since $\alpha = 2.00$, $\Delta I_a = \alpha \times \Delta C = 2.00 \times 15 =$ ₹ 30 crore. The aggregate increase in income in period 3 is ΔY = initial investment (20) + induced consumption (25) + induced investment (30) = ₹ 75 crore. The induced consumption = $MPC \times \Delta Y = 0.50 \times 75 =$ ₹ 37.50 crore in the period 4. Increase in the induced consumption, $\Delta C = 37.50 - 25 =$ ₹ 12.50. As a result, increase in the induced investment, $\Delta I_a = \alpha \times \Delta C = 2.00 \times 12.50 =$ ₹ 25 crore. Following the procedure, aggregate increase in the income in period 4 is ΔY = initial investment (20) + induced consumption (37.50) + induced investment (25) = ₹ 82.50 crore. Proceeding likewise, we observe that the induced consumption in period 5 = $MPC \times \Delta Y = 0.50 \times 82.50 =$ ₹ 41.50 crore. Increase in the induced consumption, $\Delta C = 41.50 - 37.50 =$ ₹ 3.75 crore. Therefore, induced investment, $\Delta I_a = \alpha \times \Delta C = 2.00 \times 3.75 =$ ₹ 7.50 crore. Aggregate increase in the income in period 5 is $\Delta Y = 20 + 41.50 + 7.50 =$ ₹ 68.75 crore. Note that aggregate increase in income ($\Delta Y =$ ₹ 82.50) was the maximum in period 4. It has gone down to ₹ 68.75 in period 5. Calculations of the aggregate increase in income for the subsequent periods reveal that aggregate increase in income registers a steadily declining trend after period 4.

The leverage effect initially increases the national income at a fast pace but as the process advances, the aggregate increase in income slows down steadily, even to negative values at long last.

According to Soviet economist, R. Khafizov[3] the multiplier provides only one sided picture of the investment and the consumption relationship. The multiplier explains how consumption grows as a consequence of an increase in investment. The other side of the picture is provided by the accelerator process which automatically gets going with the start of the multiplier process. To understand the mechanism of the interaction between the multiplier and the accelerator, let us refer to Table 6.3 above.

[1] Hansen, A.H., *Business Cycles and National Income,* New York (1951), p.173.

[2] Hansen, A.H., '*Business Cycles and National Income*', New York, (1951), p.173.

[3] Khafizov, R., *Theories of Regulated Capitalism* (Moscow), p. 25.

The process of income propagation through the multiplier-accelerator interaction (leverage effect) can be portrayed graphically as in Figure 6.5.

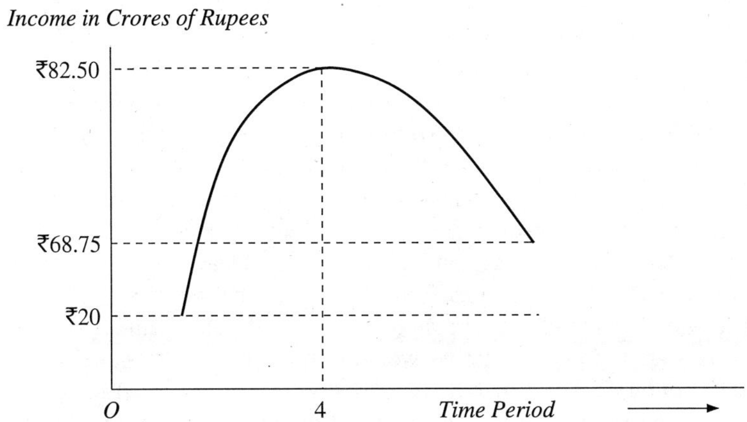

FIGURE 6.5 The process of income generation is rapid till the end of 4th period It retards thereafter at a faster pace even to negative values at long last. Accelerator thus retards the process of income propagation ultimately.

Accelerator, thus, retards the process of income generation ultimately. It would not be wrong to say that it obstructs the process of investment multiplier.

6.6 LIMITATIONS OF THE MULTIPLIER-PROCESS

The multiplier and its operation are both based on certain assumptions, non-fulfilment or partial fulfilment of which adversely affects the working of the multiplier and retards the process of income generation. Some of these assumptions are outlined below:

1. *Availability of Consumer Goods:* Availability of adequate supply of consumption goods is the basic requisite of the income propagation and multiplier process to operate. According to Dr. V.K.R.V. Rao[1], "the principle of multiplier does not work vigorously in an underdeveloped country like India on account of the inelastic nature of the consumption output curve". If the consumer goods are not available, consumers would not be able to spend their incomes on these goods and the value of *MPC* and hence that of the multiplier would be low.
2. *Maintenance of the Level of Investment:* Various increments in the investment have to be repeated at regular intervals so that the multiplier process receives its regular feed. If there is a break in the continuity of investments, national income will rapidly fall back to the original low levels.
3. *Overall Increase in the Investment:* An increase in investment in one sector should not be offset by a disinvestment in some other sector. If this happens, the overall increase in investment in the economy would be low and so will the income generation be. The multiplier would have only little to multiply.

[1] Dr. V. K. R. V. Rao, *Keynesian Economics in Underdeveloped Countries.*

4. *Induced Consumption Should Have No Adverse Affect on Investment:* Induced consumption should have no dampening effect on the investment. In other words, it is assumed that accelerator should not interfere with the working of the multiplier.

   For this, accelerator should never be less than one. If it were, $\Delta I < \Delta C$, that is, induced consumption would dampen induced investment and hence income generation.

   Retardation of the multiplier process by the accelerator has already been explained in Section 6.5.
5. *MPC should remain unchanged:* The marginal propensity to consume is assumed to remain unchanged failing which the value of the multiplier would be highly unstable.
6. *Existence of closed economy:* In order to realize the full impact of the multiplier process, it is assumed that the economy should not have any trade relations with the outside world. If the economy is open to the rest of the world, export surpluses and deficits would make the value of the multiplier either greater or smaller than its true value respectively. Export surpluses lead to income streams from the rest of the world and hence the value of the multiplier works out to be higher than its true value. In like manner, if there exist the export deficits, leakage from the multiplier would result, affecting its value adversely.
7. *Absence of the time lags between successive expenditures on consumption:* Expenditure on consumption should not lag much behind the receipt of income. Long time lags retard the process of income generation through the multiplier.
8. *Economy should be at less than full employment:* At full employment, growth of output, income and employment stagnate and the multiplier becomes very low. Some unemployment of involuntary type must exist.

6.6.1 Conditions Necessary for Working of the Multiplier

For working of the multiplier, some conditions are very necessary. A few of them are outlined below:

(i) *Existence of Involuntary Unemployment:* As stated earlier, existence of involuntary unemployment makes the investment fruitful, i.e., investment incurred helps realization of additional output through utilization of involuntarily unemployed resources.

(ii) *Existence of Industrialized Economy:* The multiplier works more freely and fully in an industrialized country. In an agricultural economy with subsistence cultivation, multiplier fails to become functional. But if agriculture is industrialized, employment of the factors leads to generation of income for the factor-owners who spend the same on consumption of goods and services.

(iii) *Existence of the Excess Capacity:* Existence of excess capacity is must so that investment may lead to an increase in production. If the plants are operating at full capacity, investment fails to increase employment, income and output.

(iv) *Existence of Elastic Supply of Capital:* An increase in investment necessitates employment of more workers as also of more capital. If supply of capital assets be inelastic, demand for additional workers would hardly arise.

6.6.2 Leakages from Multiplier

As already stated, *MPC* is seldom 1. Generally, it is less than 1 or 100 percent. In other words,

$$\frac{\Delta C}{\Delta Y} < 1.00$$

$$\Rightarrow \qquad \Delta C < \Delta Y.$$

This implies that whole of the income is not spent on consumption. That part of the income which is not spent on consumption is referred to as a leakage from it. The following are some important sources of leakage from the multiplier process:

1. *Savings:* This is the most common leakage from the circular flow of income and expenditure. In fact, the higher the propensity to save, the smaller the value of the multiplier $K = 1/MPS$ and the slower is the income propagation.
2. *Debt Cancellation:* If increase in income is used by people in paying off the old debts, consumption expenditure does not rise. *MPC* remains stagnant and so do the multiplier and its working.
3. *Taxes:* Generally whole of the income or an increase in it is not spent on consumption because a part of it is used to pay off the taxes or enhanced taxes. Thus tax is another source of leakage from income and consumption expenditure.
4. *Inflation:* When rise in prices is not neutralized by Government through dearness allowances and such other relief measures, an increase in income fails to bring about a proportionate increase in consumption. Hence, inflation is yet another source of leakage from income.
5. *Accumulation of Idle Cash Deposits:* If a part of the increased income is relocated abroad as bank-deposits, it amounts to curtailment of income from consumption and thus another source of leakage.
6. *Purchase of Old Stocks and Securities:* That part of the income which is diverted to the purchase of the old shares from others is neither spent on consumption nor does it lead to any capital formation. The act therefore serves as yet another source of leakage from income.
7. *Imports:* A part of the enhanced income is often diverted to the purchase of foreign goods due to which consumption of domestic goods fails to increase in the same proportion in which income increases. Thus, imports too are a part of the leakage from the income.

6.6.3 Reasons for Failure of the Multiplier in the Underdeveloped Countries

In underdeveloped countries, multiplier fails to operate. It is so because conditions necessary for its operation do not exist in such countries. To make the matters worse, several types of leakages from the multiplier process also persist. Apart from these, the underdeveloped countries have a peculiar socio-economic character that obstructs the multiplier process. In context to the *UDCs,* we can outline several reasons that are responsible for failure of the multiplier process or operation of Keynesian economics. Some of them are:

(1) Low Marginal Propensity to Consume: It has been shown that the higher the marginal propensity to Consume, the higher is the investment multiplier and the faster is the process of income propagation. In underdeveloped countries *(UDCs), MPC* for subsistence goods is very high, no doubt, but it is unusually low for industrial output. For the multiplier process to take off, *MPC* for industrial output should be very high. Industries produce goods mostly for trade. Division of labour and the degree of specialization help them to produce better products that sell faster. In *UDCs, MPC* is generally very low for the industrial output. It is so due to the low standard of living in these countries. A vast majority of the people in these countries depend on subsistence cultivation. Food grains they grow are mostly for self-consumption. The rural population lives in primitive conditions with little civic amenities available to them. Most of the rural regions have no electricity and hence no demand for the consumer durables. *MPC* in such countries is very high but only for food grains. The overall *MPC* in *UDCs* thus work out very low and so does the value of the multiplier. It is due to this reason that the process of income generation is extremely slow in these countries.

(2) Lack of Investment: Investment, so crucial for income generation, is scarce in the Less Developed Countries (*LDCs*)[1]. The reasons for this, are the following:

(i) *Low Level of Savings:* Savings finance investment. In *LDCs* per capita savings are very low due to low per capita income.

(ii) *Low Level of Demand:* Due to low per capita income, demand for consumption goods is also low. This serves as a disincentive to invest.

(iii) *Inadequate Mobilization of Savings:* Savings cannot be appropriately mobilized unless banking sector has a widespread and efficient network for the purpose. In most of the underdeveloped countries, banking sector has yet to reach the rural sector. Moreover, deposit attracting schemes too in the *LDCs* are either inadequate or ineffective. Rate of interest offered to the depositors on the saving deposits is too low and it has been so for ages.

(iv) *Existence of Parallel Economy:* Due to high rates of taxation, evasion of tax is a common practice in the *LDCs*. This leads to accumulation of black money, running a parallel economy of its own. Such stocks of money do not reach the banking sector of the country due to the fear of detection by the income tax authorities and get relocated abroad as bank-deposits. If invested, domestically, black money could provide a potential source of investment.

(v) *Lack of Capital Goods and Technology to Utilize the Available Resource Endowment:* Most of the underdeveloped countries have remained so due to their inability to tap the resources they possess. For instance, India, for long, has not been able to utilize its abundant soil resource due its inability to provide machines, tools, fertilizers, irrigation facilities and improved seeds. Non-availability of capital goods discourages investment.

(3) Leakages from the Circular Flow of Income and Expenditure: As stated earlier in the section, leakages from the multiplier process render the Keynesian tools of income generation and propagation totally ineffective in the underdeveloped countries. Savings, debt-cancellation, taxes, inflation, accumulation of idle cash abroad, purchase of the old shares and imports are the common leakages of the underdeveloped countries.

(4) Non-existence of the Conditions Essential for Operation of the Multiplier Process: Among the conditions necessary for the multiplier, the second and the fourth conditions, namely, non-existence of industrialized economy and that of the elastic supply of the capital goods, are more relevant in the context of the underdeveloped countries.

From the discussions above, it is evident why Keynesian economics fails in the underdeveloped or less developed countries.

6.7 DETERMINATION OF EQUILIBRIUM INCOME IN AN ECONOMY WITH THREE SECTORS

In section 6.1, we discussed determination of equilibrium level of income in an economy that has only two sectors, namely, the households' sector and the producers' sector. Such economies do not survive

[1] The expressions Underdeveloped Countries (*UDCs*) and Less Developed Countries (*LDCs*) are often used interchangeably.

in real world for long. They need a regulatory authority for their smooth functioning sooner or later. Invariably, a government sector becomes inevitable, more so, when the state is a welfare state. Apart from acting as a producer, the government of a welfare state acts as a watch dog of all the activities of production and consumption. Taxation—direct and indirect—provides a source of income for the government and public expenditure and transfer payments, as channels of its spending.

6.7.1 When Taxation is Autonomous

The aggregate demand (*AD*) for an economy with three sectors, namely, the households' sector, the producers' sector and the government sector, can be expressed as

$$AD = C + I + G \tag{6.18}$$

Here, $G \equiv$ government spending on goods and services.

$I \equiv I_a$, the autonomous investment.

(In this section, we will proceed with the assumption that investment is fixed)

The Aggregate Supply (*AS*), in the like manner, can be expressed as

$$AS = C + S + T \tag{6.19}$$

Here, $T \equiv$ tax revenue net of transfer payments. Taxation assumed fixed at T_a and the transfer payments assumed fixed at R, the tax revenue net of transfer payments, $T = T_a - R$.

$AS = Y$, as in Figure 6.2, would again lead to a 45° line while $AD = C + I_a + G$ would be a vertical displacement of $C = C_a + bY^d$, first by I_a and then by G. Here, Y^d is the disposable income given as

$$\begin{aligned} Y^d &= \text{National Income} - \text{Tax Revenue net of Transfer payments.} \\ &= Y - [T_a - R] \\ &= Y - T_a + R \end{aligned} \tag{6.20}$$

Equilibrium Level of income would refer to the condition $AD = AS$, as in Section 6.1. The reader can easily verify that the alternative equilibrium condition would stand modified to

$$I_a + G = S + T_a \tag{6.21}$$

where, $I_a + G \equiv$ injections

and, $S + T \equiv$ withdrawals.

Graphically, equilibrium is shown in Figure 6.7. The upper panel shows determination of income through the equality of *AD* and *AS* while the lower one, that of it through the equality of injections and withdrawals.

Algebraically, combining $AS = Y$ and $AD = C + I_a + G$, we have

$$\begin{aligned} Y &= C_a + b\,Y^d + I_a + G \\ &= C_a + b\,[Y - (T_a - R)] + I_a + G \\ &= C_a + b\,Y - bT_a + b\,R + I_a + G \end{aligned}$$

$$\Rightarrow \quad (1 - b)\,Y = C_a - bT_a + bR + I_a + G$$

$$\Rightarrow \quad Y = \frac{1}{(1-b)}[C_a - bT_a + bR + I_a + G] \tag{6.22}$$

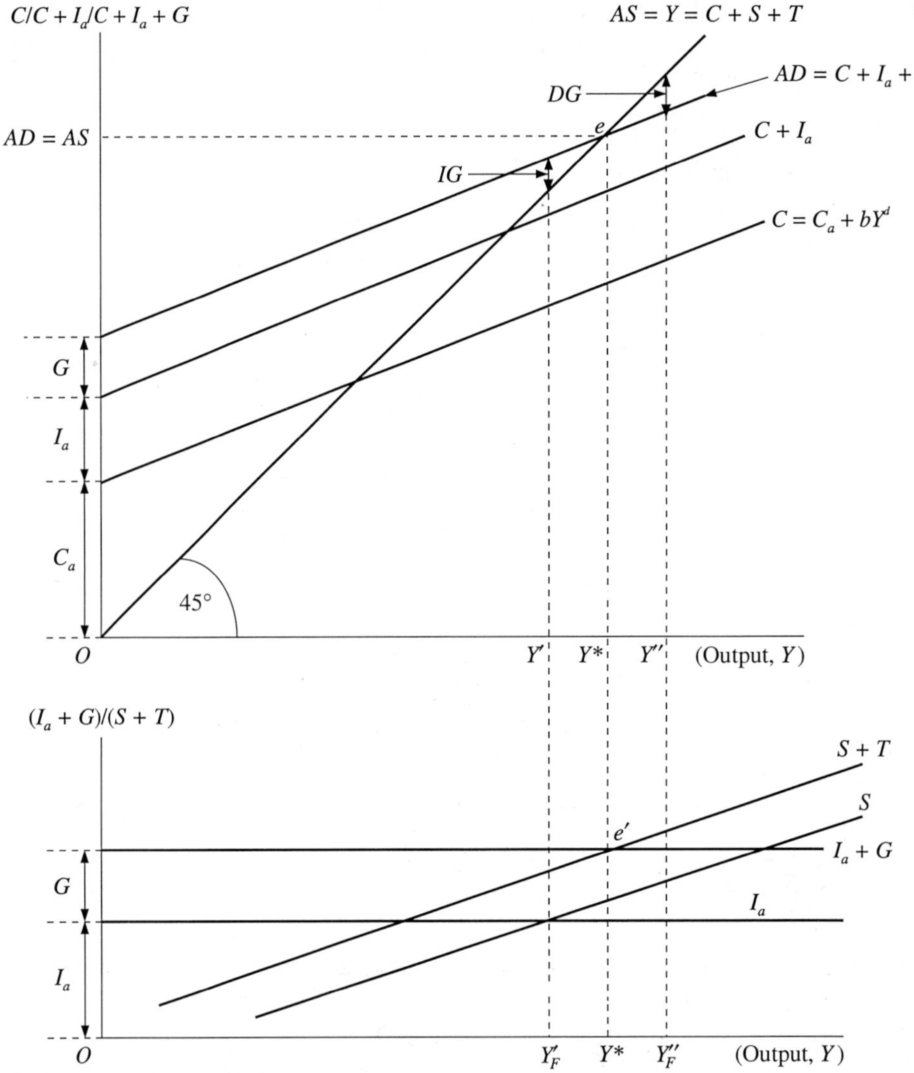

FIGURE 6.6 Determination of equilibrium level of income through $AD = AS$ (Upper Panel) and through $I_a + G = S + T$ (Lower Panel): In the upper panel, $AD = C + I_a + G$ and $AS = Y = C + S + T$ at the equilibrium. In the lower panel, $S + T = I_a + G$ at the equilibrium. Equilibrium level of income is Y^* in each case. Note how the consumption curve has been displaced vertically first by I_a and then by G to obtain the AD curve in the upper panel and how I_a and S curves have been displaced vertically by G and T respectively in the lower panel. Note also that $T = (T_a - R)$.

If full employment is reached at an income level of Y'_F ($Y'_F < Y^*$), $AD > AS$ and $AD - AS$ at Y'_F is known as the ***Inflationary Gap*** (***IG***). The name owes its origin due to emergence of inflationary tendency at this level of output (Y'_F) due the existence of the **excess demand** ($AD - AS$). There are no more factors of production available at full employment. Hence output can't be increased to the level of the aggregate demand (AD). As a result prices begin to shoot up at Y'_F.

(Contd.)

FIGURE 6.6 Contd.

As against this, if the full employment is reached at output level Y_F'' ($Y_F'' > Y^*$), $AD < AS$ and $AS - AD$ at Y_F'' is known as the ***Deflationary Gap*** (**DG**). At this level of output prices develop a tendency to fall due to ***deficient demand*** ($AS - AD$). While 'excess demand at full employment' is called the '*inflationary gap*' leading to price rise (inflation), the 'deficient demand at full employment' is called the '*deflationary gap*' leading to a fall in price (deflation). Both the situations relate to the states of disequilibrium and require a curtailment of *AD* through pruning its components of *C*, *I* and *G* in case of inflationary gap (excess demand at full employment) or an increase of *AD* through increasing the same in case of deflationary gap (deficient demand at full employment).

To correct the excess and deficient demands, economic policies are resorted to. Such policies are discussed in their requisite detail in chapters 10, 11 and 12 as monetary, fiscal and foreign trade policies.

Expression in Equation 6.22 gives the equilibrium level of income.

This expression, as evident, has been obtained from the equality of *AD* and *AS* in the upper panel of Figure 6.6. The same result can be obtained through the equality of the injections and withdrawals in the lower panel.

$$I_a + G = S + T$$
$$= -C_a + (1-b)Y^d + T$$
$$= -C_a + (1-b)[Y - T_a + R] + T_a - R$$
$$(Y^d = Y - T = Y - T_a + R \text{ and } T = T_a - R)$$
$$= -C_a + (1-b)Y - (1-b)T_a + (1-b)R + T_a - R$$
$$= -C_a + (1-b)Y - T_a + bT_a + R - bR + T_a - R$$
$$\Rightarrow \quad (1-b)Y = C_a - bT_a + bR + I_a + G$$
$$\Rightarrow \quad Y = \frac{1}{(1-b)}[C_a - bT_a + bR + I_a + G] \tag{6.23}$$

Note that the expressions in Equations 6.22 and 6.23 for the equilibrium level of income are the same. Following the expression of Equation 6.13 for investment multiplier, we can define three more multipliers, namely, the government expenditure multiplier (dY/dG), the taxation multiplier (dY/dT_a) and the transfer payments multiplier (dY/dR) as follows:

$$K_G = \frac{dY}{dG} = \frac{1}{(1-b)} \tag{6.24}$$

$$K_{Ta} = \frac{dY}{dT_a} = \frac{-b}{(1-b)} \tag{6.25}$$

$$K_R = \frac{dY}{dR} = \frac{b}{(1-b)} \tag{6.26}$$

An illustration would be in order here to explain the concepts.

ILLUSTRATION 6.3: For a hypothetically economy with three sectors, the following specifications are provided:

$$C = 20 + 0.75\,Y^d$$
$$I_a = 20$$
$$G = 25$$
$$T_a = 25$$

Determine:

(i) The equilibrium level of income through the equality of the *AS* and *AD* as well as through that of the injections and withdrawals.
(ii) Investment multiplier, Govt. expenditure multiplier and tax multiplier.
(iii) Disposable income, consumption expenditure and the level of savings at equilibrium.
(iv) Effect on the national income of each of the following changes:
    1. Investment increases to 30.
    2. Govt. expenditure increases to 40.
    3. Tax decreases to 20.

Solution:

(i) $AD = AS$ leads to Equation 6.22. We have,

$$Y = \frac{1}{(1-b)}[C_a - bT_a + bR + I_a + G]$$

Substituting data from the question, $b = 0.75$, $C_a = 20$, $G = T_a = 25$, $I_a = 20$, we have,

$$Y = \frac{1}{(1-0.75)}[20 - 0.75 \times 25 + 0.75 \times 0.00 + 20 + 25]$$

$$Y = 4.00\ [20 - 18.75 + 0.00 + 45] = 185.$$

Injections = withdrawals also leads to the same result.

(ii) From Equation 6.13, the investment multiplier, K_{Ia},

$$K_{Ia} = \frac{1}{(1-b)}$$

$$= \frac{1}{(1-0.75)}$$

$$= 4.00$$

From Equation 6.24, government expenditure multiplier, K_G can be calculated as,

$$K_G = \frac{1}{(1-b)}$$

$$= 4.00 \qquad \text{(as above)}$$

Tax multiplier, K_{Ta}, from equation 6.25, is

$$K_{Ta} = \frac{-b}{(1-b)}$$

$$= -0.75/(1-0.75)$$

$$= -3.00$$

Likewise transfer payments multiplier,

$$K_R = b/(1-b)$$

$$= \frac{0.75}{(1-0.75)}$$

$$= 3.00$$

(iii) Disposable income, Y^d, at the equilibrium,

$$Y^d = Y - T_a + R$$
$$= 185 - 25 + 0.00$$
$$= 160.$$

Consumption expenditure at the equilibrium level of income,

$$C = C_a + b\,Y^d$$
$$= 20 + 0.75 \times 160$$
$$= 20 + 120$$
$$= 140$$

Savings at the equilibrium,

$$S = -\,C_a + (1 - b)\,Y^d$$
$$= -\,20 + (1 - 0.75) \times 160$$
$$= 20$$

Even directly, savings,

$$S = Y^d - C$$
$$= 160 - 140$$
$$= 20.$$

(iv) (1) When $\Delta I_a = 30 - 20 = 10$, $K_{Ia} = 4.00$ (as calculated above in part (ii))

$$\therefore\ \Delta Y = (K_{Ia})\,\Delta I_a$$
$$= 4.00 \times 10$$
$$= 40$$

Thus an increase in investment from 20 to 30 increases income by 40.

(2) When $\Delta G = 40 - 25 = 15$, $K_G = 4.00$ (as calculated above in part (ii))

$$\Delta Y = (K_G)\,\Delta G$$
$$= 4.00 \times 15$$
$$= 60.00$$

Thus an increase in government expenditure by 15, increases national income by 60.

(3) When $\Delta T_a = 20 - 25 = -\,5.00$, $K_{Ta} = -\,3.00$ (as calculated above in part (ii)

$$\Delta Y = (K_{Ta}) \times \Delta Ta$$
$$= (-\,3.00) \times (-\,5.00)$$
$$= 15.00$$

That is a decrease in autonomous tax from 25 to 20, increases income by 15.00.

6.7.2 When Taxation is Progressive/Degressive

In our analysis of equilibrium of a three sector economy, we assumed that taxation is purely autonomous in character. The assumption was intended to simplify the model at its introduction stage. Now that the purpose is served, we relax the assumption and take taxation in its most common form, the one in which it is a function of income as shown in Equation 6.27. The equation describes it as a function of income comprising of two components, *one*, purely autonomous (T_a) and the *other*, purely progressive (tY) in character. A tax is termed as *progressive* when its rate increases with increasing taxable income. The incomes for the purpose are divided into several income slabs with the lowest slab subjected to the lowest rate of taxation and the highest, to the highest. When incomes high or low are subjected to the same rate, taxation is termed as proportional and when incomes up to a certain slab are subjected to progressive taxation and slabs thereafter, to proportional taxation , the system of taxation is termed as a degressive one. Income tax in India, for example, is a degressive tax.

The tax function in such cases can be written as,

$$T = T_a + tY \tag{6.27}$$

where, $T_a \equiv$ autonomous tax, $t \equiv$ tax rate and $Y \equiv$ income.

Aggregate demand (*AD*) under purely progressive component , tY, is given as

$$\begin{aligned} AD &= C + I_a + G \\ &= C_a + bY^d + I_a + G \\ &= C_a + b\,[\,Y - (\,T - R\,)] + I_a + G \\ &= C_a + b\,[\,Y - T + R] + I_a + G \\ &= C_a + b\,[\,Y - tY + R] + I_a + G \\ &= C_a + b\,Y - btY + bR + I_a + G \end{aligned}$$

For equilibrium, $AD = AS = Y$; simplifying for equilibrium, we have

$$(1 - b + bt)\,Y = C_a + bR + I_a + G$$

$$\Rightarrow \qquad Y = \frac{1}{(1 - b + bt)} \times [C_a + bR + I_a + G] \tag{6.28}$$

Equation 6.28 gives the equilibrium level of income with the following multipliers:

$dY/dG = 1/(1 - b + bt)$, *(Government expenditure multiplier)* (6.29)

$dY/dI_a = 1/(1 - b + bt)$, *(Autonomous investment multiplier)* (6.30)

$dY/dR = b/(1 - b + bt)$, *(Transfer payments multiplier)* (6.31)

$dY/dt = [(-b)/(1 - b + bt)^2] \times [C_a + bR + I_a + G]$. *(Tax rate multiplier)* (6.32)

Tax rate multiplier can also be written as,

$$dY/dt = [(-b)Y/(1 - b + bt)] \tag{6.33}$$

where, $Y = [1/(1 - b + bt)] \times [C_a + bR + I_a + G]$

AD with tax function of Equation 6.27, likewise, can be given as

$$\begin{aligned} AD &= C + I_a + G \\ &= C_a + bY^d + I_a + G \\ &= C_a + b\,[Y - (\,T - R\,)] + I_a + G \\ &= C_a + b\,[Y - T_a - tY + R] + I_a + G \\ &= C_a + b\,Y - bT_a - btY + bR] + I_a + G \end{aligned}$$

Subjecting it to the condition of equilibrium,

$$AD = AS = Y$$

we have,

$$Y = C_a + bY - bT_a - btY + bR + I_a + G$$

$$\Rightarrow \qquad Y = \frac{1}{(1 - b + bt)} \times [C_a - bT_a + bR + I_a + G] \tag{6.34}$$

This adds yet another multiplier, the autonomous tax multiplier, which is given as

$dY/dT_a = (-b)/(1 - b + bt)$, *(Autonomous tax multiplier)* (6.35)

6.7.3 Balanced Budget Multiplier

From Equations 6.24 and 6.25, we have

$$K_G = \frac{dY}{dG} = \frac{1}{(1-b)}, \text{ and}$$

$$K_{Ta} = \frac{dY}{dT_a} = \frac{-b}{(1-b)}$$

Adding them up, we have

$$K_G + K_{Ta} = \frac{1-b}{1-b} = 1 \tag{6.36}$$

That is, the sum of the government expenditure multiplier and tax multiplier when tax is autonomous is one.

The result is called ***unit multiplier theorem*** or ***balanced budget multiplier theorem*** elaborated below.

Under the balanced budget, $\Delta G = \Delta T_a = x$ *(say)*.

Then change in income due to a change government spending of ΔG can be given from Equation 6.24 as,

$$\Delta Y = (K_G)\, \Delta G$$
$$= 1/(1-b) \times x$$

Change in income due to a change in autonomous tax can be given from Equation 6.25 as,

$$\Delta Y = (K_{Ta})\, \Delta T_a$$
$$= [(-b)\,(1-b)] \times x$$

Thus the total change in income,

$$\Delta Y = [(1-b)/(1-b)] \times x$$
$$= x$$

Under balanced budget, change in national income is limited to the magnitude of government spending or autonomous tax. In other words, *autonomous tax financed increase in government spending can increase national income only by the amount of increase in tax or government spending.*

However, if taxation is progressive, the balanced budget multiplier is less than one and change in national income is less than the change in government spending or autonomous tax.

From Equations 6.29 and 6.35,

$$dY/dG = 1/(1-b+bt), \text{ and}$$
$$dY/dT_a = (-b)/(1-b+bt).$$

Clearly, $dY/dG + dY/dT_a = (1-b)/(1-b+bt) < 1$ (6.37)

Under the balanced budget, $dG = dT_a = x$ *(say)*

Then, change in income due to a change in government spending, x,

$$dY = 1/(1-b+bt) \times x, \text{ and}$$

Change in income due to a change in autonomous tax by the same amount, x(under a balanced budget),

$$dY = [(-b)/(1-b+bt)] \times x$$

The total change in national income when government spending is financed only by autonomous taxation (Balanced budget).

$$dY = [(1 - b)/(1 - b + bt)] \times x < x$$

ILLUSTRATION 6.4: For a hypothetical economy with following specifications,

$$C = 2000 + 0.80\ Y^d$$
$$I_a = 500$$
$$G = 400$$
$$R = 100$$
$$T = 100 + 0.25\ Y$$

Determine:

1. equilibrium level of income,
2. consumption expenditure, savings, disposable income, and tax revenue at equilibrium,
3. relevant multipliers,
4. effect on income of each of the following:
   (a) increase in government spending by 20,
   (b) increase in autonomous taxation by 20,
   (c) decrease in autonomous investment by 50,
   (d) decrease in transfer payments by 50, and
   (e) increase in tax rate by 5%.
5. budget surplus at the equilibrium.,
6. tax financed government expenditure when taxation is autonomous.

Solution:

1. Substituting the data in Equation 6.34, we have

$$Y = [1/(1 - b + bt)] \times [C_a - bT_a + bR + I_a + G]$$
$$= [1/(1 - 0.8 + 0.8 \times 0.25)] \times [2000 - 0.8 \times 100 + 0.8 \times 100 + 500 + 400]$$
$$= 2.5 \times 2900$$
$$= \mathbf{7250.}$$

2. Substituting it in tax function, we have

$$T = 100 + 0.25 \times 7250$$
$$= \mathbf{1912.50}$$

Substituting in the expression for disposable income, we have

$$Y^d = Y - T + R$$
$$= 7250 - 1950.50 + 100$$
$$= \mathbf{5437.50}$$

Substituting for Y^d in the consumption and savings functions, we have

$$C = 2000 + 0.8\ Y^d$$
$$= 2000 + 0.8 \times 5437.50$$
$$= \mathbf{6350}$$
$$S = -C_a + (1 - b) \times Y^{d.}$$
$$= -2000 + (1 - 0.8) \times 5437.50$$
$$= \mathbf{-912.50}$$

(*Note that withdrawals* = $S + T - R = -912.50 + 1912.50 - 100 =$ **900,** and injections = $I_a + G = 500 + 400 =$ **900.**

3. $dY/dG = dY/dI_a = 1/(1 - b + bt)$
$= 1/(1 - 0.8 + 0.8 \times 0.25)$
$=$ **2.50**

$dY/dR = b/(1 - b + bt)$
$= 0.8/(1 - 0.8 + 0.8 \times 0.25)$
$=$ **2.00**

$dY/dT_a = -b/(1 - b + bt)$
$=$ **– 2.00**

$dY/dt = -bY/(1 - b + bt)$
$= -0.8 \times 7250/(1 - 0.8 + 0.8 \times 0.25)$
$= -14{,}500$

4. (a) **50**, (b) – **40.00**, (c) **– 125**, (d) – 100, (e) **– 725.**
5. Budget surplus (BS) = $T_a + tY - (G + R)$
$= (100 + 0.25 \times 7250) - (400 + 100)$
$=$ **1,412.50.**
6. $\Delta T_a = \Delta G = x.$
$dY = [(-b)/(1 - b)] \times x + 1/(1 - b) \times x$
$= -4x + 5x$
$= x.$

Thus under autonomous tax, tax financed government spending increases national income only by the amount of government spending or by the tax.

6.8 DETERMINATION OF EQUILIBRIUM LEVEL OF INCOME IN AN ECONOMY WITH FOUR SECTORS

When the economy opens up to foreign trade, it is said to have the fourth sector also to deal with. The fourth sector is the *Rest of the World* (*ROW*) sector. Exports to the ROW and the imports from the *ROW* disturb the equilibrium of the economy as in the previous section.

6.8.1 When Taxation and Imports are Autonomous

Value of the exports (X) constitutes another source of income and the value of imports (M), as another channel of expenditure. Aggregate Demand (AD) and Aggregate Supply (AS) can for an economy with four sectors be expressed as:

$AD = C + I + G + X$

and, $AS = C + S + T + M$

An alternative expression for AD may be given as,

$$AD = C + I + G + (X - M) \tag{6.38}$$

and that for AS may be given as,

$$AS = C + S + T \tag{6.39}$$

To simplify the matters, let us assume again that $I = I_a$, $T = T_a$ and $M = M_a$. We know that G, R and X are already independent of income, Y. With these specifications, AD curve can be obtained by the vertical displacement of the consumption curve first by I_a, then by G and finally by $(X - M_a)$. We know that the Aggregate Supply (AS) curve representing the identity $AS = Y$ is always a straight line inclined at 45° to the x-axis, the equilibrium level of income can be determined at the equality of the AD and AS. Thus, equilibrium income is given as:

$$
\begin{aligned}
Y &= AD \\
&= C + I_a + G + (X - M_a) \\
&= C_a + bY^d + I_a + G + (X - M_a) \\
&= C_a + b[Y - T_a + R] + I_a + G + (X - M_a) \\
&= C_a + bY - bT_a + bR + I_a + G + (X - M_a)
\end{aligned}
$$

$$\Rightarrow \quad (1 - b)Y = C_a - bT_a + bR + I_a + G + (X - M_a)$$

$$\Rightarrow \quad Y = \frac{1}{(1-b)}[C_a - bT_a + bR + I_a + G + (X - M_a)] \tag{6.40}$$

The same results are obtained through the equality of the injections and the withdrawals.

Injections = withdrawals

$$
\begin{aligned}
I + G + X - M_a &= S + T_a - R \\
&= - C_a + (1 - b)Y^d + T_a - R \\
&= - C_a + (1 - b)[Y - T_a + R] + T_a - R \\
&= - C_a + Y - T_a + R - bY + bT_a - bR + T_a - R \\
&= - C_a + (1 - b)Y + bT_a - bR
\end{aligned}
$$

$$\Rightarrow \quad (1 - b)Y = C_a - bT_a + bR + I_a + G + X - M_a$$

$$\Rightarrow \quad Y = \frac{1}{(1-b)}[C_a - bT_a + bR + I_a + G + X - M_a] \tag{6.41}$$

Equations 6.40 and 6.41 both yield the same value of the equilibrium level of income.

Graphical representation of the equilibrium of a four sector model is left to the reader. What the reader needs to do is to give a further upward shift by $(X–M_a)$ to the AD curve of Figure 6.6 (upper panel). Rest of the two panels remains unchanged.

ILLUSTRATION 6.5: Consider an economy with following specifications:

$$
\begin{aligned}
C &= 80 + 0.80\,Y^d \\
Y^d &= Y - T_a + R \\
T_a &= 10 \\
R &= 20 \\
I_a &= 50 \\
G &= 50 \\
X &= 20 \\
M_a &= 28
\end{aligned}
$$

and calculate:

(i) Equilibrium level of income,
(ii) The relevant multipliers,
(iii) Effect on income of each of the following changes:

1. Increase in investment by 10,
2. Decrease in autonomous taxation by 5,
3. Increase in transfer payments by 5,
4. Increase in exports by 10,

5. Decrease in autonomous imports by 8,
6. Decrease in public expenditure by 10.

The solution is left to the reader as an exercise. Answers are provided below for reader's verification.

[**Ans:** (i) 900; (ii) $K_{Ia} = K_G = K_X = 5.00$; $K_{Ta} = -4.00$; $K_R = 4.00$; $K_{Ma} = -5.0$ (iii) **1.** + 50; **2.** + 20; **3.** + 20; **4.** + 50.00; **5.** + 40.00; **6.** – 50.00]

Besides the multipliers given in Equations 6.14, 6.24, 6.25 & 6.26; we can define yet another two as the export multiplier and the import multiplier for this model by differentiating Equation 6.41.

$$K_X = 1/(1 - b) \tag{6.42}$$

$$K_{Ma} = -1/(1 - b) \tag{6.43}$$

6.8.2 When neither Import nor Taxation is Autonomous

In our analysis of the equilibrium level of income of an economy with three and four sectors, we have oversimplified the treatment by making the following assumptions:

1. Taxes are autonomous, *i.e.*, independent of income, Y. In real world this is not so. Taxes vary directly with income and a real world tax function may be expressed as,

   $T = T_a + tY$, where t is the tax rate.

2. Imports are autonomous, *i.e.*, independent of income, Y. In real world this is not so. Imports vary directly with income and a real world import function may be expressed as,

   $M = M_a + mY$, where m is the marginal propensity to import.

3. Investment is autonomous, *i.e.*, independent of both—income (Y) and rate of interest (r). Investment varies directly with income (Y) and inversely with the rate of interest (r).

$$I = I_a + iY$$

$$I = I_a - hr$$

The objective of this oversimplification has been to give an idea to the layman of what the discipline really looks like at its fundamental stage so that the reader may not feel a complete stranger at the time of stepping into the real world situation where nothing is held as fixed. Let us modify Equation 6.28 to incorporate these changes in T, M, and I, leaving Investment as a function of rate of interest, for a latter analysis in Chapter 8.

$$Y = AD$$

$$= C + I + G + (X - M)$$

where,

$$C = C_a + bY^d$$

$$Y^d = Y - (T - R)$$

$$I = I_a + iY$$

$$X = \bar{X}$$

$$M = M_a + mY, \text{ and}$$

$$T = T_a + tY$$

The expression for AD or Y then reduces to,

$$Y = C_a + b\,[Y - (T_a + tY - R)] + I_a + iY + G + [X - (M_a + mY)]$$

Collecting and combining the terms involving Y, we have

$$Y = [1/(1 - b + bt - i + m)] \times [C_a - bT_a + bR + I_a + G + X - M_a] \tag{6.44}$$

where, i , t and m are propensities to invest, levy tax and to import.

Equation 6.44 gives the equilibrium level of income with the following multipliers:

$$\left.\begin{aligned} dY/dG &= dY/dI_a \\ &= dY/dX \\ &= 1/(1 - b + bt - i + m) \\ dY/dT_a &= (-b)/(1 - b + bt - i + m) \\ dY/dM_a &= (-1)/(1 - b + bt - i + m) \\ dY/dR &= b/(1 - b + bt - i + m) \\ dY/dt &= (-b)\,Y/(1 - b + bt - i + m) \end{aligned}\right] \quad (6.45)$$

ILLUSTRATION 6.6: Given an economy with following specifications,

Consumption, $C = 80 + 0.8\,Y^d$

$Y^d = Y - [T - R]$

Tax, $T = 60 + 0.2\,Y$

Investment, $I = 100 + 0.06\,Y$

$G = 160$

Transfers, $R = 40$

$X = 80$

$M = 50 + 0.2\,Y$

Calculate: (a) Equilibrium level of income, tax revenue, disposable income, consumption, savings and imports,

(b) Relevant multipliers,

(c) Effect on income of each of the following changes,

(i) Increase in government spending by 20,

(ii) Increase in autonomous tax by 20,

(iii) Decrease in autonomous investment by 50,

(iv) Decrease in transfer payments by 50,

(v) Increase in tax rate by 5%.

(d) Budget surplus at equilibrium.

(e) Net exports at equilibrium.

Solution: Substituting, for parameters in Equation 6.44, we have

(a) $$Y = \frac{1}{(1 - 0.8 + 0.8 \times 0.2 - 0.06 + 0.2)} \times [80 - 0.8 \times 60 + 0.8 \times 40 + 100 + 160 + 80 - 50]$$

$$= \frac{1}{0.5} \times [354]$$

$$= 2.00 \times 354$$

$$= \mathbf{708}$$

[($Y^d = 546.4$, $C = 517.12$, $T = 201.6$, $S = 29.28$, $I = 142.48$ and $M = 191.6$; Also, injections = withdrawals = 422.48)]

(b) Multipliers: $$K_G = K_X = K_{Ia} = \frac{1}{(1 - 0.8 + 0.8 \times 0.2 - 0.06 + 0.2)} \times 1$$

$$= \frac{1}{0.5}$$

$$= \mathbf{2.00}$$

$$K_{Ma} = \frac{1}{(1 - 0.8 + 0.8 \times 0.2 - 0.06 + 0.2)} \times (-1)$$

$$= \frac{1}{0.5} \times (-1)$$

$$= \mathbf{2.00}$$

$$K_R = \frac{1}{(1 - 0.8 + 0.8 \times 0.2 - 0.06 + 0.2)} \times (0.8)$$

$$= \frac{1}{0.5} \times (0.8)$$

$$= \mathbf{1.60}$$

$$K_{Ta} = \frac{1}{(1 - 0.8 + 0.8 \times 0.2 - 0.06 + 0.2)} \times (-0.8)$$

$$= \frac{1}{0.5} \times (-0.8)$$

$$= -\mathbf{1.60}$$

$$K_t = \frac{1}{(1 - 0.8 + 0.8 \times 0.2 - 0.06 + 0.2)} \times (-0.8 \times Y)$$

$$= \frac{1}{0.5} \times (-0.8 \times 708)$$

$$= -\mathbf{1132.8}$$

(c) (i) $\Delta Y = K_G \times \Delta G = 2.00 \times (+20) = \mathbf{+40}$

(ii) $\Delta Y = K_{Ta} \times \Delta T_a = (-1.60) \times (+20) = \mathbf{(-32)}$

(iii) $\Delta Y = K_{Ia} \times \Delta I_a = 2.00 \times (-50) = \mathbf{(-100)}$

(iv) $\Delta Y = K_R \times \Delta R = 1.60 \times (-50) = \mathbf{(-80)}$

(v) $\Delta Y = K_t \times \Delta t = (-1132.8) \times 0.05 = \mathbf{(-56.65)}$

(d) Budget Surplus (*BS*) = $T - G - R$ = 201.60 – 160 – 40 = (+) **1.60**

(e) Net exports (*NX*) = $X - M$ = 80 – 191.60 = (–) **111.60**

Changes in government spending (*G*), taxation (*T*), and transfer payments (*R*) influence the equilibrium of the goods market. Such changes are subject to the *fiscal policy* of the government, discussed in chapter 10.

Changes in exports (*X*) and imports (*M*) also disturb the equilibrium of the goods market. Such changes are subject to *foreign trade policy,* discussed in chapter 11.

KEY TERMS AND CONCEPTS

Aggregate Demand (*AD*): It is total demand for consumption and investment. Consumption demand refers to demand for consumer goods by the household and government sectors. Investment demand refers to the demand for the producers' goods (such as raw material, machinery, plant, equipment, etc.) by the producers. *AD* is given as the sum of C_h, C_g, *I*, and $(X - M)$.

Aggregate Supply: It is total quantity offered for sale. It also represents the money value of the output. Thus, $AS = Y$, the output. Also, *AS* is equal to $(C + S)$ in a two sector economy and to $(C + S + T)$ in economies with three and four sectors.

Condition of Equilibrium for an Economy with Two Sectors: An economy with the households and the producers' sectors is in equilibrium at the point where AD $(C + I) = AS$ $(C + S)$. This leads to the condition $I = S$; where I is the investment (often termed as injection) and S, the saving (often termed as withdrawal). In a simple version, $I = I_a$ the autonomous investment.

Condition of Equilibrium for an Economy with Three Sectors: When Government sector is included, the equilibrium condition $AD = AS$ changes to $C + I + G = C + S + T$ or $I + G = S + T$.

Condition of Equilibrium for an Economy with Four Sectors: When Rest of the World (ROW) is also included, the equilibrium condition $(AD = AS)$ changes to, $C + I + G + (X - M) = C + S + T$ or $I + G + (X - M) = S + T$.

Investment Multiplier: Investment Multiplier: It is defined as the ratio of an increase in income to an increase in investment. It can also be defined as the increase in income caused by a unit increase in investment. Symbolically, $K_{Ia} = \Delta Y/\Delta I = 1/(1 - b)$ for a two sector economy with b = marginal propensity to consume (MPC). For a three sector models, $K_{Ia} = \Delta Y/\Delta I = 1/(1 - b)$ when tax and investment are both autonomous, and $K_{Ia} = \Delta Y/\Delta I = 1/(1 - b + bt)$ when tax is degressive with t as the rate of tax and investment is autonomous. For a four sector model, $K_{Ia} = \Delta Y/\Delta I = 1/(1 - b)$ when tax, investment and imports are all autonomous and $K_{Ia} = \Delta Y/\Delta I = 1/(1 - b + bt + m)$ when none but investment is autonomous.

Government Expenditure Multiplier: Like investment multiplier, government expenditure multiplier can be defined as a ratio of an increase in income to an increase in government spending. It can also be defined as increase in income caused by a unit increase in government spending. Thus, $K_G = \Delta Y/\Delta G = 1/(1 - b)$ in a three sector economy with taxation and investment both autonomous. For a four sector economy, KG = $\Delta Y/\Delta G = 1/(1 - b)$ when taxation, investment and imports are all autonomous; $K_G = \Delta Y/\Delta G = 1/(1 - b + bt)$ when imports and investment are autonomous and $K_G = \Delta Y/\Delta G = 1/(1 - b + bt + m)$ when only investment is autonomous.

Export Multiplier: Like the government expenditure multiplier, export multiplier is defined as a ratio of an increase in income to an increase in export earnings. It can also be defined as an increase in income caused by a unit increase in export earnings. Thus, $K_X = \Delta Y/\Delta X = 1/(1 - b)$ when taxation, investment and imports are all autonomous, $K_X = \Delta Y/\Delta X = 1/(1 - b + bt)$ when investment and imports are both autonomous and $K_X = \Delta Y/X = 1/(1 - b + bt + m)$ when only investment is autonomous.

Taxation Multiplier: Also known as the tax multiplier, it is defined as a ratio of a decrease in income to an increase in taxation or as the ratio of an increase in income to a decrease in taxation. In general, it can also be defined as a change in national income per unit change in taxation. It is negative always and can be expressed as $K_{Ta} = \Delta Y/\Delta T_a = - b/(1 - b)$ when taxation, imports and investment are all autonomous, $K_{Ta} = \Delta Y/\Delta T_a = - b/(1 - b + bt)$ when tax is degressive with investment and imports both autonomous and $K_{Ta} = \Delta Y/\Delta T_a = - b/(1 - b + bt + m)$ when only investment is autonomous.

Transfer Payments Multiplier: It is defined as the ratio of an increase in income to an increase in transfer payments. It can also be defined as an increase in income per unit increase in the transfer payments. It is expressed as $K_R = \Delta Y/\Delta R = b/(1 - b)$ when taxation, investment and imports are all autonomous, $K_R = \Delta Y/\Delta R = b/(1 - b + bt)$ when investment and imports are both autonomous and $K_R = \Delta Y/\Delta R = b/(1 - b + bt + m)$.

Import Multiplier: It is defined as a ratio of an increase (decrease) in income to a decrease (increase) in imports. It can also be defined as an increase (decrease) in income per unit decrease (increase) in the imports. It is given as $K_{Ma} = - 1/(1 - b)$ when investment, taxation and imports are all autonomous, $K_{Ma} = - 1/(1 - b + bt)$ when investment and imports are autonomous and $K_{Ma} = - 1/(1 - b + bt + m)$ when only investment is autonomous.

Tax Rate Multiplier: It is defined as the ratio of decrease (increase) in income per unit increase (decrease) in tax rate and is given as $K_t = dY/dt = - b/(1 - b + bt) \times (C_a - bT_a + bR + I_a + G + X - M_a) = - b/(1 - b + bt \times Y$ when investment and imports are autonomous and $K_t = dY/dt = - b/(1 - b + bt + m)^2 \times (C_a - bT_a + bR + I_a + G + X - M_a) = - b/(1 - b + bt + m) \times Y$ when only investment is autonomous.

Disposable Income: Income net of direct taxes and transfer payments which people feel free to dispose off is known as disposable income. It is given as $(Y - T + R)$, where, T represents direct taxes and R the transfer payments.

Static and Dynamic Multipliers: All the multipliers defined above are the static multipliers. Their effect on income can't be determined before the multiplier period which is infinitely long. As against the static multipliers, the dynamic multipliers are capable of reflecting the effect on income of a change in any parameter at any point of time during the multiplier period. For instance, $K = 1/(1 - b)$ is the static investment multiplier while $K_D = (1 - b^n)/(1 - b)$ is the dynamic investment multiplier.

Marginal Propensity to Import: It is defined as a ratio of a change in imports to a change in income. It can be expressed as $(\Delta M/\Delta Y)$ or as dM/dY, where, M represents imports. It is given as m for the import function, $M = M_a + mY$.

Paradox of Thrift: It refers to contrasting implications of savings to households and economy as a whole. Saving is treated as a virtue by the households while the same is treated as a vice by an economy for causing a leakage from the circular flow of income and expenditure and hence for retarding the process of income generation.

Accelerator Principle and Leverage Effect: Accelerator is defined as a ratio of a change in investment to a change in consumption expenditure. It can also be defined as an increase in investment per unit increase in the consumption expenditure. It is expressed as $(\Delta I/\Delta C)$ or as (dI/dC). The collaborating operation of the multiplier and the accelerator is called the leverage effect.

Assumptions of the Multiplier Theory: The concept of multiplier is based on the following assumptions:

1. Availability of consumer goods
2. Maintenance of the level of investment
3. Overall increase in the investment
4. Induced consumption should have no adverse effect on investment
5. *MPC* should remain unchanged
6. Existence of closed economy
7. Absence of the time lags between successive expenditures on consumption
8. Economy should be at less than full employment

Conditions necessary for working of the multiplier: For working of the multiplier, some conditions are very necessary. For instance, the following conditions are very essential:

(i) Existence of involuntary unemployment
(ii) Existence of industrialized economy
(iii) Existence of the excess capacity
(iv) Existence of elastic supply of capital

Leakages from Multiplier: The following are the main sources of leakages from the multiplier-process:

1. Savings
2. Debt cancellation
3. Taxes
4. Inflation
5. Accumulation of idle cash deposits
6. Purchase of old stocks and securities
7. Imports

Reasons for Failure of the Multiplier in the Underdeveloped Countries: In underdeveloped countries, multiplier fails to operate. It is so because conditions necessary for its operation do not exist in such countries. To make the matters worse, several types of leakages from the multiplier process also persist there.

1. Low Marginal Propensity to Consume
2. Lack of investment, so crucial for income generation, is scarce in the Less Developed Countries (LDCs).The reasons for this, are the following:
   (i) Low level of savings
   (ii) Low level of demand
   (iii) Inadequate mobilization of savings
   (iv) Existence of parallel economy
   (v) Lack of capital goods and technology to utilize the available resource endowment
3. Leakages from the circular flow of income and expenditure
4. Non-existence of the conditions essential for the operation of the multiplier process

General condition for Goods Market Equilibrium: In general, goods market equilibrium is characterized by the equality of injections to the withdrawals as $I_a + G + X = S + T_a + M_a$. For the sake of simplicity, the expression is referred to as $I = S$ and the curve it traces as the '*IS*'-curve. [Please also see Q.43, Figure 5.9, Chapter 5 for an understanding of the '*IS*'-curve].

Excess Demand (*ED*): When aggregate Demand (*AD*) is greater than Aggregate Supply (*AS*), the excess of *AD* over *AS*, given as (*AD* – *AS*) is called the Excess Demand (*ED*).

At equilibrium, where *AD* = *AS*, *ED* = 0; elsewhere, it is non-zero.
For outputs less than the equilibrium level of output, *AD* is greater than *AS* or *ED* is greater than zero.
For outputs greater than the equilibrium level of output, *AD* is less than the *AS* or *ED* is less than zero.

Deficient Demand (*DD*): For outputs greater than the equilibrium level of output, *AD* is less than the *AS* or *ED* is less than zero. Negative excess demand is called the deficient demand. It is equal in magnitude to the excess of *AS* over *AD*. In terms of actual value, it is equal to (*AD* –*AS*) which is negative because *AS* is greater than *AD*.

Inflationary Gap (*IG*): The value of excess demand at the full employment level of output is called the Inflationary Gap (*IG*). It always takes place to the left of the equilibrium level of output. In this range of output, $AD > AS$ and excess demand is positive. The name 'inflationary gap' owes its origin to the fact that price-rise (inflation) takes place when *AD* is greater than *AS* at full employment.

Deflationary Gap (*DG*): The value of deficient demand at the full employment level of output is called the Deflationary Gap (*DG*). It always takes place to the right of the equilibrium level of output. In this range of output, $AD < AS$ and excess demand is negative or deficient demand is positive. The name 'Deflationary gap' owes its origin to the fact that price-fall (deflation) takes place when *AD* is less than *AS* at full employment.

EXERCISES

A. Short Answer Questions

1. Define the aggregate demand for an economy with two sectors. Outline its components.
2. Define the aggregate supply for an economy with two sectors. Outline its components.
3. How can an economy with two sectors attain its equilibrium? Explain with the help of a neat sketch.
4. What is investment multiplier? Explain its working when an increase in investment by 20 leads to an increase in income by 100. **[Ans:** 5.00]
5. Calculate the investment multiplier when marginal propensity to consume is 0.80. How **would** your answer change when marginal propensity to consume changes to 0.99? **[Ans:** 5.00; 100]
6. What is marginal propensity to save (*MPS*)? Calculate investment multiplier when *MPS* is (a) zero, (b) Infinite **[Ans:** (a) ∞; (b) 0.00]
7. Given annual income of a family as 300,000; tax paid = 7,500 and transfers received 2,500? What is its disposable income? **[Ans:** 2,95,000]
8. Calculate disposable income of a family whose annual income is 300,000 and merit scholarship received by a school-going child is 50000 per-annum and tax liability of the family is 5000? **[Ans:** ₹ 345,000]
9. 'In a two sector economy, savings are always equal to the investment' Is it true?
10. What is meant by paradox of thrift? Use a sketch to explain.
11. What is a balanced budget multiplier? Show that it is unitary when taxation is wholly autonomous.
12. What are the main reasons for failure of multiplier process in underdeveloped countries?
13. Explain Hansen's leverage effect with an example. Take $MPC = 0.8$ and accelerator = 2.00
14. Distinguish between inflationary gap and deflationary gap.
15. Distinguish between multiplier and accelerator. Is it correct to say that the latter is responsible for reverse operation of the former? Give reasons.

B. Long Answer Questions

16. How does the marginal propensity to consume and marginal propensity to save affect investment multiplier? Illustrate your answer with examples.
17. With the help of a neat sketch show how national income can be determined in an economy with two sectors through
    (i) the equality of aggregate demand and aggregate supply
    (ii) the equality of savings and investment?
18. 'Despite the fact that most of the people in underdeveloped countries consume whole of their incomes much before the month, the Keynesian Theory of income propagation does not operate in underdeveloped countries' Discuss.

[**Hint:** The question says that *MPC* in underdeveloped countries is very high. This must lead to a very high value of the multiplier and hence to a high value of income generation, indicating successful operation of the multiplier theory in the underdeveloped countries; but in reality, it does not. Why? Is MPC really high in the underdeveloped countries?]

19. 'Leakage from the circular flow of income and expenditure leads to depression ultimately' Discuss.

[**Hint:** If a part of income received by people doesn't reach back to the producers it would affect employment and output both. Saving which is a virtue for an individual, if not mobilized by banks or if relocated to foreign banks or if diverted to foreign products, proves a vice for the nation. Insert paradox of thrift to supplement your answer)].

20. Consider the following specifications for a hypothetical economy with two sectors:

$$C = 2000 + 0.8Y$$
$$I = 500$$

Determine:

(i) The equilibrium level of income.
(ii) Level of consumption and savings at equilibrium.
(iii) *APC*, *MPC*, *APS* and *MPS*
(iv) Investment multiplier.
(v) Change in income when:
  (a) Investment increases by 100,
  (b) Investment decreases by 100.
(vi) Suppose full employment is reached at $Y =$ ₹ 10,000. Determine *AD* and *AS*.
(vii) Suppose full employment is reached at $Y =$ ₹ 15,000. Determine *AD* and *AS*.

[**Ans:** (i) $Y =$ ₹ 12,500; (ii) $C =$ ₹ 12,000, $S = 500$; (iii) $APC = 0.96$, $APS = 0.04$, $MPC = 0.80$ and $MPS = 0.20$; (iv) $K_{Ia} = 5.00$; at the equilibrium (v) (*a*) $\Delta Y = K_{Ia} \times \Delta I = 5.00 \times 100 = 500$, (b) $\Delta Y = K_{Ia} x \Delta I = 5.00 (-100) = -500$; (vi) $AD = C + I =$ ₹ 10,500 and $AS = C + S = Y =$ ₹ 10,000. Excess demand $= AD - AS =$ ₹ (10,500 – 10,000) = ₹ 500; (vii) $AD = C + I =$ ₹ 14,500, $AS = C + S = Y =$ ₹ 15,000. Demand deficiency $= AS - AD = 15{,}000 - 14{,}500 = 500$].

21. What is meant by the leakages from multiplier? Enumerate the main sources of leakages from it and examine the role played by them in income propagation.

22. What conditions are essential for the successful operation of the investment multiplier? Do economies like ours fulfill them? Explain your answer.

23. What are the limitations of the multiplier process? What remedies would you suggest to overcome these limitations?

24. What is excess demand? What policy measures can correct it? To what extent can such measures be effective in a two sector model? Explain your answer.

[**Hint:** Policy measures to correct excess demand comprise of the monetary, fiscal and foreign trade policies. In a two sector economy absence of government sector makes it impossible to induct the fiscal and the foreign trade policies. The only policy that can be possible is the monetary policy provided private monetary institutions exist and feel concerned about economic stability. Private banking sector may have their own limitations. In sum, there is little recourse to the problem of excess demand in a two sector economy. For effective control of the problem, government sector is must. In the absence of the government sector, the remedy lies in curtailment of the consumption and investment demands only.]

25. What is deficient demand? What policy measures can correct it? To what extent can such measures be effective in a two sector model? Explain your answer.

[**Hint:** Policy measures to correct deficient demand comprise of the monetary, fiscal and foreign trade policies. In a two sector economy absence of government sector makes it impossible to induct the fiscal and the foreign trade policies. The only policy that can be possible is the monetary policy provided private monetary institutions exist and feel concerned about economic stability. Private banking sector may have their own limitations. In sum, there is little recourse to the problem of deficient demand in a two sector economy. For effective control of the problem government sector is must. In the absence of the government sector, the remedy lies in curtailment of the consumption and investment demands only.]

26. Define excess demand for a three sector economy. Briefly outline various policy instruments that can help to exercise appropriate control over the problem of excess demand.

[**Hint:** Presence of the government sector helps an effective control over the mismatch between *AD* and *AS*. Monetary and fiscal policies of government can exercise an effective control over aggregate demand (*AD*) which is made up of *C, I* and *G*. In the situation of excess demand, consumption demand can be controlled through an increase in taxation (*T*) and a decrease in transfer payments (*R*). Note that the consumption demand depends on the disposable income (Y^d), which in turn is given as a function of *T* and *R* as $Y^d = Y - T + R$. Hence through appropriate fiscal policy, government can regulate the volume of the disposable income to regulate the consumption demand. Another tool of fiscal policy is government final consumption expenditure (*G*). To control *AD*, government can curtail *G*. Thus fiscal policy of the government proves a very effective tool in regulating both the components *C* and *G* of *AD*. Here, the use of the term 'regulate' is deliberate and is intended to indicate that *AD* can be increased or decreased at will by suitable changes in *C* and *G* through appropriate fiscal measures of *T, R* and *G*. This provides a remedy not only for the problem of excess demand but also for the deficient demand. For instance, as a remedy to deficient demand, government can reduce taxes and increase transfer payments to increase private final consumption demand and can also increase government final consumption demand to boost the *C* and *G,* the components of *AD*. Exactly opposite is the change required in *T, R* and *G* to suppress the *C* and *G* components of *AD* to suppress *AD*. The last component of *AD* is the investment, *I*. It is dependent on both, the income (output) and the rate of interest. Income (output) can't be affected by the fiscal or monetary policies in the short-run but rate of interest can be increased or decreased at will through appropriate monetary policy. To decrease private investment spending with a view to decrease *AD*, rate of interest should be increased ($I = I_a - hr$). This can be accomplished by decreasing the money supply. Decreasing the money supply is known as the contractionary monetary policy. As against this, if private investment spending (*I*) is desired to be increased to increase *AD*, rate of interest *r* needs to be decreased as evident from the investment function, $I = I_a - hr$. This can be accomplished by increasing the money supply, known as expansionary monetary policy.]

27. Define deficient demand for a three sector economy. Briefly outline various policy instrument that can help to exercise appropriate control over the problem of deficient demand.

[**Hint:** Please see the hint for *Q*. 26]

28. Define excess demand for a four sector economy. Briefly outline various policy instruments that can help to exercise appropriate control over the problem of excess demand.

[**Hint:** Please see the hint for *Q*. 26 and add the treatment of the fourth component of the aggregate demand (*AD*). It is the net investment abroad (*X* – *M*). To suppress *AD*, (*X* – *M*) needs to be decreased. That is, *X* needs to be decreased while *M* needs to be increased. This can be accomplished through foreign trade policy of regulating imports and exports appropriately. In the same way, to boost *AD*, (*X* –*M*) needs to be increased. That is, *X* needs to be increased while *M* needs to be decreased. This can be accomplished through foreign trade policy of regulating imports and exports appropriately.]

29. Define deficient demand for a four sector economy. Briefly outline various policy instruments that can help to exercise appropriate control over the problem of deficient demand.

[**Hint:** Please see the hints for Q. 26 and 28.]

C. Essay Type Questions

30. Consider the following specifications for a hypothetical economy with three sectors:

$$C = 2{,}000 + 0.75\, Y^d$$
$$Y^d = Y - T + R$$
$$T = 500$$
$$I = 500$$
$$G = 200$$
$$R = 100$$

Determine:

(a) Equilibrium level of income, consumption and savings.
(b) Relevant multipliers.

(c) Given that the full employment income is ₹ 12000, what change in each of the following would help to bring about the full employment
  (i) Taxation, T
  (ii) Government expenditure, G
  (iii) Transfers, R, and
  (iv) Investment, I?

(d) AD, AS, excess or deficient demand at the full employment income of ₹ 12000.

(e) Budget surplus at equilibrium

(f) Budget surplus at full employment

[**Ans:** Following the method of illustration 6.3, equilibrium income, $\boldsymbol{Y}$ **= 9,600.** $Y^d = Y - T + R = 9600 - 500 + 100 =$ **9200**. Substituting for Y^d in the consumption function, we have, $\boldsymbol{C}$ **= 8900**. Then , $\boldsymbol{S = Y^d - C}$ **= 300**. Relevant multipliers are $K_I = 4.00 = K_G$; $K_T = -3.00$ and $K_R = 3.00$. That takes care of parts (a) and (b). As regards part (c), $\Delta \boldsymbol{Y} = 12000 - 9600 =$ **2400.** Thus, the change needed in taxation, ΔT is given as **– 800,** that needed in government spending, $\Delta \boldsymbol{G}$ **= 600;** that needed in transfer payments is $\Delta \boldsymbol{R}$ **= 800;** and the change needed in investment, $\Delta \boldsymbol{I}$ **= 600.** (d) Since full employment income is ₹ 12000, $\boldsymbol{Y = AS}$ **= 12000.** AD at this level of income is given as, $\boldsymbol{AD} = C + I + G = C_a + b\,[Y - T + R] + I + G = 2000 + 0.75 \times [12000 - 500 + 100] + 500 + 200 =$ **11400.** As $11400 < 12000$, $\boldsymbol{AD < AS}$ and the situation is one of deficient demand. The gap between the two refers to the deflationary gap (e) *Budget Surplus* can be defined as $\boldsymbol{BS}$ = Tax Revenue, net of transfer payments – government spending

$$= [T - R] - G$$
$$= [500 - 100] - 200$$
$$= \mathbf{200}$$

(f) As T is autonomous, and, R and G are both fixed, the budget surplus does not depend on output or income. It is the same whether at equilibrium or at the full employment.]

31. How would your answers to Q. 30 change if the economy opens up to foreign trade with exports (X) as 400 and autonomous imports (M_a) as 800? Estimate the trade balance and the import and export multipliers.

[**Ans:** (a) $Y = 8000$, $C = 7700$ and $S = 300$; (b) Relevant multipliers are $K_I = 4.00 = K_G$; $K_T = -3.00$, $K_R = 3.00$; $K_X = 4.00$ and $K_{Ma} = -4.00$. (c) $\Delta \boldsymbol{Y} = 12000 - 8000 =$ **4000.** Thus, the change needed in taxation, ΔT is given as **– 1333.33,** that needed in government spending, ΔG **= 1000;** that needed in transfer payments is ΔR **= 1333.33;** the change needed in investment, ΔI **= 1000;** that needed in exports is ΔX **= 1000** and the change needed in imports is ΔM_a **= – 1000.** (d) $\boldsymbol{AD}$ **= 8400** and $\boldsymbol{AS}$ **= 12000.** AD being less than AS, deficient demand exists and is equal to **3600.** (e) $\boldsymbol{BS}$ **= 200** (unchanged), (f) Answer is unchanged **Trade Balance** = $X - M = 400 - 800 =$ **– 400].**

32. Given that taxes are fixed taxes, show that increase in national income is limited to the amount of government spending or autonomous tax under a balanced budget.

33. Under the progressive taxation, show that the balanced budget multiplier is less than one and that the rise in national income is less than the government spending or autonomous taxes.

34. Explain the Keynesian process of income propagation. Why does it fail to take off in the undeveloped countries?

35. Distinguish between the excess demand and the deficient demand in each of the following cases:

(a) Economy has only two sectors, namely the household sector and the producers' sector

(b) Economy has only three sectors, namely the household sector, the producers' sector and the government sector

How can they be corrected in each case?

36. Distinguish between the inflationary gap and the deflationary gap in each of the following cases:

(a) Economy has only two sectors, namely the household sector and the producers' sector

(b) Economy has only three sectors, namely the household sector, the producers' sector and the government sector

How can they be corrected in each case?

37. Explain the multiplier-accelerator interaction and its effects on income propagation. Show that the accelerator works as an accelerator only in the initial stages of its operation.

38. 'Accelerator supports the multiplier process only to reverse it ultimately' Discuss.

39. 'An expansionary fiscal policy need not always be inflationary.' Examine the statement in the light of the inflationary gap.

[Hint: First explain the inflationary gap and the condition (attainment of full employment) responsible for its origin. Then discuss govt. expenditure (G) as a component of the AD. An increase in leads to a proportionate increase ($\Delta Y = K_G \times \Delta G$) in income until the income can no longer be increased. The only increase that takes place is in price in consequence to further increases in G caused by the expansionary fiscal policy. Hence show that inflation arises only after the attainment of full employment].

40. For an economy with following specifications:

$$C = 1000 + 0.8\,Y^d$$
$$T = 0.2\,Y$$
$$R = 100$$
$$I = I_a = 400$$
$$G = 320$$

Determine:

(i) Equilibrium level of income, tax revenue, disposable income and consumption expenditure.
(ii) Relevant multipliers.
(iii) Effect on income of each of the following changes:
  (a) Decrease in government spending by 20,
  (b) Increase in transfer payments by 20,
  (c) Increase in investment spending by 50, and
  (d) Increase in tax rate by 5%.
(iv) Budget surplus at the equilibrium level of income.

[Ans: (i) 5000; 1000; 4100; 4280
(ii) $K_G = 2.7778 = K_{Ia}$, $K_R = 2.2222$, $K_t = (-)\,11{,}111.11$.
(iii) (a) (–) 55.56, (b) 44.44, (c) 138.89, (d) (–) 555.55
(iv) 580.]

41. For a hypothetical economy with following specifications:

$$C = 1225 + 0.75\,Y$$
$$T = 100 + 0.2\,Y$$
$$I_a = 500$$
$$R = 200$$
$$G = 500$$
$$X = 200$$
$$M = 100 + 0.1\,Y$$

Determine:

(i) Equilibrium level of income, tax revenue, disposable income, consumption expenditure, imports and savings.
(ii) Relevant multipliers.
(iii) Effect on income of each of the following changes:
  (a) Increase in government spending by 50,
  (b) Increase in investment spending by 50,
  (c) Decrease in autonomous tax by 20,
  (d) Increase in exports by 50,
  (e) Increase in autonomous imports by 20,
  (f) Decrease in transfers by 50, and
  (g) Decrease in tax rate by 5%.
(iv) Budget surplus band net exports at the equilibrium level

[Ans: (i) 4800; 1060; 3940; 4180; 580; (–) 240
(ii) $K_G = 2.00 = K_{Ia} = K_X$, $K_R = 1.50$; $K_{Ta} = (-)\ 1.50$ $K_t = (-)\ 6697.67$; $K_{Ma} = (-)\ 2.00$
(iii) (a) 100, (b) 100, (c) (+) 30, (d) 100, (e) (–) 40, (f) (–) 75, (g) 334.88.
(iv) $BS = (+)\ 360$, $NX = 380$]

42. Distinguish between static and dynamic multipliers. Comment on the significance of a dynamic multiplier to a finance minister.

Chapter 7

Money, its Functions, and Money Market Equilibrium

INTRODUCTION

Ancient societies knew only two economic activities—production and consumption. Production was mostly for self-consumption. It comprised mainly of the subsistence goods. Human needs were few and societies were self-sufficient isolated units. They seldom felt the need for exchange. In case some exchange became inevitable, they worked out exchange of one commodity with another through mutual negotiations. The system of exchange, known as the ***barter system***, later gained ground with the passage of time as human activities acquired higher degree of specialization. A farmer specializing production of food grains learnt to raise surpluses with a view to exchange them with those commodities which he himself was not in a position to produce while his fellow farmers were, with some degree of specialization. Commodity exchange or the barter system was the only recourse in such societies. Barter, however, had its own drawbacks most of which stood in the way of trade and commerce. Let us cast a glance at them to understand the process and the purpose of the evolution of money.

7.1 BARTER AND ITS DRAWBACKS

Barter or commodity for commodity exchange suffered from the following drawbacks:

1. *Lack of Double Coincidence of Wants:* Quite often, two individuals do not need each other's products. For instance, a farmer, willing to exchange food grains for a cow, can't do so unless the owner of the cow is willing to accept food grains in exchange for the cow. What if the cow-owner wants goats in exchange for his cow? If he does, the farmer with food grains would have to locate another one who owns either goats or a cow and is also willing to exchange whatever he has for food grains at the same time. In case the latter owns a cow, the farmer's problem is solved. He can exchange his food grains for the cow and the matter is over. But if the latter owns goats, the farmer has to exchange his food grains for the latter's goats and then he has to lead these goats to the cow-owner to exchange them for the cow. What if the cow-owner has already concluded the deal with someone else? If he has, the farmer with goats would have to look for someone else who is willing to exchange his cow for the farmer's goats. The exchange of food grains for cow, if direct, implies existence of *double coincidence of wants*; and if indirect, it implies ***lack of double coincidence of wants.*** In the latter case, the process of exchange is a long one involving wastage of time and effort both.

2. *Lack of Divisibility of Certain Commodities:* Most often, commodities involved in exchange need not have identical values. What if the exchange involved splitting of the larger and the more valuable unit into smaller parts so that one or more parts of it may be exchanged for the smaller and the less valuable commodity? For example, the large commodity may be an elephant and the smaller one, a bunch of bananas. The owner of the elephant can't chop off the animal's earlobe to buy the fruit. Such commodities have to be given away as a whole unit even if it amounts to accepting the entire farm of bananas for which, the elephant-owner may have no desire.
3. *Lack of Common Denominator:* It is difficult to find a standard commodity as a unit of account to express the values of all the other commodities in. For instance, some measure of wheat may serve the purpose provided it possesses same value for all the individuals at all the times along with the attribute of general acceptability. Value of wheat depends on its demand, supply and quality. The attribute of its general acceptability is just non-existent because it is not required by all at all the times. A small piece of gold of a standard quality and fixed quantity may serve the purpose better as a unit of account. It also possesses the attribute of general acceptability. The only drawback it suffers from is its limited stocks possessed by nation-states.
4. *Lack of Store Value:* It is risky to store savings and surpluses in terms commodities that deteriorate in value with the passage of time. All perishable commodities lack the attribute of store value. The same is the case with animals and animal skins that age with time and require maintenance and care. Gold pieces of fixed purity and weight possess a very high ***store value.***
5. *Lack of Standard of Deferred Payments:* Contracts are often drawn in business requiring payments to be made in future (***deferred payments***) by one party to another. Commodity money fails to provide a standard unit of account in terms of which such payments be quoted in the agreements so as to arouse no uncertainty of value to be transferred at a point of time in future. For instance, if a payment is to be made 5 years hence in terms of a commodity, the agreeing parties may dispute the mode of payment (whether it should be through cows or goats or some other commodity). Then there could also be a dispute over the quantity (10 cows or 12 cows) of the commodity to be transferred. Finally, there could also be a dispute over the quality of the commodity (old cows or young cows) to be transferred. Thus, there is no standard commodity in terms of which a future payment can be agreed upon without involving an element of uncertainty of its value.

Clearly, the system of barter did initiate the exchange but failed to facilitate it with desired smoothness, acceptability and equability. With the passage of time, as human activities grew in complexity and as trade evolved as an economic activity, the need for some medium of exchange possessing the attributes of universal acceptability and measure and store of value was increasingly felt by the societies. Money of today fulfils these requirements but its evolution to its current form has preceded a number of stages and forms none of which was as perfect. Let us introduce some of these forms and stages, below.

7.1.1 Forms of Money through its Stages of Evolution

(1) Commodity as Money: Commodities of common need such as furs, skins, wheat, rice, etc. were used as money by primitive societies. Even cow, ox (in regions of warm climate), sea-shells (in coastal regions), tea (in Tibet), rice (in Japan), cattle (in Vedic India) were used as money by people.

(2) Metal Pieces as Money: Inadequacy of commodity money led to evolution of the metallic money. Pieces of copper, brass, iron, silver and gold substituted for commodity money with the passage of time. The problem of uniformity of weight, purity and fineness of precious metals to serve as money led to private and state coinage. Private coinage was done by goldsmiths who stamped their seals on pieces of metals as a mark of the quality and quantity of precious metals used in coinage. State coinage is believed to be innovated by the king of Lydia during 560 – 546 BC. Exact time of state coinage in India is not known but historical evidence shows that official coins were in circulation around 400 BC.

TABLE 7.1 Distinction Between Standard and Token Money

Standard Coin	*Token Coin*
1. It is the principal coin of a nation.	1. It is the subsidiary coin of a nation.
2. It is a full-bodied coin with the attribute that its face-value is equal to its intrinsic value.	2. It is not a full-bodied coin. The intrinsic value is less than its face-value.
3. Standard coins are made of gold or silver of a well defined weight, purity and fineness.	3. Token coins are made of inferior metals such as Nickel, Copper, Aluminium, etc.
4. Standard coins possess the attribute of free-coinage which implies that the mint is open for the public for getting their precious metals minted into standard coins.	4. Token coins don't possess the attribute of free-coinage. Public can't get the metals converted into coins.
5. Standard coins possess the property of unlimited legal tender, i.e., no one can refuse to accept value if paid in standard coins in any quantity.	5. Token coins don't possess this property. They are only limited legal tender, i.e., no one can be compelled to accept more than a certain limit.At present coin of half a rupee (50 paise) is legal tender for a sum not exceeding ten rupees and coin of any denomination not lower than one rupee is legal tender for any sum not exceeding one thousand rupees[1]. Thus all these coins are limited legal tender.
6. Standard coins possess following merits:	6. Token coins possess following merits:
(i) They inspire higher confidence in the holder.	(i) Token coins are economical as they cost less than their market value.
(ii) They provide an excellent means of storing purchasing power.	(ii) Token coins are highly elastic in supply as the metal used in their manufacture is cheaper and lighter.
(iii) There is no fear of inflation.	
7. Standard coins posses following demerits:	7. Token coins possess following demerits:
(i) They are non-economical as they cost the same as their market value.	(i) Token coins inspire less confidence in the holder.
(ii) They are less elastic in their supply which is always limited to the stocks of the precious metal.	(ii) Fear of inflation is always there.
(iii) They cause wastage of precious metal.	(iii) Token coins are unsuitable for storing wealth.
	(iv) They possess limited acceptability, particularly, abroad.
	(v) They are suitable only for smaller transactions.

[1] According to RBI's update of May 17, 2024, coins of any denomination not lower than one rupee shall be legal tender for any sum not exceeding one thousand while fifty paise coin shall be legal tender for any sum not exceeding ten rupees.

Coins issued have been of two types—***standard coins*** and ***token coins***. Standard coins are ***full bodied coins***. A full bodied coin is a coin for which the value of the metal it is made of (intrinsic value of the coin) is equal to the value marked on its face (face value of the coin). Standard coins have enjoyed ***free coinage*** and have been treated as an ***unlimited legal tender***. By free coinage we mean freedom to the common people to get their precious metals converted into coins from the mint and by unlimited legal tender we mean the legal money has to be accepted by all at its face value in unlimited quantities. Standard coin has thus been the principal coin of the nation. Token coin, on the other hand, has lacked free coinage and has served as a ***limited legal tender***. It has therefore served as a subsidiary coin of the nation. Token coins, not being full bodied, have had an attribute of lower intrinsic value than their face value. The distinction between the two types of coins is being drawn in Table 7.1.

Having gone through the distinguishing features of the two types of coins, let us come to the question whether Indian rupee is a token coin or a standard coin. Before 1893, Indian rupee used to be a standard coin. It was a full bodied coin made of silver with its face value being at par with its intrinsic value. It also enjoyed free coinage and the status of an unlimited legal tender. Thereafter, it transformed into the status of a token coin with the use of inferior metals in its manufacture. Its intrinsic value dropped much below its face value and it lost its status as an unlimited legal tender. Even the provision of free coinage was withdrawn. Today, it possesses some features of a standard coin and others of a token coin and is thus known as the ***standard token coin***. Withdrawal of both—the provision of free coinage and the status of unlimited legal tender—make it a token coin, but rapid fall of its face value and rise of its intrinsic value—both due to inflation—make it a full bodied coin. Hence, it is neither a pure standard coin nor a pure token coin. It is a blend of the two.

(3) Paper Money: Evolution of paper money traces its origin perhaps to the paper chits or receipts issued by goldsmiths to the individuals as an acknowledgement of the receipt of precious metals and other valuables for safe custody. Later, banks substituted for the goldsmiths and their promissory notes for the goldsmiths' chits or receipts. Initially, these promissory notes were convertible into precious metals at will and were thus known as the convertible paper money or simply as ***convertible currency***. In case of the issue of the convertible paper money, the issuing authority has to maintain metallic reserves to back up the conversion of currency issued. When such convertibility of paper currency into precious metals does not exist, the paper money is called as the ***inconvertible paper money*** or simply as *the* ***inconvertible currency***. Convertibility of currency into precious metals had been withdrawn by the nation-states when their currency requirements exceeded much beyond the stocks of the precious metals possessed by them. This exempted the monetary authority from the compulsion of of maintaining matching bullion reserves at the time of issuing currency.

Paper money was introduced in 9th century. The first country to use paper money was China. However, use of paper money on a large scale began in 17th and 18th centuries. In India, it started in the 19th century. It was the Bank of Bengal that first issued paper currency in 1806 in India. Paper money is classified under four heads:

1. Representative Paper Money which is fully backed by gold and silver reserves;
2. Convertible Paper Money which can be converted into standard coins or bullion at will;
3. Inconvertible Paper Money which is backed by no guarantee to convert it into standard coins or bullion; and
4. Fiat Money which is inconvertible paper currency issued only at the time of the crisis.

(4) Deposit Money: With evolution of commercial banking, another form of money called the ***deposit money*** or ***chequable deposits*** has gained ground. Commercial banks promise to honour the depositors' cheques upto the balance available in their deposit accounts with the bank.

(5) Near Money or Quasi-money: Instruments such as credit cards are known as ***near money***. They are not as good as cash or currency (money proper) in making transactions but are quite close to being that when it comes to transact goods and services. Credit cards are widely used by people while shopping. They serve as good as money in that regard. But shopping with credit cards proves a little costlier to the shoppers due to the transaction fee charged by the bank of issue. Moreover, use of the credit cards is not common everywhere. One can't use credit cards to buy vegetables and groceries from vendors nor can one use such instruments to pay the maid servant for her services. One can't buy a pencil or an eraser through it nor can one pay for the use of local transport such as taxi, rickshaw or local bus. That is, one can't make payments through it for small amounts. We need cash (money proper) for such transactions. Thus, credit card is not a perfect substitute of money proper. It is only a close substitute and hence is known as ***near money or quasi*-money.** Other instruments serving as near money are time deposits, treasury bills, bonds, debentures and bills of exchange.

A ***bill of exchange*** represents a promise to pay a fixed amount of money on a specified point of time in future. It can also be encased even earlier through the discounting process of a commercial bank.

A ***treasury bill*** is a promise of the government to pay a specified amount to the bearer after a specified period of time, usually 90 days of the issue of the bill.

Likewise, bonds and debentures represent long-term borrowings of government and commercial concerns. Even these instruments can be converted into money proper through the discounting process of the commercial banks.

Credit cards impart liquidity to the holders at specified establishments. Expenditure of the people is thus no longer limited to the stock of cash (money proper) possessed by them but it extends to include near money as well. Near money differs from money proper in two respects—*first*, it can't function as a medium of exchange without general acceptability and *second*, it has a cost to function as money which the holder has to bear in the form of transaction fees and the annual charges in respect of credit cards and discounting charges in respect of other instruments of near money.

(6) Legal Tender Money: All types of money that have legal sanction behind them are called the ***legal tender money***. It has to be accepted by all. It is called ***limited legal tender*** when no one can be forced to accept it beyond a certain limit which varies from denomination to denomination. According to RBI's update of May 17, 2024, coins of any denomination not lower than one rupee shall be legal tender for any sum not exceeding one thousand while fifty paise coin shall be legal tender for any sum not exceeding ten rupees. On the other hand, money, which a person has to accept up to any limit, is called the ***unlimited legal tender***.

(7) Optional Money: That form of money which is ordinarily accepted by people without a legal obligation to do so is called the ***optional money***. Accepting payments through the modes of cheques, *hundies* and bills of exchange is a normal practice in day-to-day business but if a recipient refuses to accept them, there is no legal provision to compel him/her for. In other words, it is the recipient's discretion to accept or to reject such modes of payment. No one, on the other hand, can refuse to accept a payment if it is made in currency, the legal tender of the nation.

(8) Fiat Money: ***Fiat money***, also called as the ***emergency currency***, is a form of inconvertible paper money, issued generally at a time of crisis. It does not require maintenance of any kind of reserves behind it. Monetary authorities have to give no assurance to convert it into any metal or metallic coins.

Imposing no compulsion of a cover on the monetary authorities, it is quite tempting to issue fiat money whenever in crisis. The risks that put a restraint on its issue are mainly twofold—*first*, it does not enjoy the confidence of public and *second*, its issue entails the danger of inflation. If issued in controlled quantities, it can stimulate economic development in underdeveloped countries.

(9) Credit Money: ***Credit money*** refers to money whose intrinsic value is less than its face value. The face value of a hundred rupee note is ₹ 100 but its intrinsic value is the value of the paper of which it is made. The value of the paper is much less than the face value of the currency note. Forms of money such as deposit money, currency notes, token coins, representative money and the like for which the value of the commodity they are made up of or the value of bullion they are backed up with fall short of their face value are all examples of credit money. ***Representative money*** refers to the paper money backed up with an equivalent amount of bullion or metallic coins.

7.2 DEFINITIONS AND FUNCTIONS OF MONEY

7.2.1 Definitions

Money has been defined in a number of ways. Some of these definitions are known as the ***narrow definitions*** while others as the ***broad definitions***. Narrow definitions focus on money as a ***medium of exchange*** through which liabilities may be discharged and transactions affected smoothly. Broad definitions, on the other hand, expect money not only to serve as a medium of exchange but also to eliminate all the drawbacks of barter that obstructed smoothness in trade and commerce. That way, money, in the broad sense, must serve as ***measure and store of value*** as also the ***standard of deferred payments*** apart from acting as a medium of exchange.

According to Harry G. Johnson[1], there are broadly four approaches to define money. Here, we provide a brief account of these for the benefit of the reader:

(1) Conventional Approach: The conventional approach, the oldest known approach to the definition of money, refers to those definitions of money which are based on certain function(s) money is expected to perform. Some of these definitions are mentioned below:

(a) "Money is what money does"–Withers.
(b) "Money is anything that possesses general acceptability" –Marshall.
(c) "Anything that is generally acceptable as a *means of exchange,* and at the same time acts as a *measure and store of value,* is money"–Crowther, Geoffrey[2].

Definition (a), however, make no mention of the essential functions of money explicitly. It leaves them to the interpreter. Definition (b) refers only to the general acceptability of money while definition (c) makes explicit reference to the functions money is to perform. Thus, definition (c) is the most comprehensive and explicit definition of money, and therefore, the best one so far.

(2) The Chicago School Approach: In this approach, some of the definitions given by the Chicago University group of the monetary theorists are included. We mention two of them below:

(a) Money is "currency plus total commercial bank deposits adjusted"–Friedman, Phillip Cagan, David Fand, David Meiselman and A. J. Schwartz.
(b) "Anything that serves the function of providing a temporary abode for general purchasing power"–Milton Friedman.

Definition (a) includes quasi-money (near money) explicitly in money while definition (b) does so implicitly. The conventional approach treats *money-proper* as money while the Chicago approach includes quasi-money too in it.

[1] Harry G. Johnson, *Monetary Theory and Policy,* American Economic Review, Volume 52, June1952, pp. 351–354.
[2] Crowther, Geoffrey, An Outline of Money, p. 20.

(3) Gurley and Shaw Approach: Like Chicago approach, this approach also includes quasi-money in money along with money-proper, but unlike the Chicago approach, it provides a broader definition of money by including the liabilities of non-bank financial intermediaries[1] in quasi-money along with the demand[2] and the time[3] deposits of the commercial banks. In their work entitled *Money in a Theory of Finance*, John G. Gurley and Edward S. Shaw define money as "*the concept of money relevant to monetary theory and policy should include the liabilities of non-bank financial intermediaries together with currency* (***money-proper***) *and commercial bank demand and time deposits* (***quasi-money***)".

(4) The Central Bank Approach: The central bank approach provides the broadest possible definition to money. It defines money in terms of ***credit funds*** *lent to borrows*. Thus, currency and all other means of financing the purchases are included in the definition of money. The approach resembles the Gurley and Shaw Approach in that it includes the near money in the definition of money but it differs from the Gurley and Shaw Approach in that it provides much broader definition to money by including credits such as overdraft and loans in the definition of money.

To sum up, Crowther's definition continues to be an ideal one as it defines money as something possessing universal acceptability as a medium of exchange and at the same time, a measure and store of value. No doubt near money constitutes a part of the purchasing power but it can't possess the attribute of universal acceptability as a medium of exchange. It is in this sense that near money should be treated as such, rather than raising it to the level of money-proper.

7.2.2 Functions of Money

Functions of money can be classified into four heads:

1. Primary or main functions of money
2. Secondary functions of money
3. Contingent functions of money
4. Other functions of money

Let us discuss them in brief for clarity of concept.

(1) Primary Functions of Money: Functions that money has essentially to perform are known as its primary functions. They are two—the medium of exchange and the measure of value.

(a) *Medium of Exchange:* One of primary functions of money is to serve as a ***medium of exchange*** for day-to-day transactions. The property of general acceptability of money was basically intended to do away with the main drawback of the barter system, *the lack of double coincidence of wants*. Under barter, the buyer and the seller both must be willing to exchange their goods, but most often, they were not. This drawback of barter adversely affected the smoothness of trade and commerce. Evolution of money was intended to serve as a medium of exchange so that trade and commerce may progress smoothly. Lack of double coincidence of wants no longer obstructs trade mainly due to this function of money.

(b) *Measure of Value:* The other primary function of money is that money must serve as a measuring rod for value of goods and services. As a ***measure of value***, money facilitates pricing of products which is so crucial for exchange. The number of money units that represent

[1] Non-bank financial intermediaries include shares, bonds, units of investment trusts, post office saving deposits, etc. all of which possess convertibility into cash to a high degree.

[2] Demand deposits, such as the current account, are deposits that can be withdrawn through cheques.

[3] Time deposits are fixed deposits made for a fixed period of time. Against such deposits, most of the banks provide cash credit facility to the depositors. Under the cash credit facility, almost 90% of the fixed deposit can be converted into cash before its maturity.

the value of a good or of a service is called its price. Thus money has come to serve as a common denominator so that value of all goods and services may be expressed in terms of its units. The barter system suffered from the *lack of common denominator*. This obstructed pricing and hence exchange. Evolution of money had intended to remove this drawback so that trade may be smooth and rewarding.

(2) Secondary Functions of Money: The following ones are known as the secondary functions of money:

(i) *Standard of Deferred Payments:* Lending and borrowing, so common and so essential in trade, could not be possible under barter system due to *lack of standard of deferred payments.* In business, payments for goods received at a point of time now are often put off to a point of time in future. Such payments are known as **deferred payments.** Use of a commodity with highly flexible value lent an element of uncertainty to the value of the repayment. This discouraged credit and loans. Evolution of money must eliminate this uncertainty and must provide a ***standard of deferred payments***.

(ii) *Store of Value:* Storing surpluses or savings involved the risk of loss of value with the passage of time under the barter system. Savings and surpluses were stored in terms of goods either perishable or susceptible to loss of value due to deterioration, infliction and such other time and age-related factors. This defeated the process of storing surpluses.

(iii) *Transfer of Purchasing Power:* Transfer of purchasing power from one place to another or from one individual to another in terms of assets under barter involved transfer-costs and transit-damages. Evolution of money had to do away with such wastages. Today, money makes it possible to move even the immovable property from one place to another through its conversion into cash at the place of its origin and then back into immovable property at the desired location.

(3) Contingent Functions of Money: In addition to the above, money performs certain additional functions in developed countries. These functions well described as the ***contingent functions*** by Prof. Kinley are as given below:

(a) *As the Basis of all Credit:* In developed and developing countries, credit plays a very important role in all economic activities. Instruments of credit, such as the ***bills of exchange,*** etc. are in extensive use in developed countries. Money forms the basis of such credit instruments.

(b) *As the Basis of Distribution of Income:* Share of each factor of production in the total output is measured in terms of money. This was exceedingly difficult under barter system. Each factor can now be duly compensated for its services in terms of money. Money thus helps distribution of income.

(c) *As the Basis of Maximization of Total Utility by the Consumer and Total Productivity by the Producer:* Money plays an important role in utility maximization by the consumer and productivity maximization by producers.

Value of goods and services expressed in terms of money makes it possible for a consumer to compare the marginal utility of a product with that of money the consumer is to forego for it. A simple mathematical treatment can show that the utility maximizing level of consumption requires equating the marginal utility of money to the marginal utility of the product.

In the same way, equating marginal productivity of a factor of production to the marginal utility of money being paid in compensation to the factor helps the cause of cost minimization and productivity maximization by the producers.

(4) Other Functions of Money: Through its mere existence, money plays the following important roles:

(i) As Guarantor of Solvency.
(ii) As Bearer of the Last Option.
(iii) As an Instrument that renders liquidity to capital.
(iv) As the Basis of the Price mechanism.

Money, due to its general acceptability, serves as a ***guarantor of solvency***.

Possession of liquidity (cash) serves as a safeguard against insolvency.

Holding wealth in the form of money imparts the last option to the holder. Suppose you enter in partnership with a person who is not as reliable as you think. He wants your contribution in the form of your building or an equivalent amount of cash. If you chose the former and committed your building by way of your share, you can't opt out of partnership without suffering loss. But if you chose your contribution in cash, you can opt out unscathed.

Choice between asset or cash in payments, it is cash that imparts the last option to the holder to go for it or to withdraw from it. An asset poses problems of valuation which under distress amounts to distress sale. But if wealth is stocked as cash, it can serve as ***bearer of the last option*** by helping the holder to choose the best among its available alternative uses.

Money is the most liquid form of the capital. It helps a variety of motives of the individuals. For instance, money provides for certain anticipated or non-anticipated transactions in day-to-day functioning of business or in day-to-day needs of domestic life. Such motives money serves are called the ***transaction motives***. In like manner, people store cash as a safeguard against unforeseen contingencies. Such motives are called the ***precautionary motives***. People hold cash for acquiring shares and such other liquid assets when their market prices crash. This they do to avoid loss of such opportunities. Prof. Keynes calls such motives as the ***speculative motives***.

TABLE 7.2 Functions of Money

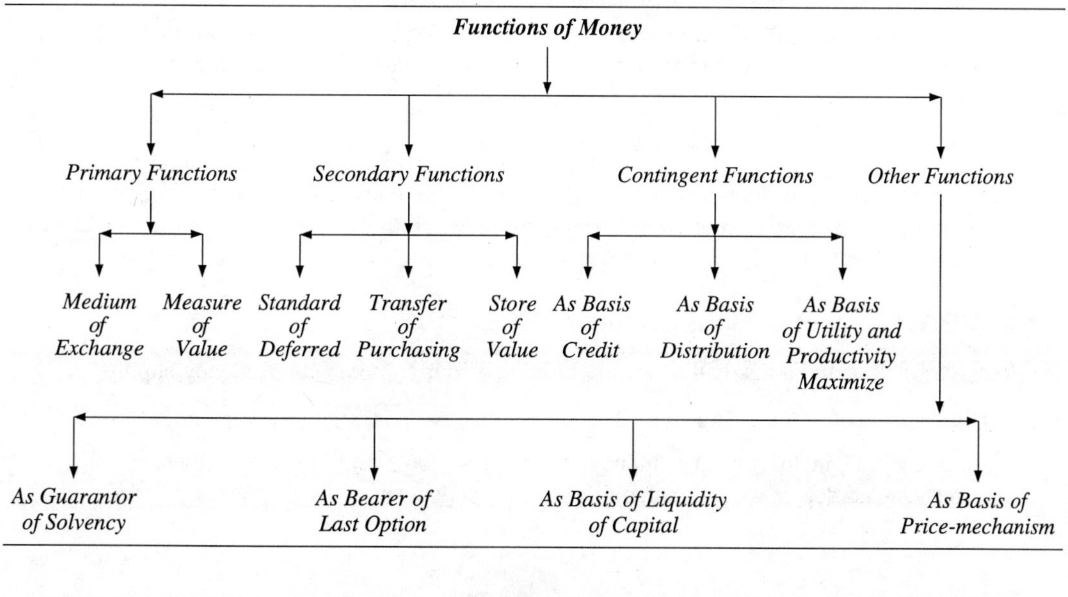

Price mechanism *can't* function without the institution of money. Prices are expressed in terms of monetary units, which forms the basis of exchange.

In sum, money was invented to serve as a medium of exchange and as a measure and store of value, but it turned out to be doing much more than that. Its contribution to the modern industrial world is so crucial that it is impossible even to think of a money-less society, leave alone the question of running it. The role of money is of identical importance in all economic systems—be it capitalistic, socialistic or mixed in nature. Table 7.2 summarizes the functions of money.

7.3 SUPPLY OF MONEY

Supply of money refers to aggregate stock of domestic money owned by public in the country. The term public refers to the private individuals and firms operating in the economy.

Cash balances held by the central and the state governments, those held by central bank, treasury and commercial banks do not comprise money supply. The reason for their exclusion from the supply of money is the fact that cash balances held by them are not in actual circulation in the country. Money supply thus refers to the total volume of money circulating in the public at a point of time (Being a stock concept, money supply always refers to a point of time).

There are mainly two concepts of money supply:

(a) *Narrow Concept:* According to this concept, all assets that serve as medium of exchange are to be included in money supply. Generally, economists consider currency and demand deposits as the two components of money supply, M^s, which can thus be expressed as:

$$M^s = C + DD \tag{7.1}$$

Here, C refers to *currency* and DD to ***net demand deposits***. The term *net* refers to that part of the demand deposits which can be withdrawn through cheques by public. Net demand deposits can be obtained by subtracting the inter-bank deposits from the total demand deposits. The inter-bank deposits refer to deposits of one bank held with the other bank(s). Such deposits can't be withdrawn by public.

(b) *Broader Concept:* The broader concept of money supply is based not only on the medium of exchange function of money but also on the store value function of it. Accordingly, all the assets possessing liquidity to serve as a store of value, along with currency and demand deposits of the public, comprise money supply in broader sense. The expression for money supply in this sense can be made as:

$$M^s = C + DD + TD \tag{7.2}$$

Here, TD refers to ***time deposits*** (fixed deposits) with commercial banks as well as with the post offices and DD, to the ***net demand deposits***. Note that the time deposits qualify as a component of money supply in broader sense.

7.3.1 RBI's Concept of Money Supply

The Reserve Bank of India has laid down the following four components of money supply:

(1) M_1 Component of Money Supply: This component of money supply refers to:

(a) Currency, C, including paper money and metallic coins of all denominations,
(b) Net demand deposits, DD, including the savings deposits with the banking sector, and

(c) Other Deposits, *OD*, refer to the deposits of quasi-government institutions with *RBI* such as Industrial Finance Corporation of India, State Finance Corporations, Industrial Development Bank of India, Agricultural Refinance and Development Corporation, deposits of International Monetary Fund (*IMF*) in Account No. 2, deposits of foreign governments and foreign central banks and the deposits of *RBI's* Employees Co-operative Credit Societies. It is to be noted that other deposits with the Central Bank here do not include the deposits of government, commercial banks and the *IMF* deposits in Account No.1.
Thus,

$$M_1 = \text{Currency} + \text{Net Demand Deposits with Banks} + \text{Other Deposits with RBI}$$

$$\boldsymbol{M_1 = C + DD + OD} \qquad (7.3)$$

M_1 as a measure of money supply has been found highly useful by the monetarists in their theoretical analysis of income, price-level, and money supply. Another argument that goes in favour of M_1 is the exclusion of time deposits from the components of money supply. Many scholars believe that time deposits should not be included in money supply due to their non-uniform maturities and their resemblance with non-money financial assets. However, exclusion of time deposits from M_1 makes it a ***narrow measure of money supply.***

(2) M_2 Component of Money Supply: This component of money supply is devised to include post office savings deposits in the M_1 component of money supply. Thus,

$$\boldsymbol{M_2 = M_1 + \textit{Post Office Savings Deposits}} \qquad (7.4)$$

Note that the time deposits remain excluded even from M_2, making it a ***narrow measure of money supply.*** In terms of liquidity, M_2 ranks next to M_1.

(3) M_3 Component of Money Supply: M_3 is the sum of M_1 and the time deposits. Hence, it represents a ***broader measure of money supply*** and is known as the ***Aggregate Monetary Resource*** (*AMR*). Thus,

$$M_3 = M_1 + \textit{Time Deposits}$$

$$= \boldsymbol{M_1 + TD} \qquad (7.5)$$

M_3 as a measure of money supply is shown preference not only by *RBI* but also by economists such as Milton Friedman. Even Chakravarty Committee has favoured M_3 to M_1 as a measure of money supply. The need for evolution of M_3 was perhaps intentional. *RBI* might have an intention to impart high level of liquidity to the time deposits at some point of time. The fact may be evidenced by its recent policy of allowing the commercial banks to grant cash credit upto 90% of the time deposits to the depositors. Under it, depositor can enjoy credit facility to the tune of 90% of the time deposit and can continue with their time deposits which they had otherwise to discontinue in the event of cash requirement. Time deposits under the circumstances, do no longer resemble the other non-money financial assets and hence should be included in the money supply. Inclusion of the time deposits in M_3 makes it a ***broader measure of money supply***. In liquidity, M_3 ranks below M_1 and M_2.

(4) M_4 Component of Money Supply: M_4 is the sum of M_3 and the Post Office Savings Deposits. It represents broader concept of money supply.
Thus,

$$\boldsymbol{M_4 = M_3 + \text{Post Office Savings Deposits}} \qquad (7.6)$$

While M_2 is an extension of M_1, M_4 is an extension of M_3. M_2 and M_4 are recent concepts. In liquidity, M_2 ranks above M_4.

RBI periodically provides estimates of money supply in terms of M_1, M_2, M_3 and M_4 to indicate varying degrees of liquidity of different components of money supply. If arranged in descending order of liquidity, the four components will follow the order M_1, M_2, M_3 and M_4.

While M_1 and M_2 provide the narrow measures of money supply, M_3 and M_4 provide its broader measures.

We have seen that money supply is a stock concept. The volume of money supply at a point of time would depend on the magnitude of constituents of a particular component (M_1 or M_2 or M_3 or M_4) being used by the economy's monetary system at that point of time. The four components have their relative merits and demerits, a comprehensive discussion of which is beyond the scope of this text. Emphasis has, however, rested on the use of M_1 or M_3 to measure money supply at a point of time. Prior to 1978, *RBI* concentrated on the use of M_1 for the purpose but thereafter, it has shifted to M_3 (*AMR*) as a measure of money supply. Hence, volume of money supply would depend on the magnitudes of the constituents of M_3, namely, currency (*C*), demand deposits (*DD*), other deposits (*OD*) and time deposits (*TD*).

In the same way, changes in the volume of money supply over a period of time would depend on changes in these constituents of M_3. Both, the magnitudes of the constituents and the changes therein, depend on *policies* of monetary institutions. We will return to the monetary policy in Chapter 10.

7.3.2 *H*-Theory of Money Supply

Concepts and measures of money supply discussed so far relate to supply of ordinary money (*M*), referring to money, as people generally understand it. Monetarists often distinguish it from what they call ***high powered money*** (*H*) while discussing the theories of money supply. According to them, the single most factor determining money supply is the high powered money (*H*) defined as money produced by the central bank and the government and held by the public and banks. It consists of:

(i) Currency, *C*, including coins and notes in circulation with the public,
(ii) Cash reserves, *R*, held by commercial banks as vault cash, and
(iii) Other deposits, *OD*, of central bank.

High powered money can thus be expressed as:

$$H = C + R + OD \tag{7.7}$$

Other deposits (*OD*) being a small proportion of total money supply, if dropped from Equation (7.7) for simplicity, the expression for *H* transforms to:

$$H = C + R \tag{7.8}$$

With '*c*' representing the currency-demand-deposit ratio (*C*/*DD*) and '*r*' representing reserve-deposit ratio (*R*/*D*), Equation (7.8) transforms to:

$$\begin{aligned} H &= c.DD + r.D \\ &= c.DD + r.\,(DD + TD) \\ &= c.DD + r.\,(DD + t.DD) \end{aligned} \tag{7.9}$$

[where, (*D*) = (*DD* + *TD*) and *TD* = *t*. *DD*, *TD* ≡ Time deposits, *DD* ≡ Demand deposits and '*t*' ≡ *TD*/*DD*]

Rewriting Equation 7.9 in terms of *DD*, we have,

$$H = [c + r\,(1 + t)].DD \tag{7.10}$$

Rewriting Equation 7.1 with money supply (M^S) denoted simply as *M*, we have

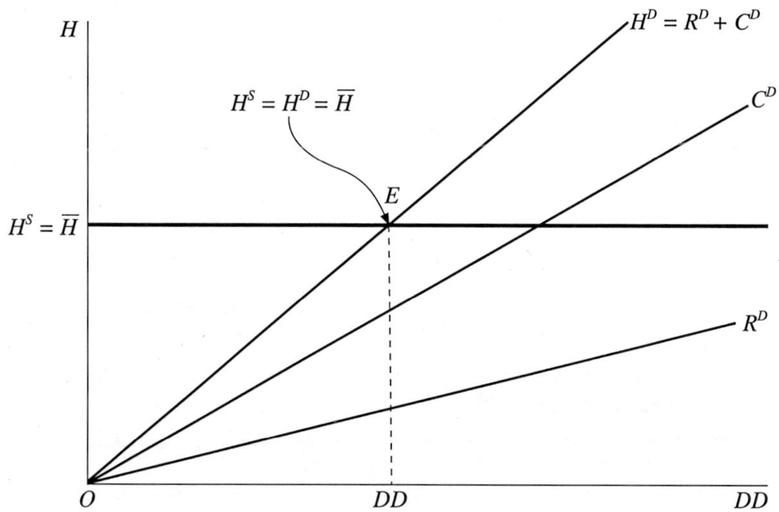

FIGURE 7.1 ***Equilibrium level of H.*** Supply of high powered money (H^S) being fixed, it yields a horizontal line described by $H^S = \overline{H}$. Demand for high powered money, H^D, comprising demands of currency and reserves, is given as the vertical summation of R^D and C^D. H^D intersects $H^S = \overline{H}$ at point E which marks the equilibrium of the H-market. Equilibrium level of demand deposits (DD, measured on x-axis) is given as DD_E and that of *high powered money* (measured on y-axis) as $H^S = \overline{H}$.

$$
\begin{aligned}
M &= C + DD \\
&= c.DD + DD \\
&= (1 + c).\ DD \\
&= [(1 + c)/\{c + r\,(1 + t)\}] \times H \qquad (7.11)
\end{aligned}
$$

(Substituting for DD from Equation 7.10) and treating TD as significantly small, implying, $t = 0$, we can have

$$
\begin{aligned}
M &= [(1 + c)/(c + r)]H \qquad (7.12) \\
&= m.H \qquad (7.13)
\end{aligned}
$$

where,

$$m = \frac{(1 + c)}{(c + r)}$$

That is, money supply is directly proportional to the high powered money. where, proportionality constant 'm' can be taken as the derivative of M with respect to H, that is, (dM/dH) and is called the ***money multiplier.***

$$dM/dH = m = [(1 + c)/(c + r)] \qquad (7.14)$$

In either case, when increase in H is not infinitesimally small, increase in M may be given as:

$$\Delta M = m \times \Delta H = [(1 + c)/(c + r)] \times \Delta H \qquad (7.15)$$

Inferences drawn from Equations 7.13 and 7.14 support the statement that *high powered money is the single most determinant of money supply, given c, r and t. It is for this reason that high powered money (H) is at times called the money base.*

Equilibrium level of high powered money can thus be determined through the interaction of its demand and supply.

At a given stock of $\bar{H}$ its supply is fixed and is given as:

$$H^S = \bar{H} \tag{7.16}$$

Likewise demand for high powered money (H^D) can be expressed as the vertical summation of demands of currency and reserves. *The expression for its demand therefore* can be given as:

$$H^D = C^D + R^D \qquad \text{[(From Equation (7.8)]} \tag{7.17}$$

Figure 7.1 shows working of the equilibrium. An illustration would drive the concept home.

ILLUSTRATION 7.1: Government purchases goods and services from public worth ₹ 90.00 crore. Given that currency deposit ratio (c) as 0.50 and reserve deposit ratio (r) as 0.10, determine deposit and money multipliers and hence calculate the volume of additional deposits and money created by the high powered money of ₹ 90.00 crore.

Solution: Govt. purchases create additional high powered money, $\Delta H = 90.00$. Given $c = 0.50$, and $r = 0.10$.

Consequential change in money supply,

$$\Delta M = \frac{(1+c)}{(c+r)} \times \Delta H$$

$$= \frac{(1+0.50)}{(0.50+0.10)} \times 90.00$$

$$= \mathbf{225.00}$$

That is, money supply increases by ₹ 225 crore. Money multiplier, m, from Equation 7.14, works out as:

$$m = \frac{(1+c)}{(c+r)}$$

$$= \frac{(1+0.50)}{(0.50+0.10)}$$

$$= \mathbf{2.50}$$

From Equation 7.9, we have

$$H = c.DD + r.\,(DD + t.DD)$$

$$= (c + r)DD \qquad \text{(treating } t = 0\text{)}$$

$$\Rightarrow \qquad DD = H/(c + r)$$

$$\Rightarrow \qquad \Delta(DD) = \Delta H/(c + r)$$

$$= 90.00/(0.50 + 0.10)$$

$$= \mathbf{150.00}$$

That is, deposits increase by ₹ 150.00 crore.

Deposit multiplier,

$$\Delta(DD)/\Delta H = 1/(c + r)$$

$$= 1/0.6$$

$$= \mathbf{1.67}$$

The mechanism of money supply through high powered money can also be explained as below without the use of the formulae developed above:

As soon as public receives ₹ 90.00 crore for sale of goods and services to the government, it makes deposit of ₹ 90.00 crore with its bank. The cheque is sent for collection by its bank and the amount lands in its account. As soon as this happens, public divides the amount between currency held and bank-deposit maintained in such a way that 50% of the bank deposit must be cash in hand ($c = 0.50$). In other words, C/DD being 0.50 and $C + DD = 90.00$, DD would work out at ₹ 60 crore while the currency held by public at ₹ 30 crore.

As soon as the bank realizes a deposit of ₹ 60 crore, it retains ₹ 6.00 crore [10% of 60, $r = 0.10$) as vault cash by way of reserve and lends the rest, ₹ 54.00 crore (60 – 6) to prospective borrowers. [Vault cash may be treated as ready cash to be maintained by the bank to meet the future cash requirement , if any, of the deposit making public]. The remainder 54 crore lent out to borrowers causes fresh deposit of ₹ 54.00 crore with the bank. The borrower would split the amount between currency and deposit in the same manner (C/DD is 0.50 and $C + DD = 54$) withdraws ₹ 18 crore as cash in hand and keeps ₹ 36 crore as demand deposit.

This creates fresh deposits of ₹ 36 crore, of which, banks would retain ₹ 3.60 crore (10% of ₹ 36 crore) as vault cash and the remainder, ₹ 32.40 (36 – 3.60) crore, they would lend out to prospective borrowers. The borrowers would split it between currency and deposit components as per $C/DD = 0.50$ and $C + DD = 32.40$ and would withdraw cash amounting to ₹ 10.80 crore leaving ₹ 21.60 Crore with their banks by way of fresh deposits.

This would lead to subsequent deposits of ₹ 21.60 crore. The process of lending and currency–deposit splitting would continue indefinitely until banks are left with nothing to lend. Additional deposits in respective rounds increase by ₹ 60 crore, 36 crore, 21.60 crore ,and so on and currency held by public by ₹ 30 crore, ₹ 18 crore, ₹ 10.80 crore, ...and so on while vault cash with banks by ₹ 6.00 crore, ₹ 3.60 crore, ₹ 2.16 crore,... and so on. Total additional deposits would work out at ₹ 150 crore, Total additional currency held by public and banks as ₹ 75 crore. Thus additional money pumped into the economy would work out at ₹ 225 crore.

7.4 DEMAND FOR MONEY

The term *Demand for Money* has been interpreted in two different senses depending on different views held in regard to the functions of money:

1. Money as a medium of exchange
2. Money as a store of value

Accordingly, there are two concepts of demand for money:

(a) Medium of exchange concept, often referred to as *the classical approach,* and
(b) Store value concept, referred to as *the Keynesian approach.*

Let us discuss them in that order.

7.4.1 Classical Approach to Demand for Money

The main exponents of this approach are J.S. Mill, Irving Fisher, Marshall, Pigou and Robertson—all grouped as the *classical economists.* They argued that money is not demanded for its own sake, that is, not for its store value but only for facilitating transactions of goods and services demanded by people to satisfy their needs. They held that the demand for money is the derived demand. *The larger the volume of the transactions of goods and services, the larger is the demand for money*. Also, the larger the volume of transactions of goods and services, the larger must be the level of income. Demand for money can thus be said to depend on the supply of exchangeable goods and services in the market or on the level of income enjoyed by the people, on which, the volume of such transactions of goods and services depend. The classical version of demand for money (M^d) is thus limited to the ***transaction demand*** (M_t) and can be expressed as

$$M^d = M_t \text{ and } M_t \propto Y$$

$$\Rightarrow \quad M^d = kY \tag{7.18}$$

where, Y is the output of goods and services in monetary units and k is the constant of proportionality.

Figure 7.2 portrays the classical version of demand for money.

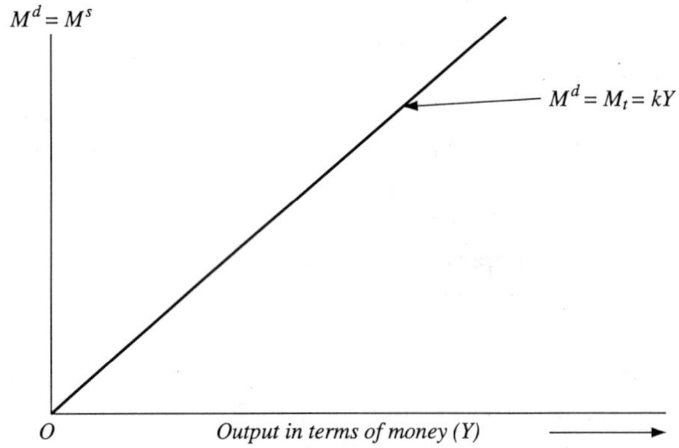

FIGURE 7.2 Representing output in terms of money as Y on the horizontal axis and demand for money solely as the transaction demand ($M^D = M_t$) on the vertical axis, classical version of demand for money given by Equation 7.18 is portrayed as a ray passing through the origin.

7.4.2 Keynesian Approach to the Demand for Money

J. M. Keynes, in his *General Theory of Employment, Interest and Money,* stressed on the store value function of money, while accounting for the demand for it. Keynes, in divergence from the Cambridge economists Marshall, Pigou and Robertson, held that money is demanded by people not only for transaction purposes but also for the precautionary and speculative purposes. Demand for money, according to him, is the sum total of its demand for all the three purposes. Demand for money for transaction motives is a function of income [Figure 7.3(a)] and is perfectly interest inelastic [Figure 7.3(b)]. The same is the case with its demand for precautionary motives [Figures 7.4(a) and (b)]. Transactory and precautionary demands are therefore clubbed together as first component, L_1, of demand for liquidity which is perfectly interest inelastic. Apart from transaction and precautionary motives, Keynes held that money is demanded for speculative motives as well. The latter, denoted as L_2, is a function of interest alone [Figure 7.6 (b)] which forms the second component of total demand for money.

Before proceeding any further with the derivation of total demand for money, let us first understand its three components discussed above.

7.4.2.1 Transaction demand for money

J.M. Keynes endorsed the classical version of the demand for money only to the extent that its demand for transactory motives is only one part of its total demand. He also endorsed the view that this demand, known as the transaction demand, depends on the volume of transactions and hence on income [(Figure 7.3(a)], but it is perfectly interest inelastic [(Figure 7.3(b)]. People set aside a portion of their incomes to give effect to the transactions they have in mind in immediate future. For example, households set aside a portion of their incomes every month and hold it in liquid (cash) form so that they may keep buying their day-to-day needs of vegetables, bread, butter, detergents, etc. through it. It is of common knowledge that they won't part with this portion of income whatever the rate of interest offered by the borrowers. It is one part of the first component of demand for money, L_1.

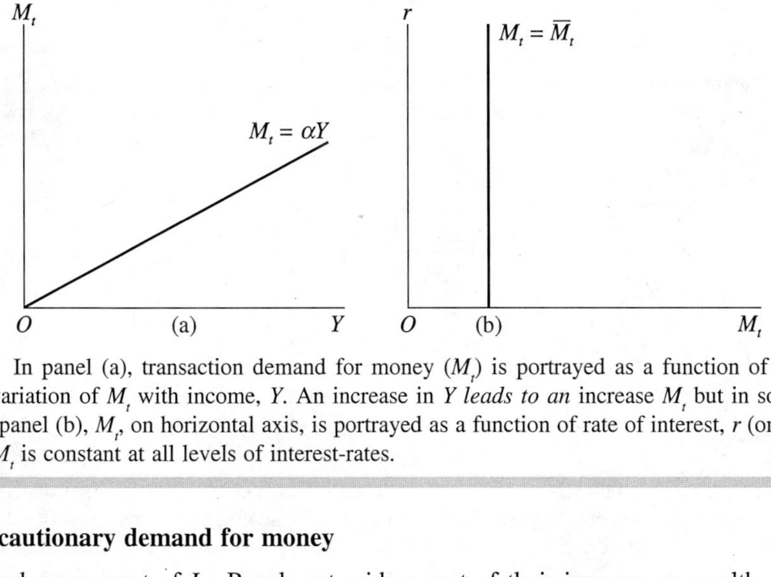

FIGURE 7.3 In panel (a), transaction demand for money (M_t) is portrayed as a function of income (Y). It shows direct variation of M_t with income, Y. An increase in Y *leads to an* increase M_t but in somewhat lesser proportion. In panel (b), M_t, on horizontal axis, is portrayed as a function of rate of interest, r (on vertical axis). It shows that M_t is constant at all levels of interest-rates.

7.4.2.2 Precautionary demand for money

It is the second component of L_l. People set aside a part of their incomes or wealth and hold it in the liquid form (as cash balances) as a safeguard against the unforeseen. Such cash balances, held by people as a precautionary measure, represent the store value concept of demand for money. Like the transaction demand, precautionary demand is also interest inelastic depending solely on the level of income. The main point of difference between the two is that the transaction demand for money is based on the medium of exchange function of money while the pre-cautionary demand for it is based on the store value function of money. The transaction demand is meant for current or short run expenditures, most of which are anticipated ones. On the contrary, precautionary demand is meant for unforeseen or non-anticipated expenditures whether in short run or in long run. Moreover, transaction demand is a recurring phenomenon while precautionary demand is not. Figure 7.4 shows variation of the precautionary demand with income as well as with rate of interest.

7.4.2.3 Reconciling transaction and precautionary components

We have seen that L_1 component of the total demand of money is income elastic but interest inelastic. As a function of income, it can be derived through a vertical summation of M_t and M_p (panel 'a' of Figure 7.5) and as a function of rate of interest (r), it can be derived as a horizontal summation of the two (panel 'b' of Figure 7.5).

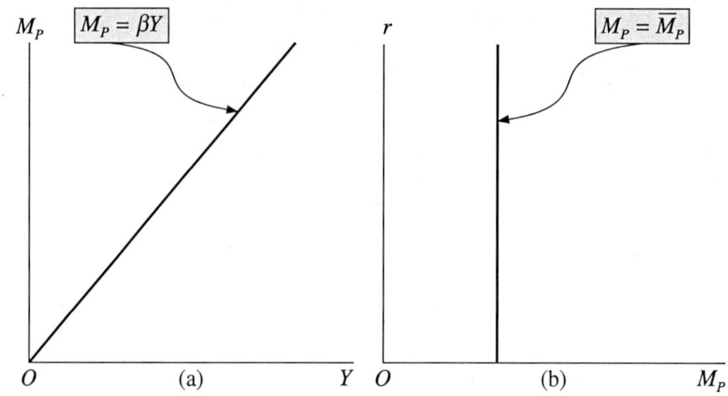

FIGURE 7.4 Just like transaction demand (Figure 7.3), the precautionary demand is perfectly interest inelastic [panel (b)] and income elastic [panel (a)].

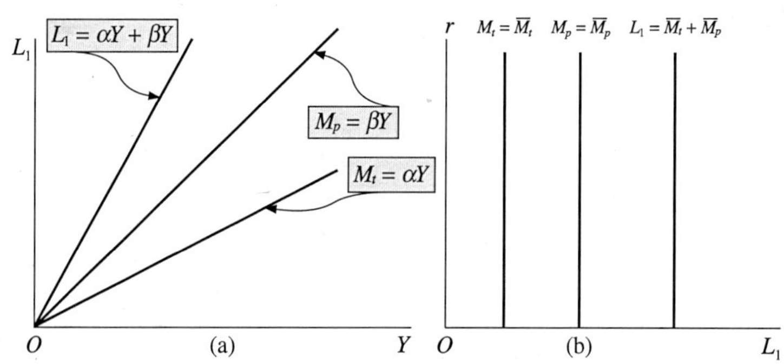

FIGURE 7.5 L_1 as a function of income is obtained as a vertical summation of M_t and M_p (panel a) and L_1 as a function of rate of interest is obtained as a horizontal summation of M_t and M_p (panel b).

In the first case,

$$\begin{aligned} L_1 &= \text{Transaction Demand} + \text{Precautionary Demand} \\ &= M_t + M_p \\ &= \alpha Y + \beta Y = (\alpha + \beta)\, Y = kY \end{aligned} \tag{7.19}$$

In the second case,

$$\begin{aligned} L_1 &= \text{Transaction Demand} + \text{Precautionary Demand} \\ &= \overline{M}_t + \overline{M}_p = \overline{M}_T, \text{ the interest inelastic total demand for transactions now or later} \end{aligned} \tag{7.20}$$

7.4.2.4 Tobin-Baumol's version of transaction demand and interest rates

J. Tobin[1] and W.J. Baumol[2] held that transaction demand for cash is not all that interest inelastic. For people with highly developed banking habits and consciousness for purchase and sale of paper

[1] See J. Tobin, "The Interest-elasticity of the Transaction Demand for Cash", *In Review of Economics and Statistics*, August 1956, pp. 241–47.

[2] W.J. Baumol, "The Transaction Demand for Cash, An Inventory Theoretic Approach", *In Quarterly Journal of Economics*, Nov.1952, pp. 645–56.

assets such as bonds and shares don't hold back cash meant for periodic transactions but keep it in significant interest bearing deposits with banks or buy bonds and shares provided they are sure of liquidity of such investments as and when desired by them. For instance, people make fixed deposits for higher rate of interest and avail liquidity against them by arranging for cash credit accounts with the same bank at slightly higher rate of interest. This they do particularly for precautionary motive so that they may withdraw cash from the cash credit account rather than break the fixed deposit (*FD*) pre-maturely and suffer loss of interest income on it. As for transaction motive, people with developed banking habits don't hold back entire cash in hand for transaction intended over a certain period (month or week at the end of which next inflow of income is expected). Depending on their convenience and cost benefit considerations, they may divide the transaction period and retain some part of cash for transactions intended in that period and entrust the rest with bank accounts for interest income. At the end of the first transaction period they may withdraw cash from bank for their transaction needs of the next transaction period and the remainder of the deposit continuing to earn interest for remaining period. To elaborate, suppose a person earns ₹ 40,000 every month. With highly developed banking habits and proximity to a bank, he may hold back ₹ 10,000 for transactions in the first week and allow ₹ 30,000 to earn interest over first week as a bank deposit. As soon as the week is over, he may withdraw another ₹ 10,000 for the second week's transactions, allowing the balance of ₹ 20,000 to continue earning interest over the second week. Continuing likewise, he can earn interest on ₹ 30,000 for first week, on ₹ 20,000 for second week, and on ₹ 10,000 for the third week. His average deposit for the month can be taken as ₹ 15,000 [(30,000 + 20,000 + 10000 + 0)/4 = 15,000], which is entitled to interest income. Such behavior of the person depends on the following factors:

1. Interest rate offered by the bank is attractive enough,
2. Banking habits of the person are highly developed, and
3. The bank is in close proximity so that he may not have incur expenditures on transport.

If digital transactions such as those through debit card, credit card or through net-banking be effective and possible, cash holding by people for prospective transaction reduces to very low levels and we can say that transaction demand may be fairly interest elastic, more so when interest rate offered by the banks is high enough to offset the cost of withdrawals. Balances for the precautionary motive are more likely to be held with banks than in hand. For such motive periodicity of cash demand is usually longer and frequency, lower. The person concerned can invest such funds in bonds, shares, etc. depending on cost and benefit considerations apart from risk element, if any, involved. Here cost refers to cost of purchasing and selling such securities and benefit refers to the premium expected on such securities. The benefit must exceed the costs and precautionary component of cash demand also turns interest elastic beyond a certain rate of return or interest.

We can thus say that these components of cash demand are interest elastic beyond certain levels of return.

Figure 7.6 (A) portrays the behavior transaction and precautionary demands for cash holding.

7.4.2.5 Speculative demand for money

Speculative demand for money occupies a strategic position in Keynesian theory of demand for money. According to Keynes, theories of interest have little meaning if speculative demand for money is overlooked. It refers to people's preference for holding assets in liquid (cash) form at a given rate of interest. The purpose is speculation. People prefer to hold liquidity so that they may not miss an opportunity to buy bonds when their market prices are either at their lowest or expected to rise in near future. The objective is to earn an appreciation on such paper titles. In due course of time when bond prices go up, the buyers sell them off earning capital gains. If prices go further down instead of

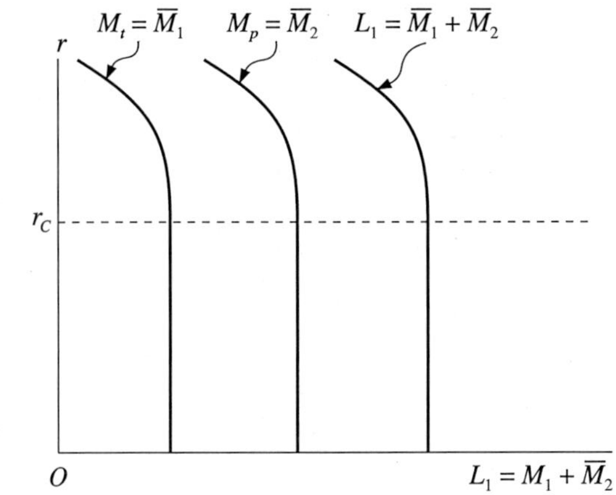

FIGURE 7.6(A) Tobin–Baumol Version of Transaction Demand for cash: L_1 is interest inelastic up to the rate of return r_C. Thereafter, it turns interest elastic as shown. A horizontal summation of M_t and M_p gives L_1.

going up, substantial losses too may accrue to them. Due to highly volatile nature of the stock (bond) markets, both gains and losses are likely to accrue to the buyers. Thus acquiring bonds for capital gains is an activity that may turn either way. It may lead to sizable profits or to colossal losses. That is the reason why sale and purchase of bonds and shares in the stock markets for capital gains are known as the ***speculative activities*** and those involved in them, as *speculators*.

Preference for holding assets in their liquid form (cash balances) is called *the* ***liquidity preference.*** It varies inversely with the rate of interest prevailing in the market. To demonstrate, suppose that government issues a perpetual bond of face value, ₹ 10,000. The rate of dividend is fixed at 10% per annum and the annual dividend is payable to the holder at the end of each year. The bond being a perpetual one, the holder can never seek its redemption from the government but is entitled to a sum of ₹ 1000 (10% of ₹ 10,000) per annum for ever.

In chapter 5, we observed that the sum of the present values (ΣPV) of fixed annual incomes of rupees 'A' per annum accruing perpetually to an investor when the market rate of interest is 'r' is,

$$(\Sigma PV) = [A/r]^1 \tag{7.21}$$

[1] Suppose an investment made now generates an income stream of $A_1, A_2, A_3, \ldots, \ldots, A_n$ respectively after 1, 2, 3, ..., ..., n years. Also suppose that the market rate of interest is fixed at r percent per annum.
The expression for the Present Value of the income stream from Equation 5.4 is

$$\Sigma PV = \frac{A_1}{(1+r)^1} + \frac{A_2}{(1+r)^2} + \frac{A_3}{(1+r)^3} + \ldots + \frac{A_n}{(1+r)^n}$$

$$= \frac{A}{(1+r)}\left[1 + \frac{1}{(1+r)} + \frac{1}{(1+r)^2} + \ldots + \frac{1}{(1+r)^{n-1}}\right]$$

Assuming annual incomes to remain same year after year at A, so that $A_1, = A_2, = A_3 = \ldots = A_n = A$; we have

$\Sigma PV = A \times [1 + R + R^2 + \ldots + \ldots + R^{n-1}]/(1 + r)$, [Substituting $(1/(1 + r) = R)$, everywhere inside the square brackets]

Sum of the first 'n' terms of a geometric progression with first term 'A' as 1 and common ratio 'R' given as $R = 1/(1 + r)$, gives:

$\Sigma PV = [A/(1+ r)] \times [R^n - 1]/(R - 1)\}$

Re-substituting for R as $1/(1 + r)$; we have

$= A/(1 + r) \times [1 - 1/(1 + r)^n]\ (1 + r)/(- r) = (A/r) \times [\{1/(1 + r)^n\} - 1]$ (On simplification)

$= A/r$ [When $n \to \infty$, $1/(1 + r)^n \to 0$]

TABLE 7.3

Rate of Interest(r)	*Perpetuity(A)*	*PV = P = A/r*	*Bond Preference*	*Liquidity Preference*
25%	1000	4000	Highest	Lowest
20%	1000	5000	Moderately high	Moderately low
15%	1000	6667	Moderately high	Moderately low
12%	1000	8333	Moderately high	Moderately low
10%	1000	10000	Lowest	Highest

Table 7.3 Suppose a perpetual bond is issued by government at its face value of ₹ 10,000. The rate of dividend is the current rate of interest, 10%. The buyers of this bond can never get it redeemed. Instead, they are entitled to a perpetual dividend of ₹ 1000 (10% of 10,000) per annum. Suppose further that the rate of interest varies from the lowest of 10% to the highest of 25%. Market prices (*PVs*) of the bond at the rates of interest from 10% to 25% as per formula 7.21 are calculated and recorded in the table. At 25%, market price is ₹ 4000 and at 10%, it is ₹ 10,000. In between these rates too the market prices are calculated and recorded in the Table 7.3. We observe that bond preference is the highest (liquidity preference lowest) at 25% and bond preference lowest (liquidity preference highest) at 10%. Bond preference is highest at 25% because its price is lowest (₹ 4000) and it is lowest at 10% because its price is ₹ 10,000. Accordingly, liquidity preference is lowest at 25% because bond's market price is (₹ 4000) is lowest and it is highest at 10% because bond's market price (₹ 10,000) is highest. When the bond price is highest, nobody would buy bonds. Instead, they would like to sell them. Likewise when bond price is lowest every speculator would like to buy it not to sell it.

The trends of the data tabulated above are portrayed in Figure 7.6(B). When the rate of interest is highest, bond price is lowest, bond preference highest and liquidity preference lowest. Opposite is the case when rate of interest is lowest.

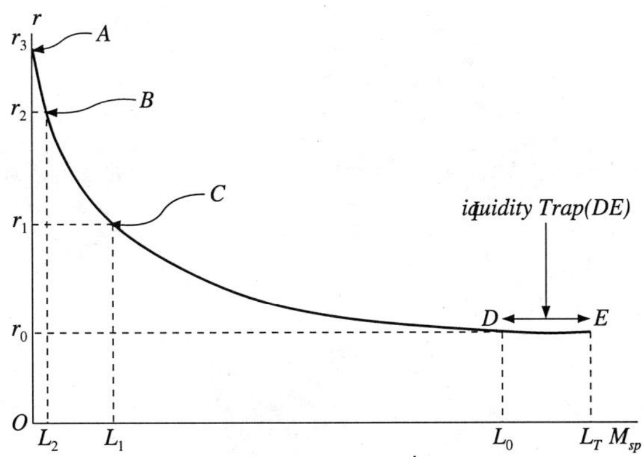

FIGURE 7.6(B): When rate of interest is r_3 (highest), liquidity preference is lowest (zero) as bond price is lowest. When rate of interest is as high as r_2, liquidity preference is moderately low as L_2. When rate of interest is r_0 (lowest) liquidity preference infinite as bond price is highest. Liquidity preference is L_0 as well as L_T or even infinite because *DE* is horizontal. Here, r_0 is the lowest possible rate of interest at which bond prices in the market are the highest and liquidity preference infinite. Liquidity preference or speculative demand for liquidity (L_2) can thus be given as a function of rate of interest as:

$$M_{sp} = L_2 = g(r) \tag{7.22}$$

where, $g(r)$ is a function of the rate of interest, *r*.

Substituting, A = ₹ 1,000, r = 10% = 0.10 in Equation 7.21, we have (ΣPV) = P = 1,000/0.10 = 10,000 and substituting r = 25%, P = ₹ 4000.

Hence, when the rate of interest is the same as the rate of dividend, the present value of the perpetual income stream, is ₹ 10,000 which is equal to the face value of the bond. Since the market price of the bond has to be equal to the present value of the perpetual income stream, the market price of this bond is ₹ 10,000. If the rate of interest rises to 25%, the market price of the bond would fall to ₹ 4000. Speculative demand for the bond is highest when its price is lowest and when it is lowest its price is highest. Liquidity preference, on the contrary, is lowest when rate of interest is highest or bond price, lowest while liquidity preference is highest when rate of interest is lowest or bond price highest.

7.4.2.6 Total demand for money

Total demand for money is the sum total of the transaction, precautionary and the speculative components of demand. Transaction and precautionary components being perfectly interest inelastic are clubbed together as such and are given by Equation 7.19. The speculative component of demand is given by Equation 7.22. Total demand for money can thus be given as

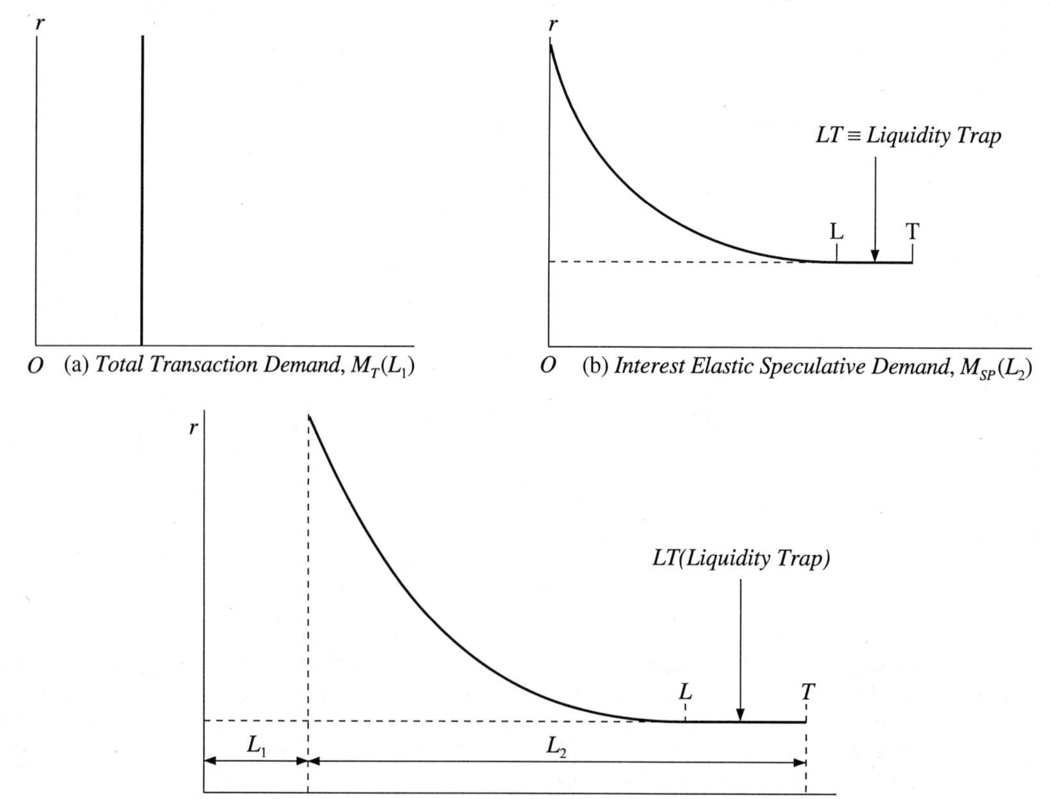

FIGURE 7.7 Part (a) is a reproduction of Figure 7.5(b) and part (b), that of Figure 7.6(B). Part (c) [Not to scale] portrays the total demand for liquidity (M^d), obtained through the horizontal summation of L_1 and L_2. Segment LT marks the liquidity trap.

$$M^d = L_1 + L_2 = (M_t + M_p) + g(r) = kY + g(r) \qquad (7.23)$$

Here, L_l is called the transaction and precautionary demand for liquidity or liquidity preference for transaction and precautionary motives while L_2 is speculative demand (M_{SP}) for liquidity or liquidity preference for speculative motives. L_1 is given by Equation 7.19 as a function of income (Y). Note that Y is in physical units representing the identity, output = income) and so are L_1 and L_2, both in real terms. To convert them in nominal terms (money value) each can be multiplied by the general price level P.

7.5 MONEY MARKET EQUILIBRIUM

Discussion of supply and demand for money in this chapter was intended to pave the way for the study of income Y as exogenous variable in ***static equilibrium*** [Figure 7.8(b)] and as endogenous variable in ***dynamic equilibrium*** (Figure 7.9 and 7.10).

7.5.1 Static Equilibrium of Money Market [Figure 7.8(b)]

Money market equilibrium is static [Figure 7.8(b)] if it relates to a point of time. If Y is constant, so is L_1. Thus total demand for money can be represented as a function of the rate of interest, r. It is the horizontal summation of L_1 and L_2. Using Figure 7.5 for L_1 and Figure 7.6 for L_2, the total demand curve can be obtained as suggested above. Thus Keynesian theory of demand, known as the liquidity preference theory of demand, leads to a demand curve as a function of the rate of interest as given in panel (c) of Figure 7.7.

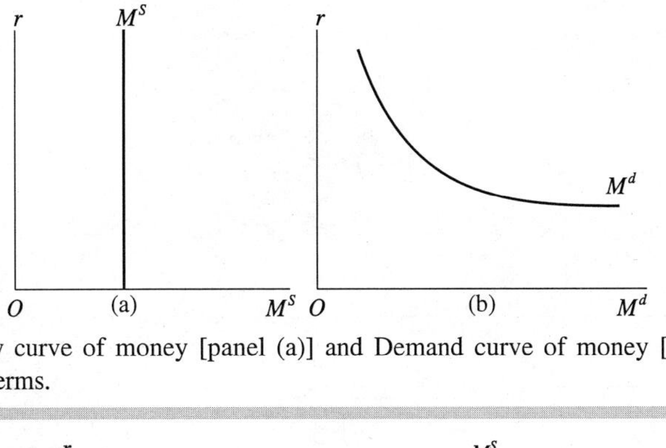

FIGURE 7.8(a) Supply curve of money [panel (a)] and Demand curve of money [panel (b)] in Keynesian theory. Both are in real terms.

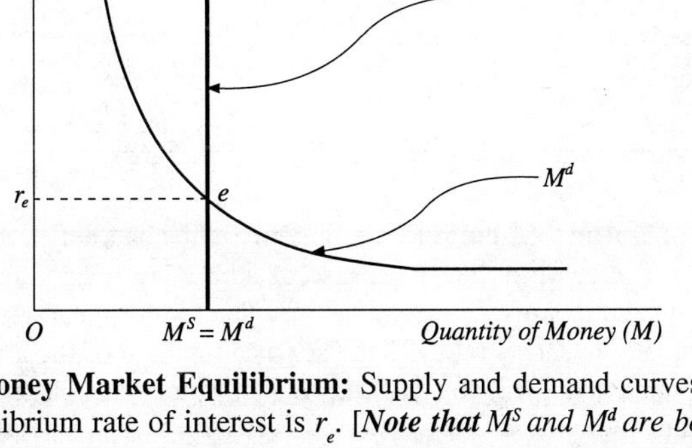

FIGURE 7 8(b) **Static Money Market Equilibrium:** Supply and demand curves intersect each other at the point e where $M^s = M^d$. Equilibrium rate of interest is r_e. [***Note that*** *M^S and M^d are both in real terms*].

Given the supply of money as fixed, its curve is perfectly interest inelastic as in panel (a) [Figure 7.8(a)]. The demand curve, as shown in Figure 7.7(c), is highly interest elastic. ***The static equilibrium of the money market** therefore refers to a point of time at which Y is exogenous.* It refers to the point of intersection of supply and demand curves drawn with rate of interest on the vertical axis and quantity of money, demanded and supplied, on the horizontal axis. Figure 7.8(b) shows the static equilibrium at point *e*, which results from superimposing supply and demand curves of Figure 7.8(a) into the same space.

7.5.2 Dynamic Equilibrium of Money Market [Figure 7.9 and 7.10]

The dynamic equilibrium has two manifestations, *first*, in which speculative demand for money is linear (Figure 7.9), and *second*, in which it is non-linear (Figure 7.10). In the former case, demand for money is an additively inverse function of rate of interest and in the latter case, it is a multiplicatively inverse function of the rate of interest. Let us discuss both. Each one gives the dynamic equilibrium in the form of *LM*-curve. In the former case, *LM*-curve is linear while in the latter, it is non-linear.

7.5.2.1 Linear LM-curve [Figure 7.9]

As regards, supply and demand functions, they can be expressed as below in this case:

$M_S^R = M$, where $M_S^R \equiv$ supply of money in real terms

$M_D^R = kY + g(r)$, where $M_D^R \equiv$ demand (L) of money in real terms and Y, income or output in physical terms

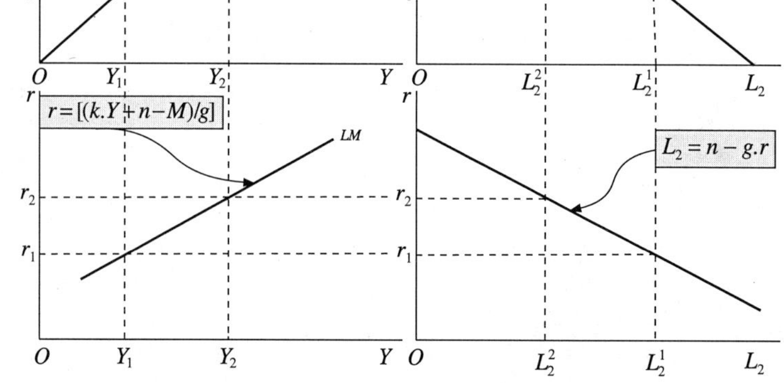

FIGURE 7.9 Derivation of linear LM-curve: The bottom right quadrant portrays speculative demand as a function of rate of interest. The curve is linear because of additively inverse relationship between the two. The top-right quadrant portrays the identity $L_1 + L_2 = L = M$. The top-left quadrant portrays L_1 as a function of Income, Y while bottom left quadrant shows rate of interest r as a function of Income Y(the *LM*-curve). See how the rates of interest r_1 and r_2 relate to L_2^1, L_2^2, $(L_1 + L_2)$, L_1^1, L_1^2, Y_1, Y_2 and back. The *LM*-curve slopes upwards as shown in bottom left quadrant.

Here, $k.Y$ *is* interest inelastic component, L_1 [Figure 7.5], and $g(r)$, interest elastic speculative demand, which is an additively inverse function of *r,* the rate of interest, expressed as:

$$g(r) = n - g.r,$$

where, n and g are constants. It yields a linear speculative demand curve [bottom-right quadrant, Figure 7.9]) leading to an upward sloping *LM*-curve (bottom-left quadrant) in the Figure.

Mathematically, equation of the *LM*-curve can be derived as outlined below.

$$g(r) = L_2 = n - g.r$$

Thus, $$M_D^R = L_1 + L_2 = k.Y + g(r) = L$$

$$= k.Y + n - g.r \quad (7.24)$$

At equilibrium, $M_D^R = M_S^R$ or $L = M$. Substituting, we have

$$\Rightarrow \quad k.Y + n - g.r = M$$

$$\Rightarrow \quad g.r = k.Y - M + n$$

$$\Rightarrow \quad r = (k/g).Y + (n - M)/g \quad (7.25)$$

Equation 7.25, gives the expression of *LM*-curve. The nomenclature originates from *equality of demand, L, and supply, M, at every point on it.* It can thus be defined as *locus of combinations of Y and r for each of which L = M.*

7.5.2.2 Non-linear LM-curve [Figure 7.10]

Figure 7.10 demonstrates the diagrammatic derivation of the non-linear *LM*-curve comprising distinct segments *AB*, *BC* and *CD*. Bottom right quadrant of the figure shows speculative demand for money. It is non-linear, reflecting speculative demand as a multiplicatively inverse[1] function of the rate of interest, expressed as:

$$g(r) = L_2 = (n/g.r)$$

Total demand of money can be expressed as,

$$M_D^R = L_1 + L_2 = k.Y + g(r) = k.Y + (n/g.r) \quad (7.26)$$

For equilibrium, $M_D^R = M_S^R$, *or* $L = M$. Substituting, we have

$$k.Y + (n/g.r) = M \Rightarrow r = n/[g(M - k.Y)] \quad (7.27)$$

Equation 7.27 gives the expression for the *LM*-curve in this case. The same is obtained by four quadrant method as in Figure 7.10. Note that *liquidity trap* is related to the Keynesian speculative demand for money as explained in Figure 7.6. The horizontal segment *AB* of *LM*, called the *Keynesian Range* of it, corresponds to this liquidity trap.

7.5.2.3 Derivation of *LM*-curve under classical theory (Figure 7.11)

According to the classical economists, money is demanded only for transaction and precautionary motives. The two, being perfectly interest inelastic, are clubbed together as L_1 component of Keynesian total demand. Speculative demand (L_2) is therefore zero in classical theory. *LM*-curve as derived in (Figure 7.11) is vertical.

It is for this reason that the vertical segment (*CD*) of *LM*-curve of Figure 7.10 is termed as *classical range* of it.

[1] There are authors who've oversimplified speculative demand as an additively inverse function of rate of interest and have still portrayed its curve as a non-linear curve for the convenience of showing the liquidity trap and also authors who've treated it as a multiplicatively inverse function of rate of interest yet portrayed it as a linear curve. The objective before them perhaps is the ease of explanation.

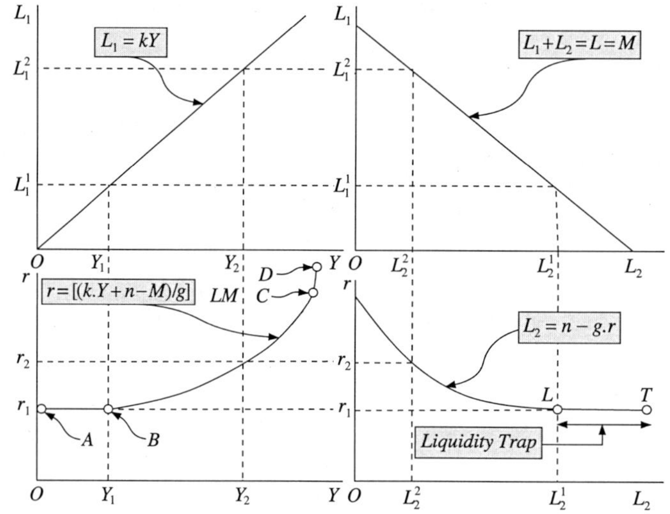

FIGURE 7.10 Derivation of Non-linear LM-curve: The bottom right quadrant portrays speculative demand as a function of rate of interest. The curve is non-linear because of multiplicatively inverse relationship between the two. The top-right quadrant portrays the identity $L_1 + L_2 = L$. The top-left quadrant portrays L_1 as a function of Income, Y while bottom left quadrant shows the rate of interest r as a function of Income Y(the *LM*-curve) See how the rates of interest r_1 and r_2 relate to L_2^1, L_2^2, $(L_1 + L_2)$, L_1^1, L_1^2, Y_1, Y_2 and back. The *LM*-curve slopes upwards as shown in bottom left quadrant. See also how the shape of L_2–curve changes the shape of the *LM*-curve and how the liquidity trap is reflected in the *LM*-curve at the lowest rate of interest, r_1. Segment *AB* of *LM*-curve represents Keynesian Range; *BC*, Intermediate Range and *CD*, Classical Range of it.

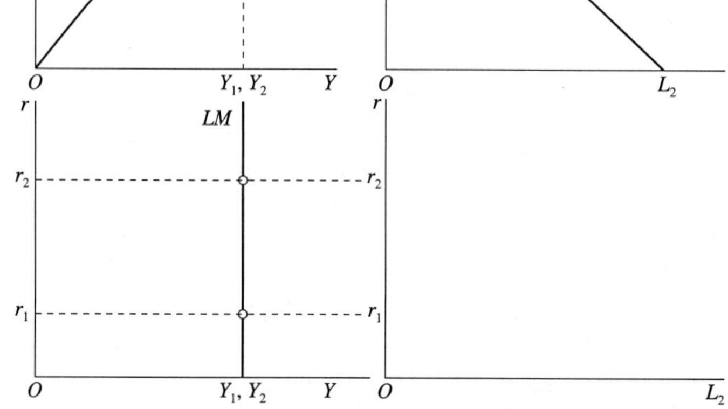

FIGURE 7.11 Derivation of *LM*-curve in Classical Theory: In absence of speculative demand, $L_1 = L = M$. No matter what the rate of interest be, *LM*-curve is vertical.

7.6 APPLICATIONS AND IMPLICATIONS OF *LM*-CURVES

In this section we will examine the effect of a change in money supply under fixed and variable prices.

7.6.1 *LM*-curve and Changes in Money Supply (Fixed Price Model, Figure 7.12)

Increase in real money supply causes a rightward shift in the *LM*-curve. Such shifts are demonstrated in Figure 7.12:

Figure 7.12 shows the effect of an increase in money supply on the *LM*-curve which shifts to right. In case of a decrease in money supply the shift in *LM*-curve would be to the left. Price level in this derivation is assumed to remain fixed. When nominal money has increased by 20%, real money supply would also rise by 20% and the *LM*-curve will shift rightwards as shown in the figure.

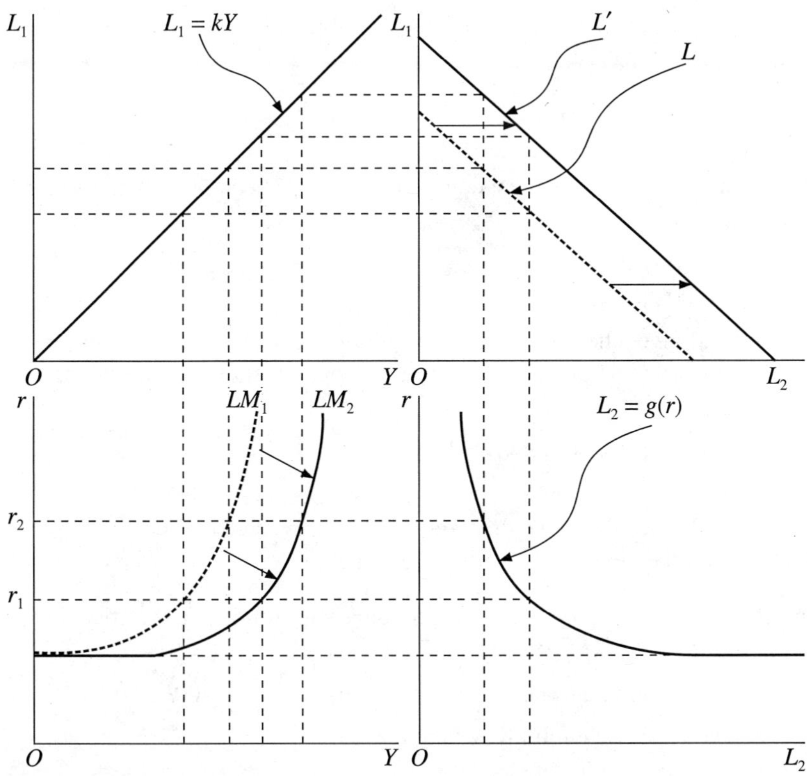

FIGURE 7.12 Effect of an increase in real money supply leads to an upward to right shift in the *LM*-curve. When money supply is *L* the *LM*-curve is LM_1 and when it is L', the *LM*-curve is LM_2. Note that money supply (*L* and *L'*) represent money supply in real terms. Note also that nominal money can be converted into real money by dividing it by the price level. To elaborate, suppose nominal money changes from 1000 to 1200, that is, by 20%. If price level is fixed at 5, the real money supply would also increase by 20% from 200 to 240. The derivation of *LM*-curves is based on the assumption of fixed price level.

Let us have a few illustrations first.

ILLUSTRATION 7.2: Given the supply of nominal money as ₹ 1600 crore, the transaction and precautionary component of demand of real money, $L_1 = 0.4Y$, while speculative component of it in real terms is $L_2 = 4000–200r$, determine the equation of the *LM*-curve when price level is fixed at $P = 4$.

Solution: Supply of money is given in nominal terms while its demand, in real terms.
To make them both in same terms, we can follow either of the following two ways:

1. Convert money supply from nominal to real terms by dividing it by the price level. That way, $M_S^R = M_S^N/P$, where $M_S^N \equiv$ nominal money supply and $M_S^R \equiv$ real money supply. $= 1600/4 = 400$.
2. Alternatively, convert demand for money from real to nominal terms by multiplying it by the price level. That way,
$M_D^N = P \times M_D^R$, where $M_D^N \equiv$ demand for nominal money and $M_D^R \equiv$ that for real money.

$$\begin{aligned} &= P \times L \\ &= 4\,(L_1 + L_2) \\ &= 4(0.4Y + 4000 - 200r) \\ &= 1.6Y + 16000 - 800r. \end{aligned}$$

Following the first approach, equation of money market equilibrium or *LM*-curve is given by:

$$M_S^R = M_D^R$$

$$\Rightarrow \quad 400 = 0.4Y + 4000 - 200r$$

$$\Rightarrow \quad r = 0.002Y + 18 \tag{7.28}$$

Equation 7.28 gives the money market equilibrium (*LM*-curve).
Following the second approach, equation of money market equilibrium or *LM* is given by:

$$M_S^N = M_D^N$$

$$\Rightarrow \quad 1600 = 1.6Y + 16000 - 800r$$

$$\Rightarrow \quad r = 0.002Y + 18 \tag{7.29}$$

Equation 7.29 gives the money market equilibrium (*LM*-curve).
Note that both the approaches lead to the same result.

ILLUSTRATION 7.3: For a hypothetical economy with following specifications,

Nominal money supply (M_S^N) = 2000

Nominal money demand (M_D^N) = $0.50Y + 400/r$

Determine the money market equilibrium or the *LM*-curve.

Solution: Since supply and demand are both in similar terms (nominal),

$$M = L$$

$$\Rightarrow \quad (M_S^N) = (M_D^N)$$

$$\Rightarrow \quad 2000 = 0.50Y + 400/r$$

$$\Rightarrow \quad r = 400/(2000 - 0.50Y) \tag{7.30}$$

ILLUSTRATION 7.4: For the data in illustration 7.3, suppose money supply is given in real terms while money demand is given in nominal terms as $L = 0.50Y - 400r$. How would your answer to the equation of the *LM*-curve change (given $P = 4.00$)?

Solution: Following the first approach for converting the two in same terms, we have

Money supply in nominal terms, $M_S^N = P \times M_S^R$
$= 4.00 \times 2000$
$= 8000$

For equilibrium,

$$\Rightarrow \quad 8000 = 0.50Y - 400r$$

$$\Rightarrow \quad r = 0.00125Y - 20 \tag{7.31}$$

Equation 7.31 gives the equation of the *LM*-curve.

Following the second approach,

$$M_S^R = 2000$$

$$M_D^R = M_D^N/P = (0.50Y - 400r)/4.00 = 0.125Y - 100r$$

For equilibrium,

$$2000 = 0.125Y - 100r$$

$$\Rightarrow \quad r = 0.00125Y - 20 \tag{7.32}$$

Both the approaches lead to the same result.

7.6.2 *LM*-curve and Changes in Money Supply (Variable Price Model, Figure 7.13)

So far we discussed the derivation of *LM*-curve assuming fixed prices. As mentioned earlier in the derivations, *L* and *M* have to be in real terms. In Figure 7.12, supply of money in nominal terms increased while price level was treated fixed. As a result, supply of real balances increased from M_1 to M_2.

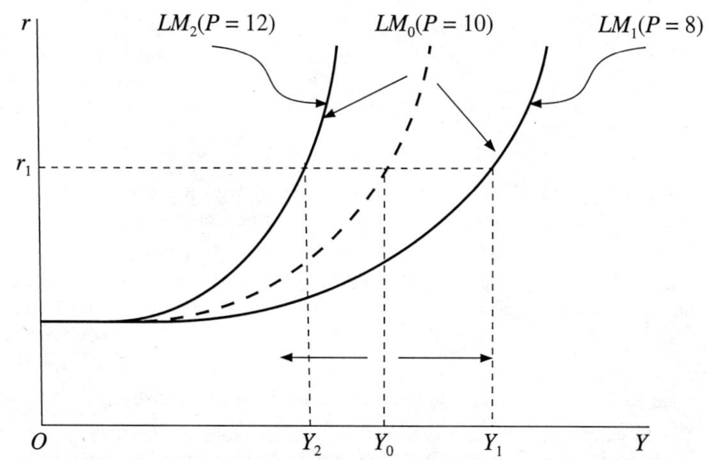

FIGURE 7.13 Supply of nominal balance being fixed, a rise in price level shifts the *LM*-curve to left and a fall in it, to right.

Now let us take supply of nominal balances as fixed and price level as variable. Derivation of the *LM*-curve is as shown in Figure 7.13.

A rise in the price level decreases the quantity of real balances and a fall in it, increases it. To demonstrate, suppose supply of nominal money is fixed at 1000. Now let the price level falls from 10 to 8. The real balances would increase from 1000/10 (that is, 100) to 1000/8 (that is, 125). The *LM* would then follow the trend of Figure 7.12 and shift downward to right.

On the other hand, let the price level rise from 10 to 12. As a result, supply of real money would fall from 100 to 83.33. The effect on *LM*-curve would be opposite. It will shift upwards to left in consequence. If price levels has a rising trend, *LM*-curve would shift upward to left each time price rises.

Figure 7.13 focuses on the shift in *LM*-curve in response to rising and falling prices when nominal money supply is fixed.

For general equilibrium, equilibrium of the money market and that of goods market are both essential. We will take up goods market equilibrium in the next chapter.

KEY TERMS AND CONCEPTS

Barter System: A system of exchange of one commodity with another. It existed prior to the evolution of money.

Drawbacks of Barter System: Barter system suffered from the following drawbacks:

1. Lack of double coincidence of wants
2. Lack of divisibility of commodity.
3. Lack of common denominator
4. Lack of store value
5. Lack of standard of deferred payments

Money: "Anything that is universally acceptable as a medium of exchange and at the same time acts as a measure and store of value" – Crowther.

Forms of Money: Money has had several forms:

1. Commodity Money
2. Metallic Money
3. Paper Money
4. Deposit Money
5. Near Money
6. Optional Money
7. Fiat Money
8. Legal Tender Money

Standard and Token Money: Standard money is full bodied money with its intrinsic value equal to its face value, whereas token money is representative money, usually made of inferior metals the value of which is much less than their face value.

Near Money: Instruments such as credit cards, bills of exchange, treasury bills, bonds and debentures are known as near money. They are not as good as cash or currency (money proper) in making transactions but are quite close to being that when it comes to transact goods and services. Near money does not possess the attribute of general or universal acceptability.

Deposit Money: Chequeable deposits that can be operated through cheques constitute deposit money.

Paper Money: It refers to currency notes. It was introduced in 9th century. The first country to use paper money was China. However, use of paper money on a large scale began in 17th and 18th centuries. In India, it started in 19th century. It was the Bank of Bengal that issued paper currency in 1806. Paper money is classified under four heads: (1) Representative Paper Money which is fully backed by gold and silver reserves; (2) Convertible Paper Money which can be converted into standard coins or bullion at will; (3) Inconvertible Paper Money which is backed by no guarantee to convert it into standard coins or bullion; and (4) Fiat Money which is inconvertible paper currency issued only at the time of the crisis.

Fiat Money: It refers to inconvertible paper money issued only at the time of crisis. It requires no reserves to back up its issue. Controlled issue of token money can help the cause of economic development of less developed countries.

Legal Tender Money: It refers to that form of money which is backed up as such by the law of the land. Such money needs no other back up. It has two types, (1) Unlimited legal tender which is to be accepted in payment in unlimited quantities, and (2) Limited legal tender which can't be forced on the recipients beyond a certain limit.

Functions of Money: Medium of exchange and measure of value are two primary functions of money while store of value, standard of deferred payments and transfer of purchasing power are its three secondary functions. Among its contingent functions are money as the basis of all credit, money as the basis of maximization of utility and productivity, money as a guarantor of solvency, money as the bearer of last option, money as a tool that renders liquidity to capital and money as the basis of functioning of the price mechanism.

Supply of Money: Supply of money refers to aggregate stock of domestic money owned by public in the country. The term public refers to the private individuals and firms operating in the economy. Supply of money is a stock concept which refers to the stock of money at a point of time.

Measures of Money Supply: There are two concepts of measurement of money supply:

1. *Narrow Concept:* Under this concept are included the components M_1 and M_2. While M_1 comprises of currency (C), net demand deposits (DD) and other deposits (OD), M_2 comprises of M_1 and the post office savings deposits.
2. *Broader Concept:* Under this concept we include the M_3 and M_4 components. M_3 includes M_1 and the time deposits while M_4 includes M_3 and the post office savings deposits. Till 1978, *RBI* used M_1 as a measure of money supply. Thereafter, it used M_3 in its place. M_3 is termed as the *Aggregate Monetary Resource* (*AMR*).

The Order of Liquidity of the Four Components of Money Supply: In order of liquidity, the four components rank as follows: (a) M_1, (b) M_2, (c) M_3, (d) M_4.

Demand for Money: There are two concepts of demand for money.

Classical View: It represents the viewpoint of the classical economists and states that money is demanded by people for transaction purposes only and is perfectly interest inelastic.

Keynesian View: Under it, money is demanded not only for transaction purposes but also for precautionary and speculative purposes. Demand for the first two purposes is perfectly interest inelastic while that for the third, a highly interest elastic.

Transaction Demand for Money: It refers to demand for money for transactions purposes and is perfectly interest inelastic. Its volume depends on the volume of transactions or on income.

Precautionary Demand for Money: It refers to that part of money which is demanded purely as a provision against the unforeseen contingencies. Its volume depends on the volume of unanticipated transactions.

Speculative Demand for Money: It refers to that part of money which is demanded for the speculative activities, i.e., for buying bonds and debentures when their market values are low.

Money Market Equilibrium (Static): It refers to a state in which demand for money equals its supply, at a point of time, income (Y) being an exogenous variable.

Money Market Equilibrium (Dynamic): It refers to a period of time. It is described by the *LM*-curve which represents various combinations of income (Y) and rate of interest (r) for each of which demand (L) is equal to supply (M). Income (Y) is endogenous in dynamic equilibrium.

EXERCISES

A. Short Answer Questions

1. What is meant by barter system? Outline its drawbacks that hampered free flow of day-to-day business.?
2. Define money that eliminated all the drawbacks of barter system.?
3. Distinguish between:
   (a) standard coin and token coin
   (b) near money and credit money
   (c) limited legal tender and unlimited legal tender

(d) convertible currency and inconvertible currency
(e) representative money and fiat money
(f) optional money and deposit money
(g) full bodied money and representative full token money
(h) time deposits and demand deposits
(i) demand deposits and net demand deposits
(j) budget surplus and trade surplus
(k) Classical and Keynesian versions of demand for money
(l) fiat money and inconvertible paper money.

4. Define money. What are its primary functions?

5. Define money. What are its secondary functions?

6. What are contingent functions of money? What other functions does it perform by way of its existence?

7. What is meant by aggregate monetary resource (*AMR*)? What are its components?

8. What are the components of *RBI's* concept of money supply? Arrange them in order of liquidity.

9. What is meant by liquidity preference? Explain with the help of examples.

10. When in particular would liquidity trap occur in respect of speculative demand for money. Elaborate.

11. Explain Tobin-Baumol's Version of Transaction Demand with help of a sketch.

12. Give an example of money serving each of the following objectives:

(a) maximization of total utility of the consumers
(b) maximization of productivity of the firms
(c) liquidity to capital assets
(d) standard of deferred payments
(e) store of value
(f) bearer of the last option
(g) guarantor of solvency
(h) basis of all credit.

13. What are the constituents of the M_3 component of money supply? How does it differ from M_1-component?

14. How does M_2 component of money supply differ from its M_1 component?

15. On what grounds should post office savings deposits be treated as a part of money?

16. Give examples to show that near money has a price to function as money proper.

17. Why is precautionary demand for money treated as a part of the transaction demand for it?

18. On what grounds should time deposits be treated as a part of money? Should they be treated as demand deposits?

19. Explain the static equilibrium of money market with a neat sketch.

B. Long Answer Questions

20. Distinguish between narrow and broad views of money supply. Outline two main views of each.

21. On what factors does the Keynesian demand for money depend? Outline them briefly.

22. What is meant by speculative demand for money? Explain with the help of illustrative sketch.

23. Comment upon the major drawbacks of the barter system. Trace the stages of evolution of money to eliminate barter system.

24. Outline some of the important forms of money with particular reference to the paper form of it.

25. Explain various functions of money with particular reference to its medium of exchange and store value functions.

26. Explain *RBI's* concept of money supply.

27. Explain the mechanism of deriving a linear *LM*-curve? How can it be treated as a dynamism of money market equilibrium.

28. Obtain the *LM*-curve for the classical theory of demand for money.

29. Derive the non-linear *LM*-curve and mark off the Keynesian and classical ranges on it.

30. Distinguish between real and nominal balances of money. How do fluctuations in price level affect money market equilibrium? Explain.

31. Account for the effect of changes in nominal balances on the *LM*-curves under fixed price level. Draw diagrammes.

32. 'Demand for money no longer depends on the volume of transactions but more so it depends on the market rate of interest.' Discuss.

[Hint: Show that transaction demand for money is not all that interest inelastic as classical theory assumed. Tobin-Baumol's version shows that transaction demand turns interest elastic at high rates of interest. Digitalization of transactions has made it even more interest elastic in recent days. Speculative demand already being highly interest elastic, demand for money can be treated as fairly interest elastic. Thus combine Tobin-Baumol's version with Keynesian speculative demand as also modern digitalization to support the statement].

C. Essay Type Questions

33. 'Necessity is the mother of invention'. Elucidate evolution of money to its present form in the light of this statement. Make a comprehensive account on money and its evolution.

34. Explain various functions of money in a modern economic set-up.

35. 'Equilibrium of the money market refers to various combinations of income (Y) and market rate of interest (r) for each of which demand for money (L) is equal to its supply (M). Discuss.

36. Money supply in nominal terms is given as,

$$M_S^N = 2000$$

while demand for the real balances is a function of Y and r given as,

$$M_D^R = 0.50\ Y - 200r$$

Given the general price level as $P = 5.00$, determine the money market equilibrium (*LM*-curve) and sketch it. If the equilibrium level of income is given as 5000, what is the market rate of interest?

[Ans: $r = 0.0025\,Y - 2$; $r = 10.5\%$**]**

37. Given the supply of money in real terms as,

$$M_S^R = 1000$$

and the demand for real balances as,

$$M_D^R = 0.60\ Y - 200r$$

Find the expression for the *LM*-curve when general price, $P = 4.00$ **[Ans:** $r = 0.003\,Y - 5$**]**

38. What is high powered money? Show that money supply is directly proportional to the volume of high powered money. Is it true to call high powered money as the money base?

39. Obtain an expression for money multiplier. Given the cash deposit ratio as 0.40 and the reserve deposit ratio as 0.10, estimate the quantum of additional deposits as also of money created by an increase of ₹ 60 crore in the high powered money. **[Ans:** ₹ 120 crore; ₹ 168 crore**]**

40. With suitable sketches, distinguish between static and dynamic equilibria of money market.

Chapter 8

Goods Market Equilibrium

INTRODUCTION

An economic system can't be in equilibrium unless goods and money markets are in simultaneous equilibrium. For instance, an increase in money supply, other things remaining the same, would lower the interest rates. In consequence, investment ($I = I_a - hr$) would increase and so would the demand for productive factors, which in turn, would raise factor prices and production costs. This would raise general price level. Thus, an increase in money supply (a disturbance in money market) would go a long way to disturb the equilibrium of the goods market as well. It does so through its immediate impact on the rate of interest. That is how J. M. Keynes explained the relationship between the general price level and money supply, rejecting the classical version of quantity theorists[1]. Keynes held that changes in money supply do cause changes in the general price level but they do so indirectly, that is, through the rate of interest.

The instance explains the interdependence of the two markets. It can be demonstrated that a disturbance in the goods market disturbs the money market as well. For instance, a fall in demand for products lowers the product-prices in the market. This affects the profit margin as also the marginal efficiency of capital (*MEC*) adversely. In consequence productive investment and demand for factors of production both fall. If sustained, these tendencies lead to retrenchment of factors, causing unemployment. Output and income too fall and so do bond prices leading to a hike in speculative demand for money, thereby, raising rate of interest to restrict which the monetary authority feels compelled to increase the money supply. Thus a disturbance in the goods market is transmitted into the money market as well.

There are several ways to establish the interdependence of the two markets. The reader can try how an increase in government spending or an increase in export-earning or even a decrease in import spending leads to an increase in national income and a decrease in the market rate of interest. In the same way how an increase in demand for money or a decrease in its supply results in a rise in interest rate and a fall in national income. Changes in the above parameters if reversed would also reverse the corresponding effects in the other market.

We have already discussed working of money market and its equilibrium at a point of time as also over a period of time in the previous Chapter. Goods market equilibrium was hinted in *Q* 31 of Chapter 5 but it was left for this chapter to take its various aspects. Let us do that now so that we can establish the conditions of equilibrium of money and goods markets simultaneously.

[1] The term refers to classical economists known for their *Quantity Theory of Value of Money*. According to this theory, general price level, a passive factor, is directly proportional to the money supply.

8.1 GOODS MARKET EQUILIBRIUM—THE *IS*-CURVE

Goods market equilibrium refers to the adequacy of the goods and services supplied to meet their demand. We have seen that an increase in thriftiness decreases employment, production and supply each and a decrease in it increases them all. In the former case, production falls and so does supply in the face of demand and in the later case, production increases and so does supply in the face of demand. Inadequacy of supply against demand causes disequilibrium in goods market and so does excess or deficient demand in the face of supply. Mismatch between the two owes its origin to leakages from the circular flow of income and expenditures or overflows in it. In the Sections that follow we will discuss the conditions necessary to keep such disequilibria at bay.

8.1.1 Algebraic Method of its Derivation

In Chapter 6, we learnt how to determine equilibrium level of income when investment is independent of interest rate, r. We observed that the condition for the goods market equilibrium is equality of the injections $(I + G + X)$ to the withdrawals $(S + T + M)$, where, I stands for investment; G for public spending; X for export earning; S for savings; T for tax revenue and M for import expenditure. In simpler terms, if withdrawals from the circular flow of income and expenditure be plugged by an equal amount of injections, unsold stocks disappear and all that is produced and supplied is sold leading to an equilibrium of the goods market. In a two sector economy, we spelled this condition as the equality of investment to savings; in a three sector model, we spelled it as the equality of $(I + G)$ to $(S + T)$ and in a four sector economy, we expressed the condition of equilibrium as the equality of $(I + G + X)$ to $(S + T + M)$. In general, we can describe goods market equilibrium by the identity $I = S$, where I would represent injections and S, withdrawals. When I is independent of interest rate (r) and S is a function of income (Y), goods market equilibrium for different models reduces to its forms discussed in Chapter 6. But when I is a function of r, tools of analysis discussed in chapter 6 prove inadequate. A separate analysis, in this case, is called for. Suppose following specifications for an economic system are provided:

$$AD = C + I + G + (X - M)$$

where,

$$\begin{aligned}
C &= C_a + bY^d \\
Y^d &= Y - (T - R) = Y - T + R \\
T &= T_a + tY \\
R &= \overline{R} \\
I &= I_a - hr \\
G &= \overline{G} \\
X &= \overline{X} \\
M &= M_a + mY
\end{aligned}$$

Symbols have their usual meaning, as in Chapter 6. The only point of difference is the one that relates to the investment function that involves r. Expression for aggregate demand (AD) can be worked out as

$$\begin{aligned}
AD &= C + I + G + (X - M) \\
&= C_a + bY^d + I_a - hr + \overline{G} + (\overline{X} - M_a - mY) \\
&= C_a + b(Y - T_a - tY + R) + I_a - hr + \overline{G} + (\overline{X} - M_a - mY) \\
&= C_a + bY - bT_a - btY + bR + I_a - hr + \overline{G} + \overline{X} - M_a - mY
\end{aligned}$$

$$= C_a - bT_a + bR + I_a - hr + \bar{G} + \bar{X} - M_a + (b - bt - m)Y$$

$$= \bar{A} + \{b(1 - t) - m\}Y - hr \qquad (8.1)$$

where, $\bar{A}$ ≡ absorption, which is independent of Y as well as of r

For equilibrium, $AD = AS$, where, AS = aggregate supply = Y. Combining this with equation 8.1, we get

$$Y = C_a + bY - bT_a - btY + bR + I_a - hr + \bar{G} + \bar{X} - M_a - mY \qquad (8.2)$$

$$\Rightarrow \quad hr = (C_a - bT_a + bR + I_a + \bar{G} + \bar{X} - M_a) - (1 - b + bt + m)Y$$

$$\Rightarrow \quad r = \frac{(C_a - bT_a + bR + I_a + \bar{G} + \bar{X} - M_a)}{h} - \frac{(1 - b + bt + m)}{h} \times Y \qquad (8.3)$$

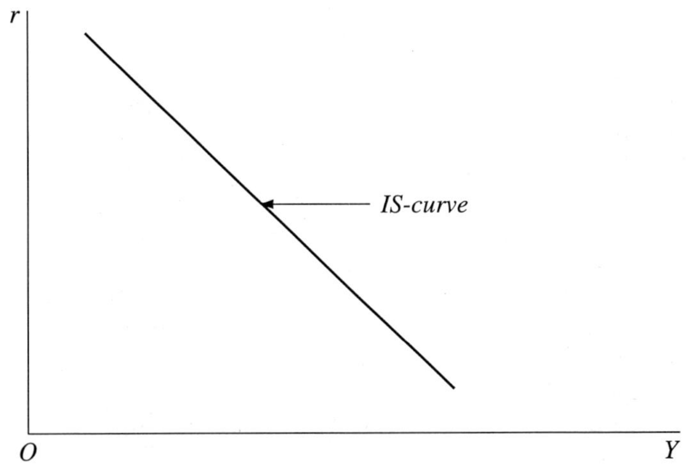

FIGURE 8.1 Derivation of *IS*-curve through Algebraic Method: Plot of Equation 8.2 gives the *IS*-curve.

Equation 8.3 spells the condition of equilibrium. It expresses rate of interest, r, in terms of income Y. If plotted with income (Y) on x-axis and rate of interest (r) on y-axis, we obtain a curve that slopes downward from left to right. The curve, called the *IS-curve,* characterizes the *goods market equilibrium.* It can be defined as *the locus of various combinations of income (Y) and rate of interest (r) for each of which I = S.*

Alternatively, taking I as Injections and S as withdrawals, we have, incorporating transfer payments R,

$$I + \bar{G} + \bar{X} = S + T + M - R$$

$$\Rightarrow \quad I + \bar{G} + (\bar{X} - M) = S + (T - R)$$

Substituting,

$$I = I_a - h.r,$$

$$M = M_a + m.Y,$$

$$T = T_a + t.\ Y, \text{ and}$$

$$S = -C_a + (1 - b)\,[Y - T_a - t.Y + R]$$

We have,

$\Rightarrow \; I_a - h.r + \bar{G} + \bar{X} - M_a - m.Y = - C_a + (1 - b)\,[Y - T_a - t.Y - R] + T_a + t.Y - R$

$\Rightarrow \; - h.r = - C_a + (1 - b)\,[Y - T_a - t.\, Y + R] + T_a + t.Y - R - I_a - \bar{G} - \bar{X} + M_a + m.Y$

$= - C_a + (1 - b)Y - (1 - b)\,T_a - (1 - b)t.Y + (1 - b)\,R + T_a + t.Y - R - I_a - \bar{G} - \bar{X} + M_a + m.Y$

$\Rightarrow \; = - C_a + Y - b.Y - T_a + b.T_a - t.Y + b.\,t.Y + R - b.R + T_a + t.Y - R - I_a - \bar{G} - \bar{X} + M_a + m.Y$

$\Rightarrow \; = [- C_a - T_a + b.T_a + R - b.R + T_a - R - I_a - \bar{G} - \bar{X} + M_a] + [1 - b - t + b.t + t + m]$

$\Rightarrow \; = [- C_a + b.T_a - b.R - I_a - \bar{G} - \bar{X} + M_a] + [1 - b + b.t + m]$

$$\Rightarrow \quad r = \frac{[C_a - b.T_a + b.R + I_a + \bar{G} + \bar{X} - M_a]}{h} - \frac{[1 - b + b.t + m]}{h} \times Y \qquad (8.4)$$

Equation 8.4 is the same as Equation 8.3.

Let us now discuss some of the implications of changes in parameters on shifts of *IS*-curve:

1. *IS*-curve shifts upwards, parallel to itself in response to
   (a) an increase in C_a, R, I_a, $\bar{G}$ and $\bar{X}$ [*IS* shift to *IS*″ as in Figure 8.2 (a)]
   (b) a decrease in T_a, h and M_a [*IS* shifts to *IS*″ as in Figure 8.2 (a)]
2. *IS*-curve shifts downwards, parallel to itself in response to
   (a) a decrease in C_a, R, I_a, $\bar{G}$ and $\bar{X}$ [*IS* shift to *IS*′ as in Figure 8.2(a)]
   (b) an increase in T_a, h and M_a [*IS* shift to *IS*′ as in Figure 8.2(a)]
3. *IS*-curve pivots upwards in response to
   (a) an increase in h and b [*IS* pivots to *IS*″ as in Figure 8.2(b)]
4. *IS*-curve pivots downwards in response to
   (a) a decrease in b, and h [*IS* pivots to *IS*″ as in Figure 8.2(b)]
   (b) an increase in $b.t$, and m [*IS* pivots to *IS*″ as in Figure 8.2(b)]

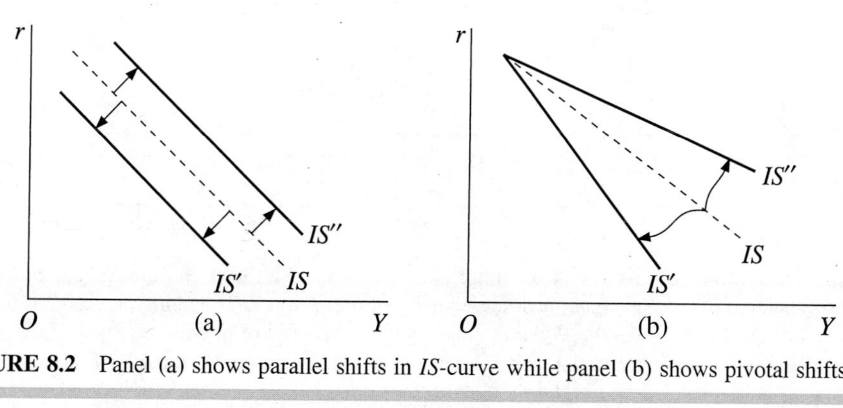

FIGURE 8.2 Panel (a) shows parallel shifts in *IS*-curve while panel (b) shows pivotal shifts in it.

8.1.2 Four Quadrant Method of its Derivation

Alternatively, we can demonstrate goods market equilibrium through four quadrant method. Figure 8.3 explains the process.

8.1.3 Two Quadrant Method of its Deriving (Figure 8.4)

Goods market equilibrium (*IS*-curve) can also be reached through two quadrant method as well. In the upper panel, we take aggregate demand and aggregate supply (output 0 as the condition of equilibrium along with actual aggregate demand as per Equation 8.1 which runs as below:

$$AD = \overline{A} + \{b\,(1 - t) - m\}Y - hr$$

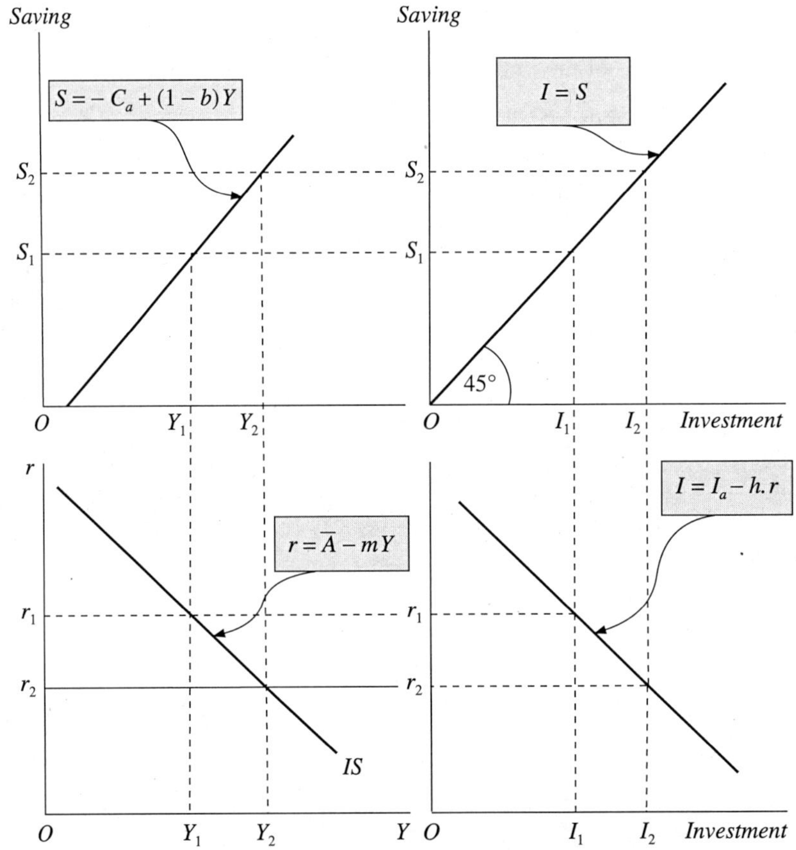

FIGURE 8.3 Derivation of *IS*-curve through Four Quadrant Method: Bottom-right quadrant portrays investment as a function of '*r*'; top-right quadrant, equality of *S* to *I*; top-left quadrant depicts *S* as a function of *Y* while bottom-left quadrant derives the *IS*-curve. Starting with two rates of interest, corresponding investments, savings and income levels are marked to reach the corresponding *IS*-curve. [*Note that* $\overline{A}/h$ *stands for* $[(C_a - b.T_a + b.R + I_a + \overline{G} + \overline{X} - M_a)]/h$ *and m, for* $[1 - b + b.t + m]/h$].

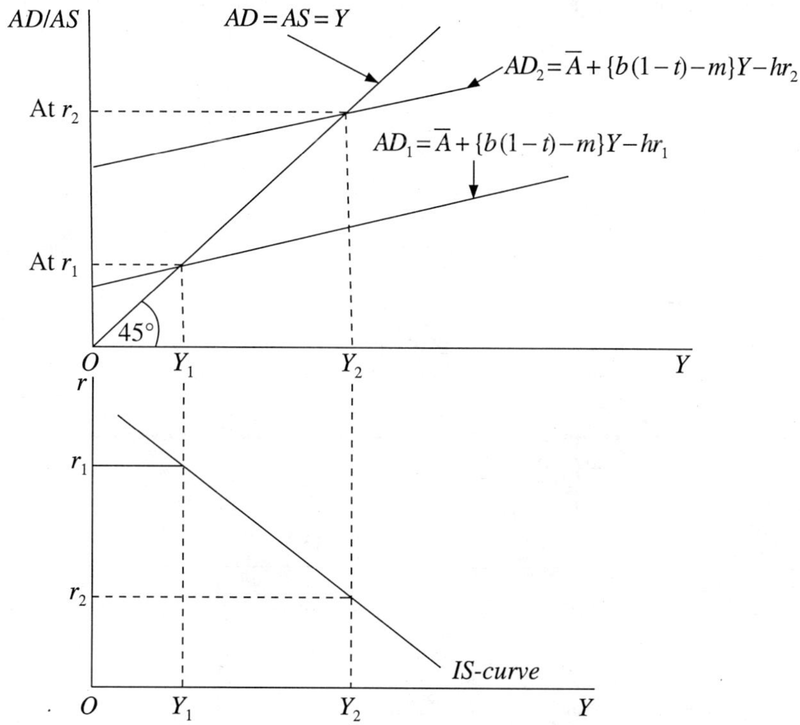

FIGURE 8.4 Derivation of Goods Market Equilibrium (*IS*-curve) through two Quadrant Method: Equilibrium condition is $AD = AS$, which is a 45° line (upper quadrant). Actual *AD*s are drawn at two different interest rates, r_1 and r_2. Intersection of *AS* with AD_1 at r_1 and AD_2 at r_2 yields corresponding outputs as Y_1 and Y_2. Projections to the lower panel give the *IS*-curve, which is a locus of various combinations of *Y* and *r* for each of which *Injections* (*I*) are equal to withdrawals (*S*).

8.2 APPLICATIONS AND IMPLICATIONS OF *IS*-CURVES

8.2.1 *IS*-curves Undergo a Parallel Shift upwards to Right when Autonomous Investment Increases (Figure 8.5)

Increase in autonomous investment (I_a) leads to an upwards to right shift in investment function ($I = I_a - hr$). The shift so caused is parallel to the original investment curve. This results in an upward to right parallel shift in *IS*-curve as worked out in Figure 8.5.

8.2.2 *IS*-curves undergo a Parallel Shift upwards to Right when Tax Financed Government Expenditures Increase (Figure 8.6)

In Figure 8.5, I_2 can be replaced by (I_1 + *G*) in the bottom right quadrant and *S* by (*S* + *T*) in the top right quadrant. As for the top left quadrant, *S* and (*S* + *T*) functions are drawn and income levels found are at r_1 and r_2 rates of interest through projections as shown in Figure 8.6. *IS*-curve shifts to right parallel to itself. In this case too but the degree and quantum of shift is different.

The reader can likewise try studying the effects on the *IS*-curve of changes in exports, transfer payments, and autonomous imports.

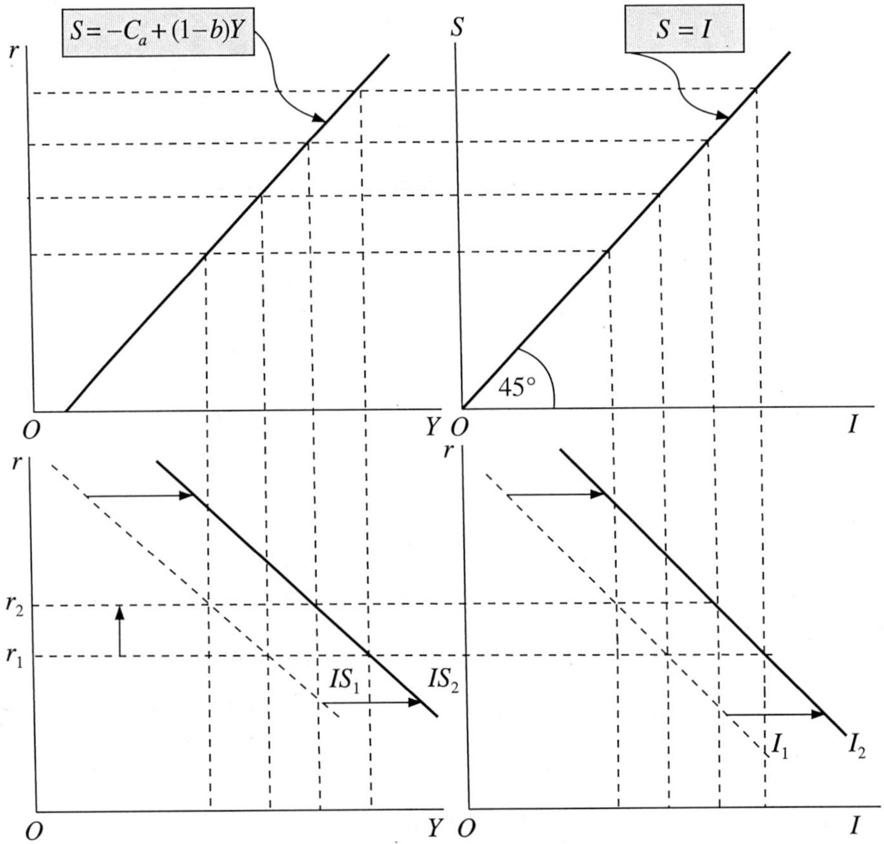

FIGURE 8.5 Effect of an Increase in Investment on IS-curve: Investment function increases from I_1 ($I_a - hr$) to I_2 ($I'_a - hr$). As a result savings equal to these levels of investments are located in the top–right quadrant which portrays equality of *S* to *I*. Levels of income, *Y*, are located in top-left quadrant. Projection from the respective points of the savings function mark off the corresponding levels of incomes and rates of interest in the bottom-left quadrant. Joining the corresponding points in the bottom-left quadrant yield the respective *IS*-curves. In consequence, when investment increases, Investment function shifts rightwards parallel to itself and so does the *IS*-curve from IS_1 to IS_2.

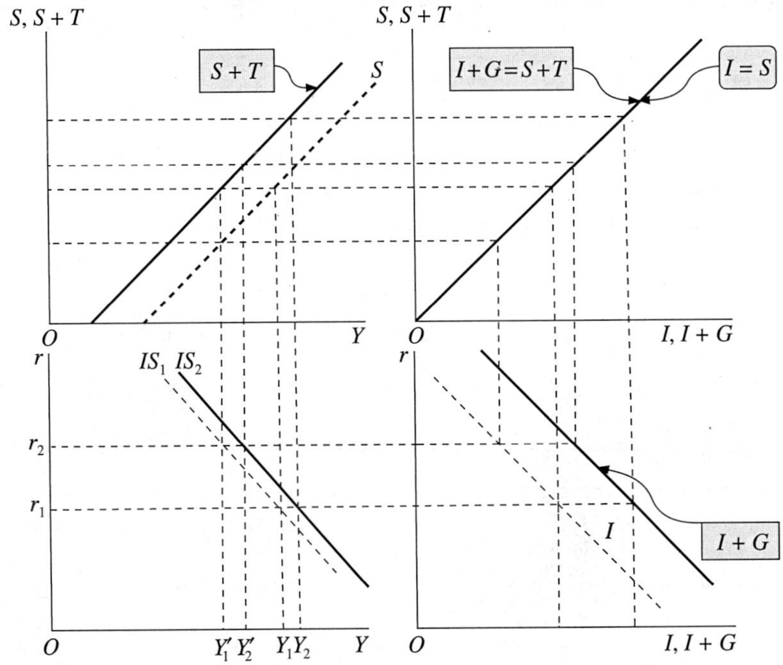

FIGURE 8.6 The bottom-right panel shows how government spending shifts injections upward to right. The top-right panel, portrays equality of injections to withdrawals, that is , I to S and $(I + G)$ to $(S + T)$. Top-left quadrant portrays both S and $S + T$, the withdrawals, as functions of income Y. Projections from the rates r_1 and r_2 of interest to meet injections in bottom-right and top-right quadrants help fixing respective values of withdrawals in top-right and top-left quadrants, which in turn, help fixing the corresponding levels of Income, Y, in the top-left and bottom-left quadrants. Joining points (Y_1, r_1) and (Y_1', r_2) gives IS_1 and points (Y_2, r_1) and (Y_2', r_2) gives IS_2. The shift is less than that in the injections. It is so because injection of government spending and withdrawals of taxation offset each other.

KEY TERMS AND CONCEPTS

Goods Market Equilibrium or *IS*-curve: The locus of various combinations of income and rate of interest for each of which $I = S$. The equation of the *IS*-curve for a four sector economy follows the format:

$$r = \alpha - \beta Y$$

Here, $$\alpha = [C_a - bT_a + bR + I_a + \overline{G} + \overline{X} - M_a]/h; \ \beta = [1 - b + bt + m]/h$$

Symbols have their usual meanings.

Absorption: Absorption (A) refers to the fixed expenditures in the economy that represent the intercept of the *IS*-curve. Thus,

$$\overline{A} = [C_a - b\,T_a + b\,R + I_a + \overline{G} + \overline{X} - M_a]$$

EXERCISES

A. Short Answer Questions

1. How is goods market equilibrium reached? Comment on its shape.
2. What causes parallel shifts in the *IS*-curve and what pivotal shifts in it? Demonstrate with the help of sketches.
3. How does the tax financed government spending affect the *IS*-curve? Explain with the help of a diagram.
4. How does an increase in autonomous investment affect the *IS*-curve? Explain with the help of a sketch.

B. Long Answer Questions

5. Suppose national income is to be increased. Can an increase in government expenditure or in export earning serve the purpose? Explain.

   [**Ans:** Yes. Use multipliers to demonstrate. Government expenditure multiplier,

   $$KG = \Delta Y/\Delta' G = 1/(1 - b + bt + m) = \Delta Y/\Delta' X = KX \Rightarrow \Delta Y = KG \times \Delta' G, \text{ and } \Delta Y = KX \times \Delta' X$$

   [See Equations 6.44 and 6. 45 (with $i = 0$), Chapter 6].
6. What do you mean by injections and withdrawals? How can they lead to goods market equilibrium?

   [**Hint:** Injections comprise I, G and X which are fed into circular flow of income and expenditure to offset the leakage of withdrawals comprising S, T, and M.]
7. Obtain the *IS*-curve from (i) two quadrant method, (ii) algebraic method, (iii) Four quadrant method.

Chapter 9

Simultaneous Equilibrium of Goods Market and Money Market (General Equilibrium)

INTRODUCTION

Equilibrium of goods and money markets is best understood through the *IS-LM* framework. It refers to macro-economic equilibrium. It is a form of general equilibrium with no restrictive conditions of ceteris paribus. The latter is traced through interdependence of a large number of economic entities. There are so many goods and services produced by so many firms employing so many factors of production in an economy. The equilibrium of all is a steady-state from which no economic entity—be it a producer, a consumer or a factor of production—feels an incentive to deviate from. Taking into account all of them is a time consuming process, which loses its sanctity due to dynamic changes in demand and supply conditions from season to season that render such equilibrium of little consequence.

However, French economist Leon Walras[1] (1834–1910) developed a model under certain assumptions to provide a feel of interdependence among various entities involved in general equilibrium. In his model, behavior of each individual unit or market is presented by a set of equations. For instance, a consumer buys goods and provides factor services. This leads to a set of equations depicting his behavior. But there are so many consumers! In a Walrasian system, there are so many markets as there are commodities and factors of production. Each market has three types of functions—***demand functions, supply functions*** and a ***market clearing functions.*** For the sake of simplicity, it'd be better to explain his general equilibrium model by assuming two consumers, say, *A* and *B*; two commodities, say, *X* and *Y*; and two factors of production, say, *L* and *K*. The pattern of changes taking place among them over time is worked out by the author[2] while explaining the general equilibrium model of Walras of 2 × 2 × 2[3] entities involving as many as 18 unknowns and 18 equations. This makes a model befitting micro-analysis only. It is solvable at micro-level as the number of equations and the number of unknowns involved is limited to 18 each. This makes Walraian model of general equilibrium only a virtual demonstration of interdependence among various entities. It does not give the complete picture of general equilibrium, which by no means can be possible at micro-level.

[1] Leon Walras, *Elements & Economie politique pure* (Lausanne,1874). First translated in English by William Jaffe (Allan & Unwin,1954).

[2] Chauhan, S.P.S., *Microeconomics, An Advanced Treatise*, 3rd Edition, PHI Learning.

[3] For a rigorous treatment of 2 × 2 × 2 model, see H.G. Johnson, *Two-Sector Model of General Equilibrium* (Aldine Press, New York, 1971).

Macroeconomic equilibrium worked out through *IS-LM* framework assumes periodic equilibrium of goods and services market on one hand and money market on the other. How such equilibria are reached over the period is of no concern. Let us therefore demonstrate them here assuming the end results.

9.1 EQUILIBRIUM THROUGH *IS-LM* FRAMEWORK

We have derived *IS* and *LM*-curves in earlier chapters. Superimposing the two in the same space yields goods and money market equilibrium as shown in Figure 9.1(a) for linear *LM* and Figure 9.1 (b) for non-linear *LM.*

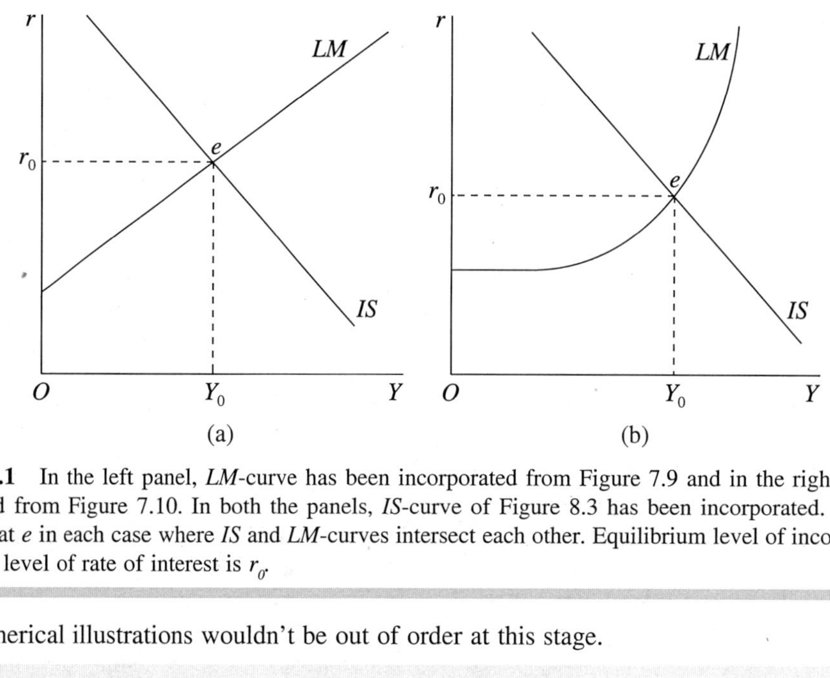

FIGURE 9.1 In the left panel, *LM*-curve has been incorporated from Figure 7.9 and in the right panel, it is incorporated from Figure 7.10. In both the panels, *IS*-curve of Figure 8.3 has been incorporated. Equilibrium takes place at *e* in each case where *IS* and *LM*-curves intersect each other. Equilibrium level of income is Y_0 and equilibrium level of rate of interest is r_0.

A few numerical illustrations wouldn't be out of order at this stage.

ILLUSTRATION 9.1: For an economy with following specifications,

Consumption, $C = 80 + 0.8Y^d$

Tax, $T = 60 + 0.2Y$

Investment, $I = 200 - 10\,r$, r = rate of interest

Transfers, $R = -40$

Govt. expenditure, $\bar{G} = 160$

Transaction and Precautionary Demands for money,

$$L_1 = 0.40\,Y$$

Speculative demand for Money,

$$L_2 = 300 - 20r,\ r = \text{rate of interest}$$

Money supply, $M = 476$

Determine:

(a) equations of *IS* and *LM*-curves
(b) equilibrium level of income and rate of interest
(c) tax revenue at the equilibrium level of income
(d) level of disposable income at the equilibrium
(e) level of consumption at the equilibrium
(f) the budget surplus.

Solution:

(a) The equation of the *IS*-curve, as given by Equation 8.3, is

$r = [(C_a - b\,T_a + b\,R + I_a + \overline{G} + \overline{X} - M_a)/h] - [(1 - b + bt + m)/h] \times Y$

$= [80 - 0.8 \times 60 + 0.8 \times (-40) + 200 + 160 + 0]/10 - [1 - 0.8 + 0.8 \times 0.2 + 0]/10 \times Y$

(Substituting data from the question)

$= [360/10] - [0.36/10] \times Y$

$= 36 - 0.036Y$ (9.1)

The equation of the *LM* –curve, as given by Equation 7.25, is

$r = (k/g)\,Y + \{(m - M)/g\}$

$= (0.4/20)\,Y + \{(300 - 476)/20\}$

$= 0.02\,Y - 8.8$ (9.2)

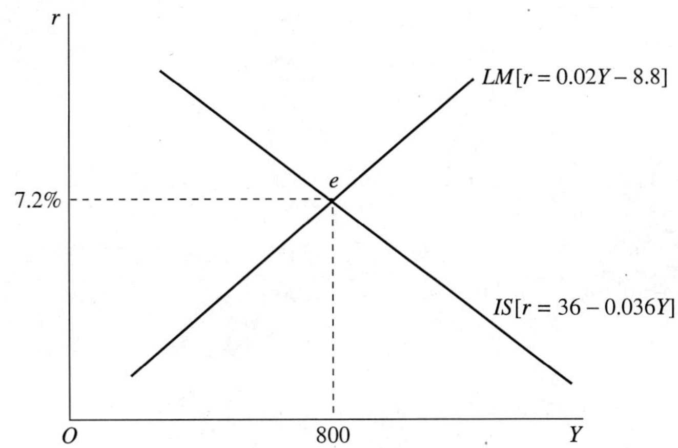

FIGURE 9.2 The *IS*-curve [$r = 36 - 0.036Y$] intersects the *LM*-curve [$0.02\,Y - 8.8$] at *e*. Equilibrium level of income *Y* and rate of interest *r* are respectively 800 and 7.2%.

Equations 9.1 and 9.2 give the equations of *IS* and *LM*-curves.

(b) Simultaneous solution of Equation 9.1 and 9.2 yields equilibrium level of income and rate of interest,

$$Y = 800;\ r = 7.2\%$$

(c) Tax Revenue,

$$T = 60 + 0.20Y$$
$$= 60 + 0.20 \times 800$$
$$= 220.$$

(d) Disposable Income,

$$Y^d = Y - T + R$$
$$= 800 - 220 + (-40)$$
$$= 540.$$

(e) Consumption Expenditure at equilibrium,

$$C = 80 + 0.80\ Y^d$$
$$= 80 + 0.80 \times 540$$
$$= 80 + 432$$
$$= 512.$$

(f) Budget Surplus,

BS = Tax revenue net of transfers – government expenditure = $T - R - \overline{G}$
$= 220 - (-40) - 160$
$= 100.$

ILLUSTRATION 9.2: Consider an economy with following specifications:

Consumption, $C = 100 + 0.90Y^d$
Income Tax, $T = 100 + 0.20\ Y$
Investment, $I = 500 - 25\ r$
Govt. expenditure, $\overline{G} = 300$
Transfers, $R = 100$
Exports, $\overline{X} = 200$
Imports, $M = 175 + 0.02\ Y$
Transaction demand for money, $L_1 = 0.40\ Y$
Speculative demand for money, $L_2 = 600 - 50\ r$
Nominal money supply, $M = 1500$
Price level, $P = 3.00$
Full employment income, $Y_F = 2000$

Determine:

(a) Equations of *IS*- and *LM*-curves
(b) Equilibrium level of income and rate of interest
(c) Tax revenue
(d) Disposable income
(e) Imports
(f) Trade surplus
(g) Budget surplus
(h) Increase in government expenditure to bring about full employment income.

Solution:

(a) From Equation 8.3, equation of The *IS*-curve is given as

$$r = [(C_a - b\ T_a + bR + I_a + \overline{G} + \overline{X} - M_a)/h] - [\ (1 - b + bt + m)/h] \times Y$$

Substituting $C_a = 100$, $b = 0.90$, $T_a = 100$, $t = 0.20$, $\overline{G} = 300$, $R = 100$, $\overline{X} = 200$, $M_a = 175$, $m = 0.02$, $h = 25$ and $I_a = 500$; we've

$$r = (100 - 0.9 \times 100 + 0.9 \times 100 + 500 + 300 + 200 - 175)/25 - [1 - 0.9 + 0.9 \times 0.20 + 0.02)/25 \times Y$$
$$= (925/25) - (0.3/25)\ Y$$
$$= 37 - 0.012Y \tag{9.3}$$

From Equation 7.25, equation of the *LM*-curve is given as,

$$r = (k/g)\ Y + \{(n - M)/g\}$$

Substituting $k = 0.40$, $g = 50$, $n = 600$ and $M = 1500/3 = 500$, we've

$$r = 0.008Y + 2 \tag{9.4}$$

(b) Simultaneous solution of Equations 8.6 and 8.7 yields,

$$Y = 1750,\ r = 16\%$$

(c) Tax,
$$T = T_a + 0.20Y$$
$$= 100 + 0.20 \times 1750$$
$$= 450$$

(d) Disposable income,
$$Y^d = Y - T + R$$
$$= 1750 - 450 + 100$$
$$= 1400$$

(e) Imports,
$$M = M_a + m\ Y$$
$$= 175 + 0.02\ Y$$
$$= 175 + 0.02 \times 1750$$
$$= 210$$

(f) Trade Balance,
$$NX = \overline{X} - M$$
$$= 200 - 210$$
$$= -10$$

(g) Budget Surplus,
$$BS = T - R - \overline{G}$$
$$= 450 - 100 - 300$$
$$= 50$$

(h) Full employment income, $Y_F = 2000$. Current income = 1750. Hence, Govt. expenditure multiplier,

$$K_{\overline{G}} = \Delta Y/\Delta\overline{G}$$
$$= 1/(1 - b + bt + m)$$
$$= 1/(1 - 0.9 + 0.9 \times 0.20 + 0.02)$$
$$= 10/3$$

To raise income to the full employment level, desired increase in income is 250 (2000 – 1750). To reach it, increase in government spending is thus given by

$$\Rightarrow \quad \Delta\overline{G} = 3 \times 250/10$$
$$= 75.$$

9.2 *IS-LM* EQUILIBRIUM UNDER FISCAL AND MONETARY INFLUENCES

Goods market equilibrium can be given by quation of *IS*-curve (Equation 8.3, Chapter 8) as,

$$Y = K_G\ (\overline{A} - hr) \tag{9.5}$$

$$\text{where, } K_G = 1/(1 - b + bt + m)$$

$$\bar{A} = (C_a - b\,T_a + bR + I_a + \bar{G} + \bar{X} - M_a)$$

and that of the money market (*LM*-curve) by Equation 7.25[1] (Chapter 7) as,

$$r = (k/g)\,Y + (n - M)/g$$

Dropping n from it for the sake of simplicity and expressing money supply $\bar{M}$ in real terms, as $\bar{M}/\bar{P}$, we've

$$r = [k\,Y - (\bar{M}/\bar{P})]/g \tag{9.6}$$

where $\bar{M}/\bar{P} \equiv$ supply of real money (M_S^R), $\bar{M} \equiv$ nominal money supply

Demand for real money is given as $[k\,Y - gr]$ and its supply as $\bar{M}/\bar{P}$

Eliminating r from Equations 9.5 and 9.6, we have

$$Y = K_G[\bar{A} - h\,\{k\,Y - (\bar{M}/\bar{P})\}/g] \tag{9.7}$$

Collecting and combining terms and solving for the equilibrium level of output, we have,

$$Y = \frac{K_G}{[1 + k\,K_G(h/g)]} \times \bar{A} + \frac{h\,K_G[(\bar{M}/\bar{P})]}{g[1 + k\,K_G(h/g)]}$$

$$= \gamma\bar{A} + \gamma(h/g)\,[(\bar{M}/\bar{P})] \tag{9.8}$$

where, $\gamma \equiv K_G/[1 + k\,K_G\,(h/g)]$

Equation 9.8 gives equilibrium level of income which depends on exogenously determined $\bar{A}$ and fiscal policy parameters $\bar{G}$, $\bar{R}$, T_a, and net exports $\bar{X}$ and M_a. Equilibrium rate of interest can be given as,

$$r^2 = \gamma(k/g)\,\bar{A} - \gamma[1/g\,K_G]\,[\bar{M}/\bar{P}] \tag{9.9}$$

On substituting for Y from Equation 9.8 in the expression of r (Equation 9.6) and simplifying. Differentiating Equation 9.8 with respect to $\bar{G}$, we get $d\,Y/d\bar{G}$, or simply, $\Delta Y/\Delta\bar{G}$ equal to γ, the ***fiscal policy multiplier.*** Note that $[\bar{M}/\bar{P}]$ is treated as fixed and that $\bar{A}$ being a function of C_a, $\bar{G}$, $\bar{R}$, T_a, I_a, $\bar{X}$, and M_a, $dY/d\bar{G} = dY/d\bar{A} \times d\bar{A}/d\bar{G}$ (Chain Rule of differentiation).

$$dY/d\bar{G} \text{ or } \Delta Y/\Delta\bar{G} = \gamma = K_G/[1 + k\,K_G\,(h/g)] \tag{9.10}$$

Note that $\bar{G}$ is a part of $\bar{A}$, the autonomous absorption (see Equation 8.2, Ch. 8).

Fiscal policy multiplier can thus be defined as increase in output/income per unit increase in government spending when real money supply is constant,

$$\Delta Y = (d\,Y/d\,\bar{G}) \times \Delta\bar{G}$$

---

[1] Based on speculative demand as an additively inverse function of rate of interest.

[2] Proof: Substituting for Y from Equation 9.8 in the expression for r (Equation 9.6), we have

$$r = (1/g)[kY - (\bar{M}/\bar{P})$$
$$= (1/g)[k\{\gamma\bar{A} + \gamma(h/g)(\bar{M}/\bar{P})\} - (\bar{M}/\bar{P})]$$
$$= (1/g)[k\{\gamma\bar{A}\} - \gamma(\bar{M}/\bar{P})\}\{(1/\gamma) - hk/g\}]$$
$$= (1/g)[\{k\gamma\bar{A}\} - \gamma(\bar{M}/\bar{P})\}\{(1 + kK_G(h/g)/K_G) - hk/g\}$$
$$= (1/g)[\{k\gamma\bar{A}\} - \gamma(\bar{M}/\bar{P})\}\{g(1 + kK_G\,(h/g) - k\,K_G\,(h/g)\}/gK_G$$
$$= (1/g)[\{k\gamma\bar{A}\} - \gamma(\bar{M}/\bar{P})\}\{g/g\,K_G\}$$
$$= (k/g)\,\gamma\bar{A} - \gamma(1/g\,K_G)\,(\bar{M}/\bar{P}).$$

$$= \gamma \times \Delta\overline{G} \qquad (9.11)$$

For the data of Illustration 9.2,

$$\gamma = K_G/[1 + k\, K_G(h/g)]$$
$$= (10/3) \div [1 + 0.4(10/3)\,(25/50)]$$
$$= 2.00$$

If a government adopts a fiscal expansion worth ($\Delta\overline{G}$) = 10, national output increases by 20, when real money supply remains unchanged.

[*Note how Government Expenditure multiplier and fiscal policy multiplier differ from each other. Fiscal policy multiplier relates to changes in equilibrium level of output / income per unit change in Government Expenditure when interest rate adjustments are taken into account as also real money supply is held constant while Government Expenditure multiplier relates simply to changes in output/ income without such considerations. That is the reason why fiscal policy multiplier is always less than Government Expenditure multiplier and why an increase in interest rate has a dampening effect on income/output. Examine Equation 9.10 to see the interrelationship between the two multipliers.*]

Likewise differentiating Equation 9.8 with respect to [$(\overline{M}/\overline{P})$], while $\overline{A}$ is constant, we can get ***monetary policy multiplier***, given by

$$dY/d\,(\overline{M}/\overline{P}) \text{ or } \Delta Y / \Delta\,(\overline{M}/\overline{P}) = (h/g)\ \gamma = (25/50) \times 2.00 = 1.00 \text{ for Illustration 9.2} \qquad (9.12)$$

9.3 TRACING PATH FROM DISEQUILIBRIUM TO EQUILIBRIUM IN *IS-LM* FRAMEWORK [Figure 9.3]

Before we proceed to some interesting implications and applications of equilibrium of *IS-LM* framework, let us see how a point of disequilibrium automatically traces its path to equilibrium (Figure 9.3)

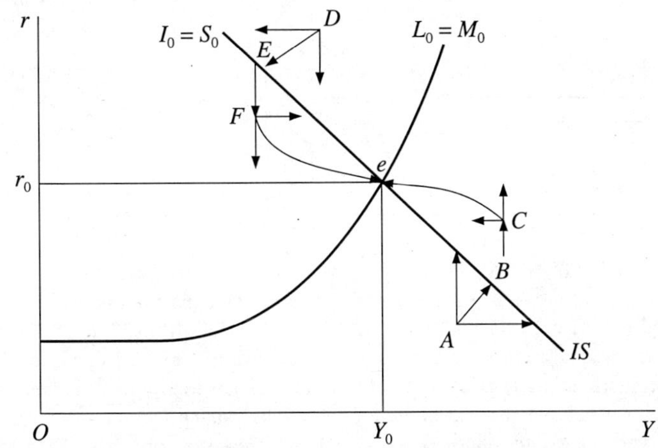

FIGURE 9.3 Point *A* falls below *LM*-curve. Demand for money [refer to Equation 7.24, Ch.7] varying inversely with interest, the tendency of point *A*, where $M^d > M^S$, is to move vertically towards the *LM*-curve so that $M^d = M^s$ at the same *Y*. This would apply to every point below the *LM*-curve. Point *A* also falls below *IS*-curve, that is, $I > S$ at *A*, it must move rightwards so that $I = S$ at same rate of interest. This would apply to every point lying below the *IS*-curve. Simultaneous pressures would lead Point *A* to move to point *B* on the *IS*-curve. But Point *B* is still below

(Contd.)

FIGURE 9.3 Contd.

the *LM*-curve [$M^d > M^S$ at *B*], it must move vertically upwards so that $M^d = M^S$ at the same *Y*. Let point *B* reach in position of point *C*. Point *C* being above the *IS*-curve, would move horizontally leftwards following a track opposite of that which point *A* took for being below *IS*-curve, and it will move upwards towards the *LM*-curve for being still below it, following the same pattern as point *A* did for being below the *LM*-curve. The simultaneous pressures on *C* would lead it to the equilibrium point *e*. Thus, tracing the path to equilibrium at *e* from points of disequilibrium, namely, *A*, *B*, and *C* is an automatic process. Similar is the process of tracing equilibrium at *e* from points of disequilibrium, namely *D*, *E* and *F*. Any point below, above or on the *IS*-curve has an automatic tendency to go to the *IS*-curve and to end up in equilibrium Likewise any point below, above or on the *LM*-curve too has an automatic tendency to move to the *LM*-curve and to end up at equilibrium.

9.4 EFFICACY OF MONETARY AND FISCAL POLICIES THROUGH *IS-LM* FRAMEWORK

The figure (Figure 9.4) depicts efficacy of monetary and fiscal policies in Keynesian, classical and intermediate ranges of *LM*-curve. In Keynesian range fiscal policy is highly effective while monetary

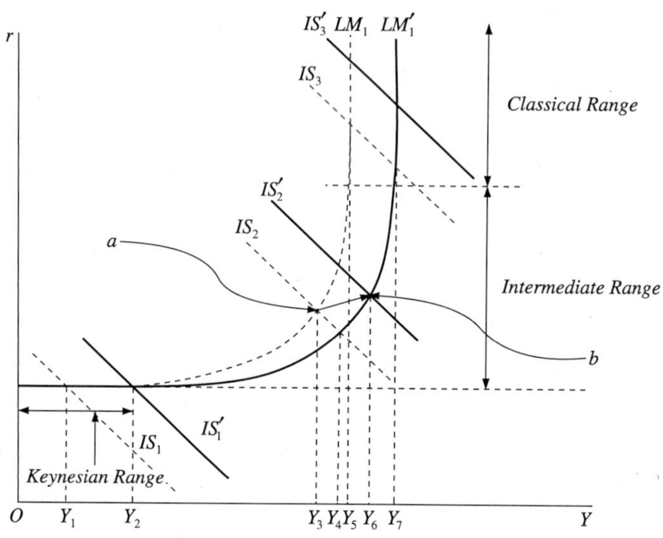

FIGURE 9.4 As explained in Figure 7.12, expansionary monetary policy shifts the *LM*-curve to right as shown. In Keynesian Range (horizontally overlapping *LM*-curves) monetary expansion is ineffective by itself in growth of income *Y* but coupled with fiscal expansion (shift in *IS*-curve to right from IS_1 to IS_1') it proves more effective than in intermediate and classical ranges by increasing income from Y_1 to Y_2. Keynesian Range corresponds to the liquidity trap. In the intermediate Range, effect of monetary expansion by itself is moderate on income (from Y_3 to Y_4) but coupled with fiscal expansion it is more effective by raising income from Y_3 to Y_6. In the Classical Range, *LM*-curve being vertical, expansionary monetary policy increases income from Y_5 to Y_7. while expansionary fiscal policy proves ineffective. The credit goes only to the monetary policy in this case.

Note that the *LM*-curve is horizontal in Keynesian Range and vertical in Classical Range. The latter owes its nature to the assumption of the classical version of demand for money which does not admit speculative component (L_2) in it. According to the classical view, money is demanded for transaction and precautionary motives only which being identically interest inelastic each individually as well as together.

[*Note that movement from point 'a' to point 'b' marks the effect of simultaneous increase in investment and money supply.*]

policy isn't effective at all. In this range expansionary fiscal policy increases income from Y_1 to Y_2 without causing any change in the interest rate. In classical range, fiscal policy is ineffective while monetary policy is effective in raising the income level fromY_5 to Y_7. Income stagnates at Y_5 in this range due to fiscal expansion. In the intermediate range, monetary and fiscal policies each effect income moderately, which rises from Y_3 to Y_4 due to monetary expansion and from. Y_3 to Y_6 due to the effect of both together.

Effect on the rate of interest, none in Keynesian range due to either of the policies while substantial in the classical range due to fiscal expansion and moderate in it due to monetary expansion. In the intermediate range effect on interest rate due to fiscal expansion is higher than that due to monetary expansion. Even the collective effect on the interest rate of the two policies is moderate.

That explains how a parallel shift in the *IS*-curve effects income and interest in the three ranges of the *LM*-curve. Let us now take the effect caused by a pivotal/non-parallel shifts in *IS*-curves. Figure 9.5 demonstrates it.

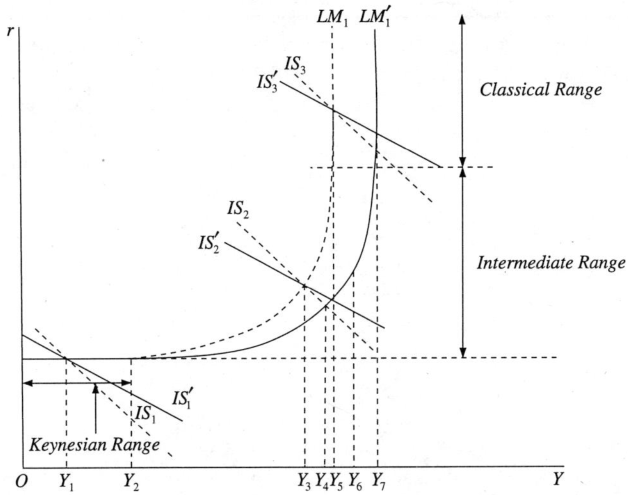

FIGURE 9.5 As against a parallel shift, a pivotal or non-parallel shift in *IS*-curve is completely ineffective in Keynesian range by itself and so is the case in other ranges too. Monetary expansion can be seen to be ineffective in Keynesian range but effective in intermediate and classical ranges. The joint effect of the two policies in the intermediate and classical ranges, however, is not insignificant.

Note that pivotal shift in *IS*-curve is caused by changes in the slope of the *IS*-curve (its elasticity), which is the coefficient of *Y* in Equation 8.3 of the previous chapter.

9.5 ASSORTED IMPLICATIONS AND APPLICATIONS

9.5.1 Derivation of Aggregate Demand under Fixed Prices

In this section, we are going to discuss cases where increase in supply of nominal money increases that of real money by the same proportion under fixed price level. To demonstrate, suppose supply of nominal money increases from 1000 to 1200, that is by 20%. Suppose further that the price level is stable at 4.00. As a result, supply of real money would increase from 250 (1000/4) to 300 (1200/4), that is, by the same proportion (20%). Increase in real money affects the *LM*-curve accordingly. It shifts rightwards as shown in Figure 9.6. Thus, increase in real money shifts the *LM*-curve upwards to right. A decrease in it will have an opposite effect.

In the first application, that is, in Subsection 9.5.1.1, we show its effect on *IS -LM* equilibrium. The figure sketches less than full employment equilibrium with aggregate supply (*AS*) behaving perfectly elastic up to full employment level of income and turning perfectly inelastic at full employment while aggregate demand (*AD*) being perfectly inelastic. Thus, Applications 9.5.1.1, 9.5.1.2, and 9.5.1.3 are all based on the following assumptions:

1. ***Aggregate supply is perfectly elastic up to full employment level and perfectively inelastic at full employment:***
   The assumption implies that supply of goods and services is unlimited at same price until full employment of factors is reached. At full employment, supply turns perfectly inelastic as production can't increase due unavailability of factors of production.
2. ***Economy operates at less than full employment:***
   Aggregate demand curve is perfectly inelastic, that is, demand is fixed whatever the level of price. With these assumptions we discuss the effect of an increase in money supply in Subsection 9.5.1.1, that of an increase in investment in Subsection 9.5.1.2, and that of an increase in government spending in Subsection 9.5.1.3.

9.5.1.1 Effect of a change in money supply on *IS-LM* equilibrium and derivation of aggregate demand (*AD*) under fixed prices [Figure 9.6]

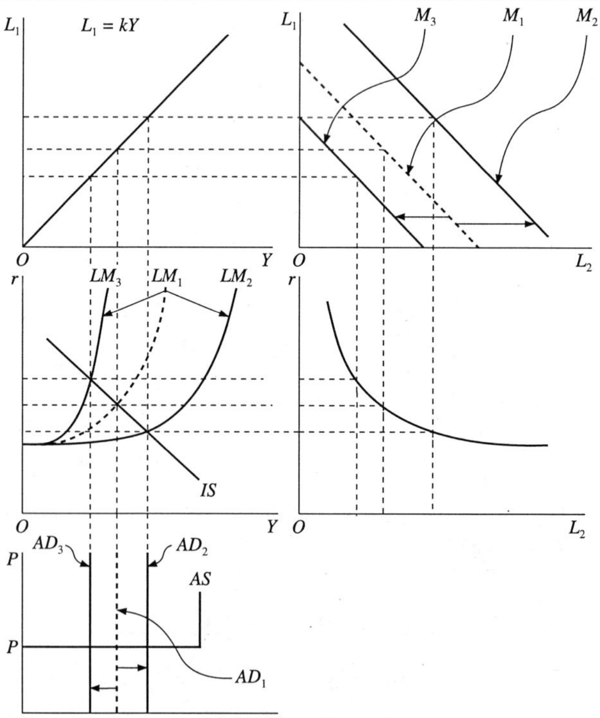

FIGURE 9.6 Increase in money supply shifts supply ($M = L$) upwards from M_1 to M_2 and a decrease in it, shifts it downwards from M_1 to M_3. The effects of these shifts reflect in the shifts of *LM*-curves as shown. *IS*-curve remains unaffected. Points of intersection of *IS*-curve with the *LM*-curves so obtained give corresponding aggregate demand curves that are vertical in fixed price model.

[*Note that aggregate supply curve is perfectly elastic until full employment and perfectly inelastic at full employment*].

9.5.1.2 Effect of a change in investment on *IS-LM* equilibrium and derivation of aggregate demand [Figure 9.7]

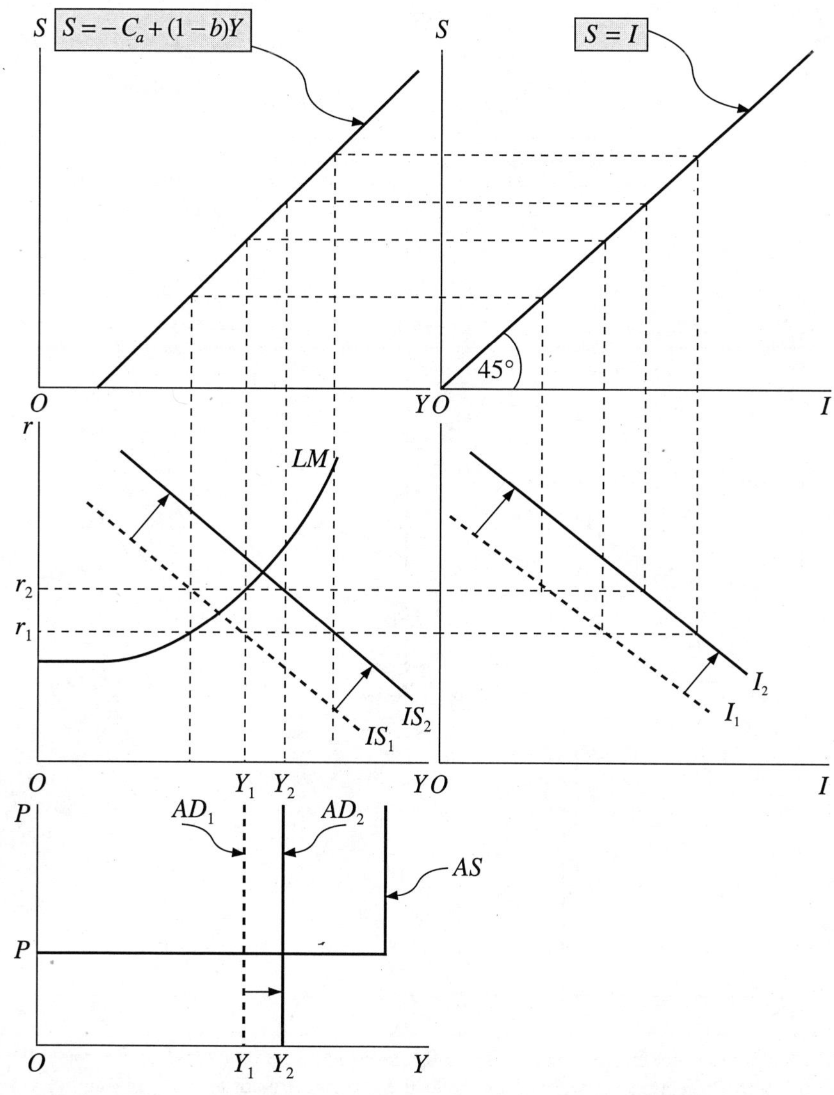

FIGURE 9.7 As investment increases from I_1 to I_2, at applicable rates of interest, r_1 and r_2 in bottom-right quadrant, the equilibrium condition of goods market ($S = I$) in upper right quadrant helps estimation of corresponding saving in upper left quadrant as a function of *Y*. Downward projections from corresponding points in upper-left quadrant to bottom left quadrant give the goods market equilibrium curves, IS_1 and IS_2. Their intersection with the *LM*-curve ascertains aggregate demands Y_1 and Y_2 each of which is perfectly inelastic in fixed price model Note the shift of IS_1 to IS_2 as also that of AD_1 to AD_2.

9.5.1.3 Effect of a change in tax financed government spending on *IS-LM* equilibrium and derivation of aggregate demand (*AD*) [Figure 9.8]

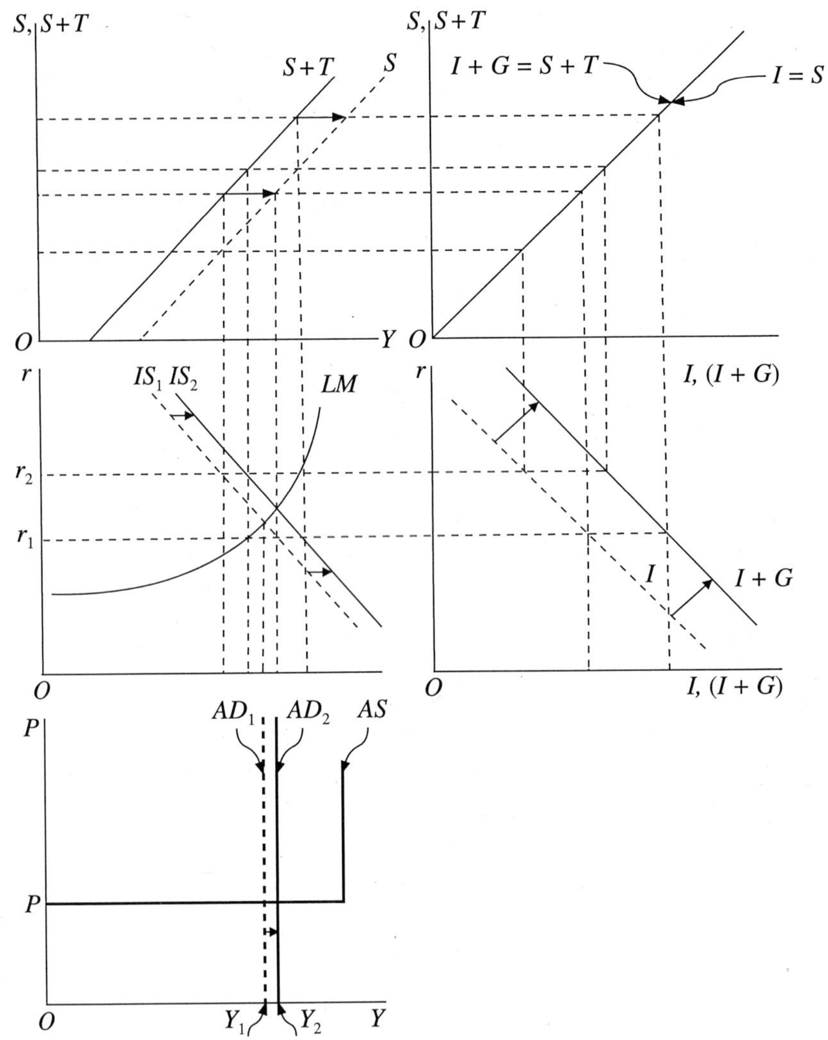

FIGURE 9.8 Increase in government spending shifts investment curve from I to $I + G$ as depicted in the bottom-right quadrant. Projections upwards from it to the top-right quadrant showing equality of S to I and $S+T$ to $I + G$ (the equilibrium condition), and then, to the top left quadrant portraying S and $S + T$ as functions of income Y, give the corresponding downward-sloping *IS*-curves in the bottom left quadrant. Projections from the points of intersection of the *IS* and *LM*-curves to the lower left quadrant intended for *AD* and *AS*, with price on its vertical axis, yields vertical *AD*-curves as shown. Note that *AS*-curve is perfectly elastic up to the full-employment level of income while *AD*-curves are vertical. Note also that the effect on *IS*-curve of a change in any parameter that shifts *IS*-curve upwards parallel to itself can be explained on the lines of Figure 9.7 above.

9.5.2 Effect on Aggregate Demand (*AD*) through *IS-LM* Framework under Variable Prices

We consider the following three cases here:

1. Nominal money is fixed in supply while price level rises/falls.
2. Nominal money supply increases/decreases and so does the price level by the same proportions.
3. Nominal money supply and price increase/decrease by a different proportion.

9.5.2.1 Nominal money is fixed in supply while price level rises/falls (Figure 9.9)

An increase or a decrease of price tends to decrease or increase real money as explained earlier. Consider the situation of Figure 7.13. Reproducing the figure with given situation of *IS*-curve, we attempt derivation of the AD curve below.

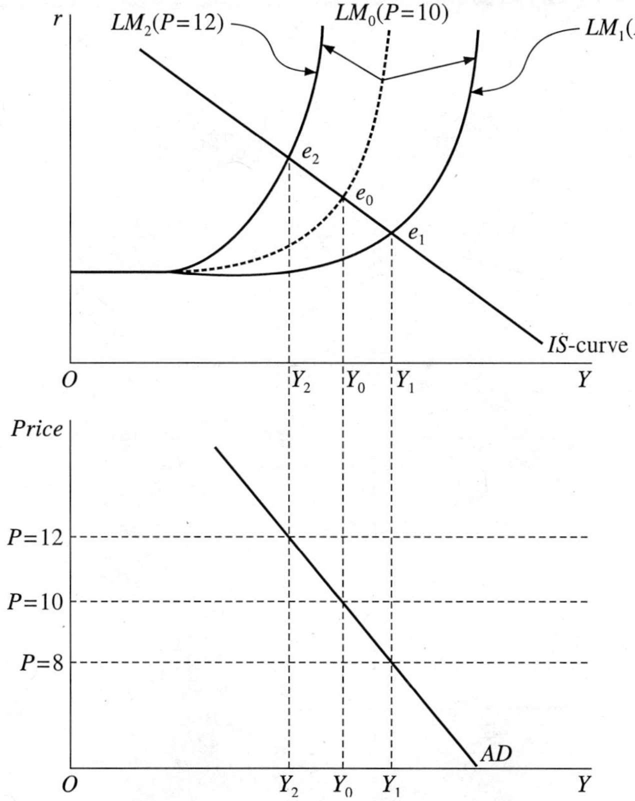

FIGURE 9.9 Supply of nominal balance being fixed, a rise in price level shifts the *LM*-curve upwards to left and a fall in it, to downward to right as shown. Output falls in response to a rise in price and it rises in response to a fall in it. The general equilibrium comprises points of intersection of *IS* and *LM*-curves. It involves points e_1, e_2 and e_0 corresponding to prices 8, 12 and 10. Projections downwards to the lower panel from these points give a downward sloping aggregate demand curve, *AD*.

9.5.2.2 Nominal money supply and prices increase/decrease by the same proportion and in the same direction so that real money supply is constant (Figure 9.10)

Changes in nominal money and prices in the same proportion do not affect real money supply. This leads to same position of the *LM*-curve. Aggregate demand curve so obtained is perfectly price inelastic as in Figure 9.10.

To elaborate, let the quantity of nominal money be 1000 while price level is 5. Quantity of real money would work out to 1000/5, that is, 200. Now let nominal money increase by 20%, that is, from 1000 to 1200. Assuming price level to increase by the same proportion, it would rise to 6. The quantity of real money would remain unchanged as 1200/6 or 200. In the same way, 20% fall in nominal money as also in the price level would leave real balances unchanged. The *LM*-curve in either case would remain unchanged. The nature of the aggregate demand curve is shown in Figure 9.10.

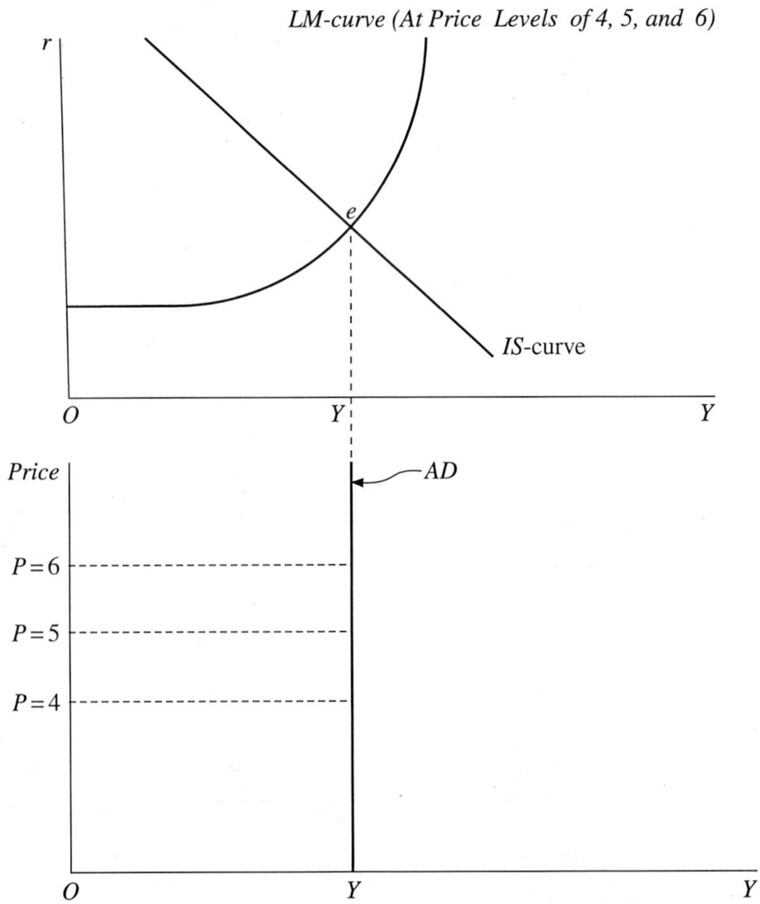

FIGURE 9.10 Derivation of *AD* when nominal money supply changes in the same proportion in the same direction in which price level does: As explained output remains same no matter what the price level be. It is thus perfectly price inelastic.

9.5.2.3 Nominal money supply and prices increase/decrease by a different proportion (Figure 9.11)

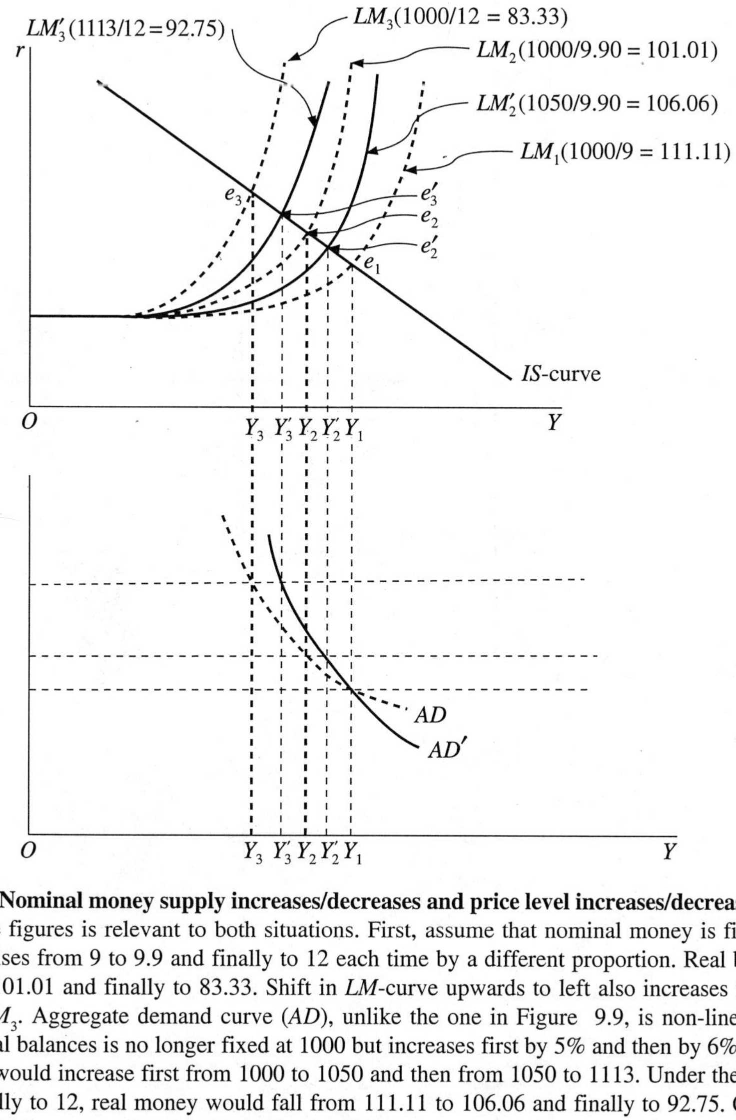

FIGURE 9.11 Nominal money supply increases/decreases and price level increases/decreases by a different proportion: The figures is relevant to both situations. First, assume that nominal money is fixed at, say, 1000 and price level rises from 9 to 9.9 and finally to 12 each time by a different proportion. Real balances decrease from 111.11 to 101.01 and finally to 83.33. Shift in *LM*-curve upwards to left also increases from LM_1 to LM_2 and finally to LM_3. Aggregate demand curve (*AD*), unlike the one in Figure 9.9, is non-linear. Now suppose supply of nominal balances is no longer fixed at 1000 but increases first by 5% and then by 6%. In consequence, nominal money would increase first from 1000 to 1050 and then from 1050 to 1113. Under the price changes of 9 to 9.9 and finally to 12, real money would fall from 111.11 to 106.06 and finally to 92.75. Carefully observe the shifts in the *LM*-curve as also the change in the *AD* curve.

The reader can try changes of the opposite nature.

9.5.3 Downward Wage-price Flexibility and the Classical Full Employment Equilibrium through *IS-LM* Framework (Figure 9.12)

In Figure 7.11 (Chapter 7) we derived the *LM*-curve under the classical assumption of demand for money comprising solely the transaction motives, that is, the speculative motives being non-existent.

In other words, L_2-component being zero, $L = L_1$. The *LM*-curve derived under the assumption was vertical without non-linearity and liquidity trap.

To obtain ***classical full employment equilibrium through IS-LM framework***, we need to derive the *AD curve.* Suppose nominal money supply *M* (say, 6000) is given and so are price levels P_3 (say, 15), P_2 (say, 12) and P_1 (*say, 10*). *LM*-curves [LM_3 (P_3 = 15), LM_2 (P_2 = 12) and LM_1 (P_1 = *10*)] corresponding to real balances of 400, 500 and 600 at prices 15, 12 and 10 are vertically linear as shown in Figure 9.12 (Upper Panel). A fall in prices boosts demand for goods but through the *IS*-curve, not directly. *IS*-curve takes into account the interest rates which falls.

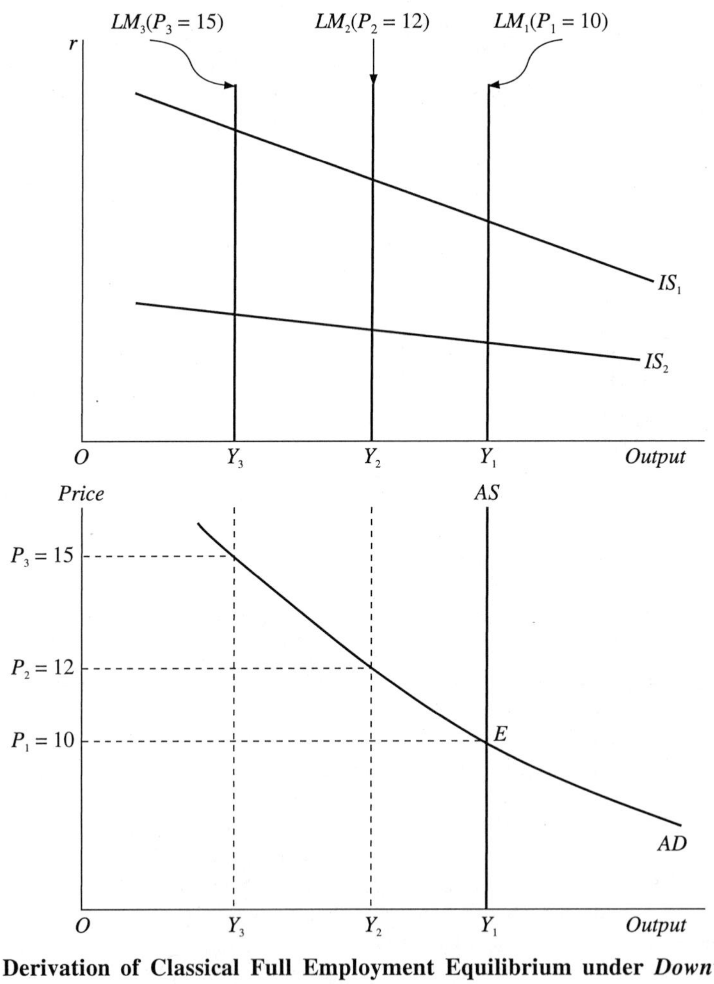

FIGURE 9.12 Derivation of Classical Full Employment Equilibrium under *Downward Wage Price Flexibility* through *IS-LM* Tools: *LM*-curves are vertical in absence of speculative demand. When Price is P_3, *LM*-curve is LM_3. When price falls to P_2, *LM* shifts to LM_2 and when it fall to P_1 *LM* shifts to LM_1. Irrespective of the elasticity of the *IS*-curves, price outputs determined through intersections of the *IS* and *LM*-curves yield the aggregate demand *AD* as shown. The intersection of aggregate demand curve with perfectly inelastic aggregate supply curve *AS* of the classical theory, full employment equilibrium is established at point *E*. Note that downward flexibility of money wages gives vertical *AS*-curve.

9.5.4 Downward Wage-price Flexibility and Less than Full Equilibrium in Keynesian Model through *IS-LM* Tools (Figure 9.13)

In Figure 3.2(a) and (b) (Chapter 3), we discussed Keynesian Model of less than full employment equilibrium under rigid wages with constant and diminishing MPP_L. *IS-LM* framework was nowhere in the picture there. Here we employ the same for derivation of the Keynesian equilibrium.

Let us derive *AD*-curve assuming fixed money supply and downwardly inflexible wages through the *IS-LM* framework. *AS*-curve, in Keynesian Theory, is assumed to be steadily rising until full employment while it is perfectly inelastic due to ***downward flexibility of money wages*** as per classical theory.

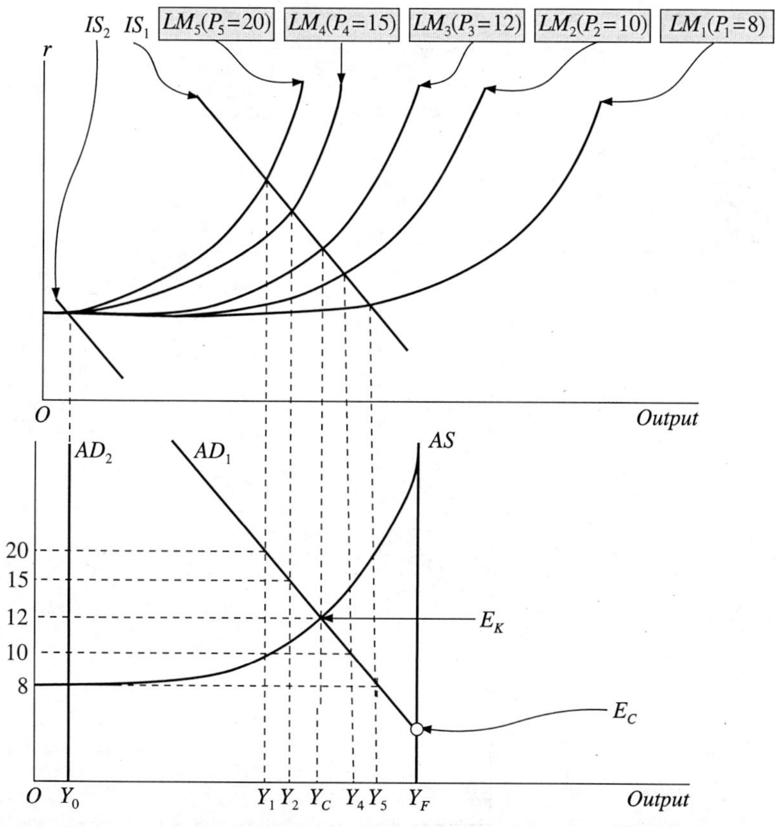

FIGURE 9.13 Equilibrium in Keynesian Model through *IS-LM* Framework: A fall in price level increases real money balances. In consequence, *LM*-curve shifts upwards to right each time. IS_2 passes through the *liquidity trap* while IS_1 passes through *LM*-curves much above the liquidity trap. The former yields a vertical *AD* while the latter, a downwardly sloping one. It is the *AS* curve that makes the Keynesian equilibrium different from the classical equilibrium. Keynesian contention that money wages are inflexible downward and *MPPL*, whether constant or diminishing, makes production costs and hence prices to continue to rise and so does employment as firms sight their profits. It is at full employment output (*YF*) that process of employing workers comes to an end as no more factors existlike to employ. As a result, *AS* curve assumes an elastic shape till full employment output (*YF*) and an inelastic one thereafter. Thus, unlike classical version which envisaged a vertical *AS* curve throughout under the assumption of downward wage price flexibility making it unsustainable, the Keynesian less than full employment equilibrium at *EK* proves to be a reality.

9.5.5 Keynesian Reasoning for Unattainability of Classical Full Employment through *IS-LM* Tools even with downward Wage-price Flexibility

J.M. Keynes attributed un-attainability of full employment to the following two reasons:

(a) **Inconsistency between Savings and Investment (Figure 9.14):** We discussed in earlier chapters how saving, a virtue for an individual, proves a vice for the nation, particularly when saving is cut off from the circular flow of income and expenditure. The deficiency so caused in investment causes unemployment and affects outputs adversely.

Under downward wage price flexibility, we can show through *IS-LM* tools how it happens. When either of the saving or investment functions shifts leftwards, the IS-curve so derived shifts downward to left.

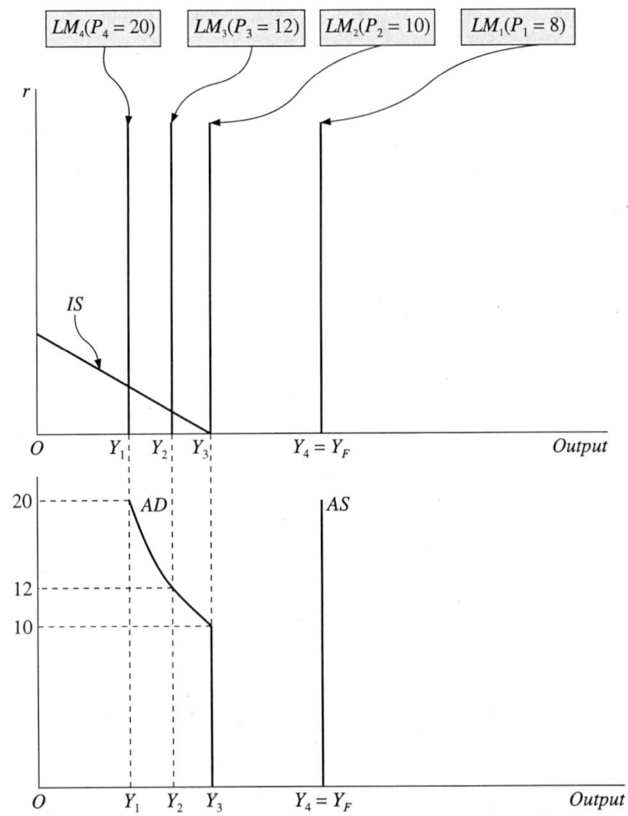

FIGURE 9.14 Unattainability of Classical Full Employment Equilibrium due to Inconsistency between Saving and Investment: Inconsistency between savings and investment implies leftward shift in savings function or downward shift in investment function so that $S > I$. This tends to push the *IS*-curve downward to left. *LM*-curve being vertical in classical theory, the *IS*-curve intersects $LM_4 (P_4 = 20)$, $LM_3(P_3 = 12)$, and $LM_2 (P_2 = 10)$ only. It meets $LM_2(P_2 = 10)$ at the point $(Y_3, 0)$ and doesn't reach the LM_1-curve which relates to classical full employment equilibrium. At Y_3, $r = 0$. This makes I maximum so that I equals S. (Note that $I < S$ at Y_4 which can't be an equilibrium output). Projections from the points of *IS-LM* intersection into the lower panel give the *AD* curve, which is partially elastic and partially inelastic as shown. It does not intersect the perfectly inelastic *AS*-curve implying unattainability of full employment equilibrium, Note again that downwardly flexible money

(Contd.)

FIGURE 9.14 Contd.

wages lead to a vertical *AS*-curve. and downwardly flexible prices boost demand for real money which in turn boosts demand for out-put but through interest rate or *IS*-curve. As soon as the rate falls to zero, *I* increases to the level of *S* and equilibrium reached is below full employment at Y_3. The output of Y_4, the full employment output, is thus unattainable.

(b) **Unattainability of Classical Full Employment due to Liquidity Trap under Downward Wage Price Flexibility (Figure 9.15):** Liquidity trap implies an interest rate below which the rate of interest does not fall. The rate is stagnant over a range of output causing an *LM*-curve to have a horizontal segment at the bottom.

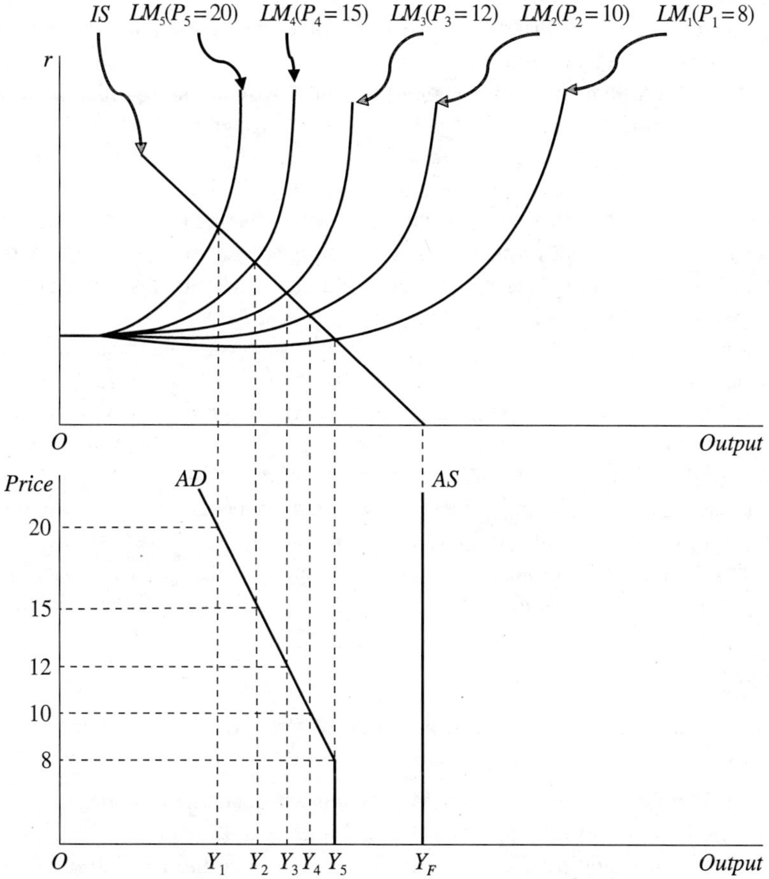

FIGURE 9.15 Unattainability of Classical Full Employment Equilibrium due to Liquidity Trap: As mentioned several times earlier, downwardly flexible money wages yield a vertical *AS*-curve as envisaged by the classical theory. Downwardly falling prices boost demand for real money. This demand for real money boosts demand for output but through the interest rate or *IS*-curve. It is the demand for capital goods that rises as liquidity trap restricts interest rate and hence investment so that maximum amount of output is restricted to Y_5. Output demanded does not reach the full employment-level of it at Y_F as envisaged by the classical theory. Note here that Keynes treated demand for real money as comprising both, L_1 and L_2.

9.5.6 Wage Price Flexibility and Pigou Effect

According to classical economists, wages are downwardly flexible and so are prices. Downwardly flexible wages lead to perfectly inelastic aggregate supply (*AS*) curve and downwardly flexible prices, to unitary elastic Aggregate Demand curve. The latter owes its origin to Quantity Theory of Money which states, $MV = PY$ where M is nominal money supply, V, its velocity of circulation, P, the price level and Y is output produced.

We have seen how J.M. Keynes rejected the possibility of full employment equilibrium on the grounds that wages are inflexible downward, due to which, Aggregate Supply (*AS*) curve is elastic before full employment and perfectly inelastic at it.

Some classical economists tried to revive the classical version. For instance, A.C. Pigou employed *IS-LM* tools to rehabilitate full employment equilibrium (Figure 9.16).

Pigou in his attempt retained the vertical (Perfectly inelastic) aggregate supply (*AS*) curve and established an elastic *AD* curve to justify attainment of full employment through the downward wage-price flexibility and its influence on interest rate.

According to Edward Shapiro[1], "An attempt to counter Keynesian argument and rehabilitate the classical theory's conclusion of automatic full employment through wage-price flexibility is found in ***Pigou-effect***[2] also known as ***real balance effect***, first advanced by Professor A. C. Pigou in the early 1940s and later, the subject of a sizable literature."

A falling investment leads to falling output and employment in the Keynesian model. Falling employment leads to falling money wages and falling wages lead to falling costs and hence falling prices. This in turn leads to falling prices of goods, buildings, land and common shares with the other prices with the result that there will be no change in their real value.

However, falling prices lead to a rise in the real value of certain assets, such as money, savings deposits and bonds, that are fixed in monetary terms. Holders of such assets won't be keen to continue to raise them any longer. They would rather tend to enjoy consumption. This would lead to an upward shift in the consumption function and a downward shift in the saving function. This would result in a rightward shift in the *IS*-curve each time prices drop (Figure 9.16).

We have already seen that falling prices lead to rising real balances in consequence to which *LM*-curve shifts rightwards. Liquidity trap sets an upper limit of Y_5 to output produced and demanded. However, allowing Pigou-effect, *IS* and *LM*-curves continue to shift rightwards each time price falls. This causes aggregate demand curve to shift from AD_1 to AD_2 establishing full employment equilibrium (Figure 9.16).

Criticism of Pigou Effect

As would appear to the reader, Pigou effect appeared to fetch lot of water until it was subjected to the following criticism:

1. As far as the rise in fixed value monetary assets are concerned, propensity to consume rises for the creditors but it falls for the debtors. Increase in the debtor's liability forces them to save more so that additional savings may finance the additional liability caused by falling prices of such assets. Increase in propensity to consume for creditors offsets the decrease in it for the debtors. The overall system remains unchanged. This renders a deadly blow to Pigovian contention. In defence, Pigou argued that fixed currency assets are to be limited

[1] Edward Shapiro, '*Macroeconomic Analysis*' Fifth Edition, 1999, Galgotia Publications (P) Ltd, pp. 273–277.

[2] A.C. Pigou,"The Classical Stationary State", *Economic Journal*, Dec. 1943, pp. 345–351, and "Economic Progress in a Stable Environment", *Economica*, August 1947, pp.180–188.

only to those assets that are issued by government. This he said would not affect debtors expenditure negatively nor would it make their propensity to consume fall to offset the rise in propensity to consume of creditors.

2. Even if we grant Pigou the viability of his defence, by how much would the propensity to consume rise due to rise in real value of private fixed currency assets of creditors to offset the fall in real value of the private fixed currency assets of debtors? How big a rise in consumption will take place so as to reduce savings sufficiently to shift *IS*-curve to right? A hyper deflation is must to satisfy the theoretical requirement of Pigou effect.
3. A minor once-and-for-all deflation may fail to grant Pigou effect any mileage. People would treat it a temporary phenomenon and would not raise their consumption.
4. Is it likely to hold that rise in consumption due to rise in real value of private fixed currency assets of the creditors would off-set the fall in it in respect of the debtors who face an additional burden of interest they have to pay on their fixed currency assets? Obviously not in that case the Pigovian effect collapses.

All said and done, Pigovian argument appears impractical as an approach to the solution of unemployment problem.

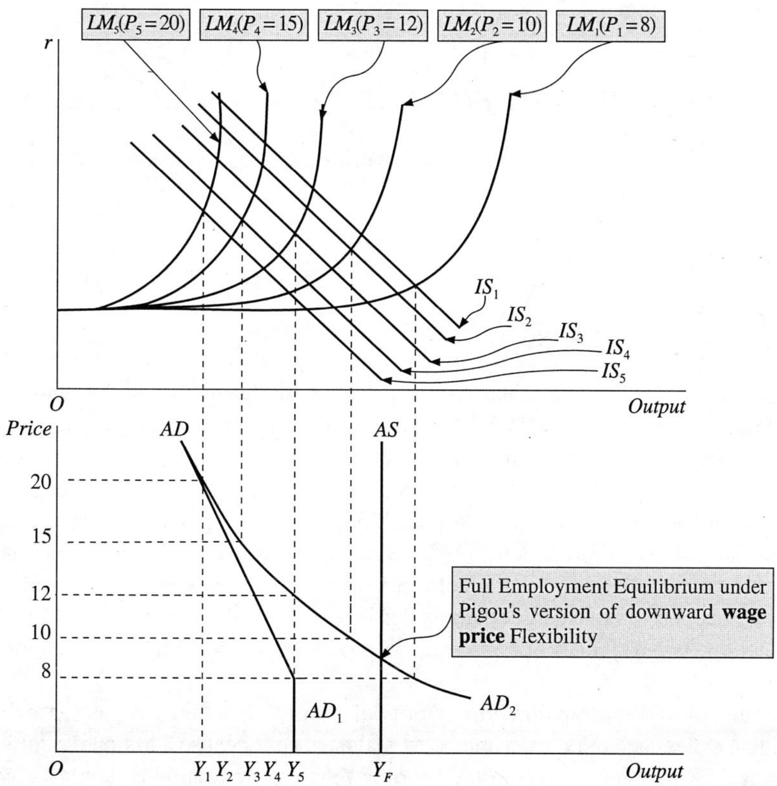

FIGURE 9.16 Wage Price Flexibility and Pigou Effect: As mentioned several times earlier downwardly flexible money wages yield a vertical *AS*-curve as envisaged by the classical theory. Downwardly falling prices boost demand for real balances, which in turn, boosts demand for output. Unlike classical version of direct link between price and demand, Pigou, accepted the Keynesian version of indirect link through rate of interest between the

(Contd.)

FIGURE 9.16 Contd.

two and hence through the *IS*-curve. If the rate of interest falls to the level of liquidity trap or even to the zero level before output can be increased to the full employment level, wage-price flexibility working through the Keynesian effect is cast off as means to achieve full employment level of output. This, however is based on the argument that the downward wage price flexibility exerts its influence through interest rate. Pigou effect thus counters the Keynesian argument and rehabilitates automatic full employment. The working of Pigou effect can be outlined as follows. Falling prices lead to a rise in the real value of assets, such as money, savings deposits and bonds, that are fixed in monetary terms. Holders of such assets won't be keen to continue to raise them any longer. They would rather tend to enjoy consumption. This would lead to an upward shift in the consumption function and a downward shift in the saving function. This would result in a rightward shift in the IS curve each time prices drop. However, allowing Pigou-effect, *IS* and *LM* curve continue to shift rightwards each time price falls. This causes aggregate demand curve to shift from AD_1 to AD_2 establishing full employment equilibrium.

In neo Keynesian model, falling prices may lead to rising values of creditors fixed currency assets due to which holders of these assets prefer to enjoy higher consumption causing saving function to shift downward and *IS* curve upwards as contended by Pigou but what about debtors who experience rising liabilities for which they tend to raise savings and their saving function? Falling savings of creditors get offset by rising savings of debtors with the result *IS* doesn't continue to shift rightwards. As seen falling prices lead to rising real balances in consequence to which *LM* curve shifts rightwards and liquidity trap sets an upper limit of Y_5 to output produced and demanded. This leads to a collapse of Pigou's version of full employment equilibrium.

9.6 SUGGESTED REMEDIES FOR THE PROBLEM OF UNEMPLOYMENT

Remedies are problem specific. One measure can't work for all economies. Nevertheless, some general measures are suggested here. They may come handy tin solving the problem.

1. Expansionary Monetary policy
2. Expansionary Fiscal policy
3. Foreign Trade policy.

Let us introduce each briefly here:

1. An increase in supply of nominal money leads to a rightward shift in the *LM*-curve under fixed and falling prices (see Figures 7.12 and 7.13). The higher the increase in nominal money the higher is the rightward shift in the *LM*-curve. We have seen how supply and demand for real balances increase and how *LM*-curve shifts to right in each case. [For its effect on national output/income, see ***monetary policy multiplier,*** Sec. 9.2}. Apart from the rightward shift in the *LM*-curve, there happen to be two other changes taking place simultaneously. *First,* rate of interest falls giving a boost to investment which in consequence shifts the *IS*-curve to right. *Second,* increase in demand/supply of real balances tends to boost employment and production. For instance, liberal credit to producers goes a long way to boost employment and output both.
2. A fiscal policy of reduction/elimination of commodity taxes or increase in government spending can reduce price level and boost real balances to cause additional rightward shift in the *LM*-curve. Reduction/elimination of corporate tax, introduction of tax holidays, contributes even further to the cause of boosting employment and production. For their effect on national output/income see ***fiscal policy multiplier***, Sec. 9.2.
3. Foreign trade can further contribute to attainment of full employment. Exports may clear surpluses on one hand and bring income on the other.

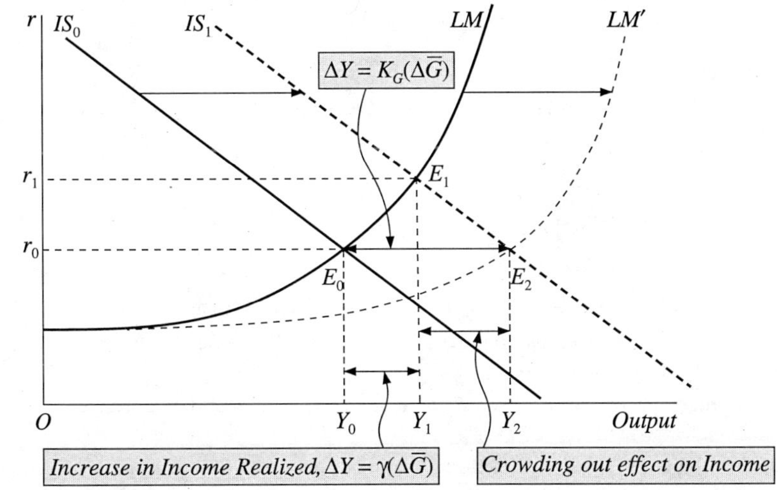

FIGURE 9.17 Crowding out of Government Spending by Private Investment: Suppose economy is at equilibrium at point E_0 when government decides to boost income/output by increasing its spending by $\Delta\bar{G}$. As a result *IS*-curve shifts rightward to the position IS_1. The new curve intersects the *LM*-curve at E_1, thereby increasing income/output from Y_0 to Y_1 while government's intention was to increase it to Y_2 through full multiplier effect. The reason for the failure to achieve the desired increase is that the private investment drops due to a rise in interest rate from r_0 to r_1. The Government spending makes a dent in private investment spending which is termed as *crowding out of investment.* As a result, only fiscal policy multiplier effect ($\gamma\,\Delta\bar{G} = Y_0Y_1$) is realized instead of full multiplier effect ($K_G\,\Delta\bar{G} = Y_0Y_2$). The effect on income so caused is called *crowding out effect on income.*

It is not difficult to see that an appropriate monetary expansion can offset the dent and help the government to realize the desired increase in income/output to the level of Y_2. For that, the *LM*-curve must be shifted rightwards through appropriate monetary expansion.

Note the difference between fiscal policy multiplier, γ, and government expenditure multiplier, K_G.

Note that no single policy can bring about the desired effect in output/income and hence in growth. The fact can be supported by the observation of crowding out of government spending by the private investment. The said effect is termed as the ***crowding out effect*** in macroeconomic literature. It is explained in Figure 9.17. Similar would be the case if certain other components of autonomous spending, $\bar{A}$.

Redistribution of income is yet another factor that may further the cause of attaining full employment.

KEY TERMS AND CONCEPTS

Goods Market Equilibrium or *IS*-curve: The locus of various combinations of income and rate of interest for each of which $I = S$. The equation of the *IS*-curve for a four sector economy follows the format:

$$r = \alpha - \beta Y$$

Here, $\alpha = [C_a - bT_a + bR + I_a + \bar{G} + \bar{X} - M_a]/h;\ \beta = [1 - b + bt + m]/h$

Symbols have their usual meanings.

Budget Surplus: It is defined as the excess of net taxes (T-R) over government expenditure ($\overline{G}$). Thus,

$$BS = (T - \overline{R}) - \overline{G}$$

Here, net taxes refer to the difference of tax revenue over the transfer payments.

Trade Balance: It is defined as the difference of the export earning over the import expenditure. Thus, balance of trade or trade surplus or net exports,

$$NX = \overline{X} - M$$

Government Expenditure Multiplier (K_G): It is defined as the ratio of a change in Y to a change in government expenditure, i.e., as $\Delta Y/\Delta\overline{G}$.

Export Multiplier (K_X): It is defined as the ratio of a change income to a change in exports, i.e., as $\Delta Y/\Delta\overline{X}$.

Investment Multiplier (K_{Ia}) or Autonomous Investment Multiplier: It is defined as the ratio of a change in income to a change in autonomous investment, *i.e.*, as $\Delta Y/\Delta I_a$.

Tax Multiplier or Autonomous Tax Multiplier (K_{Ta}): It is defined as the ratio of a change in income to a change in tax or autonomous tax, i.e., as $\Delta Y/\Delta T_a$.

Transfer Payments Multiplier (K_R): It is defined as the ratio of a change in income to a change in transfer payments, i.e., as $\Delta Y/\Delta\overline{R}$.

Import Multiplier (K_{Ma}): It is defined as the ratio of a change in income to a change in autonomous imports, i.e., as $\Delta Y/\Delta M_a$.

Fiscal policy Multiplier: Fiscal policy multiplier is defined as an change in income per unit change in government spending. It is given as,

$$\gamma = dY/d\overline{G} \text{ or } \Delta Y/\Delta\overline{G} = K_G/[1 + k\,K_G(h/g)],$$

where, $K_G = 1/(1 - b + bt + m)$, h *comes from* $I = I_a - hr$, k comes from $L_1 = kY$ and g from $L_2 = -g\,r$

Monetary Policy Multiplier: It is defined as change in income/output per unit change in real money supply. It is given as,

$$dY/d(\overline{M}/\overline{P}) \text{ or } \Delta Y/\Delta(\overline{M}/\overline{P}) = (h/g)\,\gamma$$

where, γ is fiscal policy multiplier, h comes from $I = I_a - hr$ and g from $L_2 = -g\,r$.

Downward Wage-price Flexibility: It was the main assumption of classical economists to establish full employment equilibrium (See Figure 3.2 and Figure 9.13). In simple words, it implied clearance of unsold stocks through price cuts and employment of unemployed workers through wage cuts. Workers rendered unemployed due to diminishing MPP_L regain it on their acceptance of wage cuts. Keynes rejected downward wage flexibility arguing that wages can't be flexible downward and so are prices. Downwardly inflexible wages increase production costs in the face of diminishing or constant MPP_L. This gives rise to gradually rising price levels which sharply rose at full employment.

Keynesian Less than Full Employment Equilibrium: The AD curve to Keynes was a unitary elastic rectangular hyperbola [According to quantity theory of money which stated that price level varied directly with money supply, that is $P = MV/Y$, with M standing for money supply, P for price level, V for velocity of circulation of money and Y for outputs transacted. Unlike classical view that aggregate supply (AS) is perfectly inelastic, Keynes advocated that it perfectly elastic(horizontal) so long as MPP_L is constant and upward sloping when MPP_L begins to diminish. [See Figures 3.2(a) and 3.2 (b)] In either case, equilibrium is attained below full employment.

Keynesian Arguments against Full-employment Equilibrium: J.M. Keynes attributed non-attainability of full employment to:

(a) Inconsistency between Savings and Investment (See Figure 9.13), and
(b) Liquidity trap in the LM-curve (See Figure 9.14).

Restatement of Full employment Equilibrium by Pigou: Prof. A.C. Pigou in 1940s tried to re-establish full employment equilibrium through what is known as Pigou Effect. Under down wage price flexibility, falling prices lead to a rise in the real value of assets, such as money, savings deposits and bonds, that are fixed in monetary terms. Holders of such assets won't be keen to continue to raise them any longer. They would rather tend to enjoy consumption. This would lead to an upward shift in the consumption function and a downward shift in the saving function which in turn, would result in a rightward shift in the *IS*-curve each time prices drop (Figure 9.16). This would cause *AD* curve a pivotal shift in and be more elastic to intersect with the vertical aggregate supply curve to yield full employment equilibrium.

Criticism of Pigou Effect: Pigovian contention met severe criticism. The following two points deserve special attention:

1. As far as the rise in fixed value monetary assets are concerned, propensity to consume rises for the creditors but it falls for the debtors. Increase in the debtor's liability forces them to save more so that additional savings may finance the additional liability caused by falling prices of such assets. Increase in propensity to consume for creditors offsets the decrease in it for the debtors. The overall system remains unchanged.
2. A minor once-and-for-all deflation may fail to grant Pigou effect any mileage. People would treat it a temporary phenomenon and would not raise their consumption.

Crowding out Effect: Fiscal expansion intended to bring about a certain increase in income/output succeeds only partially in its objective. This follows from upward shift in *IS*-curve which leads to a rise in interest rate and hence a fall in investment spending of the private entities (See Figure 9.17). The increase in government spending thus crowds out private investment and desired increase in output/income is not realized.

EXERCISES

A. Short Answer Questions

1. Define *IS*- and *LM*-curves. Is it possible to determine equilibrium rate of interest and income through only one of these curves? Give reasons for your answer.
2. When will an *LM*-curve be a linear sloping upwards and when non-linear with a horizontal segment? Explain.
3. Outline factors that cause parallel shift in *IS*-curve as also factors that cause pivotal shifts in it. Explain.
4. Show that *LM*-curve in classical theory is perfectly inelastic.
5. Account for the Keynesian, classical and intermediate ranges of *LM*-curves. In which one of these is fiscal expansion most effective and in which one it is least effective? Use a sketch to explain.
6. In which of the above three ranges of *LM*-curve do you think monetary expansion is most effective and in which one, it is least effective? Use a sketch to explain.
7. Assume *IS-LM*-curve to yield a disequilibrium. How would it trace its path to equilibrium? Explain with a sketch.
8. What is the effect on *IS*-curve of an increase in private investment ? Draw diagram.
9. What is the effect on *IS*-curve of an increase in tax financed government spending? Draw a diagram.
10. Account for the shift in *LM*-curve of an increase/decrease in real money supply with the help of a sketch.
11. How would *LM*-curve behave if nominal money supply changes in the same proportion in which price level does?
12. How would *LM*-curve behave if nominal money supply changes in proportions different from those in changes of price level?
13. Suppose price level is fixed. Account for the effect on *LM*-curve of the changes in nominal money supply.
14. Distinguish between fiscal policy multiplier and government expenditure multiplier.

    Given, Consumption, $C = 100 + 0.90Y^d$
    Investment, $I = 500 - 25r$,
    $L_1 = 0.4Y$ and $L_2 = 600 - 50r$
    Income Tax, $T = 100 + 0.20Y$
    Govt. expenditure, $\overline{G} = 300$
    Transfers, $R = 100$
    Exports, $\overline{X} = 200$
    Imports, $M = 175 + 0.02Y$
    Supply of nominal money, $\overline{M} = 1500$
    Price, $\overline{P} = 3$
    Full employment income, $Y_F = 2000$

(a) Find fiscal policy multiplier, γ. Estimate change in income when government expenditure increases by 50. **[Ans:** $\gamma = 2.00$, $\Delta Y = 100$]

(b) Find monetary policy multiplier when price falls to 2 while nominal money supply remains unchanged. **[Ans:** 1.00]

(c) Find change in income due to a fiscal expansion of $\Delta G = 150$ when nominal money supply increases to 1800 and price remains unchanged. **[Ans:** $\Delta Y = 150$]

15. Obtain an expression for fiscal policy multiplier. How is it related to the government expenditure multiplier? Explain with an example.

16. Obtain an expression for monetary policy multiplier. How is it related to the fiscal policy multiplier? Explain.

17. In Illustration 9.2, for the problem 14, we computed equilibrium income, $Y = 1750$, and interest rate, $r = 16\%$. Government expenditure multiplier is 10/3. To attain full employment income of 2000, government needs to increase income by 250. With the help of its expenditure multiplier, government decides to increase its spending by $\Delta\bar{G} = \Delta Y/K_G = 250 \times 3/10 = 75$. Would the policy measure serve the government's objective? What can you say about crowding out effect in this case?

18. Distinguish between government expenditure multiplier and fiscal policy multiplier. Is it true to say that a fiscal policy multier reveals what simple government expenditure multiplier fails? Use a neat sketch.

B. Long Answer Questions

19. Through *IS-LM* framework, derive aggregate demand (*AD*) curve when nominal money supply
(i) increases
(ii) decreases
while price level remains fixed.

20. Through *IS-LM* framework , derive aggregate demand (*AD*) curve when nominal money supply
(i) increases
(ii) decreases
and so does price level but in somewhat different proportion.

21. Through *IS-LM* framework, derive aggregate demand (*AD*) curve when nominal money supply
(i) increases
(ii) decreases
and so does price level in same proportion.

22. Comment on downward wage-price flexibility and the classical full employment equilibrium through *IS-LM* tools.

23. Demonstrate downward Wage-price Flexibility and Less than Full Equilibrium in Keynesian Model through *IS-LM* tools.

C. Essay Type Questions

24. Examine the efficacy of fiscal and monetary policies in the Keynesian, classical and intermediate ranges of the *LM*-curve.

25. Account for the role of elasticity of *IS*-curve from the view point of effectiveness of monetary and fiscal policies in boosting income/output.

26. Give a critical assessment of Pigou effect. How far do you agree with Pigou on the possibility of full employment equilibrium?

27. Explain Keynesian arguments of liquidity trap and inconsistency between savings and investment against full employment equilibrium. Draw diagrams in support.

28. Derive an expression for fiscal policy multiplier. How is it related to the monetary policy multiplier? Calculate each for the data of Q.14 when $I = 500 - 20r$ and $L = 0.6Y - 50r$. Is it true that the effect on national income of government expenditure multiplier is an increase of 250 while that of fiscal policy multiplier, only 138.9. What is the significance of the difference between the two?

[Ans: $\gamma = 1.852$; monetary policy multiplier = 0.741]

UNIT-4

ECONOMIC POLICIES

Chapter 10: Monetary Policy
Chapter 11: Fiscal Policy
Chapter 12: Foreign Trade Policy

Chapter 10

Monetary Policy

INTRODUCTION

In Chapter 3, we briefly mentioned the role economic policies (monetary, fiscal and foreign trade policies) while drawing the outlines of the Keynesian Theory. In Chapter 6 (Sections 6.1 and 6.7), we referred to the role played by these policies in correcting the excess and the deficient demand situations (See Figures 6.3 and 6.7 and Questions 26 and 28). On both the occasions, we contented ourselves with the workable reference to these policies, sparing their detailed discussions to Chapters 10, 11 and 12. In this Chapter, we take up the monetary policy and we reserve Chapters 11 and 12 for fiscal and foreign trade policies.

A monetary policy, in its broader sense, refers to the monetary system along with the measures undertaken to manage the money and credit supply in the economy, including steps taken from time to time, to regulate and control the interest rates. It may include even the non-monetary measures undertaken by government to influence the monetary situation in the economy. The reference here is to the measures such as those of controlling wages, prices, and budgetary operations which are non-monetary in character but influence the monetary situation in the economy indirectly.

In its narrower sense, the monetary policy covers the steps taken by government and the banking authorities to manage the money and credit supplies including steps taken from time to time to control and regulate the interest rates. A closer examination reveals that the non-monetary measures of the government do not find a place under the monetary policy in its narrower sense.

A look at the monetary policy in its broader sense calls for a discussion of the monetary measures intended to control supply of money as also credit and hence the rate of interest as one part and also for that of the functions of the monetary institutions such as the central and commercial banks as another. Pursuing the approach, we first discuss various objectives of monetary measures in Section 10.1 followed by the monetary measures themselves in Section 10.2 and by functions of the monetary institutions in Section 10.3. Finally, in Section 10.4, we take up the process and control of credit creation by the monetary institutions to wind up the monetary system in its totality.

10.1 OBJECTIVES OF MONETARY POLICY

Broadly speaking, a monetary policy aims at the following five goals, popularly known as its objectives:

(1) Neutrality of Money: Initially suggested by Wicksteed, supported later by Hayek and Robertson, the objective of neutrality of money implies that money should remain strictly neutral, causing no changes in the general price-level, output, income and employment. According to these economists, often referred to as the ***neutralists***, money should not influence economic entities such as price, output, income and employment nor should it influence the pattern of distribution in the society. In other words, money should play a passive role as a medium of exchange and store of value.

Neutrality of money is often put to *severe criticism* on following grounds:

1. It is based on the *wrong assumption* implicit in quantity theory that a change in money supply causes a direct and proportional change in the price-level. The assumption like many other postulates of classical theory was put to severe criticism by followers of Keynes.
2. It is *difficult to implement*. Neutrality of money requires that money supply should remain constant and adjustments in it should be made only to accommodate the fundamental changes in the economy.
3. It imparts *no guarantee of price-stability*. Even when money supply is kept constant, prices may change either due to bottlenecks in production or due to an increase or a decrease in demand caused by a sudden change in tastes, preferences, etc.
4. It is *self-contradictory*. On one side, neutralists assign a passive role to money while on the other, they prescribe that the monetary authority should maintain constant supply of money through frequent adjustments in it so as to accommodate fundamental changes taking place in the economy.
5. *It fails to explain the onset of depression.* Prices fall down in depression even when money supply is held constant. Moreover prices fail to rise in depression even when money supply is increased.

(2) Price Stabilization: Prof. Gustav Cassel and Lord Keynes (during the early period of his career) suggested price stabilization as a desirable objective of the monetary policy. During the decades of twenties and thirties in the last century, price stabilization as the objective of monetary policy was tried on experimental basis by several countries; but, with the passage of time, it was replaced by a more acceptable objective—the objective of full employment.

Instability of price leads to distortions in the economy. The evils of inflation and deflation disturb the economic relationships among various sections. On the other hand, stability of price eliminates cyclical fluctuations, prevents artificial prosperity, facilitates equitable distribution of income and promotes economic stability and social welfare.

But price stabilization should not be interpreted here in its literal sense. It does not imply stability of individual prices. Instead, it refers to the stability of average price, as reflected by the wholesale price index or the consumer price index.

(3) Exchange Stabilization: Another objective of the monetary policy is *stabilization of the exchange rate*. Under the gold standard, countries followed the system of proportional reserves while issuing the currency. This they did under the compulsion of convertibility of currency issued into gold. Under the circumstances, supply of money got limited to the stocks of gold the bank of issue possessed. As a result, countries followed the principle—*'expand the currency and the credit when gold comes in and contract them when it goes out.'* Supply of money thus was linked to the stock of bullion reserves of the Central Banks. Value of a currency in terms of other currencies was more or less stable and so was the exchange rate. But after the Second World War, most of the war-shattered countries felt compelled to give up the gold standard. They had to solve their problem of reconstructtion and rehabilitation but the monetary resource they possessed under the convertible currency system, being limited to the stock of gold with the mint, posed serious constraints. In consequence, they felt compelled to switch over to a currency system that allowed them to issue more currency. The ***system of minimum reserves*** came handy as it permitted them to issue unlimited currency after fulfilling the requirement of a certain minimum of the bullion reserves with the mint. This affected the value of their currency in terms of the other currencies and thus their exchange rates. Ever since the switch over to the minimum reserve system, widespread fluctuations in the exchange rates have become a common observation and a common cause of concern at the same time. Instability of the exchange rate poses several problems, a few of which may be outlined below:

1. Heavy fluctuations in the exchange rates encourage speculation in the foreign exchange markets.
2. Heavy fluctuation in the exchange rates lead to loss of confidence on the part of the foreign investors, who may, in consequence, decide to hold back their investments.
3. Heavy fluctuations in the exchange rates also produce repercussions on the internal price-level of the country concerned.
4. Heavy fluctuations in the exchange rates give a serious setback to the flow of trade between the countries concerned.

Fluctuations in the exchange rates thus have serious repercussions, but before getting carried away with them, it is necessary to examine the following arguments often put forth against exchange rate stabilization:

1. Stability of exchange rates is generally achieved at the expense of the stability in the internal price-level. Fluctuations in the internal prices hamper the economic progress of the country.
2. Under the stable exchange rates, inflation or deflation prevalent in some countries gets transmitted to the trading partners. Such transmissions jeopardize the internal stability of the latter through the ***repercussion effect***.

As is well known, International Monetary Fund (IMF) was specifically set up after Second World War with a view to stabilize exchange rates among the member-nations. This being so, the individual countries no longer attach much importance to stabilization of the exchange rate as an objective of their monetary policy.

(4) Full Employment: According to J.M. Keynes, the objective of monetary policy should be to ensure maximum utilization of the productive resources of the economy. None of the above objectives, however desirable, can promote full employment of productive resources. On the contrary it is more likely that the objectives of neutrality of money or of price and exchange stabilization may create deflationary forces and cause unemployment in the economy. Monetary policy can serve as an effective tool to secure full employment. Recall the Keynesian equation $Y = C + I + G$, where C is consumption, I is investment and G is government spending. A monetary policy to boost consumption and investment is capable of raising income, output and employment. To demonstrate, suppose government initiates a reduction in the lending rate of interest on housing loans. This would encourage home loans which in turn would boost the demand for housing. In consequence, construction industry would respond to the rising demand for housing by constructing more houses. This would create new job opportunities for masons, architects, brick layers and general labour. All along demand for building materials such as cement, granite, marble, iron, sanitary wares, electrical fittings, etc. too would rise creating fresh job opportunities in all these industries. House construction is an activity which draws inputs from a number of industries and employs man-power of all the categories-skilled or unskilled, educated or uneducated, trained or untrained—alike. Related industries too experience a boom.

A recent boom in the construction industry in the suburbs of Delhi stands a testimony to the hypothesis. A sizable reduction in the lending rate on home loans propelled housing demand sky high with the result that construction activities in and around the capital city shot up to their highest level in the entire National Capital Region. Investments even in the related industries shot up to new heights to keep pace with the construction industry. There is enough scope for researchers to study the nature and extent of correlation between the lending rate on home loans and consequential investment in construction and related industries. This may reveal the true nature of the investment function ($I = I_a - hr$) as also of the applicability of the Keynesian process of income propagation through investment multiplier in the less developed countries with massive unemployment. Investment in construction industry and the borrower friendly lending rate on home loans have both gone quite well in boosting income propagation in NCR.

(5) Economic Growth: As an objective of the monetary policy, emphasis has shifted from *full employment* to *economic growth* in the recent years There are mainly three reasons for this shift:

1. With the realization that full employment is not possible without stepping up of the economic growth, emphasis automatically shifted to economic growth.
2. A rising rate of economic growth is necessitated also by the universal desire among the people to enjoy ever-rising living standards in the developing as well as the developed countries.
3. In the modern competitive world, ever-increasing rate of economic growth is a condition essential for the survival of the developing nations.

Economic growth may be defined as *the sustained increase in real income of a country over a long period of time.* In the process, money has a very important role to play as a mobilizing agent. Many nations possess abundant human and non-human resources but somehow these resources remain unutilized due to lack of finance. Given adequate monetary support, both types of resources can be put to fuller utilization, leading, in the process to substantial increase in the size of the real output. Monetary policy can thus be considered as a stimulant of growth.

We have seen in Section 9.2, how an increase in income/output can be realized through ***monetary policy multiplier***, given by Eq. 9.12 as

$$dY/d\,(\overline{M}/\overline{P}) \text{ or } \Delta Y/\Delta\,(\overline{M}/\overline{P}) = (h/g)\,\gamma \qquad (10.1)$$

10.2 INSTRUMENTS OF MONETARY POLICY

Various methods employed by a Central Bank to regulate and control the volume of money circulating in the economy are referred to as the ***instruments of monetary policy*** or *methods of credit control.* These instruments are grouped under two broad heads:

1. Quantitative methods, and
2. Qualitative methods.

While ***quantitative methods*** affect the quantity of money in circulation directly, the ***qualitative methods***, also known as *the **selective credit control methods,*** do it indirectly. Quantitative methods are non-discriminatory in character as they tend to expand or contract the flow of money in all the channels or uses alike. Qualitative methods, on the other hand, are discriminatory in this regard. They encourage money flows in certain selected channels and check it in the others with a view to facilitate desired growth of the selected sectors only. For example, to facilitate growth of agricultural sector, money and credit may be directed to this sector at lower rates of interest while rate of interest for the rest of the economy may continue to be high. Policy of extending credit at lower rate to favoured sectors, such as that of agriculture, is called *the **cheap money policy*** while that of doing the same at higher rates to others is called *the **dear money policy***. Adoption of cheap money policy for some sectors and dear money policy for the rest at the same time is referred to as a discriminatory policy and is possible only under the qualitative or the selective credit control methods. No such discrimination is possible under quantitative methods of credit control.

The following is the layout of grouping different instruments of monetary policy under the two heads:

TABLE 10.1 Instruments of Credit Control

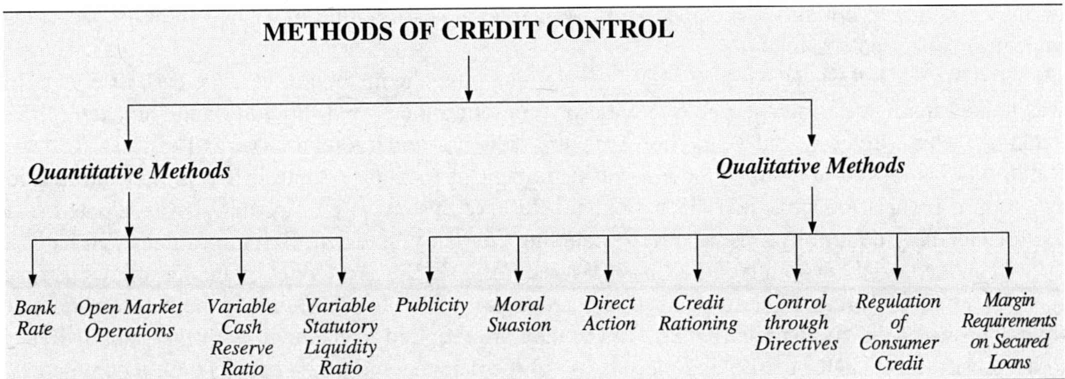

Let us discuss them in the following paragraphs:

10.2.1 Quantitative Methods

(1) Bank Rate: In narrow sense, ***bank rate*** may be defined as the official rate at which the Central Bank rediscounts the first class bills of exchange brought to it by the discount houses and the commercial banks. In its broader sense, bank rate refers to the varying terms and conditions under which the market can have temporary access to the Central Bank either in the form of rediscounts or through secured advances. It is the earliest method of credit control.

The Central Bank attempts to regulate the volume of credit through the bank rate policy by influencing both the cost as well as availability of credit. By raising the bank rate or the discount rate, the Central Bank raises the cost of credit. The bank rate policy also affects the availability of credit by changing the conditions of loans to the commercial banks. A higher bank rate increases the cost of credit and discourages rediscounting of bills of exchange by the commercial banks at the Central Bank as also their borrowings from it. This contracts or squeezes the volume of money or credit in the circulation. The process is called the ***contraction of credit.*** As opposed to it, a decrease in bank rate has an opposite effect and the process is called the ***expansion of credit.***

The mechanism of contraction or expansion of credit can be understood through the linkage of the lending rate of the commercial banks to the bank rate. The higher the bank rate charged by the Central Bank, the higher is the lending rate of the commercial banks and the lower is the people's demand for loans from the commercial banks (and so is the volume of credit in circulation). The opposite is the case when bank rate is lowered. The policy of low bank rate is termed as the ***cheap money policy*** while that of high bank rate as the ***dear money policy.*** The biggest limitation of the bank rate policy is the increasing non-dependence of the commercial banks on the central banks.

(2) Open Market Operations: *Open market operations* as an instrument of monetary control developed only after the First World War. The method refers to purchase and sale of the government securities as well as other eligible papers such as bills of exchange and securities of the private concerns by the Central Bank in open market.

Purchase by the Central Bank of such paper assets increases the volume of credit in circulation and their sale by it, decreases it. Thus purchases expand the credit and sales contract it.

The open market operations gained in popularity because they are more immediate and more direct than the bank rate policy in their effectiveness in influencing the volume of credit in the economy. That way, open market operations rank much above the bank rate policy.

Conditions necessary for the success of this instrument as a measure of credit control depends on the existence of a highly developed security market as also on that of a huge stock of securities in central bank's possession.

(3) Variable Cash Reserve Ratio (CRR): For a long time, the method of variable cash reserve ratio was looked upon as an indispensable method of promoting the overall liquidity and solvency of the banking system. In the recent years, however, the view has undergone a change. The Cash Reserve Ratio, now, is looked upon as an additional instrument of monetary control. It was first introduced as a tool of monetary control in 1933 by Federal Reserve System in USA. Later, it was adopted as a tool of monetary control by several others including Germany, Sweden, Belgium, France, etc.

To understand the working of the ***Cash Reserve Ratio*** (CRR) as a tool of credit control, let us first see what it is. CRR may be defined as a percentage part of the total volume of the net demand and time deposits of the commercial banks, which, they are required to maintain with the Central Bank. to demonstrate, let CRR be 20% and the volume of the demand and time deposits with a commercial bank, ₹ 50 lakh. The bank would therefore have to keep 20% of this or ₹ 10 lakh with the Central Bank. This will reduce their deposits only to ₹ 40 lakh. Now suppose the Central Bank intends to contract the credit. What it needs to do is to raise the CRR. In consequence, suppose it raises CRR from 20% to say 25% with the result that the volume of the demand deposits with the commercial banks falls from ₹ 40 lakh to only ₹ 37.50 lakh, leaving ₹ 2.50 lakh less of it with the commercial banks to use as the base for their credit creation (see Section 10.4). The credit creating capacity of the commercial banks would fall from ₹ 200 lakh to ₹ 150 lakh, registering a fall of ₹ 50 lakh in consequence to this change in CRR[1]. On the contrary, if the Central Bank reduces CRR from 20% to 10% in order to increase the credit supply, the resulting increase in it is as high as ₹ 250 lakh[2].

This method of credit control is effective when commercial banks possess excessive cash reserves and the demand for credit by borrowers is substantially high but it is likely to fail in its purpose when the commercial banks possess large volumes of foreign funds.

(4) Variable Statutory Liquidity Ratio (SLR): SLR or the ***Statutory Liquidity Ratio*** may be defined as a percentage part of the total volume of the net demand and the time deposits of the commercial banks, which, the commercial banks are required to keep with the Central Bank in the form of liquid assets. The liquid assets referred to here are paper assets such as government securities and bills of exchange. Such liquid assets are often used by the commercial banks for borrowing from the central

[1] Commercial banks acquire credit creating capability through the CRR (Please see next Section). The credit multiplier, given as K = 1/CRR, works out at 5.00 when CRR is 20% and at 4.00 when it is 25%.The total volume of the demand deposits created by the commercial bank, DD = K × Primary Deposits. Thus, an increase by the Central Bank in the CRR from 20% to 25% would reduce the total volume of demand deposits likely to be created by the commercial bank from 5 × ₹ 50 lakh to 4 × ₹ 50 lakh or by ₹ 50 lakh. In consequence, the volume of the credit, given as the difference of demand deposits created over the primary deposits of ₹ 50 lakh, would fall from ₹ 200 lakh (250 – 50) to ₹ 150 lakh (200 – 50). In consequence to a hike in CRR from 20% to 25%, the net fall in the supply of credit in this case is ₹ 50 lakh.

[2] When CRR is 20%, the credit multiplier is 1/0.20 = 5.00 and the volume of the demand deposits is ₹ 250 lakh (5 × 50 = 250). Credit created by the commercial bank is ₹ 200 lakh (250 – 50 = 200). When CRR is reduced to 10%, credit multiplier is 1/0.10 = 10.00 and the volume of demand deposits is ₹ 500 lakh (10 × 50 = 500). Credit created by the bank is ₹ 450 lakh (500 – 50 = 450). Thus, a fall in CRR from 20% to 10% leads to an increase in credit supply from ₹ 200 lakh to ₹ 450 lakh, registering an increase of ₹ 250 lakh (450 – 200 = 250).

bank under its rediscounting scheme (bank rate policy). To demonstrate, let the total volume of net demand deposits be ₹ 50 lakh and let SLR be 10%. The commercial bank would then have to keep liquid assets worth ₹ 5.00 lakh (10% of 50 = 5.00) with the Central Bank. Now suppose the central bank raises the SLR to 15%. As a result, the bank in question would have to keep liquid assets worth ₹ 7.5 lakh with the Central Bank instead of those worth ₹ 5 lakh kept earlier. The bank thus would have fewer liquid assets than before while borrowing from the Central Bank under its rediscounting scheme. Its borrowing capacity would fall in consequence and so would the supply of credit. Exactly opposite is the effect of a reduction in the SLR.

Liquid assets mentioned here include:

(a) Excess Reserves (*ER*), representing cash in hand plus balances with the Central Bank minus required reserves with the Central Bank.
(b) Unencumbered Securities(*I*), representing government and other securities against which no loans are yet taken by the commercial banks.
(c) Current Account Balances (*CB*) with other banks.

SLR may be given as the ratio of the total value of these liquid assets to the total net demand and time deposits (*L*). Thus,

$$SLR = (ER + I + CB)/L \tag{10.2}$$

10.2.2 Qualitative Methods

(1) Publicity: Several Central Banks have resorted to the use of publicity as an instrument of credit control. They have done so not only for influencing the credit policies of the commercial banks but also for influencing the public opinion in the economy. Publicity takes several forms. It includes publishing of the monthly reviews of the credit and business conditions and of annual reports on the operations of the business and the banking sectors.

Publicity as an instrument of monetary control has been extensively used by U.S.A. where the Federal Reserve System regularly publishes reports about the credit matters in the economy.

(2) Moral Suasion: This method of credit control involves the techniques of advice, persuasion and requests to be exercised by the commercial banks to cooperate with the Central Bank in implementation of its credit policies. The Central Bank can only use its moral influence with the commercial banks to prevail upon them to cooperate. No punitive action can be taken against the non-cooperating bank under this method.

The success of this method depends on the moral strength of the Central Bank over the commercial banks. The biggest limitation of this method is that it lacks legal force and, as such, it fails to be effective at a time when the forces of credit expansion in the economy happen to be very strong and powerful. For instance, if public is willing to borrow from commercial banks even when rate of interest charged by them is high, no amount of moral persuasion can influence the commercial banks to refrain from such lending activities.

(3) Direct Action: This method of credit control is most extensively used by the Central Banks to implement their credit control policies. The method implies the use of coercive measures against the commercial banks that do not fall in line with the credit policies of the Central Bank. Direct action of the Central Bank against the erring banks may involve one or more of the following actions—(i) refusal to grant discounting facilities to the erring banks; (ii) refusal to sanction further financial accommodation to them, and/or (iii) charging of penal rates of interest on money borrowed by them beyond the prescribed limit.

The method suffers from the limitation that the commercial banks always look upon it as a Damocles' Sword hanging over their heads and act under pressures.

(4) Credit Rationing: It implies two things—*first*, fixing up of a limit upon the rediscounting facility to a particular bank by the Central Bank, and *second*, fixing different quotas of financial accommodation for different banks by it.

This method of credit control has, however, been subjected to criticism for conflicting with the '*lender of the last resort*' function of the Central Bank.

(5) Control through Directives: Under this method of credit control, a Central Bank may enforce flow of credit in the desired direction through written directives which may include warnings or strict instructions to the commercial banks.

(6) Regulation of Consumer Credit: This method of monetary control was first introduced by the Federal Reserve System in U.S.A. in August 1941. The objective was to regulate the terms and conditions under which credit repayable in installments was being extended to consumers for the purchase of durables. Such regulation of terms and conditions of the consumer credit was deemed necessary to curb demand for the durables in short supply. This could be achieved by discouraging loans for scarce consumer durables through the introduction of more stringent terms and conditions. For instance, increase in the cash down component of the installment plan, reduction in the repayment period of the loan and increasing the rate of interest applicable to such loans are a few changes in the terms and conditions that discourage borrowing for the purchase of the scarce durables. In other words, reducing the supply of the consumer credit for the purchase of the scarce goods was the main purpose. Later, the method gained popularity with the Central Banks all over the world.

(7) Margin Requirements on Secured Loans: Secured loans refer to loans granted by the commercial banks to their customers against the mortgage of bonds, shares, ownership documents of properties, etc. The amount lent by the bank is a fraction of the market value of the security. The difference of the market value of the security offered by the borrowers over the loan amount is called the ***margin.*** A Central Bank varies this margin from time to time to regulate the volume of credit in circulation at the desired level. To demonstrate, suppose a customer approaches his commercial bank for a loan against property. The market value of the property is, say, ₹ 50 lakh. The customer has, in his possession, the relevant documents showing the exclusive ownership of the property. Now suppose the margin requirement fixed by the Central Bank is 20%. The commercial bank, in this case, can grant a loan up to a maximum of ₹ 40 lakh to the borrower. This is 80% (100 – 20 = 80) of the market value (₹ 50 lakh) of the property. In consequence, credit supply would amount to ₹ 40 lakh. Now suppose the Central Bank wants to increase the credit supply to ₹ 45 lakh. What it needs to do is to decrease the margin requirement to 10% which is nothing but [{(45 – 40)/50} × 100] % of the market value of the property. The commercial bank now would grant a maximum of 90% (100 – 10 = 90) of the market value of the property to the borrower.

Thus by changing the margin requirement, a Central Bank can regulate the volume and direction of credit outflows in the economy.

The method of fixing the margin requirements on the secured loans of the commercial banks was first introduced in U.S.A. under the Securities Exchange Act of 1934. Under the provisions of the act, the Federal Reserve System was granted power to vary the margin requirements on the secured loans of the commercial banks.

The instruments of credit control, whether qualitative or quantitative, are exercised by the Central Bank and hence are collectively known as its credit control functions.

10.3 FUNCTIONS OF THE MONETARY INSTITUTIONS

The Central Bank and its member banks including the commercial banks are collectively known as the *monetary institutions.* At the top sits the Central Bank, entrusted with a number of functions related to money matters. The most important one of them, *the credit control function*, has already been discussed above in Section 10.2. Let us discuss the rest of them also before coming to commercial banks.

10.3.1 Functions of the Central Bank

According to De Kock, the functions that are performed by the Central Bank in almost all the countries are:

(1) Issue of Currency: The Central Bank is the solitary institution of a country to issue currency. Bearing the sole liability for the currency issued, the Central Bank maintains equivalent value in terms of bullion and securities to back up the issue. Securities include domestic securities as well as foreign securities. Domestic securities comprise of treasury bills sold by the central government to the Central Bank. In the event the budgeted government expenditure exceeds its budgeted revenue, a *deficit* is said to be incurred. To finance this deficit, the government resorts to borrowing from the Central Bank by issuing documents called the treasury bills. The Central Bank issues fresh currency worth the value of these securities. This method of financing the budgetary deficit is known as ***monetizing the deficit.***

(2) Banker, Agent and Adviser to the Government: The Central Bank acts as a banker to the Central and the state governments. It performs the same functions for government as the commercial banks do for their customers. It accepts government deposits, collects cheques and drafts deposited in government accounts and transfers government funds from one account to another or from one place to another. It also advances short-term loans to government to enable government to fill the gap between its receipts and payments. In addition, Central Bank also provides foreign exchange to government to enable it to settle external debts or to purchase foreign goods.

In its capacity as agent to government, the Central Bank organizes sale of treasury bills in open market to enable the government to manage its public debt. As its fiscal agent, the Central Bank also receives taxes and other payments from public on behalf of the government.

In its capacity as Financial Adviser to government, the Central Bank provides advice to government on important economic issues such as those pertaining to devaluation of currency, commercial policies, foreign exchange policies, and budgetary policies.

(3) Banker's Bank: A Central Bank acts as a banker to the commercial banks in three ways:

(a) *As a Custodian of Cash Reserves of the Commercial Banks:* As stated earlier, the Central Bank requires all commercial banks to keep a certain proportion of their net demand and time deposits as cash reserves with it. In compliance, commercial banks maintain such reserves on behalf of the Central Bank. It is a different matter that such reserves are used by the commercial banks in times of emergency.

(b) *As **Lender of the Last Resort:*** When commercial banks are not able to secure financial accommodation from other sources, they approach the Central Bank for the same as a last resort. The Central Bank in such cases grants the desired credit against the eligible securities.

(c) *As a Bank of **Central Clearance,** Settlement and Transfers:* Since the Central Bank holds the cash reserves of the commercial banks, it becomes easier and more convenient for it to act as a clearing house for them for settling the inter-bank liabilities without involving physical cash transactions for the purpose. It is due to this function of the Central Bank that the commercial banks are able to create a large volume of credit.

(4) Custodian of Nations Gold and Foreign Exchange Reserves: All the gold and the foreign exchange reserves of the nation are kept under the custody of the Central Bank. This helps the Central Bank to minimize the fluctuations in the foreign exchange rates. To demonstrate, suppose dollar-rupee exchange rate is ₹ 40 per dollar at a point of time. Suppose further that demand for dollars increases with the result that the exchange rate rises to ₹ 50 per dollar. Under the fixed exchange rate system, the Reserve Bank of India (the Central Bank of the nation), in its attempt to retain the original rate of exchange, must supply dollars in the foreign exchange market at ₹ 40 a dollar. This results in an increase in supply of the foreign currency with the result that the exchange rate begins to fall below ₹ 50 per dollar. The trend would continue until the original level of ₹ 40 per dollar is reached. If the opposite happens, i.e., the demand for dollars falls, the exchange rate may dip down, say, to as low as ₹ 30 a dollar. To stabilize the rate, the Central Bank of the nation must start buying dollars so that dollar demand may rise and so may the exchange rate to the original level of ₹ 40 per dollar. In fact, RBI can't accomplish this commitment to International Monetary Fund if it does not possess the enough foreign exchange reserves.

Possession of gold reserves may also come handy in stabilization of rupee value in the economy in the same manner. An increase in gold reserves with the Central Bank may help it to issue more currency while a decrease, to a decrease in its issue. If the gold prices fall, the Central Bank may buy gold at specified rate so as to stabilize gold prices and hence the general price level. In the process, the Central Bank may have to issue more currency to buy the precious metal. Exactly opposite may the case be when gold prices shoot up.

(5) As a Source of Authentic Statistics about Economic Activities: In almost every country, the Central Bank collects and publishes statistics about various aspects of functioning of the national economy. This provides valuable information about the economic activities in the nation which helps the government to formulate suitable economic policies.

(6) As a Controller of Credit: As explained already in Section 10.2, a Central Bank is an apex body of a country to control and regulate the volume of credit in the nation. *Credit Control* is the most important function of a Central Bank (Section 9.2 for details).

10.3.2 Functions of a Commercial Bank

The variety of functions, a commercial bank performs is so vast in the industrial world of today that a precise definition to cover its activities is really difficult to evolve. Some of the definitions attempted by economists are given below:

According to Prof. Hart, "A banker is one who in ordinary course of his business, receives money which he repays by honouring cheques of persons from persons from whom or on whose account he receives"?

According to Kinley, "A bank is an establishment which makes to individuals such advances of money as may be required and safely made, and to which, individuals entrust money when not required by them for use".

According to Indian Banking Regulation Act, 1949, commercial banking involves, "the accepting for the purpose of lending or investment, deposits of money from the public, repayable on demand or otherwise, and withdraw able by cheque, draft, order or otherwise".

All these definitions lay emphasis on acceptance of chequable deposits from public and use them for lending as the main feature of a commercial bank. A close look at the activities of a commercial bank would reveal that neither of these two functions is sufficient by itself to characterize an organization as a commercial bank. Accepting chequable deposits from public is a necessary but by no means a sufficient function of a commercial bank. Even Post Office savings banks accept deposits of money many of which are chequable also but they don't do all those things which a modern commercial bank does today. Likewise, many institutions like the LIC, the UTI, the IDBI, etc. lend or invest money but none of them performs many other activities commercial banks do. That is why, institutions like the LIC, the UTI, the IDBI, etc. are all known as the non bank financial institutions. Thus, *accepting chequable deposits as well as lending or investing them, along with performing a host of other financial and agential services for their customers are all traditional functions of commercial banks.*

It, therefore, becomes essential to enumerate the functions of a modern commercial bank to provide an idea of what a commercial bank actually does. Here is the list of these functions:

(1) Accepting Deposits: Commercial banks accept the following three types of deposits:

(a) *Fixed or Term Deposits:* Money in the fixed deposit accounts is accepted for a fixed period, varying from a few months to a few years. The money so deposited can't be withdrawn by the depositor before the expiry of the fixed period. Interest offered by the banks on such accounts is higher than that offered on other accounts. In fact, the longer the period of the fixed deposit, the higher is the rate of interest offered. A variant of the term deposits is the recurring deposits in which deposits of specified amounts are made at regular intervals with an objective of raising a desired sum of money by a depositor at the end of the period.

(b) *Current Account Deposits:* These deposits are often made and maintained by business houses. They qualify for unrestricted withdrawals through cheques as they don't earn any interest on such accounts. Periodic statements of transactions are provided by the banks for the benefit of the depositors.

(c) *Savings Account Deposits:* Such deposits qualify for interest payments but don't enjoy unrestricted withdrawal facility. This however does not imply that they are non-chequable. Withdrawals can be made through cheques or through withdrawal-slips but under certain restrictions that vary from bank to bank. Some banks permit two or three withdrawals per week while others permit more. Depositors are required to maintain a certain minimum balance in the accounts to continue to enjoy the benefits of these deposits.

In monetary analysis, deposits were classified as the demand deposits and the time deposits. The fixed and the term deposits are classified as the time deposits while current account deposits and the savings deposits fall into the category of the demand deposits.

(2) Advancing Loans: The deposits received by the banks are not allowed to remain idle as vault cash. Banks have to pay interest on time-deposits and savings deposits for which, and also for raising funds to meet their own expenditures on running the establishments, they resort to lending or investing the deposits. For this, commercial banks grant various types of loans and advances to individuals and business houses. Some of such loans are introduced below:

1. *Cash Credit:* It refers to the credit limit granted to a borrower on the basis of his creditworthiness determined by borrower's assets such as listed shares, bonds and securities, fixed deposit certificates, LIC policies, goods-in-trade, inventory stocks, movable assets such as vehicles, and immovable assets such as land, building, etc. Usually paper assets such as securities and bills receivable of legal authenticity are pledged, movable assets such as

vehicles are hypothecated and immovable assets are mortgaged to bank by the borrower for availing such facility. The amount granted is credited in the borrower's account from which the borrower keeps withdrawing as and when need arises. He can even make deposits in the cash credit account. Bank charges interest only on the portion of the credit which is actually utilized by the borrower and only for that period for which it is utilized by the borrower. The tenure of such facility is 1 year subject to renewal year after year by the bank. Interest charged is higher when the facility is availed against goods-in-trade or inventory stocks or movable or immovable assets than that when it is availed against securities. This is so due to higher liquidity possessed by securities. Some multinational banks such as ABN Amro-Bank and Standard Chartered Bank have started granting Clean Cash Credit facility to reputed borrowers generally in the service sector without any security but the rate of interest charged is higher than even that charged on cash credit availed against movable and immovable assets.

2. *Demand Loans:* Such loans are granted against the security of financial assets, goods, or personal credit worthiness. Entire loan amount is credited to the loan account of the borrower and is chargeable to interest. It can be recalled on demand. The borrowers are usually the security brokers whose credit requirements vary from day to day. Bankers use the term 'money at call' or 'call money' for these loans in their balance sheets. In liquidity, such loans rank next only to cash-in-hand.
3. *Short-term Loans:* Such loans are meant for short periods. They include personal loans (granted as unsecured loans for a period not exceeding 5 years) and working capital loans (granted as secured loans for short periods). In respect of such loans entire loan amount is credited to the loan account of the borrower and is chargeable to interest. In case of personal loans, repayment is made through Equated Monthly Instalments (EMI's) spread over the period of loan; but in respect of the working capital loans, repayment may be made through single installment at the end.
4. *Discounting Bills of Exchange:* The most common way of extending credit to the business houses is through *discounting* their ***bills of exchange***. The tenure of the loan is the period of maturity of the document and the amount of the loan is equal to the discounted value of the bill of exchange, discounted at the standard rates. A *bill of exchange* is a document that acknowledges an amount of money owed by the issuer in consideration of the consignment of goods to be received. On receipt of the bill of exchange, the supplier of the goods may present the same before the bank for immediate encashment. The bank deducts its commission from the present value of the document and releases the rest. At the maturity of the bill, it is presented before its issuer for its encashment. Cost of such loans has two parts—*first,* the discounting bank's commission and *second,* the excess of the face value over the current value of the bill at the time of discounting.
5. *Long Term Loans:* Such loans are fully secured loans. The period of such loans is long, extending up to 25 years depending on the borrower's preference. Repayment is spread over the entire period of loan and is usually made through *EMI's*. Home loans provide an example.
6. *Overdrafts:* It refers to a temporary credit facility granted to an account holder for a period of 3 months at the maximum. It is usually done against the pledge of paper-assets such as listed shares and debentures, or even against the assignment by the borrower of the LIC policies or the fixed deposit certificates to the bank. The borrower can draw from

the account up to the overdraft-limit granted to him, over and above the current account balance. Rate of interest is charged on the credit used by the borrower but it is lower than that charged on the clean cash credit or the cash credit availed against movable and immovable assets.

In common man's language, the terms ***cash credit*** and ***overdraft*** are used inter-changeably but the two are not the same, as is clear from the discussions above. The main points of difference relate to, *first*, the tenure, which is 3 months in case of an overdraft and 1 year in case of a cash credit and, *second*, the existence of a current account with the lending bank, which is must in case overdraft but not so in case of cash credit.

(3) Investment of Funds: Commercial banks invest idle funds in government securities and in other securities approved under the Indian Banking Regulation Act, 1949. Investment in such securities by commercial banks is mandatory for them under the Statutory Liquidity Ratio (SLR) requirement of the Reserve Bank of India (RBI). Commercial banks have a tendency to overinvest in these securities despite lower returns from them, mainly for the reason of their very high liquidity. They can always avail loans against them from the RBI or can even sell them in open market whenever they need cash.

(4) Agency Functions of the Commercial Banks: Commercial banks act as agents of their customers in following matters:

1. *Remittance of Funds:* Commercial banks help their customers in sending money from one place to another through drafts, mail transfers and telegraphic transfers at nominal charges.
2. *Collection of Funds:* Commercial banks help their customers in collection of funds through cheques, drafts, hundis and bills.
3. *Sale and Purchase of Shares:* Commercial banks help their customers by undertaking sale and purchase of shares on behalf of their customers.
4. *Collection of Dividends:* Commercial banks help their customers by collecting dividends and interests accruing on their shares and debentures.
5. *Payments of bills:* Commercial banks help their customers by making payments of their bills and insurance premia.
6. *Execution and trusteeship of will:* Commercial banks act as executors and trustees of the customer's will.
7. *Tax Consultancy:* Commercial banks undertake to act as income tax consultants to their customers and also to make tax payments on behalf of them.
8. *Collection of Documents:* Commercial banks collect documents showing dispatch of consignments through air and sea passages. This is convenient not only to the customers but also to the bank. For example, collection of documents of loading the consignments if entrusted to the bank helps the bank as well as the customers at the time of discounting the letters of credit.
9. *Sale and Purchase of Foreign Exchange:* Commercial banks undertake to buy and sell foreign exchange for their customers.
10. *Safe Custody of Valuables:* Commercial banks provide lockers for safe custody of customer's valuables.
11. *Purchase of movable and immovable Assets:* Commercial banks represent their customers in sale purchase of assets so that the authenticity of title deeds and their transfer may be ascertained to avoid the chances of cheating in the deal.

12. *Underwriting Activities:* Commercial banks act as underwriters of share capital issued by the customer companies. An underwriter is usually a business house of high repute or a commercial bank prepared to buy the unsold portion of the new issue of the share capital.

From the discussions above, it is clear that commercial banks not only deal in money matters but also perform a number of activities in the interest of their customers. A modern business can't run without cooperation of the commercial banks.

To provide an idea to the reader about various forms of the commercial banks we resort to the following tree-diagram:

TABLE 10.2

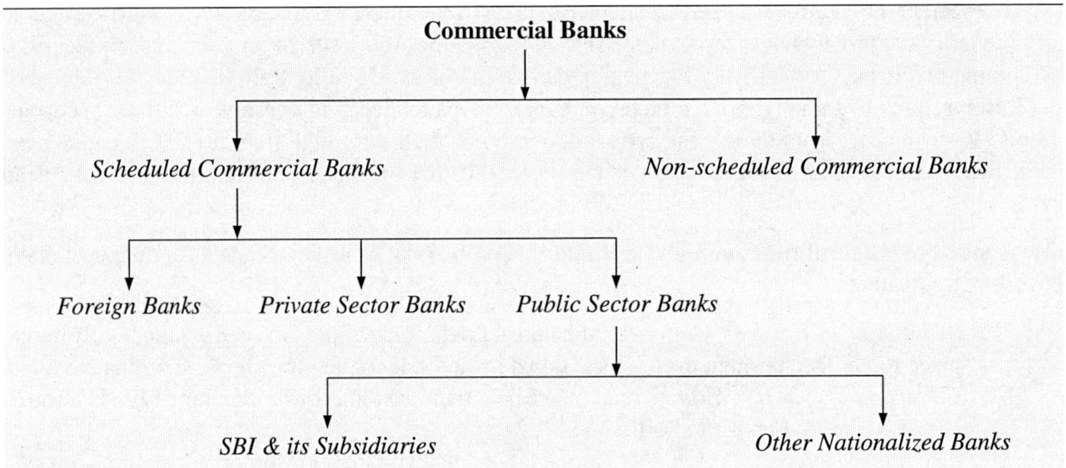

10.3.3 Balance Sheet of a Commercial Bank

A look at the balance sheet of a commercial bank may provide an idea of what the commercial banks prefer to do and how they hold their assets and liabilities. Here we list items on the asset and liability sides of their balance sheets for the benefit of the keen reader.

TABLE 10.3 Balance Sheet of a Commercial Bank

Capital and Liabilities	*Property and Assets*
1. Capital	1. Cash
2. Reserve Funds and Other Reserves.	2. Balances with Other Banks
3. Deposits and Other Accounts	3. Money at Call or Short Notices
4. Borrowings from Other Banking Companies, Agents, etc.	4. Investments
5. Bills Payable	5. Advances
6. Other Liabilities	6. Premises less Depreciation
7. Profit and Loss	7. Furniture and Fixtures less Depreciation
	8. Other Assets
	9. Non-banking Assets acquired in satisfaction of claims.

A close look at the asset side of the balance sheet reveals that commercial banks follow a particular pattern to reconcile the conflict between the liquidity and the profitability. Assets are arranged in order of decreasing liquidity but increasing profitability. *Cash-in-vault* is most liquid but least profitable while ***non-banking assets** in satisfaction of claims* is least liquid but most profitable. The banks aspire for both—the profitability and liquidity. A higher profitability requires lower liquidity but a higher liquidity reduces profitability. How can banks earn higher profits if they don't resort to lending and how can they maintain higher liquidity if they lend every rupee for the sake of earning higher profits? The banks strike a balance between the two by preferring their assets in decreasing order of liquidity lor increasing order of profitability.

10.4 COMMERCIAL BANKS—CREATION AND CONTROL OF CREDIT

In this section, we explain the process of credit creation by commercial banks and also the mechanism of control on it as exercised by a Central Bank.

10.4.1 Process of Credit Creation by Commercial Banks

(i) Under Monopoly Bank or Single Bank System: To begin with, let the Cash Reserve Ratio (*R*) be 20%. Further, let the initial deposit (Primary Deposit, *PD*) made with a commercial bank by depositor '*A*' be ₹ 10,000. The commercial bank is required to retain 20% of the deposit as vault cash to encash the cheques of depositor '*A*' and the rest, 80% of it, it lends to borrower, '*B*'. Thus, it retains only ₹ 2000 (R % of $PD = r.\ PD$) and lends out the rest, ₹ 8000 [$(1 - R)$ % of $PD = (1 - r).\ PD$] to the borrower. Here, $r = R/100$. The loan amount of ₹ 8000 is credited in *B*'s account by the bank. This creates a secondary deposit of ₹ 8000 with the bank. Borrower '*B*' is issued a cheque book to make withdrawals from his account as and when he likes. The Total Deposits (*TD*) with the bank increases by ₹ 8000. The bank has to maintain another cash reserve of ₹ 1600 [20% of ₹ 8000 or $r.(1 - r)\ PD$] for *B*'s cheques. The total cash reserve now is ₹ 3600 (₹ 2000 for *A's* cheques and ₹ 1600 for *B*'s cheques). The bank now feels free to lend 80% [$(1 - r)$] of *B's* deposit of ₹ 8000 [$(1 - r)$ of *PD*], which it lends to borrower '*C*'. This creates a third deposit of ₹ 6400 [$(1 - r).(1 - r) \times PD = (1 - r)^2.\ PD$] in the name of '*C*' to maintain which the bank has to retain yet another cash reserve of ₹ 1280 [$r.(1 - r)^2 \times PD$]. The total cash reserve in the bank's vault rises to ₹ 4880 (₹ 2000 for *A*'s cheques, ₹ 1600 for *B*'s cheques and ₹ 1280 for *C*'s cheques). The third deposit of ₹ 6400 [$(1 - r)^2.\ PD$] entitles the bank to lend 80% [$(1 - r)$] of it, i.e., ₹ 5120 [$(1 - r).(1 - r)^2.\ PD = (1 - r)^3.\ PD$] to some other borrower, '*D*'. The process of lending by the commercial bank continues indefinitely until the bank is left with nothing to lend or it has the whole of the primary deposit as cash reserve in its vault. The lending process can be summarized as in Table 10.4.

TABLE 10.4 [$PD = 10000$, $r = 0.20$]

No. of Deposit (n)	*Deposit* $= (1 - r)^{n-1}.\ PD$	*Required Cash Reserves* $= r.\ (1 - r)^{n-1}.\ PD$	*Loanable Funds with the Bank* $= (1 - r).\ (1 - r)^{n-1}.\ PD$
1	$(1 - 0.20)^{1-1}.10000$ ₹ 10000	$0.20\ (1 - 0.20)^{1-1}.10000$ = ₹ 2000	$(1 - 0.20)(1 - 0.20)^{1-1}.10000$ = ₹ 8000
2	$(1 - 0.20)^{2-1}.10000$ = ₹ 8000	$0.20\ (1 - 0.20)^{2-1}.10000$ = ₹ 1600	$(1 - 0.20)(1 - 0.20)^{2-1}.10000$ = ₹ 6400
3	$(1 - 0.20)^{3-1}.10000$ = ₹ 6400	$0.20\ (1 - 0.20)^{3-1}.10000$ = ₹1280	$(1 - 0.20)(1 - 0.20)^{3-1}.10000$ = ₹ 5120

(Contd.)

No. of Deposit (n)	*Deposit* $= (1 - r)^{n-1}.\, PD$	*Required Cash Reserves* $= r.\,(1 - r)^{n-1}.\, PD$	*Loanable Funds with the Bank* $= (1 - r).\,(1 - r)^{n-1}.\, PD$
4	$(1 - 0.20)^{4-1}.10000$ = ₹ 5120	$0.20\,(1 - 0.20)^{4-1}.10000$ = ₹1024	$(1 - 0.20)(1 - 0.20)^{4-1}.\,10000$ = ₹ 4096
...	...	... ...	... ...
	...	... ...	... ...
n	$(1 - 0.20)^{n-1}.10000$	$0.20\,(1 - 0.20)^{n-1}.10000$	$(1 - 0.20)(1 - 0.20)^{n-1}.\,10000$
∞	0.00	0.00	0.00
Total	**₹ 50,000**	**₹ 10,000**	**₹ 40,000**

The totals reached follow from the formulae:

$$\text{Total Deposits } (TD) = (PD/r)^1 \quad (10.2)$$

$$\text{Loanable Funds created} = TD - PD = [(1/r) - 1].\, PD \quad (10.3)$$

$$\text{Total Cash Reserves} = PD \quad (10.4)$$

The formulae 10.2, 10.3 and 10.4 follow from the sum to infinity of the geometric progression with common-ratio,

$$`t' = (1 - r)^2$$

Thus, Total Deposit, $TD = PD/r$ = 10,000/0.20 = ₹ 50,000
Loans Created = $PD\,[(1 - r)/r]$ = 10,000 [0.80/0.20] = ₹ 40,000
Required Cash Reserves = PD = ₹ 10,000

Note that the commercial bank ends up retaining the entire primary deposit as vault cash, and at the same time, it succeeds in creating loans (credit) worth as much as ₹ 40,000, with total deposits rising from ₹ 10,000 to as high as ₹ 50,000. All this has been possible due people's faith in the banking system. Had people insisted on cash loan, the deposit in consequence to the loan would never have occurred and bank's credit creating capacity would have been checked. Thus, highly developed banking habits play an important role in credit creation by commercial banks.

(ii) Credit Creation by Commercial Banks under Multi-bank System or under Competitive Banking: The process of credit creation by commercial banks under multiple bank system differs from that in the single bank system basically in one respect—the subsequent or the derivative deposits

---

[1] Reciprocal of cash reserve ratio ($1/r$) is identified by some economists as credit multiplier or primary deposit multiplier.

[2] To obtain expression 10.2 for Total Deposits (TD) with the commercial bank caused by the primary deposit, including the primary deposit, express TD as

$TD = \Sigma(1 - r)^{n-1}.\, PD,\ n = 1, 2, 3, \ldots,$ to ∞ [Note that $(1 - r)$, the common ratio, can be denoted as t. It is < 1]
$= [(1 - r)^{1-1}.\, PD] + [(1 - r)^{2-1}.\, PD] + [(1 - r)^{3-1}.\, PD] + [(1 - r)^{4-1}.\, PD] + [(1 - r)^{5-1}.\, PD] + \ldots + \ldots$ to ∞
$= [PD] + [(1 - r)^1.\, PD] + [(1 - r)^2.\, PD] + [(1 - r)^3.\, PD] + [(1 - r)^4.\, PD] + \ldots + \ldots$ to ∞
$= PD.\, [1 + (1 - r) + (1 - r)^2 + (1 - r)^3 + (1 - r)^4 + \ldots + \ldots + \ldots$ to ∞]
$= PD.\, [1 \times (1 - r)^n/\{1 - (1 - r)\}]$
$= PD/r.$ [Since, $Lim_n \to \infty\,(1 - r)^n = 0$ as $|(1 - r)| < 1$]

In the same way, Loans Created $= TD - PD$
$= PD/r - PD$
$= PD.\, [(1/r) - 1]$
$= PD.\, [(1 - r)/r]$

Required Cash Reserves $= \Sigma\,[r.\,(1 - r)^{n-1}.\, PD],\ n = 1, 2, 3, \ldots$
$= r.\,\Sigma\,[(1 - r)^{n-1}.\, PD],\ n = 1, 2, 3, \ldots \ldots$
$= r.\, PD/r$
$= PD$

(Secondary deposits, tertiary deposits, etc.) need no longer return to the bank of the primary deposit. Presence of other banks in the banking sector provides alternatives to the public to choose from. They may choose a bank of their own convenience which need not be the bank from which they have borrowed. The derivative deposits thus may arise in banks other than those where the primary deposits originated. But the total volume of credit generated remains unaffected. The figure below shows the flow of deposits in a multiple bank system. Suppose there are three banks—A, B and C from which a depositor has to make his choice for making his deposit. If the bank chosen by him is bank A, the deposit made in the bank is the primary deposit if the same is the first one from this person. The first loan granted to an individual by bank A from this deposit may go to any of the three banks, including bank A. If it goes to bank A, it will form the secondary deposit, else, if it lands in bank B or bank C, it will form the primary deposit. The arrows show various possibilities for primary and derivative deposits.

The total volume of credit created by the commercial banks in a multi-bank system remains same as that in a single bank system.

10.4.2 Limitations to Credit Creation by Commercial Banks

We have seen how commercial banks multiply credit. The way they go they might create much more than what the economy can sustain. After all, the process generates income for them. The reality, however, is different. Commercial banks, despite their intentions to generate an infinite credit, are

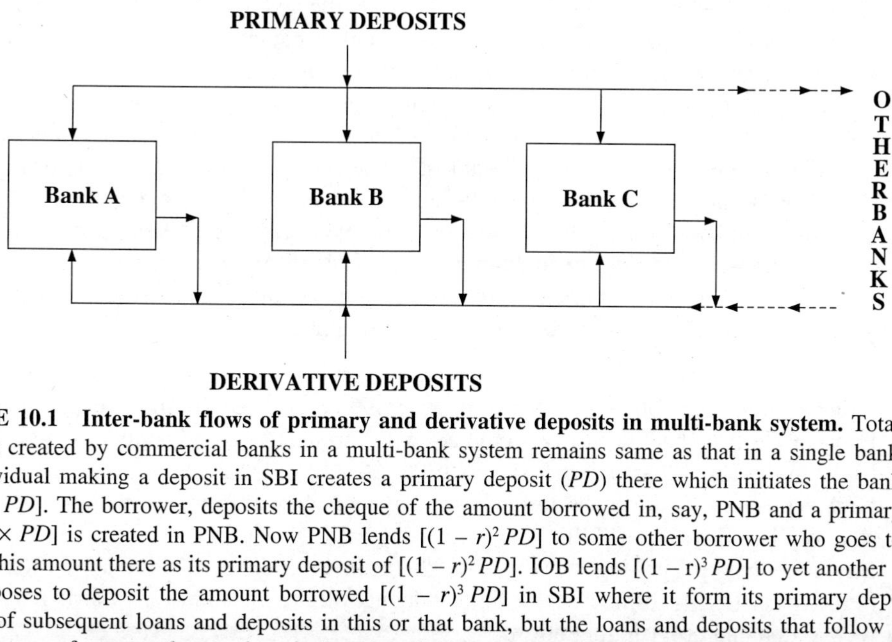

FIGURE 10.1 Inter-bank flows of primary and derivative deposits in multi-bank system. Total volume of credit created by commercial banks in a multi-bank system remains same as that in a single bank system. An individual making a deposit in SBI creates a primary deposit (*PD*) there which initiates the bank to lend [(1 – *r*). *PD*]. The borrower, deposits the cheque of the amount borrowed in, say, PNB and a primary deposit [(1 – *r*) × *PD*] is created in PNB. Now PNB lends $[(1 - r)^2 PD]$ to some other borrower who goes to IOB to deposit this amount there as its primary deposit of $[(1 - r)^2 PD]$. IOB lends $[(1 - r)^3 PD]$ to yet another borrower who chooses to deposit the amount borrowed $[(1 - r)^3 PD]$ in SBI where it form its primary deposit. The process of subsequent loans and deposits in this or that bank, but the loans and deposits that follow the same trend in terms of amounts lent or deposited as they did in a single bank system. The net effect is that the initial primary deposit at SBI generates the same amount of total deposits [*PD*/*r*] in the banking sector as it would have under the single bank system in SBI had it been the only bank in the sector. The same goes for the loans created.

always constrained by the credit control measures of the Central Bank. Through an appropriate blend of *instruments of monetary policy* (Section 10.2), a Central Bank exercises an effective control over the commercial banks in their credit expansion. For instance, the Central Bank may choose to increase the *CRR* to twice as high a level (Say, 40%) with a view to curtail the credit expansion to half as much (to ₹ 25000 instead of ₹ 50000 at a *CRR* of 20%). In the same way, it may vary the *SLR* or the bank rate or the credit quotas or any other of the quantitative or qualitative instruments or any combination of them or even all of them to effectively control the process.

Apart from these instruments of credit control, credit expansion depends also on the banking habits of the people and the level of economic activities in the economy. If the people do not possess highly developed banking habits or the level of economic activity is primitive, the commercial banks can't do much even when prompted by the Central Bank for the same. Their credit expansion capacity is thus not unlimited. Instead it is subject to a number of constraints of several types.

10.5 PRIVATIZATION AND MODERNIZATION OF INDIAN BANKING

Indian banking system, like most others in the developing countries, is characterized by the coexistence of different ownership groups—public and private. Banks in public sector have passed through several stages of existence. The first one was of nationalization of the Imperial Bank of India and seven other banks of the princely states in fifties. This led to emergence of State Bank of India and its seven associate banks.

The second stage comprised the two phases of nationalization of major private banks in 1969 and 1980. Non-nationalized private and foreign banks were allowed to coexist with the public sector banks. Their activities were, however, restricted through entry regulation and strict branch licensing policies. As a result, public sector banks dominated banking business, accounting for nearly 90% of the total deposits and advances in 1990-91. Non-nationalized private and foreign banks shared the residual of 10%. There were 27 public sector banks, 23 private sector banks and 23 foreign banks in operation in India in 1990–91. They were all subject to the central bank (RBI) regulations.

In 1991–92, RBI launched major banking sector reforms aiming at creating a more profitable, efficient and sound banking system. Based on the recommendations of Narasinhan committee on financial system reforms, these reforms sought to make the banking system more responsive to changes in market conditions. As a result an era of deregulation of entry, branch licensing and interest rates dawned upon Indian banking industry in the form of privatization and modernization This led to following repercussions:

1. Permission to the public sector banks to raise 49% of their equity in the capital market.
2. Entry of 6 private banks, mostly promoted by government owned institutions, and 3 foreign banks in the Indian banking industry in 1994–95.
3. Higher profitability to banks through gradual reduction in cash reserve ratio (*CRR*) and statutory liquidity ratio (*SLR*).
4. Strengthening of banking system through the institution of the Bank of International Settlements (BIS) norm of 8% capital adequacy ratio in addition to stringent income recognition and provisioning norms.
5. Creation of level playing field for domestic and foreign banks.
6. Requirement from the foreign banks to earmark 32% of their total credit to the priority sector in India with effect from 1993. Prior to the reforms, they were exempted from such requirement while all the domestic banks, whether public or private, were by contrast, required to earmark 40% of their total credit to the priority sector.

Disinvestment in the public sector banks and deregulation of Indian banking industry as a whole have increased competition in the banking industry through increased private participation.

Privatization of Indian banking industry coupled with information technology revolution in India in general has modernized Indian banking with higher competitiveness. RBI's Monetary and Credit policy (2003–04) provides an insight into the current developments and prospective technology up-gradation in Indian financial sector. Substantial progress has been made for developing a modern, efficient, integrated and secure payment and settlement system Modernization of clearing and settlement through MICR (Magnetic Ink Character Recognition) based cheque clearing, popularization of electronic clearing services (ECS) and integration of RBI-EFT scheme with electronic funds transfer (EFT) scheme, introduction of centralized funds management system (CFMS) are a few significant milestones in this regard. Real time gross settlement (RTGS) environments improve the effectiveness of asset-liability management. Core banking system (CBS) and cheque truncation system (CTS), the recent developments, in multicity banking that replaced the existing system of remittances that used to cost time and money both.

KEY TERMS AND CONCEPTS

Monetary Policy: A monetary policy, in its broader sense, refers to the monetary system along with the measures to manage supply of money and credit in an economy, including steps taken from time to time, to regulate and control interest rates.

Objectives of Monetary Policy: One after another economists came up with their suggestions about the objectives of monetary policy.

1. *Neutrality of Money:* The first one was that monetary policy such that doesn't affect general price-level, output, income and employment.
2. *Price Stabilization:* The next one was stabilization of price level.
3. *Exchange Stabilization:* Then emphasis shifted stabilization of exchange rate thereafter.
4. *Full Employment:* Maximum utilization of productive resources was yet another one in the line.
5. *Economic Growth:* The emphasis finally shifted onto economic growth in the recent years,

Instruments of Credit Control: Various methods employed by a Central Bank to regulate and control the volume of money circulating in the economy are referred to as instruments of monetary policy or of credit control. These instruments are grouped under two broad heads:

1. Quantitative methods that influence the volume of credit directly such as bank rate, open market operations, cash reserve ratio (CRR), statutory liquidity ratio (SLR).
2. Qualitative methods that influence the volume of credit indirectly such as publicity, moral suasion, direct action, credit rationing, directives, regulation of consumer credit, margin requirement.

Functions of Central Banks: A central bank performs the following functions:

1. *Issue of Currency:* The Central Bank is the solitary institution of a country to issue currency.
2. *Banker, Agent and Adviser to the Government.*
3. *Banker's Bank:* A central Bank acts as a banker to the commercial banks in three ways:
   (a) As a Custodian of Cash Reserves of the Commercial Banks.
   (b) As Lender of the Last Resort.
   (c) As a Bank of Central Clearance, Settlement and Transfers.
4. *Custodian of Nations Gold and Foreign Exchange Reserves.*
5. *As a Source of authentic Statistics about Economic Activities.*
6. *As a Controller of Credit.*

Functions of the Commercial Banks: The essential functions of a modern commercial bank are:

1. *Accepting Deposits:* Commercial banks accept the following three types of deposits:
   (a) Fixed or Term Deposits
   (b) Current Account Deposits
   (c) Savings Account Deposits
2. *Advancing Loans:* Some of such loans are:
   (a) Cash Credit
   (b) Demand Loans
   (c) Short-term Loans
   (d) Discounting Bills of Exchange
   (e) Long-term Loans
   (f) Overdrafts
3. *Investment of Funds*
4. *Agency Functions of the Commercial Banks*

Balance Sheet of a Commercial Bank: Capital and liabilities on one side must balance the assets of the commercial bank on the other side. To strike a reconciliation between profitability and liquidity, commercial banks prefer to arrange their assets in decreasing order of liquidity or increasing order of profitability.

Process of Credit Creation by Commercial Banks: Commercial banks create credit through credit multiplier (1/CRR).When CRR = 20%, credit multiplier = 5.00. Commercial banks thus multiply the primary deposits by 5, generating 5 times as much volume of credit.

Process of Credit Control: All the instruments of the monetary policy of the Central Bank help the Central Bank to control the credit creation by the commercial banks.

EXERCISES

A. Short Answer Questions

1. Define monetary policy in its broader and narrower perspectives. Briefly outline its objectives.

2. Arrange the objectives of a monetary policy for its relevance to a developing country. Which one of them is most important for your country?

3. Briefly explain the major instruments of monetary control as exercised by a Central Bank.

4. Briefly explain the functions of a central bank.

5. Distinguish between:

6. (a) CRR and SLR
(b) Quantitative and qualitative methods of credit control

7. Suggest a scheme to:

8. (a) Regulate consumer credit

9. (b) Margin requirement on secured loans

10. Can ministry of finance issue currency? If yes, up o what denomination? Give reasons for your answer.

11. Outline the essential functions of a commercial bank.

12. What is meant by credit multiplier? What are the limitations to credit creation of a commercial bank?

13. How would the volume of credit created by the commercial bank be affected, if:

(a) CRR is raised to 25% from the existing one of 20%. Assume primary deposit to be 10,000?

[Ans: Volume of credit would fall to ₹ 40,000]

(b) Primary deposit is raised to ₹ 20000 from the initial level of 15,000? Assume a CRR of 10%?

[Ans: Volume of credit would rise to ₹ 200,000]

14. Liquidity and profitability of a commercial bank are opposed to each other. How does a commercial bank reconcile them?

15. Comment on the evolution of Indian banking industry since independence.

B. Long Answer Questions

16. Explain the process of credit creation of a commercial banks with specific reference to CRR and Primary deposits.
17. Explain various instruments of the monetary policy.
18. Explain the financial functions of a commercial bank.
19. On what factors does the credit creation of a commercial bank depend? How does a central bank exercise control on credit creating capacity of commercial banks?

C. Essay Type Questions

20. 'Objectives of the monetary policy have always been under review'. Discuss.
21. 'As compared to the quantitative methods, the qualitative methods are more immediate in their effect on monetary control'. Discuss.
22. 'Commercial banks do much more than just dealing with cash'. Discuss.
23. Obtain an expression for primary deposit multiplier. How is it related to *CRR*? How do commercial banks use it to create credit money? Demonstrate.
24. 'Be it the single bank system or the multi-bank system, volume of credit created by the commercial bank (s) remains same so long as the CRR, the magnitude of primary deposit and the banking habits of the people remain unchanged'. Discuss. Are the limitations to credit creation also the same in both types of banking systems?

Chapter 11

Fiscal Policy

INTRODUCTION: MEANING AND EVOLUTION OF FISCAL POLICY

Fiscal policy may be defined as that part of the economic policies of a government which deals with public revenue (taxation), public expenditure and public debt along with its management. All budgetary policies are included in fiscal policy. It is an indispensable instrument of public finance in the hands of a modern state striving to achieve its cherished goals of economic growth, full employment and economic stability in the economy. Underdeveloped countries strive for high rate of economic growth while the developed ones strive for full employment and economic stability. Like a monetary policy, fiscal policy also concerns itself with the flow of funds in the economy. Taxation diverts funds from the private sector to the government sector while public expenditure, on the contrary, diverts them from the government sector to the private sector. Management of public debt involves floating of government loans, payment of interest thereon and retirement of matured debts. Fiscal policy thus has a powerful bearing on the working of an economy in respect of its output, income and employment.

Evolution of fiscal policy has passed through three distinct stages:

1. ***Classical Stage:*** In this stage, fiscal policy was confined to its limited operations with small but balanced budgets. The philosophy underlying such limited role of fiscal policy was the classical thought that the state should not intervene in the economic matters of the society. Classical economists believed that the law of markets automatically took care of output, income and employment. Existence of full employment and absence of under-consumption or over-production were the two implications of the law. State therefore had to focus only on the maintenance of law and order in the society.
2. ***Neo-classical Stage:*** In this stage, role of fiscal policy extended substantially, discarding its garb of non-intervention in the economic activities of people. Economic thinkers like Marshall and Pigou held that classical stage of fiscal policy is responsible for accentuating and perpetuating the widespread social inequalities It was realized that maximization of social welfare can't be possible in a *laissez-faire* capitalistic system through the policy of non-intervention in the economic affairs of the people. State has to step in to promote general well-being of public. The neo-classical stage thus shifted emphasis from *laissez-faire* capitalistic mode of production (production without government intervention) to one with welfare orientation of state in which government had to intervene whenever investment concentrated in sectors not conducive to maximization of social welfare. Fiscal policies of subsidy and indirect taxation were considered handy to give a desired tilt in the direction of investment. This required enlargement of fiscal operations and government budget.

3. ***Keynesian Stage:*** In this stage, fiscal policy was assigned a role totally different from that it played in earlier stages. To compensate for the deficiency of private investment during the period of depression, fiscal policy was required, even if it led to budgetary deficit, to provide for huge government expenditures on public works and other utility projects. Budgetary deficit refers to the excess of government's planned expenditures over its expected income from taxation. To finance the excess expenditures, printing of currency was treated as an integral part of the fiscal policy. This was the only way to raise Keynesian effective demand during depression. In Keynesian theory, depression was a consequence of demand deficiency which, in turn, was a consequence of low private investment.

Fiscal policy thus assumed maturity in its Keynesian stage. It has been thereafter cast into several moulds to cater to the specific needs. A.P. Lerner refined it to a form called ***functional finance*** which means a fiscal policy that is contra-cyclical in nature. That is, it should steer the economies clear of the hazards of trade cycles. Accordingly, the government budget should never be a balanced one. Instead, it should be a ***deficit budget*** when massive unemployment exists (as in the period of depression) and a *surplus budget* when overemployment exists (as in the period of *boom*). A surplus budget implies excess of revenue over expenditure. The objective of functional finance should be economic stability.

Another form of fiscal policy for economic stability is its features of ***built-in-stabilizers.*** For instance, if taxation is progressive, that is, if tax rate rises with rising levels of income, the fiscal policy is said to possess an automatic or built in stabilizer. Progressive tax is one such stabilizer. To see how it works, suppose national income increases. Under the progressive taxation, tax revenue of government increases automatically as a higher number of tax payers enter higher income slabs. Opposite is the case when national income falls.

Discretionary fiscal policy is yet another form of fiscal policy. It means deliberate government action to alter tax structure or expenditure to bring about economic development in the underdeveloped countries. Public borrowing and forced savings are some tools of discretionary fiscal policy.

11.1 OBJECTIVES OF FISCAL POLICY

Objectives of the fiscal policy vary from country to country depending on whether the economy is a developed one or an underdeveloped one. This is so because the problems of the two types of economies differ in nature and character from each other. For instance, developed countries are concerned with attainment and maintenance of full employment and economic stability while the underdeveloped ones worry about economic development, growth, and eradication of unemployment, poverty, hunger, epidemics and the like.

(a) Objectives of Fiscal Policy in a Developed Country: As mentioned above, fiscal policy in a developed capitalist economy has two broad objectives—*first,* maintenance of full employment, and *second,* economic stability. Both these objectives can be realized through ***compensatory spending*** of government (popularly known as ***compensatory fiscal policy***) to supplement private investment. When private investment is low, so is each one of the factor demand, output, income and employment. In case the trend of low investment continues, even a decline in each one of these may soon begin as low level of investment drifts the economy to depression. In such situations, the government should supplement private investment through its compensatory variation in its public expenditure even if it requires deficit financing. This creates an expansionary effect on the sagging economy (See also Section 9.5).

In like manner, policy of ***surplus budgeting*** helps dealing with the inflationary situations. When tax revenue is higher than government spending, net inflow of public money into the economy is negative. This has a depressing effect on private investment which helps to check inflation. Policy of ***deficit budgeting,*** on the other hand, helps to check the deflationary pressures. When public expenditure is higher than the tax revenue, net inflow of government money into the economy is positive. This supplements the private investment which helps to check deflation.

Thus, policies of surplus and deficit budgeting bring about economic stability in a developed economy. Whatever the nature of an economy, a fiscal policy aims at growth of income. In Section 9.2 we saw how ***fiscal policy multiplier*** can serve the purpose. Nevertheless, its effect is of limited consequence without proper monetary management. We have seen the fact through ***crowding out*** of private investment by public spending leading to failure of public spending in realization of full multiplier effect on income (See Section 9.5).

(b) Objectives of Fiscal Policy in an Underdeveloped Country: Fiscal policy, in an underdeveloped country, as stated above, aims at growth, economic development, reduction in income inequalities and eradication of poverty, hunger, epidemics unemployment and the like.

Objectives of economic development, attainment of full employment and economic growth—both require heavy investment. Private investment in underdeveloped countries being already at low levels. A *compensatory variation* in public expenditure through deficit financing generally proves somewhat effective in attainment of these objectives but not to the desired level unless it is supported by an appropriate monetary expansion (See Section 9.5, Figure 9.17). Supported appropriately by monetary expansion through monetary policy multiplier[1], private investment can help the cause of development, growth and employment. The objective of reduction in income inequalities, a discretionary fiscal policy with a tilt in favour of the weaker sections of the society proves highly effective. Taxing the rich and diverting the proceeds towards public works and such other public utility projects generate employment opportunities for the weaker sections. As regards economic stability, it comes later in respect of the underdeveloped countries. Whenever it does, deficit and surplus budgeting can prove as useful as they do in case of the developed world.

11.2 INSTRUMENTS OF FISCAL POLICY

Taxation, public expenditure, public borrowing and forced savings are various instruments of fiscal policy. We will discuss each one of them in brief.

(1) Taxation: It is an important source of government revenue. There are two types of taxes—direct taxes and indirect taxes. ***Direct taxes*** are those whose incidence and impact both fall on the same source, that is, they are non-shiftable. Such taxes are to be paid by the very source on which they are levied. Personal income tax is an example. The individual who pays it and the individual on whom it is levied is the same person. Corporate profit tax is another example of a direct tax. It is levied on the net profits of a firm. Property tax is yet another tax, levied on propertied class. Wealth tax and inheritance tax are other examples of direct taxes. ***Indirect taxes***, such as goods and services taxes, are those taxes whose impact and incidence do not fall on the same entity. Excise duties, sales tax, and custom duties are three important commodity taxes. Excise duty is a tax levied on production of goods and are shiftable in part or in full on the buyers. Sales tax is levied on the sale of goods. Custom duty is levied on import and export of goods. When levied on imports, it is called the import duty or import

[1] For monetary policy multiplier, see Equation 10.1 and for its working, see Equation 9.12.

tariff and when levied on exports, it is called the export duty or export tariff. Service taxes are other examples of indirect taxes. They are levied on services and are shared between provider and receiver of the services. A commodity tax is also known as ***unit tax***. It is levied at a fixed rate on each unit. The value of tax may also manifest as a percent of the price of the unit. In the later case it is called a ***percent tax*** and serves as a built-in-stabilizer as tax revenue automatically goes up when prices do.

Apart from the above classification, taxes are also classified as proportional, progressive, digressive and regressive taxes. A ***proportional tax*** is a fixed proportion of income or of value. For example, taxation of income in India between ₹ 3,00,001 and ₹ 7,00,000, as per the provisions of the Central Budget 2024–25, is a proportional tax. It is levied at 5% of the precise value of taxable income is subjected to tax. To demonstrate, tax liability at taxable income of 4,00,000 would be ₹ 20,000 and that at taxable income of ₹ 6,00,000, ₹ 30,000. That is tax liability is a fixed proportion of the precise value of taxable income. On the other hand, a ***progressive tax*** is one in which tax rate varies with rise in income slabs. It is high for the high slabs. For instance, if taxable income fall in the income slab of ₹ 7,00,001 to 10,00,000, the rate of taxation is 10% of the precise taxable income and if it is between ₹ 10,00,001 to 12,00,000, the tax liability is 15% as per the provisions of the Central Budget 2024–25.Tax liability is proportional within a slab but progressive in between the slabs. A tax, such as this, which is proportional within a slab and progressive between the slabs is known as a **digressive tax.** Indian income tax is thus digressive in nature. A ***regressive tax*** is opposite in nature to the progressive tax. The tax burden is heavier on for low income people and lighter for high income people. Excise on production of liquor is an example. It is levied at higher rates on country made liquor and at lower rates on superior brands of whisky in India. The policy of taxation such as this is intended to discourage production and consumption of country made liquor which is believed to be injurious to human health. Such inferior liquor is consumed by the vast majority of the low income people in India. They are the ones who bear the burden of higher tax rates. Another example if a regressive tax is the salt tax which was levied in British Period. The poor were the major consumers of salt while the rich, minor ones.

(2) Public Borrowing: Public borrowing is yet another instrument of fiscal policy. To borrow, government floats bonds and securities through the Central Bank. Financial institutions dealing with public funds turn out the main sources of such loans to the government. Interest and dividends are the costs of such loans. Funds so raised by government form a part of its productive expenditures.

(3) Public Expenditure: Expenditures of government are called *public expenditures*. Apart from maintenance of law and order, the government of a welfare state has to do many more things for people. It has to provide infrastructure for development and has also to act as producer of a number of goods and services in the public interest. Ever since its transition to a welfare state, the expenditures of the state have always been on the rise.

(4) Deficit Financing or Forced Savings: ***Forced savings,*** or more popularly, *deficit financing* is yet another tool of fiscal policy. As explained in Section 11.2 under ***compensatory fiscal policy***, a government resorts to deficit budgeting either to steer clear of depression or to further the causes of economic development and employment generation. In such cases, excess of public expenditure over its revenue is financed by printing of currency by the government. In fact, such currency is printed by the Central Bank under the instructions of the government. The process of financing the budgetary deficit created deliberately by government for supplementing the sagging private investment is called ***monetization of the deficit***.

11.3 GOVERNMENT BUDGET AND ITS TERMINILOGY

In the beginning of every financial year, government presents before the parliament an estimate of its receipts and expenditures for the coming financial year. The statement, generally comprising of two parts, is called the *government budget*. The *first part* of the budget presents the financial performance of the government in the financial year just concluded and the *second part* of it, financial plans of the government for the year just commenced. Government budget being an integral part of its fiscal policies, it spells its objectives and instruments resorted to in the year past or those being proposed for the year to come. To understand the terminology of the budget, we begin with the ***revenue budget*** and the ***capital budget,*** into which the budget of the Central Government is divided.

11.3.1 Revenue Budget

This part of the budget comprises of the revenue receipts and the revenue expenditures. Revenue receipts finance revenue expenditures. When revenue expenditure exceeds revenue receipts, the revenue budget is said to be in *deficit*, when opposite is the case, it is said to be in *surplus* and when the two are equal, the revenue budget is said to be in balance. Thus,

BOX 11.1 Revenue Budget
Revenue Expenditure – Revenue Receipts = Revenue Deficit Revenue Receipts – Revenue Expenditure = Revenue Surplus Revenue Receipts = Revenue Expenditure ⇒ Balanced Budget

11.3.1.1 Revenue receipts

Revenue receipts comprise of tax and non-tax revenues. *Tax revenue* is revenue from direct as well as indirect taxes. We have already discussed them in Section 11.2.

Non-tax revenue comprises of (a) commercial revenue, and (b) administration revenue. ***Commercial revenue*** refers to receipts from the sale of tangible or intangible government products. For example, receipts from sale of postages, interest receipts on funds lent by government credit corporations, receipts from sale of services such as electricity and railways, dividend receipts on investments made by government etc. constitute commercial revenue. ***Administrative revenue*** comprises of receipts such as *license fee* for grant of permission or privilege, *college fee* in government colleges, *registration fee* on registration of automobiles and fire-arms, *fines and penalties* levied on infringement of law, *surety forfeitures* on failure to comply with orders or on failure to fulfil contracts and ***escheats*** meaning claims made by government on property of individuals who die without any legal heirs or without leaving a will. Thus,

$$\text{Revenue Receipt} = \text{Tax Revenue} + \text{Non-tax Revenue} \tag{11.1}$$

11.3.1.2 Revenue expenditure

It refers to all those expenditures of government that do not result in creation of assets. Government expenditures on running its departments and those on providing various services, paying national debt interest and paying subsidies granted constitute revenue expenditures. All grants to the state governments are treated as revenue expenditure even though some of them may be meant for creation of assets. Thus,

$$\text{Revenue Expenditure} = \text{Running Expenditures of Departmental undertakings} + \text{Interest Payments} + \text{Subsidies} + \text{Grants-in-aid to States} + \text{Provision for Services such as Defence} \quad (11.2)$$

11.3.2 Capital Budget

This part of the budget comprises of capital receipts and capital expenditures. Let us cast a look at the constituents of the two.

11.3.2.1 Capital receipts

Capital receipts include *loans* raised by government from different sources, *repayments (recoveries) of loans* granted to states and union territories in the past, *borrowings* from small savings of the people and from deposits in the public provident funds (*PPF*) and *funds realized* from disinvestment in Public Sector Undertakings (*PSUs*). Loans raised from different sources comprise loans from public, borrowings from RBI through sale of treasury bills, loans raised from foreign governments and international financial institutions such as *IBRD* (World Bank), *ADB* (Asian Development Bank), etc. *PSU*-disinvestment refers to the government withdrawal from maintaining its investment, in part or in full, in *PSUs*. The act releases government funds back to the government. Thus,

$$\text{Capital Receipts} = \text{Recovery of Loans} + \text{Receipts from } PSU\text{-disinvestment} + \text{Borrowings and Other Liabilities} \quad (11.3)$$

11.3.2.2 Capital expenditure

Capital expenditures comprise expenditures made on acquisition of assets like land, building, plant, equipment, machinery, etc. or giving loans to state and union territories, corporations, joint stock companies for the same or making investments in issue capital of *PSUs*.

11.3.3 Overall Budget

Overall budget, whether a deficit budget or a surplus or even a balanced budget, can be understood by taking into account the overall budget receipts and overall budget expenditures. While overall receipts comprise of revenue and capital receipts, overall expenditures comprise of revenue and capital expenditures. Overall expenditures can also be expressed as the sum of plan and non-plan expenditures as also as developmental and non-developmental expenditures.

BOX 11.2 Budget Receipts and Expenditures

Budget Receipts = Revenue Receipts + Capital Receipts
Budget Expenditures = Revenue Expenditures + Capital Expenditures
= Plan Expenditure + Non-plan Expenditure
= Developmental Expenditure + Non-developmental Expenditure
Budget Deficit = Budget Expenditures – Budget Receipts

Plan expenditure refers to government expenditures on current development and investment arising out of plan proposals. On the other hand, ***non-plan expenditures*** are expenditures other than the plan expenditures.

Developmental expenditure, as the name suggests, refers to plan expenditure for development purposes. It includes plan expenditure on departmental and non-departmental commercial undertakings. Expenditure incurred on departmental undertakings like Railways, Posts, Telecommunications, etc. and that incurred on non-departmental commercial undertakings by way of loans, grants-in-aid, etc. are examples. ***Non-developmental expenditures***, on the other hand, refer to expenditures on certain essential services such as defence, police, tax-collection, general administration, interest payments on national debt, pension payments, expenditure on relief work, expenditure on payment of food subsidy, etc.

11.3.4 Concept of Budget Surplus

When the ***budget receipts*** fall short of ***budget expenditures***, the budget is said to be a ***deficit budget***; when budget receipts exceed the budget expenditures, the budget is said to be a ***surplus budget*** and when budget receipts are just equal to the budget expenditures, the budget is said to be a ***balanced budget.***

Denoting budget expenditure as G, net budget receipts as $(T - R)$, where T is tax revenue and R the transfer payments, and budget surplus as BS, we have

$$
\begin{aligned}
BS &= T - R - G \\
&= tY - R - G \qquad (11.4)
\end{aligned}
$$
[1]

(t is tax rate, Y is income)

If $BS > 0$, the budget is a surplus budget

If $BS < 0$, the budget is a deficit budget

If $BS = 0$, the budget is a balanced budget

In Section 11.1, we discussed the role of fiscal policy in influencing income and employment. We have seen how compensatory fiscal policy or deficit budgeting gives a boost to both. A little needs to be mentioned here to correlate the concept of the budget surplus to income and employment.

To avoid complications, let $R = 0$ in Equation 11.4 so that $BS = T - G$. Assume further that taxation is autonomous so that $T = T_a$. Now $BS = T_a - G$. Suppose the economy has so far been on a balanced budget with the result that $T_a = G$. If it wishes to continue with balanced budget, an increase in G (say, ΔG) would have to be matched by an equal increase in taxation (say, ΔT_a). How would these changes affect Income?

Illustration 6.3 (Section 6.7, Chapter 6) answers the question. The balanced budget multiplier being unitary, income increases by as much as the increase in G or in T despite the reality that injection (ΔG) is equal to withdrawal (ΔT_a). Please refer to part (v) of the illustration. Increase in income due to ΔG=10 with MPC of 0.75 is 40 [{1/(1 – 0.75)} × 10 = 40]. Decrease in income due to ΔT_a = 10

---

[1] Equation 11.4, at full employment income, can be rewritten as

$$
\begin{aligned}
BS^* &= T^* - R - G \\
&= tY^* - R - G \qquad (1)
\end{aligned}
$$

[star (*) indicates budget surplus at full employment income, Y^*]

From Equations 11.1 and 11.2, we have

$$BS^* - BS = t(Y^* - Y) \qquad (2)$$

Equation 11.3 leads to following implications:

If output is below full employment, the full employment surplus exceeds the actual surplus.

The full employment surplus (BS^*), also known as *high employment surplus,* indicates directional changes in fiscal policies to attain full employment. For instance, if BS^* exceeds the actual surplus (BS), persistent use of fiscal expansion provides a solution to the problem of unemployment.

with same MPC is 30 $[\{-0.75/(1 - 0.75)\} \times 10 = -30]$. The net increase in income is 40 – 30 = 10, which is the same as the value of ΔG or ΔT_a.

In the same way, if it is a surplus budget with $\Delta T_a = 20$, [Delta $Y = -\{0.75/(1 - 0.75)\} \times 20 = -60$], $\Delta G = 10$ and $MPC = 0.75$; the net increase in income can be seen to be – 20 (40 – 60 = – 20). This shows that a surplus budget decreases income and employment in the economy.

To see how a deficit budget influences income and employment, let $\Delta G = 20$ and $\Delta T_a = 10$. The net increase in income (with the same MPC as before) is 50 (80 – 30 = 50).

That illustrates the role of the fiscal policies in influencing the income and the employment in the economy.

11.3.5 Types of Deficits

The term *deficit* has four variations. They are:

(a) Budget deficit,
(b) Revenue deficit,
(c) Fiscal deficit, and
(d) Primary deficit.

Let us see what each one implies.

(a) Budget Deficit: ***Budget deficit***, as given in Box 11.2, refers to the excess of budget expenditure over the budget receipts. Thus,

$$\text{Budget deficit} = \text{Budget Expenditure} - \text{Budget Receipts} \tag{11.5}$$

(b) Revenue Deficit: As is evident, ***revenue deficit*** refers to the excess of revenue expenditure over the revenue receipts. Thus,

$$\text{Revenue Deficit} = \text{Revenue Expenditure} - \text{Revenue receipt} \tag{11.6}$$

(c) Fiscal Deficit: ***Fiscal Deficit*** is defined as the sum of the budget deficit and borrowings and other liabilities. Thus,

BOX 11.3

Fiscal Deficit = Budget Deficit + Borrowings and Other Liabilities
= Budget Expenditure – Budget Receipts
+ Borrowings and Other Liabilities
= Budget Expenditure – Revenue Receipts – Capital Receipts
+ Borrowings and Other Liabilities
= Budget Expenditure – Revenue Receipts – Recovery of Loans
– Receipts from PSU-disinvestment
– Borrowings and Other Liabilities
+ Borrowings and Other Liabilities
(From Equation 11.3)
= Budget Expenditure – Revenue Receipts – Recovery of Loans
– Receipts from PSU-disinvestment (11.7)

(d) Primary Deficit: ***Primary deficit*** may be defined as the excess of fiscal deficit over interest payments. Thus,

BOX 11.4

Primary Deficit = Fiscal Deficit – Interest Payments
= Budget Deficit + Borrowings and Other Liabilities – Interest Payments
= Budget Expenditure – Budget Receipts + Borrowings and Other Liabilities – Interest Payments
= Budget Expenditure – Revenue Receipts – Capital Receipts + Borrowings and Other Liabilities – Interest Payments
= Budget Expenditure – Revenue Receipts – Recovery of Loans – Receipts from PSU-disinvestment – Borrowings and Other Liabilities + Borrowings and Other Liabilities – Interest Payments
(From Equation 11.3)
= Budget Expenditure – Revenue Receipts – Recovery of Loans – Receipts from PSU-disinvestment – Interest Payments (11.8)

To demonstrate, let us take up an illustration.

ILLUSTRATION 11.1: Consider the data below from the Central Budget for 2002–03:

	Item	*Amount (₹ in crores)*
(i)	Tax revenue	= 172965
(ii)	Non-tax Revenue	= 72140
(iii)	Recovery of Loans	= 17680
(iv)	Receipts from PSU-Disinvestment	= 12000
(v)	Borrowing and Other Liabilities	= 135524
(vi)	Revenue Expenditure	= 340482
(vii)	Capital expenditure	= 69827
(viii)	Plan Expenditure	= 113500
(ix)	Non-plan Expenditure	= 296809
(x)	Interest Payments	= 117390
(xi)	Subsidies	= 38923
(xii)	Defence Expenditure	= 43589

Determine: (a) Budget Deficit, (b) Revenue Deficit, (c) Fiscal Deficit, and (d) Primary Deficit.

Solution:

(a) *Budget Deficit:* From Equation 11.5,
Budget Deficit = Budget Expenditure – Budget Receipts
= [Revenue Expenditure + Capital Expenditure] – [Revenue Receipts + Capital Receipts]
= [(vi) + (vii)] – [(i) + (ii) + (iii) + (iv) + (v)]
= [340482 + 69827] – [172965 + 72140 + 17680 + 12000 + 135524]
= [410309] – [410309]

= 0

(b) *Revenue Deficit:* From Equation 11.6,

Revenue Deficit = Revenue Expenditure – Revenue Receipts
= [(vi)] – [(i) + (ii)]
= [340482] – [172965 + 72140]
= 340482 – 245105
= 95377

(c) *Fiscal Deficit:* From Equation 11.7,

Fiscal Deficit = Budget Deficit + Borrowings and Other Liabilities
= 0 + (v)
= 0 + 135524
= 135524.

(d) *Primary Deficit:* From Equation 11.8,

Primary Deficit = Fiscal Deficit – Interest Payments
= 135524 – (x)
= 135524 – 117390
= 18134.

11.4 ASSORTED CONSEQUENCES OF DIRECT AND INDIRECT TAXES

In a lighter vein, it is said that a tax is an unpleasant levy for those who pay it and a pleasant one for those who levy it.

Be it whichever way it be looked at, it is not only an essential source of revenue for government but also a tool to regulate production, consumption, economic growth and development. Indirect taxes raise cost of production and hence product-prices. This affects production and consumption both adversely. On one hand, it reduces *GDP* by reducing output and employment and on the other, it causes ***deadweight loss*** to society. A negative indirect tax (subsidy) however has effects exactly opposite of those an indirect tax. A direct tax affects disposable income of the consumers adversely and thus sales and consumption adversely. Here, we demonstrate the effects to drive the concepts home with the assumption that demand curve portrayed is total demand and supply curve, total supply of the economy.

11.4.1 Effect of Taxes and Subsidies on (GDP), Employment and Prices

Let us demonstrate these through estimated demand of a hypothetical economy.

ILLUSTRATION 11.2: Demand and supply functions of a *TVs* in a small economy are as given below:

$$Q^d = 150{,}000 - 3P, \text{ and}$$
$$Q^S = 7P \text{ respectively.}$$

Equilibrium output and price of the *TV* are 105,000 and 15,000. How would the output, price and government revenue be affected by:

(i) the levy of unit tax of 20% of the market clearing price (that is, by ₹ 3000 per unit),
(ii) the grant of unit subsidy of 20% of the market clearing price, and
(iii) the levy of a direct tax that shifts the demand schedule to

$$Q^d = 120{,}000 - 3P.$$

Solution:[1]

(a) *Effect of unit tax:*

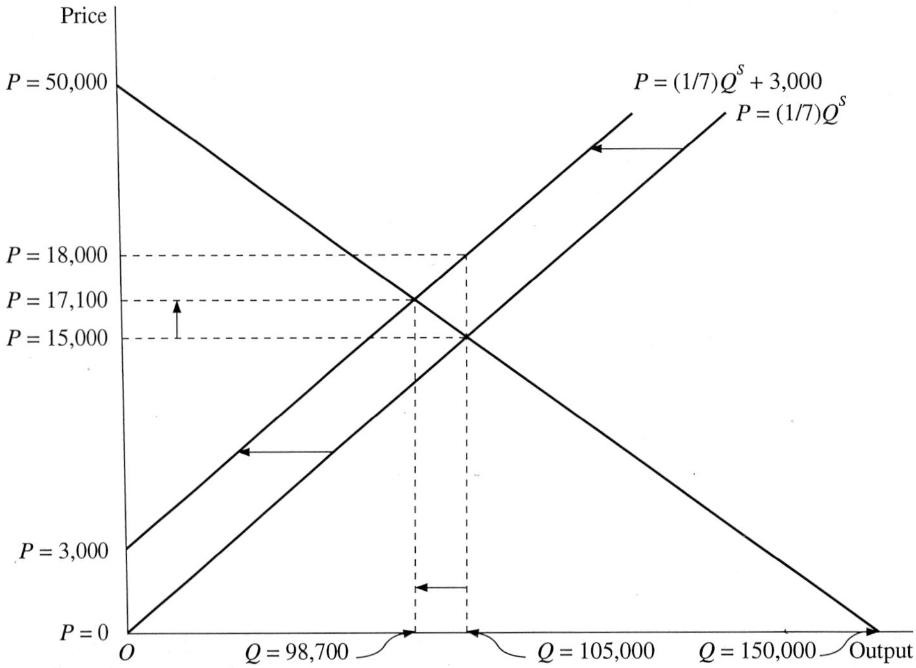

FIGURE 11.1 Effect of Unit Tax: Demand and supply schedules of the economy intersect at point (105,000, 15000). Levy of unit tax shifts the supply schedule from $P = (1/7)\,Q^S$ to $P = (1/7)\,Q^S + 3{,}000$, thereby, intersecting the demand schedule at (98,700; 17,100).

Clearly, output falls from 105,000 to 98,700, registering a fall of 6% [= (6300/105000) × 100]. Price rises from 15,000 to 17,100 registering a rise of 14% [= (2100/15,000) × 100].

If the data relate to an economy, the *GDP* of the economy would fall by 6% and its price level would go up by 14%. Fall in *GDP* may imply a fall in employment as well. Government revenue from unit tax is 3000 × 98700 = 296,100,000.

Thus, all indirect taxes tend to lower GDP and to raise price level.

(ii) *Effect of unit subsidy:* Grant of unit subsidy has exactly opposite effects on *GDP* and Price level (Figure 11.2).

Equilibrium output and price before the grant are 105,000 and 15,000 respectively. A 20% subsidy would amount to 3000 and would shift the supply curve downward to right from $P = (1/7)\,Q^S$ to $P = (1/7)\,Q^S - 3000$. Equilibrium resulting after the grant is (111, 300; 12 900).

The ultimate effects on *GDP* and price level comprise a 6% rise in *GDP* and a 14%

[1] See also , Chauhan, S.P.S., *Forces of demand and supply in action, Chapter 2, Microeconomics—An Advanced Treatise,* 3rd Edition, PHI Learning.

fall in price level. The cost of unit subsidy to government would work out at 3000 × 111300 = 333,900,000.

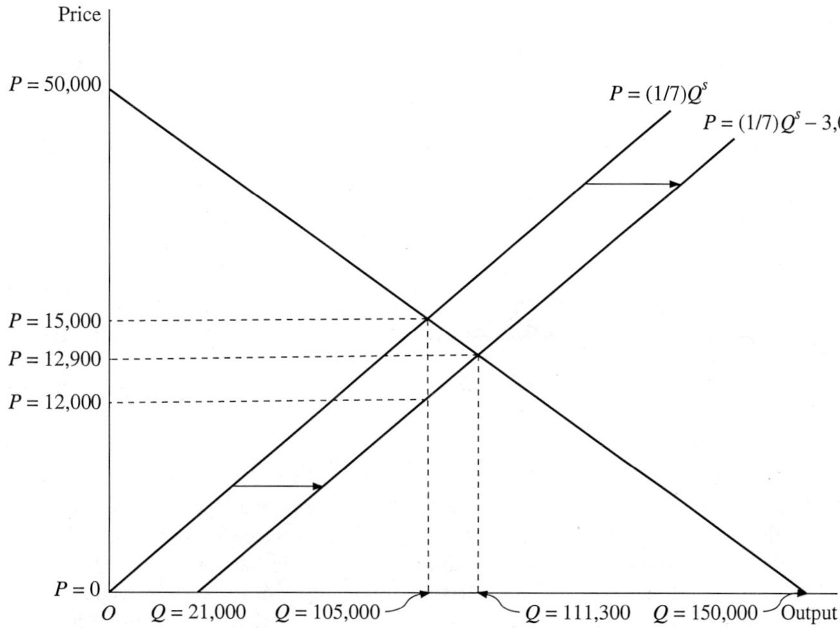

FIGURE 11.2 Effect of Unit Subsidy: Demand and supply schedules of the economy intersect at point (105,000, 15000). Grant of unit subsidy shifts the supply schedule from $P = (1/7)Q^S$ to $P = (1/7)Q^S - 3000$, thereby, intersecting the demand schedule at (111,300, 12,900).

Clearly, output increases from 105,000 to 111,300, registering a fall of 6% [= (6300/105000) × 100]. Price falls from 15,000 to 12,900 registering a fall of 14% [= (2100/15,000) × 100].

If the data relate to an economy, the *GDP* of the economy would increase by 6% and its price level would fall by 14%. Increase in *GDP* may imply an increase in employment as well. Loss of government revenue from the grant of subsidy is 3000 × 111300 = 333,900,000.

Thus, all unit subsidies tend to increase GDP and to lower price level.

(iii) *Effect of a Direct Tax:* The levy of a direct would shift the economy's demand schedule downward to left. Supply schedule would remain unchanged. *GDP* and market price both will fall depending on the levy of direct tax whether it is autonomous or progressive. If it is such that shifts demand schedule downward to left from 150,000 – 3*P* to 120,000 – 3*P*, *GDP* would register a fall of [(84,000 – 105000)/105000] × 100, that is, of 20% and so will the market price, a fall of 20%. Government revenue from the levy of Unit tax (indirect tax) was 296,100,000 while loss of it from the direct tax (autonomous) would work out at 3000 × 84000, that is, 252,000,000.

11.4.2 Direct Tax and Laffer's Curve

As regards the levy of direct tax, American economist Arthur Laffer developed a bell-shaped curve in 1974 depicting the relationship between direct tax rates and the corresponding tax revenues to government.

Rate percent of the personal tax on the horizontal axis and total tax revenue accruing in consequence to government on vertical axis depicted a perfect bell-shaped curve according to the economist.

A tax cut increases disposable income of the taxpayers. This results in an increase in demand for goods and services, which in turn, increases production and employment Before further discussion, let us have a look on the Laffer 's Curve[1] (Figure 11.3).

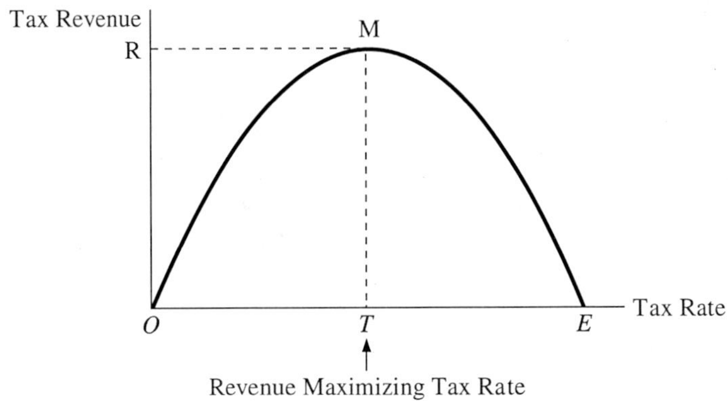

FIGURE 11.3 Laffer's Curve: When tax rate is raised from *O* to *T*, revenue receipts of government rise to a maximum of *OR*. If it be increased further revenue receipts of government begin to decline. It is so because tax payers divert their funds to foreign countries rather than investing them in the domestic territory. Tax evasion so resulting affects domestic production and employment adversely. Government therefore reduces tax rate from *E* first to *T* and then towards *O* as a measure to retain tax payers funds within the domestic territory. If revenue maximization is the government's objective, it must hold tax rate at *T* but if it is maximization of *GDP* and employment, tax rate must be below point *T*. Striking a balance is not easy. Much depends on the agenda of government.

As appears from the figure, choice of an ideal rate of taxation is a matter of debate. Revenue receipts must be as high as possible for government expenditures and so must be domestic production and employment. Lower tax rates (below point *T*) incentivise investment and production and give a boost to employment and trickle down.

11.4.3 Principle of Maximum Social Advantage in Taxation

We have referred the Principle of Maximum Social Advantage (MSA) as a tool of the public sector decision making policies in Chapter 1 of Microeconomics—An Advanced Treatise as also in Chapter

[1] Arthur Laffer presented his ideas in 1974 to staff members of President Gerald Ford's administration. Most believed at the time that an increase in tax rates would increase tax revenue Laffer countered that taking more money from a business in the form of taxes means the less money the business will be willing to invest. A business will find ways to protect its capital from taxation or to relocate all or a part of its operations overseas. Workers lose the incentive to work harder when they see a greater portion of their paychecks taken for taxation.

Laffer argued that this means less total revenue as tax rates rise and that the economic effects of reducing incentives to work and invest by raising tax rates would damage an economy.

Laffer argued that this means less total revenue as tax rates rise and that the economic effects of reducing incentives to work and invest by raising tax rates would damage an economy.

Laffer's findings influenced President Ronald Reagan's economic policy known as Reaganomics, based on supply-side and trickle-down economics. It resulted in one of the biggest tax cuts in history. Yet annual federal government current tax receipts still grew during Reagan's time in office. (**Source:** https://www.investopedia.com/terms/l/laffercurve.asp).

1 of this book. Here comes its appropriate place to discuss. Western authors have confined their discussions on taxation by mentioning its characteristic traits (Dalton's Canons of taxation) and by deliberating on tax revenue maximizing tax rate (Laffer's Curve as in last Subsection) but rarely has a discussion come up on the extent to which taxes can be levied in a welfare state. We focus a bit on this aspect as its relevance to such states.

Taxes are levied by government and paid by people. They serve as an unpleasant levy to the taxpayers and a pleasant one to the finance ministers. For tax payers it is a sacrifice they make and for a finance ministers, it is the most important source of revenue. All public utilities/amenities and government expenditures are financed by this revenue. Arthur Laffer deliberates on how to maximize tax revenue while Dalton enumerates characteristics of a good tax through his canons of taxation According to Dalton, a good tax must possess among others, the following canons:

1. Canon of economy
2. Canon of convenience
3. Canon of elasticity
4. Canon of equity
5. Canon of productivity
6. Canon of certainty

To an appreciable extent, these canons are not opposed to the principle of maximum social advantage but they are not explicitly in favour of it too as would be clear from the discussions below.

The principle has in main two components:

1. **Marginal Social Benefit (MSB):** It can defined as a change in social benefit per unit of tax paid. Like the marginal utility of a commodity to a consumer, marginal social benefit (MSB) too has a diminishing trend with successive units of benefit created by the expenditure of tax revenue. If social benefit be represented on the vertical axis and tax rupees on the horizontal axis, the *MSB* diminishes with increasing units of tax financed public amenities created.
2. **Marginal Social Sacrifice (MSS):** It can be defined as change in sacrifice of a tax payer per additional unit of tax paid. The marginal social sacrifice increases with increasing burden of tax. Thus *MSS* has a rising trend if it is measured on the vertical axis and taxes paid on the horizontal axis.

The optimal tax revenue is determined at the point where *MSB* intersects *MSS* as shown in Figure 11.4.

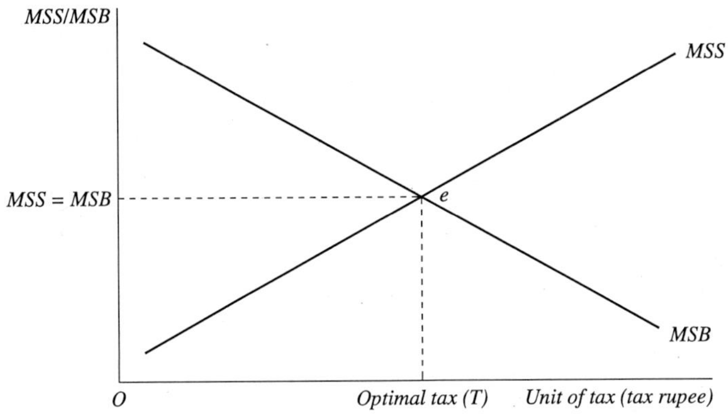

FIGURE 11.4 Principle of Maximum Social Advantage—*MSB* and *MSS* intersect each other at point *e* which serves as the point of optimality of taxation. An *y* levy beyond *OT* is rented.

KEY TERMS AND CONCEPTS

Fiscal Policy: Fiscal policy may be defined as one of the economic policies of a government. It deals with taxation, expenditure, borrowing and management of public debt in the economy. All budgetary policies are included under fiscal policy.

Laissez-faire System: It is a system in which government does not intervene in the economic affairs of the people. For instance, *laissez-faire* trade is free trade. State does not intervene in free flow of goods and services whether within the domestic territory or beyond it.

Functional Finance: A.P. Lerner refined fiscal policy to a form called *functional finance* . It is contra-cyclical in nature. That is, it should steer the economies clear of the trade cycles.

Built-in-stabilizers: Also known as automatic stabilizers, the built-in-stabilizers refer to fiscal measures that start functioning automatically to restore economic stability whenever destabilizing forces raise their heads. For instance, taxation of income, if progressive, would automatically take care of increasing government revenue whenever income of the people increases.

Discretional Fiscal Policy: It refers deliberate government action to alter tax structure or public expenditure to bring about economic development in the underdeveloped countries.

Compensatory Fiscal Policy: It refers to a compensatory variation in public expenditure with a view to supplement private investment to give the desired tilt to the direction of the economic activities. During depression, private investment is unusually low. A fiscal expansion to finance public works and such other public utility projects raises the level of injections and helps to generate employment and income.

Surplus Budgeting: It refers to a fiscal policy of heavier taxation so that tax revenue collected is much higher than the public expenditure incurred. In other words, it is a contractionary fiscal policy intended to reduce injections $(I + G + X)$ or to increase withdrawals $(S + T + M)$.

Deficit Budgeting: It refers to a fiscal policy of heavier public expenditure so that the tax revenue collected is much lower than the public expenditure . In other words, it is an expansionary fiscal policy intended to increase injections $(I + G + X)$ or to reduce withdrawals $(S + T + M)$.

Instruments of Fiscal Policy: Taxation, public borrowing, public expenditure and deficit financing are the major instruments of fiscal policy.

Direct and Indirect Taxes: Taxes such as income tax are direct taxes as their incidence and impact both fall on the same entity. Direct taxes are non-shiftable. Indirect taxes, on the other hand are taxes whose incidence and impact do not necessarily fall on the same entity. Indirect taxes are therefore shiftable fully or partially.

Progressive, Proportional, Digressive and Regressive Taxes: A progressive tax refers to a tax in which tax rate is higher for higher income slabs and lower for lower ones. On the other hand, a proportional tax is one in which tax rate is fixed for all levels of income within a slab. When tax is progressive up to certain level of income and proportional thereafter, it is called a digressive tax. A regressive tax is one whose burden is heavier on low-income people and lighter on high-income people.

Public Borrowing: It refers to a practice of government to borrow from public or from financial institutions with public funds through the issue of treasury bills or bonds. The Central Bank of the land executes the process as an agent of the government.

Public Expenditure: Expenditure incurred by government on running departmental and non-departmental undertakings, on paying national debt interest, on providing services such as police, defence, general administration, on paying subsidies, etc. are collectively termed as Public expenditure. Such expenditures may be developmental or non-developmental, plan or non-plan expenditures.

Deficit Financing: It refers to the process of financing the budgetary deficit. When governments resort to printing of currency for the purpose, the process is called monetizing the deficit. Since this is the only way left with the modern states, deficit financing or monetizing the deficit are generally taken as synonyms.

Overall Budget of the Government: It is a statement of budget receipts and budget expenditures. Budget receipts comprise revenue receipts and capital receipts while budget expenditures comprise revenue expenditure and capital expenditure. Mismatch between the two may form budget surplus (when receipts exceed expenditures) or budget deficit (when expenditures exceed revenue). A budget deficit is preferred for underdeveloped economies due to their development orientation.

Revenue Budget: A revenue budget refers to revenue receipts and revenue expenditures. Revenue receipts comprise receipts from tax revenue and non-tax revenue. Revenue expenditure comprise running expenditures of departmental undertakings and those on payments of interest, subsidies, grants-in-aid to States and on making provision for services such as defence. When revenue expenditures exceed revenue receipts, revenue budget is said to be in deficit, else, when revenue receipts exceed revenue expenditures, the revenue budget is said to be in surplus.

Capital Budget: Capital budget comprises capital receipts and capital expenditures. Capital receipts consist of recovery of loans, receipts from PSU-disinvestment, borrowings & Other Liabilities. Capital expenditures, on the other hand, comprise expenditures made on acquisition of assets like land, building, plant, equipment, machinery, etc. or giving loans to state and union territories, corporations, joint stock companies for the same on investments in issue capital of *PSUs*.

Plan and Non-plan Expenditures: Budget expenditures are classified also as the plan and non-plan expenditures. Plan expenditure refers to government expenditure on current development and investment arising out of plan proposals. On the other hand, non-plan expenditures are expenditures other than the plan expenditures.

Developmental and Non-developmental Expenditures: Budget expenditures are classified also as the developmental and non-developmental expenditures. Developmental expenditure, as the name suggests, refers to plan expenditure for development purposes. It includes plan expenditure on departmental and non-departmental commercial undertakings. Expenditure incurred on departmental undertakings like Railways, Posts and Telecommunications, etc. and that incurred on non-departmental commercial undertakings by way of loans, grants-in-aid, etc. are examples. Non-developmental expenditures, on the other hand, refer to expenditures on certain essential services such as defence, police, tax-collection, general administration, etc., expenditure on interest payments on national debt, expenditure on pension payments, expenditure on relief work, expenditure on payment of food subsidy, etc.

Budget Deficit: It is defined as the excess of budget expenditure over budget receipts.

Revenue Deficit: It is defined as the excess of revenue expenditures over revenue receipts.

Fiscal Deficit: It is defined as the sum of the budget deficit and the borrowings and other liabilities.

Primary Deficit: It is defined as the excess of the fiscal deficit over the interest payments.

Escheats: Reverting to government property of a person who dies without leaving a heir.

Laffer's Curve: Relationship between rates of direct taxes and corresponding evenue receipts of government take the bell-shape according to American economist Arther Laffer. Raising tax rates up to a certain point can raise government revenue but raising it further has an adverse effect on government receipts. To evade high taxation, people relocate their funds to foreign contries leaving the domestic territory dry.

Canons of Taxation: Dalton defined a good tax as one that has features of economy, elasticity, equity, convenience and productivity.

Principle of Maximun Social Advantage: The point where marginal social benefit curve intersects that of marginal social sacrifice is the point of maximum social benefit.

EXERCISES

A. Short Answer Questions

1. Define fiscal policy. Trace its evolution to its current form.
2. What is meant by functional finance? Elucidate its role in a depression hit economy with examples.
3. What are built-in-stabilizers? Which one of the progressive and proportional taxes do you think is a better built-in-stabilizer? Use examples to elaborate.
4. What is a discretionary fiscal policy? Why is it considered a must for the undeveloped countries? Substantiate with examples.
5. Outline major objectives of fiscal policy in a developed country.
6. Outline major objectives of fiscal policy in an underdeveloped country.
7. What are various instruments of fiscal policy? Which one would you recommend for an inflation hit economy and why?
8. What is a compensatory fiscal policy? Explain with examples.
9. Distinguish between:
   (a) Revenue budget and capital budget
   (b) Deficit budget and surplus budget
   (c) Fiscal deficit and primary deficit
   (d) Net direct tax and net indirect tax
   (e) Unit tax and unit subsidy
   (f) Plan expenditure and non plan expenditure
   (g) Developmental expenditure and non-developmental expenditure
   (h) Progressive tax and proportional tax
   (i) Progressive tax and regressive tax
   (j) Fiscal policy multiplier and monetary policy multiplier
10. What is meant by forced savings? Explain with examples.
11. What is meant by escheats? Which form of fiscal instrument is an escheat?
12. Is a fiscal policy multiplier same as a government expenditure multiplier? Comment upon their significance.
   [Hint: No. See Equation 9.10, (Chapter 9), its application to crowding out effect (Figure 9.17), and *Q* 31(Chapter 9)].

B. Long Answer Questions

13. Distinguish between direct and indirect taxes with examples. Which one has the attribute certainty of revenue?
14. Explain the significance of budget deficit. Why should a state prefer a deficit budget during depression?
15. How does a surplus budget help in checking deflationary pressures? Explain.
16. Write a comprehensive note on Laffer's Curve. Comment on its significance.
17. It is said that 'a tax is an unpleasant levy for those who pay it and a pleasant one for those who levy it'.
   [Hint: Taxes levied beyond taxable capacity of tax payers are unjust. Marginal social sacrifice (*MSS*) of a rupee of tax must not exceed marginal social benefit (*MSB*) of it. *MSS* schedule rises with every rupee of tax levied while *MSB* schedule fall with it. The point of intersection of the two schedules where, *MSS* = *MSB*, determines the level of tax.

In their bid to raise revenue, governments violate this principle of taxation. They go on levying tax beyond the point of equality of *MSS* and *MSB*. No wonder if tax payers resent it. Even otherwise, tax paid by an individual may not provide commensurate benefit to him because benefits provided by governments impart non-rival and non-exclusive consumption. Quite a few tend to evade taxes because they don't find any direct benefit coming to them].

C. Essay Type Questions

18. 'Government spending to boost national income/output may bring about full multiplier effect if it is financed through printing of currency (deficit financing)'. Discuss.

[Hint: See fiscal policy multiplier (Equation 9.10, Ch.9) and crowding out effect (Figure 9.17, Ch. 9)**].**

19. Distinguish between full employment budget surplus and actual budget surplus. Discuss various implications of the full employment budget surplus being greater than the actual budget surplus.

20. Discuss various implications of deficit financing in a developing economy. Can it be employed to fulfil the developmental requirements of the underdeveloped economies?

21. Revised budget estimates for the year 2001–02 are as given below. Estimate budget deficit, revenue deficit, fiscal deficit and primary deficit. Revenue receipts = 212572, Capital receipts = 148060, Revenue expenditure = 304305, Capital expenditure = 69826, Interest payments = 107257, Borrowings and other liabilities = 131721.

[Ans: Refer to Illustration 11.1 Budgetary Deficit = 13499, Fiscal Deficit = 145220, Primary Deficit = 37963, Revenue Deficit = 91733.]

CASE STUDY

Suppose Figure 11.1 relates to imposition of goods and services tax (*GST*) of 20% of the market clearing price and the demand and supply equations of Illustration 11.2 relate to an economy that produces a composite product instead of *TVs*. Suppose further that market clearing price of the product before the levy is 15000 per unit and 105,000 units of the product are produced and sold in a year. Gross domestic product (*GDP*) being 157,50,00,000. Which falls to 168,77,79,000 after the levy.

Comment on the effects of the levy on *GDP* and inflation.

Compare the effect with that of the grant of subsidy of equal percentage under same demand and supply conditions. Would you infer from your computations that a high *GST* is highly harmful for an underdeveloped economy from the view point of *GDP* growth and inflation while an equal subsidy is highly gainful on both counts?

Chapter 12

Foreign Trade Policy

INTRODUCTION

In Chapter 6, we have seen how aggregate demand (*AD*) in a four sector model depends on *C, I, G,* and (*X-M*). Equation 6.5 (Section 6.8) shows that *AD* is greater by (*X-M*) in a four sector model than in a three sector model. This shows that an economy suffering from demand deficiency in its domestic territory need no longer produce sub-optimal size of its output but by opening itself up to foreign trade, it can enjoy the fruits of optimality in utilization of its full capacity. It can export its surplus product to other countries and raise its income. This would help it to cut unit cost too and to improvise its competitiveness in the domestic as well as in the international markets. Foreign importers too can share the benefits by helping themselves to cheaper goods. Opening up to the rest of the world (*ROW*) may also help the country to have an easier access to cheaper foreign goods with the help of the foreign currencies earned through exports. It is for this reason that the countries prefer to enter in foreign trade.

Countries buying our exports have to pay for them in our currency, that is, they have to buy Indian currency with theirs in order to pay for products bought from us. To demonstrate, suppose US buys cottons worth ₹ 100,000 from India. To settle the payment, US has to buy ₹ 100,000 from the international money market with its own currency which is dollar. Assuming the currency exchange rate as ₹ 40 per dollar, US would have to shell out as much as $2,500 (100,000/40 = 2,500) to buy Indian currency. This amount ultimately reaches the vaults of the Central Bank of India (*RBI*). The exporter receives payment in rupees. In the same way, suppose an Indian firm decides to buy some machine components from US priced in US at $3,000. Indian buyer will then have to buy this amount of dollars at the rate of ₹ 40 per dollar, spending in the process a sum of ₹ 120,000 for the purpose. If these be the only foreign transactions made by India this year, India's *balance of trade* as also its *balance of payments* would be equal to the net receipts from the trade, that is, (–) ₹ 20,000.

As the net receipts from the trade are negative, India's balance of trade as also that of its payments is said to be unfavourable or adverse. In such circumstances, Indian government may decide to restrict imports through a levy of tax, called import tariff, on its imports. In case, the balance is favourable, the Indian government may or may not like to restrict our exports for obvious reasons. If for some reasons, it decides to restrict exports, it can do so through the levy of ***export tariff*** on its exports.

Levy of tariffs on imports or exports is a part of a nation's *foreign trade policy.* Such policies are based mainly on two things:

(a) Foreign Exchange Rates
(b) Balance of Trade or of Payments

Let us discuss them in brief here in that order.

12.1 FOREIGN EXCHANGE RATES

12.1.1 Nominal Exchange Rates

The rate at which currencies are exchanged for each other is called *nominal exchange rate,* denoted by 'e'. In the example above, the US-based importer of Indian cottons had to avail Indian currency at the rate of \$0.025 per rupee (₹ 40 per dollar). This is dollar-rupee exchange rate. Such rates of currency exchange if fixed between the trading partners can promote trade between them to a marked extent. For instance, if the exchange rate in the example above were ₹ 50 per dollar, US buyer has to spend only \$2,000 now instead of \$2,500 for Indian cottons. In other words, US-import of Indian cottons would turn cheaper at ₹ 50 per dollar than at ₹ 40 per dollar. On the contrary, Indian import of machinery from US, priced at \$3,000 in US, would turn costlier at ₹ 50 per dollar than at ₹ 40 per dollar. The Indian importer has to pay now ₹ 150,000 instead of ₹ 120,000. Under the changed exchange rate, *trade deficit* or the adversity of balance of trade or of payments has worsened from that of ₹ 20,000 to ₹ 50,000. This may prompt Indian government to adopt even stricter tariff measures to restrict import of the machine. Thus fluctuations in foreign exchange rates influence not only the volumes of trade between the trading partners but also the extent of trade deficits or trade surpluses. It is therefore important to discuss the mechanism of determining the exchange rate as also the factors that influence it.

12.1.2 Real Exchange Rates

Real exchange rate (R) is related to the nominal exchange rate (e) through the following relationship:

$$R = \frac{eP_f}{P_d} \tag{12.1}$$

To elaborate, let the rupee dollar exchange rate (nominal) be ₹ 40 per dollar, that is, e = ₹ 40 per dollar. Further, let the price of a drink in *US* be \$1.50 per piece while in India, ₹ 10 per per piece. The real exchange rate,

$$R = \frac{(₹\ 40/\$) \times (\$1.50/\text{unit})}{₹\ 10/\text{unit}}$$

$$= 6.00$$

Note that real exchange rate is a ratio which can be defined as the ratio of foreign to domestic prices. It measures a country's competitiveness in the international market. In the above example, $R = 6$ denotes that *US* price of the drink is 6 times the Indian price of it, and that India has much higher competitiveness than US on it.

If for any pair of countries, $R = 1.00$ for the same product, their currencies are said to possess equal purchasing power or same purchasing power parity (*PPP*) or same competitiveness. On the other hand, if $R = 0.20$, the foreign country's price of the product is 1/5th of that at home and that foreign country has higher competitiveness than home country.

Market forces prevent the exchange rate from moving too far away from *PPP.*

Before taking up the process of determination of the foreign exchange rate, let us have a look at different types of foreign exchange markets and the nature of transactions therein, first.

12.1.2.1 Types of foreign exchange markets: Spot and forward markets

Foreign exchange markets are classified as ***spot market*** and ***forward market*** depending on whether foreign exchange transactions are *spot* or *forward.*

A spot market refers to that part of the foreign exchange market in which sale and purchase of foreign currencies are settled within *two days* of the deal. The rate of exchange of currencies in the spot market is called the ***spot rate** of exchange* or the ***current rate of exchange.***

Spot rate of exchange refers to that exchange rate which balances the current account of the external transactions with rest of the world (*ROW*). Relative prices of goods and services between the countries influence the exchange rate significantly. Thus ***Purchasing Power Parity (PPP) theory*** forms the basis of this measure. *PPP*-theory has two versions—***absolute purchasing power parity*** and ***relative purchasing power parity***. The former holds that commodities have the same price all over the world when same currency is used to measure it. The latter relates inflation rate to the rate of exchange between two countries.

A forward exchange market refers to that part of the foreign exchange market in which deals for sale and purchase of foreign currencies at a pre-settled exchange rate are agreed upon for their execution in future after 90 days of the deal. The exchange rate settled between the buyers and the sellers for future sale and purchase of currencies is called the **forward exchange rate.**

Nature of Transactions

Foreign exchange transactions are classified as hedging, arbitrage and speculation.

Hedging is a feature of the forward exchange market. When exporters and importers agree to buy and sell goods at a future date at current price and rate of exchange, the arrangement is called ***hedging***. It is a safeguard against a likely loss due to possible fluctuations in exchange rate and prices of goods. Hedging takes place through banks dealing with forward sale and purchase of currencies. Such banks guarantee payment to the exporters and supply foreign exchange to the importers at the exchange rate agreed upon.

Arbitrage refers to an act of simultaneous sale and purchase of foreign currencies in different exchange markets with a view to take advantage of different rates of exchange prevailing in different markets. It helps to stabilize the exchange rate in different markets by transferring the currency from the markets where its value in terms of other currencies is low to the markets where it is high. For example, purchasing of dollars in a market where it costs ₹ 30 per dollar and selling it in another where it fetches ₹ 45. It leads to a gain of ₹ 15 per dollar and helps to stabilize the value of a dollar in the two markets. Supply of dollars increases in the market where rupee price of dollars is high and it decreases in the market where rupee price of dollars is low. In consequence, dollar price falls in the high price market and it rises in the low price market until it reaches the same level in the two. The practice however requires absence of controls or barriers.

Speculation refers to deliberate attempt to bear risks under the expectation of profits. For example, when an individual buys dollars at a price of ₹ 30 per dollar under the expectation that the price will rise to, say, ₹ 40 in near future and that he will make a profit of ₹ 10 per dollar in consequence, the individual for sure is a speculator. Rupee price of dollar may even fall in near future leading to a loss to the speculator. The activity is thus highly risky. Speculator prefers taking risks under the belief that risk bearing always pays pay-off.

12.1.2.2 Determination of exchange rate

We will discuss determination of exchange rate under:

(a) Fixed exchange rate system, and
(b) Flexible or floating exchange rate system.

Determination of Exchange Rate under Fixed Exchange Rate Regime

Under the fixed exchange rate regime, the monetary authority of a country fixes the official value of its currency in terms of a *reserve currency* (usually the US dollar) or a basket of *key currencies* of the world. The value of currency so determined is known as its *par value* and the exchange rate so determined is called ***pegged exchange rate.***

Under the ***gold standard*** (1880–1914), value of each currency was defined in terms of quantity of gold of a fixed purity and the exchange rates were determined accordingly. To demonstrate, suppose the value of an Indian rupee is 0.60 mg of gold of given purity and that of a dollar is 24.00 mg of gold of the same purity, the rupee-dollar exchange rate would be ₹ 40 = \$1.00.

After the collapse of the gold standard in 1920's, an alternative system was introduced by International Monetary Fund (*IMF*) on its creation at Bretton Woods in 1944. The system known as the Bretton Woods System, made the US dollar directly convertible into gold at a fixed price and the currencies of the member countries were required to be expressed in terms of US dollar. Under the normal circumstances, a flexibility of ± 1% was prescribed by IMF. This determined the upper and the lower limits to the fixed exchange rate of the currency of a member nation and came to be known as the ***adjustable peg.*** The ultimate link of currencies to gold remained intact though indirectly.

The basic purpose of adopting the fixed exchange rate system was to ensure stability in foreign trade and capital movements. To ensure stability of the fixed exchange rate, the Central Banks were required to undertake to buy and sell foreign currencies at the exchange rate so fixed. For example, when value of a dollar falls (say, from ₹ 40 to ₹ 30) for dollar sellers, the Central Bank of India (RBI) would start buying dollars at the rate of ₹ 40 per dollar and when it rises (say, from ₹ 40 to ₹ 50) for dollar buyers, RBI would start selling dollars at the rate of ₹ 40 per dollar. Such sale-purchase of dollars through rupees at ₹ 40 per dollar goes a long way to stabilize the exchange rate. The Bretton Woods system and the fixed exchange created by it however broke down in 1971.

Determination of Exchange Rate under Flexible Exchange Rate System

Exchange rate in a free exchange market or in a flexible or floating exchange rate system is determined through the interaction of market demand and market supply of the foreign currency. To demonstrate, suppose we have to determine rupee-dollar exchange rate (i.e., rupee price of a dollar) in a free exchange market. What we need, for the purpose, are

(i) the dollar demand as a function of its price in rupees, and
(ii) the dollar supply as a function of its price in rupees.

Demand for dollars varies inversely with the rupee price of a dollar, that is, the higher the rupee price of a dollar, the lower is its demand in the Indian market. The demand curve for dollars, therefore, slopes downwards from left to right as shown in Figure 12.1.

Supply of dollars, on the other hand, varies directly with the rupee price of a dollar, that is, the higher the price of a dollar, the higher is their supply in the Indian market. The supply curve of dollars, therefore, slopes upwards from left to right.

The point of intersection of the two is the point of market equilibrium. The equilibrium quantity of dollars is Q_e and the equilibrium rupee price of a dollar is P_e (Figure 12.1).

The figure explains how an increase in demand for dollars increases the equilibrium rate of exchange and how the original rate of exchange is restored through an increase in supply of dollars. The figure also explains the factors that cause an upward to right shift in demand for the foreign currency as also the factors that cause a downward to right shift in supply of the foreign currency. When rupee price of a dollar increases, rupee is said to have *depreciated* and when rupee price of a dollar falls, rupee is said to have *appreciated.* To demonstrate, rupee is said to depreciate when rupee-dollar exchange rate rises from, say, ₹ 30 per dollar to ₹ 40 per dollar and it is said to appreciate if the opposite happens.

The system of ***flexible exchange rate*** requires a free market system to operate.

Presence of barriers to trade or that of the regulatory authorities, like Central Bank and the government obstruct its operation. Its biggest advantage is its role in boosting the efficiency of resource allocation in the economy but its disadvantages include uncertainty caused by it in trade, foreign investment, employment and balance of payment.

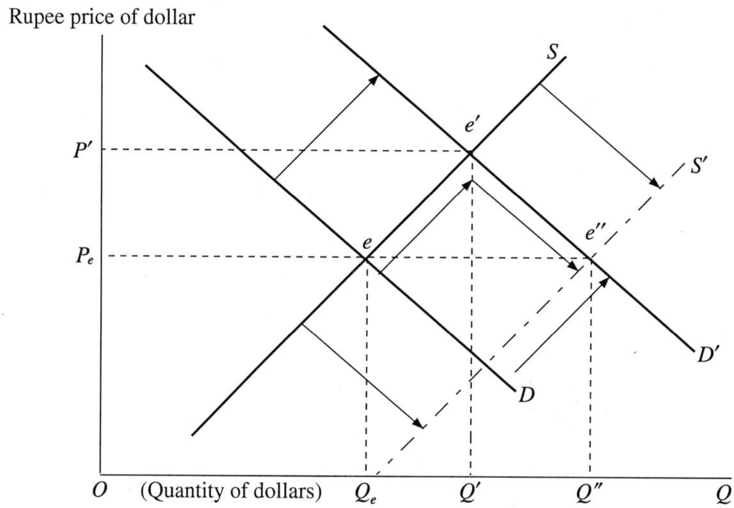

FIGURE 12.1 Determination of exchange rate under flexible system: Downward slope of demand curve for dollars shows that quantity of dollars demanded is low when rupee price of dollars is high and it is high when the rupee price of dollars is low. In the same way, upward slope of the supply curve for dollars shows that quantity supplied of dollars is high when rupee price of dollars is high and it is low when rupee price of dollars is low. The demand and the supply curves intersect each other at *e* which is the point of equilibrium. Quantity of dollars transacted at this point is Q_e and the equilibrium exchange rate is P_e.

Now suppose demand for dollars increases with the result that the demand curve shifts upwards to right from position *D* to *D*′. The increase in demand for dollars may be a result of an increase in demand for American products, or of an increase in Indian investments in *US*, or an increase in speculation in India over dollars. Whatever the cause, equilibrium shifts from *e* to *e*′, quantity of dollars transacted increases from Q_e to *Q*′ and exchange rate rises from P_e to *P*′. If the exchange rate is to be restored to the original level, supply of dollars needs to be increased so that the new supply curve passes through *e*″, as shown. The factors that contribute in increasing the dollar supply may include an increase in American demand for Indian goods, or an increase in American investment in India or an increase in speculation in US over rupees.

Some supporters of market mechanism believe that under the regime of the flexible exchange rates, the markets would be cleared and the balance of payments would be automatically adjusted. *IMF* was created at Bretton Woods in 1944, and under its system, called the ***Bretton Woods system***, the world trade followed the ***fixed exchange rate regime***. The system collapsed in 1971 and so did the fixed exchange rate regime. The period from 1971 to 1976 can be described as one of ***informal flexible exchange rates***. US dollar got devalued a number of times and several major currencies began to float during this period. In January, 1976, Jamaica Agreement formalized flexible exchange rates. We have been in the flexible exchange rate regime ever since.

In practice, most of the countries adopt a ***dual exchange rate system.*** For all official transactions, fixed exchange rate is employed while for all private transactions, flexible exchange rate is used.

A number of hybrid systems have also been suggested from time to time to take advantages of both the systems. Some of them are introduced below:

Wider Bands

The proposed ***wider band*** requires reintroduction of the fixed exchange rate with a wider adjustable peg of 10% to be in force instead of the old one of 1%. This is believed to serve the cause of easy adjustment of balance of payments. To demonstrate, suppose rupee-dollar exchange rate is fixed at ₹ 40 per dollar. A 1% adjustable peg allows variations between ₹ 39.60 and ₹ 40.40 per dollar. If India uses ₹ 40.40 per dollar as the exchange rate, its goods priced at ₹ 500 each would cost $12.38 to US buyer but if it is allowed to use ₹ 44.00 (with 10% peg), the goods would cost only $11.36 each to the US buyer. This would increase competitiveness of Indian goods in US and would boost Indian export without affecting the profitability of the Indian exporter who gets same rupee price for his products.

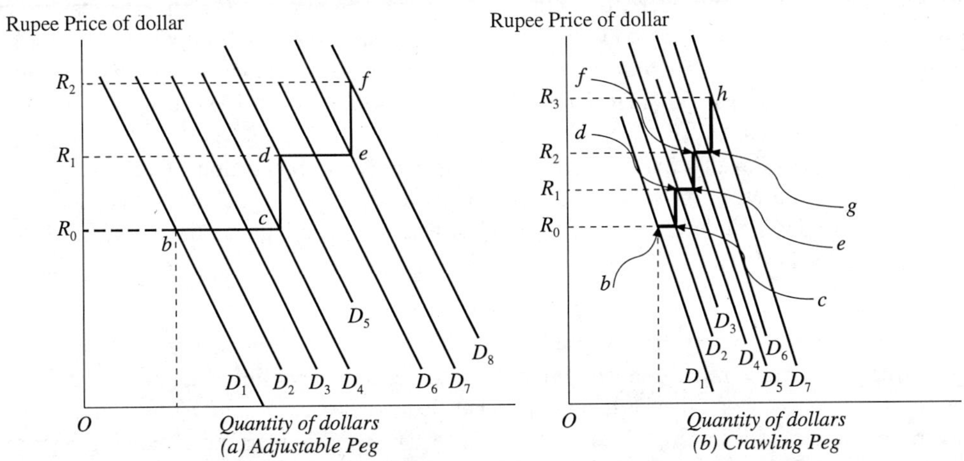

FIGURE 12.2 Adjustable and Crawling pegs: In panel (a), RBI supplies dollars at ₹ R_0 per dollar along segment '*bc*' under its fixed exchange rate regime despite increasing dollar demand (from D_1 to D_4). At point *c*, *RBI's* dollar reserves exhaust. It can no longer supply dollars at R_0. If demand for dollars further rises, government has to devalue rupee as a part of its adjustable peg so that the exchange rate rises to R_1. Dollars are now supplied at R_1 along '*de*' despite increasing dollar demand (from D_5 to D_7). At point *e*, *RBI's* dollar reserves again exhaust. Dollar supply can't be increased unless a further devaluation of rupee is executed by government to raise the exchange rate to R_2. Since periodic adjustments are not made under the adjustable peg, large and sudden devaluations of the currency become unavoidable.

In panel (b), dollars are supplied at ₹ R_0 per dollar at *b*. Even when demand increases from D_1 to D_2, dollar supply continues to be made at R_0 along '*bc*'. If demand further increases to D_3, a small devaluation is executed by government despite the fact that dollar reserves of the RBI have not exhausted yet. Exchange rate gets pegged at R_1 in consequence and remains so along the segment '*de*'. A further hike in demand for dollars to D_5 calls for further devaluation of rupee, raising the exchange rate to R_2. The process of this type of small devaluations at short intervals, called the crawling peg, continues even when dollar reserves are not exhausted. In fact, the purpose of the crawling peg is to delay the exhaustion of the foreign exchange reserves. Note that small variations at short intervals are subject to the ceiling and floor limits so as to impose a discipline on a government in its exercise of crawling peg. However, crawling peg system is closer to the flexible exchange rate system while adjustable peg system is closer to the fixed exchange rate system.

At the same time, Indian imports from US would get discouraged. A product from US priced at \$100.00 would cost Indian buyer ₹ 4040 at ₹ 40.40 per dollar and ₹ 4400 at ₹ 44.00 per dollar. This would discourage.

Indian imports. Higher exports and lower imports help to improve the balance of payments position.

Crawling Peg

We have mentioned how adjustable peg lends some flexibility to the fixed rate of exchange. Permissible variations in the exchange rate may take place in two ways—*first*, large variations at long intervals, known as ***adjustable peg,*** and *second*, small and regular variations at short intervals, known as ***crawling peg.***

Suppose RBI, under fixed exchange rate regime, supplies dollars at a fixed price of ₹ 40 per dollar and demand for dollars is on the rise in leaps and bounds at regular intervals. If the bank continues to sell dollars at this rate, the time may soon arrive when it runs out of steam. Its dollar reserves exhaust. The bank, under the circumstances, has no other recourse but to use its permissible peg to raise the rupee-price of dollars as high as possible. This provides an example of *adjustable peg* or 'large variations at long intervals' in the exchange rate. Figure 12.2(a) demonstrates the point.

Under adjustable peg, devaluation is called for when dollar reserves get fully exhausted. It brings a large variation in the exchange rate. Under crawling peg, frequent devaluations of the home currency are executed at small intervals in small amounts with a view to delay the exhaustion of the nation's foreign exchange reserves.

To demonstrate, a devaluation of rupee by about 5% at the exhaustion of the dollar reserves would comprise a large variation under adjustable peg while that of 1% each time made five times at shorter intervals to delay the exhaustion of the dollar reserves. The latter is the ***crawling peg*** while the former, the ***adjustable peg***.

Managed Floating

Managed floating refers to a system of gradual adjustments in the exchange rate which take place through government intervention. Managed floating resembles the crawling peg but for the difference that the band in it is wider and the settlements quicker than what they are in the crawling peg system. Moreover, crawling peg has a built in bias in favour of stability, but managed floating hasn't. The system of ***managed floating***, at times, is referred to as the ***dirty floating*** in the event of the government intervention to harvest the advantages of high demand of its currency. In contrast, an exchange rate fluctuating freely is known as the ***clean floating.***

12.2. STRENGTH OF A COUNTRY'S CURRENCY IN RELATION TO THE CURRENCIES OF ITS TRADING PARTNERS

In modern world of specialization, a country trades with a number of other countries each of which has its own currency, its own level of trade and its own general price level. Generally, the currency of a trading country appreciates in relation to the currency of its trading partner when its exports to the latter go up or its imports from the latter go down, other things remaining the same. The same may or may not be the case with its currency when it trades with any of the other trading partners. The currency of a trading country may appreciate in relation to the currencies of some trading partners and may depreciate in relation to those of the rest. The way the currency exchange rate between two trading partners shuffles between appreciation and depreciation, it becomes very difficult to draw a single conclusion about the performance of a country's currency and its trade in relation to those of its trading partners. Data pertaining to the past reveal a mixed bag of performance. It reveals gain of strength by a currency in relation to another in one year but a loss of the same by it in the other year or gain of strength by one currency in relation to that of one partner while a loss of the same by it in relation to the currency (currencies) of the other partner (partners).

The Nominal Effective Exchange Rate (*NEER*) and the Real Effective Exchange Rate (*REER*) are two such measures of a currency's strength or weakness in general in relation to the currency basket of all the trading partners at a time. This reveals overall performance of a currency vis-à-vis the currencies of all the trading partners at a point of time.

NEER provides a measure of a currency's strength at a point of time in nominal terms while *REER* does the same but in real terms, that is, after eliminating the effects of price changes. *NEER* is defined as below,

$$NEER = \sum_{i=1}^{n} [R^i_{index}][W_i] \tag{12.1}$$

Where, $NEER \equiv$ nominal effective exchange rate (in monetary terms),

$[R^i_{index}] \equiv$ exchange rate index of the domestic currency with respect to the currency of ith trading partner

$= [R^i_a/R^i_b] \times 100$; where, $R^i_a \equiv$ exchange rate in year '*a*', $R^i_b \equiv$ exchange rate in the base year '*b*',

$W_i \equiv$ ratio of the volume of the domestic trade with i^{th} partner to the total volume of trade of the domestic country with all the trading partners

$= (X_i + M_i)/(X_{Total} + M_{Total})$

here, $X_i \equiv$ exports to i^{th} partner,

$M_i \equiv$ imports from i^{th} partner,

$X_{Total} \equiv$ Total domestic exports,

$M_{Total} \equiv$ Total domestic imports.

While REER is defined as below,

$$REER = \sum_{i=1}^{n} [RER^i_{index}][W_i] \tag{12.2}$$

Where,

$REER \equiv$ real effective exchange rate

$RER^i_{index} \equiv$ real exchange rate index for the ith partner.

$$R^i_a \times \frac{\text{(price index in country } i \text{ in year '}a\text{' with base ear as '}b\text{'}}{\text{(price index in the domestic country in the year '}a\text{' with base year as '}b\text{')}}$$

To illustrate, suppose India trades only with 2 countries, namely, UK and US.

Clearly, $n = 2$. For UK, $i = 1$ and for US, $i = 2$. India's exports to and imports from UK are respectively ₹ 100 crore and ₹ 200 crore, total exports and imports with both the trading partners are respectively ₹ 400 crore and ₹ 600 crore. Then,

$$W_1 = (X_1 + M_1)/(X_{Total} + M_{Total}) = (100 + 200)/(400 + 600) = (3/10)$$

$$W_2 = (X_2 + M_2)/(X_{Total} + M_{Total}) = (300 + 400)/(400 + 600) = (7/10)$$

Suppose further that year '*a*' is the year 2005 and the base year '*b*' is year 2001. Now let the following changes in value of rupee in terms of Pound (UK) and Dollar (US) over the period 2001–05 be given as,

Years:	2001	2002	2003	2004	2005
₹/£:	60	62	65	63	65
₹/$:	40	40	42	41	45

(The exchange rates are hypothetical, assumed to simplify the calculations of the respective nominal and real effective exchange rates). For the year 2001,

$$R_a^1 = ₹\ 60 \text{ per pound and } R_b^1 = ₹\ 60 \text{ per pound. Then,}$$

$$\begin{aligned}[R^1_{index}] &= [R^1_a/R^1_b] \times 100\\ &= [60/60] \times 100\\ &= 100\\ [R^2_{index}] &= [R^2_a/R^2_b] \times 100\\ &= [40/40] \times 100\\ &= 100\end{aligned}$$

Let us further assume that the ratios of the volumes of trade with these countries remain unchanged during the period 2001–05, that is, $W_1 = 3/10$ and $W_2 = 7/10$.

Then, *NEER* for the year 2001, 2002, 2003, 2003, 2004, and 2005 are given as,

$$\begin{aligned}NEER_{2001} &= \sum_{i=1}^{2}[R^i_{index}][W_i]\\ &= [100]\ [3/10] + [100][7/10]\\ &= [300/10] + [700/10]\\ &= [1000/10]\\ &= 100\end{aligned}$$

$$\begin{aligned}NEER_{2002} &= \sum_{i=1}^{2}[R^i_{index}][W_i]\\ &= [62/60] \times 100 \times [3/10] + [40/40] \times 100 \times [7/10]\\ &= [31] + [70]\\ &= 101\end{aligned}$$

$$\begin{aligned}NEER_{2003} &= \sum_{i=1}^{2}[R^i_{index}][W_i]\\ &= [65/60] \times 100 \times [3/10] + [42/40] \times 100 \times [7/10]\\ &= [32.5] + [73.5]\\ &= 106\end{aligned}$$

$$\begin{aligned}NEER_{2004} &= \sum_{i=1}^{2}[R^i_{index}][W_i]\\ &= [63/60] \times 100 \times [3/10] + [41/40] \times 100 \times [7/10]\\ &= [31.5] + [71.75]\\ &= 103.25\end{aligned}$$

$$\begin{aligned}NEER_{2005} &= \sum_{i=1}^{2}[R^i_{index}][W_i]\\ &= [65/60] \times 100 \times [3/10] + [45/40] \times 100 \times [7/10]\\ &= [32.5] + [78.75]\\ &= 111.25\end{aligned}$$

Since *NEER* changes from 100 to 101 in 2002, to 106 in 2003, to 103.25 in 2004 and to 111.25 in 2005, it is clear to deduce that rupee *depreciated* over 2001 to 2002; depreciated further over 2002 to 2003; *appreciated* over 2003 to 2004 and *depreciated* again over 2004 to 2005 in relation to the currency basket of the trading partners UK and US.

In the same way, *REER* can be calculated. For that we need to the price indices of the three countries with that of the base year (2001) as 100 for each. Let them be given as 100, 120, 130, 140 and 150 for India; 100, 110, 120, 125, 130 for UK and 100, 110, 115, 120, 125 for US over the period 2001–2005. Then,

$$REER_{2001} = \sum_{i=1}^{2}[RER^{i}_{\text{index}}][W_i]$$
$$= (60/60) \times 100 \times [(100/100)][(3/10) + (40/40) \times 100 \times [(100/100)(7/10)]$$
$$= 100$$

$$REER_{2002} = \sum_{i=1}^{2}[RER^{i}_{\text{index}}][W_i]$$
$$= (62/60) \times 100 \times [(110/120)][(3/10) + (40/40)\times 100 \times [(110/120)(7/10)]$$
$$= 28.4166 + 64.1666$$
$$= 92.5832$$

$$REER_{2003} = \sum_{i=1}^{2}[RER^{i}_{\text{index}}][W_i]$$
$$= (65/60)\times 100 \times [(120/130)][(3/10) + (42/40) \times 100 \times [(115/130)(7/10)]$$
$$= 30 + 65.019$$
$$= 95.0192$$

$$REER_{2004} = \sum_{i=1}^{2}[RER^{i}_{\text{index}}][W_i]$$
$$= (63/60) \times 100 \times [(125/140)][(3/10) + (41/40) \times 100 \times [(120/140)(7/10)]$$
$$= 28.125 + 61.5$$
$$= 89.625$$

$$REER_{2005} = \sum_{i=1}^{2}[RER^{i}_{\text{index}}][W_i]$$
$$= (65/60)\times 100 \times [(130/150)][(3/10) + (45/40) \times 100 \times [(125/150)(7/10)]$$
$$= 28.1666 + 65.625$$
$$= 93.791.$$

Since *REER* changes from 100 to 92.333 in 2002, to 92.0192 in 2003, to 89.625 in 2004 and to 93.791 in 2005, it is clear to deduce that in real terms rupee appreciated over 2001 to 2002; depreciated over 2002 to 2003; *appreciated* over 2003 to 2004 and depreciated again over 2004 to 2005 in relation to the currency basket of the trading partners UK and US.

12.3 BALANCE OF TRADE AND BALANCE OF PAYMENTS

Foreign trade is a common economic activity of the modern world. Gone are the days when a country could produce and consume in isolation. Countries better equipped for certain production, specialize that production with the result that they export the surplus to others which are not so suited for such production. The importers of such goods thus reap the benefits of specialized large-scale production of goods they themselves are not suited for and focus on production of what they themselves best at. This benefits other countries in the same way. In an ideal situation, a country's exports must buy its imports. Most of the countries, therefore, strive for a *balance of trade* or, more so, for a *balance of payments.*

Balance of trade of a country shows its aggregate exports and imports of visible transactions with the rest of the world during the course of a year. The visible exports and imports are those that are actually recorded at the ports. If the money value of the exports exceeds that of the imports, the trade is said to be favourable to the country. On the contrary, if the money value of the exports is less than that of the imports, the balance of trade is said to be unfavourable for the country.

Balance of payment of a country, on the other hand, shows aggregate exports and imports of visible as well as invisible items with the rest of the world during the course of a year. Invisible items are those which are not recorded at the ports. These items refer to services rendered by shipping, insurance, and banking companies, debt repayment and payment of interest expenditures by tourists, payment of dividend on capital invested by foreigners, war indemnities, etc. While balance of trade takes into account only the receipts and payments on account of visible exports and imports; balance of payments takes into account receipts and payments on account of both, the visible and the invisible exports and imports. Thus, balance of payments is a wider and more comprehensive concept than the balance of trade. Here, we present the structure of a country's balance of payments account in Table 12.1.

TABLE 12.1 Account of a Country's Balance of Payments

Receipts (Credit)	*Amount (Crores of ₹)*	*Payments (Debit)*	*Amount (Crores of ₹)*
(1) Exports of goods	500	(1) Imports of goods	700
(2) Exports of services	200	(2) Imports of services	100
(3) Unilateral receipts (gifts, indemnities, etc., from foreigners)	50	(3) Unilateral Payments (gifts, indemnities, etc., to foreigners)	20
(4) Capital receipts	100	(4) Capital payments	200
(5) Export of gold	170	(5) Imports of gold	00
Total receipts	**1020**	**Total payments**	**1020**

Exports appear as receivables (credit entry) while imports as payables (debit entry) in a balance of payments (BOP) account. It is so because money value is received for exports and paid for imports. Import and export of visible items (tangible goods) constitute the ***balance of trade account*** while those of the visible items (tangible goods) as well as the invisible items (intangible services) taken together constitute the ***balance of payments account***. In Table12.1, country's balance of visible items (excess of exports over imports of goods) is (–) 200 (500 – 700 = – 200). Balance of trade therefore is in deficit and hence unfavourable. Balance of invisible services along with that of unilateral transfers is however in surplus [(200 + 50) – (100 + 20) = + 130] but it is not large enough to offset the deficit of the balance of trade. A deficit of 70 in balance of trade still persists. Balance of visible goods, invisible services and unilateral transfers (i.e., balance of the first three entries) is known as the ***balance of the current account*** because receipts and payments on account of first three entries constitute the current account. Thus, a deficit of 70 exists on the current account. The deficit on current account can be settled either by a surplus on the capital account (capital receipts – capital payments) or through an export of monetary gold. A look at the capital account (Table 12.1) shows that it is in deficit by 100

(100 – 200 = – 100) itself. Total deficit of current and the capital accounts works out at 170 [(500 + 200 + 50 + 100 – (700 + 100 + 20 + 200) = 170]. This is offset by an export of gold worth 170.

The simple illustration of BOP account (Table 12.1) leads to the following observations:

1. Balance of visible items (excess of exports over imports of goods), known as balance of trade is in deficit of 200 (500 – 700 = – 200).
2. Balance of invisible items (excess of exports over imports of invisible services and unilateral transactions) is in surplus by 130(250 – 120 = + 130).
3. Balance of current account [balance of (1) and (2) above taken together is in deficit by 70 (– 200 + 130 = – 70).
4. Balance of capital account (excess of exports over imports of capital) is in deficit by 100(100 – 200 = – 100).
5. Balance of current and capital accounts taken together [balance of (3) is in deficit by 170 (– 70 – 100 = – 170).
   It is settled by export of gold worth 170.

Structure of the current account may thus be presented as in Table 12.2.

TABLE 12.2 Balance of Payments: Current Account

Receipts (Credit)	*Amount (Crores of ₹)*	*Payments (Debit)*	*Amount (Crores of ₹)*
(1) Exports of goods	500	(1) Imports of goods	700
(2) Exports of services	200	(2) Imports of services	100
(3) Unilateral receipts (gifts, indemnities, etc., from foreigners)	50	(3) Unilateral Payments (gifts, indemnities, etc., to foreigners)	20
Deficit on current A/c	70		
Total receipts	**820**	**Total payments**	**820**

Unilateral transfers are unrequited transfers including receipt of gifts, remittances, foreign aid, etc. which have no obligation of any return, i.e., no *quid pro quo.* Deficit on current account is a balancing entry. It appears on the opposite side on the capital account.

Structure of capital account may thus be presented as in Table 12.3

TABLE 12.3 Balance of Payments: Capital Account

Receipts (Credit)	*Amount (Crores of ₹)*	*Payments (Debit)*	*Amount (Crores of ₹)*
(1) Capital receipts	100	(1) Deficit on current account	70
(2) Export of gold	170	(2) Capital payments	200
Total receipts	**270**	**Total payments**	**270**

Capital receipts and payments involve the following:

1. ***Private transactions:*** All non-government transactions influencing the assets and the liabilities of non-government entities.
2. ***Official Transactions:*** All government transactions influencing the assets and liabilities of the government entities.

3. ***Direct Investment:*** All acquisitions and controls of assets by one country in another country.
4. ***Portfolio Investment:*** All acquisitions of assets (paper assets such as shares and bonds) by one country from another.

Net value of capital flows is known as the balance on capital account. Exports and imports of monetary gold represent the balance on the capital account. If the entry appears as the net export (exports–imports) of gold and is positive, the capital account is said to be in deficit, else in surplus.

In the discussions of the balances in the *BOP* account, economists use terms such as autonomous and accommodating items.

Autonomous items or ***above the line items*** refer to international transactions which take place on some economic purpose and have nothing to do with the state of a nation's balance of payments. That way, all the non-balancing items on the current and the capital accounts (items 1, 2, 3 and 4 in Table 12.1) are autonomous or the 'above the line' items. If autonomous receipts exceed autonomous payments, the *BOP* account is said to be in surplus, else in deficit. All entries on a *BOP* account except those of deficit or of surplus are of autonomous nature.

Accommodating items or ***below the line items*** refer to balancing transactions (item 5 in Table 12.1) made in official settlement of the deficit and surplus on the BOP account. For instance, financing of the BOP deficits or receiving of the BOP surpluses by the monetary authority of a country in their settlement through net monetary transactions are accommodating items.

12.4 DISEQUILIBRIUM IN BOP—INTERNAL AND EXTERNAL IMBALANCES

Balance of payments is said to be in disequilibrium when receipts fail to match international payments. It is characterized by deficit (or a surplus) on the *BOP*-account. While a surplus is always welcome, a deficit is a cause of worry. Let us represent balance of payments (*BP*) by the equation,

$$BP = NX(Y, Y_f, R) + CS(r - r_f), \tag{12.3}$$

where, net exports or balance of visible trade (NX) = $X(Y_f,R) - M(Y,R)$ = Exports (X) – Imports (M), ***Surpluses on capital account*** (CS) = $CS(r - r_f)$. Note that exports is a function of foreign income (Y_f) and real exchange rate (R) while import (M), that of domestic income (Y) and real exchange rate (R) and surplus on capital account (CS) is a function of interest differential of domestic rate of interest over foreign rate of interest ($r - r_f$). In the *IS-LM* framework, we can show the mechanism of $BP = 0$ under perfect capital mobility and fixed exchange rate by dividing the *IS-LM* space into four quadrants (Figure 12.3).

12.4.1 The Mundell-Fleming-Model—Perfect Capital Mobility under Fixed Exchange Rates

The *IS-LM* model applied to the open economy under perfect capital mobility can be termed as the *Mundell-Fleming model*. Nobel laureate Robert Mundell[1] of Columbia University and Marcus Fleming a researcher at the International Monetary Fund developed this model in 1960s much before the inception of the flexible exchange rate.

The original Mundell-Fleming model discussed here remains intact as a way of understanding how policies work under perfect capital mobility. It states:

[1] See Robert Mundell's books: *International Economics* (New York, Macmillan, 1967) and *Monetary Theory* **(Pacific Palisade, CA,** Goodyear, 1971).

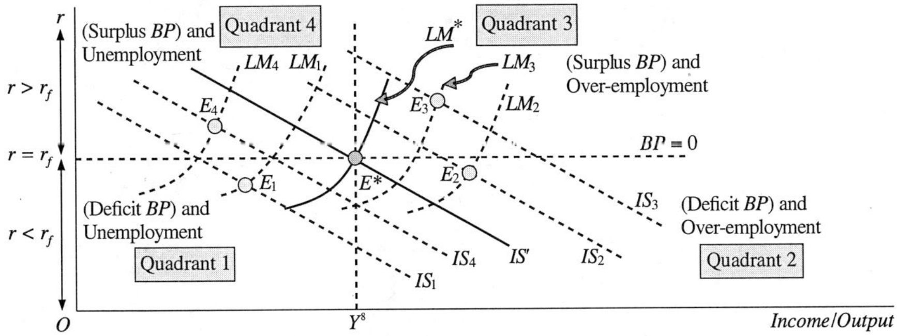

FIGURE 12.3 State of Employment, *BOP*, Fixed Exchange Rate and Perfect Capital Mobility: When $r = r_f$, $BP = 0$ as surplus on capital account is zero. The *BP* schedule is a horizontal line. To understand the mechanism of attainment of balance of payments in an open economy, that is, under perfect capital mobility and fixed exchange rate, let us segment the *IS-LM* space into four quadrants. The first and second quadrants relate to $r < r_f$ (below $BP = 0$ schedule). Points E_1 and E_2 are located in them establishing *IS-LM* equilibrium of deficit *BP* at both, unemployment at E_1 and over-employment at E_2. The 3rd and 4th quadrants relate to $r > r_f$ (above $BP = 0$ schedule). Points E_4 and E_3 are located in them establishing *IS-LM* equilibrium of surplus *BP* at both, unemployment at E_4 and over-employment at E_3.

Under perfect capital mobility and fixed exchange rate, *BP* can't remain in deficit or in surplus for long. For $r < r_f$, capital outflows get initiated which depreciate domestic currency in relation to foreign currency. Exchange rate depreciates forcing central bank's intervention to keep it fixed. It will therefore tighten the domestic currency issue for purchase of the foreign currency. On the contrary, for $r > r_f$, capital inflows get initiated which appreciate domestic currency in relation to the foreign currency. Exchange rate appreciates, forcing central bank's intervention to maintain it at fixed level.

If the economy is to the left of $Y = Y^*$, that is, if economy is at E_1 or E_4, there is a situation of unemployment. To raise employment, it requires rightward shifts in the *LM*–and-*IS* curves. This calls for expansionary monetary and fiscal policies. Their mechanism follows in next sub-section.

Under perfect capital mobility and fixed exchange rate, no central bank can pursue an independent monetary policy.

To understand, suppose a central bank intends to raise the interest rate (r), through monetary contraction, above the world level (r_f). This it does to attract foreign capital. The central bank tightens its monetary policy for the purpose. Wealth holders abroad shift their stocks for higher return of (r). This boosts demand for domestic currency, which in consequence, appreciates in relation to the foreign currencies. In other words, exchange rate of domestic currency appreciates. The central bank due to its commitment to fixed exchange rate regime, feels compelled to intervene. It therefore buys foreign currencies in exchange for domestic money at predetermined fixed exchange rate. This increases supply of domestic currency in the domestic territory. The interest rate (r) falls to the original level in consequence and the initial monetary contraction gets reversed. Thus an independent monetary policy of central bank proves to no avail under perfect capital mobility and fixed exchange rate. In sub-section 12.4.1.1, we will demonstrate efficacy of monetary policy in somewhat greater detail and in sub-section 12.4.1.2, we will examine that of a fiscal policy.

12.4.1.1 Ineffectiveness of monetary policy

Suppose a central bank is mandated to expand money supply with a view to boost output/income and employment. Further, suppose it is at point *E* when it acts as per the requirement. The *LM*-curve shifts to *LM′* in consequence-as shown in Figure 12.4.

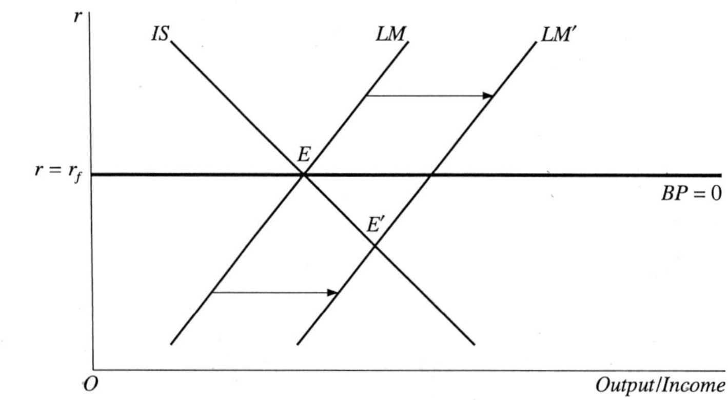

FIGURE 12.4 Ineffiveness of Monetary Policy on Income/Output under Perfect Capital Mobility and Fixed Exchange Rate: Economy is at point *E*, the initial equilibrium when expansionary monetary policy is adopted by the central bank to boost output/income. The *LM*-curve shifts to *LM*′ in consequence. The new equilibrium is established at *E*′ which falls below the *BP* = 0 schedule. The balance of payments turns into deficit and the domestic interest rate, *r*, drops below r_f. Under perfect capital mobility capital outflows take place as a result of which domestic currency depreciates in relation to the foreign currencies implying depreciation of the exchange rate. The central bank has to sell foreign currencies in exchange with domestic currency. This results in contraction of domestic money, which causes the domestic interest rate to rise to point *E*. The *LM*-curve retracts back to *LM*-curve from its temporary position of *LM*′. *Thus monetary policy proves ineffective in its objective of boosting income under perfect capital mobility and fixed exchange rate.*

12.4.1.2 Effectiveness of fiscal policy

As against monetary policy, a fiscal policy is highly effective in the objective of boosting income/ output and employment. Figure 12.5 demonstrates the mechanism.

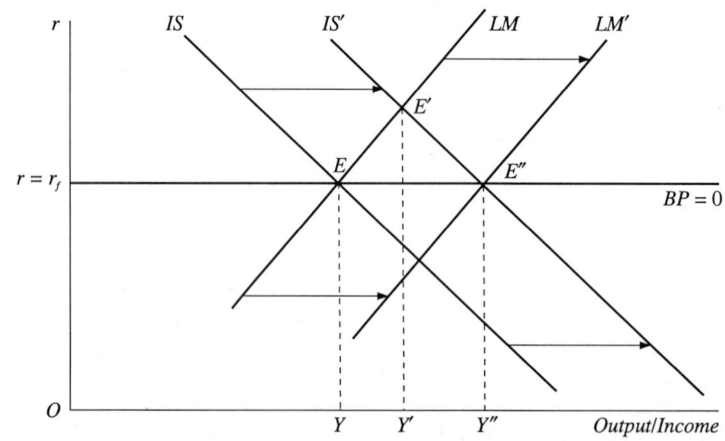

FIGURE 12.5 Effectiveness of Fiscal Policy on Income/Output under perfect Capital Mobility and Fixed Exchange Rate: Expansionary fiscal policy shifts the *IS*-curve to right as shown. The equilibrium shifts from *E* to *E*′ thereby raising the interest rate, as also, the output which rises from *Y* to *Y*′. Capital inflows, tempted by higher returns follow,

(Contd.)

FIGURE 12.5 Contd.

implying appreciation of the domestic currency and hence the exchange rate. Even balance of payments position turns to surplus. The central bank due to its commitment to fixed exchange rate buys foreign currency with the domestic currency at the predetermined fixed exchange rate. The *LM*-curve shifts rightwards to *LM′* which restores interest rate and balance of payments to the initial level at point *E″*. In the process output/income rises further from *Y′* to *Y″*. *Thus a fiscal expansion, coupled with the monetary expansion maintains interest rate and BP yet raises output/income substantially.*

12.4.2 Mundell-Fleming Model—Perfect Capital Mobility under Flexible Exchange Rates

Assuming domestic price level fixed when exchange rate is fully flexible, we employ Mundell-Fleming model to explore efficacy of monetary and fiscal policies. As evident, central bank has no business to intervene in the foreign exchange market. Instead, foreign exchange rate must adjust itself to the market forces of demand and supply of foreign exchange so that *BP* schedule is zero. Current account deficits must be financed by private capital inflows and the current account surplus by capital outflows. Adjustments in the exchange rate make sure that the sum of the current and capital accounts is zero. However, the central bank can set the money supply at will.

All said and done, there is only one interest rate at which balance of payments balances under perfect capital mobility, that is,

$$r = r_f \tag{12.4}$$

At the rate other than r_f huge capital flows take place and disturb the balance of payment-balance.

Representing goods market equilibrium by domestic spending, we can represent an *IS*-curve as below:

$$\begin{aligned} \text{Spending on domestic goods} &= (DS) + (NX) \\ &= C + I + G + (X - M) \\ &= IS\,(Y, r) \end{aligned} \tag{12.5}$$

Equations 12.3, 12.4 and 12.5 help understanding of the effect of flexible exchange rates on aggregate output/income. Figure 12.6 explains it.

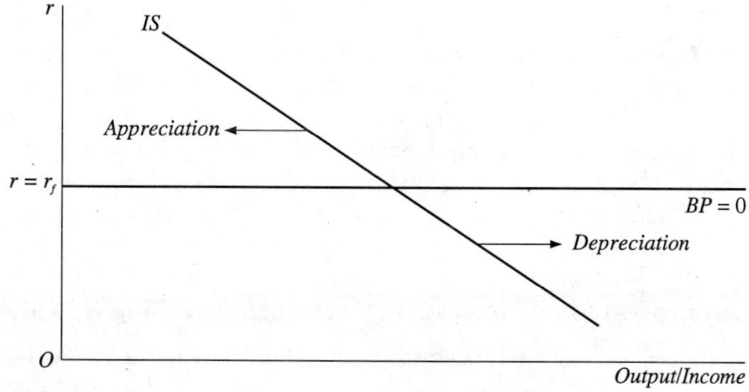

FIGURE 12.6 Appreciation/Depreciation of Home Currency and Change in Competitiveness of domestic Goods: When $r < r_f$, capital outflows make the home currency depreciate. Given domestic and foreign prices, home products become more competitive abroad. Let a product be priced at home at 1000. Since home currency

(Contd.)

FIGURE 12.6 Contd.

depreciates in relation to the foreign currency, foreigners have to pay less for our products. If the home currency depreciates from ₹ 40 per dollar to ₹ 50 per dollar, foreigners would have to pay \$20 instead of the \$25 for our product. After depreciation of home currency, home products turn cheaper to foreigner making their demand for our goods rise. In consequence home exports rise and *IS* curve shifts to rightward as shown by the arrow.

Exactly opposite is the case when $r > r_f$. Capital inflows appreciate home currency in relation to foreign currencies. This makes foreign goods cheaper for the home buyers giving rise to home imports to rise. This makes the *IS*-curve shift leftwards as shown by the arrow.

12.4.2.1 Adjustment process to an increase in exogenous exports

Let the economy be in equilibrium at *E* (Figure 12.7). Now suppose Foreign demand for domestic goods rises. The rise in demand exceeds domestic supply at *E,* which calls for excess production that would result in a shift the *IS*-curve upwards to right, increasing output/income in the process. All along, rate of interest would also go up as the economy proceeds towards *E*′. This rise in the rate of interest must be followed by (a) lowering of the private investment, (b) capital inflows, and (c) appreciation of the exchange rate. Fall in private investment pushes the *IS*-curve back to the initial equilibrium at *E.* Thus what was initiated by excess export demand for domestic goods, is simultaneously reversed and the new equilibrium at *E*′ can't be reached.

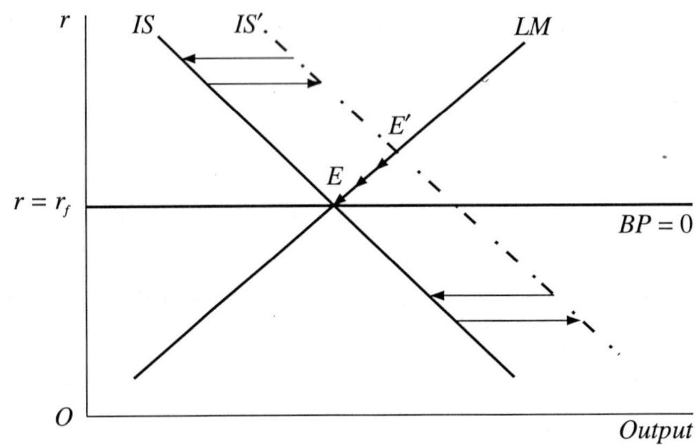

FIGURE 12.7 Effect of Increase in Exogenous Exports: New foreign demand for domestic goods sets the *IS* curve to shift rightwards to some position at *E*′ but the same doesn't come into being because of a rise in the interest rate ($r > r_f$), which triggers three things, (a) fall in private investment, (b) capital inflows, and (c) appreciation of exchange rate. The first one itself tends to bring the *IS* curve back to the initial position at *E.* The backward shift of the *IS*-curve is gradual. Each time interest goes up, it follows with the result that attainment of the new equilibrium at *E*′ turns infeasible.

12.4.2.2 Adjustment process to an increase in government spending (Fiscal expansion)

The treatment draws a parallel with that of sub-section 12.4.2.1 (Figure 12.7). The reader can try it on the same lines.

12.4.2.3 Adjustment process to an increase money stock

Given the product prices, an increase in $\overline{M}$ amounts to an increase in $(\overline{M}/\overline{P})$ which is followed by a rightward shift in the *LM*-curve (Figure 12.8) to set equilibrium at *E′*. This sets (a) interest rate to fall, (b) capital outflows to follow $(r < r_f)$, and (c) exchange rate to depreciate. The first one tends to raise the private investment but not so much due to capital outflows. Depreciation of exchange rate makes domestic products more competitive to the foreign buyers. Their demand gets a boost and this complements the outward shift in the *IS*-curve caused by private investment. The *IS*-curve now shifts significantly outwards to right. Economy reaches its equilibrium at *E″* as shown. A possible implication of this is the improvement of the current account through the induced depreciation.

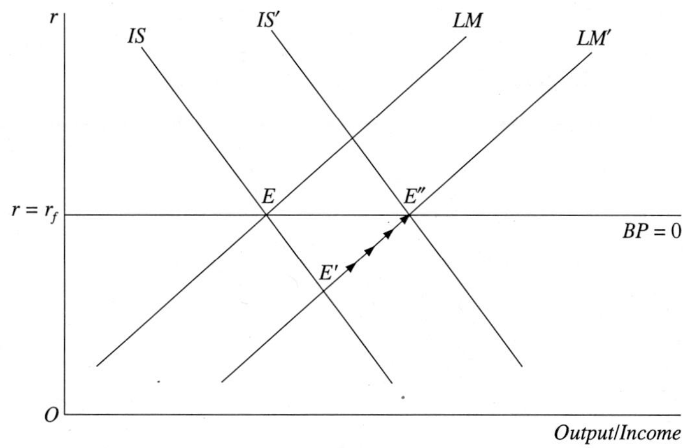

FIGURE 12.8 Adjustment Process of an Increase in Real Money Stock: Given the product prices, an increase in $\overline{M}$ amounts to an increase in $(\overline{M}/\overline{P})$ which is followed by a rightward shift in the *LM*-curve to set equilibrium at *E′*. This sets (a) interest rate to fall, (b) capital outflows to be-gin $(r < r_f)$, and (c) exchange rate to depreciate. The first one tends to raise the private investment to shift the *IS*-curve upwards to right. Depreciation right, depreciation of domestic currency in relation to the foreign currencies makes the domestic products cheaper to the foreign buyers. As a result foreign demand for domestic products rises. This results in consequential shift in the *IS*-curve outwards. Economy reaches its equilibrium at *E″* as shown. A possible implication of this is the improvement of the current account through the induced depreciation of exchange rate.

12.5 TRILEMMA AND ITS IMPOSSIBILITY

*The theorem states that a situation of **trilemma** arises before every economy while making a choice of any two from the three combinations, namely, Combination 'a', Combination 'b' and Combination 'c'.*

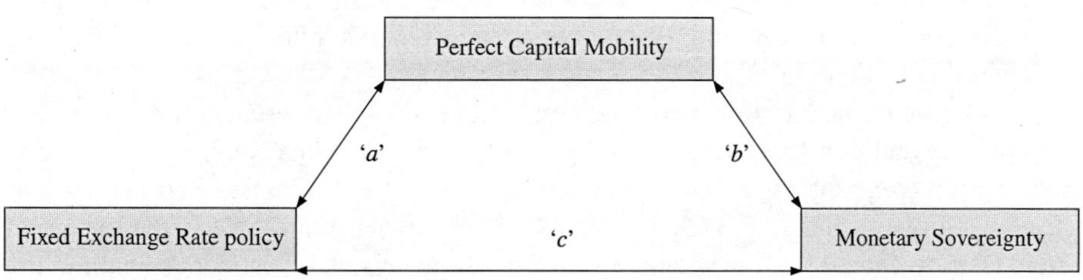

If a country follows Combination '*a*', it has to employ ***'perfect capital mobility'*** with the policy of '*fixed exchange rate*' and to sacrifice that of ***'monetary sovereignty'***.

If it follows the Combination '*b*', it has to adopt the policy of ***'perfect capital mobility'*** with the ***'policy of monetary sovereignty'*** sacrificing that of ***'fixed exchange rate'***.

If the country follows Combination '*c*', it chooses the policy of '*fixed exchange rate*' with the policy of '*monetary sovereignty*' sacrificing the policy of '*perfect capital mobility*'.

The three alternative options to boost *GDP*, constitute the famous *trilemma*, also called the ***Impossible Trinity*** or ***Unholy Trilemma***, getting out of which, is difficult if not impossible for the world economies according to many economists.

Currently some of the Euro-zone members are pursuing '*a*', sacrificing '*monetary sovereignty* while most other countries follow '*b*' , sacrificing the '*policy of fixed exchange rate*'. Dani Rodrix, a Harward economist, advocates '*c*', in his book 'Globalization Paradox', emphasizing that world *GDP* grew fastest during the Bretton Wood's Era when perfect capital mobility was sacrificed.

The *IS-LM* framework (Figure 12.9) demonstrates the efficacy of Combination '*c*'.

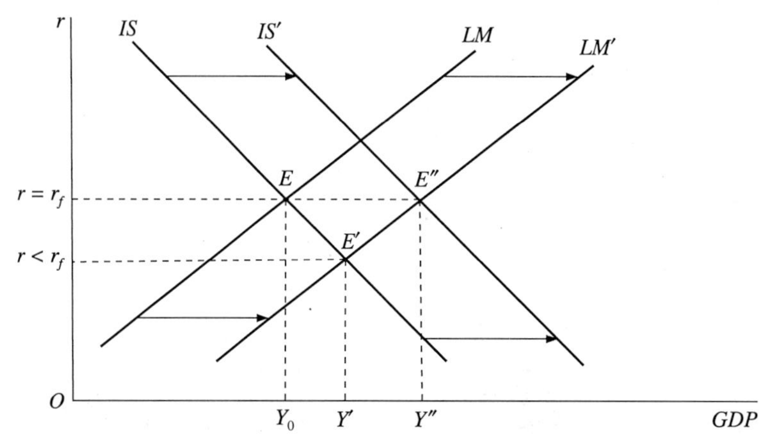

FIGURE 12.9 Option 'c' Implying Combination 'Fixed Exchange Rate and Monetary Sovereignty leads to faster growth of *GDP*: To under-stand, suppose the economy is at *E* when it expands money supply, $\overline{M}$, with a view to boost its *GDP*. Given the price level, $\overline{P}$, real balances increase leading to a rightward shift in the *LM*-curve as shown. Equilibrium shifts from *E* to *E*′. The rate of interest falls and private investment rises ($I = I_a - hr$) in consequence. This brings in a shift in the *IS*-curve outward to right. The new equilibrium is set up at *E*″ bringing about an increase in *GDP* from Y_0 *to Y*″. Even the *BOP* is to balance. That way, Dani Rodrix has proved his point.

Dani Rodrix argues that perfect capital mobility or financial globalization is the cause of economic crisis in both—the developed and the developing countries.

We have discussed at length combinations '*a*' and '*b*' in various forms. Both involve perfect capital mobility, which gives rise to economic crises in developed and developing economies as held also by Dani Rodrix. Combinations '*a*' and '*c*' involve 'fixed exchange rate', which is of little relevance as an alternative due to floating of currencies after seventies.

After the collapse of the Bretton Woods agreement in early seventies and adoption of the flexible rate regime in late seventies after its ratification by *IMF* in 1976, only one combination, namely, perfect capital mobility and ***monetary sovereignty*** remained open for the economies. Expansionary monetary policy causes a rightward shift in the *LM*-curve, resulting in lower interest rate. Due to perfect capital mobility, this leads to capital outflows rather than of boosting private investment spending. In absence of any shift in *IS*-curve, the *LM*-curve retracts back to its original position at *E*. The trilemma thus no longer offers an alternative and is therefore termed as ***impossible trilemma*** or ***impossible trinity*** or even as ***unholy trilemma***.

12.6 CONCLUDING NOTE

Balance of payments and deficits therein owe their origin to the following factors in general:

(1) Economic Factors: Economic factors responsible for the *BOP* deficit include the following:

(a) Large-scale imports of capital and technology for economic development make the import bills heavy for most of the developing nations. Heavy imports on one hand and low export demand on the other, build up a huge deficit on the BOP account for such countries. This is the plight of the underdeveloped and developing nations. Their exports always lag behind due to lack of competitiveness of their products in the international markets. Moreover, most of their exports comprise of primary goods which fetch low prices everywhere. For example, India has suffered a lot from the chronic problem of the BOP deficit caused by its heavy imports and low exports.

(b) Trade cycle, in particular its phase of depression, is yet another important factor responsible for trade imbalances. Demand falls and so do output, income and employment. Economic activity drops to its lowest ebb and trade gets distorted.

(c) Inflation and deflation influence the direction of trade. A country in the grip of inflation imports more and exports less.

(d) Development of better or cheaper substitutes through innovations, new and better sources of supply or technological breakthrough leading to cost advantages change the volume and direction of trade. Countries with these advantages raise trade surpluses while those lacking them suffer trade deficits.

(2) Political Factors: Political instability in a country not only discourages foreign investors, it also causes capital outflows. This affects output, employment and income of the country adversely, and above all, it distorts its trade completely at times.

(3) Social Factors: Changes in tastes, preferences, fashions, customs, lifestyles, habits, etc. affect the volume and direction of trade significantly. For example, popularity of western lifestyle in India may increase Indian imports of many western products.

Remedies

There is no easy way out of the problem of BOP deficits. The traditional solutions of *import substitution* and *export promotion* have been tried by many countries time and again but the fact remains. A developing nation can hardly afford import substitution. It costs the nation its cause of modernization and growth. Modernization of technology and growth of income are both crucial for development. In the like manner export promotion is very difficult to realize without enhancing competitiveness of products in the international markets. This requires low production costs with high product quality, which, in turn, require a contemporary technology, if not a better one. This necessitates import of technology. Import substitution therefore fails to serve the purpose. India too attempted import substitution at the initial stages of its planned development. The lesson it learnt led to a shift in emphasis from import substitution to export promotion. The latter was considered possible through export production, export quality and export packaging. All the imports deemed essential for the purpose were treated unavoidable. Another solution to the problem of *BOP* deficits tried by Indian government with effect from 1991 has been to attract direct foreign investment. The objective has been to curtail the heavy import bills. India can gain substantially also through its exports of tourism. What it needs for the purpose is to market it. India possesses huge potential for it, no doubt.

KEY TERMS AND CONCEPTS

Import Tariff: It is a tax levied on imports. The purpose is to restrict imports or to make them costlier to the domestic buyer.

Export Tariff: It is a tax levied on exports. The purpose is to restrict exports or to make them costlier to the foreign buyer.

Exchange Rate: it refers to the rate at which currencies are exchanged for each other. For example, the rupee-dollar exchange rate of ₹ 40 per dollar implies that each of the two currencies can be converted into the other at this rate.

Spot Market: A spot market refers to that part of the foreign exchange market in which sale and purchase of foreign currencies are settled within *two days* of the deal. The rate is called the *spot exchange rate* or the *current exchange rate.*

Forward Market: A forward exchange market refers to that market in which deals for sale / purchase of foreign currencies at a pre-settled exchange rate are executed in future after 90 days of the deal. The rate is called the *forward exchange rate.*

Purchasing Power Parity Theory (PPP- theory): The theory provides a measure of the purchasing powers of two currencies. For any pair of currencies, if real exchange rate $(R) = 1.00$, the currencies have equal purchasing power or possess purchasing power parity (*PPP*) or equal competitiveness. On the other hand, if $R = 0.20$, the foreign country's price is $1/5^{th}$ of the domestic price, that is, the foreign country is cheaper than domestic country or it is said to have higher competitiveness than the domestic country. Likewise, if real exchange rate is greater than one, say 6, the foreign country is 6 times costlier than the domestic country.

Hedging: It is a feature of the forward exchange market. When traders agree to trade goods at a future date at current prices and current rate of exchange in the international market, the arrangement is called *hedging*. It is a safeguard against a likely loss due to possible fluctuations in exchange rate and prices of goods.

Arbitrage: It refers to an act of simultaneous sale and purchase of foreign currencies in different exchange markets with a view to take advantage of different rates of exchange prevailing in different markets. It helps to stabilize the exchange rate in different markets by transferring the currency from the markets where its value in terms of other currencies is low to the markets where it is high.

Speculation: It refers to deliberate attempt to bear risks under the expectation of profits. Buying of currencies for trading them for profit is an example of speculation. Speculators buy currencies under the belief that their prices will go up and they will make profits by selling them at higher prices. But what if the prices fell instead and losses accrue in consequence? Well, that is the risk the speculators take.

Fixed Exchange Rate: When price of a currency is officially fixed by the monetary authority of a country in terms of a reserve currency (Usually dollar) or a basket of key currencies of the world, the exchange rate so determined is called the fixed exchange rate or the *pegged* exchange rate. The monetary authority of a country undertakes to maintain the rate through transacting at it irrespective of the fluctuations.

Flexible Exchange Rate: Exchange rate determined through the market forces of demand and supply of a currency in the free market is called the flexible exchange rate or the floating exchange rate.

Adjustable Peg: Under normal circumstances, some flexibility in the fixed exchange rate is permitted by the *IMF*. It is called the adjustable peg. This is usually executed through devaluation at the exhaustion of the foreign exchange reserves of a country.

Crawling Peg: Flexibility in the fixed exchange rate by small amounts at short intervals executed with a view to delay the exhaustion of the foreign exchange is called the crawling peg.

Devaluation of Currency: When government of a country officially lowers the external value of its currency either within the limits of the adjustable peg or with a prior approval from the *IMF*, the act is known as devaluation of the currency. In other words, it is the official and deliberate depreciation of the external value of the currency. Its immediate effect on the price of a foreign currency in terms of the domestic currency is an increase in it. For instance,

1% devaluation of rupee would change the exchange rate from ₹ 40.00 per dollar to ₹ 40.4040 per dollar. An act opposite to devaluation is called ***revaluation.***

Depreciation of Currency: Loss of external value by a currency in a free exchange market is called its depreciation. It is a result of market forces. Its effect on the exchange rate is similar to that of devaluation. Opposite of currency depreciation is called currency *appreciation.*

Managed Floating or Dirty Floating : It refers to a system of gradual adjustments in the exchange rate which take place through government intervention. Managed floating resembles the crawling peg but for the difference that the band in it is wider and the settlements quicker than what they are in the crawling peg system. Moreover, crawling peg has a built in bias in favour of stability, but managed floating hasn't. The system of managed floating, at times, is referred to as the *dirty float* due to deliberate absence of the government intervention to smoothen out the ups and downs in the exchange rate. In contrast, an exchange rate fluctuating freely is known as the *clean float.*

Balance of Trade (*BOT*): It is a statement of visible transactions of a country with the rest of the world. Balance of trade of a country shows its aggregate exports and imports of visible transactions with the rest of the world during the course of a year. The visible exports and imports are those that are actually recorded at the ports.

Balance of Payments (*BOP*): Balance of payment of a country shows aggregate exports and imports of visible as well as invisible items with the rest of the world during the course of a year. Invisible items are those which are not recorded at the ports.

Trade Deficit: When exports of the visibles lag behind the imports of the visibles, the balance of trade is said to be in deficit. In the opposite case, when exports of the visibles exceed their imports, the balance of trade is said to be in surplus.

***BOP* Deficit:** When exports of the visibles and invisibles taken together lag behind the imports of the visibles and invisibles taken together, the balance of payments is said to be in deficit. In the opposite case, when exports of the visibles and invisibles taken together exceed their imports taken together, the balance of payments is said to be in surplus.

***BOP* Current Account:** The statement of exports of visible goods and invisible services including the unilateral transactions of a country with the rest of the world on the credit side and imports of the same in respect of the same country on the debit side is called the current account of the balance of payments. The difference between the two sides is called the balance on the current account. If the credit side exceeds the debit side, the difference is called the surplus on current account and is recorded on the debit side as such to balance the two sides. If the debit side exceeds the credit side, the difference is called the deficit on current account and is recorded on the credit side as such to balance the two sides.

***BOP* Capital Account:** The statement of exports of visible and invisible items of capital transactions of a country with the rest of the world on the credit side and imports of the same in respect of the same country on the debit side is called the capital account of the balance of payments. The difference between the two sides is called the balance on the capital account. If the credit side exceeds the debit side, the difference is called the surplus on capital account and is recorded on the debit side as such to balance the two sides. If the debit side exceeds the credit side, the difference is called the deficit on capital account and is recorded on the credit side as such to balance the two sides. The deficit on the capital account may be treated either as 'net incurrence of foreign financial liability' or as 'net external borrowings' and may be requited through an export of gold while the surplus on the capital account may be treated either as 'net acquisition of foreign financial assets' or as 'net lending to the rest of the world (ROW)' and may be requited through import of gold. Note that deficit on current account (appearing on the credit side of the current account) reappears as such on the debit side of the capital side and the surplus on the current account (appearing on the debit side of the current account) reappears as such on the credit side of the capital account.

***BOP* Account:** Compiling the current and the capital accounts to constitute the BOP account reveals that the *BOP* account is automatically balanced. The balancing entry of the current account reappears as contra entry on the capital account and the balancing entry of the capital account incorporated as the deficit or surplus on capital account to balance the capital account automatically balances the *BOP* account.

Autonomous or Above the Line Items: All the items, except the balancing item, which constitute the current and the capital accounts (items 1, 2, 3 and 4 in Table 11.1) are commercially or economically motivated and are referred to by the economists as the autonomous or the 'above the line items'.

Accommodating or Below the Line Items: All the balancing items or transactions (item 5 in Table 11.1) made in official settlement of the deficit and surplus on the BOP account are referred to by the economists as the accommodating or the 'below the line' items. For instance, financing of the BOP deficits or receiving of the BOP surpluses by the monetary authority of a country in their settlement through net monetary transactions or net exports of gold are accommodating items.

Factors Responsible for Disequilibrium of BOP: The factors that lead to BOP disequilibrium include, apart from the economic factors, the social and political factors as well.

Monetary Sovereignty: A country exercising independent monetary policies.

Perfect Capital Mobility: A state of investment in which **a** country feels free to regulate capital flows across borders.

Impossible Trilemma: It is impossible to pursue perfect capital mobility, fixed exchange rate and monetary sovereignty at the same time. Currently some of the Euro-zone members are pursuing fixed exchange rate and perfect capital mobility, sacrificing 'monetary sovereignty while most other countries follow perfect capital mobility and monetary sovereignty, sacrificing the policy of fixed exchange rate. Dani Rodrix, a Harvard economist, advocates fixed exchange rate with monetary sovereignty sacrificing perfect capital mobility in his book 'Globalization Paradox', emphasizing that world *GDP* grew fastest during the Bretton Wood's Era when perfect capital mobility was sacrificed.

EXERCISES

A. Short Answer Questions

1. Distinguish between:
   (a) Import and export tariffs
   (b) Spot and forward exchange rates
   (c) Fixed and flexible exchange rates
   (d) Adjustable and crawling pegs
   (e) Nominal and real exchange rates
   (f) Depreciation and devaluation of currencies
   [Hint: A fall in value of a currency against currencies of the currency basket in free market (flexible exchange rate regime is called its depreciation. For example, let the rupee dollar exchange rate at a point of time be ₹ 40 per dollar. After some time, if the exchange rate changes to ₹ 50 per dollar, rupee is said to have depreciated. As against this, if Indian government officially lowers the value of rupee against foreign currencies under fixed exchange rate regime, it is called devaluation. A 10% devaluation of rupee changes the exchange rate from ₹ 40 per dollar to ₹ 44 per dollar. That is, India will have to pay ₹ 44 for a dollar worth of import while US will have to pay 40 dollars buy from India a product priced at ₹ 1760. Before devaluation, US paid dollars 44 for it. Thus, Indian imports from US turn costlier and hence get discouraged while Indian exports to US buyers turn cheaper and hence get encouraged.]
   (g) Dirty float and clean float
   (h) Above line transactions and below the line transaction
   (i) Spot market and forward market
   (j) Arbitrage and speculation of currency markets
   (k) Devaluation and revaluation of currencies
   [Hint: Revaluation is to appreciation as devaluation is to depreciation]
   (l) Depreciation and appreciation of currencies
   (m) Balance of trade and balance of payments
   (n) Free float and managed float
2. Define hedging. Outline some of its advantages.
3. Explain the real exchange rate with an example. How is it related to purchasing power parity theory?

B. Long Answer Questions

4. Distinguish between import and export tariffs. What role can they play in improving country's trade balance?
5. Distinguish between spot and forward markets of foreign exchange. What role does a forward market play in foreign trade?
6. Distinguish between fixed and flexible exchange rates. Why do countries follow dual exchange rates?
7. Distinguish between adjustable and crawling pegs. Which one is more suitable in general and why?

8. Distinguish between crawling peg system and managed floating system. What conditions would you impose on countries preferring managed floating system so that they may not resort to dirty floating?
9. Explain the mechanism of determining the flexible exchange rate. How does an increase in imports affect the exchange rate?
10. Explain the mechanism of determining the flexible exchange rate. How does a decrease in imports affect the exchange rate?
11. Explain the mechanism of determining the flexible exchange rate. How does an increase in exports affect the exchange rate?
12. Explain the mechanism of determining the flexible exchange rate. How does a decrease in exports affect the exchange rate?
13. Explain the mechanism of determining the flexible exchange rate. How does a decrease in exports affect the exchange rate?
14. Distinguish between devaluation and depreciation of currency. How do they affect imports and exports of a country?
15. Distinguish between balance of trade and balance of payments. Can *BOP* be favourable when *BOT* is in deficit? Explain your answer.
16. Draw the structures of current and capital accounts of external transactions and estimate:
    (i) Deficit on current account
    (ii) *BOP* deficit

    when,

    Exports of goods = 300
    Imports of goods = 500
    Exports of services = 250
    Imports of services = 150
    Unilateral transfers (receipts) = 200
    Unilateral transfers (payments) = 100
    Capital receipts = 300
    Capital payments = 200 **[Ans:** (i) 0.00; (ii) 100.00 see tables 12.2 and 12.3]
17. (i) Distinguish between autonomous and accommodating transactions.
    (ii) What is meant by perfect capital mobility? Explain.

    [Hint: When capital is free to move across the borders for higher rates of return, it is said to be perfect capital mobility]
18. Suppose rupee-dollar exchange rate is ₹ 40 per dollar. Indian government devalues rupee by 5%. How would the rupee-dollar exchange rate change in consequence? How would it affect India's foreign trade? Explain your answer.
19. Describe the causes of *BOP* disequilibrium. Briefly explain each.
20. What is the remedy to the problem of *BOP* deficits? What measures would you recommend for solving India's problem of *BOP* deficits and why?
21. (a) What is meant by real exchange rate? How can it account for purchasing power parity (*PPP*) between two countries?
    (b) Suppose that the rupee-dollar exchange rate in nominal terms is ₹ 80 per dollar . Suppose further that price of Coke in *US* is \$2.00 per bottle while in India it is ₹ 20 per bottle. Calculate real exchange rate between India and *US*. What is its unit?

    [Ans: (b) Real exchange rate is given as,

$$R = \frac{eP_f}{P_d}$$

    Making substitutions, we have

$$R = \frac{(₹\ 80/\$) \times (\$2.00/\text{unit})}{₹\ 20/\text{unit}}$$

$$= 8.00$$

Note that real exchange rate is a ratio that can be defined as the ratio of foreign to domestic prices. It measures a country's competitiveness in the international market. In the above example, $R = 8$, denotes that *US* price is 8 times higher than Indian price and that India has much higher competitiveness than US. If for any pair of countries, $R = 1.00$, their currencies have equal purchasing power or possess purchasing power parity (*PPP*) or equal competitiveness. On the other hand, if $R = 0.20$, the foreign country's price is $1/5^{th}$ the domestic price and the foreign country is cheaper than domestic country or it has higher competitiveness than the domestic country.]

22. It is desired to compare true *GDP* per capita of two countries, namely, Richland and Poorland. Assuming that per capita products comprise *TVs* and Haircuts only and the actual per capita consumption is 1 *TV* and 10 Haircuts only. Employ the purchasing power parity exchange rate to estimate the true *GDP* per capita of Poorland in relation to that of the Richland from the data on respective outputs and prices of the two goods as given in the table below:

Country	*Production of TVs per capita*	*Price of a TV in local currency*	*Production of Haircuts per capita*	*Price of a Haircut in local currency*	*GDP per capita in local currencies*
Richland	4	10	40	2	120
Poorland	1	10	10	1	20

[**Ans:** As it appears, *GDP* per capita of Poorland is 20/120 or $(1/6)^{th}$ of the *GDP* per capita of Richland. Burt under *PPP* exchange rate, an artificial rate, one basket per capita in Richland comprises one *TV* and 10 Haircuts the cost of which is \$30 (= 10 + 2 × 10) and in Poorland it is \$20 (= 10 + 10). That means *GDP* per capita of \$30 of Richland is equal to GDP per capita of \$20 of Poorland. Under the system, *GDP* per capita of 120 of Richland is equivalent to *GDP* per capita of \$30 of Poorland. Thus, GDP per capita of Poorland = $(1/4)^{th}$ of *GDP* per capita of Richland.]

C. Essay Type Questions

23. Write a comprehensive note on examining the strength of a currency via-a-via other currencies of the world.

24. Examine the interrelationship among rate of interest, perfect capital mobility and fixed exchange rate through *IS-LM* tools.

25. 'Under perfect capital mobility and fixed exchange rate, no central bank can pursue an independent monetary policy' Discuss.

26. 'Under perfect capital mobility and fixed exchange rate, show that monetary policy proves ineffective in boosting national income/output while fiscal policy proves highly effective' Discuss.

27. Make a comprehensive case for applying *Mundell-Fleming* model to boost national income /output under perfect capital mobility and flexible exchange rate.

28. Give a comprehensive account of the impossible trilemma.

29. Indian currency has significantly weakened against dollar over the last decade or so. One reason is relocation of its huge amounts to foreign banks and the other is falling demand of Indian goods abroad. The latter has affected India's BOT and BOP both' Discuss.

CASE STUDY

An Indian producer has availed projections of US demand for one of its products.. The demand function for the said product as per the US based consultant is highly price sensitive and is given as:

$$Q = 75000 - 96P$$

where, $Q \equiv$ the number of units demanded at price P in dollars.

Consultant's fee for the projection is \$18,000 and the dollar equivalent of the variable cost per unit of the product is \$718.75 inclusive of all expenses of packaging, marketing, and transportation. Rupee-dollar exchange rate relevant to all these estimates is ₹ 75 per dollar.

Determine:

(i) number of units to be produced,
(ii) profit maximizing price in dollars as also in rupees,
(iii) producer's profits in dollars as also in Indian currency,
(iv) would you advise the producer to prefer setting price in dollars or in rupees? Give reasons.

[Ans: (i) profit maximizing number of units = 3000,
(ii) profit maximizing price in dollars = $750 and in rupees ₹ 56,250,
(iii) producer's profit in dollars = $75,750; and in rupees = ₹ 56,81,250],
(iv) Either way, it does not make a difference.]

Further, suppose that capital outflows from India continue to soar. As a result, rupee-dollar exchange rate rises to ₹80 per dollar by the time the product hits the US markets.

Determine:

(i) number of units to be produced,
(ii) profit maximizing price in dollars as also in rupees,
(iii) producer's profit in dollars as also in rupees,
(iv) Would you advise the producer to prefer setting price in dollars or in rupees? Give reasons.

[Ans: (i) profit maximizing number of units = 3000,
(ii) profit maximizing price in dollars= $750; and in rupees= ₹ 60,000,
(iii) producer's profit in dollars = $75,750; and in rupees = ₹ 60,60,000.]
(iv) Preference to continue with rupee price in the event of rupee depreciation would boost product's competitiveness in US. The buyer would have to pay less ($703.13 instead of $750 per unit) leading to a rise in product 's demand in US.]

Now suppose the producer feels no constraints in boosting production to match the rise in US demand with the result that variable cost per unit also falls from $718.75 to $700.00.

Determine:

(i) number of units to be produced,
(ii) profit maximizing price in dollars as also in rupees,
(iii) producer's profits in dollars as also in rupees,
(iv) Would you advise the producer to prefer setting price in dollars or in rupees? Give reasons.

[Ans: (i) profit maximizing number of units = 3900,
(ii) profit maximizing price in dollars = $740.63; and in rupees = ₹ 59,250,
(iii) producer's profit in dollars = $1,40,400; and in rupees = ₹ 1,12,32,000,
(iv) Setting price in rupees boosts competitiveness and profitability both.]

Do you agree with the proposition that setting price in the domestic currency enhances competitiveness and profitability of the products abroad? Give reasons for your answer.

UNIT-5

MONEY-EROSION IN ITS VALUE: INFLATION

Chapter 13: Inflation: Meaning, Theories, Causes and Effects

Chapter 13

Inflation: Meaning, Theories, Causes and Effects

INTRODUCTION: MEANING OF INFLATION

The term *'inflation'* originates from the Latin word, *'inflare'* which means 'to blow into' or 'inflate' just as we blow air into the tyres. In simple terms if you inflate the economy with currency to the extent that it stands out of proportion with the goods and services produced, prices in general would rise due to a spurt in demand. Inflation so resulting is called ***demand-pull inflation.*** Too much money chasing too few goods and services is the trait of demand-pull inflation. As the saying goes, 'general price level once up, never down'. It is compared to a spiral that springs up and up. This gives the name of ***price spiral*** to persistently rising prices. It happens when production, a time consuming process, fails to keep pace with money supply. The boost in demand so caused prompts producers to hire more factors of production thereby raising factor prices as also production cost. By the time producers are able to produce enough to match the initial level of demand, unit costs increase and so do prices giving rise to what is called the ***cost-push inflation***. Thus, demand-pull inflation leads to cost-push inflation. Likewise, cost-push inflation leads to that, demand-pull. The latter, can be understood from the fact that higher costs crop up due to higher factor payments which boost the disposable income of the factor owners and hence their demand for goods and services. This, in turn, results in raising their prices. That 's how the two get intertwined. We will demonstrate the process diagrammatically in Section 13.3. Here one thing we can safely conclude with, that is, inflation is a persistent rise in general prices of goods and services It should not be confused with ***high prices***.

13.1 DEFINITIONS OF INFLATION

Inflation can't be restricted to a single definition. Economists and institutions have defined it in a number of ways. Some of them are outlined below.

According to the Chambers Twentieth Century Dictionary, inflation is an "undue increase in quantity of money in proportion to its buying power, as on an excessive issue of fiduciary money"

Gardner Ackley[1] has defined inflation as a "persistent and appreciable rise in the general level or average of prices". Elaborating it further, Ackley states, " we define inflation as rising prices, not as

[1] Gardner Ackley, *Macroeconomic Theory, 1961, p. 422.*

high prices. In some sense, then inflation is a disequilibrium state , it must be analyzed dynamically rather than with the tools of statics."[1]

According to Crowther[2], "inflation is a state in which the value of money is falling, *i.e.,* prices are rising." According to Pigou[3], inflation exists, "when money income is expanding relatively to the output or work done by the productive agents for which it is the payment"

In sum, inflation is a sustained rise in general level of prices, brought about by the high rate of expansion in aggregate money supply. It is a state of persistently rising prices and not just of high prices.

13.2 THEORIES OF INFLATION

Among the theories of inflation, we take up the prominent ones:

1. Quantity theory of value of money theory,
2. Cost-push and Demand-pull theories, and
3. Monetization of unforeseen expenditures of government theory

Let us take them up in that order.

13.2.1 Quantity Theory of Value of Money Theory

Classical economists attributed the cause of inflation to money supply. According to them, an increase in money supply leads to currency depreciation (a fall in value of currency) while stock of goods and services remains static.

Economist Jean Bodin was the first one to discover the relationship between general price level and quantity of money supplied. The theory passed through several reviews and revisions by writers and economists like Dudley North in 1661, Isaac Gervaise in 1720, Richard Cantillon in 1730, and Jacob Vanderlint in 1734 with varying degrees of correctness and completeness until it acquired the status of an important doctrine. In its earlier versions, a positive relationship between quantity of money supplied and the general level of prices was established to the tune that an increase in the former always led to a rise in the latter. However, the relationship was not one of strict proportionality. Subject to these limitations, it was stated that the general price level is less than equiproportional to the quantity of money, M , or more appropriately, MV. Figure 13.1 portrays the relationship.

The later classical and neo-classical economists stated the relationship between changes in money supply (MV) and changes in general level of prices, P, (Figure 13.2), as also the relationship between changes in money supply (MV) and changes in value of money,1/P, (Figure 13.3) in terms of the rigid proportionality.

The entire exercise, however amounted to a vain attempt as it amounted price -change as a function of change in money supply. This implied that doubling the volume of money in circulation, amounts to reducing its value to half as much and raising the general price level to twice as much.In the same way, restricting the volume of money supply to half as much amounts to raising its value to twice as much and lowering the general price level to half as much. The conclusion was based on the assumption of full employment, given the output.

If classical theory be true then, problem of control of inflation must pose no problem. No government would have to strain as much as they do to control inflation. They can then easily regulate prices by regulating the volume of money supply.

---

[1] Gardner Ackley, *Ibid.*

[2] Geoffrey Crowther, *An outline of Money, Revised Edison, 1948, Reprinted 1958, p. 107.*

[3] A.C. Pigou, *The Veil of Money,* 1949, *p.34.*

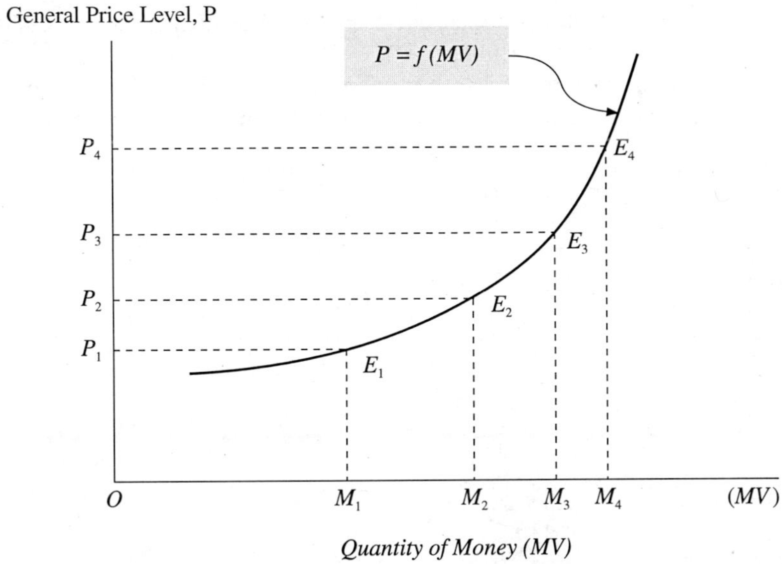

FIGURE 13.1 Non-linear plot of $P = f(MV)$ depicts less than equi-proportional variation between P and MV. Note that M is quantity of money while V is velocity of its circulation However, quantity theorists could not provide appropriate definition of V nor could they attach appropriate units or methodology of its measurement.

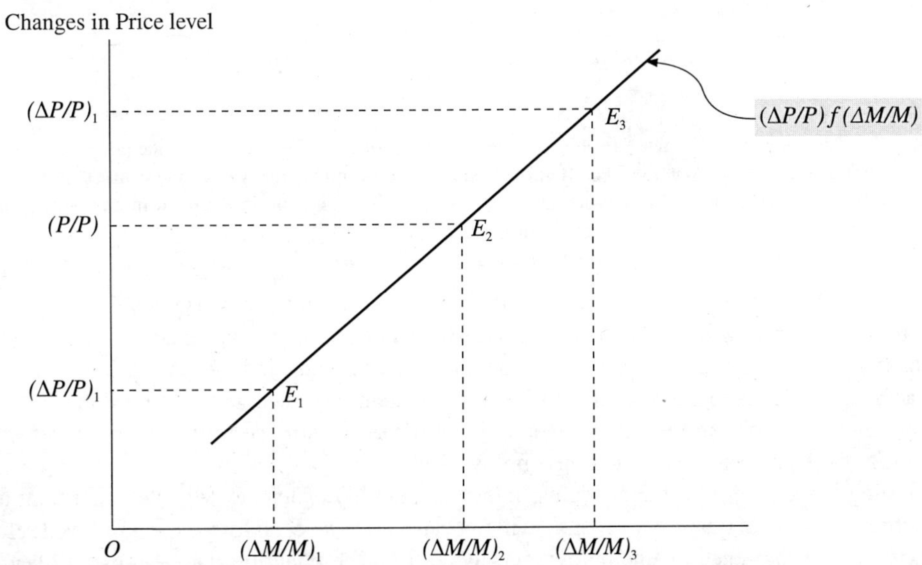

FIGURE 13.2 Change in general price level is being portrayed as a function of changes in money supply. The relationship is linear, indicating direct variation. It also reflects that changes in money supply can regulate changes in price level. Reader must be wondering why then governments can't control inflation by controlling money supply? Had it been possible, governments would not have allowed inflation to persist.

Later several forms of quantity equations were suggested. The two most familiar ones were:

1. Cash Transactions Equation of Exchange or Fisher's Equation of the form, $MV = PT$, where T stands for volume of transactions
2. Cash Balances Equation of Exchange of the form s, $M = kPT$, $M = kPO$ *or* $M = kY$. Here, k is constant of proportionality, T and O stand for output transacted and output.

American Economist Irving Fisher[1] is credited for the first form while Cambridge Economists[2] such as Alfred Marshall, A.C. Pigou, D.H. Robertson and J.M. Keynes[3], to the second form.

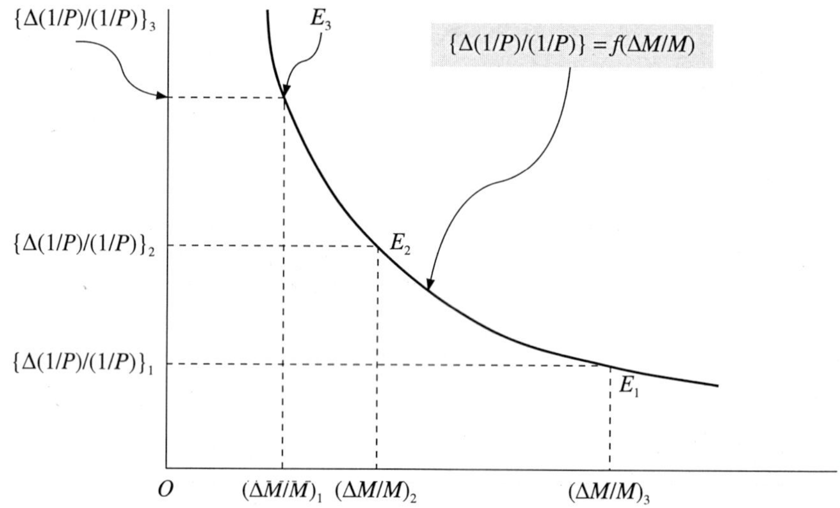

FIGURE 13.3 Value of a unit of currency is defined as the reciprocal of price. To illustrate, let the price of a pen be ₹ 10. Then the value of a rupee is 1/10 of the pen. If money supply be doubled, the value rupee must drop to half as much (to 1/20) and the price would rise twice as high to ₹ 20 a pen. Thus an increase in money supply leads to a decrease in the value of money or an increase in the price level.

However, J.M. Keynes, at a later stage, criticized classical inferences. He developed a reformed quantity theory integrating the theory of prices with the general theory of value and output. He rejected direct causal relationship between increase in the quantity of money and the rise in the level of prices as long as unemployed resources are in existence in the economy. According to him, the effect of an increase in money supply on the rise in general level of prices is made up of two other effects-*one,* effect on the wage unit and *two*, effect on employment.

Assuming homogeneity of factor inputs (interchangeability efficiency-wise) and constant returns in production, increase in quantity of money will not raise price level so long as unemployed resources are in existence. In presence of unemployment, increase in the quantity of money would lead to an equiproportional increase in employment of the unemployed resources.

---

[1] Irving Fisher, *The Purchasing Power of Money,* 1926, p. 24.

[2] J.M. Keynes taught in Cambridge University. Cambridge economist did much to develop the Equation, it is known as Cambridge Equation.

[3] J.M. Keynes, *A treatise on Money,* Volume 1, 1930, pp. 235–236.

At full employment of resources (if possible) an increase in quantity of money may lead to a direct equi-proportional increase in the general level of prices. Even then the first thing to get affected would be the rate of interest, not the price level directly.

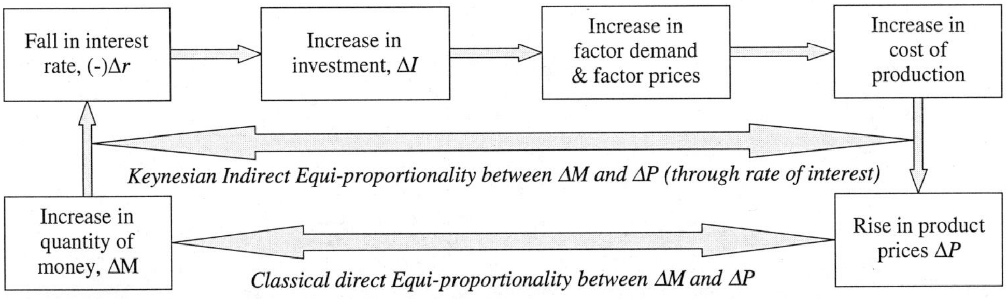

FLOW CHART 13.1 Comparison of proportionality between increase in money supply and rise in general level of prices (Keynesian and Classical Versions): J.M. Keynes rejected the classical direct causal relationship between increase in the quantity of money and rise in the level of prices so long as unemployed resources were in existence in the economy. According to him, increase in quantity of money would affect price level indirectly through the rate of interest. First rate of interest would fall leading to a rise in investment ($I = Ia - hr$). This in turn would boost factor demand and factor prices. As a result, production costs rise and so do product prices.

Note that Keynes denied existence of full employment and held that increase in quantity of money would lead to equi-proportional increase in employment of the unemployed resources while classical economists believed in existence of full employment, in which case, increase in quantity of money, they asserted, would lead to a direct equi-proportional increase in general level of prices.

Note also that even under Keynesian denial of existence of full employment, price level would rise in consequence to increase in quantity of money. This is so due to time-lags between the act of employment of the unemployed resources and the act of supply of goods and services

13.2.2 Cost-Push and Demand-Pull Theories

13.2.2.1 Cost-push inflation

Cost-push factors lead to an upward shift in the aggregate supply (*AS*) curve. Such factors include wage-hikes and profit hikes. Higher wages raise production cost, thereby, shifting the *AS* curve upwards. Similar is the case when higher profit margins are desired by producers. In both the cases, *AS* curve shifts upwards raising the product price up. When price rises due to wage hikes, the resulting inflation is termed as ***wage-push inflation*** and when it rises due to profit hike, it is termed as ***profit push inflation*** The two account for the ***supply side of inflation*** The general name given to the two is ***cost-push inflation.***

There is a third supply side factor , namely, the ***supply shock*** factor. The inflation resulting from it is called the ***supply-shock inflation***. The mechanism of the supply shock inflation is the same as that of wage-push or of the profit push inflations. The *AS* curve is pushed upwards just as it is in case of wage-push or profit push inflations. The point of difference of the supply shock factors from the wage-push or profit push factors is that supply shocks crop up from factors beyond anybody's control. For instance crop failures due to natural calamities affect supply of food grains adversely and lead to inadvertent rise in food grain prices. Another example may be the exercise of market power by external factors. An example is provided by pricing policies of *OPEC* countries. Petroleum products being a world wide necessity, their pricing policies affect world prices with no respite. Supply shock inflation is exogenously created and hence beyond the control of the concerned sufferers. Figure 13.4 demonstrates the mechanism of cost-push inflation as also of the process of its control.

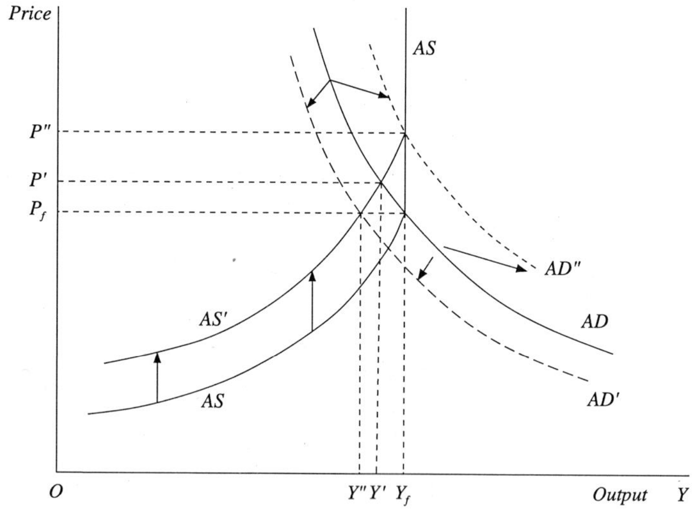

FIGURE 13.4 Cost-push Inflation and its Control: Output Y_f and price P_f are determined at the point where aggregate demand (*AD*) intersects aggregate supply (*AS*) . Now suppose cost-push factors push the aggregate supply (*AS*) curve upwards to *AS*′. In consequence, output falls from Y_f to *Y*′ and price rises from P_f to *P*′. This affects not only the output but also the employment of productive factors . If attempts to restore price be made through contractionary fiscal and monetary measures, price can be restored at the level of *Pf*, by forcing *AD* downwards to *AD*′. This would lower the output even further to *Y*”. Even employment will go further down.

[But if full employment is to be restored, AD must shift upwards to AD”. This would have to be accomplished at a price higher than P′. Clearly, there has to be a trade-off between full employment and price control].

13.2.2.2 Demand-pull inflation

Demand-pull factors include ***real factors*** (Figure 13.5) and ***monetary factors*** **(Figure 13.6).**

(a) **Real factors (Figure 13.5):** Real factors include all those factors that cause a rightward shift in the *IS* curve. Have a look at the Equation of *IS* curve (Equation 8.3, Chapter 8). Such shifts may be caused by an increase in I_a, $\overline{G}$, $\overline{X}$, *R* or by a decrease in T_a or in M_a. The affect of such shifts in the initial set of three *IS* curves from IS_1, IS_2 and IS_3 to IS_1', IS_2' and IS_3' with a set of three *LM* curves corresponding to a given nominal money supply at the three price levels P_1, P_2 and P_3 are employed in Figure 13.5 to obtain the shift in aggregate demand from *AD* to *AD*′. The rise in price that results is from P_1 to P_2.

(b) **Monetary Factors (Figure 13.6):** Monetary factors initiating demand-pull inflation include the decrease in demand for money or increase in its supply. However, it is supply of money that is usually found of an overriding importance. The mechanism of accounting for the demand-pull inflation resembles very much with Figure 13.5. Initial set of *IS* curves (IS_1, IS_2 and IS_3) at prices (P_1, P_2 and P_3) intersect with the initial set of the *LM* curves (LM_1, LM_2 and LM_3) at prices (P_1, P_2 and P_3) to give the *AD* curve The same set of *IS* curves at same set of prices intersects with outwardly shifted *LM* curves (LM_1', LM_2' and LM_3') due to decrease in demand for money or increase in its supply yielding a vertically shifted *AD*′ curve. Inflation so caused is $P_2 - P_1$ (Figure 13.6).

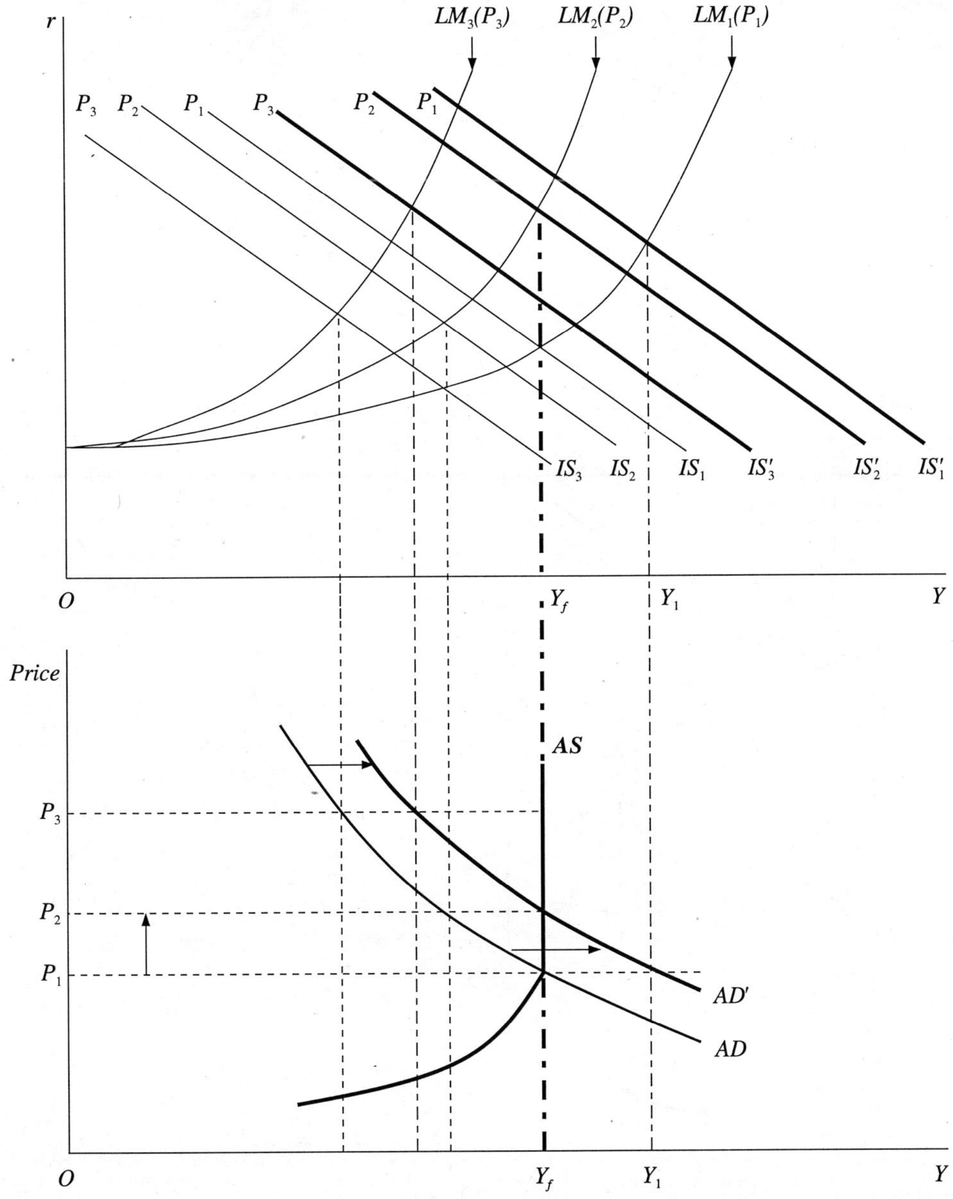

FIGURE 13.5 Demand-Pull Inflation due to Real Factors: Increase in any of the real factors I_a, $\overline{G}$, $\overline{X}$, R or decrease in any of T_a or M_a or simultaneous increase in all the former factors and decrease in all the latter factors shifts the *IS* curves IS_1, IS_2 and IS_3 to IS'_1, IS'_2 and IS'_3 upwards to right. The affect of such shifts with the three *LM* curves corresponding to a given nominal money supply at the three price levels P_1, P_2 and P_3 are employed to obtain the initial *AD* curve as also the shifted one *AD'* in consequence to the shifts in the *IS* curves. The rise in price that results from P_1 is P_2.

Intersection of Is_1, Is_2 and Is_3 With Lm_1, Lm_2 and Lm_3 *Gives Ad* Curve and that of IS'_1, IS'_2 and IS'_3 with them Gives *Ad'* Curve.

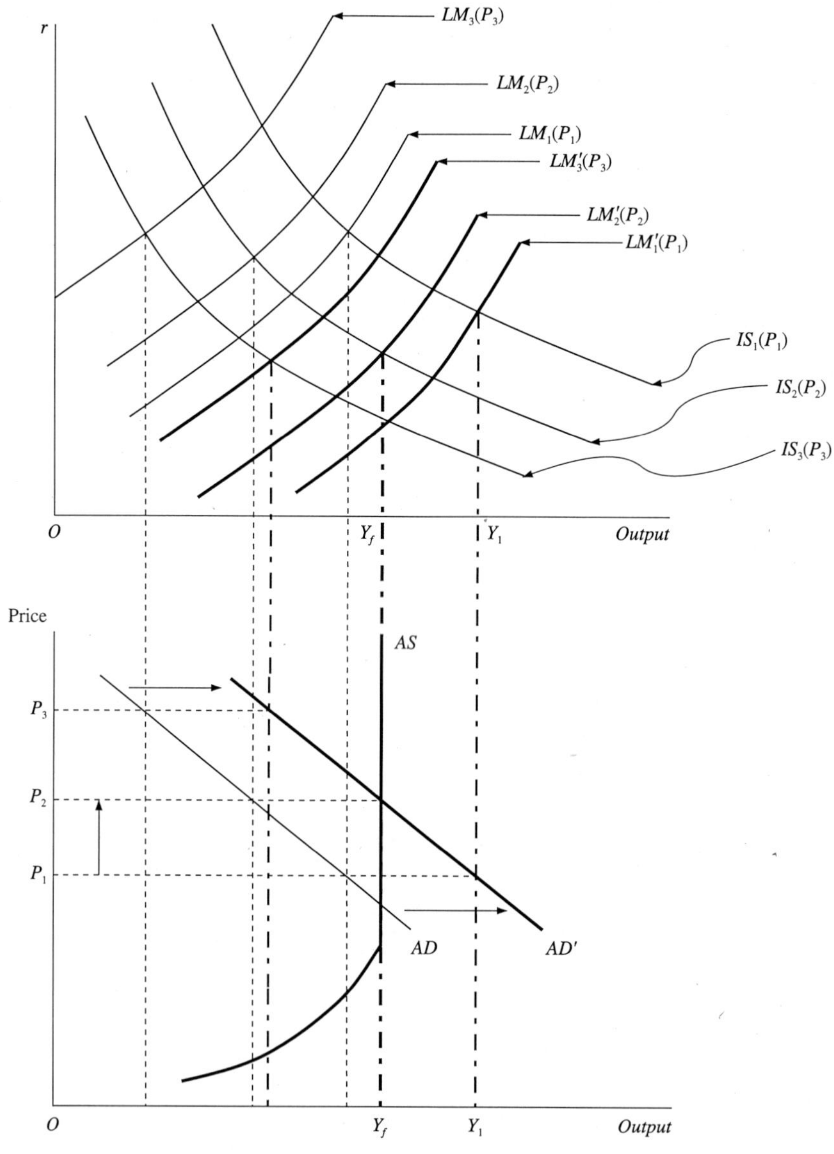

FIGURE 13.6 Demand-Pull Inflation due to Monetary Factors: Initial set of *IS* curves (IS_1, IS_2 and IS_3) at prices (P_1, P_2 and P_3) intersects with the initial set of the *LM* curves (LM_1, LM_2 and LM_3) at prices (P_1, P_2 and P_3) to give the *AD* curve. The same set of *IS* curves at same set of prices intersects with outwardly shifted *LM* curves (LM'_1, LM'_2 and LM'_3) due to decrease in demand for money or increase in supply of it and yields *AD'* curve which is a vertically shifted one. Inflation so caused is $P_2 - P_1$.

Unlimited expansion of money supply will imply unlimited rise in price-level.

Economists are in agreement on this count but in high disagreement over the real factors initiating and sustaining persistent rise in prices. Some of the economists agree with Milton Friedman[1] in his assertion that 'inflation is always everywhere as a monetary phenomenon'. Others will agree with J.R. Hicks[2] who assigns only a supporting role to money in this regard.

Monetary factors include decreasing demand for money or, more importantly, increasing supply of money. The latter shifts the *LM* curves downward to right as shown in Figure 13.6.

13.2.2.3 Demand-pull and cost-push—do they feed each other (Figure 13.7)?

We have discussed the two in complete isolation to each other. The discussions so far sounded dichotomous The question is-are they really unrelated or mutually intertwined ? Do they feed each other? We will seek answers to these questions in this section. The dichotomy that inflation is either demand-pull or cost-push , not both, is subjected to debate by many economists. They argue that inflation contains some elements of cost-push and some of demand-pull.

In many cases, excess demand may give rise to demand-pull inflation even when no cost-push factors are at work. In the same way, wage-push and profit push factors lead to cost-push inflation even when no demand-pull factors are in operation.

There are cases in which cost-push leads to demand-pull and demand-pull to cost-push. In other words, they feed each other. The figure below demonstrates the point (Figure 13.7).

Economists who subscribe to the dichotomy between demand-pull and cost-push inflations think that employment can't be increased at full employment and therefore despite producers' temptation of helping themselves to profits, they can do nothing in this regard. Thais is not wholly true. They can pay overtime wages to their workers for producing more. This would raise the cost of additional output. This explains how demand-pull leads to cost-push . In the same way higher costs (caused by wage push or profit push factors) generate more income for workers as well as for producers to boost demand for goods and services. That explains how demand-pull inflation leads to cost-push inflation.

13.2.2.4 Deficit financing, unforeseen expenditures on calamities & wars etc.

There are yet other potential sources of inflation. Budgetary deficits are usually monetized. This contributes to monetary as well as real factors of demand-pull inflation. Commodity taxes like goods and services taxes (*GST*) raise price level significantly.

War finance is yet another potential source of inflation. Salaries and wages of the armed personnel get hiked and domestic resources get diverted to war front. The latter causes scarcity of goods and services at the domestic world.

Natural and man-made calamities call for relief work which cost government a sizable part of their revenue. Quite ften, government final consumption expenditures go up inadvertently. This contributes further to inflation.

Developmental needs of the developing nations force them to print additional currency due to non availability of aid or public borrowing. This adds yet another plank in government spending. All these factors contribute to the rise in the general price level, at times, through cost-push factors, at others through demand-pull factors. Inflation in such developing nations turns out to be a necessary evil.

---

[1] Milton Friedman, The counter *Revolution in Monetary Theory*, Occasional Paper No. 33, Institute of Economic Affairs, London, 1970, p. 24.

[2] J.R. Hicks, "The Permissive Economy" in crisis '75..? Occasional Paper Special No. 43, Institute of Economic Affairs, London, 1975, p. 17.

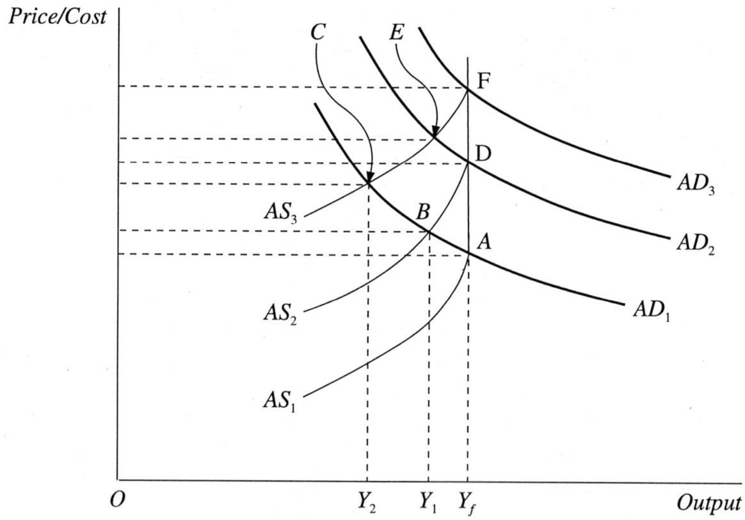

FIGURE 13.7 Demand-pull feeds cost-push and cost-push , demand-pull : Consider point *A* at which AD_1 intersects AS_1. Output is full employment output, Y_f. Now let higher wages and profits push the cost so that aggregate supply shifts upwards to AS_2. The new equilibrium *is* reached at point *B* which corresponds to output Y_1, which is less than the full employment output Y_f and to a price higher than that at point *A*. Higher wages and profits increase households' incomre which in turn increases their demand for goods and servicess. As a result agrregate demand curve shifts to AD_2 and equilibrium to point *D*. At this point, output is full employment output and price, much higher than that at points *A* or at point *B*. Firms see their chance of even higher profits. They decide to boost output but there are no more workers available for employment. What firms can still do is to prompt their workers for overtime work. This gives workers a chance to earn higher than normal wages. Additional work at additional wages increases costs due to which aggregate supply shifts further up to the position AS_3. Increase in costs leads to highes disposable incomes with the households' sector which in turn boosts aggregate demand to the position AD_3. Equilibrium shifts to point *F* and price *to* even higher level. Everytime costs increase so does the disposable income of the consumers as also their demand for higher level of consumption. This shows that cost-push inflation leads to demand-pull inflation.

To show how demand-pull inflation leads to cost-push inflation, suppose demand increases from AD_1 to AD_2. Equilibrium and price shift from point *A* to point *D* implying higher profit margins for there producers. Tempted so producers decide in favour of overtime work to produce more at full employment. This implies higher costs. AS_1 shifts to AS_2, Thus demand-pull inflation results in cost-push inflation. The process is an ongoing one making cost-push and demand-pull inflations intertwined.

13.3 INFLATION: TERMINOLOGIES

We have already had a fair idea of ***cost-push inflation*** caused by ***wage push, profit push and supply shock factors*** as also of ***demand-pull inflation*** caused by ***expansionary monetary and real factors.***

On the basis of the rate at which prices rise per year, inflation is termed as ***creeping inflation***, ***walking inflation, running inflation*** and **galloping inflation**. Galloping inflation is also termed as ***hyperinflation*** while running inflation, as ***trotting inflation.***

Creeping inflation refers to a sustained rise of about 2% per annum in the general price level. As against it, ***hyperinflation*** refers to a rise of over 50% per month in the general price level. Walking and running inflations refer to the situations of milder price-rise, the former referring to a price rise of 8–10% per annum while the latter, the running inflation, to that of higher percent points (two digits) per annum.

Figure 13.8 depicts the rate based terminology diagrammatically.

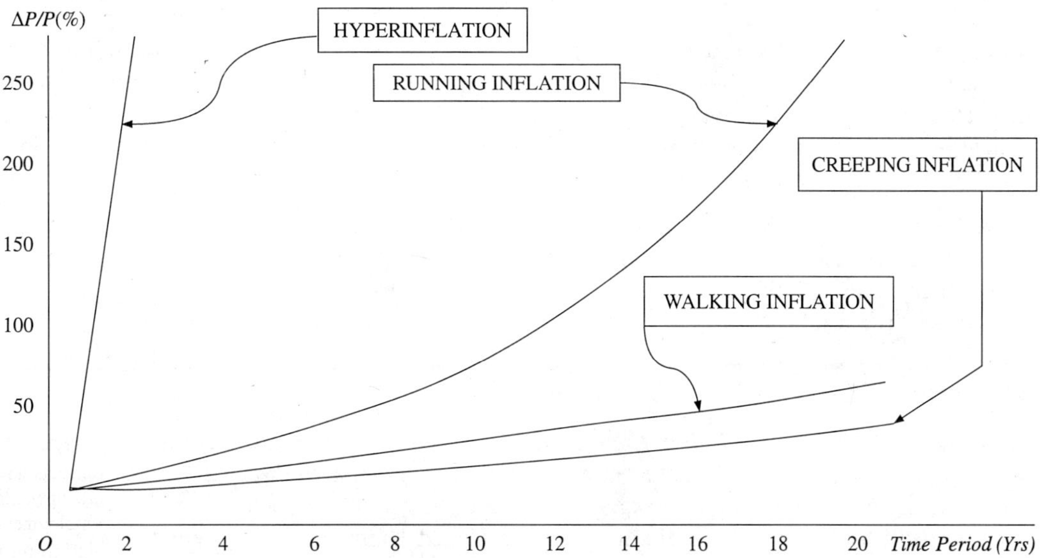

FIGURE 13.8 Terminology of Inflation on the Basis of Rate of Rise in the General Price **Level.**

Apart from the rate based terms used for inflation, there are quite a few other terms characterizing different situations of cause and effects . Let us introduce them now:

(1) Open and Suppressed Inflation: Inflation in an economy may be open or suppressed. It is said to be open when government takes no measures to control it or is completely unconcerned with its speed. According to Milton Friedman, ***open inflation*** is an "inflationary process in which prices are permitted to rise without being suppressed by government price control or similar techniques " Post war inflation is usually an open inflation in most of the war shattered countries.

Suppressed or repressed inflation refers to the conditions of effective price control and rationing of essential commodities and grant of subsidies to suppress the menace . To be noted is the point that prices so controlled spring up as if in vengeance the moment such measures of control are relaxed. Note also that the measures adopted to suppress inflation cost the government dearly which makes the government run out of steam sooner than it thinks.

(2) International Inflation: Imports from a country suffering from inflation bring in inflation all along to the importer. That way, the importer is said to be importing inflation along with the merchandise. Inflation from one country spreads to all its trading partners and is often referred to as ***international inflation***.

(3) Stagflation: The term is derived from the combination of two terms. The first one is *stagnant* and the second, evidently, *inflation* . It refers to a state of sustained hyperinflation to which government has openly surrendered. The economy is marked for low economic growth, hyperinflation and high unemployment Deflation can serve as a remedy to the problem of inflation , not to that of ***stagflation.***

It is so because slow economic growth and high unemployment that exist in such economies force them to heavy monetization. Stagflation was a relatively a common occurrence in late 1970s and 1980s. Even US was inflicted with stagflation in 1970s. The reasons in main were monetization of budgetary deficits related to social spending and Vietnam war.

(4) Ratchet Inflation: ***Ratchet inflation*** refers to that state of inflation in which overall inflation in the economy remains unchanged while its certain sectors experience it while certain others don't. Aggregate Demand is so distributed in an economy that it is excessive in certain sectors of it and deficient in others. The ones with excessive demand experience inflation while others deficient in it, do not, yet the overall price level, in general, remains unchanged.

(5) Mark-up Inflation: When a mark up by an appropriate percentage of production cost is added to the production cost with a view to meet some sales targets or to ensure a certain percentage of return desired by share-holders or to allow desired wage hike to workers or profit hike to producers, ***mark-up inflation*** results.

13.4 PHILLIPS CURVE AND INFLATION

In this section, we employ ***Phillips Curve***, ***Modified Phillips Curve*** and ***Inflationary Pressure Curve*** to determine the inflation rate as also to derive the ***long-run Phillips curve.*** The analysis of the relationship between the rate of wage increase and the rate of unemployment was first carried out by the British economist A.W. Phillips[1] for the United Kingdom and is therefore named after him as Phillips curve. The relationship, as mentioned , correlates the unemployment rate with the rate of wage hike without commensurate hike in labour productivity[2]. In the event of high rate of unemployment, workers can't ask for or realize a high hike in their wages. The reason is simple. If they do, their threat of agitation can be matched by a counter threat of retrenchment from their employers who have the advantage of availability of the unemployed hands to replace them. When rate of unemployment is low, workers are in an advantageous position as their employers can't replace them due to non availability of the unemployed hands. Employers in this case have to concede desired wage hike to workers under the same condition of working hours and labour productivity.

Thus, the rate of wage hike ($\Delta W/W$) is inversely related to the rate of unemployment, as depicted in Figure 13.9. Phillips Curve focused on the relationship between the unemployment rate and the rate of wage hike with no compulsion on workers to increase their productivity. This raises production cost and hence product price. Such wage hikes, $\Delta W/W$, are therefore inflationary establishing a link between $\Delta W/W$ and rate of inflation, $\Delta P/P$. which is so close that the Phillips Curve can be portrayed in a modified form as in Figure 13.10 and termed as ***modified Phillips Curve***. As pointed out, this is so because the wage hikes are allowed to workers without any compulsion of commensurate hike in labour productivity.

---

[1] A.W. Phillips,"The relationship between Unemployment and the Rate of Change of Money Wages in United Kingdom,1861–1957," Economica, Nov.1958.

[2] Dornbusch, Fisher and Startz in their work "Macroeconomics", McGraw Hill Education (India) Edition. 2015, p.121; portray the relationship as a curvilinear one (Figure 6.2) but describes it as a linear one (Equation 2) as $g_w = -\varepsilon(u - u^*)$, where $g_w \equiv$ growth of nominal wages, $u \equiv$ rate of actual unemployment, $\varepsilon \equiv$ responsiveness and $u^* \equiv$ rate of natural unemployment. (*Note that the additively inverse relationship seems an over simplification of the multiplicatively inverse relationship. Note also that u^*, the natural rate of unemployment, is the actual rate of unemployment, u, at which $g_w = 0$ or wage inflation is zero, a situation of equality of actual inflation to the expected inflation.*

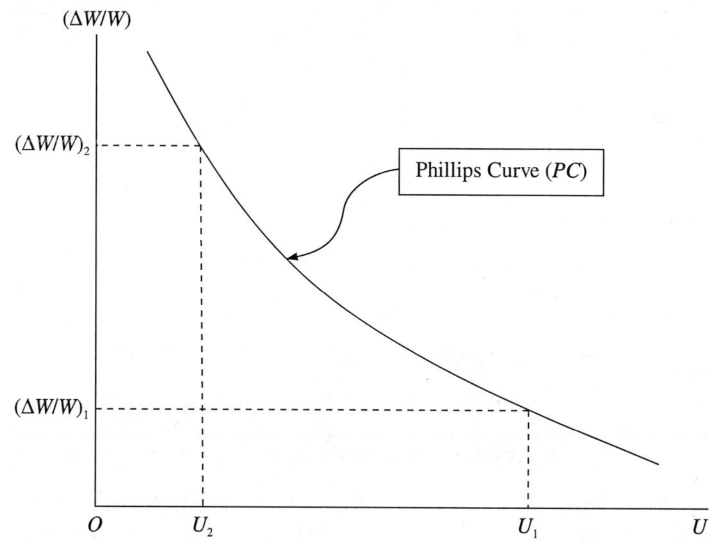

FIGURE 13.9 Phillips Curve Depicting the Inverse Variation Between the Rate of Unemployment (*U*) and the rate of wage hike ($\Delta W/W$).

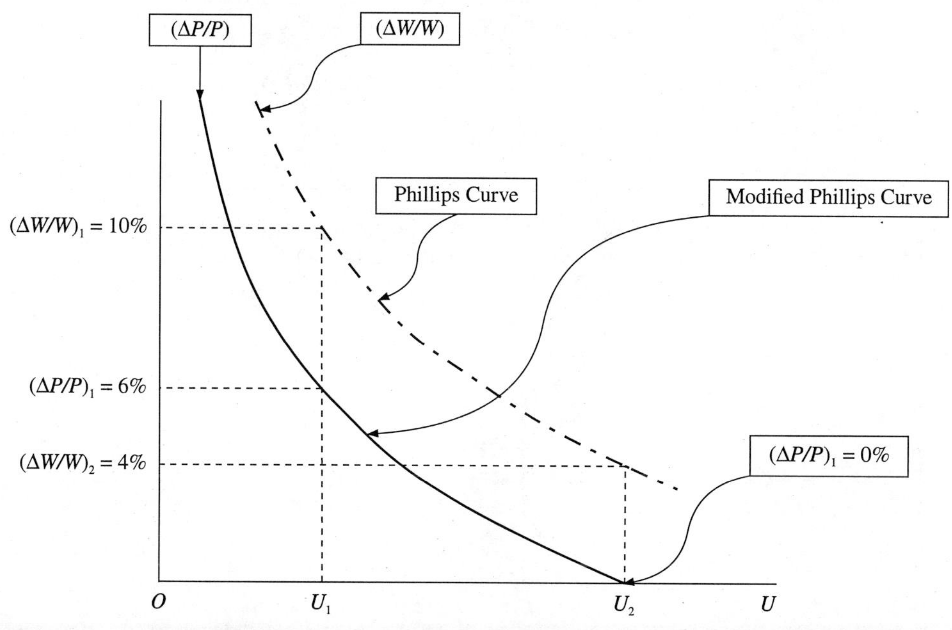

FIGURE 13.10 *Modified Phillips Curve:* Upper curve is Phillips Curve portraying ($\Delta W/W$) as a function of *U* while the lower curve is modified Phillips curve portraying ($\Delta P/P$) as a function of *U*. To demonstrate, suppose labour productivity is 4% per year. If U_2 =10%, rate of increase in wage rate is also 4%, rate of inflation ($\Delta P/P$) is zero percent . Note that wage hike is matched by labour productivity. No rise in cost means no change in price. If unemployment rate is U_1 = 7%, and rate of wage hike ($\Delta W/W$), 10%, labour productivity remaining unchanged, the increase in the price level would be, $(\Delta P/P)_1$ = 6%.

Inflationary Pressure curve (IPC) relates unemployment rate to the rate of inflation but in a different way. It is based on inverse variation of real output with the price, which is quite different from the modified Phillips curve The modified Phillips curve relates inflation rate caused by wage hikes of labour without commensurate increase in their productivity while inflationary pressure curve, on the other hand, relates inflation rate to growth of real output and hence to the rate of unemployment. Let the real output be Y, nominal income X, and price P. Then real output Y can be given as

$$Y = X/P \tag{13.1}$$

Logarithmic transformation of Equation 13.1 gives

$$\text{Log } Y = \text{Log } X - \text{Log } P \tag{13.2}$$

Differentiating Equation 13.2 with respect to t, the time period, we have

$$(1/Y)\,(dY/dt) = (1/X)\,(dX/dt) - (1/P)\,(dP/dt)$$

$\Rightarrow$ $dY/Y = dX/X - dP/P$ [Treating time period dt as one year]

$\Rightarrow$ Growth of real output = growth of nominal income – growth of price level (13.3)

In other words, rise in inflation rate ($\Delta P/P$) varies inversely with the growth of real output (dY/Y) and hence directly with the rate of unemployment. That is, a decrease in rate of unemployment (U) is associated with a decrease in the inflation rate ($\Delta P/P$) and an increase in it, with an increase in the inflation rate. Thus, inflationary pressure curve is a positively sloped curve between rate of inflation and rate of unemployment as portrayed in Figure 13.11.

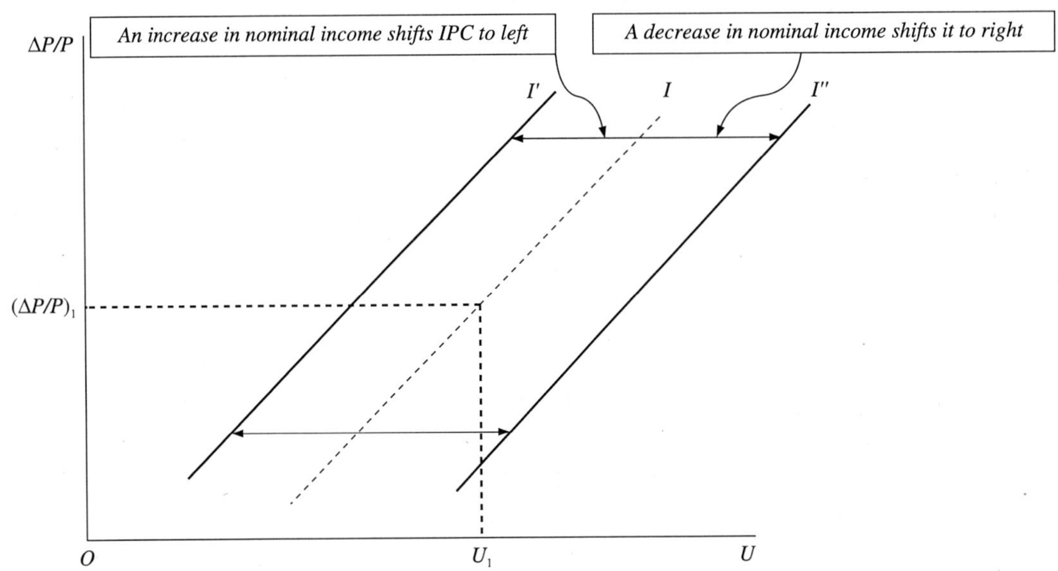

FIGURE 13.11 Inflationary Pressure Curve: As explained above, the curve has a fixed positive slope of approximately 2.5, implying direct variation of inflation rate ($\Delta P/P$) with the rate of Unemployment (U). Its position depends on the shift in it caused by changes in the growth rate of nominal income, an increase in which shifts the curve to left and a decrease, to right, as shown.

Determination of Inflation Rate and Changes in it

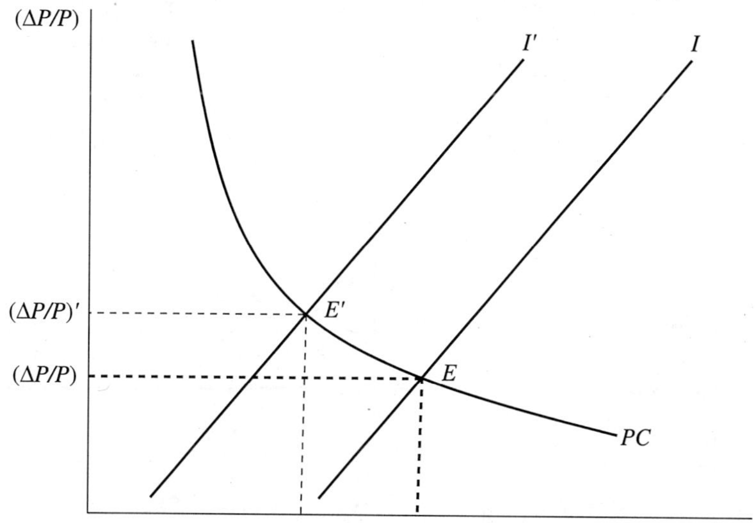

FIGURE 13.12 Inflationary Pressure curve, *I*, is drawn on the assumption that the rate of unemployment is *U* and nominal money supply, *X*. It intersects the modified Phillips curve at *E*. The corresponding rate of inflation is ($\Delta P/P$). Now let the nominal money supply increase to X' ($X' > X$). The *IPC* shifts to I'. It intersects the *PC* at E' giving the rate of inflation as $(\Delta P/P)'$ and the rate of unemployment as U'.

The inflationary pressure curve thus has a positive slope which according to Economist A.M. Okun, is approximately, 2.5 implying a 1% change unemployment rate leads to 2.5% change in total output of the economy relative to its potential output and approximately 2.5 % change in the rate of inflation. The observation is named after the economist as ***Okun's Law***[1]. The law has been quite sturdy for *US* economy but it lacks the precision-associated with laws of economics.

Slope of the curve is unchanged but its position can change due a shift caused in it by a change in the growth rate of the nominal income ($\Delta X/X$), an increase in it shifts the curve to left and a decrease, to right. In short-run, unemployment and output are also closely linked. According to Okun's law, 1 extra percent point of unemployment would cost the economy 2.5% of *GNP*[2].

---

[1] A.M.Okun, *Potential GNP, Its Measurement and Significance in 1962 Proceedings of the Business and Economic Statistics Section of the American Statistical Association,* reprinted in W.L. Smith and R.L. Teigen, eds, *Readings in Money, National Income, and Stabilization Policy,* 3rd ed. Richard D. Irwin, 1974, pp.285–92.

[2] Dornbusch, Fischer and Startz, define natural rate of unemployment through the Equation, $\pi = \pi_e = -\varepsilon (u - u^*)$, which they call 'as the modern version of Phillips curve' or 'inflation-expectations-augmented Phillips curve'. Here, $\pi \equiv (\Delta P/P)$, $\pi_e \equiv (\Delta P/P)_e$, $\varepsilon \equiv$ constant of proportionality, $u \equiv U$ and $u^* \equiv U_n$, the natural rate of unemployment. The authors deduce that $u = u^*$ when $\pi = \pi_e$. Thus, natural rate of unemployment is the rate of unemployment at which actual rate of inflation is equal to the expected rate of inflation.

The authors began with the relationship, $(\Delta W/W) = \varepsilon (u - u^*), = g_w$, where $g_w \equiv$ wage inflation or rate of change of wages. From this inverse relationship, they proceed to the relationship $(\pi - \pi_e) = -\varepsilon (u - u^*)$, and to the definition of the natural rate of inflation as that rate of unemployment at which $\pi = \pi_e$.

From here they derive Okun's law as $dY/Y = -\omega (u - u^*)$ to state that growth of GDP $(dY/Y) = -\omega$ at natural rate of unemployment, leaving so many gaps and oversimplifications unexplained. The conclusion reached by them is $\omega = -2$ percent points for 1 percent point increase in $(u - u^*)$.

Long-run Phillips Curve and Natural Rate of Unemployment

Long-run Phillips Curve is no longer downward sloping. Instead, it is vertical at the rate of unemployment, called the ***natural rate of unemployment***. Figure 13.13 demonstrates the point. Let us first define the natural rate of unemployment. It is that rate of unemployment below which the inflation rate tends to rise and above which it tends to fall (See the shape of *PC*). In the figure, natural rate of unemployment is U_n. At this rate there is no tendency for inflation to accelerate or to decelerate and the actual rate of inflation can be treated to be equal to the expected rate of inflation.

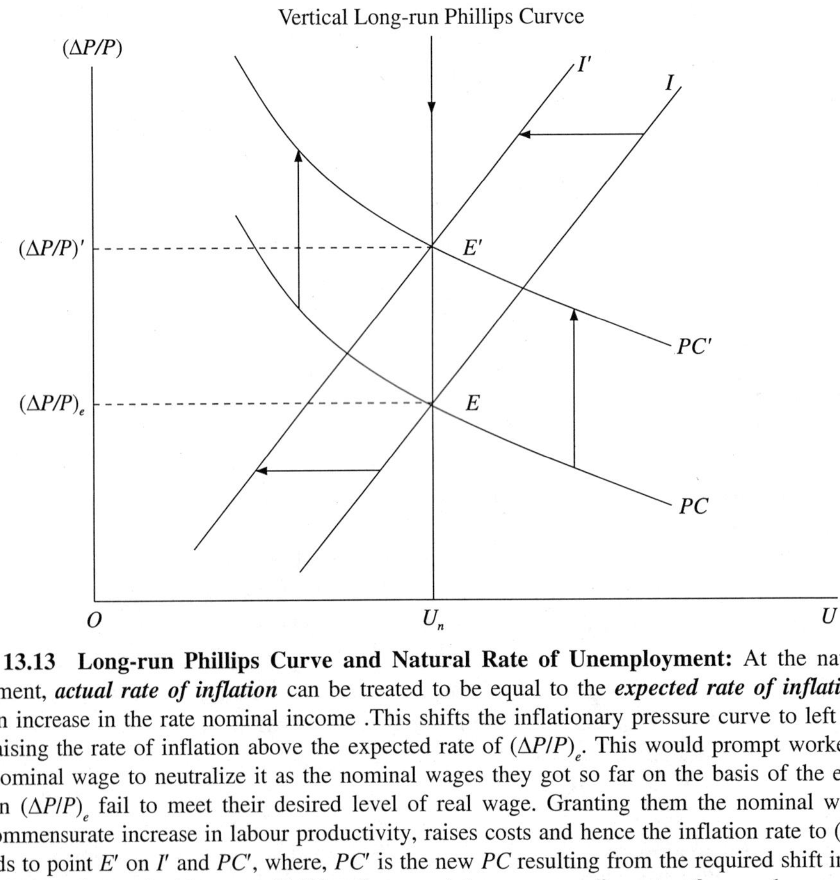

FIGURE 13.13 Long-run Phillips Curve and Natural Rate of Unemployment: At the natural rate of unemployment, ***actual rate of inflation*** can be treated to be equal to the ***expected rate of inflation***. Now let there be an increase in the rate nominal income .This shifts the inflationary pressure curve to left from *I* to *I*′, thereby, raising the rate of inflation above the expected rate of $(\Delta P/P)_e$. This would prompt workers to ensure a higher nominal wage to neutralize it as the nominal wages they got so far on the basis of the expected rate of inflation $(\Delta P/P)_e$ fail to meet their desired level of real wage. Granting them the nominal wage increase without commensurate increase in labour productivity, raises costs and hence the inflation rate to $(\Delta P/P)'$. This corresponds to point *E*′ on *I*′ and *PC*′, where, *PC*′ is the new *PC* resulting from the required shift in it. The join of *E* and *E*′ gives the vertical long-run Phillips Curve and the corresponding rate of unemployment, U_n , is the *natural rate of unemployment*.

Now suppose there is an increase in the rate of nominal income. As a result, inflationary pressure curve shifts to left from *I* to *I*′ thereby raising the rate of inflation above the expected rate of $(\Delta P/P)_e$. This would prompt workers to ensure a higher nominal wage rate to neutralize it because nominal wages they got on the basis of $(\Delta P/P)_e$ fail to meet their desired level of real wages. Granting them the nominal wage increase without commensurate increase in labour productivity, raises costs and hence price-level to $(\Delta P/P)'$ which corresponds to point *E*′ on *I*′. This causes an upward shift in the

PC to *PC′*. New equilibrium is reached at *E′* exactly above *E*. The join of *EE′* is the ***vertical long-run Phillips Curve*** and the corresponding rate of unemployment, U_n, is the ***natural rate of unemployment***.

13.5 MEASURES OF INFLATION

We take up the following four measures of inflation:

(i) **The Consumer Price Index (CPI):** This index is designed to reflect changes in prices of a *market basket.* The basket comprises a variety of goods and services purchased by urban consumers. The basic data are collected from stores and reporters. A single index is calculated for all goods and services in the basket as also separate indices for a group of items like food, housing, apparel, transportation, etc.

Each item in the *market basket* is assigned a weight according to its importance in consumer's budget. The data collection is done each time constituent items in the basket get changed. It is common knowledge that some items get dropped from the basket and some others added to it with passage of time either because of changes in consumers' tastes and preferences or because of changes in their prices. These changes of items in the basket or in their prices differ from country to country. Items included and the weights assigned to each reflect the spending pattern of the consumers during the period in between the surveys.

The price index suited for the purpose is the Laspeyre's price index given by

$$P_{01}^{La} = \frac{\Sigma\, p_1 q_0}{\Sigma\, p_0 q_0} \times 100 \tag{13.4}$$

Here, subscript '0' is used for the base year or the year of the last estimates while subscript '1' is used for the estimates in current state of change or year. $\Sigma p_1 q_0$ represents expenditure on base year's quantity q_0 at current year's price p_1 while $\Sigma p_0 q_0$ represents base year's expenditure on base year's quantity q_0 at base year's price p_0.

To demonstrate suppose *PLa* for the year 2011 averages 276.6 (Base year 2001 = 100) which implies that 2011 cost of the basket is 276.6% of the cost in 2001 and that for 2007 that averages at 256.4, implies that 2007 cost of the basket is 256.4% of the cost in 2001 (base year 2001 = 100). This implies that the cost of consumption basket in 2001 was 100, that in 2007 was 256.4% of it and the cost of the consumption basket in 2011 is 276.6% of it. In other words, the cost of the consumption basket increased by 156.4 during 6 years (2001–2007and by 176.6 during 10 years (2001 – 2011). The percent increase in the cost over 2007-2011 (4 years) works out at 20.2% at an average increase per year of 5.05%.

(ii) **The Producer Price Index (PPI):** ***Producer price index***, also called wholesale price index at times, resembles consumer price index(*CPI*) in its construction. It measures money value of a basket of products at the level of prices that existed at their first commercial transaction. Note that the basket here doesn't include services and that the product prices are prices at the first commercial transaction which need not be same as the wholesale prices. The name, wholesale price index was thus a misnomer of the producer price index because the prices involved in it are not the prices applicable to the wholesalers.

Interpretation of *PPI* and determination of inflation rate are similar to those for *CPI.* To demonstrate suppose *PPI* for the year 2011 averages at 276.6 (Base year 2001 = 100) which implies that 2011 value of the product-basket is 276.6% of its value in 2001 on an average and that for the year 2007 averages at 256.4, which implies that 2007 value is 256.4 % of its value in 2001 (base year 2001 = 100). This indicates that the value of product-basket in 2001 was 100, that in 2007 was 256.4% of it and the value of the product-basket in 2011 is 276.6% of it. In other words, the value of the product basket increased by 156.4 during 6 years (2001-2007and by 176.6 during 10 years (2001–2011). The percent increase in the value over 2007-2011 (4 years) works out at 20.2% at an average increase per year of 5.05%.

(iii) **The GNP Implicit Price Deflator:** A byproduct of deflation process is a price index called ***GNP implicit price deflator***. The term implicit implies that it is not obtained directly like *CPI* or *PPI* but is calculated by dividing Current rupee *GNP* by constant rupee *GNP*. For its meaning, calculation and interpretation of the *GNP* implicit price deflator as also to calculate the rate of inflation , see Section 2.4 (Chapter 2, Boxes 2.33 and 2.34) of this book and the illustration that follows them there (pp. 34–37)[1].

GNP implicit price deflator is thus the ratio of Current Year's GNP at current prices / current year's *GNP* at constant prices multiplied by 100

(iv) **The PCE Implicit Price Deflator:** The ***personal consumption expenditure (PCE) implicit price deflator*** is an index of price change for all the goods and services included in personal consumption expenditure. Recall that *PCE* is a component of *GNP,* that is, C_h. The other components are Government Final Consumption Expenditure (C_g), Gross Domestic Capital Formation (GDCF)and Net Investment Abroad . *PCE* or C_h is just one of the four (See Table 2.3, p. 49 and Account no. 1, page 54) of Chapter 2[2].

The procedure for *PCE* implicit price deflator is the same as that of *GNP* implicit price deflator. It is given as the ratio of *PCE* of the year at current prices/*PCE* of the same year at constant prices multiplied by 100.

13.6 EFFECTS OF INFLATION

Effects of inflation can viewed as:

1. Non-economic effects, and
2. Economic Effects

13.6.1 Non-Economic Effects of Inflation

Such effects cluster around socio-political effects of inflation. Among political effects, the worst ones focus on toppling of governments if inflation goes on unabated to pinch people's pocket severely. When inflation widens the gap between the rich and poor or when life becomes difficult to live for the common people, government is usually held responsible for it. People vote the government out of power in the election.

Even social effects are as bad as the political ones if inflation divides the society into groups of haves and havenots or masters and slaves. This boosts crime rate which is given a steep rise by the have-nots who resort to criminal activities such as robbing, way-laying, dacoities etc. Social miseries convert into social anguish which ultimately affects the survival of the government.

13.6.2 Economic Effects of Inflation

As pointed out above, socio-political effects of inflation are off-shoots of economic effects. Let us outline them below for a detailed insight

[1] *Chauhan, S.P.S "Macroeconomics..." Ibid.*

[2] *Ibid.*

(a) Effect of inflation on distribution of income and wealth
(b) Effect of inflation on output and employment
(c) Effect of inflation on economic growth
(d) Effect of inflation on economic development

13.6.2.1 Effect of inflation on distribution of income and wealth

Income as we know from what we have learnt so far is income in its narrow sense. It includes salaries, wages, interests, dividends, rents, royalties and earnings of the self-employed. From the view point of the ***effects of inflation on distribution of income***, we include government transfer payments, unemployment compensations, private and government pensions also in the aforesaid. Taken together, they define ***income in the narrow sense*** which has a specified period of time for its reference. This definition of income is used by U.S. Census Bureau in its income distribution data.

The ***broader definition of income*** includes not only the above but also changes therein during the time period in a households ***net worth***. Such changes reflect changes in a household's assets and liabilities over the said period.

In its narrow sense, income distribution is affected by inflation to the extent that it alters the way in which flow of the total income is distributed in the income class. If this remains unchanged, inflation is said not to affect the distribution of income. For example, suppose there are three individuals in a community with nominal incomes of 10000, 20000 and 30000. Suppose further that prices get doubled and so do the nominal incomes of the three. Whatever be the real income levels before doubling of prices they remain unchanged after it. Under the narrow definition, inflation thus causes no change in the distribution of income.

Now suppose nominal incomes of the three change to 18,000; 38,000 and 33,000 instead of changing to twice as much. Doubling of the prices does not result in doubling of the real incomes.. Evidently, inflation has affected the distribution of income adversely .

As regards the implications of the broader definition of income which relates to changes over time in the net worth of the individual, given the real balances with them during the same period, we have to consider the change in the difference of assets over liabilities (Net worth = Assets – Liabilities) in post inflation period. Assets refer to fixed value assets as well as variable value assets. The same is the case with liabilities that are of fixed value or of variable value. The fixed value assets and liabilities don't change even after nominal income and price level are both doubled. But, variable value assets and liabilities do change in value. The negative or positive balance of the change in net worth gives the effect of inflation as far as the broader concept of income is concerned. If the net worth is negative the effect of inflation is bad and if it is positive, the effect of inflation is good. To elaborate, let an individual possess a fixed value asset of 10,000 and variable value asset of 8000. Likewise let his fixed value liability be worth 12000 and variable value liability be worth 6000. The net worth before inflation is zero [(10000 + 8000) – (12000 + 6000)]. In the post inflation period fixed value assets and liabilities remain unchanged while variable value assets and liabilities drop to half as much in real terms due to doubling of prices. The net worth after 100% inflation therefore is (–)1000[(10,000 + 4000) – (12000 + 3000) as inflation reduces the value of variable assets and liabilities to half as much while that of the fixed value assets and liabilities remains unchanged.

13.6.2.2 Effect of inflation on output and employment

If an economy is below full employment (producing less than its potential) and inflation is an anticipated one, employment of workers will increase pushing the economy closer to its potential output. As soon as full employment is reached no workers are available (?) in short-run under anticipated inflation of creeping or crawling type but if the gap between *AD* and *AS* (*IG or AD-AS*) is wide enough (See Figure 6.6, Ch. 6) the creeping inflation gets converted into walking inflation followed by running inflation. If it is unanticipated, employment of workers will not increase in any manner but if it is anticipated, over employment of workers gets initiated. This type of unemployment is usually a feature of underdeveloped or developing economies. Producers tempted by higher profit margins resulting from higher prices would tend to produce more even if it costs them overtime wages to the existing work-force.

This, however, is subject to the cost benefit analysis of producers. If rise in price is not high enough to off-set overtime wage, output produced may not increase due to the disincentivised production through overtime work. On the contrary, if rise in price is high enough and is anticipated to continue like that, overtime work is a certainty in developing underdeveloped economies and over employment through overtime wages turns profitable to all concerned.

In long-run if prices continue to sour over employment continues to survive as long as cost is less than price, if not, cost saving techniques and technologies provide the only solution unless cheaper imports are resorted to or foreign direct investment (*FDI*) be attracted . Even government may decide to step into production or grant subsidies to the producers.

13.6.2.3 Effect of inflation on economic growth

Economic growth refers to year-end increase in output expressed as a percentage of output in the beginning of the year. It is expressed as $[(\Delta Y/Y) \times 100]$. Such growth requires more productive factors if they exist or higher efficiency of production or optimizing resource allocations. In the event of running or hyperinflation, the need for full and efficient utilization of productive factors apart from diversion of resources to more productive sectors of the economy is called for. Resources must be allocated to such production in which capital output ratio (K/Y) and incremental capital output ratio must both be lower. Normally, a high rate of inflation promotes a high growth rate no matter how is it realized. Import of superior technology, adapting workers to work with it, and attracting foreign direct investment are all essential for underdeveloped developing economies.

A high growth rate is essential because it generates surpluses that can be deployed for economic development.

13.6.2.4 Effect of inflation on economic development

Development refers to improvements in physical quality of human life in which there is no poverty, no epidemics no superstitious beliefs, no hunger, no servitude, low infant mortality, low illiteracy and high status of women. Better and adequate medical facilities, better and adequate educational institutions, nutritional food, better housing, are all very essential for this.. They all cost dearly. It doesn't matter whether cost of living is low or high so long as it is affordable to people. A high rate of inflation raises cost of living so much so that cost of living turns unaffordable. In the event of hyperinflation, cost of living rises and economic development suffers. A high growth generates surpluses to provide for. In fact, development is qualitative growth of a nation. Economic growth leads to economic development provided it is adequate. That is why they say every growth does not give rise to ***economic development*** but adequate development certainly leads to adequate economic growth. A high quality worker, a high quality planner, a high quality government-bring about high rate of economic growth as also of economic development.

13.7 CONTROL OF INFLATION

Control of inflation has been a big problem for all the economies whether underdeveloped or developed. Classical economists tried to control inflation through monetary measures. They made it look too simple to execute. According to them , reduce the money supply to half as much and cut price-level to half as much. It sounded nothing more than a theory. Those who tried it, didn't get far.

Nevertheless, monetary and fiscal measures are the only measures that can help. The other ones are increasing production of goods and services. Neither one is instrumental nor easy. We can safely conclude that there exist no direct methods for the purpose. However some indirect methods are there. If executed properly they can serve the purpose to an appreciable extent.

More production

Increasing output of goods and services with a view to match their demand at the existing prices is a way out. This would require more of the resources along with more of collaborating factors. They may all lead to raise the production cost and hence raise prices even further. In this regard, efficient and full utilization of the existing factors only can serve. Particular attention be given to cut wastages of all types. Resources must be allocated and reallocated in such a manner that production of essentials gets encouraged. Apart from this, ***grant of unit subsidy*** is a very good measure to check product price on the one hand and to boost output on the other. Another way to increase output is elimination or reduction of ***unit taxes*** (***Goods and Services Tax***)[1]. Both these measures of increasing output are termed as ***reflation***. Techniques and technologies that are more efficient must be employed for large scale production so that unit cost falls to low levels. Moreover, stock of inflation sensitive commodities must be maintained as ***buffer stocks*** either through its procurement and distribution policies under ***public distribution system (PDS)***[2] by government or through import from foreign countries.

Monetary Measures

Money supply, in particular, printing of currency for final consumption should be avoided. Governments often get more such currencies printed from the central bank for their consumption. The demand so risen raises price level. ***Monetizing budgetary deficits*** increases price level. Likewise, grant of ***supplementary income***[3] to the weaker sections also has the same effect. Government must rafrain from such measures if they intend to curtail prices. Instead of supplementary income, government should resort to ***subsidy***[4] on essentials to help the weaker sections to buy them without cash or with less of it.. Many countries have done this and have helped the cause of price control to some extent. ***Food stamp programme of US***[5] provides an example. Besides distribution of subsidised essentials through ***rationing or fair price shops***[6] proves very helpful in this regard. In sum, measure to use as less money as possible is a way out in this case.

Fiscal Measures

Commodity taxes must be kept as low as possible because they form a part of the production cost or output price. ***Unit taxes (Goods and services taxes)*** boost inflation unabatedly. They should be avoided or kept as low as possible. Government should rely more on direct taxes. Such taxes have some inherent advantages for the government in terms of revenue certainty over indirect taxes. Besides, direct taxes make a dent in consumers disposable income and curtail their demand and hence price. Most often governments monetize ***nonproductive expenditures*** which are highly inflationary. This should be avoided. Quite often, governments resort to ***strategic production*** or strategic imports

[1] See Chauhan, S.P.S., Microeconomics-An Advanced Treatise, 3rd Edition, PHI Learning, [Figure 2.42(a) 2.42(d)].
[2] See Chauhan, S.P.S., Microeconomics-An Advanced Treatise , 3rd Edition, PHI Learning, (Figures. 2.40 & 2.41).
[3] See Chauhan, S.P.S., Microeconomics-An Advanced Treatise , 3rd Edition, PHI Learning, (Figure 4.79).
[4] See Chauhan, S.P.S., Microeconomics-An Advanced Treatise , 3rd Edition, PHI Learning, (Figure 4.79).
[5] See Chauhan, S.P.S., Microeconomics-An Advanced Treatise , 3rd Edition, PHI Learning, p. 176.
[6] See Chauhan, S.P.S., Microeconomics-An Advanced Treatise , 3rd Edition, PHI Learning, Figure 4.80, 4.81, 4.82, 4.83.

allocating a sizable part of their revenue. This they do to keep up with the Joneses. The same is the case with ***war finance.***

Such resource if spent on production and distribution of essential goods, directly or indirectly, may keep the prices in check. ***Grant of subsidy*** does wonders in this regard as already pointed out. Inflation has become a necessary evil for all, in particular, for underdeveloped and developing economies.

Unlike the ***Quantity Theory of Money*** that implied direct impact of money supply on price, most other measures are case specific. A judicial mix can be of immense help in abating inflation.

KEY TERMS AND CONCEPTS

Inflation: A state of sustained and persistent price rice. The term owes its origin from the Latin word *inflare* meaning '*blowing into*'. Just as air is blown into a tyre, when too much money is pumped into the economy, general price goes up. The definition seems to be in line with quantity theorists who held that price level depends on quantity of money supplied .When too much money chases too few good , persistent price rise results, according to them.

Demand-Pull Inflation: When supply of goods and services fails to match demand the resulting inflation is termed demand-pull. It is the time lag between increasing demand and static supply that is responsible at the core.

Cost-Push Inflation: When rise in production costs reflects in product prices. This characterizes cost-push inflation.

Cost-Push Inflation Feeds Demand-Pull Inflation: Increase in production costs leads to cost-push inflation. Higher costs result in higher factor incomesleading to higher demand and higher prices if output remains stagnant. Such increase in prices is called demand-pull inflation which is an offshoot of cost-push inflation.

Demand-Pull Inflation Feeds Cost-Push Inflation: Rising demand for goods and services leads to rising demand for productive factorsas also their prices . This increases cost giving rise to cost-push inflation. It is an offshoot of demand-pull inflation.

Quantity Theory of Inflation: Quantity theorists held that increases in money supply raises the general price level. According to them, 'double the money supply and the general price level will get doubled' Their theory became a sizable part of subsequent literature on economics. For instance, rejecting such direct variation of price level with quantity of money, J.M. Keynes held that the variation is not direct. Instead it is indirect, through the rate of interest.

Components of Cost-Push Inflation: Wage push, profit push and supply shock inflations are the three components of cost-push inflation.

Wage Push Inflation: Hike in nominal wages to match the real wage-level of workers without affecting their productivity adds to the costs of production leading to wage push inflation.

Profit Push Inflation: Higher profit margins desired by producers add to the costs and cause cost-push inflation.

Supply Shock Inflation: When supply fails due to factors beyond control (External factors) supply shock inflation results. For example, failure of crops is a supply shock and so is the discriminatory pricing policy of the OPEC countries.

Components of Demand-Pull Inflation: Demand-pull inflation has two components-inflation due to real factors and that due to monetary factors.

Real Factors: Rise in parameters like I_a ,$\overline{G}$, $\overline{X}$, R or fall in those like T_a or in M_a shift the goods market equilibrium (*IS* Curve) upwards to right and affect the price level.

Monetary Factors: A decrease in demand for money or an increase in it causes shifts in the *LM* curve thereby shifting the *AD* curve vertically upwards and affecting the price level.

Deficit Financing (Monetizing the Budgetary Deficit): It makes too much money chasing too few goods. It causes inflation. Same is the effect of war finance.

Creeping Inflation: When price rise is mildest, that is, about 2% per annum, inflation is called creeping inflation.

Walking Inflation and Running Inflation: Milder price rise to the tune of 8% to 10% per annum is called walking inflation while that to the tune of higher two digit percent points per annum, running inflation.

Galloping Inflation (Hyperinflation): When price rise over 50% per month, the unbearable form of inflation is called hyperinflation or galloping inflation.

Open Inflation: When rise in price becomes an open reality with no efforts made to control it, it is called open inflation.

Suppressed Inflation: It refers to the conditions of effective price control through rationing of essential commodities and grant of subsidies to suppress inflation.

International Inflation: Inflation that spreads from inflicted nation's exports to the importing nations is categorized as international inflation.

Stagflation: It refers to a state of sustained running or hyperinflation to which government has openly surrendered. The term is coined from the join of stagnant and inflation.

Ratchet Inflation: It refers to that state of inflation which exists only in certain sectors of economy while overall effect is nil. When aggregate demand is so distributed in an economy that it is excessive in certain sectors of it and inadequate in others, the ones with excessive demand experience rise in prices while the others deficient in it, low prices. The overall price level in general remains unchanged

Mark-up Inflation: When a mark up by an appropriate percentage of production cost is added to the production cost with a view to meet some sales target or to ensure a certain percentage of return desired by share-holders on their investment or to allow desired wage hikes to workers, the inflation that results is called mark-up inflation.

Phillips Curve: It refers to the relationship between the rate of unemployment and the rate wage hike workers can enforce without commensurate productivity. The relationship is inverse indicating that workers bargaining power for higher wage-hikes without commensurate productivity is high when rate of unemployment is low and low when rate of unemployment is high. .

Modified Phillips Curve: Wage hikes enforced by workers without commensurate productivity increase production cost and hence product price. This gives a close relationship between the rate of price rise (inflation) and the rate of unemployment which is called modified Phillip curve.

Inflationary Pressure Curve: The curve portraying a direct variation of inflation rate with the rate of unemployment is termed as in factionary pressure curve. The curve depicts a lower rate of inflation at a lower rate of unemployment and a higher one at higher rate of unemployment . The curve has a positive slope and is linear in nature.

Okun's Law: The inflationary pressure curve thus has a positive slope which according to Economist A.M. Okun, is approximately, 2.5 implying a 1% change in unemployment rate leads to 2.5% change in total output of the economy relative to its potential output and approximately 2.5 % change in the rate of inflation The law has been quite sturdy for *US* economy but it lacks the precision associated with laws of economics.

Expected rate of Inflation: It is the rate of inflation at which inflationary pressure curve intersects the modified Phillips curve in equilibrium

Long-run Phillips Curve: In the long-run, Phillips curve turns vertical at natural rate of unemployment indicating an inflation rates independent of the rate of unemployment.

Natural Rate of Unemployment: It is the rate of unemployment at which workers' nominal wages conform to their real wages desired by them and the output , to the potential output of the economy. In other words, it is that rate of unemploment at which modified Phillips curve is vertical.

Consumer Price Index: It is the Laspeyre's price index that expresses a consumer's expenditure on base year's basket at current year's prices as a percentage of base year's expenditure at base year's prices.

Producer Price Index: Also called wholesale price index at times, resembles consumer price index(*CPI*) in its construction. It measures money value of a basket of products at the prices of their first commercial transaction. Note that the basket here doesn't include services. and that the product prices are prices at the first commercial transaction which need not be same as the wholesale prices.

GNP Implicit Price Deflator: It is a byproduct of deflation process. The term implicit implies that it is not obtained directly like *CPI* or *PPI* but is calculated by dividing Current *GNP* at current prices by *GNP* at constant prices.

PCE Implicit Price Deflator: is an index of price change for all the goods and services included in personal consumption expenditure. Recall that *PCE* (*Ch*) is a component of *GNP* by expenditure method. The procedure for *PCE* implicit price deflator is the same as that of *GNP* implicit price deflator. It is given as the ratio of *PCE* of the year at current prices to *PCE* of the same year at constant prices multiplied by 100.

Net Worth: Net worth refers to the difference total assets over total liabilities.

Deflation: It is opposite of inflation. Reduction prices is what it means.

Reflation: Increasing output through unit subsidy and elimination or lowering of unit taxes (Goods and Services Tax, *GST*). Reduction in unit taxes and granting unit subsidies both lower the cost and price and increase output. The measures are called reflationary measures.

Income in National Income Accounts: It refers to income earned through quid-pro-quo. It includes salaries wages, mixed incomes and operating surplus.

Income from the View Point Income Distribution-Narrow Sense: Income in this sense includes income in the sense of national income accounts as also income by way of government transfer payments, unemployment compensation, private and government pensions and such other unilateral receipts.It is in relation of effect of inflation on income distribution before and after inflation.

Income from the View Point Income Distribution-Broad Sense: Apart from distribution of income in its narrow sense, distribution of income in its broad sense includes changes in the net worth of individuals. Effect of inflation on its distribution is done by measuring changes in it before and after the incidence of inflation.

EXERCISES

A. Short Answer Questions

1. Differentiate among inflation, deflation and reflation with examples.
2. What is supply shock? How can it be held responsible for inflation?
3. What is international inflation? Can you suggest a way to optimize it in a developing country?
4. State Okun law. Is it true to say that the law lacks precision associated with laws of economics
5. How does inflation affect output and employment?
6. How does inflation affect economic growth and economic development ?
7. Distinguish between:
   (a) Cost-Push Inflation and demand-pull inflation
   (b) Wage push inflation and profit push inflation
   (c) Demand-pull inflation caused by real factors and demand-pull inflation caused by monetary factors
   (d) Open inflation and suppressed inflation
   (e) Stagflation and ratchet inflation
   (f) Expected rate of inflation and actual rate of inflation
   (g) Economic and non economic effects of inflation
   (h) Consumer price index and producer price index
   (i) *GNP* implicit price deflator and *PCE* implicit price deflator
   (j) Narrow sense of income and broad sense of income
   (k) Subsidy and supplementary income
8. Comment on the effect of inflation on income distribution in each of the following cases :
   (a) Annual nominal incomes of three households are respectively 500,000; 750,000 and 1000,000. Price level doubles from 250 to 500. over the year and so do the nominal incomes of the individuals.
   [Ans: No effect on Income distribution]
   (b) Annual nominal incomes of three households are respectively 500,000; 750,000 and 1000,000. Price level doubles from 250 to 500 over the year and the nominal incomes of the individuals change to 600,000; 1000,000 and 1500,000.
   [Ans: Nominal incomes failing to double with doubling prices, inflation has affected income distribution. Since the nominal incomes get less than doubled, inflation has had an adverse effect on income distribution]
   (c) Before and after doubling of the price level, values of the fixed-value-assets and liabilities of two households were as given in the table below:

	Before		*After*	
	Assets	*Liabilities*	*Assets*	*Liabilities*
First Household	100,000	80,000	100,000	120,000
Second Household	200,000	160,000	200,000	240,000
Total	300,000	240,000	300,000	360,000

If assets were fixed value assets and liabilities, variable value liabilities, estimate the effect of inflation on the net worth of the two households

[Ans: Net worth before price change = [total value of assets-total value of liabilities] of both the households
= [(100,000 + 200,000 + 100,000 + 200,000) – (80,000 + 160,000 + 120,000 + 240,000)]
= 6,000 – 6,000
= 0

Net worth after price change = [(100,000 + 200,000 + 100,000 + 200.000) – (40,000 + 80,000 + 60,000 + 120,000)]
= 6,000 – 3000,
= 300, 000

Thus effect of inflation on change in net worth
= + 300,000 – 0
= + 300,000

Thus, inflation has improvised net worth by 300,000]

(d) In part (c) above, how would your answer change if assets were of variable value while liability were of fixed value? **[Ans: (–) 300,000.** The households got worse off due to doubling of prices]

(e) In part (c) above how would your answer change if assets and liabilities were both variable in value?

[Ans: Inflation will reduce both, assets and liabilities of both the households, to half as much. Net worth will remain unchanged therefore]

9. The nominal *GNP* for the year 1992–93 was ₹ 61897 billion and the real *GNP* for the same year, ₹ 21870 billion. The figures of the nominal and real *GNP* for the previous financial year were ₹ 54269 billion and 20979 billion. Compute:

(a) *GNP* implicit price deflator for 1091–92 and 1992–93
(b) Rate of inflation over 1991–92 to 1992–93.

[Ans: (a) *GNP* implicit price deflator for 1091–92
= Nominal *GNP* for the year 1991–92/Real *GNP* for the same year
= 54269/20979
= 2.587

GNP implicit price deflator for 1092–9
= Nominal *GNP* for the year 1992–93/Real *GNP* for the same year
= 61897/21870
= 283.02]

(b) Approximate Price Index number for1992–93
= GNP implicit price deflator for the year × 100.
= 2.8302 × 100
= 283.02

Approximate Price Index number for1991–92
= GNP implicit price deflator for the year × 100.
= 2.587 × 100
= 258.7

Rate of inflation over 1991–92 to 1992–93

$$\frac{\text{Price index for (1992–93)} - \text{Price Index for (1991–92)}}{\text{Price Index for (1991–92)}} \times 100$$

$$\frac{283.02 - 258.7}{258.7} \times 100$$

B. Long Answer Questions

10. General price level depends directly on money supply' Do you agree? Discuss..
11. With the help of a diagram, demonstrate the mechanism of cost-push inflation and it control.
12. With the help of a neat sketch, show how real factors lead to demand-pull inflation.
13. With the help of a neat sketch, show how monetary factors lead to demand-pull inflation.
14. With the help of a diagram, show that cost-push and demand-pull inflations feed each other
15. 'Monetization of budgetary deficits is a necessary evil for underdeveloped developing countries'. Discuss.
16. 'War finance as also financing strategic production is an undesirable activity for every country' Discuss.
17. Differentiate among creeping inflation, walking inflation, running inflation and galloping inflation with the help of a sketch.
18. Differentiate among mark-up inflation, wage push inflation, profit push inflation and supply shock inflation
19. With the help of a diagram show the genesis of Phillips curve and modified Phillips curve.
20. Show that an inflationary pressure curve has a fixed positive slope . What causes shifts in it? Use a neat sketch.
21. 'Every growth doesn't lead to development but every development leads to growth' Discuss.

C. Longer Answer Questions

22. With the help of a diagram, establish the relationship between natural rate of unemployment and long-run Phillips curve.
23. What are various measures of inflation.
24. Explain ways and means you would recommend to control inflation in an underdeveloped developing economy.
25. With the help of illustrations, explain effect of inflation on income distribution.

UNIT-6

GROWTH AND DEVELOPMENT

Chapter 14: Economic Growth and Development

Chapter 14

Economic Growth and Development

INTRODUCTION

Economic growth refers to periodic increase in ***real output***. The period here refers to the time period between the start of the growth process and its termination. Usually it is a year, the financial year. Real output in relation to an economy is *GNP* at constant prices. If Y be the real *GNP*, ΔY, the increase in it over the period of one year then economic growth can be defined as a percent of Y as

$$\text{Economic Growth} = (\Delta Y/Y) \times 100$$

A high growth rate is believed essential for the multiplying millions. All economies whether developed or underdeveloped strive for it. Developed countries with adequate resources and cost saving technologies don't face many problems while the undeveloped ones suffer from both, the inadequacy of resources and lack of cost saving technologies. There is, therefore, a separate theory of growth for each—***balanced growth theory*** for the *haves* and ***unbalanced growth theory*** for the *have-nots*. Let us have a brief introduction of each.

Balanced growth theory requires simultaneous growth of all the sectors. The theory was pioneered by economist Ragnar Nurkse (1907–1959). It hypothesized that an economy needs a huge investment (big push) for simultaneous growth of all the sectors. Nurkse advocated balanced growth of agriculture and industry simultaneity.

Unbalanced growth theory suits underdeveloped countries as it requires investment in selected sectors and leaves the other ones to catch up on their own. Economists like Singer, Kindleberger and Streeten have spoken quite a lot about unbalanced growth theory but its systematic development goes to economist Hirschman.

Let us demonstrate the working of the two theories diagrammatically before proceeding further.

For the purpose, we take up the process of balanced growth of an economy that has sectors of agriculture and industry as hypothesized by Ragnar Nurkse It can be portrayed through the tool of production possibility curves (PPCs) that represent different combinations of outputs of agriculture and industry that are possible to be produced with full and efficient utilization of available resources under given technology.

The theory is also known as ***Big Push Theory*** due to the size of investment required in it. Figure 14.1 demonstrates its working.

In respect of unbalanced growth doctrine, due to paucity of investment, focus of investment is laid on one sector and the other sector is expected to catch up. Agricultural sector is more important for such economies because its outputs feed the manufacturing sector as the latter's inputs. The manufacture sector therefore is left to catch up.

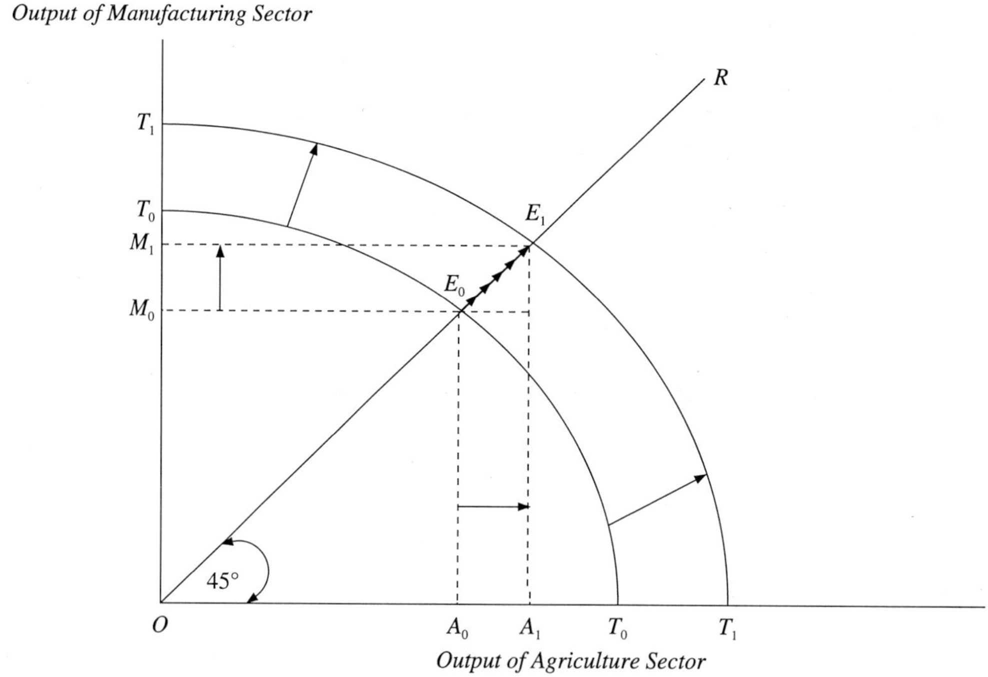

FIGURE 14.1 Essentials of Balanced Growth of Agriculture and Manufacturing Sectors: T_0T_0 represents the production possibilities of the two sectors in the beginning of the year while T_1T_1, in its end after adequate investment. Under balanced growth, T_0T_0 blows out uniformly to T_1T_1. A ray *OR* drawn from origin at 450 to *x*-axis depicts balanced growth along it if the slope of E_0E_1 segment of *OR* is one (tan 450 = 1) which is equal to the ratio of M_0M_1/A_0A_1. In case growth pattern continues likewise, even T_1T_1 will blow out uniformly with identical traits.

The unbalanced growth process is portrayed in Figure 14.2. It is highly recommended for developing economies that lack resources. For example, consider the manufacturing sector that lacks infrastructure such as roads, railways, and means of communications that obstruct its growth. If focus be laid on the growth of infrastructure manufacturing sector is likely to take off automatically and grow due to facility made available to it by infrastructure development by government.

14.1 NEED FOR ECONOMIC GROWTH

Multiplying millions multiply demand for food, housing, medicines, clothing, schooling, hospitals, jobs, transport and the like, without which, it is difficult to sustain life. This is the case with every economy be it an advanced, underdeveloped or a developing one. Growth is therefore as much or even more talked about a problem of modern economies than is that of inflation.

One thing more. Realization of growth is no less difficult than control of inflation. If growth is possible to realize inflation would perhaps be easier to combat. If community basket desired by an economy is attainable through growth, nothing like it. Let us use a community indifference curve and the existing *PPC* to highlight the point.

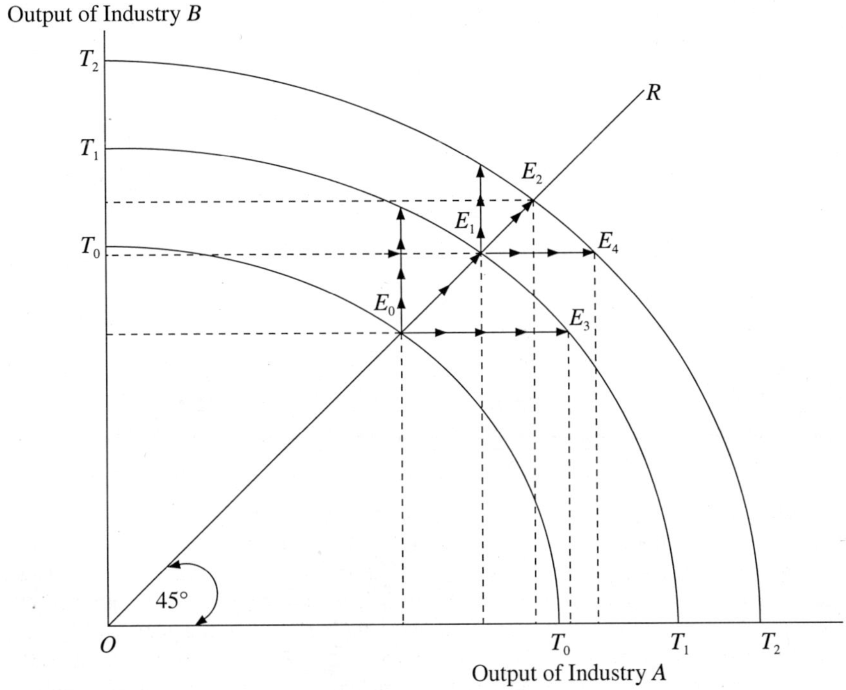

FIGURE 14.2 Unbalanced Growth: Investment is made in Industry *A,* leaving Industry *B* to catch up. According to unbalanced growth doctrine, output of Industry *A* increases along E_0E_3 while that of Industry *B* too begins to increase, may be because some of its inputs easily come from Industry *A*. For instance, an investment on infrastructure makes regions unapproachable now approachable to Industry *B* which thus begins catching up with Industry *A*. Industry *A*. In the figure Industry *A* is grown along E_0E_3 and Industry *B* moves along E_0E_5 to realize simultaneous growth along E_0E_1. The pattern continues with the result that growth of the economy takes place along the ray *OR*.

See Figure. 14.3 for an illustration

Shift in *PPC* indicates growth. This requires production of more of both the goods either in the same proportion for balanced growth or in unequal proportion for uneven or unbalanced growth. For more of either prod uct, more of resources are needed, given technology, efficiency and full utilization. At times, inefficiency and less than full employment are reasons for lower location of *PPC*. Obsolete technology is yet another reason for that. For growth, therefore, more of labour, more of capital and cost saving technology is required apart from efficient and full utilization of resources. Misallocation of resources amounts for their ***inefficient allocation***.

From the foregone discussion, it is clear that growth is must for better living conditions of the people. It raises their level of well being as also of satisfaction.

Besides, growth generates surpluses to be deployed by government for creation of better amenities for people. These amenities include transport, telecommunication, educational institutions , hospitals, housing, nutritional food, and above all , job opportunities for all so that each one may lead a life of dignity.

Growth may provide a solution to the problem of inflation. Adequate supply prevents prices from rising. By this time, the reader is aware of what we need for satisfactory growth rate and why.

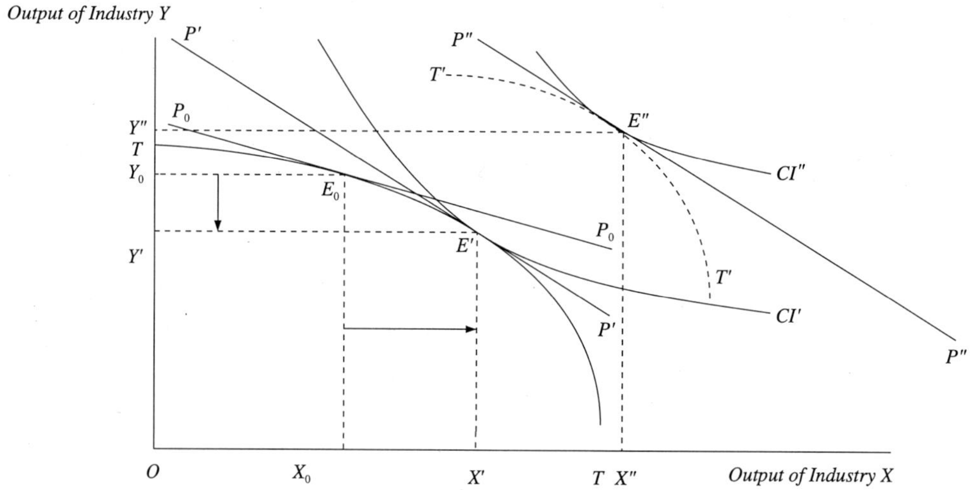

FIGURE 14.3 Outputs Desired by the Community and Outputs Produced in the Economy: Economy is producing (X_0, Y_0) at E_0 on production possibility curve *TT*. The economy charges prices given by price line P_0P_0. The community at *TT* wants to consume (X', Y') at E' at prices given by price line $P'P'$. This requires the economy to reallocate resources against *Y* and in favour of *X*. However, suppose community desires much more, say, (X'', Y'') at E'' of both the goods at the same prices as at $P'P'$. This would require the *PPC* to shift to $T'T'$, price line $P'P'$ to shift parallel to itself to $P''P''$ (Why?) and community indifference curve CI' to shift to CI''. This can't be possible without growth of both the industries in some what simultaneous manner, may be in a balanced manner. At E'', production and consumption are both higher than those at E' and at the same price as at $P'P'$. That is the reason growth is aspired for by every country whether it underdeveloped , developing or developed.

14.2 SOURCE OF ECONOMIC GROWTH

Growth needs additional labour and capital apart from cost saving technology and natural resources. Assumed here is that production is efficient and resources are under full utilization.

For our analysis, let us assume that production follows Cobb Douglas production function,

$$Q = A\, L^{\alpha} K^{\beta} \tag{14.1}$$

where, $Q \equiv$ output, $L \equiv$ labour, $K \equiv$ capital, $A \equiv$ a constant, a shift factor, α and $\beta \equiv$ shares of L and K used. Suppose further that constant returns accrue in production, that is, $\alpha + \beta = 1$

As far as A is concerned, it represents a host of things that shift the isoquant, Q. They may be technological changes, changes in natural resources etc. Let us attempt an expression for growth. Taking logarithm (Eq.14.1), we've

$$\log Q = \log A + \alpha \log L + \beta \log K \tag{14.2}$$

Differentiating Equation 14.2 with respect to time period, t, we have

$$(1/Q) \times dQ/dt = (1/A) \times dA/dt + \alpha\,(1/L) \times dL/dt + \beta\,(1/K) \times dK/dt$$

$$\Rightarrow \qquad dQ/Q = (dA/A) + \alpha\,(dL/L) + \beta(dK/K)$$

(treating $dt = 1$, for measuring growth rate on year to year basis)

$\Rightarrow$ Rate of growth of Q = rate of growth of A + $\alpha \times$ rate of growth of L + $\beta \times$ rate of growth of K.

$$\Rightarrow \qquad g = s + \alpha \times l + \beta \times k \qquad (14.3)$$

where, $g \equiv$ growth rate of output, $s \equiv$ growth rate of A, $l \equiv$ growth of labour force and $k \equiv$ growth of capital. Growth rate is thus the sum of growth rate of A, growth rate of L, and growth rate of K. Let us have a brief discussion on each.

14.2.1 Technology and Resources (A)

In Equation 14.1, A represents states of technology and natural resources which characterize an economy. If A is higher for one economy than for another, the isoquant of the economy will be located above that of the economy with lower value of it or if the economy with lower value of A manages to raise it through import of cost saving technology or finds a few petroleum, mineral and metal deposits under its soil, which it needed earlier but lacked them, its own isoquant will shift outwards. As you have studied in microeconomics[1], an isoquant represents various combinations of labour (L) and capital (K) each of which produces same quantity of output, Q. For demonstration, consider production functions with different specifications,

1. $Q = A\, L^{\alpha} K^{\beta}$, with $A = 100$, $L = 100$, $K = 64$, $\alpha = 1/2$ and $\beta = 1/2$
2. $Q' = A'\, L'^{\alpha} K'^{\beta}$, with $A' = 400$, $L' = 25$, $K' = 16$, $\alpha = 1/2$ and $\beta = 1/2$
3. $Q'' = A'\, L^{\alpha} K^{\beta}$, with $A = 400$, $L = 100$, $K = 64$, $\alpha = 1/2$ and $\beta = 1/2$

The third production function differs from the first only in the value of A. second from it in the values of all the three.

A simple calculation depicts $Q' = Q$ while Q'' is greater than either one of them.

$$Q = (100) \times (100)^{1/2} \times (64)^{1/2} = 100 \times 10 \times 8 = 8{,}000$$
$$Q'' = (400) \times (100)^{1/2} \times (64)^{1/2} = 400 \times 10 \times 8 = 32{,}000$$
$$Q' = (400) \times (25)^{1/2} \times (16)^{1/2} = 400 \times 5 \times 4 = 8{,}000$$

The illustration explains the role of shift factor, A. With same labour and capital a higher Value of A leads to higher output $Q''(Q'' > Q)$ and with higher value of A, much lower amounts of labour and capital are capable of producing quantity, $Q'(Q' = Q)$. Note that Q'' greater than Q and Q' both but when plotted, isoquant of Q' lies below that of Q and that of Q'', above those of Q and Q' both (see Figure 14.4).

The state of technology and natural resources is thus an external factor that varies from economy to economy. Those economies that have a higher A produce a higher output Q with same quantities of labour and capital. A is also called ***exogenously determined total factor productivity residual*** (*TFP*[2]). *TFP* refers to total productivity of factors labour and capital.

14.2.2 Labour (L)

Labour is the second resource of growth. Efficient and sufficient labour with high labour productivity is an important source of growth. If growth of such labour ($\Delta L/L$ *or* dL/L) is low with its supply depending on external factors , it can be and usually is an exogenous factor like efficiency parameter ,A. Workers of some countries are less productive than those of other countries. Labour in such countries can be clubbed with the ***exogenously determined total factor productivity residual*** and given the name of ***labour augmented total factor productivity residual.*** Besides, some countries that have characteristically less labour than capital, growth of labour relative to that of capital is low. Also, it is low in developed countries because of high tech cost saving technology and it is low in developing

[1] See Chauhan, S.P.S., Microeconomics—An Advanced Treatise, pp. 232, 253, Chapter 5, 3rd Edition , *PHI* Learning.
[2] See Chauhan, S.P.S., Microeconomics—An Advanced Treatise, p. 257, Chapter 5, 3rd Edition , *PHI* Learning.

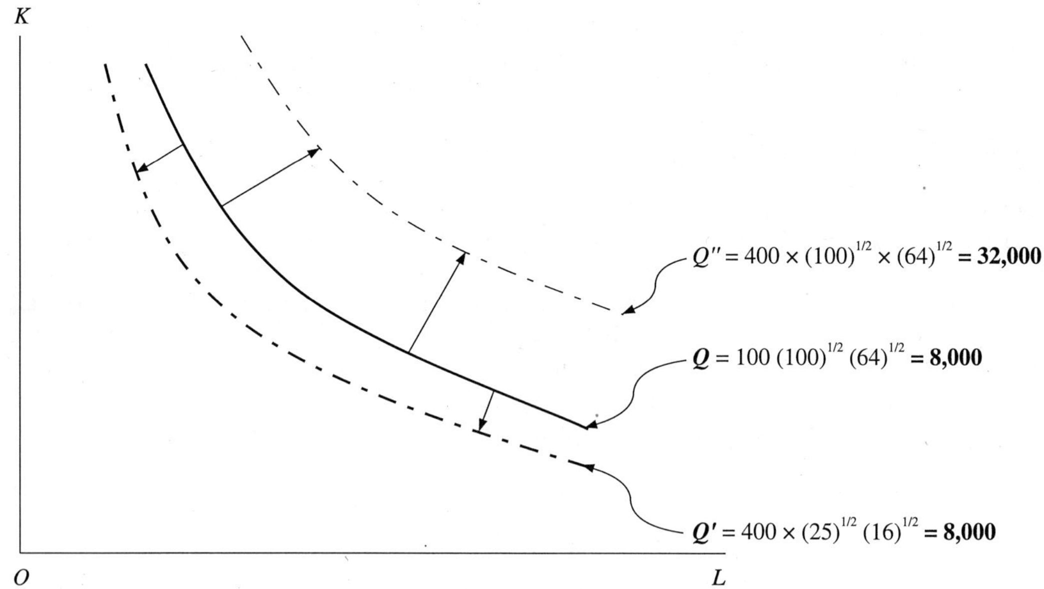

FIGURE 14.4 Role of Total Factor Productivity Residual, *A*: Same quantity of output (Q' = 8,000) can be produced with 25 units of labour and 16 units of capital when A = 400 as that of output (Q = 8000) with 100 units of labour and 64 units of capital when A = 100. If labour (L = 100) and capital (K = 64) were used with A = 400, output realized would grow to 400 × 10 × 8 = 32,000. Here, same labour (100 units) and same capital (K = 64 units) produce 32,000 units of output when A = 400 while they produce only 8000 units of output when A = 100. Study the curves and equations closely and see what inferences are there for you to draw.

countries too because of its low productivity and slow growth of industrialization In situations like these, labour augmented total factor productivity residual may be taken as $R = (AL^{\alpha})$ and the production function as

$$Q = RK^{\beta}. \tag{14.4}$$

We spare the discussion on Equation 14.4 for Subsection 14.3. Right now we take up an illustration to demonstrate working of Equation 14.3.

ILLUSTRATION 14.1: If 'l'= + 3% and k = + 8%, $\alpha = \beta = ½$, s = 0, by how much would you expect the *GDP*-growth rate to rise?

Solution: Making substitutions in Equation 14.3, we have

$$\begin{aligned} g &= s + \alpha \times l + \beta \times k \\ &= 0 + 1/2 \times 0.03 + 1/2 \times (+)\ 0.08 \\ &= (+)\ 0.055 \text{ or } 5.5\ \%\ \text{growth}. \end{aligned}$$

14.2.3 Capital (K)

The problem of growth in less developed economies (*LDCs*) relates not as much with labour or technology as does with capital formation. It is not that governments can't shell out the needed funds, but it is the leakage from it of a sizable part for conspicuous imports or its relocation abroad. Capital leaked out thus gets spent on non-productive activities. Each year, planners allocate increasing amounts of financial capital and expect to touch the target rate of growth which they never realize due to its leakage[1] or dilution.

For a feel of things, think of a nation that shells out 1000, 1200 and 1500 millions in each of the three consecutive years and expects growth rates of 6%, 7% and 8% respectively. What the nation realizes in consequence are rates of 4%, 5% and 6% for the respective years. Assume the capital allocated to be in real terms

The data from banks reveal emergence of non-performing loans (*NPLs*) to the tunes of 200, 300 and 300 millions in real terms in these years. The borrowings were for working capital needs or for sinking new facilities.

Let us tabulate data for clearer understanding:

Year	$K_{inducted}$	*NPLs*	$K_{Operative}$	g_t	g_m	g_p
1.	1000	200	800	6%	4%	5%
2.	1200	300	900	7%	5%	6.67%
3.	1500	300	1200	8%	6%	7.5%

Notes: 1. *K ≡ GDCF at constant prices in millions*
2. *NPLs ≡ Non Performing Loans at constant prices in millions*
3. *Operative K ≡ K-NPL*
4. g_t *≡ Targeted growth rate*
5. g_m *≡ Measured growth rate*
6. g_p *≡ Potential rate of growth.*

Government targeted growth rates of 6%, 7% and 8% on the basis of capital inducted 1000, 1200, and 1500 but realized 4%, 5% and 6% due to leakages by 200, 300, 300 respectively. Capital that actually operated was thus 800, 900, and 1200

From a simple unitary method, a growth rate of 4% was measured in Year 1 through inducted real capital of 1000 or operative capital of 800. Had *NPLs* been non-existent, the growth rate would have been 5% (= 1000 × 4/800) in Year 1, 6.67% (= 1200 × 5/900) in Year 2, and 7.5% (1500 × 6 /1200) in Year 3.

In sum, *NPLs* affect capital inducted adversely and so do they affect growth rates of *GDP*.

For a formal treatment for potential growth rate (g_p), let us go back to Equation 14.4, where *R* is the labour weighted *TFP* residual; *K*, the capital inducted and *b* is the share of *K* in total output (*Q*). This is as good as assuming that *AL*a remains unchanged in their contribution to *GDP*. Then it is the role of operative capital, which is the difference of capital inducted over *NPLs*.

Transforming Equation 14.4 logarithmically, we have

$$\text{Log } Q = \text{Log } R + b \text{ Log } K \tag{14.5}$$

Differentiating Equation 14.5 with respect to time period *t*, we've

$$\frac{dQ/dt}{Q} = \frac{dR/dt}{R} + \beta\frac{dK/dt}{K} \tag{14.6}$$

[1] Prof. Chauhan, S.P.S., & Dr. Sharma, G.L, Impact of *Non Performing Assets on Growth of Indian GDP,* Research Paper, published in Financial System Reforms & Economic Growth-Issues & Challenges, 2017 Issue, McGraw Hill Education(India) pvt.ltd Chennai.

Rewriting Equation 14.6 with $dt = 1$ to refer to the time period of one year for year to year growth, and changes in Q, R and K on yearly basis taken as discrete, we have,

$$(\Delta Q/Q) = (\Delta R/R) + \beta\ ((\Delta K/K) \tag{14.7}$$

That is, *GDP* growth, $\Delta Q/Q$, is directly related to the growth of capital, $(\Delta K/K)$, given exogeneity of growth of $(\Delta R/R)$. Denoting $(\Delta Q/Q)$ as 'g_m', the measured growth rate; $\Delta R/R$ as 'r' and $(\Delta K/K)$ as '$k_{operative}$' we can rewrite Equation 14.7 as

$$g_m = r + \beta \times k_{operative} \tag{14.8}$$

Equation 14.8 for potential growth rate g_p would have been

$$g_p = r + \beta \times k_{inducted}. \tag{14.9}$$

To demonstrate, let $\beta = 0.50$, $k_{inducted} = 0.20$ (20%), and $r = 5\%$, 'g_p' 0.15 (15%) where g_p is potential growth rate (in absence of *NPLs*). Now let $k_{inducted}$ be reduced by *NPLs* from 20% to 15%. As a result, g_p falls from 15% to 12.5%, which is the measured growth rate, g_m. It falls short of g_p by 2.5%.

Representing *NPL*-diluted capital as $k_{operative}$ given by $(k_{inducted} - n)$ where n is $[(N/K_{inducted}) \times 100]$ and *NPL, N;* measured growth rate g_m can be given as

$$\begin{aligned} g_m &= r + \beta \times k_{operative} \\ &= r + \beta \times (k_{inducted} - n) \\ &= r + \beta \times (k_{inducted}) - \beta \times n \\ &= g_p - \beta \times n \end{aligned}$$

$\Rightarrow$ $$g_p = g_m + \beta \times n$$

Thus, $$g_p = g_m + \beta \times n. \tag{14.10}$$

where, $$g_p = \text{'}r\text{'} + \beta \times (k_{operative}) + \beta \times \text{'}n\text{'}) \tag{14.11}$$

In simple words, potential growth rate exceeds the measured growth rate by $(\beta \times n)$

ILLUSTRATION 14.2: The measured *GDP* growth rates of a country for the period 2011–12 to 2015–16 were 5.6%, 6.6%, 7.2%, and 7.6% per annum respectively and the corresponding growth rates of real *GDCF* over the same period were 4.3%, 2.1%, 5.6%, and 5.3%. If growth of n were 0.82%, 1.0%, 1.4%, and 1.4%, calculate labour augmented *TFP* residual (r) in each case and show that the potential rate of growth of *GDP* would work out at 6.01%, 7.10%, 7.9%, and 8.3% [Take $\beta = 0.50$.]

Solution: **Calculation of r and that of g_p through Equations 14.10 and 14.11**

Year	g_m %	$k_{inducted}$ %	β	n %	$k_{operative} = (k_{inducted} - n)$	$r = g_m - \beta \times k_{operative}$	$g_p = g_m + b \times n$	$g_p = r + b(k_{operative} + n)$
2011–12	–	–	–	–	–	–	–	–
2012–13	5.6	4.3	0.5	0.82	4.3−0.82 = 3.48	3.86	5.6 + 0.5 × 0.82 = **6.01**	3.86 + 0.5(3.48 + 0.82) = **6.01**
2013–14	6.6	2.1	0.5	1.00	2.1−1.00 = 1.10	6.05	6.6 + 0.5 × 1.00 = **7.10**	6.05 + 0.5(1.10 + 1.00) = **7.10**
2014–15	7.2	5.6	0.5	1.40	5.6−1.40 = 4.20	5.10	7.2 + 0.5 × 1.40 = **7.90**	5.10 + 0.5(4.20 + 1.40) = **7.90**
2015–16	7.6	5.3	0.5	1.40	5.3−1.40 = 3.90	5.65	7.6 + 0.5 × 1.40 = **8.30**	5.65 + 0.5(3.90 + 1.40) = **8.30**

Are the differences between g_m and g_p insignificant? Relevant statistical test can answer the question[1].

The sources of growth therefore are (1) natural resources, (2) technology, (3) work force and (4) capital. Except natural resources, all the rest require a sizable investment, called ***net investment***, which can be defined as gross investment *less* depreciation.

In the next section we are going to discuss some of the theories of growth. Implicit is the assumption of absence of any leakage or dilution from capital.

14.3 THEORIES OF GROWTH

In this section we take up some of the theories of growth which have captured a sizable part of growth literature all over the world. Let us outline them below:

1. Harrod-Domar Theory of Growth.
2. Neoclassical Theories of Growth:
   (i) Solow's per capita growth theory, and
   (ii) Lewis Structural Change Theory of Growth.
3. Rostov's Theory of Growth
4. International Dependence Theory of Growth
5. Indian Growth Models: Mahalanobis's Model of growth and Vakil & Brahmananda Model of Wage Goods.

Let us introduce these models in their requisite detail in Sub-sections 14.3.1, 14.3.2, 14.3.3, 14.3.4 and 14.3.5.

14.3.1 Harrod-Domar Theory of Growth

The core factor emphasized by Harrod-Domar and incorporated by most of the modern theories of growth is the dual effect of net investment, comprising ***demand effects and capacity effects***.

The ***demand effect*** of net investment implies increase in demand for producer goods like plant, equipment, machinery, bricks, steel etc demanded for factory establishment. The demand effect creates productive capacity (capacity effect) in the current period which boosts aggregate demand of output in the next period. If net investment is financed by net savings, it buys that part of the output, which is not bought by consumers. For simplicity,consider a two sector economy with the households as

[1] Statistical test relevant here is the student's t-test , calculation of which is shown below:

Year	g_p	g_m	$d = (g_p - g_m)$	$d - \bar{d}$	$(d - \bar{d})^2$
2011–12	–	–			
2012–13	6.01	5.60	0.41	– 0.1675	0.0281
2013–14	7.10	6.60	0.50	– 0.0775	0.00
2014–15	7.90	7.20	0.70	+ 0.1225	0.0150
2015–16	8.30	7.60	0.70	+ 0.1225	0.0150
			$\Sigma d = \mathbf{2.31}$	$\Sigma(d - \bar{d})^2 = 0.0641$	

$\bar{d} = 0.5775$; and , $\bar{d} = \sqrt{0.0641/4} = 0.1266$

$= (0.5775 - 0)/0.0731 = \mathbf{7.901}$. ($t_{0.05}$ for 3-digrees of freedom = 2.3534)

Thus $t_{observed} > t_{0.05}$. Null Hypothesis is rejected. The difference between measured g and potential g is significant. Thus apparently small looking differences between g_m and g_p are significantly different.

one sector and producers as the other. If Y represents output, C, Consumption, I, investment and S, savings then $Y = C + I$ is aggregate demand (AD) and $Y = C + S$, aggregate supply (AS). This implies that investment (I) = savings (S). Goods not bought by consumers are thus equivalent to their savings. Producers treat them as a part of their capital stock (unsold stocks), which can be treated by them as a part of the future production. Net investment in the current period may be given as a difference of current investment over unsold stocks. The latter may be treated as a part of the output of next period. If fixed net investment of the value ΔI be planned period after period, then the values of the outputs in the subsequent periods will not be affected by the unsold stocks of the previous periods. Output produced (Y_r) in any period may be less than that supplied in next period. To demonstrate, suppose output produced and supplied in one period is1000 units while consumers buy only 800 units with the result producers may be prompted to produce 200 units less in the next period but if net investment planned and made be worth 200 units of additional output each period, that is, worth 1000 units, then the unsold stock of the previous period will not affect subsequent period's output that will amount to 800 plus 200 or 1000 units in the next period which work out as 1200 units including 200 units of the unsold stock. Thus real output (Y_r) this period (1000 units) would be less than the potential output (Y_p) of 1200 next period.

The model assumes fixed net investment period after period and fixed planned output, Y_r, of 1000 units period after period regardless of the unsold stocks of the previous period. Potential output each period would grow by the unsold stock of the previous period which may imply a growth rate of 20% in the current period over that of the previous period. Consumers' income from production of 1000 units next period would be higher than that from production of 800 units next period, which would have been the case if the investment 200 units worth be neither planned nor made.

In a two sector model, the multiplier effect is given by

$$\Delta Y_r/\Delta I = 1/MPS = 1/s,$$

$$(\text{where,} \quad s \equiv \Delta S/\Delta Y_r)$$

$$\Rightarrow \quad \Delta Y_r = \Delta I/s$$

$$\text{Now,} \quad \Delta Y_p = \sigma \times I \tag{14.12}$$

(where $\sigma \equiv$ capital productivity, given as Y_p/K or $\Delta Y_p/\Delta K$ and $I \equiv$ total investment)

In equilibrium state , when Aggregate Demand (AD) = Aggregate Supply (AS) in the subsequent periods, we've

$$\Delta Y_r = \Delta Y_p = \Delta Y$$

$$\Rightarrow \quad \Delta I/s = \sigma \times I \tag{14.13}$$

Multiplying by s both sides of Equation 14.13, we have

$$\Delta I = \sigma \times I \times s \tag{14.14}$$

Dividing by I on both sides of Equation 14.14, we've

$$\Delta I/I = \sigma \times s \tag{14.15}$$

Now growth rate of output is given as

$$\Delta Y/Y = \Delta I/I = \sigma \times s \tag{14.16}$$ [1]

[1] Note that $\Delta Y > \Delta I$, the growth rate of actual output, $\Delta Y_r/Y_r$ must be the same as $\Delta I/I$. In equilibrium, since $\Delta Y_r = \Delta Y_p = \Delta Y$ and since $\Delta Yp = \sigma \times I$ and $\Delta Y_r = \Delta I/s$, we have $\sigma \times I = \Delta I/s$, implying $\Delta I/I = \sigma \times s = \Delta Y/Y = g$, the growth rate. Note also that changes from one period to another are designated with Δ while fixed value in a period without Δ. For a 2 sector model, aggregate demand (AD), is given as $Y = C_a + (1 - b)I$ & $\Delta Y = (1 - b)\Delta I$. Dividing corresponding sides of the latter by those of the former, we've, $\Delta Y/Y = \Delta I/I$.

$$\Rightarrow \quad g = \sigma \times s = s/k \quad (14.17)$$

(where, $g \equiv \Delta Y/Y$, $k \equiv 1/\sigma$ or capital output ratio, K/Y)

Critical Assessment of Harrod-Domar Model

The model is based on the assumption that savings worth the unsold stocks need to be invested whether by the producers or by those who save. The model collapses if savings remain stuck up in the household sector, that is, not mobilized by the banks or the producer does not plan fixed investment each period. Like Keynesian theory, the model has little relevance to developing third world countries. Implicit assumptions of fixed *MPS* (*s*) and fixed Capital productivity are unrealistic. Moreover, exclusion of government and foreign sectors from the model makes it highly restrictive in its applicability.

Despite limited applicability of the model, the model signifies that over investment causes capital scarcity and under investment leads to excess capacity.

14.3.2 Neoclassical Theories of Growth—Solow's per capita Growth Theory and Lewis Structural Change Theory of Growth

In this section we take neoclassical theories of growth. The ones we take up are :

1. Solow's Per Capita Growth Theory
2. Lewis dual sector Structural Change Theory of Growth

Let us introduce them in that order.

14.3.2.1(A) Solow's Per Capita Growth Theory[1] without technological progress

The model takes on Cobb Douglas function to define total output under constant returns to scale. That is, Output Y is given as

$$Y = A \times L\,(1 - \alpha) \times K^{\alpha} \quad (14.18)$$

where, $A \equiv$ Technology Factor or Total Factor Productivity
$L \equiv$ *Labour,*
$K \equiv$ *Capital,*
$(1 - \alpha) \equiv$ Share of Labour, and
$\alpha \equiv$ Share of Capital

Growth of output can be obtained through logarithmic differentiation of Equation 14.18,

$$\Delta Y/Y = \Delta A/A + (1 - \alpha) \times \Delta L/L + \alpha \times K \quad (14.19)$$

Denoting output per capita by lower case letter '*y*' and its growth rate by $\Delta y/y$, expressions for the two can be given as

$$y = Y/L$$
$$= [A \times L^{(1-\alpha)} \times K^{\alpha}]/L$$
$$\Rightarrow \quad \log y = \log A + (1 - \alpha) \log L + \alpha \log K - \log L \quad \text{(On logarithmic transformation)}$$
$$\Delta y/y = \Delta A/A + (1 - \alpha)\, \Delta L/L + \alpha \times \Delta K/K - \Delta L/L$$
$$= \Delta A/A + \alpha \times \Delta K/K - \alpha \times \Delta L/L$$

[1] R. Solow, "A Contribution to the Theory of Economic Growth," (Quarterly Journal of Economics, February 1956).

$$= \Delta A/A + \alpha \times (\Delta K/K - \Delta L/L)$$
$$= \Delta A/A + \alpha \times \Delta k/k^1 \qquad (14.20)$$

where, $\Delta k/k = \Delta K/K - \Delta L/L \equiv$ growth rate of capital per worker or of capital labour ratio per worker. Equation 14.20 gives that ***per capita growth rate*** of output depends on two elements:

1. $\Delta A/A$, which is improvement in technical progress or change in total factor productivity
2. $\Delta k/k$, which is the rate of change in capital-labour ratio.

In the first case, if technological progress is negligible or zero ($\Delta A/A = 0$), output growth per worker can be given as

$$\Delta y/y = \alpha \times \Delta k/k \qquad (14.21)$$

[On substituting $\Delta A/A = 0$ Equation 14.20]

Equation 14.21 portrays per capita growth as a function of $\Delta k/k$. We can portray the relationship through Figure 14.5.

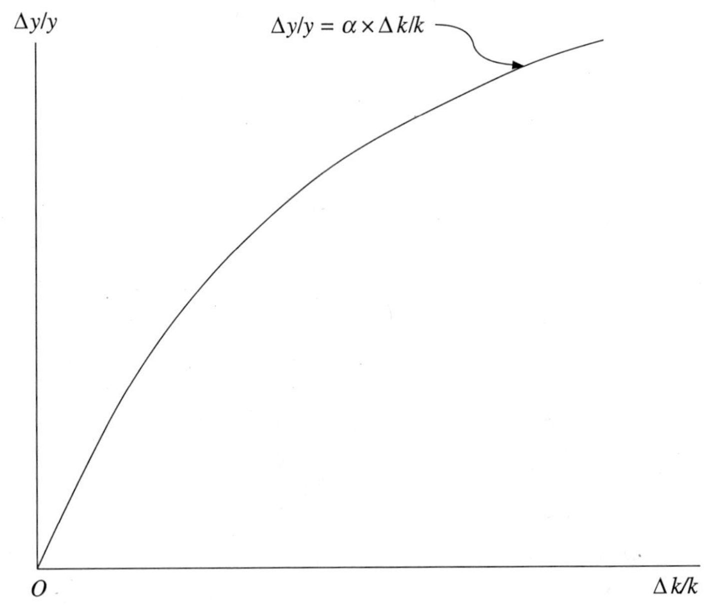

FIGURE 14.5 Growth rate of per capita output without technological progress As portrayed in the figure, growth rate per capita is proportional to the growth of capital labour ratio.

14.3.2.1(B) Solow's per capita Growth with Technological progress

In the presence of technological progress the threshold value of per capita growth rate is given by the *residual,*

[1] Expression $\Delta k/k$ is rate of growth k, which is rate of growth of K/L

$$k = K/L$$

$\Rightarrow$ $\log k = \log K - \log L$ (On logarithmic transformation)

$\Rightarrow$ $\Delta k/k = \Delta K/K - \Delta L/L$ (On differentiation)

$$1 - \frac{\alpha \times \Delta k/k}{\Delta y/y} \qquad (14.22)$$

which may also be called the technological progress residual and can be obtained by dividing both the sides of Equation 14.20 by $\Delta y/y$ as

$$1 = \frac{\Delta A/A}{\Delta y/y} + \frac{\alpha \times \Delta k/k}{\Delta y/y}$$

$$\Rightarrow \qquad \frac{\Delta A/A}{\Delta y/y} = 1 - \frac{\alpha \times \Delta k/k}{\Delta y/y} \qquad (14.23)$$

CRITICAL ASSESSMENT OF SOLOW'S THEORY OF GROWTH

Like Harrod-Domar Theory of Growth, Solow's per capita growth Theory too has little relevance to the underdeveloped developing countries. Solow's theory , as designated by Solow as ***'per capita growth'*** must mean 'growth of output divided by population' but Solow's work-out of the theory is based on ***'output growth per worker'.*** There would hardly be any country in which each and every individual of the population is a working-individual leave alone the question of underdeveloped developing countries The theory, in the opinion of this author, doesn't qualify for attention it has acquired in the literature of Growth and development.

14.3.2.2 Lewis Dual Sector Structural Changes Model of Growth

The Lewis two sector Structural Change Model is a model involving one sector with surplus labour and the other , labour deficient industrial sector. The former is usually the rural sector with traditional subsistence level of cultivation while the latter, the modern urbanized manufacturing and services sector. The model characterizes underdeveloped but developing economies.

According to W.A. Lewis, the underdeveloped economies have the following traits:

(a) Over populated traditional rural sector characterized by surplus labour with zero MP_L.
(b) A labour deficient but highly productive urban industrialized sector.

Labour surplus rural sector is a low wage sector while labour scarce urban sector, a high wage sector. The model deals with transfer of labour from low wage regions to the high wage regions.

Given the supply of capital, K_1, demand for collaborating labour is determined by the falling part of the marginal product of labour (MP_L) and is denoted as $D_1(K_1)$. Equilibrium level of employment at this level of capital is determined at the point F where $D_1(K_1)$ is intersected by the perfectly elastic labour supply of rural labour, $w = w_u$. At F, OL_1. labour is employment. Total output of the industry is OD_1FL_1, the area under the demand curve, $D_1(K_1)$ (See Figure 14.6). Profit accruing to the industry is $F\,w_u\,D_1$, which needs reinvestment.

CRITICAL ASSESSMENT OF DUAL SECTOR MODEL OF LEWIS

Although the model is in conformity with historical experiences of economic growth as realized in the west, yet , some of its implicit assumptions do not fit into the institutional and economic realities of most of the contemporary third world countries. They are:

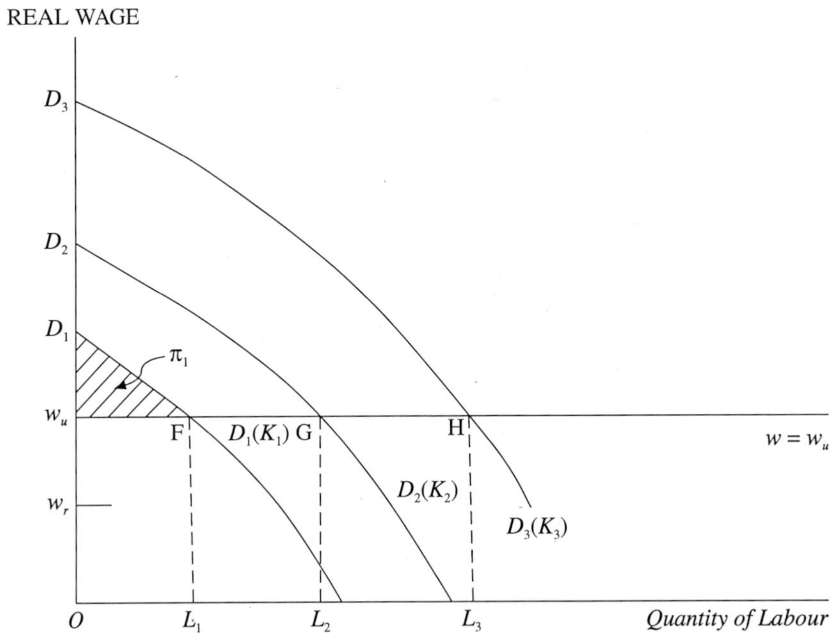

FIGURE 14.6 Lewis Two Sector Structural Change Model—Quantity of labour is measured on x-axis while real wages on y-axis. Level of wage in rural community is w_r . $D_1(K_1)$, $D_2(K_2)$ and $D_3(K_3)$ are MP_L curves at capital levels of K_1, K_2, and K_3 They represent labour demand at these levels ($K_1 < K_2 < K_3$) of capital. Labour supply curve for the industry is $w = w_u$, which is perfectly elastic. Labour employed at F is OL_1. Labour surplus rural sector wage, w_r is much lower than w_u. It is natural for the surplus rural labour to be lured by higher wages in urban industry. $Fw_u D_1$ (shaded) is the profit accruing to the industry initially. This profit if reinvested, capital stock would rise to K_2, thereby, shifting the MP_L curve upward to right as shown. This leads to a new equilibrium at G, where OL_2 labour is employed. Industry profit at G rises to G $w_u D_2$, raising capital stock to K_3 and employment to OL_3.

The process of growth of output and employment continues until entire surplus labour from rural sector is absorbed in the modern industrial sector. Disappearance of the surplus labour from the rural sector increases rural wage thereafter. Supply curve of labour therefore is no longer perfectly elastic. It begins to slope upwards as more of the workers will comply demand only at higher wages.

Implicit Assumption 1

The first implicit assumption is that the rate of labour transfer and creation of employment in modern sector is proportional to the rate of capital accumulation. In the modern sector, the faster is the rate of capital accumulation the higher must be the growth rate of the modern sector and faster must be the rate of job creation. But what if the capitalists' profits are reinvested in sophisticated labour saving capital equipments rather than in just duplicating the existing capital as is assumed implicitly by the model.? Or, what if the profits are relocated abroad as a form of capital outflow, to be added to the deposits of the foreign banks?

As demonstrated in Figure 14.7, demand curves fail to shift uniformly. They rather intersect at a point cutting short labour employment.

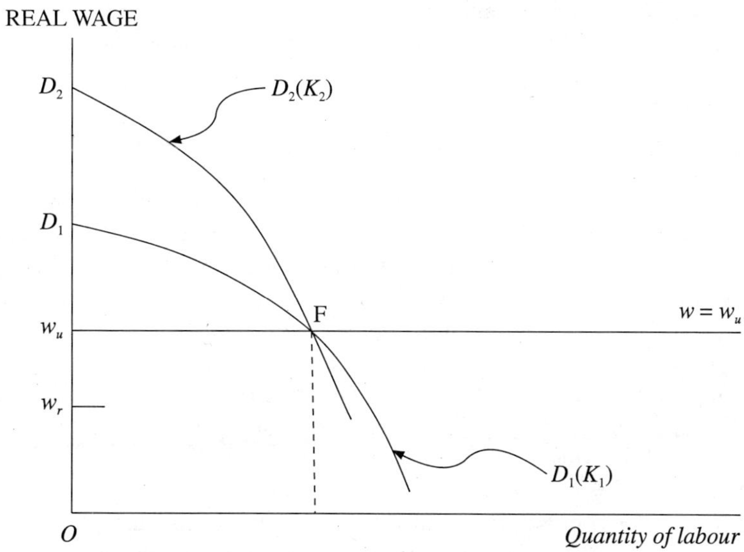

FIGURE 14.7 The dual sector growth model collapses when profits get relocated abroad or when allocated to acquisition and use of sophisticated labour saving capital equipments. In such cases demand curves intersect at *F* curtailing the labour demand, instead, of depicting a uniform shift.

Implicit Assumption 2

The second questionable assumption is that the surplus labour exists only in rural agricultural sector and that urban industrial sector is at full employment. According to western economists, the assumption of urban surplus labour is found more valid than that rural surplus labour, but there is a widespread disagreement with this view mong the econmists of the third world countries.

Implicit Assumption 3

The third implicit assumption is the existence of a competitive modern sector in labour market due to which constant real wages exist until the point where supply of labour gets exhausted.

Concluding Note

Despite criticism as above, Lewis dual sector model appears to fetch more water than the models of Harrod-Domar and Solow as far as growth of underdeveloped developing world are concerned . This is so because most of the underdeveloped countries have a labour surplus agricultural sector. Flight of labour from rural to urban sectors in search of greener pastures is a common sight in such countries.

14.3.3 Rostow's Theory of Growth

A ccording to Rostow, transition from low growth to high growth involves the following stages, called ***Rostow's stages of growth:***

1. **Traditional Society:** When society follows traditional methods of production, the growth process is at its lowest level.

2. **The Precondition for take off:** Among several things needed as its precondition, growth requires adequate amount of savings as a must to feed it.
3. **Self Sustaining Growth:** A self sustaining Growth process leads to stable growth. In case it is subject to uncertain external factors, it may suffer in its way due to waning of the external factors .
4. **Drive to Maturity:** Political will and people's resolve to bring about growth are two essentials to lead it to its maturity.
5. **High Mass Consumption:** A high level of mass consumption of goods and services produced leads to speedy back flow of funds to the producers to raise production and thus to keep capital output ratio constant or non-diminishing A high level of consumption implies a low level of savings and hence of investment but absence of unsold stocks is a point of no bother as production of output can be maintained at the same or a higher pace. In this case, same capital investment may lead to a higher output thereby lowering the capital output ratio. According to Rostow, a 15 to 20% rate savings may help an economy to take off into the growth process. It can be elaborated through Harrod-Domar Equation (Equation 14.17) as below:

   Growth rate, $g = \Delta Y/Y = s/k$,

   where, $\Delta Y/Y \equiv$ proportionate increase in output or growth,

   $s \equiv S/Y$, the average propensity to save or marginal propensity to save, $\Delta S/\Delta Y$

   and $k \equiv K/Y$, or capital output ratio.

   If $s = 15\%$ and $k = 3$, then from Harrod-Domar equation,

   $$g = s/k = 15\%/3 = 5\%$$

14.3.4 International Dependence Theory

Growing disenchantment with the western theories of growth led the economists and intellectuals of the third world to the ridding of he international dependence theories. These theories view the third world countries as beset by institutional, political and economic rigidities as also by the international dependence and dominance to the rich countries. Within this general approach, there are two major streams of thought prevalent:

1. **Neo Colonial Dependence Theory:** This theory is an outgrowth of Marxist thinking. It attributes existence and continuance of the underdevelopment of the third world countries to the unequal international capitalist system of the rich nation-poor nation relationships. Revolutionary struggles or at least major restructuring of the world capitalist system is therefore required to free dependent third world nations from direct and indirect economic control by the first world.
2. **The False Paradigm Theory:** This theory attributes the third world underdevelopment to faulty and inappropriate advice provided by well meaning but often ill-informed/uninformed international expert advisers of the developed countries' assistance agencies and *MNC* donors. These experts offer sophisticated concepts, elegant theoretical structures and complex economic models of development that often lead to inappropriate or simply, incorrect policies.

   The leading university intellectuals, economists and other civil servants—all get their training in developed countries/institutions where they are unwittingly served an unhealthy dose of alien concept and elegant but inapplicable theories. They have little or no knowledge to enable the third world to grip the real developmental problems.

14.3.5 Indian Growth Models: Mahalanobis's Model of Growth and Vakil and Brahmananda Model of Wage Goods

Two models of growth deserve special mention here. The first one is ***Mahalanobis Model of capital goods*** Based on Feldman's model, Mahalanobis divided the economy into two sectors:

1. Capital Goods sector
2. Consumer Goods Sector

The emphasis was on determination of investment in each sector. To start with, India decided to lay emphasis on capital Goods.sector.in their initial phase of growth and development

The second model was ***Vakil and Brahnananda's Model of wage goods.*** According to this model, emphasis shifted from capital goods to ***wage goods***. It was production of these goods that was given top preference.

Conclusion

In the initial stages of growth, India emphasized on import substitution. This meant production of capital goods rather than of importing them. Such production cost India significantly. Later, it was felt that India could import such goods at much lower cost than that it incurred on their production.

Subsequently emphasis shifted on export promotion to buy the necessary capital goods and technology, instead of attempting their production which was quite expensive at home. The reason for higher costs at home was India's small scale of production and lack of technical know how. Thus specializing production of such goods India was better poised and exporting them turned out the motto. Export earnings had to be used for importing capital goods and technology.

14.4 ECONOMIC DEVELOPMENT AND ITS REQUISITES

Although growth and development are related concepts, development is far different from growth in many respects. While growth refers to the rate of annual increase in output/income, development is cumulative change in quality of life. It is the way we think, the way we look at life and the way we react to changes. One can say it a matter of outlook people acquire for rest of the world. Are we rational or superstitious, do we live a life frequented by hunger, poverty, servitude epidemics or do we suffer from high mortality, illiteracy, low levels of income and a high growth rate of population ? Answers to these questions determine whether we are developed or undeveloped. Existence of illiteracy, poverty, hunger, epidemics, superstitious beliefs, servitude, population explosion, traditionalism in production, inequality of income distribution, low status of women and high rate of infant mortality—all these characterize under development or no development. Let us examine the following that can throw some light on causes and cures of underdevelopment so that we can understand it better as also its difference from growth:

1. **Illiteracy:** Illiteracy or lack of education is the main cause of irrationality or superstitious beliefs and traditionalism. Spread of education and educational institutions can cure the evils. Education can provide a cure for many other evils such as population explosion, low status of women, servitude and low productivity of workers.

   A wide and sincere network of education has a high cost that can be financed through a high rate of growth of income. That provides one reason why nation states strive for a high growth of income and output.

2. **Health Hazards:** Non availability of medical facilities coupled with lack of people's awareness of health hazards and hygiene are responsible for epidemics, high rate of infant mortality and low levels of workers' productivity as also of population explosion.

   A wide network of health care centres can cure the evils. Again, costs are heavy and a high growth rate of income and output is must to finance them.
3. **Low per Capita Income:** Low levels of income are responsible for hunger, malnutrition, poverty and servitude apart from high growth of population. It may be caused by low growth rate of income as also by inequality of income distribution.

   The cure is population control and high labour productivity. Labour participation in work needs to be improvised.
4. **Biased Distribution of productive Resources:** Concentration of productive resources in the hands of a few is responsible for mass poverty, inequality of income distribution, servitude and such other evils.

   Creation of job opportunities for have-nots can provide a cure. For this, a strong public sector is a must.

   These are only a few hazards to developmental process. The purpose of highlighting them here was to give a clear distinction between growth and development. A high growth is aspired for high level of development. Every growth can't lead to development but every development can raise the growth rate. Growth and development are not inter-changeable terms therefore as most of the laymen treat them.

   To sum up, growth refers to the rate at which *GNP* of a country increases from period to period, usually of one year. Development, on the other hand, refers to a state of general well being of the people in which social evils such as disease, hunger, poverty, illiteracy, epidemics, superstitions stand eradicated and people lead a life of dignity and self-esteem[1]. Development has more to do with quality of life than with quantity of materialistic achievements.

14.4.1 Measurement of Development

For measurement of development, several indicators have been used from time to time. Some of them were discussed in Section 2.8 (Chapter 2) Let us have a brief review of them here.

GNP per capita

GNP per capita has been treated as an indicator of economic development and social welfare for quite some time. A high *GNP* per capita has implied a high level of social welfare and economic development particularly in respect of some advanced countries. The obsession of realizing a higher growth of *GNP* had been so strong that a number of developing countries have prepared themselves to give up the very objective of social welfare in order to pursue a high *GNP* growth. Creation of employment opportunities, for instance, is a social objective of such economies. It is to fulfill such objectives only that a high *GNP* growth has been and also is targeted by them. Unfortunately, Some of them have turned to high capital intensive methods in their desperation to boost *GNP* growth, oblivious of their sacrifice of the social objective of employment generation in the process. No doubt a high *GNP* may help the nation-states in improving the standard of living of the people provided it leads to quality changes in the economy. Let us see what these quality changes are that make *GNP* growth imply economic development of a nation.

[1] A dopted from Denis Goulet, *The Cruel Choice: A New Concept in the Theory of Development* (New York), 1971, pp. 87–94.

Development, as stated above, refers to an increase in availability of the life-sustaining goods such as food, shelter, protection from epidemics; enhancement of facilities of education for improvement of cultural and humanistic values as also of freedom from servitude and dependence not only in relation to the other people and nation- states but also to the forces of ignorance and human misery. In sum, development relates to the improvement in the quality of life of people.

Evidently, a high *GNP* per capita may ensure development if it percolates among the masses equitably. Kuwait has a very high *GNP* per capita but lacks in equitability of its distribution. Many countries lack in general level of education, balanced growth of agriculture and industry and in health and medical facilities. They can't be treated as developed countries so long as they lack in diversification of their *GNP* on the improvement of the living conditions of the people.

Observations such as those about countries like Kuwait, have led to widespread disillusionment of the economists about *GNP* per capita as a measure of economic development and social welfare. The hunt for alternative yardsticks for measurement of economic development has led to the evolution of a wide range of socio-economic indicators for the purpose.

William Nordhaus and James Tobin[1] developed a ***Measure of Economic Welfare*** (*MEW*) which was adopted by Samuelson[2] and reshaped into what is known as the ***Net Economic Welfare*** (*NEW*). Samuelson's *NEW* can be calculated by subtracting from *GNP* the hidden costs of disamenities of industrialization and by adding to it the values of such items as leisure and housewife's services.

PQLI

A better-known indicator in this regard is the ***Physical Quality of Life Index*** (*PQLI*). It was developed by David Morris, an American economist, for Overseas Development Council in the late 1970s[3].

According to J.R. Hicks[4], "The purpose of income calculation—is to give people an indication of the amount they can consume without impoverishing themselves.

HDI

Another index, ***Human Development Index (HDI)***[5] reported by the United Nations Development Programme **(*UNDP*)** is based on the human development approach, developed by Pakistani economist Mahbub-ul-Haq anchored in Amartya Sen's work on human capabilities, and often framed in terms of whether people are able to "be" and "do" desirable things in life. Examples include–being: well fed, sheltered, and healthy; doing: work, education, voting, and participating in community life. The freedom of choice is central – someone choosing to be hungry (e.g. when fasting for religious reasons) is quite different from someone who is hungry because they cannot afford to buy food, or because the country is passing through a famine. The index does not take into account several factors, such as the net wealth per capita or the relative quality of goods in a country. This situation tends to lower the ranking of some of the most developed , such as the G7 members and others.

Critical Assessment

Disenchantment about *GNP per capita* as a measure of economic development laid emphasis on indicators that employ qualitative measures of development. That way, *PQLI* emerges as the best indicator as it doesn't incorporate *GNP per capita. HDI,* though commonly used by economists

[1] William Nordhaus and James Tobin, *Is Growth Obsolete*, quoted by Paul A. Samuelson, *Economics* (12th edition) p. 119.

[2] Paul A. Samuelson, *Economics* (12th edition) p. 119.

[3] For detailed analysis of *PQLI*, and its computation, see Section 2.8 (Chapter 2) of this book.

[4] J.R. Hicks,*Value and Capital* ,Oxford University Press, 1975, p. 172.

[5] For detailed analysis and computation, see Section 2.8 (Chapter 2 of this boo).

of the developed world as a measure of economic development, incorporates *GNI per capita* in its computation, which imparts it a bias in favour of high income countries. As discussed above, countries with very high *GNP per capita* show a high *HDI* but lack in development due to inequalities of income distribution and absence of welfare measures.

KEY TERMS AND CONCEPTS

Real Output: It is output in physical units **or at constant prices**

Growth Rate: It is increase in real *GNP* in a year expressed as a percent of the value *GNP* in the beginning of the year.

Balanced Growth Theory: It refers to simultaneous growth of all the sectors of an economy. It requires a big push and called a big push theory as well.

Unbalanced Growth Theory: A theory that prescribes investment in selected sectors and leaves the rest to catch up. It practiced when amount of investment is insufficient for all the sectors

Inefficient Allocation: It refers to misallocation of resources against most productive or desirable sectors . Purchase of weapons for war is inefficient allocation when agricultural sector awaits it for fertilizers, irrigation facilities and better seeds.

Total Factor Productivity Residual (TFP): In a production function sources of production other than labour and capital, such as technology, natural resources etc, are called total factor productivity residual as they are external to the output of labour and capital. For cobb-Douglas production function, $Q = A\ L^{1-\alpha} K^{\alpha}$, A is the total factor productivity residual Being exogenously determined, it is also called exogenously determined total factor productivity residual. Since it causes shifts in the isoqunts of labour and capital, it is also called shift factor.

Labour Augmented Total Factor Productivity Residual: Given unchanged or fixed labour factor, A and $L^{1-\alpha}$ of $Q = A\ L^{1-\alpha}\ K^{\alpha}$ get clubbed together to give labour augmented total factor productivity residual .

Net Investment: It is gross investment less depreciation .Here it is additional investment made each year.

Demand Effect: It is one of the dual effects of net investment. It causes demand for inputs like land, building, plant, equipment etc.

Capacity Effect: Inputs bought and installed create new capacity of production. It is called the second effect of net investment. Output of this new capacity may be available in the next period.

Harrod Domar Model: This model expresses growth rate as a ratio of *MPS* **to** Capital output ratio, (s/k), where s is *MPS*, and k, capital output ratio.

Solow's Per Capita Growth Rate (without Technological Progress): It is given as $(\alpha \times \Delta k/k)$, where, α is share of capital in *GNP*, and $\Delta k/k$ is growth rate of capital per worker.

Solow's Per Capita Growth Rate with Technological Progress: It given as $(\Delta A/A)/(\Delta y/y)$ which is $[1 - (\alpha \times \Delta k/k)/\Delta y/y]$, where, α is the share of capital in *GNP*, $\Delta k/k$ is growth rate of capital per worker, $\Delta y/y$ is growth rate of *GNP* per worker with technological progress and $\Delta A/A$ is growth of technological progress per worker

Dual Sector Lewis Structural Change Model of Growth: The model befits the growth aspirations of underdeveloped economies that have two sectors-one labour surplus agricultural sector and the other, labour scarce manufacturing sector. Flight of labour from labour surplus rural sector, where wage rate is low, to the urban industrial sector, where labour is deficient and wage rate high, causes growth. The Modern industry employs new labour at the existing wage rate. This causes profits to the industry which reinvests them for acquiring more capital and realizing higher output.

Rostow's Stages of Growth Theory: Rostow defines 5 stages of growth and fixes the minimum rate of savings (S/Y) to be 15 to 20% for an economy to take off into the process of growth.

International Dependence Theories of Growth: An outgrowth of Marxist thinking, economists and intellectuals dismissed the theories of West as unsuitable for the third world**'s** developmental needs on the grounds that the western models caught up the third world in the dependence and dominance of the capitalist system and that *MNC* donors provided complex and inapplicable models with no relevance to receiver's needs. The economists and intellectuals of the third world recommended that the third world must set itself free from such dependence and devise its own models befitting its own conditions.

Indian growth Models: The first Indian growth model was Mahalanobis Model of growth which divided the economy into two sectors, namely, capital goods sector and consumer goods sector. It recommended emphasis of investment on capital goods sector to start within its initial phase of growth. The second model was Vakil and Brahmananda's model which emphasized wage goods. It was production of these goods that was given top preference.

Development: It refers to a state of well being of people in which social evils, such as, poverty, illiteracy, superstitious beliefs , hunger and servitude as also health hazards, such as, epidemics stand eradicated and people lead a life of dignity and self esteem.

Yard-stick of Development: Development is measure *d* through indices of physical quality of life index (*PQLI*) and human development index (*HDI*) These indices blend infant mortality rate, literacy rate life expectancy rate in respect of *PQLI* and life expectancy index, education index and income index in respect of *HDI.* The former is an arithmetic mean of the said rates while *the latter,* a geometric mean of the said index numbers.

EXERCISES

A. Short Answer Questions

1. Define growth. Which type of growth–balanced or unbalanced—would you recommend for a developing economy and why?
2. What are the advantages/disadvantages of unbalanced growth theory in a developing economy?
3. 'It is the difference between output desired by a community and output produced by it that calls for economic growth' Elucidate.
4. What is meant by inefficiency of resource allocation? How is it responsible for slow growth as also for slow development
5. Are economic growth and economic development one and the same thing? Give reasons in support?
6. Outline various sources of growth. What role does technological progress play in economic growth?
7. What is meant by total factor productivity residual? Is it the same as labour augmented total factor productivity? Explain
8. A firm is producing 8000 tons of cement using 100 units of labour and 64 units of capital. Another firm produces same quantity of cement with 25 units of labour and 16 units of capital. Each firm employs Cobb Douglas production function with $\alpha = \beta = 1/2$ Can you explain the discrepancy in factor employment of the two for the same output?.
9. Given that growth of capital is 8% and that of labour employment, 5%; $\alpha = \beta = 1/2$ and technological progress (i) 0%, (ii) 10%

   Calculate growth rate in each case. **[Ans:** (i) 6.5%, (ii) 16.5%]
10. What is labour augmented total factor productivity residual? If growth of capital be 9%, calculate growth rate in each of the following cases:
    (i) Labour augmented total factor productivity residual = 2%, $\alpha = 1/3$ and $\beta = 2/3$
    (ii) Labour augmented total factor productivity residual = 0%, $\alpha = 1/3$ and $\beta = 2/3$
    (iii) Labour augmented total factor productivity residual = 10%, $\alpha = 1/3$ and $\beta = 2/3$

    [Ans: (i) 8%, (ii) 6%, (iii) 16%]
11. How would your answers to Q.10 change if capitalists relocate capital to foreign banks so that capital growth is reduced to 6%? **[Ans:** (i) 6%, (ii) 4%, (iii) 14%]
12. Obtain the expression for Harrod-Domar growth rate and use it to calculate it when capital productivity is 1/4 and marginal propensity to save is 20%. **[Ans:** Derive $g = \sigma \times s$, 5%]
13. Obtain an expression for Solow's per capita growth rate without technological progress.
14. Obtain an expression for Solow's per capita growth rate with technological progress.

15. What are various stages of growth according to Rostow? If the rate of savings during the year is 18% and capital output ratio, 3; what would be the growth rate of the economy? **[Ans: 6%]**
16. Why do economists and intellectuals of the third world countries advise them to set themselves free from international dependence and dominance models of Growth?
17. Introduce the Indian models of growth. How does Mahalanobis model differ from Vakil and Brahmananda's model?
18. In what respects does Lewis dual sector model capture the growth problem of an underdeveloped economy?
19. Human Development Index (*HDI*) incorporates Life Expectancy Index (*LEI*), Education Index (*EI*) and Income Index (*II*) all over the world with effect from 2011. Given below the relevant data for countries *A* and *B*, compare them on their *HDIs*: LEI of country A = 65.5 years,
Mean schooling years in Country *A* = 12 years.
Expected schooling years in country *A* = 15 years.
GNI per capita in Country *A* = $1500
LEI of country *B* = 69.5 years,
Mean schooling years in Country *B* = 14 years.
Expected schooling years in country *B* = 16 years.
GNI per capita in Country *B* = $750

[Ans: HDI for Country A = $[LEI \times EI \times II]^{1/3}$

where, $$LEI = \frac{65.5 - 20}{85 - 20} = \frac{45.5}{65} = \mathbf{0.70}$$

$$EI = \frac{(12/15) + (15/18)}{2} = \mathbf{0.8617}$$

$$II = \frac{\text{Log}_e 1500 - \text{Log}_e 100}{\text{Log}_e 75000 - \text{Log}_e 100} = \frac{2.7081}{6.6200} = 0.4090$$

Substituting, *HDI* of Country *A* = $[0.70 \times 0.8167 \times 0.4090]^{1/3} = [\mathbf{0.2338}]^{1/3} = \mathbf{0.6161}$
Calculate *HDI* of Country *B* as an exercise. It is 0.**4715]**

20. Distinguish between:
    (i) Growth and development,
    (ii) Capital goods and wage goods,
    [Capital goods refer to productive assets like plant, equipment, machinery etc. while wage goods refer to basic necessities like milk, food, rice, cloth and the like that workers need to survive]
    (iii) GNP per capita growth and GNP per worker growth rate,
    (iv) Total Factor productivity residual and labour augmented total factor productivity residual,
    (v) Demand and capacity effects of net investments
21. 'Every growth doesn't lead to development but every development leads to growth', discuss with illustrative examples.

B. Long Answer Questions

22. Critically analyze Harrod -Domar theory of growth.
23. Provide a comprehensive account of Solow's per capita growth rate with and without technological progress
24. Explain Lewis Dual Sector Structural Change Model of Growth. Account for its advantages and disadvantages.

C. Essay Type Questions

25. 'All the western growth models are based on concepts irrelevant to the developing third world. They subject the third world to dependence and dominance of the rich countries apart from contributing little or nothing to the cause of developing nations'. Discuss.

Index

Absolute consumption, 105
Absolute income, 105
hypothesis, 108
Absolute purchasing power parity, 286
Accelerator, 149
Accommodating items or below the line items, 296
Actual rate of inflation, 328
Adjustable peg, 287, 290
Adjustment process to an increase in exogenous exports, 300
Adjustment process to an increase money stock, 301
Adjustment process to an increase in government spending, 300
Administrative revenue, 270
A firm's investment decisions, 121
Aggregate demand (AD), 137, 229
Aggregate demand function(*ADF*), 85
Aggregate demand under fixed prices, 225
Aggregate monetary resource (*AMR*), 185
Aggregate supply, *AS*, 137
Aggregate supply function (*ASF*), 85
Aggregative problems, 4
Annuities, 124, 125
APC ≡ average propensity to consume (C/Y), 99
Appreciated, 287
APS ≡ average propensity to save (*S/Y*), 99
Arbitrage, 286
Assumptions of the psychological law of consumption, 98
Autonomous consumption, 94
Autonomous investment, 120
Autonomous items or above the line items, 296
Average propensity to consume (APC), 95
Balanced budget, 272
Balanced budget multiplier, 161
Balanced budget multiplier theorem, 161
Balanced growth theory, 341
Balance of payment, 294
Balance of payments, 284
Balance of payments account, 294
Balance of payments: Capital account, 295
Balance of payments: Current account, 295
Balance of the current account, 294
Balance of trade, 284, 294
Balance of trade account, 294
Balance sheet of a commercial bank, 258
Barter and its drawbacks, 175
Barter system, 175
Bearer of the last option, 183
Big push theory, 341
Bills of exchange, 179, 182, 256
Boom, 77
Bretton Woods system, 288
Broad definitions, 180
Broader definition of income, 331
Broader measure of money supply, 185
Budget deficit, 273
Budget expenditures, 272
Budget receipts, 272
Buffer stocks, 333
Built-in-stabilizers, 267, 269

Canons of taxation, 279
Capacity effects, 349
Capital account, 294
Capital accumulation, 119
Capital and finance account, 58
Capital budget, 270, 271

Capital expenditures, 271
Capital formation, 119
Capital goods, 28
Capital receipts, 271
Capital stock and desired capital stock, 129
Capital stocks and the marginal efficiency of capital, 126
Cash credit and overdraft, 257
Cash reserve ratio (CRR), 250
Central clearance, 253
Changes in stocks of inventories (ΔS), 138
Characteristics of a good tax, 279
Cheap money policy, 248, 249
Chequable deposits, 178
Circular flow in a two-sector-economy, 30
Circular flows of incomes, expenditures and the products, 32
Classical full employment equilibrium through *IS-LM* framework, 232
Clean floating, 290
Closing stock, 23
Commercial Banks, 259
Commercial revenue, 270
Compensation of employees, 16, 18
Compensatory fiscal policy, 267, 269
Compensatory spending, 267
Competitiveness, 285
Conditions necessary for working of the multiplier, 152
Consumer goods, 27
Consumption and saving over life cycle, 111
Consumption demand (*C*), 137
Consumption function, 94
Consumption of fixed capital, 21
Contingent functions, 182
Contraction of credit, 249
Convertible currency, 178
Corporate profit tax, 41
Cost-push inflation, 313, 317, 322
Crawling peg, 290
Creation and control of credit, 259
Credit funds, 181
Credit money, 180
Credit multiplier, 149
Creeping inflation, 322
Crowding out effect, 239
Crowding out effect on income, 239
Crowding out of government spending by private investment, 239
Crowding out of investment, 239
Crowding out of private investment, 268
Current rate of exchange, 286
Cyclical unemployment, 78

Deadweight loss, 275
Dear money policy, 248, 249
Deduction, 8
Deductive method, 5, 8
Deferred payments, 176, 182
Deficient demand, 157
Deficient demand ($AD < AS$), 142
Deficit budget, 267, 272
Deficit budgeting, 268
Deficit financing, 3
Deficit or budget deficit, 3
Deflation, 37
Deflationary gap (*DG*), 142, 157
Deflation of the national income, 37
Demand effect, 349
Demand-pull inflation, 313, 322
Demand-pull inflation due to monetary factors, 320
Demand-pull inflation due to real factors, 319
Demonstration effect, 105
Deposit money, 178
Depreciated, 287
Depreciation, 34
    allowance, 120
Depression, 77
Desired capital stock, 129
Determination of equilibrium income in an economy with three sectors, 154
Determination of equilibrium level of income in an economy with four sectors, 163
Determination of equilibrium level of income in a two sector economy, 138
Devaluations, 289
Developmental expenditure, 272
Digressive tax, 269
Direct investment, 296
Direct tax and Laffer's curve, 277

Direct taxes, 268
Dirty floating, 290
Discounting factors, 126
Discretionary fiscal policy, 267
Disguised unemployment, 80
Dissaving, 103
Domestic factor income, 17
Domestic investment demand of foreign productive goods as M, 138
Double counting, 16, 22, 23
Downswing, 77
Downward wage price flexibility, 85
Dual exchange rate system, 289
Durable producers, 27
Durables, 27
Dynamic equilibrium, 197
Dynamic equilibrium of money market, 198
Dynamic multiplier, 147

Economic activities, 3
Economic development, 332
Economic growth, 332
Economic problem, 3
Education index (*EI*), 47
Effective demand (*ED*), 85
Effectiveness of fiscal policy, 298
Effectiveness of fiscal policy on income/output under perfect capital mobility, 298
Effect of a direct tax, 277
Effect of increase in exogenous exports, 300
Effect of taxes and subsidies on (*GDP*), 275
Effects of inflation on distribution of income, 331
Efficacy of monetary and fiscal policies, 224
Emergency currency, 179
Empirical estimates for long-run consumption function, 104
Empirical estimates for short-run consumption function, 104
Empirical estimates of consumption function, 104
Escheats, 270
Evolution of fiscal policy, 266
Excess demand, 156
Excess demand (*AD* > *AS*), 142
Exogenously determined total factor productivity residual (*TFP*), 345
Expansionary monetary, 322
Expansion of credit, 249
Expected rate of inflation, 328
Expected years of schooling, 47
Export multiplier, 143
Export tariff, 284
External transactions account, 58

Factor income, 16, 17
Factors influencing consumption demand, 100
Factors influencing *MEC*, 128
Factors influencing *NPV*, 125
Factors of production, 16
Fiat money, 179
Final goods, 16
Final product, 57
Fiscal deficit, 273
Fiscal policy multiplier, 222, 238, 268
Fiscal policy multiplier effect, 239
Fiscal policy multiplier, γ, 239
Fisher's time preference, 108
Fixed exchange rate, 302
Fixed exchange rate regime, 287, 288
Flexible exchange rate, 288
Flexible exchange rate system, 287
Food stamp programme of *US*, 333
Forced savings, 269
Foreign investment demand, 138
Foreign trade policy, 284
Forms of money, 176
Forward exchange rate, 286
Forward market, 285
Free coinage, 178
Frictional unemployment, 78
Full bodied coins, 178
Full employment equilibrium of classical theory, 82
Full multiplier effect, 239
Functional finance, 267
Functions of a commercial bank, 254
Functions of the central bank, 253

Galloping inflation, 322
General equilibrium, 5, 6, 89

Generalization, 8
Globalization paradox, 302
GNP implicit deflator or implicit price deflator, 38
GNP implicit price deflator, 330
GNP per capita, 42
Gold standard, 246, 287
Goods market equilibrium, 89
Government expenditure multiplier, K_{G}., 143, 239
Government final consumption expenditure (C_g), 27, 28
Grant of subsidy, 334
Grant of unit subsidy, 333
Gross and net investment, 119
Gross domestic capital formation (*GDCF*), 27, 28, 138
Gross domestic fixed capital formation (*GDFCF*), 138
Gross domestic product and expenditure account, 58
Guarantor of solvency, 183

Hedging, 286
High powered money (H), 186
H-theory of money supply, 186
Human development index (*HDI*), 47, 359
Hyperinflation, 322

Implications of Keynesian Theory, 88
Implications of the classical theory of employment, 84
Implications of the psychological law of consumption, 99
Implicit price deflator, 330
Import tariff, 284
Impossible trilemma, 303
Impossible trinity, 303
Imputed interest, 18
Imputed rent, 18
Income, 15
Income from property and entrepreneurship, 18
Income in the narrow sense, 331
Inconvertible currency, 178
Inconvertible paper money, 178
Indexed infant mortality rate, 45
Indexed life expectancy, 45
Indirect taxes, 268
Indirect taxes less subsidies, 21
Induced investment, 120
Induction, 8
Inductive method, 5, 8
Industry of origin, 16
Ineffectiveness of monetary policy, 297
Inefficient allocation, 343
Ineffiveness of monetary policy, 298
Inflare, 313
Inflation, 313
Inflationary gap (*IG*), 142, 156
Inflationary pressure curve (*IPC*), 324, 326
Informal flexible exchange rates, 288
Input-output table, 52
Instruments of monetary policy, 248
Interest, 18
Intermediate consumption, 22
Intermediate goods, 16, 28
Internal and external imbalances, 296
International inflation, 323
Investment, 99
  demand (*I*), 137
  function, 121
  multiplier, 143

Keynesian model of less than full employment, 233
Keynesian psychological law of consumption, 98
Keynesian reasoning for unattainability of classical full employment, 234

Labour augmented total factor productivity residual, 345
Lack of common denominator, 176
Lack of divisibility of certain commodities, 176
Lack of double coincidence of wants, 175
Lack of store value, 176
Leakage from the circular flow of income and expenditure, 94
Leakages from multiplier, 152
Legal tender money, 179
Lender of the last resort, 253

Less than full employment equilibrium of Keynesian theory, 82, 83
Leverage effect, 150
Life-cycle hypothesis, 107
Life expectancy index (LEI), 47
Limitations of the multiplier-process, 151
Limited legal tender, 178, 179
Liquidity and the profitability, 259
Liquidity preference, 194
Long-run consumption function, 96
Long-run factors, 128
Long-run Phillips curve, 324, 328
Long-run Phillips curve and natural rate of unemployment, 328
Lumping method, 6

Macroeconomics, 4
Macro problems, 4
Mahalanobis model of capital goods, 357
Managed floating, 290
Marginal efficiency of capital (*MEC*), 89, 125
Marginal efficiency of investment (*MEI*), 131
Marginal propensity to consume (*MPC*), 96
Marginal propensity to invest, 121
Marginal propensity to save (*MPS*), 99, 103
Marginal rate of time preference, 109
Marginal return over cost, 109
Marginal social benefit (*MSB*), 279
Marginal social sacrifice (*MSS*), 279
Margin requirements, 252
Mark-up inflation, 324
Mean years of schooling, 47
Measure and store of value, 180
Measured income, 105
Measure of economic welfare (*MEW*), 45, 359
Measure of value, 181
MEC and *MEI*, 130
MEC-schedule, 127
Medium of exchange, 180, 181
Methods of credit control, 248
Microeconomic analysis, 5
Microeconomics, 3
Micro problems, 3
Mixed incomes, 19
Modified Phillips curve, 324, 325
Monetary factors, 318
Monetary policy multiplier, 223, 238, 248
Monetary sovereignty, 302
Monetization of the deficit, 269
Monetizing the deficit, 253
Money market equilibrium, 89
Money multiplier, 187
Money-proper, 181
Most common form of the consumption function, 97
Multiplier, 143
Mundell-Fleming model, 296
Mundell-Fleming model: perfect capital mobility under flexible exchange rates, 299

Narrow definitions, 180
Narrow measure of money supply, 185
National, 16
National debt interest, 40
National disposable income and its appropriation account, 58
National expenditure, 17
National income, 16, 21
National income aggregates, 32
National income at constant prices, 37
National income at current prices, 37
National income deflator, 38
National product, 16
Natural rate of unemployment, 328, 329
Near money, 179
Negative indirect tax (subsidy), 275
Net demand deposits, 184
Net direct taxes, 95
Net domestic capital formation (*NDCF*), 27
Net domestic fixed capital formation (*NDFCF*), 27
Net domestic product at factor cost (*NDPFC*), 25
Net economic welfare (*NEW*), 45, 359
Net factor income from abroad (*NFIA*), 17, 34
Net foreign investment demand can be given as $(X - M)$, 138
Net indirect tax (*NIT*), 21, 33
Net investment, 349
Net investment abroad, 29
Net investment spending, 131
Net national product at factor cost (*NNPFC*), 25

Net other current transfers from *ROW*, 40
Net value added at factor cost (*NVAFC*), 25
Net worth, 331
Neutralists, 245
Neutrality of money, 84, 245
Nominal exchange rate, 285
Non-banking assets, 259
Non-developmental expenditures, 272
Non-linear consumption function, 96
Non-plan expenditures, 271
Nonproductive expenditures, 333
Non-tax revenue, 270
Normal resident, 16, 19

Official transactions, 295
Okun's law, 327
Open inflation, 323
Opening stock, 23
Open market operations, 249
Operating surplus, 18
Optional money, 179
Output growth per worker, 353
Overall budget, 271

Paradox of thrift, 148, 149
Partial equilibrium, 6
Partial equilibrium analysis, 5
Pegged exchange rate, 287
Per capita growth, 353
Per capita growth rate, 352
Percent tax, 269
Perfect capital mobility, 302
Permanent consumption component, 106
Personal consumption expenditure (PCE), 330
Personal disposable income, 42
Personal income, 41
Phillips curve, 324, 325
Physical quality of life index (*PQLI*), 45, 359
Pigou-effect, 236
Plan expenditure, 271
Plugging the leakages, 94
Portfolio investment, 296
Precautionary motives, 183
Present value, 123
Present value of a capital asset, 129
Price mechanism, 4, 184
Primary deficit, 273
Principle of maximum social advantage, 4
Principle of maximum social advantage in taxation, 278
Private final consumption expenditure (C_h), 27
Private income, 40
Private investment, 121
Private transactions, 295
Problem of growth and development, 4
Problem of inefficiency, 4
Problem of inflation, 4
Problem of unemployment, 4
Producers' boundary, 57
Producer's goods, 27
Profit, 18
Profit-push inflation, 317
Progressive tax, 269
Proportional tax, 269
Public distribution system (*PDS*), 333
Public expenditure or government spending, 3
Public expenditures, 269
Public investment, 121
Public revenue, 3
Purchasing power parity (*PPP*), 285
Purchasing power parity (*PPP*) theory, 286

Qualitative methods, 248
Quantitative methods, 248
Quantity theory of money, 334
Quasi-money, 179, 181

Ratchet effect, 105
Ratchet inflation, 324
Rate of inflation, 39
Rationing or fair price shops, 333
Real balance effect, 236
Real exchange rate, 285
Real factors, 318, 322
Real output, 341
Reasons for failure of the multiplier in the under-developed countries, 153
Recovery, 77

Reflation, 333
Regressive tax, 269
Relative income hypothesis, 105
Relative purchasing power parity, 286
Repercussion effect, 247
Representative money, 180
Reserve ratio, *r*, 149
Resource gap, 3
Retained earnings, 18
Revenue budget, 270
Revenue deficit, 273
Revenue receipts, 270
Royalty, 18
Running inflation, 322

Saving function, 102
Say's law of markets, 84, 85
Seasonal unemployment, 79
Selective credit control methods, 248
Semi-durables, 27
Short-run consumption function, 94
Short-run factors, 128
Single use consumer goods, 27
Slicing method, 6
Speculation, 286
Speculative activities, 194
Speculative motives, 183
Speculators, 194
Spot market, 285
Spot rate of exchange, 286
Stagflation, 323
Standard coins, 178
Standard of deferred payments, 180, 182
Standard token coin, 178
Static equilibrium of the money market, 198
Static investment multiplier, 146
Statutory liquidity ratio, 250
Stocks and Flows, 29
Store of value, 182
Strategic production, 333
Structural unemployment, 79
Subjective factors, 102
Subsidy, 33, 333
Supplementary income, 333
Supply shock factor, 317
Supply-shock inflation, 317
Supply side of inflation, 317
Suppressed or repressed inflation, 323
Surplus budget, 267, 272
Surplus budgeting, 268
Surpluses on capital account, 296
System of minimum reserves, 246

The consumer price index (*CPI*), 329
The *GNP* implicit price deflator, 330
The life cycle hypothesis, 107
The Mundell-Fleming-model: Perfect capital mobility under fixed, exchange rates, 296
The objective factors, 101
Theories of inflation, deflation and reflation, 7
The permanent income hypothesis, 105
The producer price index (*PPI*), 329
The willingness curve, 111
Time deposits, 184
Time preference theory of interest, 108
Tobin-Baumol's version of transaction demand and interest rates, 192
Token coins, 178
Trade deficit, 285
Transaction demand (M_t), 190
Transaction motives, 183
Transfer of purchasing power, 182
Transfer payments (*R*), 31, 40, 95
Transformation curves (TCs), 111
Transitory components, 105
Transitory consumption component, 106
Treasury bill, 179
Trilemma and its impossibility, 301
Trotting inflation, 322

Unattainability of classical full employment due to liquidity trap, 235
Unattainability of classical full employment equilibrium due to inconsistency between saving and investment, 234
Unattainability of classical full employment equilibrium due to liquidity trap, 235
Unbalanced growth theory, 341
Underemployment, 79
Under variable prices, 229

Underwriting activities, 258
Undistributed profits, 18, 41
Unholy trilemma, 303
Unilateral transactions, 31
Unilateral transfers, 95
Unit multiplier theorem, 161
Unit taxes (Goods and services taxes), 333
Unlimited legal tender, 178, 179
Upswing, 77
Urban unemployment an offshoot of rural unemployment, 80

Vakil and Brahnananda's model of wage goods, 357
Value added method, 22
Value addition, 16
Vertical long-run Phillips curve, 329
Voluntary unemployment, 78

Wage goods, 357
Wage price flexibility and Pigou effect, 236, 237
Wage-push inflation, 317
Wage push, profit push and supply shock factors, 322
Walking inflation, 322
War finance, 334
Wider band, 289
Willingness curve, 110
Willingness curve (WC_F), 109
Willingness curve (WC_P), 109
Withdrawals, 99